Yale Agrarian Studies Series
James C. Scott, series editor

The Agrarian Studies Series at Yale University Press seeks to publish outstanding and original interdisciplinary work on agriculture and rural society—for any period, in any location. Works of daring that question existing paradigms and fill abstract categories with the lived-experience of rural people are especially encouraged.

—JAMES C. SCOTT, *Series Editor*

The Art of
Not Being Governed

An Anarchist History of Upland Southeast Asia

James C. Scott

Yale University Press NEW HAVEN & LONDON

Published with assistance from the Mary Cady Tew Memorial Fund.

Designed by James J. Johnson and set in Ehrhardt type by Tseng Information Systems, Inc.
Printed in the United States of America.

The Library of Congress has cataloged the hardcover edition as follows:

Scott, James C.
The art of not being governed : an anarchist history of upland Southeast Asia / James C. Scott.
    p.   cm.
Includes bibliographical references and index.
ISBN 978-0-300-15228-9 (cloth : alk. paper) 1. Ethnology—Southeast Asia. 2. Peasantry—
Southeast Asia—Political activity. 3. Southeast Asia—Politics and government—1945-.
4. Southeast Asia—Rural conditions. I. Title.
DS523.3.S36 2009
305.800959—dc22

                                                                                    2009003004

ISBN 978-0-300-16917-1 (pbk.)

A catalogue record for this book is available from the British Library.

10   9   8

It is said that the history of peoples who have a history is the history of class struggle. It might be said with at least as much truthfulness, that the history of peoples without history is a history of their struggle against the state.

—Pierre Clastres, *La société contre l'état*

Contents

Preface

Zomia is a new name for virtually all the lands at altitudes above roughly three hundred meters all the way from the Central Highlands of Vietnam to northeastern India and traversing five Southeast Asian nations (Vietnam, Cambodia, Laos, Thailand, and Burma) and four provinces of China (Yunnan, Guizhou, Guangxi, and parts of Sichuan). It is an expanse of 2.5 million square kilometers containing about one hundred million minority peoples of truly bewildering ethnic and linguistic variety. Geographically, it is also known as the Southeast Asian mainland massif. Since this huge area is at the periphery of nine states and at the center of none, since it also bestrides the usual regional designations (Southeast Asia, East Asia, South Asia), and since what makes it interesting is its ecological variety as well as its relation to states, it represents a novel object of study, a kind of transnational Appalachia, and a new way to think of area studies.

My thesis is simple, suggestive, and controversial. Zomia is the largest remaining region of the world whose peoples have not yet been fully incorporated into nation-states. Its days are numbered. Not so very long ago, however, such self-governing peoples were the great majority of humankind. Today, they are seen from the valley kingdoms as "our living ancestors," "what we were like before we discovered wet-rice cultivation, Buddhism, and civilization." On the contrary, I argue that hill peoples are best understood as runaway, fugitive, maroon communities who have, over the course of two millennia, been fleeing the oppressions of state-making projects in the valleys—slavery, conscription, taxes, corvée labor, epidemics, and warfare.

Most of the areas in which they reside may be aptly called shatter zones or zones of refuge.

Virtually everything about these people's livelihoods, social organization, ideologies, and (more controversially) even their largely oral cultures, can be read as strategic positionings designed to keep the state at arm's length. Their physical dispersion in rugged terrain, their mobility, their cropping practices, their kinship structure, their pliable ethnic identities, and their devotion to prophetic, millenarian leaders effectively serve to avoid incorporation into states and to prevent states from springing up among them. The particular state that most of them have been evading has been the precocious Han-Chinese state. A history of flight is embedded in many hill legends. The documentary record, although somewhat speculative until 1500, is clear enough after that, including frequent military campaigns against hill peoples under the Ming and Qing dynasties and culminating in the unprecedented uprisings in southwestern China in the mid-nineteenth century that left millions seeking refuge. The flight from both the Burmese and Thai slave-raiding states is also amply documented.

My argument will, I hope, have some resonance beyond the already broad swath of Asia with which it is immediately concerned.

The huge literature on state-making, contemporary and historic, pays virtually no attention to its obverse: the history of deliberate and reactive statelessness. This is the history of those who got away, and state-making cannot be understood apart from it. This is also what makes this an anarchist history.

This account implicitly brings together the histories of all those peoples extruded by coercive state-making and unfree labor systems: Gypsies, Cossacks, polyglot tribes made up of refugees from Spanish *reducciones* in the New World and the Philippines, fugitive slave communities, the Marsh Arabs, San-Bushmen, and so on.

The argument reverses much received wisdom about "primitivism" generally. Pastoralism, foraging, shifting cultivation, and segmentary lineage systems are often a "secondary adaptation," a kind of "self-barbarianization" adopted by peoples whose location, subsistence, and social structure are adapted to state evasion. For those living in the shadow of states, such evasion is also perfectly compatible with derivative, imitative, and parasitic state forms in the hills.

My argument is a deconstruction of Chinese and other civilizational discourses about the "barbarian," the "raw," the "primitive." On close inspection those terms, practically, mean ungoverned, not-yet-incorporated. Civilizational discourses never entertain the possibility of people voluntarily going over to the barbarians, hence such statuses are stigmatized and ethnicized. Ethnicity and "tribe" begin exactly where taxes and sovereignty end—in the Roman Empire as in the Chinese.

Usually, forms of subsistence and kinship are taken as given, as ecologically and culturally determined. By analyzing various forms of cultivation, particular crops, certain social structures, and physical mobility patterns for their escape value, I treat such givens largely as political choices.

The mountains as a refuge for state-fleeing people, including guerrillas, is an important geographical theme. I develop the idea of the friction of terrain, which is a new way of understanding political space and the difficulties of state-making in premodern societies.

I'm the only one to blame for this book. I did it. Let's get that out of the way before I begin making apologies and trying, in vain, I know, to make a few preemptive strikes against some of the criticism I can, even as I write this, see bearing down on me.

I've often been accused of being wrong but rarely of being obscure or incomprehensible. This book is no different. There's no denying that I make bold claims about the hill peoples of mainland Southeast Asia. I think, naturally, that my claims are broadly correct, even if I may be mistaken in some particulars. Judgment of whether I am right is, as always, now out of my hands and in that of my readers and reviewers. There are, however, three things about these claims that I wish to assert emphatically. First, there is nothing original here. I repeat, there is not a single idea here that originates with me. What I surely have done is to see a kind of immanent order or argument in a good many of the sources I canvassed and to draw that argument out to see how far it would take me. The creative aspect, if there was any, was to make out this gestalt and to connect the dots. I realize that some of those whose arguments and speculations I have made use of will think I have gone too far—a few of them have told me so and, mercifully for me, others are no longer in a position to complain. They are no more responsible for what I have done with their ideas than I will be for what use others make of what I have written here.

To my mild astonishment, I find that I have become a kind of historian—not a particularly good one, perhaps, but a historian nonetheless. And an ancient historian at that: ancient in both senses of the term. I am familiar with the occupational hazard of historians, namely that a historian preparing herself to write, say, about the eighteenth century ends up writing mostly about the seventeenth century because it comes to seem so fundamental to the question at issue. Something like that happened to me. Here I was reading ethnographies of hill peoples and reports on human rights abuses by the Burmese military in minority areas only to find myself drawn inexorably back to the coercive state-making of the classical mandala kingdoms. I owe my renewed study of precolonial and colonial Southeast Asia to two independent graduate reading courses. One was devoted to foundational texts in Southeast Asian studies and designed as a kind of intellectual boot camp in which we read all those basic works most scholars had on their shelves but would be embarrassed to admit that they had never read, beginning with the two volumes of the *Cambridge History of Southeast Asia*. It was bracing for all of us. The second was a reading course on Burma, starting from the same premise.

This brings me to my second emphatic assertion. What I have to say in these pages makes little sense for the period following the Second World War. Since 1945, and in some cases before then, the power of the state to deploy distance-demolishing technologies—railroads, all-weather roads, telephone, telegraph, airpower, helicopters, and now information technology—so changed the strategic balance of power between self-governing peoples and nation-states, so diminished the friction of terrain, that my analysis largely ceases to be useful. On the contrary, the sovereign nation-state is now busy projecting its power to its outermost territorial borders and mopping up zones of weak or no sovereignty. The need for the natural resources of the "tribal zone" and the desire to ensure the security and productivity of the periphery has led, everywhere, to strategies of "engulfment," in which presumptively loyal and land-hungry valley populations are transplanted to the hills. So if my analysis does not apply to late-twentieth-century Southeast Asia, don't say I didn't warn you.

Finally, I worry that the radical constructionist case made here about ethnogenesis will be misunderstood and taken as a devaluation, even denigration, of ethnic identities for which brave men and women have fought and died. Nothing could be further from the truth. *All* identities, without exception, have been socially constructed: the Han, the Burman, the American, the Danish, all of them. Quite often such identities, particularly minority identities, are at first imagined by powerful states, as the Han imagined the Miao, the British colonists imagined the Karen and the Shan, the French the Jarai.

Whether invented or imposed, such identities select, more or less arbitrarily, one or another trait, however vague—religion, language, skin color, diet, means of subsistence—as the desideratum. Such categories, institutionalized in territories, land tenure, courts, customary law, appointed chiefs, schools, and paperwork, may become passionately lived identities. To the degree that the identity is stigmatized by the larger state or society, it is likely to become for many a resistant and defiant identity. Here invented identities combine with self-making of a heroic kind, in which such identifications become a badge of honor. In the contemporary world in which the nation-state is the hegemonic political unit, it is not surprising that such self-assertion should usually take the form of ethnonationalism. So for those who risk everything so that the Shan, the Karen, the Chin, the Mon, the Kayah may achieve some form of independence and recognition, I have only admiration and respect.

I owe an enormous intellectual debt to at least five "dead white men"— whose ranks I shall join in due course. They were the pioneers of the trail along which I plod here; I wouldn't even have found it without them. The earliest was Pierre Clastres, whose daring interpretation of state-evading and state-preventing native peoples in post-Conquest South America in *La société contre l'état* has come, in the wake of subsequent evidence, to seem clair-voyant. Owen Lattimore's deep and ambitious insights into the relationship between Han-Chinese states and their pastoralist periphery helped me to see that something similar might hold for China's southwest frontier. Ernest Gellner's analysis of Berber-Arab relations helped me grasp that where sovereignty and taxes stopped, there precisely, "ethnicity" and "tribes" began, and that *barbarian* was another word states used to describe any self-governing, nonsubject people. No one who plods the route I have taken gets anywhere without a sustained intellectual encounter with Edmund Leach's *Political Systems of Highland Burma*. There are few books that are so "good to think with." Finally, I am in debt to James G. Scott, aka Shwe Yoe, military commander, colonial official, compiler of the *Gazetteer of Upper Burma* and author of *The Burman*. He is no relative, but as I have learned so much from his acute observations and as we are both, according to Burmese astrological reckoning, entitled to Burmese names of the same sort, I have adopted his Burmese name, Shwe Yoe, in a bid to please his ghost.

I have been inspired and instructed by work that reexamined how out-of-the-way people came to be out of the way in the first place, while radically questioning the civilizational discourse applied to them by their self-described superiors. Gonzalo Aguirre Beltrán's small classic, *Regions of*

Refuge, published nearly thirty years ago, made a more general claim than Clastres for much of the Latin American continent, and subsequently Stuart Schwartz and Frank Salomon examined that claim in more careful, illuminating detail. Closer to my own geographic focus, Robert Hefner's study of the Tengger Highlands of Java and Geoffrey Benjamin's work on Malaysia's *orang asli* were convincing and brilliant case studies that encouraged me to see Zomia in this light.

The term *Zomia* I owe entirely to Willem van Schendel, who was perceptive enough to realize that this huge upland border area stretching in the west to India (and well beyond, in his view) was distinctive enough to merit its own designation. In sketching out an intellectual case for "Zomia studies" as a field of research, he called into question the routine ways in which we think about *area* or *region.* I enrolled as a foot soldier in the Zomia army (psychological warfare branch) immediately after reading his persuasive argument for the term. Willem and I and several colleagues look forward to the day we are able to convene the first International Zomia Studies Conference. Van Schendel's work on the Bengal borderland is already an example of what might be achieved if we took his advice to heart.

Had I the patience and even more of an impulse to comprehensiveness, there would and should have been a chapter on watery regions of refuge. I mention them only in passing and regret that I haven't been able to do them justice. The numerous *orang laut* (sea nomads, sea gypsies) in insular Southeast Asia are clearly a seagoing, archipelago-hopping variant of swiddeners dwelling in mountain fastnesses. Like many hill people they also have a martial tradition and have moved easily between piracy (seaborne raiding), slave-raiding, and serving as the naval guard and strike force of several Malay kingdoms. Poised strategically at the edge of major shipping lanes, able to strike and disappear quickly, they conjure up a whole watery Zomia that deserves a place here. As Ben Anderson noted while urging me in this direction, "The sea is bigger, emptier than the mountains and the forest. Look at all those pirates still easily fending off the G-7, Singapore, etc., with aplomb." But as any reader will note, this book is already too long, and I must leave this theme to others more competent to pursue it: a task already excellently begun by Eric Tagliacozzo.

There are four scholars whose work falls smack in the middle of my own concerns and without which this book would scarcely be conceivable. I don't know how many times I have read and reread the, in effect, collected works of F. K. L. (Lehman) Chit Hlaing and Richard O'Connor for their deep insights and what they might mean for my own argument. Victor Lieberman, the premier historian of Southeast Asia state-making in a comparative frame, and Jean Michaud, who raised the banner of Zomia (or what he would call the Southeast Asian massif) well before the rest of us, have been key interlocutors. All four of these scholars have shown me an intellectual large-spiritedness of a very high order, even, and especially, when they disagreed with me. They may dissent from much of what I say here, but they should know that they have made me smarter, though not quite as smart as they may have hoped. I am, in addition, indebted to Jean Michaud for generously allowing me to use passages from his *Historical Dictionary of the Peoples of the Southeast Asian Massif* for my glossary.

There is a large number of colleagues who, having better things to do with their time, nevertheless read part or all of the manuscript and gave me their frank advice. I hope they see, here and there, evidence of their impact as I bobbed and weaved my way to a more nuanced and defensible argument. They include, in no particular order, Michael Adas, Ajay Skaria, Ramachandra Guha, Tania Li, Ben Anderson, Michael Aung-Thwin, Masao Imamura, the historians U Tha Htun Maung and U Soe Kyaw Thu, the archaeologist U Tun Thein, the geologist Arthur Pe, Geoffrey Benjamin, Shan-shan Du, Mandy Sadan, Michael Hathaway, Walt Coward, Ben Kerkvliet, Ron Herring, Indrani Chatterjee, Khin Maung Win, Michael Dove, James Hagen, Jan-Bart Gewald, Thomas Barfield, Thongchai Winichakul, Katherine Bowie, Ben Kiernan, Pamela McElwee, Nance Cunningham, Aung Aung, David Ludden, Leo Lucassen, Janice Stargardt, Tony Day, Bill Klausner, Mya Than, Susan O'Donovan, Anthony Reid, Martin Klein, Jo Guldi, Ardeth Maung Thawnghmung, Bo Bo Nge, Magnus Fiskesjö, Mary Callahan, Enrique Mayer, Angelique Haugerud, Michael McGovern, Thant Myint U, Marc Edelman, Kevin Heppner, Christian Lentz, Annping Chin, Prasenjit Duara, Geoff Wade, Charles Keyes, Andrew Turton, Noburu Ishikawa, Kennon Breazeale, and Karen Barkey. Wait! I have secreted in this list four colleagues who failed to send their comments. You know who you are. For shame! If, on the other hand, you collapsed trying to carry the manuscript from the printer to your desk, my apologies.

I want to acknowledge a small number of collegial debts that are not easy to categorize. Hjorleifur Jonsson's uniquely perceptive book *Mien Relations* was very influential in my thinking, especially with respect to the pliability of hill identities and social structure. Mikael Gravers has taught me a great deal about the Karen and the cosmological basis of their millenarian proclivities. Eric Tagliacozzo read the manuscript with unprecedented care and assigned me a reading program that I am still trying to complete. Finally, I have learned a great deal from five colleagues with whom I set out to study "vernacular and official identities" many years back: Peter Sahlins, Pingkaew Luanggaramsri, Kwanchewan Buadaeng, Chusak Wittayapak, and Janet Sturgeon, who is, *avant la lettre,* a practicing Zomianist.

Some time back, in 1996, my colleague Helen Siu persuaded me to attend, as discussant, a conference on China's borders and border peoples. Organized by Helen, Pamela Crossley, and David Faure, this conference was so provocative and lively that it served to germinate a good many of the ideas found here. The book arising from that meeting and edited by Pamela Crossley, Helen Siu, and Donald Sutton, *Empire at the Margins: Culture, Ethnicity, and Frontier in Early Modern China* (Berkeley: University of California Press, 2006), is packed with original history, theory, and ethnography.

There are a good many institutions that harbored and supported me over the past decade while I ever so slowly found my bearings. I started background reading on upland Southeast Asia and on the relationship between states and itinerant peoples generally at the Center for Advanced Study in the Behavioral Sciences in Palo Alto, where Alex Keyssar, Nancy Cott, Tony Bebbington, and Dan Segal were boon intellectual companions. That reading continued in the spring of 2001 at Oslo's Centre for Development and the Environment, where I was the beneficiary of the intellect and charm of Desmond McNeill, Signe Howell, Nina Witoczek, and Bernt Hagvet and began Burmese lessons in earnest at the Democratic Voice of Burma radio station under the tolerant eye of Khin Maung Win. I finished the first draft of this manuscript while visiting the Department of Society and Globalization of the Graduate School of International Development Studies at Roskilde University. I want to record my warm thanks to Christian Lund, Preben Kaarsholm, Bodil Folke Frederiksen, Inge Jensen, and Ole Brun for an intellectually bracing and thoroughly enjoyable stay.

For the past two decades my real intellectual sustenance has come from the Program in Agrarian Studies at Yale University. The agraristas, fellows, speakers, graduate students, and associated faculty with whom I have taught have continually renewed my faith in the possibility of an intellectual venue that is both convivial and challenging, welcoming and tough. Kay Mansfield has always been, and continues to be, the heart and soul of the program, the compass from which we take our bearings. My colleagues K. Sivaramakrishnan (aka Shivi), Eric Worby, Robert Harms, Arun Agrawal, Paul Freedman, Linda-Anne Rebhun, and Michael Dove have all taken a liberal hand in my continuing education. Michael Dove and Harold Conklin have, between them, taught me everything I know about swidden cultivation that plays such an important role in my analysis.

I have had a series of research assistants of such initiative and talent that they have saved me many months of futile toil and many errors. They will, I am confident, make names for themselves in short order. Arash Khazeni, Shafqat Hussein, Austin Zeiderman, Alexander Lee, Katie Scharf, and Kate Harrison helped turn this project into something creditable.

Those many Burmese friends who refereed my struggles with the Burmese language deserve at least hazardous duty pay and perhaps sainthood — or perhaps that would be deva-hood in the Theravada context. I want to thank Saya Khin Maung Gyi, my longest-serving, most battle-scarred, and most patient teacher, as well as his entire family, including San San Lin. Let Let Aung (aka Viola Wu), Bo Bo Nge, KaLu Paw, and Khin Maung Win courageously braved painfully slow and misshapen conversations. Kaung Kyaw and Ko Soe Kyaw Thu, though not formally teachers, nonetheless, in befriending me, pushed me forward. Finally, in Mandalay and on various travels, Saya Naing Tun Lin, a natural teacher, invented a pedagogy suited to my modest talents and pursued it rigorously. We often had lessons on the spacious fourth-floor balcony of a small hotel. When I massacred, for the fourth or fifth time, the same tone or aspirate, he would abruptly rise and walk away to the edge of the balcony. I feared more than once that he would hurl himself over the railing in despair. He didn't. Instead he would come back, sit down, take a very deep breath, and resume. I would not have gotten through without him.

While I was casting around for an appropriate title, a friend mentioned that Jimmy Casas Klausen, a political scientist at the University of Wisconsin, Madison, was teaching a course in political philosophy titled The Art of Not Being Governed. Klausen generously agreed to let me use the title for my book, for which I am very grateful indeed. I await the day when he will no doubt put a philosophical footing under this whole enterprise with a book of his own on the subject.

The maps in this volume were created with skill and imagination by Stacey Maples at the Yale Map Collection of Sterling Library. He gave cartographic shape to my understanding of the spatial issues in Southeast Asian statecraft.

Where it seemed appropriate I have added Burmese words and occasionally a phrase to the text. As there is no universally agreed upon system for transliterating Burmese into roman letters, I have adopted the system devised by John Okell at the School of Oriental and African Studies, University of London, and explained in his *Burmese: An Introduction to the Spoken Language*, Book 1 (DeKalb: Northern Illinois University, Center for Southeast Asian Studies, 1994). To avoid any confusion, where the Burmese term seems important, I have added it in Burmese script.

I could not have asked for a more supportive and talented editor for this, and for the other titles in the Agrarian Studies Series, than Jean Thomson Black. Nor could Yale University Press ask for a more inspired editor. My manuscript editor, Dan Heaton, combined a respect for the text with a firmness about my errors and excesses that has greatly improved what the reader will encounter.

Last, and by no means least, I couldn't have thought or lived my way through this manuscript without the insights and companionship of my high altitude muse.

The Art of Not Being Governed

CHAPTER 1

Hills, Valleys, and States

An Introduction to Zomia

I open with three diagnostic expressions of frustration. The first two are from would-be conquering administrators, determined to subdue a recalcitrant landscape and its fugitive, resistant inhabitants. The third, from a different continent, is from a would-be conqueror of souls, in some despair at the irreligion and heterodoxy that the landscape appears to encourage:

> Making maps is hard, but mapping Guizhou province especially so. . . . The land in southern Guizhou has fragmented and confused boundaries. . . . A department or a county may be split into several subsections, in many instances separated by other departments or counties. . . . There are also regions of no man's land where the Miao live intermixed with the Chinese. . . .
>
> Southern Guizhou has a multitude of mountain peaks. They are jumbled together, without any plains or marshes to space them out, or rivers or water courses to put limits to them. They are vexingly numerous and ill-disciplined. . . . Very few people dwell among them, and generally the peaks do not have names. Their configurations are difficult to discern clearly, ridges and summits seeming to be the same. Those who give an account of the arterial pattern of the mountains are thus obliged to speak at length. In some cases, to describe a few kilometers of ramifications needs a pile of documentation, and dealing with the main line of a day's march takes a sequence of chapters.
>
> As to the confusion of the local patois, in the space of fifty kilometers a river may have fifty names and an encampment covering a kilometer and a half may have three designations. Such is the unreliability of the nomenclature.[1]

The hilly and jungly tracts were those in which the dacoits held out long-est. Such were [*sic*] the country between Minbu and Thayetmyo and the terai [swampy lowland belt] at the foot of the Shan Hills and the Arakan and Chin Hills. Here pursuit was impossible. The tracts are narrow and tortuous and ad-mirably suited for ambuscades. Except by the regular paths there were hardly any means of approach; the jungle malaria was fatal to our troops; a column could only penetrate the jungle and move on. The villages are small and far between; they are generally compact and surrounded by dense, impenetrable jungle. The paths were either just broad enough for a cart, or very narrow, and, where they led through the jungle were overhung with brambles and thorny creepers. A good deal of the dry grass is burned in March, but as soon as the rains recommence the whole once more becomes impassible.[2]

The surface has been minutely trenched by winding streams. So numerous are the creeks that the topographical map of a single representative county of 373 square miles indicated 339 named streams, that is, nine streams for each ten square miles. The valleys are for the most part "V"-shaped, with rarely more level space along the banks of a stream for a cabin and perhaps a garden patch. . . . The isolation occasioned by methods of travel so slow and difficult is in-tensified by several circumstances. For one thing, the routes are round-about. Travel is either down one branch along a creek and up another branch, or up a stream to a divide and down another stream on the further side of the ridge. This being the case, married women living within ten miles of their parents have passed a dozen years without going back to see them.[3]

Behind each lament lies a particular project of rule: Han rule under the Qing, British rule within the Empire, and finally, the rule of orthodox Protestant Christianity in Appalachia. All would style themselves, unself-consciously, as bearers of order, progress, enlightenment, and civilization. All wished to extend the advantages of administrative discipline, associated with the state or organized religion, to areas previously ungoverned.

How might we best understand the fraught dialectical relations between such projects of rule and their agents, on the one hand, and zones of relative autonomy and their inhabitants, on the other? This relationship is particu-larly salient in mainland Southeast Asia, where it demarcates the greatest social cleavage that shapes much of the region's history: that between hill peoples and valley peoples or between upstream (*hulu* in the Malay world) and downstream (*hilir*) peoples.[4] In tracing this dialectic with some care, I believe it also traces a path to a novel historical understanding of the global process of state formation in the valleys and the peopling of the hills.

The encounter between expansionary states and self-governing peoples is hardly confined to Southeast Asia. It is echoed in the cultural and administrative process of "internal colonialism" that characterizes the formation of most modern Western nation-states; in the imperial projects of the Romans, the Hapsburgs, the Ottomans, the Han, and the British; in the subjugation of indigenous peoples in "white-settler" colonies such as the United States, Canada, South Africa, Australia, and Algeria; in the dialectic between sedentary, town-dwelling Arabs and nomadic pastoralists that have characterized much of Middle Eastern history.[5] The precise shape of the encounters is, to be sure, unique to each case. Nevertheless, the ubiquity of the encounter between self-governing and state-governed peoples—variously styled as the raw and the cooked, the wild and the tamed, the hill/forest people and the valley/cleared-land people, upstream and downstream, the barbarian and the civilized, the backward and the modern, the free and the bound, the people without history and the people with history—provides us with many possibilities for comparative triangulation. We shall take advantage of these opportunities where we can.

A World of Peripheries

In the written record—that is to say, from the beginning of grain-based, agrarian civilizations—the encounter we are examining can fairly be said to preoccupy rulers. But if we stand back and widen the historical lens still further, seeing the encounter in human rather than state-civilization terms, it is astonishing how recent and rapid the encounter has been. *Homo sapiens sapiens* has been around for something like two hundred thousand years, and only about sixty thousand, at the outside, in Southeast Asia. There the region's first small concentrations of sedentary populations appear not earlier than the first millennium before the common era (CE) and represent a mere smudge in the historical landscape—localized, tenuous, and evanescent. Until shortly before the common era, the very last 1 percent of human history, the social landscape consisted of elementary, self-governing, kinship units that might, occasionally, cooperate in hunting, feasting, skirmishing, trading, and peacemaking. It did not contain anything one could call a state.[6] In other words, living in the absence of state structures has been the standard human condition.

The founding of agrarian states, then, was the contingent event that created a distinction, hence a dialectic, between a settled, state-governed population and a frontier penumbra of less governed or virtually autonomous peoples. Until at least the early nineteenth century, the difficulties of transportation, the state of military technology, and, above all, demographic realities placed sharp limits on the reach of even the most ambitious states. Operating in a population density of only 5.5 persons per square kilometer in 1600 (compared with roughly 35 for India and China), a ruler's subjects in Southeast Asia had relatively easy access to a vast, land-rich frontier.[7] That frontier operated as a rough and ready homeostatic device; the more a state pressed its subjects, the fewer subjects it had. The frontier underwrote popular freedom. Richard O'Connor captures this dialectic nicely: "Once states appeared, adaptive conditions changed yet again—at least for farmers. At that moment, mobility allowed farmers to escape the impositions of states and their wars. I call this tertiary dispersion. The other two revolutions—agriculture and complex society—were secure but the state's domination of its peasantry was not, and so we find a strategy of 'collecting people . . . and establishing villages.'"[8]

The Last Enclosure

Only the modern state, in both its colonial and its independent guises, has had the resources to realize a project of rule that was a mere glint in the eye of its precolonial ancestor: namely to bring nonstate spaces and people to heel. This project in its broadest sense represents the last great enclosure movement in Southeast Asia. It has been pursued—albeit clumsily and with setbacks—consistently for at least the past century. Governments, whether colonial or independent, communist or neoliberal, populist or authoritarian, have embraced it fully. The headlong pursuit of this end by regimes otherwise starkly different suggests that such projects of administrative, economic, and cultural standardization are hard-wired into the architecture of the modern state itself.

Seen from the state center, this enclosure movement is, in part, an effort to integrate and monetize the people, lands, and resources of the periphery so that they become, to use the French term, *rentable*—auditable contributors to the gross national product and to foreign exchange. In truth, peripheral peoples had always been firmly linked economically to the lowlands and to world trade. In some cases, they appear to have provided most of the products valued in international commerce. Nevertheless, the attempt to fully incorporate them has been culturally styled as development, economic progress, literacy, and social integration. In practice, it has meant something else. The objective has been less to make them productive than to ensure that their economic activity was legible, taxable, assessable, and confiscatable or, failing that, to replace it with forms of production that were. Everywhere they could, states have obliged mobile, swidden cultivators to settle in permanent villages. They have tried to replace open common-property land tenure with closed common property: collective farms or, more especially, the individual freehold property of liberal economies. They have seized timber and mineral resources for the national patrimony. They have encouraged, whenever possible, cash, monocropping, plantation-style agriculture in place of the more biodiverse forms of cultivation that prevailed earlier. The term *enclosure* seems entirely appropriate for this process, mimicking as it does the English enclosures that, in the century after 1761, swallowed half of England's common arable land in favor of large-scale, private, commercial production.

The novel and revolutionary aspect of this great enclosure movement is apparent if we open our historical lens to its widest aperture. The very earliest states in China and Egypt—and later, Chandra-Gupta India, classical Greece, and republican Rome—were, in demographic terms, insignificant. They occupied a minuscule portion of the world's landscape, and their subjects were no more than a rounding error in the world's population figures. In mainland Southeast Asia, where the first states appear only around the middle of the first millennium of the common era, their mark on the landscape and its peoples is relatively trivial when compared with their oversized place in the history books. Small, moated, and walled centers together with their tributary villages, these little nodes of hierarchy and power were both unstable and geographically confined. To an eye not yet hypnotized by archeological remains and state-centric histories, the landscape would have seemed virtually all periphery and no centers. Nearly all the population and territory were outside their ambit.

Diminutive though these state centers were, they possessed a singular strategic and military advantage in their capacity to concentrate manpower and foodstuffs in one place. Irrigated rice agriculture on permanent fields was the key.[9] As a new political form, the padi state was an ingathering of previously stateless peoples. Some subjects were no doubt attracted to the possibilities for trade, wealth, and status available at the court centers, while others, almost certainly the majority, were captives and slaves seized in warfare or purchased from slave-raiders. The vast "barbarian" periphery of these small states was a vital resource in at least two respects. First, it was the source of hundreds of important trade goods and forest products necessary to the prosperity of the padi state. And second, it was the source of the most important trade good in circulation: the human captives who formed the working capital of any successful state. What we know of the classical states such as Egypt, Greece, and Rome, as well as the early Khmer, Thai, and Burmese states, suggests that most of their subjects were formally unfree: slaves, captives, and their descendants.

The enormous ungoverned periphery surrounding these minute states also represented a challenge and a threat. It was home to fugitive, mobile populations whose modes of subsistence—foraging, hunting, shifting cultivation, fishing, and pastoralism—were fundamentally intractable to state appropriation. The very diversity, fluidity, and mobility of their livelihoods meant that for an agrarian state adapted to sedentary agriculture, this ungoverned landscape and its people were fiscally sterile. Unless they wished to trade, their production was inaccessible for yet another reason. Whereas the early states were nearly everywhere the creature of arable plains and plateaus, much of the more numerous ungoverned population lived, from a state perspective, in geographically difficult terrain: mountains, marshland, swamps, arid steppes, and deserts. Even if, as was rarely the case, their products were in principle appropriable, they were effectively out of range owing to dispersal and the difficulties of transportation. The two zones were ecologically complementary and therefore natural trading partners, but such trade could rarely be coerced; it took the form of voluntary exchange.

For early state elites, the periphery—seen frequently as the realm of "barbarian tribes"—was also a potential threat. Rarely—but memorably, in the case of the Mongols and the Huns and Osman and his conquering band— a militarized pastoral people might overrun the state and destroy it or rule in its place. More commonly, nonstate peoples found it convenient to raid the settlements of sedentary farming communities subject to the state, sometimes exacting systematic tribute from them in the manner of states. Just as states encouraged sedentary agriculture for its "easy pickings," so, too, did raiders find it attractive as a site of appropriation.

The main, long-run threat of the ungoverned periphery, however, was that it represented a constant temptation, a constant alternative to life within the state. Founders of a new state often seized arable land from its previous occupants, who might then either be incorporated or choose to move away. Those who fled became, one might say, the first refugees from state power, joining others outside the state's reach. When and if the state's reach expanded, still others faced the same dilemma.

At a time when the state seems pervasive and inescapable, it is easy to forget that for much of history, living within or outside the state—or in an intermediate zone—was a choice, one that might be revised as the circumstances warranted. A wealthy and peaceful state center might attract a growing population that found its advantages rewarding. This, of course, fits the standard civilizational narrative of rude barbarians mesmerized by the prosperity made possible by the king's peace and justice—a narrative shared by most of the world's salvational religions, not to mention Thomas Hobbes.

This narrative ignores two capital facts. First, as we have noted, it appears that much, if not most, of the population of the early states was unfree; they were subjects under duress. The second fact, most inconvenient for the standard narrative of civilization, is that it was very common for state subjects to run away. Living within the state meant, virtually by definition, taxes, conscription, corvée labor, and, for most, a condition of servitude; these conditions were at the core of the state's strategic and military advantages. When these burdens became overwhelming, subjects moved with alacrity to the periphery or to another state. Under premodern conditions, the crowding of population, domesticated animals, and the heavy reliance on a single grain had consequences for both human and crop health that made famines and epidemics more likely. And finally, the early states were warmaking machines as well, producing hemorrhages of subjects fleeing conscription, invasion, and plunder. Thus the early state extruded populations as readily as it absorbed them, and when, as was often the case, it collapsed altogether as the result of war, drought, epidemic, or civil strife over succession, its populations were disgorged. States were, by no means, a once-and-for-all creation. Innumerable archeological finds of state centers that briefly flourished and were then eclipsed by warfare, epidemics, famine, or ecological collapse depict a long history of state formation and collapse rather than permanence. For long periods people moved in and out of states, and "stateness" was, itself, often cyclical and reversible.[10]

This pattern of state-making and state-unmaking produced, over time, a periphery that was composed as much of refugees as of peoples who had never been state subjects. Much of the periphery of states became a zone of refuge or "shatter zone," where the human shards of state formation and rivalry accumulated willy nilly, creating regions of bewildering ethnic and linguistic complexity. State expansion and collapse often had a ratchet effect as well, with fleeing subjects driving other peoples ahead of them seeking safety and new territory. Much of the Southeast Asian massif is, in effect, a shatter zone. The reputation of the southwestern Chinese province of Yunnan as a "museum of human races" reflects this history of migration. Shatter zones are found wherever the expansion of states, empires, slave-trading, and wars, as well as natural disasters, have driven large numbers of people to seek refuge in out-of-the-way places: in Amazonia, in highland Latin America (with the notable exception of the Andes, with their arable highland plateaus and states), in that corridor of highland Africa safe from slave-raiding, in the Balkans and the Caucasus. The diagnostic characteristics of shatter zones are their relative geographical inaccessibility and the enormous diversity of tongues and cultures.

Note that this account of the periphery is sharply at odds with the official story most civilizations tell about themselves. According to that tale, a backward, naïve, and perhaps barbaric people are gradually incorporated into an advanced, superior, and more prosperous society and culture. If, instead, many of these ungoverned barbarians had, at one time or another, elected, as a political choice, to take their distance from the state, a new element of political agency enters the picture. Many, perhaps most, inhabitants of the ungoverned margins are not remnants of an earlier social formation, left behind, or, as some lowland folk accounts in Southeast Asia have it, "our living ancestors." The situation of populations that have deliberately placed themselves at the state's periphery has occasionally been termed, infelicitously, secondary primitivism. Their subsistence routines, their social organization, their physical dispersal, and many elements of their culture, far from being the archaic traits of a people left behind, are purposefully crafted both to thwart incorporation into nearby states and to minimize the likelihood that statelike concentrations of power will arise among them. State evasion and state prevention permeate their practices and, often, their ideology as well. They are, in other words, a "state effect." They are "barbarians by design." They continue to conduct a brisk and mutually advantageous trade with lowland centers while steering clear of being politically captured.

Once we entertain the possibility that the "barbarians" are not just "there" as a residue but may well have chosen their location, their subsistence practices, and their social structure to maintain their autonomy, the standard civilizational story of social evolution collapses utterly. The temporal, civilizational series—from foraging to swiddening (or to pastoralism), to sedentary grain cultivation, to irrigated wet-rice farming—and its near-twin, the series from roving forest bands to small clearings, to hamlets, to villages, to towns, to court centers: these are the underpinning of the valley state's sense of superiority. What if the presumptive "stages" of these series were, in fact, an array of social options, each of which represented a distinctive positioning vis-à-vis the state? And what if, over considerable periods of time, many groups have moved strategically among these options toward more presumptively "primitive" forms in order to keep the state at arm's length? On this view, the civilizational discourse of the valley states—and not a few earlier theorists of social evolution—is not much more than a self-inflating way of confounding the status of state-subject with civilization and that of self-governing peoples with primitivism.

The logic of the argument made throughout this book would essentially reverse this logic. Most, if not all, the characteristics that appear to stigmatize hill peoples—their location at the margins, their physical mobility, their swidden agriculture, their flexible social structure, their religious heterodoxy, their egalitarianism, and even the nonliterate, oral cultures—far from being the mark of primitives left behind by civilization, are better seen on a long view as adaptations designed to evade both state capture and state formation. They are, in other words, political adaptations of nonstate peoples to a world of states that are, at once, attractive and threatening.

Creating Subjects

Avoiding the state was, until the past few centuries, a real option. A thousand years ago most people lived outside state structures, under loose-knit empires or in situations of fragmented sovereignty.[11] Today it is an option that is fast vanishing. To appreciate how the room for maneuver has been drastically curtailed in the past millennium, a radically schematic and simplified fast-forward history of the balance of power between stateless peoples and states may be helpful.

The permanent association of the state and sedentary agriculture is at the center of this story.[12] Fixed-field grain agriculture has been promoted by the state and has been, historically, the foundation of its power. In turn, sedentary agriculture leads to property rights in land, the patriarchal family enterprise, and an emphasis, also encouraged by the state, on large families. Grain farming is, in this respect, inherently expansionary, generating, when not checked by disease or famine, a surplus population, which is obliged to move and colonize new lands. By any long-run perspective, then, it is grain agriculture that is "nomadic" and aggressive, constantly reproducing copies of itself, while, as Hugh Brody aptly notes, foragers and hunters, relying on a single area and demographically far more stable, seem by comparison "profoundly settled."[13]

The massive expansion of European power, via colonialism and white-settler colonies, represented a vast expansion of sedentary agriculture. In the "neo-Europes" such as North America, Australia, Argentina, and New Zealand, Europeans reproduced, as far as possible, the agriculture with which they were familiar. In colonies with preexisting states based on sedentary agriculture, the Europeans replaced the indigenous overlords as sovereigns, collecting taxes and encouraging agriculture as had their predecessors, but more effectively. All other subsistence patterns, except when they provided valuable trade goods (for example, furs), were, fiscally speaking, considered sterile. Thus foragers, hunters, shifting-cultivators, and pastoralists were bypassed and ignored or driven from potentially arable farmland into territories considered wastelands. Nevertheless, as late as the end of the eighteenth century, though they were no longer a majority of the world's population, nonstate peoples still occupied the greater part of the world's land mass—forest lands, rugged mountains, steppes, deserts, polar regions, marshes, and inaccessibly remote zones. Such regions were still a potential refuge for those who had reason to flee the state.

These stateless peoples were not, by and large, easily drawn into the fiscally legible economy of wage labor and sedentary agriculture. On this definition, "civilization" held little attraction for them when they could have all the advantages of trade without the drudgery, subordination, and immobility of state subjects. The widespread resistance of stateless peoples led directly to what might be called the golden age of slavery along the littoral of the Atlantic and Indian Oceans and in Southeast Asia.[14] From the perspective adopted here, populations were forcibly removed en masse from settings where their production and labor were illegible and inappropriable and were relocated in colonies and plantations where they could be made to grow cash crops (tea, cotton, sugar, indigo, coffee) which might contribute to the profits of landowners and the fiscal power of the state.[15] This first step of enclosure required forms of capture and bondage designed to relocate them from nonstate spaces where they were generally more autonomous (and healthy!) to places where their labor could be appropriated.

The final two stages of this massive enclosure movement belong, in the case of Europe, to the nineteenth century and, in the case of Southeast Asia, largely to the late twentieth century. They mark such a radical shift in the relationship between states and their peripheries that they fall largely outside the story I tell here. In this last period, "enclosure" has meant not so much shifting people from stateless zones to areas of state control but rather colonizing the periphery itself and transforming it into a fully governed, fiscally fertile zone. Its immanent logic, unlikely ever to be fully realized, is the com-

plete elimination of nonstate spaces. This truly imperial project, made possible only by distance-demolishing technologies (all-weather roads, bridges,
railroads, airplanes, modern weapons, telegraph, telephone, and now modern
information technologies including global positioning systems), is so novel
and its dynamics so different that my analysis here makes no further sense in
Southeast Asia for the period after, say, 1950. Modern conceptions of national
sovereignty and the resource needs of mature capitalism have brought that
final enclosure into view.

The hegemony, in this past century, of the nation-state as the standard
and nearly exclusive unit of sovereignty has proven profoundly inimical to
nonstate peoples. State power, in this conception, is the state's monopoly of
coercive force that must, in principle, be fully projected to the very edge of its
territory, where it meets, again in principle, another sovereign power projecting its command to its own adjacent frontier. Gone, in principle, are the large
areas of no sovereignty or mutually canceling weak sovereignties. Gone too,
of course, are peoples under no particular sovereignty. As a practical matter,
most nation-states have tried, insofar as they had the means, to give substance
to this vision, establishing armed border posts, moving loyal populations to
the frontier and relocating or driving away "disloyal" populations, clearing
frontier lands for sedentary agriculture, building roads to the borders, and
registering hitherto fugitive peoples.

On the heels of this notion of sovereignty came the realization that
these neglected and seemingly useless territories to which stateless peoples
had been relegated were suddenly of great value to the economies of mature
capitalism.[16] They contained valuable resources—oil, iron ore, copper, lead,
timber, uranium, bauxite, the rare metals essential to the aerospace and
electronics industries, hydroelectric sites, bioprospecting and conservation
areas—that might in many cases be the linchpin of state revenue. Places that
long ago might have been desirable for their deposits of silver, gold, and gems,
not to mention slaves, became the object of a new gold rush. All the more
reason to project state power to the nethermost reaches of these ungoverned
regions and bring their inhabitants under firm control.

Occupying and controlling the margins of the state implied a cultural
policy as well. Much of the periphery along national borders of mainland
Southeast Asia is inhabited by peoples linguistically and culturally distinct
from the populations that dominate the state cores. Alarmingly, they spill
promiscuously across national frontiers, generating multiple identities and
possible foci of irredentism or secession. Weak valley states have permitted,
or rather tolerated, a certain degree of autonomy when they had little choice.

Where they could, however, all states in the region have tried to bring such peoples under their routine administration, to encourage and, more rarely, to insist upon linguistic, cultural, and religious alignment with the majority population at the state core. This meant, in Thailand, encouraging, say, the Lahu to become Thai-speaking, literate, Buddhist subjects of the monarchy. In Burma it meant encouraging, say, the Karen to become Burmese-speaking Buddhists loyal to the military junta.[17]

Parallel to policies of economic, administrative, and cultural absorption has been the policy, driven by both demographic pressure and self-conscious design, of engulfment. Huge numbers of land-hungry majorities from the plains have moved, or been moved, to the hills. There, they replicate valley settlement patterns and sedentary agriculture, and, over time, they demographically dominate the dispersed, less numerous hill peoples. The combination of forced settlement and engulfment is nicely illustrated by a series of Vietnamese mobilization campaigns in the 1950s and 1960s: "Campaign to Sedentarize the Nomads," "Campaign for Fixed Cultivation and Fixed Residence," "Storm the Hills Campaign," and "Clear the Hills by Torchlight Campaign."[18]

Culturally, this reduction and standardization of relatively autonomous, self-governing communities is a process of long historical lineage. It is an integral theme of the historical consciousness of each of the large mainland Southeast Asian states. In the Vietnamese official national narrative, the "march to the south" — to the Mekong and the trans-Bassac Deltas — inaccurate though it is as a description of the historical process, vies with the wars of national liberation for pride of place.[19] Burmese and Thai history are no less marked by the movement of population from their more northern historical cores of Mandalay, Ayutthaya, and what is now Hanoi into the Irrawaddy, Chao Praya, and Mekong river deltas, respectively. The great cosmopolitan, maritime cities of Saigon (now Ho Chi Minh City), Rangoon, and Bangkok that grew to serve this onetime frontier, delta, hinterland have come, demographically, to dominate the earlier inland capitals.

Internal colonialism, broadly understood, aptly describes this process. It involved the absorption, displacement, and/or extermination of the previous inhabitants. It involved a botanical colonization in which the landscape was transformed — by deforestation, drainage, irrigation, and levees — to accommodate crops, settlement patterns, and systems of administration familiar to the state and to the colonists. One way of appreciating the effect of this colonization is to view it as a massive reduction of vernaculars of all kinds: of vernacular languages, minority peoples, vernacular cultivation techniques, vernacular land tenure systems, vernacular hunting, gathering, and forestry techniques, vernacular religion, and so on. The attempt to bring the periphery into line is read by representatives of the sponsoring state as providing civilization and progress—where progress is, in turn, read as the intrusive propagation of the linguistic, agricultural, and religious practices of the dominant ethnic group: the Han, the Kinh, the Burman, the Thai.[20]

The remaining self-governing peoples and spaces of mainland Southeast Asia are much diminished. We shall, for the most part, concentrate on the so-called hill peoples (often mistakenly called tribes) of mainland Southeast Asia, particularly Burma. While I will clarify what I mean by the awkward term *nonstate spaces,* it is not simply a synonym for hills or for higher altitudes. States, being associated with concentrated grain production, typically arise where there is a substantial expanse of arable land. In mainland Southeast Asia, this agro-ecology is generally at low elevations, allowing us to speak of "valley states" and "hill peoples." Where, as in the Andes, most easily cultivable land under traditional conditions is located at high elevations, it is the other way around. The states were in the hills and nonstate spaces were downhill in the humid lowlands. Thus the key variable is not so much elevation per se as the possibility for concentrated grain production. *Nonstate space,* by contrast, points to locations where, owing largely to geographical obstacles, the state has particular difficulty in establishing and maintaining its authority. A Ming emperor had something like this in mind when he described the southwest provinces of his kingdom: "The roads are long and dangerous, the mountains and rivers present great obstacles, and the customs and practices differ."[21] But swamps, marshes, mangrove coasts, deserts, volcanic margins, and even the open sea, like the ever growing and changing deltas of Southeast Asia's great rivers, all function in much the same way. Thus it is difficult or inaccessible terrain, regardless of elevation, that presents great obstacles to state control. As we shall see at great length, such places have often served as havens of refuge for peoples resisting or fleeing the state.

The Great Mountain Kingdom; or, "Zomia"; or, The Marches of Mainland Southeast Asia

One of the largest remaining nonstate spaces in the world, if not *the* largest, is the vast expanse of uplands, variously termed the Southeast Asian *massif* and, more recently, Zomia.[22] This great mountain realm on the marches of mainland Southeast Asia, China, India, and Bangladesh sprawls across roughly 2.5 million square kilometers—an area roughly the size of Europe. As one of the first scholars to identify the massif and its peoples as a single object of study, Jean Michaud has traced its extent: "From north to south, it includes southern and western Sichuan, all of Guizhou and Yunnan, western and northern Guangxi, western Guangdong, most of northern Burma with an adjacent segment of extreme [north]eastern India, the north and west of Thailand, practically all of Laos above the Mekong Valley, northern and central Vietnam along the Annam Cordillera, and the north and eastern fringes of Cambodia."[23]

Rough calculations would put Zomia minority populations alone at around eighty million to one hundred million.[24] Its peoples are fragmented into hundreds of ethnic identities and at least five language families that defy any simple classification.

Lying at altitudes from two hundred or three hundred meters above sea level to more than four thousand meters, Zomia could be thought of as a Southeast Asian Appalachia, were it not for the fact that it sprawls across eight nation-states. A better analogy would be Switzerland, a mountain kingdom at the periphery of Germany, France, and Italy that itself became a nation-state. Borrowing Ernest Gellner's felicitous phrase referring to the Berbers of the High Atlas Mountains, this huge hilly zone might be seen as a "pervasive Switzerland without cuckoo clocks."[25] Far from being a hilly nation, however, this upland belt lies on the marches, far from the main population centers of the nations it traverses.[26] Zomia is marginal in almost every respect. It lies at a great distance from the main centers of economic activity; it bestrides a contact zone between eight nation-states and several religious traditions and cosmologies.[27]

Scholarship organized historically around the classical states and their cultural cores and, more recently, around the nation-state is singularly ill-equipped to examine this upland belt as a whole. Willem van Schendel is one of a handful of pioneers who have argued that these cumulative nation-state "shards" merit consideration as a distinctive region. He has gone so far as to give it the dignity of a name of its own: Zomia, a term for highlander common to several related Tibeto-Burman languages spoken in the India-Bangladesh-Burma border area.[28] More precisely, *Zo* is a relational term meaning "remote" and hence carries the connotation of living in the hills;

Map 1. Mainland Southeast Asia

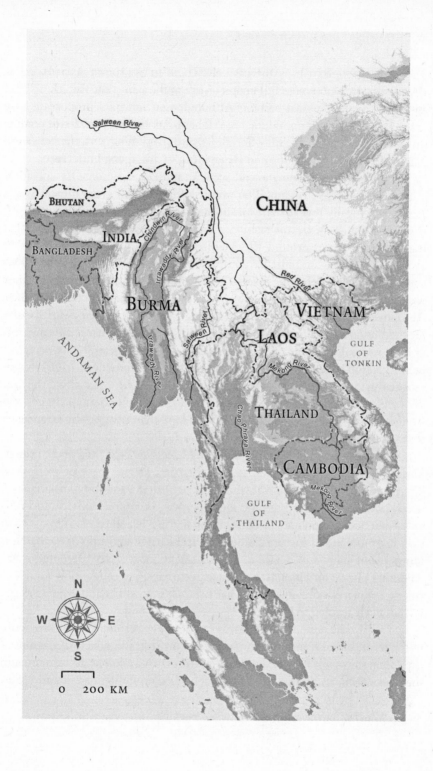

Mi means "people." As is the case elsewhere in Southeast Asia *Mi-zo* or *Zo-mi* designated a remote hill people, while at the same time the ethnic label applies to a geographical niche.[29] Although van Schendel proposes a bold expansion of Zomia's boundaries to Afghanistan and beyond, I will confine my use of the term to the hilly areas eastward, beginning with the Naga and Mizo hills in northern India and Bangladesh's Chittagong Hill Tracts.

Zomia, at first glance, would seem an unlikely candidate for consideration as a distinctive region. The premise for calling a geographical area a region is typically that it shares important cultural features that mark it off from adjacent areas. In this fashion, Fernand Braudel was able to show that the coastal societies around the Mediterranean Sea constituted a region, owing to their long and intense commercial and cultural connections.[30] Despite political and religious chasms between, say, Venice and Istanbul, they were integral parts of a recognizable world of exchange and mutual influence. Anthony Reid has made a similar, and in many respects, more powerful claim for the Sunda Shelf littoral in maritime Southeast Asia, where trade and migration were, if anything, easier than in the Mediterranean.[31] The principle behind region-making in each case is that, for the premodern world, water, especially if it is calm, joins people, whereas mountains, especially if they are high and rugged, divide people. As late as 1740 it took no more time to sail from Southampton to the Cape of Good Hope than to travel by stagecoach from London to Edinburgh.

On these grounds, hilly Zomia would seem to be a "negative" region. Variety, more than uniformity, is its trademark. In the space of a hundred kilometers in the hills one can find more cultural variation—in language, dress, settlement pattern, ethnic identification, economic activity, and religious practices—than one would ever find in the lowland river valleys. Zomia may not quite attain the prodigious cultural variety of deeply fissured New Guinea, but its complex ethnic and linguistic mosaic has presented a bewildering puzzle for ethnographers and historians, not to mention would-be rulers. Scholarly work on the area has been as fragmented and isolated as the terrain itself seemed to be.[32]

I will argue not only that Zomia qualifies as a region in the strong sense of the term, but also that it is impossible to provide a satisfactory account of the valley states without understanding the central role played by Zomia in their formation and collapse. The dialectic or coevolution of hill and valley,

---

Map 2. "Zomia," on the mainland Southeast Asian massif

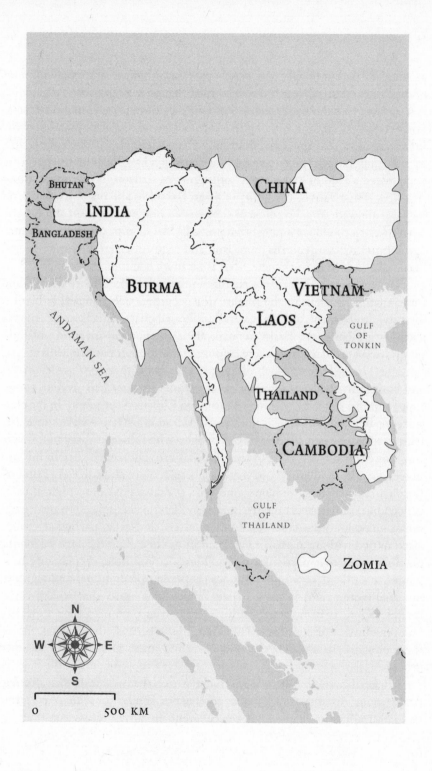

as antagonistic but deeply connected spaces, is, I believe, the essential point of departure for making sense of historical change in Southeast Asia.

Most of what the hills share as physical and social spaces marks them off fairly sharply from the more populous lowland centers. The population of the hills is far more dispersed and culturally diverse than that of the valleys. It is as if the difficulties of terrain and relative isolation have, over many centuries, encouraged a kind of "speciation" of languages, dialects, dress, and cultural practices. The relative availability of forest resources and open, if steep, land has also allowed far more diverse subsistence practices than in the valleys, where wet-rice monocropping often prevails. Swiddening (or slash-and-burn agriculture), which requires more land and requires clearing new fields and occasionally shifting settlement sites, is far more common in the hills.

As a general rule, social structure in the hills is both more flexible and more egalitarian than in the hierarchical, codified valley societies. Hybrid identities, movement, and the social fluidity that characterizes many frontier societies are common. Early colonial officials, taking an inventory of their new possessions in the hills, were confused to encounter hamlets with several "peoples" living side by side: hill people who spoke three or four languages and both individuals and groups whose ethnic identity had shifted, sometimes within a single generation. Aspiring to Linnaean specificity in the classification of peoples as well as flora, territorial administrators were constantly frustrated by the bewildering flux of peoples who refused to stay put. There was, however, one principle of location that brought some order to this apparent anarchy of identity, and that was its relation to altitude.[33] As Edmund Leach originally suggested, once one looks at Zomia not from a high-altitude balloon but, rather, horizontally, in terms of lateral slices through the topography, a certain order emerges.[34] In any given landscape, particular groups often settled within a narrow range of altitudes to exploit the agro-economic possibilities of that particular niche. Thus, for example, the Hmong have tended to settle at very high altitudes (between one thousand and eighteen hundred meters) and to plant maize, opium, and millet that will thrive at that elevation. If from a high-altitude balloon or on a map they appear to be a random scattering of small blotches, this is because they have occupied the mountaintops and left the midslopes and intervening valleys to other groups.

Specialization by altitude and niche within the hills leads to scattering. And yet long-distance travel, marriage alliances, similar subsistence patterns, and cultural continuity help foster coherent identities across considerable distances. The "Akha" along the Yunnan-Thai border and the "Hani" in the upper reaches of the Red River in northern Vietnam are recognizably the same culture, though separated by more than a thousand kilometers. They typically have more in common with each another than either group has with valley people a mere thirty or forty miles away. Zomia is thus knitted together as a region not by a political unity, which it utterly lacks, but by comparable patterns of diverse hill agriculture, dispersal and mobility, and rough egalitarianism, which, not incidentally, includes a relatively higher status for women than in the valleys.[35]

The signal, distinguishing trait of Zomia, vis-à-vis the lowland regions it borders, is that it is relatively stateless. Historically, of course, there have been states in the hills where a substantial fertile plateau and/or a key node in the overland trade routes made it possible. Nan Chao, Kengtung, Nan, and Lan-na were among the best known.[36] They are the exceptions that prove the rule. While state-making projects have abounded in the hills, it is fair to say that few have come to fruition. Those would-be kingdoms that did manage to defy the odds did so only for a relatively brief, crisis-strewn period.

Such episodes aside, the hills, unlike the valleys, have paid neither taxes to monarchs nor regular tithes to a permanent religious establishment. They have constituted a relatively free, stateless population of foragers and hill farmers. Zomia's situation at the frontiers of lowland state centers has contributed to its relative isolation and the autonomy that such isolation favors. Lying athwart state borders where multiple competing sovereignties abut one another has itself afforded its peoples certain advantages for smuggling, contraband, opium production, and the "small border powers" that negotiate a tenuous, high-wire act of quasi-independence.[37]

A stronger and, I believe, more accurate political description is that the hill populations of Zomia have actively resisted incorporation into the framework of the classical state, the colonial state, and the independent nation-state. Beyond merely taking advantage of their geographical isolation from centers of state power, much of Zomia has "resisted the projects of nation-building and state-making of the states to which it belonged."[38] This resistance came especially to light after the creation of independent states after World War II, when Zomia became the site of secessionist movements, indigenous rights struggles, millennial rebellions, regionalist agitation, and armed opposition to lowland states. But it is a resistance with deeper roots. In the precolonial period, the resistance can be seen in a cultural refusal of lowland patterns and in the flight of lowlanders seeking refuge in the hills.

During the colonial era, the autonomy of the hills, politically and culturally, was underwritten by the Europeans for whom a separately administered hill zone was a makeweight against the lowland majorities resentful of colonial rule. One effect of this classic divide-and-rule policy is that, with a few exceptions, hill peoples typically played little or no role—or an antagonistic one—in the anticolonial movements. They remained, at best, marginal to the nationalist narrative or, at worst, were seen as a fifth column threatening that independence. It is partly for such reasons that the postcolonial lowland states have sought fully to exercise authority in the hills: by military occupation, by campaigns against shifting cultivation, by forced settlements, by promoting the migration of lowlanders to the hills, by efforts at religious conversion, by space-conquering roads, bridges, and telephone lines, and by development schemes that project government administration and lowland cultural styles into the hills.

The hills, however, are not simply a space of political resistance but also a zone of cultural refusal. If it were merely a matter of political authority, one might expect the hill society to resemble valley society culturally except for their altitude and the dispersed settlement that the terrain favors. But the hill populations do not generally resemble the valley centers culturally, religiously, or linguistically. This cultural chasm between the mountains and the plains has been claimed as something of a historical constant in Europe as well, until quite recently. Fernand Braudel acknowledged the political autonomy of the hills when he approvingly quoted Baron de Tott to the effect that "the steepest places have always been the asylum of liberty." But he carried the argument much further, asserting the existence of an unbridgeable cultural gap between plains and mountains. He wrote: "The mountains are as a rule a world apart from civilizations which are an urban and lowland achievement. Their history is to have none, to remain always on the fringes of the great waves of civilization, even the longest and most persistent, which may spread over great distances in the horizontal plane but are powerless to move vertically when faced with an obstacle of several hundred meters."[39] Braudel was, in turn, only echoing a much older view captured by the great fourteenth-century Arab philosopher Ibn Khaldun, who noted that "Arabs can gain control only over flat territory" and do not pursue tribes that hide in the mountains.[40] Compare Braudel's bold assertion that civilizations can't climb hills to a nearly identical assertion made by Oliver Wolters, quoting Paul Wheatley, about precolonial Southeast Asia: "Many people lived in the distant highlands and were beyond the reach of the centers where records survive. The *mandalas* [court centers of civilization and power] were a phenomenon of the lowlands and even there, geographical conditions encouraged under-government. Paul Wheatley puts it well when he notes that 'the Sanskritic tongue was stilled to silence at 500 meters.'"[41]

Scholars of Southeast Asia have been struck again and again by the sharp limits the terrain, particularly altitude, has placed on cultural or political influence. Paul Mus, writing of Vietnam and echoing Wheatley, noted of the spread of the Vietnamese and their culture that "this ethnic adventure stopped at the foot of the high country's buttresses."[42] Owen Lattimore, best known for his studies of China's northern frontier, also remarked that Indian and Chinese civilizations, like those cited by Braudel, traveled well across the plains but ran out of breath when they encountered rugged hills: "This kind of stratification extends far beyond China itself into the Indochinese peninsula, Thailand and Burma with the influence of the ancient high civilizations reaching far out over the lower levels where concentrated agriculture and big cities are to be found, but not up into the higher altitudes."[43]

Though Zomia is exceptionally diverse linguistically, the languages spoken in the hills are, as a rule, distinct from those spoken in the plains. Kinship structures, at least formally, also distinguish the hills from the lowlands. This is in part what Edmund Leach had in mind when he characterized hill society as following a "Chinese model" while lowland society followed an "Indian" or Sanskritic model.[44]

Hill societies are, as a rule, systematically different from valley societies. Hill people tend to be animists, or, in the twentieth century, Christians, who do not follow the "great tradition" salvation religions of lowland peoples (Buddhism and Islam in particular). Where, as occasionally happens, they do come to embrace the "world religion" of their valley neighbors, they are likely to do so with a degree of heterodoxy and millenarian fervor that valley elites find more threatening than reassuring. Hill societies do produce a surplus, but they do not use that surplus to support kings and monks. The absence of large, permanent, surplus-absorbing religious and political establishments makes for a sociological pyramid in the hills that is rather flat and local when compared with that of valley societies. Distinctions of status and wealth abound in the hills, as in the valleys. The difference is that in the valleys they tend to be supralocal and enduring, while in the hills they are both unstable and geographically confined.

This characterization obscures a great deal of variation in the political

structure of hill societies. The variation is not by any means simply a function of "ethnicity," although some hill peoples, such as the Lahu, Khmu,
and Akha, seem strongly egalitarian and decentralized. It is just as common,
however, to encounter groups that defy such generalizations. Among Karen,
Kachin, Chin, Hmong, Yao/Mien, and Wa, for example, there seem to be
both relatively hierarchical subgroups and relatively decentralized, egalitarian subgroups. What is most striking and important is that the degree of
hierarchy and centralization is not constant over time. The variation, so far
as I can make out, depends largely on a kind of imitative state-making. That
is, it is either a kind of short-term war alliance or a sort of "booty-capitalism"
for slave-raiding and extracting tribute from lowland communities. Where
hill groups are in a tributary relationship with a valley kingdom—which does
not imply political incorporation or, necessarily, inferiority—it may be an
expedient to control a lucrative trade route or to safeguard privileged access
to valuable markets. Their political structures are, with extremely rare exceptions, imitative in the sense that while they may have the trappings and rhetoric of monarchy, they lack the substance: a taxpaying subject population or
direct control over their constituent units, let alone a standing army. Hill polities are, almost invariably, redistributive, competitive feasting systems held
together by the benefits they are able to disburse. When they occasionally
appear to be relatively centralized, they resemble what Barfield has called the
"shadow-empires" of nomadic pastoralists, a predatory periphery designed
to monopolize trading and raiding advantages at the edge of an empire. They
are also typically parasitic in the sense that when their host-empires collapse,
so do they.[45]

Zones of Refuge

There is strong evidence that Zomia is not simply a region of resistance to
valley states, but a region of refuge as well.[46] By "refuge," I mean to imply
that much of the population in the hills has, for more than a millennium and
a half, come there to evade the manifold afflictions of state-making projects
in the valleys. Far from being "left behind" by the progress of civilization in
the valleys, they have, over long periods of time, chosen to place themselves
out of the reach of the state. Jean Michaud notes, in this connection, that
what he calls nomadism in the hills can be "an escape or survival strategy"
and sees the unprecedented series of massive rebellions in the latter half of
the nineteenth century in central and southwest China as having pushed the

millions of refugees streaming south into the more remote highlands. He is sympathetic to the view adopted here that Zomia is best seen historically as a region of refuge from states, most especially the Han state. "It is probably fair to say," he concludes, "that the highland populations who migrated from China to the . . . highlands over the past five centuries were, at least in part, pushed from their homelands by aggression from more powerful neighbors, including especially Han expansion."[47]

Detailed and unambiguous documentary evidence of the conflicts generated by Han expansion and the migratory flights it provoked is abundant from the early Ming Dynasty (1368) onward, becoming even more abundant under the Qing. Earlier documentation is harder to come by and more ambiguous, owing to the great fluidity of ethnic and political labels. The general pattern, however, seems to be as follows: as the reach of the Chinese state grew, peoples at the point of expansion were either absorbed (becoming, in time, Han) or moved away, often after a failed revolt. Those who left became, at least for a time, distinct societies that could be said to have "self-marginalized" by migration.[48] As the process was repeated again and again, culturally complex zones of refuge sprang up in the hinterlands of the state. "The history of the various non-state peoples of this region" can, Fiskesjö believes, be written as the bifurcation between those who had long been in the hills (for example, the Wa people) and those who sought refuge there: "Among those who left [the zone of Chinese state power], we find many Tibeto-Burman ethnolinguistic formations (Lahu, Hani, Akha, etc.) as well as Miao or Hmong speakers, and other peoples . . . described as 'hill tribes out of China' with a 'heritage of defeat' that has led many of them during the past few centuries, into the northern parts of the modern states of Thailand, Burma, Laos, and Vietnam where many of them are still regarded as newcomers."[49]

There, in regions beyond the states' immediate writ and, thus, at some remove from taxes, corvée labor, conscription, and the more than occasional epidemics and crop failures associated with population concentration and monocropping, such groups found relative freedom and safety. There, they practiced what I will call escape agriculture: forms of cultivation designed to thwart state appropriation. Even their social structure could fairly be called escape social structure inasmuch as it was designed to aid dispersal and autonomy and to ward off political subordination.

The tremendous linguistic and ethnic fluidity in the hills is itself a crucial social resource for adapting to changing constellations of power, inasmuch as it facilitates remarkable feats of identity shape-shifting. Zomians are not as a rule only linguistically and ethnically amphibious; they are, in their strong inclination to follow charismatic figures who arise among them, capable of nearly instantaneous social change, abandoning their fields and houses to join or form a new community at the behest of a trusted prophet. Their capacity to "turn on a dime" represents the ultimate in escape social structure. Illiteracy in the hills can, more speculatively, be interpreted in the same fashion. Virtually all hill peoples have legends claiming that they once had writing and either lost it or that it was stolen from them. Given the considerable advantages in plasticity of oral over written histories and genealogies, it is at least conceivable to see the loss of literacy and of written texts as a more or less deliberate adaptation to statelessness.

The argument, in short, is that the history of hill peoples is best understood as a history not of archaic remnants but of "runaways" from statemaking processes in the lowlands: a largely "maroon" society, providing that we take a very long historical view. Many of the agricultural and social practices of hill peoples can be best understood as techniques to make good this evasion, while maintaining the economic advantages of the lowland connection.

The concentration of people and production at a single location required some form of unfree labor when population was sparse, as it was in Southeast Asia. All Southeast Asian states were slaving states, without exception, some of them until well into the twentieth century. Wars in precolonial Southeast Asia were less about territory than about the seizure of as many captives as possible who were then resettled at the core of the winner's territory. They were not distinctive in this respect. After all, in Periclean Athens, the population of slaves outnumbered full citizens by five to one.

The effect of all state-making projects of this kind was to create a shatter zone or flight zone to which those wishing to evade or to escape bondage fled. These regions of refuge constituted a direct "state effect." Zomia simply happens to be, owing largely to the precocious early expansion of the Chinese state, one of the most extensive and oldest zones of refuge. Such regions are, however, inevitable by-products of coercive state-making and are found on every continent. A few of them will figure as comparative cases in what follows, but here I want to enumerate several examples to suggest how common they are.

The forced-labor characteristic of Spanish colonization in the New World provoked the widespread flight of native peoples out of range, often to hilly or arid places where they could live unmolested.[50] Such areas were marked by great linguistic and ethnic diversity and occasionally by a simplification of social structure and subsistence routines—foraging, shifting cultivation—to increase mobility. The process was repeated in the Spanish Philippines, where, it is claimed, the cordillera of northern Luzon was populated almost entirely by lowland Filipinos fleeing Malay slave raids and the Spanish *reducciones*.[51] As peoples adapted to hill ecology, a process of ethnogenesis followed, after which highland Filipinos were later misrepresented as the descendants of separate, prehistoric migrations to the island.

The Cossacks on Russia's many frontiers represent another striking example of the process. They were, at the outset, nothing more and nothing less than runaway serfs from all over European Russia who accumulated at the frontier.[52] They became, depending on their location, different Cossack "hosts": the Don (for the Don River basin) Cossacks, the Azov (Sea) Cossacks, and so on. There at the frontier, copying the horseback habits of their Tatar neighbors and sharing a common open-land pasture, they became "a people," later used by the tsars, the Ottomans, and the Poles as cavalry. The history of the Roma and Sinti (Gypsies) in late-seventeenth-century Europe provides a further striking example.[53] Along with other stigmatized itinerant peoples, they were subject to two forms of penal labor: galley slavery in the Mediterranean basin and, in the northeast, forced conscription as soldiers or military porters in Prussia-Brandenburg. As a result they accumulated in a narrow band of territory that came to be known as the "outlaw corridor," the one location between the catchment areas of these twin, mortal dangers.

Inasmuch as the captivity and bondage associated with early state-making generate, in their wake, flight and zones of refuge, slavery as a labor system produced many "Zomias" large and small. It is possible, in this context, to delineate an upland, remote zone of West Africa that was relatively safe from the five hundred–year–long worldwide slave-raiding and trade that caught tens of millions of in its toils.[54] This zone of refuge grew in population despite the difficulties of the terrain and the necessity for new subsistence routines. Many of those who failed to evade the slave raids in Africa, once transplanted to the New World, promptly escaped and created fugitive slave (maroon) settlements wherever slavery was practiced: the famous highland "cockpit" of Jamaica; Palmares in Brazil, a maroon community of some twenty thousand inhabitants; and Surinam, the largest maroon population in the hemisphere, are only three illustrations. Were we to include smaller scale "refugia" such as marshes, swamps, and deltas, the list would multiply many-fold. To mention only a few, the great marsh on the lower Euphrates (drained under Saddam Hussein's rule) was for two thousand years a refuge from state control. So, on a smaller scale, were the storied Great Dismal Swamp on the North Carolina–Virginia border, the Pripet Marshes in Poland, now on the Belarus-Ukraine border, and the Pontian Marshes near Rome (drained finally by Mussolini) known as zones of refuge from the state. The list of such refugia is at least as long as the list of coercive labor schemes that inevitably spawn them.

Hill societies in mainland Southeast Asia, then, for all their riotous heterogeneity, have certain characteristics in common, and most of these characteristics distinguish them sharply from their valley neighbors. They encode a pattern of historic flight and hence a position of opposition if not resistance. If it is this historical, structural relation that we hope to illuminate, then it makes no sense whatever to confine ourselves to a nation-state framework. For much of the period we wish to examine there was no nation-state and, when it did come into being late in the game, many hill people continued to conduct their cross-border lives as if the state didn't exist. The concept of "Zomia" marks an attempt to explore a new genre of "area" studies, in which the justification for designating the area has nothing to do with national boundaries (for example, Laos) or strategic conceptions (for example, Southeast Asia) but is rather based on certain ecological regularities and structural relationships that do not hesitate to cross national frontiers. If we have our way, the example of "Zomia studies" will inspire others to follow this experiment elsewhere and improve on it.

The Symbiotic History of Hills and Valleys

Histories of the classical lowland court-states, taken in isolation, risk being unintelligible or vastly misleading. Lowland states (mandala or modern) have always existed in symbiosis with hill society.[55] By *symbiosis,* I mean to invoke the biological metaphor of two organisms living together in more or less intimate association—in this case, social organisms. The term does not specify, nor do I wish to do so here, whether this mutual dependence is antagonistic, or even parasitic, or whether it is mutually beneficial, "synergistic."

It is not possible to write a coherent history of the hills that is not in constant dialogue with lowland centers; nor is it possible to write a coherent history of lowland centers that ignores its hilly periphery. By and large, most students of hill societies have been sensitive to this dialectic, stressing the deep history of symbolic, economic, and human traffic between the two societies. The same typically cannot be said of work—even the most distinguished—on lowland centers.[56] The pattern is hardly surprising. Treatment of lowland cultures and societies as self-contained entities (for example, "Thai civilization," "Chinese culture") replicates the unreflective structure of scholarship and, in doing so, adopts the hermetic view of culture that lowland elites themselves wish to project. The fact is that hill and valley societies have to be read against each other to make any sense. I attempt just such a reading here.

Writing an account of valley population centers without including the hills would be like writing a history of colonial New England and the Middle Atlantic States without considering the American frontier. It would be like writing a history of antebellum slavery in the United States while leaving out the freedmen and the lure of freedom in Canada. In each case, an external frontier conditioned, bounded, and in many respects constituted what was possible at the center. Accounts of lowland states that miss this dimension do not merely "leave out" the hills; they ignore a set of boundary conditions and exchanges that make the center what it is.

The constant movement back and forth between the valleys and the hills—its causes, its patterns, its consequences—will preoccupy us. Many valley people are, as it were, "ex–hill people," and many hill people are "ex–valley people." Nor did movement in one direction or the other preclude subsequent moves. Depending on the circumstances, groups have disengaged themselves from a state and then, later, sought to affiliate themselves (or been seized by!) the same or another state. A century or two later, they might again be found outside that state's grasp, perhaps because they had moved away or perhaps because the state in question had itself collapsed. Such shifts were often accompanied by a shift in ethnic identity, broadly understood. I will argue for a radically "constructionist" understanding of the so-called hill tribes of mainland Southeast Asia. They are best understood, at least as a first approximation, as a fugitive population that has come to the hills over the past two millennia. This flight was not only from the Burman, Tai, and Siamese states but also, and most especially, from the Han Empire during the expansionary phases of the Tang, Yuan, Ming, and Qing dynasties, when its forces and settlers pressed into southwest China. In the hills they might have moved several times subsequently, pressed by other, stronger fugitives or threatened by a new state expansion, or in search of new land and autonomy. Their location and many of their economic and cultural practices could again fairly be termed a state effect. This picture is radically at odds with older prevailing assumptions of a primeval population in the hills abandoned by those who moved downhill and developed civilizations.

By the same token, the valley centers of wet-rice cultivation may profitably be seen as constituting a hill effect in the following ways. The valley states are, of course, new structures historically speaking, dating back to roughly the middle of the first millennium CE. They were formed from an earlier ingathering of diverse peoples, some of whom may have adopted fixed-field agriculture, but who were, by definition, not previously part of an established state.[57] The very earliest mandala states were less engines of military conquest than cultural spaces available to all those who wished to conform to their religious, linguistic, and cultural formats, whatever their origin.[58] Perhaps because such identities were newly confected from many cultural shards, the resulting valley self-representations were at pains to distinguish their culture from populations outside the state. Thus if hill society could be termed a state effect, valley culture could be seen as a hill effect.

Most of the terms that we would translate as *crude, unrefined, barbaric,* and, in the Chinese case, *raw* refer directly to those who live in the hills and forests. "Forest dweller" or "hill person" is shorthand for "uncivilized." Thus, despite a centuries-old, brisk traffic in people, goods, and culture across the very permeable membrane between the hills and valleys, it is striking how stark and durable the cultural divide remains in lived experience. Valley and hill peoples generally have an essentialist understanding of the differences between them that appears to be at odds with the historical evidence over the long run.

How can we make sense of this paradox? Perhaps the first step is to emphasize that the relationship between valley states and hill society is not just symbiotic but also both contemporaneous and quasi-oppositional. In older understandings of hill "tribes," not to mention popular folklore today, they are considered to be the historical remnants of an earlier stage of human history: what we were like before we discovered wet-rice agriculture, learned to write, developed the arts of civilization, and adopted Buddhism. While this "just-so" story treats valley cultures as later, and higher, achievements of civilization, raised from the muck of tribalism, as it were, it grossly distorts the historical record. Valley states and hill peoples are, instead, constituted in each other's shadow, both reciprocal and contemporaneous. Hill societies have always been in touch with imperial states in the valleys directly or via maritime trade routes. Valley states, by the same token, have always been in touch with the nonstate periphery—what Deleuze and Guattari call "the local mechanisms of bands, margins, minorities, which continue to affirm the rights of segmentary societies in opposition to the organs of state power." Such states are, in fact, "inconceivable independent of that relationship."[59]

Precisely the same case has been made about the relationship between itinerant peoples—including pastoral nomads—and states. Thus Pierre Clastres argues persuasively that the so-called primitive Amerindian societies of South America were not ancient societies that had failed to invent settled agriculture or state forms but rather previously sedentary cultivators who abandoned agriculture and fixed villages in response to the effects of the Conquest: both disease-induced demographic collapse and colonial forced labor.[60] Their movement and subsistence techniques were designed to ward off incorporation into the state. On the steppes of Central Asia the most ancient nomads, Griaznov has shown, were former sedentary cultivators who similarly left cultivation behind for political and demographic reasons.[61] Lattimore reached the same conclusion, insisting that pastoral nomadism arose after farming and drew in sedentary cultivators at the edge of the grasslands who "had detached themselves from farming communities."[62] Far from being successive stages in social evolution, such states and nomadic peoples are twins, born more or less at the same time and joined in a sometimes rancorous but unavoidable embrace.

This pattern of paired symbiosis and opposition is a staple of Middle Eastern history and anthropology. In the Maghreb it takes the form of structural opposition between Arabs and Berbers. Ernest Gellner's classic *Saints of the Atlas* captures the dynamic I have in mind. Gellner, too, emphasized that the political autonomy and tribalism of the Berber population in the High Atlas is "not a tribalism 'prior to government' but a political and partial rejection of a particular government combined with some acceptance of a wider culture and its ethic."[63] Sharing elements of a larger culture and a faith in Islam, such tribal opposition is explicitly political and deliberately so. Until very recently, Gellner claims, Moroccan history could be written in terms of the opposition between the land of *makhazen* (the pale) and the land of *siba* (beyond the pale). *Siba* could be defined as "institutional dissidence," though it has sometimes been translated as "anarchy." In practice, *siba* means "ungoverned," a zone of political autonomy and independence, while *makhazen* means "governed," subordinated to the state. Political autonomy was, Gellner insists, a choice, not a given.

To those groups that have self-consciously elected to move or to stay beyond the pale, Gellner applies the term *marginal tribalism* to emphasize that their marginality is a political stance:

> Such tribesmen know the possibility . . . of being incorporated in a more cen-
> tralized state. . . . Indeed, they may have deliberately rejected and violently
> resisted the alternative. The tribes of the High Atlas are of this kind. Until the
> advent of the modern state, they were dissident and self-consciously so. . . .
> "Marginal" tribalism . . . [is] the type of tribal society which exists at the edge
> of non-tribal societies. It arises from the fact that the inconveniences of sub-
> mission make it attractive to withdraw from political authority and the balance
> of power, the nature of the mountainous or desert terrain make it feasible. Such
> tribalism is politically marginal. It knows what it rejects.

In the Maghreb, as in Zomia, the distinction between a zone of state rule and a marginal, autonomous zone was geographical and ecological as well as political. There is a "rough tie-up between high-ground, Berber speech and political dissidence," such that "gorges and mountains were a clear dividing line between the land of the government (*bled el-makhazen*) and the land of dissidence (*bled-es-siba*)."[64]

The Berber case is instructive for two reasons. First, Gellner makes it abundantly clear that the demarcation line between Arab and Berber is not, essentially, one of civilization, let alone religion. Instead, it is a political line distinguishing the subjects of a state from those outside its control. Assum-ing, as Gellner does, historical movement back and forth across this divide, what becomes intriguing is that a distinction in political status is ethnically coded as if it were a fundamental difference in kinds of people and not a po-litical choice. It means that all those who had reason to flee state power, for whatever reason, were, in a sense, tribalizing themselves. Ethnicity and tribe began, by definition, where sovereignty and taxes ended. The ethnic zone was feared and stigmatized by state rhetoric precisely because it was beyond its grasp and therefore an example of defiance and an ever-present temptation to those who might wish to evade the state.

Gellner's analysis of Berber-Arab relations is also noteworthy as a long overdue corrective to what might be called "the view from the valley" or "the view from the state center." On that view the "barbarian periphery" is a diminishing remnant, drawn sooner or later and at varying speeds into the light of Arab civilization. In Southeast Asia and the Maghreb this view gains credibility because, in the past century, the ungoverned periphery has increasingly been occupied by the modern nation-state. Up until then, however, the view from the valley—the idea of a luminous and magnetic center aligning and drawing in peripheral peoples like so many iron filings—is, at the very least, half wrong. Up until then a life outside the state was both more available and more attractive. Oscillation rather than one-way traffic was the rule. If the account elaborated here emphasizes state avoidance, it is not because that is the whole truth. Rather, it is the largely untold story that has unfortunately had no legitimate place in the hegemonic narrative of civilization, despite its historical importance.

This model of symbiosis and opposition, of political choice and geographical facilitation, is, roughly speaking, applicable to the historical relationship between hill peoples and valley states in mainland Southeast Asia. In Southeast Asia, as in the Maghreb, the distinction between the "governed" and the "ungoverned" is an apparent social fact, but it is even more firmly installed in linguistic usage and popular consciousness. Depending on the particular cultural context, the connotations of the pairs "cooked" and "raw," "tame" and "wild," "valley people" and "hill people" carry the same weight as *makhazen* and *siba*—that is to say, "governed" and "ungoverned.' The linkage between being civilized and being a subject of the state is so taken for granted that the terms *subject peoples* on the one hand or *self-governing peoples* on the other capture the essential difference.

The classical states of Southeast Asia were, as in the Middle East, ringed by relatively free communities: by nonstate spaces and peoples. Such autonomous peoples lived not only in the hills but also in the marshes, swamps, mangrove coasts, and labyrinthine waterways of estuarial regions. This marginal population represented, at one and the same time, an indispensable trading partner of valley kingdoms, a zone of refuge from state power, a zone of relative equality and physical mobility, a source of slaves and subjects for valley states, and an ecocultural identity that was nearly a mirror image of lowland identities. Thus, while our attention here is trained on the uplands of Zomia, we are, more generally, concerned with the relationship between state spaces and extrastate spaces. The focus on Zomia as a vast interstate massif, in particular, arises simply because of its importance as the most significant complex catchment zone for refugees from state-making projects in the valleys. The inhabitants of this zone have come, or remained, here largely because it lies beyond the reach of the state. Here, the geographical expression *Southeast Asia,* as conventionally understood as stopping at the borders of Southeast Asian nations, is again an impediment to our understanding. Over the past two millennia, Zomia has been peopled by countless migrations of populations from well beyond its borders—many of them onetime sedentary cultivators. They have fled west and southward from Han, and occasionally Tibetan, rule (the Tai, the Yao/Mien, the Hmong/Miao, the Lahu, and the Akha/Hani) or northward from Thai and Burman rule. Their geographic location is a political, cultural, and, often, military decision.

I argue further that hill peoples cannot be understood in isolation, say, as tribes, but only relationally and positionally vis-à-vis valley kingdoms. Ethnic distinctions and identity in the hills are not only quite variable over time but also usually encode a group's relative position vis-à-vis state authority. There are, I would hazard, hardly "tribes" at all, except in this limited relational sense of the word. The subsistence practices, the choice of crops to grow, are, by the same token, selected largely with an eye to how they facilitate or thwart state appropriation. Finally, as noted earlier, even the social structures and residence patterns in the hills may be usefully viewed as political choices vis-à-vis state power. Certain egalitarian social structures reflect, I believe, a Southeast Asian variant of Berber practice: "Divide that ye be not ruled."[65] Far from being sociological and cultural givens, lineage practices, genealogical reckoning, local leadership patterns, household structures, and perhaps even the degrees of literacy have been calibrated to prevent (and in rare cases to facilitate) incorporation in the state.[66] A bold case along these lines is subject to many qualifications and exceptions. I venture it, nevertheless, not simply to be provocative but because it seems so much more in keeping with the evidence than the older traditions of relatively self-contained hill tribes left behind by civilization and progress.

Toward an Anarchist History of Mainland Southeast Asia

What blocks a clear view of the peoples of mainland Southeast Asia for most of their history is the state: classical, colonial, and independent. While a state-centric view of, say, the past fifty years might be justified, it represents a gross distortion of earlier periods. The earlier the period, the greater the distortion. For most of its history, Southeast Asia has been marked by the relative absence even of valley states. Where they arose, they tended to be remarkably short-lived, comparatively weak outside a small and variable radius of the court center, and generally unable systematically to extract resources (including manpower) from a substantial population. Indeed, *interregna*, far from being uncommon, were more protracted than *regna*, and, before the colonial period, a welter of petty principalities allowed much of the population to shift their residences and loyalties to their advantage or to move to a zone of no sovereignty or of mutually canceling sovereignties.

Where and when they did exist, the states of mainland Southeast Asia lurched from solicitous measures designed to attract subjects to those designed to capture them and extract as much grain and labor as possible. Manpower was the key. Even in those cases where the bulk of the crown's revenue derived from trade, that revenue was ultimately dependent on the state's ability to mobilize the manpower to hold and defend an advantageous position along trade routes.[67] The state was tyrannical, but episodically so. Physical flight, the bedrock of popular freedom, was the principal check on state power. As we shall see in some detail, subjects who were sorely tried by conscription, forced labor, and taxes would typically move away to the hills or to a neighboring kingdom rather than revolt. Given the vagaries of war, succession struggles, crop failures, and monarchical delusions of grandeur, such crises of state-building were unpredictable but, sooner or later, inevitable.

Earlier debates over the writing of Southeast Asian history were about how the history of states should be written — not about whether states should have been the center of attention in the first place. Thus scholars criticized Georges Coedès's *Indianized States of Southeast Asia* for missing the purposeful importation and adaptation of Indian cosmology in the court centers of Southeast Asia.[68] To the distortions of Indian-centric histories were added, later, Eurocentric colonial histories in which the local societies were observed from "the deck of a ship, the ramparts of the fortress, the high gallery of the trading house."[69] The call was subsequently issued for an "autonomous" history of Southeast Asia that might avoid both distortions.[70] And yet until very recently indeed, virtually all the responses to that call have themselves been histories, however learned and original, of the Southeast Asian *state*.

Why this should be so, why the histories of states should have so persistently insinuated themselves in the place that might have been occupied by a history of *peoples*, merits reflection. The reason, in a nutshell, I believe, is that state centers, even the tenuous and evanescent Indic-style classical states, are the political units that leave the most concentrated volume of physical evidence. The same is the case for sedentary agricultural settlements, characteristic of state centers. While they are not necessarily any more complex than foraging or swiddening societies, they are far denser — in the case of irrigated rice, one hundred times denser — than foraging societies, and hence they leave far more concentrated rubble in the form of middens, artifacts, building materials, and architectural ruins.[71] The larger the pile of rubble you leave behind, the larger your place in the historical record! The more dispersed, mobile, egalitarian societies regardless of their sophistication and trading networks, and despite being often more populous, are relatively invisible in the historical record because they spread their debris more widely.[72]

The same logic applies with a vengeance once it comes to the written record. Much of what we know about the classical states of Southeast Asia comes from the stone inscriptions and, later, paper trails they left behind in the form of land grants, memorials, tax and corvée records, religious donations, and court chronicles.[73] The thicker the paper trail you leave behind, the larger your place in the historical record. With the written record, the distortions also multiply. The traditional words in Burmese and Thai for history, *yazawin* and *phonesavadan*, respectively, both literally mean "the history of rulers" or "chronicle of kings." It becomes difficult, in this context, to reconstruct the life-world of nonelites, even if they are located at the court center. They typically appear in the record as statistical abstractions: so many laborers, so many conscripts, taxpayers, padi planters, so many bearers of tribute. Rarely do they appear as historical actors, and when they do, as in the case of a suppressed revolt, you can be sure that something has gone terribly wrong. The job of peasants, you might say, is to stay out of the archives.

Hegemonic histories centered on courts and capital cities introduce other distortions as well. They are, forcibly, histories of "state spaces"; they neglect or ignore altogether both "nonstate spaces" beyond their reach and the long periods of dynastic decline or collapse when there is hardly a state at all. In a truly evenhanded, year-by-year, chronology of precolonial, mainland Southeast Asian states, most of the pages would be blank. Are we to pretend, along with the official chronicles, that because there was no dynasty in control, there was no history? Beyond the problem of blank pages, however, the nature of the official histories of the court center systematically exaggerates the power, the coherence, and the majesty of the dynasty.[74] The court documents that survive are largely tax and land records on the one hand and hymns of praise, assertions of power, and claims to legitimacy on the other; the latter are meant to persuade and to amplify power, not to report facts.[75] If we take the cosmological bluster emanating from the court centers as indicative of facts on the ground, we risk, as Richard O'Connor has noted, "impos[ing] the imperial imaginings of a few great courts on the rest of the region."[76]

The independent nations of mainland Southeast Asia add a new layer of historical mystification. As the successor states, ethnically and geographically, to the classical kingdoms, they have their own interest in embellishing the glory, continuity, and beneficence of their ancestors. Furthermore, the histories of the classical states have been mined and distorted in the interest of identifying a protonation and a protonationalism that could be of use against contemporary enemies, both foreign and domestic. Thus early artifacts such as Dong Son drums (large bronze ceremonial objects dating from roughly 500 BCE to the beginning of the common era and found throughout highland Southeast Asia and southern China) or local uprisings have been appropriated as national and/or ethnic achievements when, at the time, such identities made no sense at all. The result is an historical fable that projects the nation and its dominant people backward, obscuring discontinuity, contingency, and fluid identities.[77] Such accounts serve, as Walter Benjamin reminded us, to naturalize the progression and necessity of the state in general and the nation-state in particular.[78]

The inadequacies of mandala, dynastic, capital-city, text-based histories are so manifest, even when read skeptically, that they are chiefly useful as self-interested descriptions and cosmological claims. During the greater part of the historical record, and especially in the uplands, there was no state or "hardly-a-state." What states there were tended to be personal creations that were tenuous and fragmented, and that seldom outlasted their founder by long. Their cosmological claims and ideological reach were far greater than their practical control over human labor and grain.[79]

Here it is crucial to distinguish the "hard" power of the state from its economic and symbolic influence, which was far wider. The precolonial state, when it came to extracting grain and labor from subject populations, could project its power only within a fairly small radius of the court, say, three hundred kilometers, and that undependably and only during the dry season. The economic reach of the precolonial state, on the other hand, was far wider but based on voluntary exchange. The higher the value and smaller the weight and volume of the commodity (think silk and precious gems as opposed to charcoal or grain), the greater the reach. The symbolic reach of the state—its regalia, titles, costumes, its cosmology—traveled far and wide as ideas that have left a deep impression in the hills, even as they were often deployed in revolts against valley kingdoms. While the valley kingdom's hard power was a minute fraction of its expansive imperial imaginings, its reach as a market of physical or, especially, symbolic commodities was far greater.

What if we replaced these "imperial imaginings" with a view of Southeast Asian history as dominated by long periods of normative and normalized statelessness, punctuated by occasional, and usually brief, dynastic states that, when they dissolved, left in their wake a new deposit of imperial imaginings? In a critique of overly state-centric histories, Anthony Day points us in just this direction: "What would the history of Southeast Asia look like, however, if we were to take the turbulent relations between families as normative rather than a departure from the norm of the absolutist state which must 'deal with disorder'?"[80]

The Elementary Units of Political Order

Abandoning the tunnel vision of the court-state view, as urged by Day and O'Connor and actually pursued some considerable distance by Keith Taylor, we attempt an account of the elementary units of political order in mainland Southeast Asia.[81] I emphasize the term *political order* to avoid conveying the mistaken impression that outside the realm of the state lay mere disorder. Depending on the location and date, such units might range from nuclear families to segmentary lineages, bilateral kindreds, hamlets, larger villages, towns and their immediate hinterlands, and confederations of such towns. Confederations appear to constitute the most complex level of integration that had any stability at all. They consisted of small towns located on terrain favorable to wet-rice cultivation, with its concentration of population, together with an allied population in the adjacent hills. Alliances of such "wet-rice archipelagoes" were common, although they too were short-lived and their constituent members rarely surrendered their freedom of action. Traces of these patterns survive in place names throughout the entire region: Xishuang Banna ("twelve village rice fields") in Yunnan, Sipsong Chutai ("twelve Tai lords") along the Vietnamese-Laotian border and Negri Sembilan ("nine realms") in western Malaysia, and Ko Myo ("nine towns") in Burma's Shan states. In this respect, the largest quasi-permanent building blocks in the region were the Malay *negeri/Negara*, the Tai *muang*, and the Burmese *main* (မိုင်း), each of which represented a potential fund of manpower and grain, located, in the most favorable cases, athwart a valuable trade route.

Assembling such potential nodes of power into a political and military alliance was itself a small, and usually evanescent, miracle of statecraft. Bringing many such units together under central rule was exceptionally rare and normally short-lived. When the political confection it represented disintegrated, it tended to fragment into its constituent units: the petty statelets, small villages, hamlets, and lineages. New agglomerations might arise, orchestrated by a new and ambitious political entrepreneur, but they were always a contingent alliance of the same elementary units. The symbolic and ideological format for state-making was known and observed by ambitious local leaders with even the slightest pretense to wider power. State mimicry — what I have called cosmological bluster — was copied from the Chinese or Indic high forms, with rudimentary materials and in miniature, right down to the most petty village chiefs.

If larger political units were radically unstable, the elementary units themselves were hardly timeless blocks of building material. We must see these units themselves as in almost constant motion: dissolving, splitting, relocating, merging, and reconstituting. The households and individuals within a hamlet or lineage were themselves in motion over time. A settlement might remain in place over, say, half a century, but because of residents coming and leaving, their linguistic and ethnic identification might shift dramatically.[82] Here demography played a central role, the population density in Southeast Asia being, in 1600, one-sixth that of India and one-seventh that of China. The existence of an open frontier operated like an automatic brake on what the state could extract. Motivated by factors as disparate as epidemics, famines, taxes, corvée labor, conscription, factional conflict, religious schism, shame, scandal, and the desire to change one's luck, it was relatively simple for households and entire villages to move. Thus, over time, the membership of any elementary unit was in flux, as was the very existence of the unit itself. If there was an element of stability here, it resided in the ecology and geography of places favorable to human settlements. A well-watered plain situated on a navigable river or a trade route might occasionally be abandoned, but it was just as likely to be reinhabited when conditions permitted. Such locations were, of course, the typical cores of the negeri, the muang, the main.

Fluid as they were, these elementary units were the only building blocks available to the would-be state-maker. In the absence of an ambitious strongman, or when the wider polity inevitably shattered, the "remains" were once again the elementary units. Is an intelligible history possible under such circumstances? I believe that it is, although it is surely not a dynastic history. The units in question do have a history, do observe a rough logic in formation, combination, and dissolution, and do exhibit a certain autonomy vis-à-vis dynastic or modern states. They have a history, but that history is on a different plane from state or dynastic history. For all their fluidity, they are the relatively constant features of the landscape, while the successful dynastic state is rare and ephemeral. The contingency of the "state" invites us to treat it less as a unity than as a "complex web of contractual mutualities."[83] For when it does splinter, as Akin Rabibhadana observed about the early nineteenth-century Siamese state, "the component parts of the system tended to split off in order to save their own lives."[84]

Making sense of innumerable small units, seemingly in constant move-ment, might seem impossible. It is surely more daunting than dynastic his-tory, but we are not without guidance from those who have sought to under-stand comparable systems. In the case of Southeast Asia, there are many studies of social structure that seek to grasp the logic behind the fluidity. First, most famous, and most controversial among them is Edmund Leach's *Political Systems of Highland Burma.* Subsequent work along these lines in the highlands, not to mention studies of the Malay world, where shifting petty states, a mobile population, and a distinction between upstream and downstream, unruled and ruled populations also is at work, is richly sugges-tive. Beyond Southeast Asia, however, we may look again to the encounter between states and nomadic, stateless populations in the Middle East. The case for beginning with the elementary unit of the household and treating villages, tribes, and confederations as provisional and shaky alliances has also been used to brilliant effect for eighteenth-century North American society in the Great Lakes region by Richard White.[85] And, finally, we may profita-bly look back to Thucydides' *Peloponnesian War,* which describes a world of peoples, some with kings, some without, whose fickle loyalties and unreliable cohesion is a source of constant anxiety to the statesmen of each of the major antagonists: Athens, Sparta, Corinth, and Syracuse—each of them, in turn, a confederation.[86]

One challenge for a non-state-centric history of mainland Southeast Asia consists in specifying the conditions for the aggregation and disaggre-gation of its elementary units. The problem has been succinctly put by one observer of a somewhat comparable flux between states and their autonomous hinterlands: "There comes a time when one realizes that one is dealing, really, with molecules which sometimes unify in the form of a vague confederation, sometimes, just as easily, disaggregate. Even their names offer no consistency or certainty."[87] If the fluidity of the molecules themselves is an inconvenience for anthropologists and historians, imagine the problem it poses for the dy-nastic official or would-be state-builder, the colonial official, and the modern state functionary. State rulers find it well nigh impossible to install an effec-tive sovereignty over people who are constantly in motion, who have no per-manent pattern of organization, no permanent address, whose leadership is ephemeral, whose subsistence patterns are pliable and fugitive, who have few permanent allegiances, and who are liable, over time, to shift their linguistic practices and their ethnic identity.

And this is just the point! The economic, political, and cultural organization of such people is, in large part, a strategic adaptation to avoid incorporation in state structures. These adaptations are all the more feasible in the mountainous hinterlands of state systems: that is to say, in places like Zomia.

> Here [Sumatra] I am the advocate of despotism. The strong arm of power is necessary to bring men together, and to concentrate them into societies. . . . Sumatra is, in great measure, peopled by innumerable petty tribes, subject to no general government. . . . At present people are as wandering in their habits as the birds of the air, and until they are congregated and organized under something like authority, nothing can be done with them.[88]

In the early nineteenth century, as in the classical mainland states, Sir Stamford Raffles, quoted above, understood that the precondition of colonial rule was the concentration of population and sedentary agriculture. He required a nonfugitive people whose labor and production were legible and hence appropriable by the state. We turn our attention next, then, to an understanding of the logic and dynamics behind the creation of state spaces in mainland Southeast Asia.

CHAPTER 2

State Space
Zones of Governance and Appropriation

The Geography of State Space and the Friction of Terrain

Put vegetables in the basket.
Put people in the *muang*.
— Thai proverb

I magine, for a moment, that you are a Southeast Asian counterpart of Jean-Baptiste Colbert, chief minister to Louis XIV. You, like Colbert, are charged with designing the prosperity of the kingdom. The setting, like that of the seventeenth century, is premodern: overland travel is by foot, cart, and draft animals, while water transportation is by sail. Let us finally imagine that, unlike Colbert, you begin with a blank slate. You are free to conjure up an ecology, a demography, and a geography that would be most favorable to the state and its ruler. What, in those circumstances, would you design?

Your task, crudely put, is to devise an ideal "state space": that is to say, an ideal space of appropriation. Insofar as the state depends on taxes or rents in the largest possible sense of the term (foodstuffs, corvée labor, soldiers, tribute, tradable goods, specie), the question becomes: what arrangements are most likely to guarantee the ruler a substantial and reliable surplus of manpower and grain at least cost?

The principle of design must obviously hinge on the geographical concentration of the kingdom's subjects and the fields they cultivate within easy reach of the state core. Such concentration is all the more imperative in premodern settings where the economics of oxcart or horse-cart travel set sharp limits to the distance over which it makes sense to ship grain. A team of oxen, for example, will have eaten the equivalent of the cartload of grain they are pulling before they have traveled 250 kilometers over flat terrain. The logic, albeit with different limits, is captured in an ancient Han proverb: "Do not make a grain sale over a thousand *li*" — 415 kilometers.[1] The non-grain-producing elites, artisans, and specialists at the state's core must, then, be fed by cultivators who are relatively near. The concentration of manpower in the Southeast Asian context is, in turn, particularly imperative, and particularly difficult, given the historical low population-to-land ratio that favors demographic dispersal. Thus the kingdom's core and its ruler must be defended and maintained, as well as fed, by a labor supply that is assembled relatively close at hand.

From the perspective of our hypothetical Colbert, wet-rice (*padi*, *sawah*) cultivation provides the ultimate in state-space crops. Although wet-rice cultivation may offer a lower rate of return to labor than other subsistence techniques, its return per unit of land is superior to almost any other Old World crop. Wet rice thus maximizes the food supply within easy reach of the state core. The durability and relatively reliable yields of wet-rice cultivation would also recommend it to our Colbert. Inasmuch as most of the nutrients are brought to the field by the water from perennial streams or by the silt in the case of "flood-retreat agriculture," the same fields are likely to remain productive for long periods. Finally, and precisely because wet rice fosters concentrated, labor-intensive production, it requires a density of population that is, itself, a key resource for state-making.[2]

Virtually everywhere, wet rice, along with the other major grains, is the foundation of early state-making. Its appeal to a hypothetical Colbert does not end with the density of population and foodstuffs it makes possible. From a tax collector's perspective, grains have decisive advantages over, for example, root crops. Grain, after all, grows aboveground, and it typically and predictably all ripens at roughly the same time. The tax collector can survey the crop in the field as it ripens and can calculate in advance the probable yield. Most important of all, if the army and/or the tax collector arrive on the scene when the crop is ripe, they can confiscate as much of the crop as they wish.[3] Grain, then, as compared with root crops, is both legible to the state and relatively appropriable. Compared to other foodstuffs, grain is also relatively easy to transport, has a fairly high value per unit of weight and volume, and stores for relatively long periods with less spoilage, especially if it is left unhusked. Compare, for example, the relative value and perishability of a cartload of padi, on the one hand, and a cartload of, say, potatoes, cassava, mangoes, or green vegetables. If Colbert were called on to design, from scratch, an ideal state crop, he could hardly do much better than irrigated rice.[4]

No wonder, then, that virtually all of the premodern state cores in Southeast Asia are to be found in ecological settings that were favorable to irrigated rice cultivation. The more favorable and extensive the setting, the more likely a state of some size and durability would arise there. States, it should be emphasized, did not typically, at least until the colonial era, construct these expanses of padi fields, nor did they play the major role in their maintenance. All the evidence points to the piecemeal elaboration of padi lands by kinship units and hamlets that built and extended the small diversion dams, sluices, and channels required for water control. Such irrigation works often predated the creation of state cores and, just as frequently, survived the collapse of many a state that had taken temporary advantage of its concentrated manpower and food supply.[5] The state might batten itself onto a wet-rice core and even extend it, but rarely did the state create it. The relationship between states and wet-rice cultivation was one of elective affinity, not one of cause and effect.

The realpolitik behind this elective affinity is evident in the fact that "for European governors and Southeast Asian rulers alike, large settled populations supported by abundant amounts of food were seen as the key to authority and power."[6] Land grants in ninth- and tenth-century Java, for which we have inscriptional evidence, were made on the understanding that the recipients would clear the forest and convert shifting, swidden plots into permanent irrigated rice fields (sawah). The logic, as Jan Wisseman Christie notes, is that "*sawah* . . . had the effect of anchoring populations and increasing their visibility, and making the size of the crop relatively stable and easy to calculate."[7] No effort was spared, as we shall see in more detail, to attract and hold a population in the vicinity of the court and to require it to plant padi fields. Thus Burmese royal edicts of 1598 and 1643, respectively, ordered that each soldier remain in his habitual place of residence, near the court center, and required all palace guards not on duty to cultivate their fields.[8] The constant injunctions against moving or leaving the fields fallow are, if we read such edicts "against the grain," evidence that achieving these goals met with a good deal of resistance. When such goals were approximated, however, the result was an impressive "treasury" of manpower and grain at the monarch's disposal. Such seems to have been the case at Mataram, Java, in the mid-seventeenth century, when a Dutch envoy remarked on "the unbelievably great rice fields which are all around Mataram for a day's travel, and with them innumerable villages." The resources of manpower at the core were not only crucial for food production; they were militarily essential to the defense and expansion of the state against its rivals. The decisive advantage of agrarian states of this kind against their maritime competitors appears to have rested precisely on their numerical superiority in fielding soldiers.

The friction of terrain set up sharp, relatively inflexible limits to the effective reach of the traditional agrarian state. Such limits were essentially fixed, as noted earlier, by the difficulty of transporting bulk foodstuffs. Assuming level terrain and good roads, the effective state space would have become tenuous indeed beyond a radius of three hundred kilometers. In one sense, the difficulty of moving grain long distances, compared with the relative ease of human pedestrian travel, captures the essential dilemma of Southeast Asian statecraft before the late nineteenth century. Provisioning the state's core population with grain ran up against the intractable limits of distance and harvest fluctuations, while the population sequestered to plant that grain found it all too easy to walk beyond the reach of state control. Put another way, the friction and inefficiencies of the oxcart worked to constrict the food supply available to the state core, whereas the relatively frictionless movement of its subjects by foot—a movement the premodern state could not easily prevent—threatened to deprive it of grain growers and defenders.[9]

The stark statistical facts of premodern travel and transportation make the friction-of-distance comparisons between water and land abundantly clear. As a rule of thumb, most estimates of travel by foot, assuming an obligingly flat, dry terrain, converge around an average of twenty-four kilometers (fifteen miles) a day. A strong porter carrying a thirty-six-kilogram (eighty-pound) load might move nearly as far under very favorable conditions. Once the terrain becomes more rugged or the weather more challenging (or both), however, this optimistic figure is dramatically reduced. The calculus is slightly modified in premodern Southeast Asia, and particularly in warfare, by the use of elephants, which could carry baggage and negotiate difficult terrain, but their numbers were modest and no military campaign depended essentially on them.[10]

What might be called state travel through difficult hilly terrain was considerably slower. One of the rare surviving documents (860 CE) from the Tang dynasty's expansion into the mountainous areas of mainland Southeast Asia begins with the critical military information about travel times, expressed in day-stages, between population centers that were nodes of imperial control.[11] A millennium later, the same preoccupation is apparent. A representative example is the trip made by Lieutenant C. Ainslie in January (the dry season) 1892 through the eastern Shan states to assess the political loyalties of the chiefs and to survey routes of march. He was accompanied by one hundred military policemen, five Europeans, and a large number of pack mules, together with their drivers. He used no wheeled transport, presumably because the tracks were too narrow. Ainslie prospected two parallel routes between Pan Yang and Mon Pan, a nine-day trip. He reported on the difficulty of each day's stage and the number of rivers and streams that had to be crossed, noting in passing that the route was "impassible in the rains."[12] The daily average distance covered was barely more than thirteen kilometers (eight miles), with considerable daily variation: a maximum of less than twenty kilometers and a minimum of barely seven.

A bullock cart can, of course, carry anywhere from seven to ten times (240–360 kilograms) the load of a fit individual porter.[13] Its movements, however, are both slower and more restricted. Where the porter requires only a footpath, the bullock cart requires a broader track. In some terrain, this is impossible; anyone familiar with the deeply rutted cart tracks in backcountry Burma will appreciate how slow and laborious the going is even when such travel is possible. For a trip of any length the carter must either carry his own fodder, thereby reducing the payload, or adjust the route to take advantage of fodder growing along it.[14] Until a century or two ago, even in the West, the overland transport of bulk commodities "has been subject to narrow and essentially inflexible limits."[15]

These geographical givens of movement of people and goods set limits to the reach of any landward state. Extrapolating from a more generous estimate of 32 kilometers a day by foot, F. K. Lehman estimates that the precolonial state's maximum size could not have been much more than 160 kilometers in diameter, although Mataram in Java was considerably broader. Assuming a court roughly in the center of a circular kingdom with a diameter of, say, 240 kilometers, the distance to the kingdom's edge would be 120 kilometers.[16] Much beyond this point, even in flat terrain, state power would fade, giving way to the sway of another kingdom or to local strongmen and/or bandit gangs. (See map 3 for an illustration of the effect of terrain on effective distances.)

Water transport, however, is the great premodern exception to these limits. Navigable water nullifies much of the friction of distance. Wind and currents make it possible to move bulk goods in large quantities over distances that are inconceivable using carts. In thirteenth-century Europe, according to one calculation, shipping costs by sea were a mere 5 percent of the cost by land. The disparity was so massive as to confer a large strategic and trade advantage on any kingdom near a navigable waterway. Most Southeast Asian precolonial states of any appreciable size had easy access to the sea or to a navigable river. In fact, as Anthony Reid notes, the capitals of most Southeast Asian states were located at river junctions where oceangoing ships had to transfer their cargoes to smaller craft plying the upstream reaches of the river. The location of nodes of power coincided largely with the intersecting nodes of communication and transportation.[17]

The key role of water transportation before the construction of railroads is evident in the great economic significance of canals, where the draft power was often the same—horses, mules, oxen—but the reduction of friction made possible by barges moving over water allowed for huge gains in efficiency. River or sea transportation takes advantage of "routes of least friction," of least geographical resistance, and thereby vastly extends the distances over which food supplies, salt, arms, and people can be exchanged. In epigrammatic form, we could say that "easy" water "joins," whereas "hard" hills, swamps, and mountains "divide."

Before the distance-demolishing technology of railroads and all-weather motor roads, land-bound polities in Southeast Asia and Europe found it extremely difficult, without navigable waterways, to concentrate and then project power. As Charles Tilly has noted, "Before the later nineteenth century, land transport was so expensive everywhere in Europe that no country could afford to supply a large army or big city with grain and other heavy goods without having efficient water transport. Rulers fed major inland cities such as Berlin and Madrid only at great effort and great cost to their hinterlands. The exceptional efficiency of waterways in the Netherlands undoubtedly gave the Dutch great advantages at peace and war."[18]

The daunting military obstacles presented by travel over very rugged terrain, even in the mid-twentieth century, was never more evident than in the conquest of Tibet by the China's People's Liberation Army in 1951. Tibetan delegates and party representatives who signed the agreement in Beijing traveled back to Lhasa via "the quicker route": namely by sea to Calcutta, then by train and horseback through Sikkim. Travel from Gongtok, Sikkim, to Lhasa alone took sixteen days. Within six months the PLA

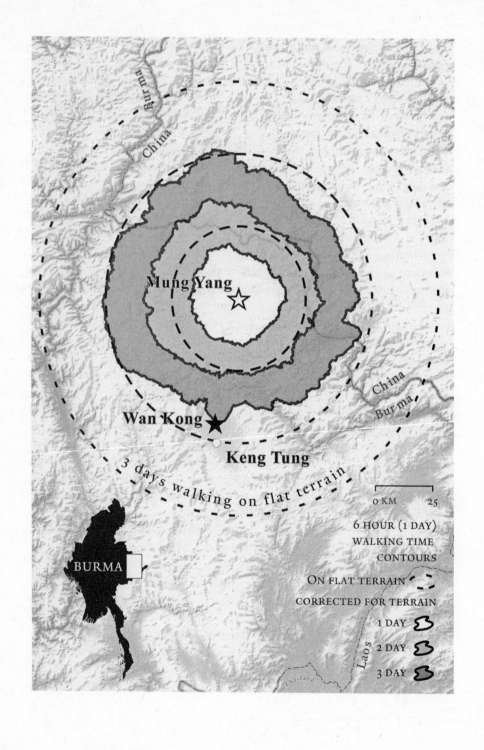

Mung Yang

Wan Kong

Keng Tung

3 days walking on flat terrain

BURMA

China
Burma

Burma
China

Laos

Thailand

0 KM   25

6 HOUR (1 DAY)
WALKING TIME
CONTOURS

ON FLAT TERRAIN

CORRECTED FOR TERRAIN

1 DAY

2 DAY

3 DAY

advance force in Lhasa was in danger of starving, and three thousand tons of rice was dispatched to them, again by ship to Calcutta and thence by mule over the mountains. Food came as well from Inner Mongolia to the north, but this required the astounding mobilization of twenty-six thousand camels, more than half of whom perished or were injured en route.[19]

The standard modern maps, in which a kilometer is a kilometer no matter what the terrain or body of water, are therefore profoundly misleading in this respect. Settlements that may be three hundred or four hundred kilometers distant over calm, navigable water are far more likely to be linked by social, economic, and cultural ties than settlements a mere thirty kilometers away over rugged, mountainous terrain. In the same fashion, a large plain that is easily traversed is far more likely to form a coherent cultural and social whole than a small mountainous zone where travel is slow and difficult.

Were we to require a map that was more indicative of social and economic exchange, we would have to devise an entirely different metric for mapmaking: a metric that corrected for the friction of terrain. Before the mid-nineteenth century revolution in transportation, this might mean constructing a map in which the standard unit was a day's travel by foot or oxcart (or by sailing vessel). The result, for those accustomed to standard, as-the-crow-flies maps, would look like the reflection in a fairground funhouse mirror.[20] Navigable rivers, coastlines, and flat plains would be massively shrunken to reflect the ease of travel. Difficult-to-traverse mountains, swamps, marshes, and forests would, by contrast, be massively enlarged to reflect travel times even though the distances, as the crow flies, might be quite small. Such maps,

---

Map 3. The striking constriction of state space imposed by rugged landscape may be illustrated by a map that compares walking times from a central place, depending on the difficulty of the terrain. Here we have selected Mung (Muang) Yang, a Shan town near the Burma-Chinese border, for illustrative purposes. The walking-time isolines shown here are based on Waldo Tobler's "hiker function," an algorithm that estimates the rate of travel possible based upon the slope at any given point on the landscape. These isolines show the travel distance possible assuming a six-hour walking day. The travel distances possible on flat terrain, based upon the Tobler algorithm, are shown in dotted lines for comparison. Setting out from Mung Yang, a traveler takes three days to cover the distance that, were the land flat, one could cover in a day and a half or two days. Travel is more difficult to the south and northwest than to the east. If we assume that the span of control varies directly with the ease of travel, than the total area under control of a hypothetical statelet centered on Mung Yang would be less than one-third of what it might be over level terrain.

however strange to the modern eye, would be far superior guides to contact, culture, and exchange than the ones to which we have grown accustomed. They would also, as we shall see, help demarcate the sharp difference between a geography more amenable to state control and appropriation (state space) and a geography intrinsically resistant to state control (nonstate space).

A map in which the unit of measurement is not distance but the time of travel is, in fact, far more in accord with vernacular practices than the more abstract, standardized concept of kilometers or miles. If you ask a Southeast Asian peasant how far it is to the next village, say, the answer will probably be in units of time, not of linear distance. A peasant quite familiar with watches might answer "about half an hour," and an older farmer, less familiar with abstract time units, might reply in vernacular units, "three rice-cookings" or "two cigarette-smokings"—units of duration known to all, not requiring a wristwatch. In some older, precolonial maps, the distance between any two places was measured by the amount of time it took to travel from one to the other.[21] Intuitively this makes obvious sense. Place A may be only twenty-five kilometers from place B. But depending on the difficulty of travel, it could be a two-day trip or a five-day trip, something a traveler would most surely want to know. In fact, the answer might vary radically depending on whether one was traveling from A to B or from B to A. If B is in the plains and A is high in the mountains, the uphill trip from B to A is sure to be longer and more arduous than the downhill trip from A to B, though the linear distance is the same.

A friction of distance map allows societies, cultural zones, and even states that would otherwise be obscured by abstract distance to spring suddenly into view. Such was the essential insight behind Fernand Braudel's analysis of *The Mediterranean World*. Here was a society that maintained itself by the active exchange of goods, people, and ideas without a unified "territory" or political administration in the usual sense of the term.[22] On a somewhat smaller scale, Edward Whiting Fox argues that the Aegean of classical Greece, though never united politically, was a single, social, cultural, and economic organism, knit together by thick strands of contact and exchange over easy water. The great "trading-and-raiding" maritime peoples, such as the Viking and Normans, wielded a far-flung influence that depended on fast water transport. A map of their historical influence would be confined largely to port towns, estuaries, and coastlines.[23] Vast sea spaces between these would be small.

The most striking historical example of this phenomenon was the Malay world—a seafaring world par excellence—whose cultural influence ran all the way from Easter Island in the Pacific to Madagascar and the coast of Southern Africa, where the Swahili spoken in the coastal ports bears its imprint. The Malay state itself, in its fifteenth- and sixteenth-century heyday, could fairly be called, like the Hanseatic League, a shifting coalition of trading ports. The elementary units of statecraft were ports like Jambi, Palembang, Johor, and Melaka, and a Malay aristocracy shuffled between them depending on political and trade advantages. Our landlocked sense of a "kingdom" as consisting of a compact and contiguous territory makes no sense when confronted with such maritime integration across long distances.

An agrarian kingdom is typically more self-contained than a maritime kingdom. It disposes of reserves of food and manpower close to home. Nevertheless, even agrarian kingdoms are far from self-sufficient; they depend for their survival on products outside their direct control: hill and coastal products such as wood, ores, protein, manure from pastoralists' flocks, salt, and so on. Maritime kingdoms are even more dependent on trade routes to supply their necessities, including, especially, slaves. For this reason, there are what might be called spaces of high "stateness" that do not depend on local grain production and manpower. Such locations are strategically situated to facilitate the control (by taxes, tolls, or confiscation) of vital trade products. Long before the invention of agriculture, those societies controlling key deposits of obsidian (necessary for the best stone tools) occupied a privileged position in terms of exchange and power. More generally there were certain strategic choke points on land and water trade routes, the control of which might confer decisive economic and political advantages. The Malay trading port is the classical example, typically lying athwart a river junction or estuary, allowing its ruler to monopolize trade in upstream (*hulu*) export products and similarly to control the hinterland's access to trade goods from downstream (*hilir*) coastal and international commerce. The Straits of Malacca were, in the same fashion, a choke point for long-distance trade between the Indian Ocean and China and thus a uniquely privileged space for state-making. On a smaller scale, innumerable hill kingdoms sat astride important caravan routes for salt, slaves, and tea, among other goods. They waxed and waned depending on the vagaries of world trade and commodity booms. Like their larger Malay cousins, they were, at their most peaceful, "toll" states.

Positional advantages of this kind are only partly a matter of the terrain and sea lanes. They are, especially in the modern era, historically contingent on revolutions in transport, engineering, and industry: for example, rail and road junctions, bridges and tunnels, coal, oil, and natural gas deposits.

Our crude first approximation of state space as the concentration of grain production and manpower in a manageable space must then be modified. The distance-demolishing properties of navigable water routes and the existence of nodes of power represented by choke points and strategic commodities can compensate for deficiencies in grain and manpower close at hand, but only to a point. Without sufficient manpower, it is frequently difficult for toll states to hold onto the site that confers a positional advantage. In the case of a showdown, agrarian states have generally been able to prevail over maritime or "trade-route" states by force of numbers. The disparity is highlighted by Barbara Andaya's comparison of the Vietnamese Trinh (an agrarian state) and Johore (a maritime state) at the beginning of the eighteenth century: "The point can be made clearly by comparing the armed forces of Johore, the most prestigious of the Malay States, but one without any agrarian base, with those of the Trinh. In 1714, the Dutch estimated that Johor could bring into battle 6,500 men and 233 vessels of all types. In Vietnam, by contrast, the Nguyen army was tallied at 22,740 men, including 6,400 marines and 3,280 infantry."[24] The earliest cautionary tale of maritime-state vulnerability is, of course, Thucydides' *Peloponnesian War*, in which a resolutely maritime Athens is, finally, undone by its more agrarian rivals, Sparta and Syracuse.

Mapping State Space in Southeast Asia

State-building in precolonial mainland Southeast Asia was powerfully constrained by geography. Here, in a rough and ready way, I shall attempt to outline those major constraints and their effects on the location, maintenance, and power dynamics of such states.

The necessary, but by no means sufficient, condition for the rise of a substantial state was the existence of a large alluvial plain suitable for the cultivation of irrigated rice and hence capable of sustaining both a substantial and concentrated population. Unlike maritime peninsular Southeast Asia, where the ease of movement over the calm waters of the Sunda Shelf permitted the coordination of a far-flung thalassocracy on the order of Athens, mainland states had to contend with far higher levels of geographical friction. Because of the generally north-south direction of mountain ranges and major rivers in the region, virtually all of the classical states were to be found along the great north-south river systems. They were, moving from west to east, the Burman classical states along the Irrawaddy near its confluence with the Chindwin (Pagan, Ava, Mandalay) or along the Sittang not far to the east (Pegu, Toungoo); the Thai classical state (Ayutthaya and, much later, Bangkok, along the Chao Phraya); the Khmer classical state (Angkor and its successors) near the great lake of Tonle Sap, a tributary of the Mekong; and finally, the early heartland of the Kinh (Trinh) classical state along the Red River in the vicinity of Hanoi.

The common denominator here is that all such states have been created near navigable water courses, but above the flood plain, where a flat, arable plain and perennial streams made wet-rice cultivation possible. It is striking that none of the early mainland states was located in the delta of a major river. Such delta regions—the Irrawaddy, the Chao Phraya, and Mekong—were settled in force and planted to wet rice only in the early twentieth century. The reasons for their late development, apparently, are that 1) they required extensive drainage works to be made suitable for rice cultivation, 2) they were avoided because they were malarial (especially when newly cleared), and 3) the annual flooding was unpredictable and often devastating.[25] This bold generalization, however, needs to be clarified and qualified. First, the political, economic, and cultural influence emanating from such centers of power, as Braudel would have predicted, spread most easily when least impeded by the friction of distance—along level terrain and navigable rivers and coastlines. Nothing illustrates this process more strikingly than the gradual, intermittent displacement of Cham and Khmer populations by the Vietnamese. This expansion followed the thin coastal strip southward, with the coast serving as a watery highway leading, eventually, all the way to the Mekong Delta and the trans-Bassac.

The economic reach of such state centers was almost always greater than their political reach. While their political control was limited by their degree of monopoly access to mobilized manpower and food supplies, their influence on trade might reach considerably farther. The friction of distance is at work here too; the greater the exchange value of a product vis-à-vis its weight and volume, the greater the distance over which it might be traded. Thus precious commodities such as gold, gemstones, aromatic woods, rare medicines, tea, and ceremonial bronze gongs (important prestige goods in the hills) linked peripheries to centers on the basis of exchange rather than political domination. On this basis, the geographical scope of certain forms of trade and exchange, requiring no bulk transport, was far more extensive than the comparatively narrow range within which political integration might be achieved.

I have thus far considered only the major classical states in mainland Southeast Asia. The key condition for state formation was present elsewhere as well: a potential heartland of irrigated rice cultivation that might constitute a "fully-administered territorial nucleus, having a court capital at its

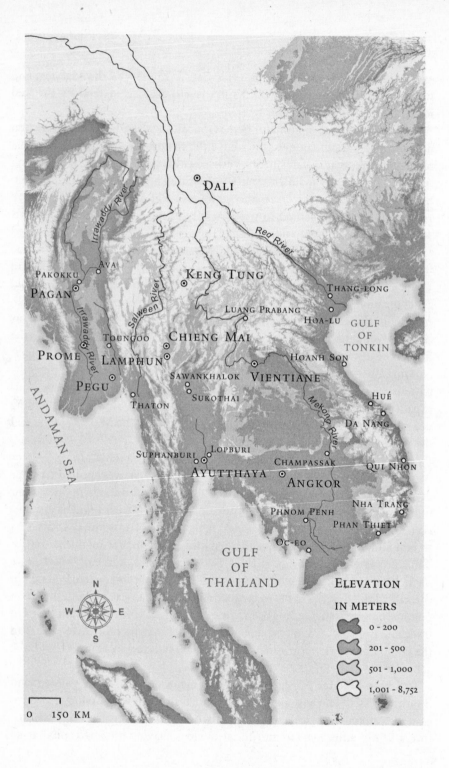

DALI

Red River

KENG TUNG

THANG-LONG

AVA

PAKOKKU

HOA-LU

PAGAN

LUANG PRABANG

GULF
OF
TONKIN

TOUNGOO

CHIENG MAI

PROME

LAMPHUN

HOANH SON

SAWANKHALOK

VIENTIANE

PEGU

SUKOTHAI

HUÉ

THATON

DA NANG

SUPHANBURI

LOPBURI

CHAMPASSAK

QUI NHON

AYUTTHAYA

ANGKOR

NHA TRANG

PHNOM PENH

PHAN THIET

OC-EO

GULF
OF
THAILAND

ELEVATION

IN METERS

0 - 200

201 - 500

501 - 1,000

1,001 - 8,752

ANDAMAN SEA

Irrawaddy River

Salween River

Irrawaddy River

Mekong River

N
W E
S

0   150 KM

center."[26] The difference was purely a matter of scale. Where the heartland of irrigated rice was large and contiguous, it might, under the right conditions, facilitate the rise of a major state; where the heartland was modest, it might, also under the right conditions, give rise to a modest state. A state on this account would be a fortified town of, say, at least six thousand subjects plus nearby hill allies, situated on wet-rice plain and having, in theory at least, a single ruler. Scattered throughout mainland Southeast Asia, often at fairly high altitudes, one finds the agro-ecological conditions that favor state formation, usually on a more Lilliputian scale. Most such places were at one time or another the sites of small Tai statelets. More rarely, leagues or confederacies of such statelets might combine, briefly, to forge a more formidable state. State formation around wet-rice cores, large or small, was always contingent and, typically, ephemeral. One might emphasize with Edmund Leach the fact that "the riceland stayed in one place" and thus represented a potential ecological and demographic strong point, which a clever and lucky political entrepreneur might exploit to create a new, or revived, state space. Even a successful dynasty was by no means a Napoleonic state; it was rather a shaky hierarchy of nested sovereignties. To the degree that it held together, the glue was a prudent distribution of spoils and marriage alliances and, when necessary, punitive expeditions for which, in the final analysis, control over manpower was vital.

Our conception of what constituted precolonial Burma must therefore be adjusted according to these basic principles of appropriation and span of control. Under a robust, flourishing dynasty, "Burma," in the sense of an effective political entity, consisted largely of wet-rice core areas within a few days' march from the court center. Such wet-rice areas need not necessarily be contiguous, but they had to be relatively accessible to officials and soldiers from the center via trade routes or navigable waterways. The nature of the routes of access was itself crucial; an army on its way to collect grain or to punish a rebellious district had to provision itself en route. This meant

---

Map 4. Rivers and classical states of Southeast Asia: The coincidence of classical states with navigable water courses is the general rule, as the map illustrates. The Salween/ Nu/Thanlwin River spawned only one classical state, Thaton, at its estuary. For much of its long course, the Salween runs through deep gorges and is not navigable. It is, solely for this reason, an exception. Keng Tung and Chiang Mai are also exceptions in the sense that neither is located close to a major navigable river. Each, however, commands a large, arable plain suitable for padi cultivation and hence for state-making.

locating a route of march through territory sufficiently rich in grain, draft animals, carts, and potential recruits for the army to sustain itself.

Thus marshes, swamps, and, especially, hilly areas, though they might be quite close to the court center, were generally not a part of "political, directly administered Burma."[27] Such hills and marshes were sparsely populated and, except in the case of a substantial plateau suitable for irrigated rice, their population practiced a form of mixed cultivation (dispersed swiddens for hill rice, root crops, foraging, and hunting) that was difficult to assess, let alone appropriate. Areas of this kind might have a tributary alliance with the court specifying the periodic renewal of oaths and the exchange of valuable goods, but they remained generally outside the direct political control of court officials. As a rule of thumb, hilly areas above three hundred meters in elevation were not a part of "Burma" proper. We must therefore consider precolonial Burma as a flatland phenomenon, rarely venturing out of its irrigation-adapted ecological niche. As Braudel and Paul Wheatley noted in general, political control sweeps readily across a flat terrain. Once it confronts the friction of distance, abrupt changes in altitude, ruggedness of terrain, and the political obstacle of population dispersion and mixed cultivation, it runs out of political breath.

Modern concepts of sovereignty make little sense in this setting. Rather than being visualized as a sharply delineated, contiguous territory following the mapmaking conventions for modern states, "Burma" is better seen as a horizontal slice through the topography, taking in most areas suitable for wet rice below three hundred meters and within reach of the court.[28]

Imagine a map constructed along these lines, designed to represent relative degrees of potential sovereignty and cultural influence. One way of visu-

---

Map 5. Elevation in central Burma: The "reach" of the precolonial state, at its most robust, stretched most easily along the low elevation plains and navigable river courses. All of the upper Burma kingdoms hugged the Irrawaddy above or below its confluence with the Chindwin. The Shan Hills to the east of Mandalay and Ava, though closer as the crow flies than the downriver towns of Pokokku and Magway, were outside the effective limits of the kingdom. The precolonial state also skirted the north-south Pegu-Yoma range of modest but rugged hills that bisected the rice plain. These hills remained effectively outside state control in the precolonial period, in much of the colonial period, and in independent Burma, where they were the redoubt of communist and Karen rebels until 1975. It is a striking example of how even relatively modest changes in the friction of terrain can impede state control.

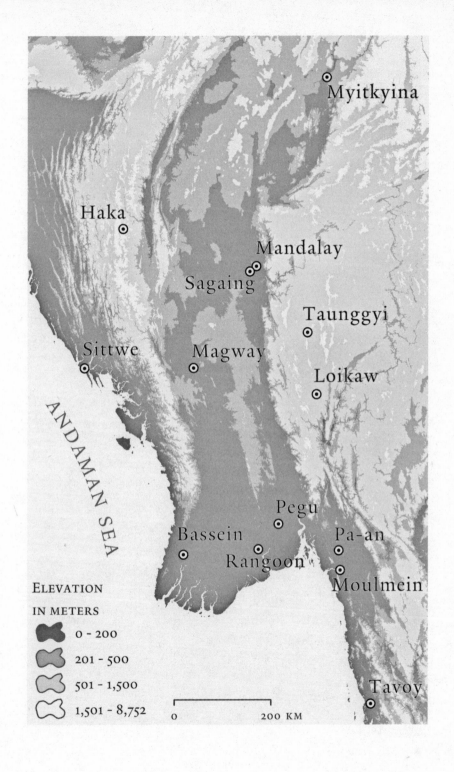

Myitkyina

Haka

Mandalay

Sagaing

Taunggyi

Sittwe

Magway

Loikaw

ANDAMAN SEA

Pegu

Bassein

Pa-an

Rangoon

Moulmein

ELEVATION
IN METERS

0 - 200

201 - 500

501 - 1,500

1,501 - 8,752

0   200 KM

Tavoy

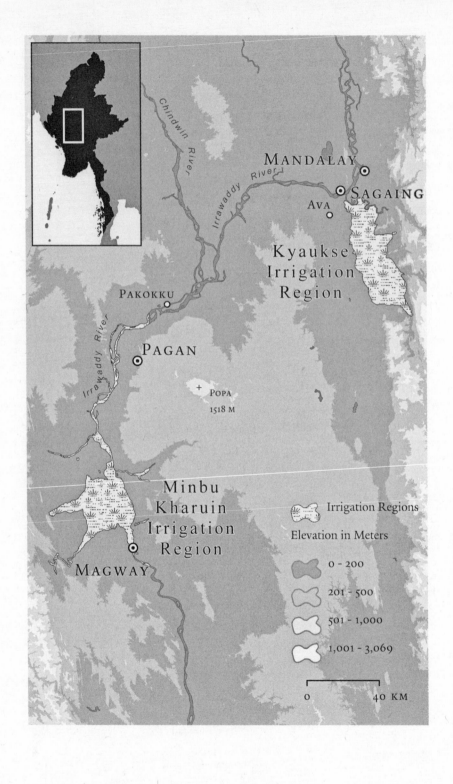

CHINDWIN RIVER

IRRAWADDY RIVER

MANDALAY

SAGAING

AVA

Kyaukse
Irrigation
Region

PAKOKKU

PAGAN

IRRAWADDY RIVER

+ POPA
1518 M

Minbu
Kharuin
Irrigation
Region

MAGWAY

Irrigation Regions

Elevation in Meters

0 – 200

201 – 500

501 – 1,000

1,001 – 3,069

0   40 KM

alizing how the friction of distance might work is to imagine yourself holding a rigid map on which altitudes were represented by the physical relief of the map itself. Further, let's imagine that the location of each rice-growing core is marked by a reservoir of red paint filled to the very brim. The size of the reservoir of paint would be proportional to the size of the wet-rice core and hence the population it might accommodate. Now visualize tilting this map, now in one direction, now in another, successively. The paint as it spilled from each reservoir would flow first along level ground and along the lowland water courses. As you increased the angle at which the map was tilted, the red paint would flow slowly or abruptly, depending on the steepness of the terrain, to somewhat higher elevations.

The angle at which you had to tilt the map to reach particular areas would represent, very roughly, the degree of difficulty the state would face in trying to extend its control that far. If we assume that the intensity of the red fades both in proportion to the distance it has traveled and the altitude it has attained, we have an approximation, again very roughly, of the diminishing influence and control or, alternatively, the relative cost of establishing direct political control in such areas. At higher elevations, the red would give way to white; if the terrain there was both steep and high, the transition would be quite abrupt. From above, depending on the number of hilly areas near the court center, this depiction of sovereignty would reveal a number of ir-regular white spots against a dark or pale red background. The population that inhabited the white blotches, although it might often be in a tributary relation to the court center, was rarely if ever directly ruled. If political con-

---

Map 6. Minbu Kharuin (K'à yaín) and Kyaukse irrigation works: These two main irrigation zones were the rice basket of precolonial states in upper Burma. The Minbu Kharuin irrigation works considerably predate the Pagan kingdom's rise in the ninth century CE. These two rice cores formed the repository of manpower and grain necessary to state formation and its inevitable accompaniment, warfare. (The term *k'à yaín*—အရိုင်—often transliterated *kharuin*, means "district" and connotes a walled town, as in the famous "nine K'à yaín" making up classical Kyaukse. It is the equivalent in most respects of the Shan term *maín*—မိုင်း—or the Thai *muang*.) Outside these two zones, on the plain, there was rain-fed, arable land, but the yields were neither as reliable nor as bounteous as those from the irrigated lands. In the north salient of the Pegu Yoma—Mount Popa and the elevated hills extending from it—population and agricultural production were even sparser. And the population and produce present were difficult to appropriate.

trol weakened suddenly before the daunting hills, cultural influence weakened as well. Language, settlement patterns, kinship structure, ethnic self-identification, and subsistence practices in the hills were distinctly different from those in the valleys. For the most part, hill peoples did not follow valley religions. Whereas the valley Burmans and Thais were Theravada Buddhists, hill peoples were, with some notable exceptions, animist and, in the twentieth century, Christians.

The color scheme of this fantasy friction-of-distance map would also offer a rough and ready guide to patterns of cultural and commercial, but not political, integration. Where the red color spreads with the least resistance, along river courses and flat plains, there one is likely to find more homogeneity in religious practices, language dialects, and social organization as well. Abrupt cultural and religious changes are likely to occur at the same places where there is, as with a mountain range, an abrupt increase in the friction of distance. If the map could also show, like a time-lapse photograph, the volume of human and commercial traffic across a space as well as the relative ease of movement, we would have an even better proxy for the likelihood of social and cultural integration.[29]

Our metaphorical map, like any map, though it serves to foreground the relationships we wish to highlight, obscures others. It cannot easily account, in these terms, for the friction of distance represented, say, by swamps, marshes, malarial zones, mangrove coasts, and thick vegetation. Another caution concerns the "pot of paint" at the state core. It is purely hypothetical; it represents the plausible reach of influence of a vigorous, ambitious state core under the most favorable conditions. Few state cores even came close to realizing this degree of sway over their hinterlands.

None of these state cores, large or small, had the terrain to itself. Each existed as one unit among a galaxy of waxing and waning contending centers. Before colonial domination and the codification of the modern territorial state vastly simplified the terrain, the sheer numbers of state centers, mostly Lilliputian, was bewildering. Leach was not exaggerating when he noted that "practically every substantial township in 'Burma' claims a history of having been at one time or another the capital of a 'kingdom' the alleged frontiers of which are at once both grandiose and improbable."[30]

How might we represent, again schematically, this plurality of state centers? One alternative is to invoke the Sanskritic term *mandala* ("circle of kings"), much used in Southeast Asia, in which the influence of a ruler, often claiming divine lineage, emanates from a court center, almost always located on a rice plain, out into the surrounding countryside. In theory, he rules over lesser kings and chiefs who recognize his claim to spiritual and temporal authority. The anachronistic metaphor of a light bulb with varying degrees of illumination to represent the charisma and sway of a ruler, first suggested by Benedict Anderson, captured two essential features of mandala-style political centers.[31] Its dimming suggested the gradual diminution of power, both spiritual and temporal, with distance from the center, and its diffuse glow avoided any modern assumption of "hard" boundaries within which 100 percent sovereignty prevailed and beyond which it disappeared altogether.

In figure 1 I attempt to depict some of the striking complexities of sovereignty in a plural mandala system. In order to do so, I have represented a number of mandala (*negara, muang, maín, k'à yaín*) by fixed circles with power concentrated at the center and fading gradually to zero at the outer circumference. This requires us, for the moment, to overlook the massive influence of terrain. We assume, in effect, a plain as flat as a pancake. Burmese authorities in the seventeenth century also made such simplifying assumptions in their own territorial order: a province was imagined as a circle and specified to have an administrative radius of exactly one hundred *tiang* (one tiang equals 3¼ kilometers), a big town a radius of ten tiang, a medium town five tiang, and a village two and a half tiang.[32] The reader should imagine how geographical irregularities — say, a swamp or rugged terrain — would truncate these circular shapes or how a navigable river might extend their reach along the waterway. More egregious, still, the very fixity of the representation of space completely ignores the radical temporal instability of the system: the fact that "centers of spiritual authority and political power shifted endlessly."[33] The reader should rather imagine these centers as sources of light that blaze, go faint, and are in time extinguished altogether, while new sources of light, points of power, suddenly appear and glow brighter.

Each circle represents a kingdom; some are smaller, others are larger, but the power of each recedes as one moves to the periphery, as represented by the diminishing density of icons within each mandala. The purpose of this rather facile graphic is merely to illustrate some of the complexities of power, territory, and sovereignty in precolonial mainland Southeast Asia, worked out in considerably more detail by Thongchai Winichakul.[34] In theory, the lands within a mandala's sway provided an annual tribute (which might be reciprocated by a gift of equal or greater value) and were obliged to send troops, carts, draft animals, food, and other supplies when required. And yet, as the graphic indicates, many areas fell within the ambit of more than one overlord.

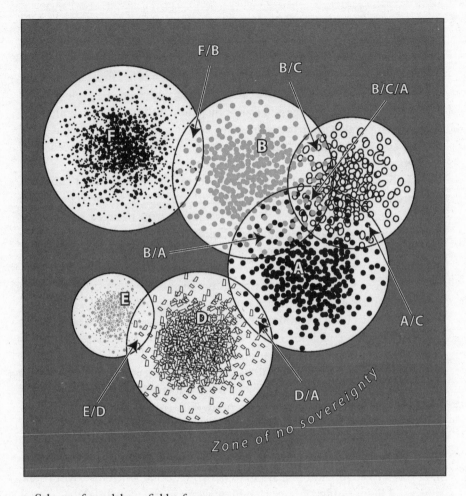

1. Schema of mandalas as fields of power

Where dual sovereignty, as in the area D/A, was located at the periphery of both kingdoms, it might well represent a case of mutually canceling, weak sovereignty, affording local chiefs and their following great autonomy in this buffer area. Where it affected much of the kingdom, as in B/A or A/C, it might be the occasion of competing exactions and/or punitive raids by the center on noncompliant, disloyal villages. Many hill peoples and petty chief-taincies strategically manipulated the situation of dual sovereignty, quietly sending tributary missions to two overlords and representing themselves to their own tributaries as independent.[35] Calculations of tribute were not an all-or-nothing affair, and the endless strategic choices of what to send, when to send it, when to delay, when to withhold manpower and supplies were at the very center of this petty statecraft.

Outside the central core of a kingdom, dual or multiple sovereignty or, especially at higher elevations, no sovereignty, was less an anomaly than the norm. Thus Chaing Khaeng, a small town near the current borders of Laos, Burma, and China, was tributary to Chiang Mai and Nan (in turn, tributary to Siam) and to Chiang Tung/Keng Tung (in turn, tributary to Burma). The situation was common enough that small kingdoms were often identified as "under two lords" or "under three lords" in the Thai language and its Lao dialect, and a "two-headed bird" in the case of nineteenth-century Cambodia's tributary relationship to both Siam and Dai Nan (Vietnam).[36]

Unambiguous, unitary sovereignty, of the kind that is normative for the twentieth-century nation-state, was rare outside a handful of substantial rice-growing cores, whose states were, themselves, prone to collapse. Beyond such zones, sovereignty was ambiguous, plural, shifting, and often void altogether. Cultural, linguistic, and ethnic affiliations were, likewise, ambiguous, plural, and shifting. If we add to this observation what we understand about the friction of terrain and altitude in projecting political power, we can begin to appreciate the degree to which much of the population, and most especially the hill peoples, were, though never untouched by the court centers of the region, hardly under their thumb.

Even the most robust kingdom, however, shrank virtually to the ramparts of its palace walls once the monsoon rains began in earnest. The Southeast Asian state, in its precolonial mandala form, its colonial guise, and, until very recently, as a nation-state, was a radically seasonal phenomenon. On the mainland, roughly from May through October, the rains made the roads impassable. The traditional period for military campaigns in Burma was from November to February; it was too hot to fight in March and April, and from May through much of October it was too rainy.[37] Not only were armies and tax collectors unable to move far in any force, but travel and trade were reduced to a trivial proportion of their dry-season volume. To visualize what this meant, we would have to consider our mandala map as a dry-season representation. For the rainy season, we would have to shrink each kingdom to something like a quarter to an eighth of its size, depending on the terrain.[38] As if some semiannual flood tide virtually marooned the state as the rains began and then released its watery grip when they stopped, state space and nonstate space traded places with meteorological regularity. A hymn of praise to a fourteenth-century Javanese ruler notes the periodicity of rule: "Every time at the end of the cold season [when it is quite dry] he sets out to roam through the countryside. . . . He shows the flag especially in remote areas. . . . He displays the splendor of his court. . . . He receives homage from all and sundry, collects tribute, visits village elders, checks land registers and examines public utilities such as ferries, bridges and roads."[39] Subjects knew roughly when to expect their ruler. They also knew roughly when to expect armies, press-gangs, military requisitions, and the destruction of war. War, like fire, was a dry-season phenomenon. Military campaigns, such as the several invasions of Siam by the Burmese, always began after the end of the rainy season, when the tracks were again passable and the crops ripening.[40] Any thorough examination of traditional state-making would have to give almost as large a place to weather as to pure geography.

Colonial regimes, though they worked mightily to construct all-weather roads and bridges, were thwarted in much the same way as the indigenous states they replaced. In the long, arduous campaign to occupy upper Burma, the progress made by colonial troops (mostly from India) in the dry season was often undone by the rains and, it seems, by the diseases of the wet season as well. An account of the effort in 1885 to clear Minbu, in upper Burma, of rebels and bandits, revealed that the rains forced a withdrawal of British troops: "And by the end of August the whole of the western part of the district was in the hands of the rebels and nothing remained to us but a narrow strip along the river-bank. The rains and the deadly season which succeeds them in the water-logged country at the foot of the Yoma [Pegu-Yoma mountain range] . . . prevented extended operations from being undertaken before the end of the year [again the dry season]."[41] In the steep, mountainous terrain along the Thai border where the Burmese army today fights a war without mercy against its ethnic adversaries, the rainy season remains a major handicap to regular armed forces. The typical offensive "window" for Burmese troops has been exactly that of the former kings of Pagan and Ava: November through February. Helicopters, forward bases, and new communications gear have allowed the regime to mount, for the first time, wet-season offensives. Nevertheless, the capture of the last major Karen base on Burmese territory took place on January 10, 1995, just as the earlier pattern of seasonal warfare would have dictated.

For those wishing to keep the state at arm's length, inaccessible mountain redoubts constituted a strategic resource. A determined state might mount a punitive expedition, burning houses and aboveground crops, but long-term occupation was beyond its reach. Unless it had hill allies, a hostile population need only wait for the rains, when supply lines broke down (or were easier to cut) and the garrison was faced with starvation or retreat.[42] Thus the physical, coercive presence of the state in the remotest, hilly areas was episodic, often to the vanishing point. Such areas represented a reliable zone of refuge for those who lived there or who chose to go there.

CHAPTER 3

Concentrating Manpower and Grain
Slavery and Irrigated Rice

It is true, I admit, that [the Siamese Kingdom] is of greater extent than mine, but you must agree that the King of Golconda [India] rules over men, while the king of Siam only rules over forests and mosquitoes.
—King of Golconda to Siamese visitor, circa 1680

The State as Centripetal Population Machine

The concentration of manpower was the key to political power in premodern Southeast Asia. It was the first principle of statecraft and the mantra of virtually every history of precolonial kingdoms in the region. Creating such state space was easiest where there was a substantial expanse of flat, fertile land, watered by perennial streams and rivers and, better yet, not far from a navigable waterway. Tracing the far-reaching logic of state spaces will help distinguish the fundamental differences between manpower-poor, land-rich political systems on the one hand and land-poor, manpower-rich systems on the other.

In its crudest version, the formula goes something like this: Political and military supremacy requires superior access to concentrated manpower close at hand. Concentrated manpower, in turn, is feasible only in a setting of compact, sedentary agriculture, and such agro-ecological concentrations are possible, before the twentieth century in Southeast Asia, only with irrigated rice. These relationships are, however, not deterministic. Padi fields are easier to create and maintain in river valleys and well-watered plateaus. But they can and have been created, through prodigious feats of terracing, in steep mountainous areas where we might least expect them, such as among the Hani along the upper reaches of the Red River in Vietnam, among the Ifugao in northern Luzon, and in Bali. Similarly, there are ecological settings suitable for padi fields where they have not been developed. Nor, as we have seen, is the link between padi fields and states invariable. States are easier to create around a wet-rice core, but there are wet-rice cores without states and, occasionally, states without wet-rice cores. Irrigated rice, then, is best understood politically as the most convenient and typical means of concentrating population and foodstuffs. Without a substantial wet-rice core, such concentration would have had to be achieved by other means—by slavery, for example, or by tolls on trade routes, or by plunder.

The need to concentrate population and, at the same time, the difficulty of doing so was inscribed in the demographic given that Southeast Asia's land mass was only one-seventh as populated as was that of China in 1600. As a consequence, in Southeast Asia control over people conferred control over land, while in China control over land increasingly conferred control over people. The abundance of arable land in Southeast Asia favored shifting cultivation, a pattern of farming that often yielded higher returns for less labor and produced a substantial surplus for the families practicing it. What constituted an advantage for the cultivators, however, was profoundly prejudicial to the ambitions of would-be state-makers. Shifting cultivation requires far more land than irrigated rice and therefore disperses population; where it prevails, it appears to "impose an upper limit of population density of about 20–30 per square kilometer."[1] Once again, concentration is the key. It matters little how wealthy a kingdom is if its potential surplus of manpower and grain is dispersed across a landscape that makes its collection difficult and costly. "Effective strength often came down to a polity's core, not the realm's total size or wealth," as Richard O'Connor has put it. "Irrigated wet-rice created stronger heartlands. . . . It not only supported a denser population, but grain-supported villagers would have been easier to mobilize."[2] The very name of the northern Thai kingdom—Lanna, "one million padi fields"—amply reflects this fiscal and manpower obsession.

Conditions in a flourishing wet-rice heartland, then, were favorable to the development of what might be called the premodern state's ideal subjects. That ideal is represented by densely packed cultivators of permanent grain fields who produce a considerable annual surplus. Having put considerable labor into their padi fields, over generations, perhaps, they are reluctant to pack up and leave. They and their rice fields are, above all, fixed in space, legible, taxable, conscriptable, and close at hand. For the court and its officials, the advantages are obvious.[3] It is in recognition of this process of "in-gathering" that Georges Condominas coined the term *emboîtement* ("containerization" or "bundling" might be the best translation) to describe the evolution of the Tai *muang*.[4] For the "ideal subject," unlike the shifting cultivator, living in a "state space," being emboîtée, meant an additional and often unpredictable claim on his labor, his grain, and, in the case of war, his very life.

The successful premodern Southeast Asian state strove constantly to assemble the population it needed and to hold it in place. Demography was not on its side. Natural disasters, epidemics, crop failures, war, not to mention an ever-beckoning frontier, constantly threatened a tenuous state. A Chinese manual on governance, from more than a millennium earlier, when China's demography, too, was unfavorable to state-making, put the danger starkly: "If the multitudes scatter and cannot be retained, the city-state will become a mound of ruins."[5] Archeologists working in Southeast Asia find no shortage of such mounds.

Discerning the precise balance of social and economic forces holding such agglomerations of power together and those tearing them apart is exceptionally difficult for two reasons. First, the balance was exceptionally volatile from year to year and from region to region. A war, an epidemic, a run of good harvests, a famine, the collapse of a trade route, a mad monarch, a civil war among claimants to the throne could tip the balance one way or the other. Second, we must be exceptionally wary of the written royal court records and even local chronicles that are strong on dynastic self-idealization and weak on hard information.[6] To take these last at face value would credit "the king's peace," prosperity, religious patronage, and divine providence with the power to attract and bind a critical mass of people around the state core. Taken with a large grain of salt, this image is not entirely false. There is repeated evidence of kings and their officials enticing settlers to open padi fields by providing working capital of grain and draft animals and waiving taxes for a time. Thus a Burmese official near Pegu boasted in his 1802 revenue report that he "fed and supported those who were pleased to come from distant towns and villages in the desert[ed] places of high jungle and tall grass."[7] A peaceful and prosperous reign did, in fact, draw in migrants fleeing unsettled conditions elsewhere and hoping to farm, work, and trade near the capital. It is this depiction of a largely peaceful and gradual ingathering of hitherto stateless peoples, attracted to a luminous and thriving court center, that is the narrative conjured by dynastic histories and contemporary schoolbook idealizations of the precolonial state. As such, it is a wildly distorted narrative. It mistakes the exception as the rule; it fails utterly to explain the frequent collapse of precolonial kingdoms; it ignores, above all, the essential role that war, slavery, and coercion played in the creation and maintenance of these states. If I slight the occasions on which a Whiggish account of the flourishing dynasties might be tenable, it is because such moments are already much storied, are comparatively rare, and grossly distort the basic characteristics of state-making in mainland Southeast Asia.

If demography and an open frontier limited the effectiveness of pure coercion, it is nevertheless abundantly clear that the use of force was instrumental in creating and maintaining the "thickly-settled clumps" of people on which the state depended.[8] The accumulation of population by war and slave-raiding is often seen as the origin of the social hierarchy and centralization typical of the earliest states.[9] Most powerful kingdoms constantly sought to replenish and enlarge their manpower base by forcibly resettling war captives by the tens of thousands and by buying and/or kidnapping slaves. Just as the key measure of a state's power was the manpower it could muster, so was manpower the key measure of the comparative standing of officials, aristocrats, and religious orders that competed for dependents, bondsmen, and slaves. The context of many royal decrees betrays both the effort to force the core population to stay put and, if we read between the lines, a hint of failure. If a majority of tsarist decrees of the eighteenth century concern runaway serfs, then we can safely surmise that the flight of serfs was a common problem. Similarly, the number of royal orders forbidding subjects to flee, to change residence, or to cease cultivating is a fair indication that absconding subjects were a constant preoccupation of rulers. Throughout much of the mainland, subjects were tattooed and sometime branded to indicate their status and their master. How effective such measures were is hard to tell, but they do reflect the attempt to hold the heartland population in place by force.

This overwhelming concern for obtaining and holding population at the core is shot through every aspect of precolonial statecraft. What Geertz says about Balinese political rivalries—that they were "a struggle more for men than for land"—could apply equally to all of mainland Southeast Asia.[10] This principle animated the conduct of warfare, which was less a grab for distant territory than a quest for captives who could be resettled at the core. Wars were, for this reason, not particularly sanguinary. Why would one want to destroy the main prize of victory? The logic was most powerful for the inland agrarian states, which relied more on core agricultural production than on the profits of long-distance commerce. But even the raiding-and-trading states of peninsular Southeast Asia were preoccupied with seizing and holding manpower. Early European officials were frequently astounded by the extremely vague demarcations of territories and provinces in their new colonies and puzzled by an administration of manpower that had little or nothing to do with territorial jurisdiction. As the British surveyor James McCarthy "noted with puzzlement: 'It was a particular custom [of the Siamese] in which power over individuals and land was separated.'" As Thongchai Winichakul's insightful book shows, the Siamese paid more attention to the manpower they could summon than to sovereignty over land that had no value in the absence of labor.[11]

The primacy of population control was embedded in the terminology of administration. Thai officials bore titles that referred directly to the number of people they could, in theory, muster: *Kun Pan* meant "Lord of a Thousand Men"; *Kun Saen* meant "Lord of a Hundred Thousand Men," not "Duke of such-and-such a place," which would have been the case in Europe.[12] The territorial designations that did exist in the area ruled by Bangkok in the late eighteenth century were essentially classed by their effective manpower rating. Thus provinces were ranked by the degree of power Bangkok exercised over them in declining order, fourth class corresponding to direct power and first class corresponding to weakest power (for example, Cambodia at the time). A province's size was then calibrated by a standardized total of manpower it could plausibly be expected to muster when summoned. Distant provinces, where Bangkok's sway was weak, tended to be both sparsely populated and much larger; the idea being that each province would yield a roughly equal number of conscripts for work or for war.[13]

The paramount importance of manpower rested, in the final analysis, on military considerations. Occupation of a fertile rice plain, of an important temple complex, of a choke point along vital trade routes was of little avail if it could not be successfully defended. This homely fact goes to the very heart of the analysis of power in such premodern political systems. Rather than wealth begetting power, as it might in Lockean systems, where the state's first duty is to defend citizens' life and property, in premodern systems only power can guarantee property and wealth. And power, before the technological revolution in warfare, was largely a matter of how many men a ruler could field; power, in other words, boiled down to manpower.

The logic of manpower operated at every level of the precolonial political systems of Southeast Asia. Princes, aristocrats, merchants, officials, village headmen, all the way down to the heads of households held their positions by virtue of the allies whose labor and support they could rely upon when challenged. The logic is captured well by Anthony Reid: "The political context made it dangerous for a small man to show his wealth unless he had sufficient dependents to defend and legitimate it. . . . Capital, therefore, had first to be deployed in obtaining people—through buying slaves, lending to those in need, marital and military alliances, and feasting."[14] Anyone bent on accumulating power in this context would, perforce, engage in behavior that would seem anomalous or profligate in a Lockean system. The Machiavellian strategy under these conditions is to surround yourself with the largest number of allies who are obligated to you; this requires a judicious liberality with gifts, loans, and feasting. Some allies can literally be bought. As a sixteenth-century visitor reported, the people of Melaka believed "that it is better to have slaves ['bondsmen' would be a better translation] than to have land, because slaves are a protection to their masters."[15]

My assertion here is not so much that manpower was wealth as that it was the only means by which wealth could be securely held. In fact, one could argue, as Reid convincingly does, that maritime and overland trade were far more lucrative than squeezing the surplus out of a sedentary peasantry, even in the sixteenth and seventeenth centuries. Even the largely agrarian state of upper Burma depended quite heavily on the taxes and tolls its strategic position on the Irrawaddy allowed it to levy on precious commodities destined for markets in China, India, and beyond.[16] Such goods were often easy to store, and their high value per unit weight and volume (like opium today) more than offset transportation costs. To reap the rewards of such trade, however, required that a kingdom defend its monopoly position on a river or athwart a mountain pass, or to enforce its claim to tribute by force if need be; in that case, the main currency of competition was, again, manpower.

It is this decisive advantage in manpower, Victor Lieberman argues, that over the long haul favored the hegemony of Southeast Asia's "agrarian" kingdoms over maritime kingdoms. "In an era of limited military specialization when the number of conscripted cultivators offered the best single indication of military success, the north [of Burma] was the natural center of political gravity," Lieberman writes. "In the central mainland and Java as well, we shall find easily cultivated dry, but irrigable, areas enjoyed an early demographic advantage over wetter, maritime districts."[17] Viewed in a crude synoptic fashion, over time a handful of larger maritime powers (Srivijaya, Pegu, Melaka) eclipsed their smaller maritime rivals; they were in turn eclipsed by more manpower-heavy agrarian states (Mataram, Ayutthaya, Ava), which had likewise eclipsed their smaller agrarian rivals (Vientiane, Lan Na, Chiang Mai). Everything we know about statecraft in Ava and Ayutthaya suggests a constant effort, by no means always successful, to hold a dense population at the core and augment it when possible.[18]

The process described above accords nicely with much of the literature on European state-making and political consolidation. Here, too, what Charles Tilly aptly called the "coercion-rich and capital-poor," "landward" agrarian states and empires (for example, Russia, Brandenburg Prussia, Hungary, Poland, and France) enjoyed an advantage in manpower, usually a decisive one, over their maritime rivals (Venice, the Netherlands, Genoa, Florence). Less reliant on volatile trade, more hierarchical, more insulated from food-supply crises, and capable of feeding quite massive armies, these agrarian states might lose a battle or even a war, but their staying power over the long haul tended to prevail.[19]

Population as the principal measure of statecraft finds abundant expression in the sayings and admonitions that infuse the courtly literature of Southeast Asia. Nowhere is the relative weight of manpower vis-à-vis territory more evident than in this epigram from the Early Bangkok Period in Siam: "To have too many people [as subjects to a lord] is better than to have too much grass [uncultivated land]."[20] The epigram is echoed, almost precisely, by one from the Burmese *Glass Palace Chronicle,* compiled at about the same time: "Yes, a soil, but no people. A soil without people is but a wilderness."[21]

Two additional Siamese sayings emphasize that wise rule requires both preventing people from fleeing the heartland and attracting new settlers to cultivate the land:

> In a large house with many servants, the door may safely be left open; in a small house with few servants, the doors must be shut.

> The governor should appoint loyal officials to go out and persuade them to come and settle down in an inhabited area so that the area will be wealthy.[22]

The collapse of a kingdom was, in turn, seen as a failure of the monarch to husband his population wisely. Queen Saw's admonition to the Burmese King Narahihapate is a dramatic illustration: "Consider the state of the realm. Thou hast no folk or people, no host of countrymen and countrywomen around thee. . . . Thy countrymen and countrywomen tarry and will not enter thy kingdom. They fear thy dominion, for thou, oh King Alaung art a hard master. Therefore I, thy servant, spoke to thee of old but thou wouldst not hearken. . . . I said bore not thy country's belly, abase not thy country's forehead." Warfare as a contest for control over cultivators rather than arable land is also evident in this praise for a Siamese military commander who not only put down rebellion but delivered his captives to the crown: "From that day forward, he sent Anantathuriya, whenever there were thieves, cutthroats, rioters, or rebels in border places and purlieux. And wheresoever he went, he caught numbers of his foes alive and brought them back to the king."[23] Even in the absence of such explicit statements, the centrality of manpower is everywhere evident in the constant emphasis on what might be called "entourage politics." It is common, whenever an official is mentioned in the court histories, to list the size and distinction of his followers.[24] Whenever a victorious military campaign is reported, it is generally the number of surviving captives rounded up and marched back to the capital that receives most attention. Although I have concentrated here on the evidence from the mainland, the same preoccupation with manpower is, if anything, more striking in peninsular Southeast Asia and the Malay world in particular.[25]

The imperative of concentrating population and grain production, in fact, confronts all would-be state-makers who must operate in an environment where open land is abundant and military technology simple. Some means must be devised to counteract the tendency of the populace to disperse widely so as to take full advantage of the hunting, foraging, and less labor-intensive farming techniques available to them. A range of incentives—from commercial exchange to reliable irrigation to participation in military plunder to the desire for sacred knowledge—might be at work. Such advantages, however, had to outweigh the burdens of taxation, conscription, and epidemics always associated with state space if the concentration was to be achieved without resistance. They seldom did. The use of force to supplement these advantages, and often to replace them altogether, was ubiquitous.

Here it is worth recalling that the political systems of classical antiquity in the West were, manifestly, coercive systems of this kind. Athens and Sparta, Thucydides tells us, fought not over ideology or ethnicity but over tribute. That tribute was measured in grain and, above all, in manpower. The populace of a surrendered town was rarely butchered; rather, its citizens and slaves were taken into captivity by the victors and by individual soldiers who had captured them. If their fields and homes were burned, it was largely to prevent them from returning.[26] The major tradable commodity on the Aegean—more valuable than grain, olive oil, or wine—was slaves. Athens and Sparta were both slave societies, although in Sparta, which was more agrarian, helots accounted for more than 80 percent of the population. In imperial Rome as well, the most important commodity transported along its fabled road system was slaves; they were bought and sold under government monopoly.

China and India, well before they became so populated that control of arable land alone ensured control of their land-starved subjects, faced similar problems of statecraft. At about the same time as the Peloponnesian War, the early Chinese state was doing everything in its power to prevent the dispersal of population. Manuals of statecraft urged the king to prohibit subsistence activities in the mountains and wetlands "in order to increase the involvement of the people in the production of grain."[27] The subtext of this and other pronouncements was that, given a choice in the matter, the king's subjects would abandon sedentary agriculture and strike out on their own. Such resistance was seen as a moral failing. If the state has "the unique power over the mountains and marshes, then the common people who detest farming, are lazy, and want doubled profits, will have nowhere to find something to eat. If they have nowhere to find something to eat, they will be obliged to engage in the cultivation of the fields."[28] The objective of this policy was, it seems, to starve the population into grain farming and subjecthood by separating them from the open commons. Somehow, the shrill tone of the advice suggests that the policy was not a complete success.

The dilemma for statecraft in settings of low population densities finds a more contemporary and instructive parallel in Africa south of the Sahara. In 1900 the population density there was not much greater than that of Southeast Asia in 1800, and, as a consequence, the problem of bundling a population at the state core was the crux of precolonial politics.[29] The theme of manpower concentration permeates the literature on indigenous politics: "The drive to acquire relatives, adherents, dependents, retainers, and subjects and to keep them attached to oneself as a kind of social and political 'capital' has often been remarked upon as characteristic of African political processes."[30] The similarities are so striking that many of the adages of rule can be transposed to Southeast Asia with no loss in intelligibility. As a Sherbro proverb has it, "One cannot be a chief and sit alone." The link between cleared, permanent fields and the foundation of a kingdom was also invoked in this advice to an ancient Malian king: "Cut the trees, transform the forests into fields, for then only will you become a true king."[31] As in Southeast Asia there was little emphasis on sharp territorial boundaries, and the important rights were rights over people, not over places, except for particular ritual sites. The competition for followers, kinsmen, and bondsmen operated at every level. Given demography so favorable to potential subjects, they had more often to be enticed rather than coerced to settle under a ruler. The relative autonomy of subjects found expression in the proliferation of titles, in feasting, in rapid assimilation and mobility for captives and slaves, in special paraphernalia and medicines to bind retainers, and above all, in the flight of unhappy subjects. This balance of power, according to Igor Kopytoff, gave subjects the distinct sense they it was they who had created the ruler and not the other way around.[32]

The Shaping of State Landscapes and State Subjects

Taxes ate the valleys, honor ate the hills.
— Afghan proverb

A premodern ruler in mainland Southeast Asia would have been less interested in what today would be called the gross domestic product (GDP) of his kingdom than what we might call its "state-accessible product" (SAP!). In a premonetary setting, products that come from any considerable distance would have to be quite valuable per unit weight and volume to justify the transportation costs. Such products existed—for example, aromatic woods, tree resins, silver and gold, ceremonial drums, rare medicines. The greater the distance they traveled, the greater the likelihood they were part of a gift or voluntary trade, for the court's capacity to compel such goods diminished more or less geometrically with distance. What mattered most were the food, livestock, and manpower—including skilled manpower—that could be conveniently seized and put to use. The state-accessible product had to be easy to identify, monitor, and enumerate (in short, assessable), as well as being close enough geographically.

State-accessible product and gross domestic product are not simply different; they are, in many respects, at odds with each other. Successful state-building is directed toward the maximization of the state-accessible product. It profits the ruler not at all if his nominal subjects flourish, say, by foraging, hunting, or shifting agriculture at too great a distance from the court. It similarly profits the ruler little if his subjects grow a diverse suite of crops of different maturation or crops that spoil quickly and are therefore hard to assess, collect, and store. Given a choice between patterns of subsistence that are relatively unfavorable to the cultivator but which yield a greater return in manpower or grain to the state and those patterns that benefit the cultivator but deprive the state, the ruler will choose the former every time. The ruler, then, maximizes the state-accessible product, if necessary, at the expense of the overall wealth of the realm and its subjects. So it is that the premodern state attempts to so arrange its subjects and to sculpt the landscape around it in order to make it a legible field of appropriation. When successful, the result in mainland Southeast Asia has been the social creation of a uniform agro-ecological landscape based on irrigated wet rice: what Richard O'Connor has called the "paddy-state."[33]

The chief advantage of padi rice is that it makes possible a concentrated density of both population and of grain. Here it is worth emphasizing the way irrigated rice fixes people in space. No other cultivar could have placed so many people within a three- or four-day march of the court center. The superior productivity of wet rice per unit of land permits enormous population densities, and the relative permanence and reliability of padi rice, so long as the irrigation system is functioning well, helps ensure that the population itself will remain in place. Each padi field — representing as it does many years of "sunk" labor costs in bunding, leveling, terracing, weir and channel construction — is not lightly abandoned. "One major problem" of the Kon-baung kings, writes Thant Myint U, "was the difficulty of the central state in gaining accurate information on the number of households in a particular locality."[34] This might be called the problem of "legibility," which was the indispensable condition of making resources accessible.[35] Compared with subsistence patterns that favored dispersal and autonomy, the social ecology of wet rice greatly simplified this problem by placing a relatively stable and dense population at the doorstep of the tax man and the military press-gang.

Fixed-point production by a sedentary peasantry in the padi state meant that the ruler and his entourage of specialists and officials could also remain in one place. Without a reliable, accessible surplus of food, fodder, and firewood, the court would have had to shift to another site, just as the English and French courts of the thirteenth century did, once they had exhausted the food supply (and forbearance!) in any one district. The size of the noncultivating elite was, of course, constrained by the size of the grain surplus; the larger the core, the more numerous and well provisioned the entourage. Only padi cultivation on a substantial scale gave an agrarian state a sporting chance at persisting.

The cultivation of a single staple grain was, in itself, an important step in legibility and, hence, appropriation. Monoculture fosters uniformity at many different levels. In the case of irrigated rice, cultivators were bound to roughly the same rhythm of production. They depended on the same, or comparable, sources of water; they planted and transplanted, weeded, cut, and threshed their crop at roughly the same time and in roughly the same way. For the maker of a cadastral survey, a tax map, the situation was nearly ideal. Most land values could be calibrated to a single metric; each harvest both was compressed in time and involved a single commodity; the mapping of open fields demarcated by bunds was relatively straightforward, although matching the land to the appropriate taxpayer was not quite so straightforward. The uniformity in the field, in turn, produced a social and cultural uniformity expressed in family structure, the value of child labor and fertility, diet, building styles, agricultural ritual, and market exchange. A society shaped powerfully by monoculture was easier to monitor, assess, and tax than one shaped by agricultural diversity. Imagine, once again as an Asian Colbert, organizing a tax system for a diverse polyculture of, say, several grains, fruits, nuts, root crops, livestock, fishing, hunting, and foraging. Such diversity would give rise, at a minimum, to different land values, family arrangements, work cycles, diets, domestic architecture, dress, tools, and markets. The existence of so many products and "harvests" would, by itself, make far more intractable the creation of any tax system, let alone an equitable one. I have, for the purposes of analytical clarity, drawn the comparison too sharply; none of the mainland agrarian states was a pure monoculture. But to the degree that it approximated one, it radically simplified the consolidation of a manageable state space.

It is in this context that the strenuous efforts of successful Burmese dynasties to maintain and extend the irrigated riceland within the dry zone should be understood. Outside these padi cores lay a less productive and more diverse agricultural landscape that posed difficulties for the tax man. The district revenue reports (*sit-tàns*) invariably list the padi land of the district first and make it clear that the revenue from nonpadi lands—millet, sesamum, cattle, fishing, coconut palms, and handicrafts—was both more difficult to collect and, compared with padi income, negligible.[36] Collecting revenue from a population that was more dispersed, that was generally poorer, and whose subsistence routines were much more varied was singularly unrewarding. What was collected, moreover, was more easily concealed from crown officials and monopolized by local strongmen. The colonial regime in Burma was no less dependent on irrigated ricelands, even when the tax on them was collected in cash. John Furnivall sees it as the "staple" of the colonial fiscal diet: "What rice is to the mild Hindoo, and to the anything but mild Burman, what macaroni is to the Italian, beef and beer to the Englishman, all that and more than that, is land revenue to *Leviathan Indicus,* the species of Leviathan that inhabits India; it is his victuals, his sustenance. Income tax, customs duties, excise receipts and so on . . . he could in a pinch do without them, but without land revenue he would starve to death."[37]

Here again the distinction between gross domestic product and state-accessible product is at work. As a general rule, the agriculture organized by and for states and enterprises with appropriation, above all, in mind, is likely to bear the marks of legibility and monocropping. Monoculture plantations, the now defunct collective farms of the socialist bloc, cotton share-cropping in the postbellum U.S. South, not to mention the coercive agricultural landscapes created by counterinsurgency campaigns in Vietnam or Malaya, are cases in point. They are rarely models of efficient or sustainable agriculture, but they are, and they are intended to be, models of legibility and appropriation.[38]

The policy of encouraging or imposing legible, agrarian landscapes of appropriation seems hard-wired to state-making. It was only such landscapes that were directly beneficial and accessible. Little wonder, then, that the efforts to sedentarize populations through fixed (usually rice) cultivation represents a striking continuity between the precolonial states and their contemporary descendants. The Vietnamese Emperor Minh Mang (1820–41) "used every method available to encourage the cultivation of new fields of rice. These included permitting a man who cleared land himself to use it as his own private field, or encouraging rich people to come forward and recruit tenants to set up new village settlements. The state's principal aim was the maintenance of control over the population. Vagrancy was discouraged and displaced people were fixed to a plot of land where they could be turned into reliable sources of taxation, corvée labour and military service."[39]

For its part, the French colonial regime was interested in turning open land into revenue-yielding, legible crops, in particular, rubber grown on plantations. The French desired to transform the fiscally sterile hills into a space that would be *rentable* and *utile.* Socialist Vietnam, up to the present, remains devoted to "fixed cultivation and fixed settlement" (*dinh canh dinh cu*), with the emphasis returning to wet rice, even in places where it is ecologically unsound. An older vision of the padi state has been married to a utopian view of the conquest of nature by heroic socialist labor. It looks lyrically forward to "a tomorrow [in which] Tay Bac's forested hills and grassy expanses will be flattened and immense fields of rice, fields of corn will be opened up." As another brave slogan had it, "With the strength of the people, even stones turn into rice."[40] One aspect of this vast policy of resettlement has been the understandable desire of the lowland Kinh to reproduce the agricultural landscape and human settlements with which they are familiar. As is so often the case, the attempt by migrants to apply techniques of cultivation that are utterly ill-suited to their new setting has resulted in ecological damage and human suffering. The other aspect of this utopian aspiration, however, has been the attempt by the Vietnamese state to re-create the landscapes of legibility and appropriation that had sustained its precolonial ancestors since at least the Le Dynasty.

Eradicating Illegible Agriculture

> Hostile nature, obstinate and fundamentally rebellious, is in fact represented in the colonies by the bush, by mosquitoes, natives and fever, and colonization is a success when all this indocile nature has finally been tamed.
> —Franz Fanon, *The Wretched of the Earth*

My only quarrel with Franz Fanon's acid insight into the colonial project is that his observation, at least with respect to "the bush" and "natives," might as easily be applied to the precolonial and postcolonial eras.

The expansion and peopling of legible state space was intrinsically difficult, given the open frontier. If it was occasionally achieved, it was due as much to the closing off of alternatives as to the inherent attractions of state space. The major alternative to irrigated padi cultivation in mainland Southeast Asia, historically, and even today in much of the region, is shifting agriculture (also known as swidden or slash-and-burn agriculture). Inasmuch as it involves population dispersal, mixed cropping (including roots and tubers), and periodic opening of new fields, swiddening has been anathema to all state-makers, traditional or modern.

As by far the most precocious state in the region, the Chinese state since at least the Tang Dynasty has been stigmatizing shifting cultivation and eradicating it when it could. Though shifting-cultivation agriculture might provide a higher return to the cultivator's labor, this was a form of wealth that was inaccessible to the state. And, especially if it was advantageous to the cultivator, it represented, at the fringes of an often heavily taxed, rice-growing peasantry, a constant temptation as an alternative subsistence. Along China's southwestern frontier, shifting cultivators were encouraged, and sometimes forced, to abandon their shifting agriculture for sedentary grain production. The Chinese seventeenth-century euphemism for incorporation into state space was "to enter the map." It meant becoming a subject of the emperor, proclaiming loyalty, and setting out on a cultural journey that would, in Han eyes, eventually lead to assimilation. Above all, however, the passage from nomadic agriculture to sedentary grain growing meant becoming a registered household that now figured in the official tax rolls.[41]

The state fiscal imperatives that lay behind the desire of Vietnam's Emperor Minh Mang or China's officials to eradicate shifting cultivation have been reinforced in the modern era by two further considerations: political security and resource control. Because shifting cultivators were not incorporated into the state administration, because they spilled promiscuously across national boundaries, and because they were seen as ethnically distinct, they were seen as potentially subversive. In Vietnam this has led to vast campaigns of forced resettlement and sedentarization. Another contemporary reason given for prohibiting shifting cultivation is that it is environmentally unsound, destroying soil cover, promoting erosion, and wasting valuable timber resources. To some considerable degree this rationale was a direct policy inheritance from the colonial period. Its premise, we now understand, is wrong, except under special circumstances. The overriding reason behind such policies, it appears, has been the state's need to use such land for permanent settlement, to realize for itself the revenue from the extraction of natural resources, and to bring such nonstate peoples finally to heel. As one government ethnographer informed a foreign colleague, the purpose of his study of the hill economy "was to see how 'nomadic' slash-and-burn agriculture can be eradicated among the minorities."[42] The "campaign to sedentarize the Nomads," begun in 1954, has, in one guise or another, remained a steadfast policy.

Much the same continuity in policy, if not in consistent enforcement, has typified the Thai state for much of its existence. Nicholas Tapp, an ethnographer of the Hmong, claims that the policies of sedentarization, permanent agriculture, political control, and "Thaiization" "represent highly conservative strategies which have characterized relations between state populations and upland developing minorities of the region for several centuries."[43] The attempts to stop swiddening became significantly more brutal at the height of the cold war in the 1960s, after a Hmong rebellion was crushed by General Prapas by means of artillery, military assaults, and napalm. Despite the fact that Vietnam and Thailand feared subversion from diametrically opposite points of the ideological compass, their policies were remarkably similar. The Hmong were to stop shifting cultivation and, as a policy document noted, officials were to "persuade the hill tribes, living scatterdly [*sic*] to move into project areas and settle down permanently."[44] State space had, under the circumstances, acquired additional meaning, but the new meaning only strengthened the reasons to eradicate shifting agriculture.[45]

Perhaps the most long-standing violent campaign against shifting cultivation, designed to force the people who practice it into what amount to concentration camps around military bases or, failing that, to force them over the border into Thailand, is the Burmese military regime's campaign against the Karen. Armed columns are sent out before swidden fields are harvested to burn the grain or to beat it down and to lay land mines in the fields. Knowing how crucial a successful "burn" is to the swidden harvest, the army also sends units to burn the slash prematurely so as to ruin the chances for a good crop. By eradicating shifting cultivation and not a few of its practitioners, they minimize the chances for survival outside state spaces.[46]

Such coincidence of policy across several centuries and, in the modern period, across very different types of regime is prima facie evidence that something fundamental about state-making is at work.

E Pluribus Unum: The Creole Center

Whatever concentration of population around the court the padi state managed to achieve was a hard-won victory against considerable demographic odds. Statecraft with both eyes fixed on the accumulation of manpower could hardly be particular about whom it incorporated. A "manpower state" in this sense is, in principle, the enemy of hard and fast cultural distinctions and exclusiveness. Put more accurately, such states had great incentives to incorporate whomever they could and to invent cultural, ethnic, and religious formulas that would allow them to do so. This fact, true of all the padi states of mainland and maritime Southeast Asia, is rich in consequences for each of these lowland civilizations.

The emphasis on inclusion and absorption was such that it would surely be mistaken to see the classical Burman or Thai state as endogenous, monoethnic expressions of cultural development. It is closer to the mark to see each such state core as a social and political invention, an alloy, an amalgam that bears traces of ingathering from many diverse sources. The culture of the center was a provisional work in progress, a kind of contingent vector sum of the various peoples and cultures who chose to identify with it or who were incorporated by force. Many of the formulas of incorporation were, one might say, "on loan" from the Indian subcontinent, in the form of Shaivite cults, Brahminical rituals, Hindu court rituals, and Buddhism—first Mahayana and then Theravada. Their value, as Oliver Wolters and others have suggested, lay in the fact that they both reinforced the claims to supernatural powers and legitimacy of local power holders and provided a universalizing framework for creating a new state-based identity from many ethnic and linguistic shards.[47]

If this explicitly political perspective has any merit, its effect is to radically decenter any essentialist understanding of "Burmanness" or "Siameseness" or, for that matter, "Hanness."[48] Identity at the core was a political project designed to weld together the diverse peoples assembled there. Bondsmen of allied strongmen, slaves captured in warfare or raids, cultivators and merchants enticed by agricultural and commercial possibilities: they were in every case a polyglot population. The premium on incorporation meant that assimilation, intermarriage, and social mobility across permeable social barriers were relatively easy. Identity was a matter more of performance than of genealogy.[49] Each of the numerous padi states that came and went in the classical period represented something of a "career open to talent." The culture each of them codified over time varied with the largely imported cultural and human material it had to work with. If there was a cultural attractiveness to the precolonial court centers, it was surely this capacity to absorb migrants and captives and, in two or three generations, to fashion them and their practices into an encompassing Burman or Thai cultural amalgam. A brief look at this process of amalgamation in the Thai padi state, in the Malay zone, and in classical Burma will sharpen our appreciation of the hybridity of the manpower state.[50]

The central plain of what would become Siam was, in the thirteenth century, a complex mix of Mon, Khmer, and Tai populations who were an "ethnicity-in-the-process-of-becoming" Siamese.[51] Victor Lieberman claims that by the mid-fifteenth century in the Ayutthaya Period, a distinctive "Siamese" culture had emerged among an administrative elite (munnai)—and, it appears, only among them. Although their courtly culture drew on Khmer and Pali texts, the commoners, when the Portuguese Tome Pires wrote about them at the very beginning of the sixteenth century, were speakers of Mon dialects, not Tai, and cut their hair like the Mons of Pegu. The ingathering practices of the manpower state were very much in evidence at the end of the seventeenth century, when it is claimed that more than a third of the people in central Siam were "'foreigners' descended chiefly from Lao and Mon captives."[52] Again in the early nineteenth century, the court redoubled its efforts to make good the massive losses of population during the Burmese wars. As a result, "All told, Laos, Mons, Khmers, Burmese and Malays may have equaled the number of self-identified Siamese in the central basin. Phuan, Lao, Cham, and Khmer peasant units formed the backbone of the standing army and navy around Bangkok. On the Khorat plateau after Anuvong's revolt of 1827 so many Lao deportees were resettled that they may have been as numerous as Siamese speakers within the Kingdom as a whole."[53]

What was true for the Chao Praya basin was also true for the veritable archipelago of smaller Tai/Shan padi states scattered here and there farther north among the hills. The consensus is that the Tai/Shan statelets were a politicomilitary invention—Condominas's *système à emboîtement*—in which the Tai were rather thin on the ground. This view matches the evidence that the Burmans were, themselves, also thin on the ground and that they constituted a pioneer, military elite with experience and skills at state-building. That the conquering lords should have been few in number and yet ultimately hegemonic should not surprise those familiar with British history, inasmuch as the conquering Norman elite that came after 1066 to dominate Britain consisted of a mere two thousand families.[54] The Tai/Shan conquerors grew by virtue of a talent for allying, absorbing, adapting, and syncretizing a confected kingdom out of the peoples available to them. The process involved incorporating remnants of preexisting political systems (Mon, Lawa, Khmer) and, above all, absorbing large numbers of upland peoples. Condominas argues that captured hill peoples might start out as bondsmen but, over time, became Tai commoners entitled to hold padi land. Those who were lucky or skilled enough to seize the muang itself would be expected to adopt a Tai noble name, thus bringing their genealogy retrospectively in line with their personal achievement.[55] A majority of the population of most such states was composed of non-Tai peoples, and even many of those who had become Tai and Buddhist continued to use their own languages and customs.[56] Although today it is customary to believe that many Kachin are becoming Shan, the Kachin graduate student who attempted to show that most Shan were at one time Kachin was probably not far off the mark.[57] Shan society, Edmund Leach believed, was not so much a "'ready-made' culture sweeping down from southwest China, as an indigenous growth resulting from an economic interaction of small-scale military colonies with an indigenous hill population over a long period." He adds: "There are various other kinds of evidence which support the view that large sections of the people we now know as Shans are descendants of hill tribesmen who have in the recent past been assimilated into the more sophisticated ways of Buddhist-Shan culture."[58] Similarly designed, but on a far smaller scale, these padi states were ethnically plural, economically open, and culturally assimilationist. Shan identity is, in every case, tied to padi cultivation and, in turn, to being a subject of a Shan state.[59] Through the medium of wet-rice cultivation, "Shanness" and stateness are firmly linked. It is wet-rice cultivation that ensures a fixed, sedentary population which is the basis for military superiority, for an accessible surplus, and for a political hierarchy.[60] Shifting cultivation, by contrast, implies non-Shan identity and, virtually by definition, living at a distance from the state.[61]

The Burman states which have arisen since the eleventh century in upper Burma have almost defined the contours of the classical agrarian, manpower state. Their agro-ecological settling was (along with the Red River in Vietnam) perhaps the most favorable location for the concentration of manpower and grain production. The state-building core, which each dynasty had to control, consisted of six districts, four of which (Kyaukse, Minbu, Shwebo, and Mandalay) had perennial streams allowing extensive, year-round irrigation. Kyaukse, whose very name implies wet-rice cultivation, was the richest of these districts. As early as the twelfth century, there were areas where three crops could be grown annually.[62] By the eleventh century, Lieberman estimates, there were several hundred thousand people within an eighty- to one hundred–mile radius of the court.[63]

Like the Tai kingdoms, Pagan was a political mechanism for the accumulation of manpower and grain production. As such, it welcomed, or seized, settlers wherever they could be found and tied them to the court as subjects. Mid-thirteenth-century Pagan, inscriptions suggest, was an ethnic mosaic including, in addition to Mons, Burmans, Kadus, Sgaws, Kanyans, Palaungs, Was, and Shans.[64] Some were there for the opportunities that a growing empire provided and, for some, perhaps, the move represented a "voluntary assimilation of bilingual peoples eager to identify with the imperial elite."[65] There was, however, little doubt that a considerable portion of the population, particularly the Mon, was the "prize" of raiding, war, and forced resettlement.

Holding together a state core of this magnitude, given the demography, was a tenuous enterprise. The temptations of a land frontier coupled with the burdens of life in state space (taxes, conscription, bondage) meant that the inevitable leakage had constantly to be replenished by military campaigns for captives and forced migration to the center. If the center, once established, managed to hold its own demographically until the mid-thirteenth century, the exodus after that—perhaps because the rice plain offered such a concentration of booty to the Mongol invaders—became a hemorrhage and the empire collapsed.

The last (Kon-baung) dynasty before British rule was, like the earlier dynasties, a manpower-obsessed state. It was understood by its rulers to be a polyglot kingdom in which an oath of loyalty and payment of tribute signaled incorporation. Like the Burmans, the Mon, Siamese, Shan, Laos, Palaungs, and Pa Os were Theravada Buddhists. But judging from the Muslim and Christian communities with their own quarters, mosques, and churches, religious conformity was not a condition of political affiliation. Estimates of what proportion of the early Kon-baung (late-eighteenth-century) population consisted of captives and their descendants necessarily involve a great deal of guesswork. Nevertheless, it seems that they represented between 15 and 25 percent of the realm's roughly two million subjects.[66] The bondsmen, as one might expect, were heavily concentrated near the court center and organized into royal service corps responsible for, say, boat building, weaving, infantry duty, arms making, cavalry, artillery. As *ahmudan* (literally, "task-carriers"), they were distinguished from the *athi,* or commoners, on the one hand, and from the personal bondsmen of private individuals on the other. In the immediate environs of the court, the royal service population (many of them Manipuri) amounted to at least a quarter of the population.

The undifferentiated term *manpower* doesn't begin to do justice to the discriminating accumulation of captives and "guests" selected with an eye to their usefulness. To cite the most celebrated instance, Hsinbyushin, after sacking Ayutthaya in 1767, brought back as many as thirty thousand captives, including officials, playwrights, artisans, dancers, and actors, much of the royal family, and many of the court's literati. The result was not just a renaissance in Burmese art and literature but the creation of a new hybrid court culture. The court entourage included a cosmopolitan collection of valuable specialists: surveyors, gun founders, architects, traders, shipwrights, and accountants, as well as drillmasters from Europe, China, India, the Arab world, and the rest of Southeast Asia. When it came to skilled manpower as well as foot soldiers and cultivators, the need for their services precluded rigid cultural exclusion.

The combination of an elaborate status hierarchy and rapid mobility and assimilation was as characteristic of Kon-baung Burma as it was of early Bangkok Siam. Most Burmans were at some point in their recent ancestry hyphenated Burmans of Shan, Mon, Thai, Manipuri, Arakanese, Karen, or other hill-group backgrounds. If one goes back far enough, one could make a credible argument that many, if not most, Burmans were a cultural amalgam of the earlier Pyu-Burman encounter. Slaves, both debt-bondsmen and captives, were, as elsewhere in Southeast Asia, likely over time to become commoners. Father Sangermano, who lived for more than twenty-five years in Ava and Rangoon at the turn of the nineteenth century, reported the great elaboration of Burmese legal codes covering different forms of bondage. He observed, however, that "this slavery is never perpetual."[67]

Perennial manpower concerns favored easy assimilation and rapid mobility and, in turn, made for very fluid, permeable ethnic boundaries. Lieberman makes an utterly convincing case that what is often seen as a Burman-versus-Mon war between Ava and Pegu was no such thing. In bilingual areas of lower Burma, ethnic identity was more a political choice than a genealogical given. A change of dress, hairstyle, and perhaps residence, and, voilà!—one's ethnic identity had also shifted. Ironically, the force the Burmese court at Ava sent against Pegu had more Mons than Burmans and those sent later (1752) by the Peguans against Alaungpaya were largely Burman. The Ava-Pegu war is thus best understood as a regional conflict in which loyalty to the kingdom trumped all other considerations and in which, in any case, identity was relatively negotiable.[68]

In each of the three kingdoms we have examined, considerations of religion, language, and ethnicity did play a role in stratification within the political system. What is crucial for our purposes, however, is that they were no barrier to membership in the political system. Each of these criteria was, furthermore, subject to transformation rather rapidly and invariably over two generations. The manpower imperative was, everywhere, the enemy of discrimination and exclusion.[69]

The precolonial state we have been examining is, in a sense, a special, limiting case of state-making in challenging demographic and technological conditions. If a state was to arise at all, its rulers would have to concentrate its subjects within a relatively narrow geographical area. Such principles of state space—namely, legibility and appropriateness—are at work in virtually all projects of rule, whether by states or by nonstate institutions. Plantation agriculture with its monoculture and workers' barracks and the mission station with its belltower and the congregants settled in its shadow are distinct forms of control, but each requires legibility and monitoring. It is a rare development project that does not also reshape the landscape and the patterns of residence and of production to achieve a greater degree of legibility and control. The early colonial regimes, in their pacification campaigns, used forced settlement, the destruction of swiddens, and the concentration of subjects. It was only gradually that all-weather roads, railroads, telegraph lines, and a reliable currency allowed a greater dispersal of population and production with little loss of control. Only in counterinsurgency strategies do we see, in miniature, the attempt to closely concentrate a feared population in legible space, occasionally to the point where it comes to resemble an actual concentration camp.

Techniques of Population Control

Slavery

Without slavery, no Greek state, no Greek art and science; without slavery, no Roman Empire. . . . We should never forget that our economic, political and intellectual development presupposes a state of things in which slavery was as necessary as it was universally recognized. In this sense we are entitled to say: without the slavery of antiquity, no modern socialism.
—Karl Marx

Where did the people living in "state space" in the precolonial era come from? Earlier theories, increasingly discredited, held that massive numbers of Tai and Burmans came from the north to displace earlier populations. Instead, it appears that rather modest numbers of Tai and Burmese established their political hegemony over the wet-rice zones that suited them.[70] These padi states undoubtedly absorbed preexisting populations such as the Pyu and Mon as well as, in times of peaceful expansion, attracting immigrants seeking position, work, and trading opportunities. What is most striking, however, is that none of these padi states flourished except by slave-raiding on a substantial scale. Formulaically, and paraphrasing an observation by Karl Marx about slavery and civilization, there was no state without concentrated manpower; there was no concentration of manpower without slavery; hence all such states, including especially the maritime states, were slaving states.

Slaves, it is fair to say, were the most important "cash crop" of precolonial Southeast Asia: the most sought-after commodity in the region's commerce. Virtually every large trader was, simultaneously, a slave-raider or a buyer. Every military campaign, every punitive expedition was, at the same time, a campaign for captives who could be bought, sold, or held. So familiar was the pattern that when Magellan was murdered on his second voyage, the Filipinos responsible rounded up what was left of his crew and sold them off in the islands. When the Burmese captured the port city of Syriam from Portuguese adventurers in the early seventeenth century, they grabbed the surviving Europeans and forcibly resettled them in villages near the capital, Ava. Southeast Asian kingdoms were remarkably broad-minded when it came to the acquisition of manpower.

Only by scouring its periphery was a growing padi state able to achieve the concentration of population required to dominate and defend its core. The process of scouring was a pan–Southeast Asian phenomenon with systematic characteristics. Anthony Reid, author of the most important analysis of slavery, explains the pattern: "Before indentured labour was developed in the nineteenth century, the movement of captive peoples and slaves was the primary source of labour mobility in Southeast Asia. Typically it took the form of transferring people from weak, politically fragmented societies to stronger and wealthier ones. The oldest, and demographically most important, form of movement was the border raiding against animist swidden cultivators and hunter-gatherers by stronger wet-rice cultivators of the river valleys."[71] Another way of describing the process is the systematic removal of captives from nonstate spaces, particularly the hills, in order to deposit them at, or nearby, state spaces. The pattern could be discerned in Cambodia in 1300 and continued in some areas (for example, Malaysia) well into the twentieth century. Gibson claims that until roughly 1920, the majority of the urban Southeast Asian population were either captives or their descendants (often in the past two or three generations).[72]

The evidence is pervasive. In the Tai world, by way of illustration, fully three-quarters of the kingdom of Chiang Mai's population in the late nineteenth century consisted of war captives. Chiang Saen (Kaing Hsen), another Tai statelet, had nearly 60 percent slaves; in Lamphun seventeen thousand of a total of thirty thousand subjects were slaves. Rural elites also held slaves as part of their labor force and entourage. Such slaves were captured directly in war or were purchased from slave-raiding parties that combed the hills kidnapping whomever they could.[73] To read any of the court histories or chronicles of Tai or Burman kingdoms is to be treated to a long series of accounts of raids whose success is typically measured by the number and skills

of the captives. Rebellion, or failure to send the appropriate tribute, was frequently punished by the sacking and burning of the disobedient district and
the deportation of its subjects to the victor's court center. When the ruler of
Songkhla, after first refusing, finally came to Ayutthaya to present tribute, the
king arranged for all of Songkhla's inhabitants to be carried off into slavery
nearer the capital. The magnitude of slaving is less obscure than many other
subjects to historians precisely because the taking of captives was the public
purpose of statecraft.

There were, of course, many other ways than by capture to become a
slave in these political systems. Debt bondage was common, in which the
debtor and/or members of his family became "slaves" of the creditor until
the debt was acquitted. Children were sold into bondage by their parents, and
convicted criminals were condemned to slavery as punishment. If, however,
such mechanisms constituted the major social origin of slavery, one would
expect that most slaves would be culturally similar to their masters, except
for the formal status difference. But this was not the case, as Katherine Bowie
shows for northern Thailand. The majority of slaves, here and elsewhere, appear to come from culturally distinct hill populations and to have been taken
in slave raids as prizes of war.[74]

The scale of slaving and its effects are hard to imagine.[75] Slaving expeditions were a regular, dry-season commercial venture in much of the mainland.
Between freebooting expeditions, small-scale kidnapping, and the larger-
scale deportations (for example, the six thousand families removed forcibly
to Thailand after the Siamese capture of Vientiane in 1826), whole regions
were largely stripped of their inhabitants. Bowie quotes the late-nineteenth-
century observer A. C. Colquhoun, who captures something of the extent
and human impact:

> There is little doubt that the sparsity of hill tribes in the hills neighboring
> Zimme [Chiang Mai] has been chiefly caused by their having been, in the olden
> time, systematically hunted like wild cattle, to supply the slave market. . . .
>   The slaves who are captured become slaves in the fullest sense of the
> word; they are carried off with no hope of deliverance save death and escape.
> Trapped by ambush, and driven off after capture, like fallow-deer, by the man-
> hunters, they are torn from their forests, chained, and taken to the chief places
> of the Shan country [Chiang Mai], Siam, and Cambodia for disposal.[76]

As different agro-ecological zones, the hills and lowland valleys were
natural trading partners. Alas, however, the most important hill commodity

for expansive valley states was its manpower.[77] This kind of manpower hunting and gathering was so lucrative that hill people and not a few hill societies
as a whole became deeply implicated in the trade. Alongside war captives and
punitive resettlement, lowland populations were augmented by what were
essentially commercial slaving expeditions. Societies in the hills could often
be classified into weak, fragmented societies that served as the sources of slave
raids, the prey, and highland groups that organized slave raids and frequently
held slaves themselves, the predators. The Akha, the Palaung, and the Lisu,
for example, seem to fit in the first category and, at times, the Karenni and
Kachin in the second. Capturing and selling slaves was such a mainstay of
the Kachin economy that an early colonial official could declare that "slavery
is a national custom among the Kachins."[78] The Karen, by contrast, appear
sometimes as prey and sometimes as predator.[79]

As is so often the case with a major commodity, slaves became virtually
the standard of value by which other goods were denominated. A slave in
the Chin Hills in the late nineteenth century was worth four head of cattle,
a good gun, or twelve pigs. "Slaves were current coin in the hills, and passed
from hand to hand as easily as a bank-note in more civilized regions."[80] The
tight association between hill peoples and the social origin of most slaves is
strikingly indexed in the fact that the terms for slaves and hill peoples were
often interchangeable. At the bottom of a Tai kingdom, Condominas reports,
were the *Sa* or *xa* in Vietnamese, like its equivalent *kha* in the Lao and Siamese languages. The term "can be either translated as 'slave' or 'mountain
tribe,' according to the context."[81] Similarly, the term for savage or barbarian
in Vietnamese, *moi*, has indelible servile connotations and, in precolonial
time, the Central Highlands were called *rung moi* or "forests of the savages."
The Khmer term for barbarian, *phnong*, has similar connotations.[82]

The memory of slave raids permeates many contemporary hill societies.
It is present in legend and myth, in accounts of abduction that the present
generation has heard from parents and grandparents, and, in some cases,
in personal memories of the elderly. Thus the Pwo Karen tell of repeated
abductions from the area around Mawlamyine and their forced relocation as
slaves in Tai kingdoms. When Karens want to make their children behave,
they scare them by saying that a Thai will come and carry them off.[83] The
Lamet, in what is now Laos, have a collective memory of Burmese slave raids
in which their hair was colored with lime to make them easily identifiable. In
response, they remember retreating to ridge villages surrounded by pits to
avoid being taken.[84] The culture of some groups, it appears, has been funda-

mentally shaped by a fear of slavery and by the measures taken to avoid it. Leo Alting von Geusau makes this case convincingly for the Akha of the Thai-Yunnan border region, whose curing rituals recapitulate the experience of lowland captivity and eventual freedom. They, like the Lamet, see themselves as a relatively powerless group which must live by its wits and stay well clear of lowland power centers.[85]

The difference between slave-raiding and warfare, in this context, becomes almost a theological issue. Large-scale warfare was conducted against other kingdoms in which the existence of the realm and its dynasty were often at stake. In the smaller wars, less was at stake, but in each case the losing side could expect to have much of its population swept up and carried back to the victor's core region. In the case of expeditions into the hills to hunt slaves, warfare gave way to something like a manhunt directed at less organized peoples whose only option was guerrilla-style self-defense or flight. The prize in all three cases was manpower: a war was a dangerous wholesale gamble for manpower; slave raids were a less dangerous, though armed, retail enterprise. Just as one could fairly call the Burmese and Tai states "warfare states," it would be just as accurate to describe them as "slaving states."

The taking of captives was not just the major strategic objective of warfare; it was the personal objective of the officers and men serving in the army. These were armies with both eyes fixed on the loot. Of the spoils, only elephants, horses, arms, and ammunition were reserved explicitly for the Burmese crown. The rest—children, women, men, cattle, gold, silver, apparel, and foodstuffs—was the property of the soldiers who had seized it, to dispose of as they pleased. The Glass Palace Chronicle of the Kings of Burma reports that during the late-eighteenth-century attack on Linzin (Vientiane) an infantryman leading back forty captives as his personal booty sold one of them to the king, who thought the man would make a good soldier.[86] One must see these armies not as unified bureaucratic organizations collectively obeying the will of their commander but rather as something like a joint trading venture, albeit a dangerous one, from which the various investors and participants expect to make a profit. The pattern conforms to Max Weber's description of certain forms of premodern warfare as "booty capitalism": a speculative, for-profit war in which there is an understanding among the investors about how the proceeds will be distributed if the enterprise succeeds. When we consider that such armies also had to provision themselves en route to their military objective, we can appreciate how destructive and feared they must have been. The armies, some of which were apparently quite large, would require carts, oxen, water buffaloes, porters, rice, meat, and recruits (to replace deserters!) all along the way. When plunder is added to the requirements of "living off the land," and the need to destroy the crops and dwellings of captives to discourage them from returning, one appreciates that this sort of warfare could be utterly ruinous without necessarily being very sanguinary.[87]

A certain proportion of the captives forcibly taken back to the victor's territory thus came as personal property rather than crown property. Manpower was not simply an end of statecraft; it was also an important mark of status, reflected in the size of one's personal entourage. Elites jockeyed to accumulate a critical mass of dependents through debt bondage and purchase that would ensure their status and wealth. The crown, prominent families, and religious establishments (for example, Buddhist abbeys) all competed against one another for the available manpower resources. At a higher level, the padi states were in competition with one another for population that represented the only guarantee of their power. Thus the Siamese and Burmans were, once Pegu had fallen, in constant conflict over which of them would come to monopolize the Mon and Karen populations that lay between them. Ava and Chiang Mai competed over the Lawa and Karen who lay between them. Their competition was not always warlike. From time to time, like real estate agents in a buyer's market with a high vacancy rate, they would offer favorable terms to those who would agree to settle under their wing. Thus Northern Thai leaders offered the Lawa and Karen exemption from corvée and taxes as long as they would permanently settle in a designated area and provide annual tribute in valuable mountain products. In the teeth of rapacious district officials, military commanders, and slave-raiders, however, even the well-intentioned ruler was unlikely to be able to keep such a promise. In this context, the Chiang Mai ruler's curse—"May those who oppress the Lawa be destroyed"—may fairly be read against the grain to indicate how relatively powerless he was to enforce his wish.[88]

When the manpower machine was working well, when a dynasty was attracting or, more likely, capturing population at a rate that far exceeded its losses, it was perforce becoming more cosmopolitan at the same time. The greater the diversity of peoples it absorbed, the more its metropolitan culture bore the linguistic and cultural traces of its hybridity. In fact, such cultural hybridity was a condition of its success. Just as the Malay coastal state, underneath its shared Malay language and the profession of Islam, was appreciably different depending on the cultural streams it had incorporated, so did the Tai and Burman padi states reflect the cultures of those they had accepted or seized under a cultural portmanteau of Theravada Buddhism and a dominant language.

The padi states' project of amassing population was a perilous, shaky enterprise for several reasons. First, of course, the demography was working against it. Population was always, for reasons we shall explore in more detail, leaking away. Much of the history of any particular padi state could well be written in terms of the oscillation over time between ingathering and exodus. Whenever the crown was unable to replenish its population through a combination of capture by warfare, slaving expeditions, and the attractions of commerce and culture at the center, it risked a fatal erosion of its demographic and military strength. The decline of the Restored Taung-ngu Kingdom after 1626 and that of the Kon-baung Kingdom after 1760 can be traced to similar disequilibria. Following the conquests of the early Restored Taung-ngu kings, an extended period of peace meant that there were not enough new captives to offset the losses of subjects fleeing the "over-exploitation" of the "nuclear area." In the 1780s the unraveling of the Kon-baung Kingdom under King Bò-daw-hpaya was less due to passivity than to failed invasions of neighbors and unprecedented labor drafts for public works that turned the normal trickle of subjects leaving the core into a crippling mass exodus.[89]

The second obstacle was simply that, looked at comprehensively, the mad scramble for manpower was essentially a zero-sum game. This was painfully obvious in the case of wars between padi states in which the gains of the victor tended to equal the losses of the defeated. Even in the case of slave-raiding expeditions to the hills, a small number of petty kingdoms were competing for the same limited pool of captives. Finally, the rulers of the padi states were systematically losing much of their accessible grain and population through their inability to overcome the combined fiscal resistance and evasion of their own elites and commoners. We turn then to this last dilemma of rule and the paradox that, when such resistance was crushed, it provoked a massive exodus, with consequences for the state that were typically even more catastrophic.

Fiscal Legibility

An efficient system of taxation requires, first and foremost, that the objects of taxation (people, land, trade) be made legible. Population rolls and cadastral maps of productive land are the key administrative tools of legibility. As in the case of our earlier distinction between gross domestic product and state-accessible product, there is an important distinction to be made here between the total population and what James Lee calls the "fiscal population"—the population which is administratively legible.[90] A similar distinction might be made between actual cultivated land and total trade on the one hand and "fiscal landholding" and "fiscal trade" on the other. It is, of course, only the registered ("fiscal") land and population that are assessed and, hence, accessible. The degree of slippage between fiscal resources and off-the-books resources is a rough measure of the efficiency of a tax system. In premodern political systems that slippage was substantial.

An effort at fine-mesh record keeping was made on Burmese King Tha-lun's order in the early seventeenth century, "to list the land under cultiva-tion and thus taxable; the people's names, ages, sex, birthdays, and children; the members and lands of the various crown service groups; the local officials and their service lands, and the boundaries of their jurisdiction."[91] The king wanted, in effect, a complete inventory of his taxable resources. Like all such records, even if it was accurate when compiled, it was a static snapshot that was soon overtaken by land transfers, population movement, and inheritance, among other things. Other decrees aimed at preserving the validity of the records by prohibiting certain kinds of social change that would make them invalid. Subjects were forbidden to move without explicit permission, and were barred from changing their civil status from commoner or royal ser-vicemen to bondsmen. The relative permanence of irrigated padi fields and a standardized "fiscal" family under a male head of household were also aids to legibility at the core.[92]

Above and beyond the inherent difficulties of premodern fiscal admin-istration, the monarch faced a more systematic and intractable structural problem. He was in direct competition with his own officials, nobles, and clerics for manpower and grain. Although the royal crown service population (ahmudan) was the most accessible manpower base for the crown, its ranks were being constantly eroded. It was in the interest of such servicemen to change their status to a less onerous and less legible one. Several options were open: to be a commoner (athi), a private client to a powerful patron, or a debt bondsman, or to join a large, undocumented "floating" population. It was, at the same time, very much in the interest of the king's officials and prominent nobles to abet, in every way possible, this shift in fiscal status, for it allowed them to sequester these resources for their own entourages and tax bases.[93] Many of the Kon-baung legal codes are devoted to thwarting this drift toward fiscal invisibility and hence into the hands of other elites. Reading this litany of prohibitions again against the grain suggests that the crown was less than completely successful.

The rulers of the Thai kingdoms struggled against the same tendency for officials, nobles, and religious authorities to appropriate the crown's fiscal resources for themselves. Thus the founder of the northern Thai kingdom of Lan Na, King Mangrai, declared the "deserters from the king's service who try to avoid their obligations, should not be allowed to become slaves [of others than the king]."[94]

Both the Thai and Burman crowns, in the era before internal passports and identity papers, hit on the device of tattooing much of the male population to indelibly mark one's status. Soldiers recruited—or press-ganged—into the Kon-baung army were tattooed with symbols showing that they were liable for military service.[95] The Thais tattooed as well. Thai slaves and bondsmen were tattooed on the wrist with a mark indicating whether they belonged to the king or to a noble. If a slave belonged to a noble, that particular noble was indicated in the tattoo in much the same way a cattle brand is used to indicate livestock ownership.[96] Karen prisoners of war were tattooed to indicate their status as war captives. The system of tattoos gave rise to bounty hunters, who coursed the forests looking for runaways to return to their "rightful" owners. Such measures not only indicated that the monitoring of manpower was, in most respects, more important than the registration of land, but that it was also more difficult.

The king's officials and local power holders also had more banal reasons for any sleight of hand that would remove resources from the crown so that they could be "privatized" and plundered. Thus the population rolls were, as the first colonial censuses documented, greatly understated. Officials removed land from the land registers for a fee, appropriated poorly documented crown lands themselves, underreported tax receipts, and left households off the tax rolls altogether. William Koenig estimates that anywhere from 10 to 40 percent of crown revenue was lost in this fashion. He cites an instance after an 1810 fire in Rangoon when officials were directed to conduct a new housing census. They omitted one thousand of the twenty-five hundred houses from the new register.[97] The net result was anything but an easing of the tax burden on commoners. Rather, it was a shift in the division of the spoils of state that was potentially ruinous for the crown and for commoners as well.

Faced with the steady evaporation of its tax base through outright flight and through the fiscal invisibility we have just described, the ruler of the padi state was hard put to hold the realm together. One of the few options open to him was a military campaign for captives to replenish those he was steadily losing. The advantage of new war prisoners was that many of them would become crown servicemen and hence owe service, at least initially, directly to the crown. This may, speculatively, help explain the tendency of such padi states to become warfare states. Only through warfare could the ruler stand a chance on making good, at one stroke, his continuing loss of manpower.

Smaller-scale slave raids into the hills and attacks on peripheral villages carried less risk, but the yield in manpower was correspondingly small. Larger-scale wars could bring in many thousands of captives. As noted, though, while this may have been a rational strategy for a particular ruling dynasty, it was systemically irrational. In a war between two padi states, the loser was likely to suffer a catastrophic diminution of its population.

State Space as Self-Liquidating

The most thoughtful historians of premodern states in Southeast Asia have been struck by their fragility, by the boom-and-bust quality of their growth and collapse. Victor Lieberman has described them as having a "convulsive quality," whereas Oliver Wolters has applied the term *concertina*.[98] In this final section, I want to endorse and expand on Lieberman's argument that there are systematic, structural reasons behind this fragility and oscillation.

The straightforward logic of "self-liquidation" can, for the purposes of illustration, be seen at work in the counterinsurgency policy of the contemporary military tyranny in Burma. Military units are attempting to control more of the insurgent border region while, at the same time, being told by their financially strapped commanders that they must provision themselves locally. Thus, a little like the premodern state, military units must find the labor, cash, building material, and foodstuffs to sustain themselves in a rugged and hostile environment. They do this, typically, by essentially capturing and concentrating a substantial civilian population around their base, which becomes their available pool of manpower, grain, and revenue. The civilians try to flee, first and foremost among them the poorest, who cannot buy their way out of forced labor or afford to provide the grain and taxes extorted from them. As a Karen schoolteacher put it to a human rights researcher, "Along the road . . . down in the plains, there used to be many villages, but the big villages have become small and the small villages have become forest. Many people have gone to the [other] towns or come up here [to the mountains], because the SPDC [military government] demands so many taxes from them and forces them to do all kinds of labour."[99] The consequences for those left behind are predictable: "As the abuses continue, focusing on fewer people, the less vulnerable become progressively more vulnerable and are gradually forced into flight themselves."[100]

Variations of essentially this argument have been made about the pre-modern Tai and Burman states by Rabibhadana, Lieberman, and Koenig.[101] The heartland or core region of the padi state is the most legible and accessible concentration of grain and manpower. Other things being equal, it is this population from which it is easiest and most efficient to extract the resources necessary to sustain the state and its elite. The fiscal temptation was to press heaviest on this core population and, as a result, it was likely to be the most beleaguered. Thus, under the Kon-baung kings, those in the Mandalay-Ava area were the most "combed over" for corvée and grain, whereas those at a greater remove were able to get away with more nominal tribute. If we recall that a considerable portion of the core population itself had been sequestered by officials and private notables, then it is clear that the burden fell disproportionately on the crown-service population, many of whom were descended from captives and commoners who figured on the tax rolls. This population operated like something of a homeostatic device for the state as a whole: the greater the pressure exerted on it, the more likely it would simply flee out of range or, in some cases, rebel.

Lieberman offers many examples of this pattern—of the padi state, in effect, killing the goose that lays the golden egg. The late-sixteenth-century king of Pegu (the son of the famous Bayin-naung), deserted by many outlying military tributaries, was compelled to press with desperation on his core population, forcing monks into the army and executing deserters. The harder he pressed the more population he lost. Cultivators disappeared en masse to become private retainers and debt bondsmen or defected to the hills and other kingdoms. Deprived of its grain producers and soldiers, Pegu was, at the end of the century, sacked by its enemies.[102] Perhaps the most notable instance of near collapse was at the turn of the nineteenth century. Although the kingdom was blessed with the captives that Alaungpaya's conquests and his dispossession of his opponents had added, the fiscal pressure on this population, aggravated by a drought and a failed invasion of Siam, resulted in a great exodus.[103] The breakdown of the Trinh in the early eighteenth century fits this pattern as well. Increasingly, the autonomy of local notables had allowed them to escape taxes themselves and appropriate labor and property that would otherwise have been available to the state. As a result, "the burden was carried by ever fewer people who were at the same time the ones least able to pay."[104] Flight and rebellion on a large scale followed.

The king's counselors surely knew, implicitly or explicitly, the structural problems they faced. The proverbs about manpower, their efforts to prevent the loss of manpower and grain to their own officials, their attempts at a more rigorous inventory of the resources they did have, and their search for other forms of revenue tell us as much. Knowing this, one might have expected statecraft to consist in sailing as close to the wind as they could: that is, in extracting resources just short of the point at which they would provoke flight or rebellion. Short of a series of very successful wars-for-captives and slave-raiding, this would be the most reasonable strategy.[105]

There are at least three reasons why the premodern state was unable to calibrate its extractions in this way. Their relative importance is hard to determine and, in any event, might vary from case to case. The first reason is simply that states did not have the kind of structural information that would allow them to make such a fine-grained judgment, especially since many of their officials had their own reasons to deceive the crown. The crop was in principle legible, but the officials were not. Second, the fiscal capacity of the population varied widely, as it would in any agrarian economy, from season to season depending on harvest fluctuations due to weather, pests, and crop diseases. Even theft and banditry could be a factor here: concentrated above-ground grain crops were just as big a temptation to gangs of thieves, rebels, or rival kingdoms as they were to the state. Allowing for the great variation in the cultivators' capacity to pay year by year would have required the crown to sacrifice its own fiscal demands for the welfare of its peasantry. All the evidence suggests that, quite to the contrary, the precolonial and colonial states tried to guarantee themselves a steady take, at the expense of their subjects.[106]

There is evidence, which we shall explore in more detail, that the demography and agro-ecology of state space, in fact, makes it more vulnerable to instability in food supply and to illness. Very briefly, fully occupied monocultures seem less environmentally resilient than dispersed, mixed cultivation. They are more prone to crop disease; they have less of an environmental buffer in case of crop failure; and they promote the multiplication of their obligate pests. Much the same might be said about the concentration of people together with livestock and poultry as well. We know that most epidemic diseases are zoonotic, moving between domestic animals and humans;

we know that urban populations in the West did not successfully replace themselves reproductively until the mid-nineteenth century; we know that the grain diet of early agrarian societies was nutritionally inferior to the mixed diet it replaced; and, finally, we have ample evidence of crop failures, famines, and cholera outbreaks in precolonial Southeast Asia. Although somewhat speculative, it is likely that the concentrations of rice and men in state spaces carried their own substantial risks.

The third reason, however obvious it might seem, was the tremendous capriciousness introduced by a political system in which the king was, at least in theory, all powerful. There is no rational accounting for Bò-daw-hpaya's ruinous invasion of Siam on the heels of a famine, nor is there one for his massive use of corvée around 1800 to build hundreds of pagodas, including one at Mingun that was to have been the largest in the world.[107] After all the structural and ecological reasons for the instability of precolonial dynasties have been accounted for, there is the added factor of arbitrary, tyrannical rule that is not institutionalized.

It is little wonder that the padi state was a fragile and evanescent affair. Given the demographic, structural, and personal obstacles in its path, what is remarkable, on a long view, is that it did occasionally coalesce long enough to create a defining cultural tradition.

CHAPTER 4

Civilization and the Unruly

Why this sudden restlessness, this confusion?
(How serious people's faces have become)
Why are the streets and squares emptying so rapidly?
Everyone's going home lost in thought
Because night has fallen and the barbarians have not come
And some who have just returned from the border say
There are no barbarians any longer
And now, what's going to happen to us without barbarians?
They were, those people, a kind of solution.
—C. Cavafy, "Waiting for the Barbarians," 1914

In effect the essential thing is to gather into groups this people which is everywhere
and nowhere; the essential thing is to make them something we can seize hold of. When
we have them in our hands, we will then be able to do many things which are quite
impossible for us today and will perhaps allow us to capture their minds after we have
captured their bodies.
—French officer, Algeria, 1845

This people have never turned their attention to agricultural pursuits, nor can it be
expected of them until they are placed upon a reservation. . . . If they are not provided
with such a home, they are destined to remain outside of those influences which are
calculated to civilize or Christianize them . . . [and] render [them] useful members of
society. Wild Indians, like wild horses, must be corralled upon reservations. There they
can be brought to work.
—Bureau of Indian Affairs agent to the Shoshone, 1865

T he permanent settlement of populations is, along with taxes, perhaps the oldest state activity. It has always been accompanied
by a civilizational discourse in which those who are settled are
presumed to have raised their cultural and moral level. While the
rhetoric of high imperialism could speak unself-consciously of "civilizing"
and "Christianizing" the nomadic heathen, such terms strike the modern ear
as outdated and provincial, or as euphemisms for all manner of brutalities.
And yet if one substitutes the nouns *development, progress,* and *modernization,*
it is apparent that the project, under a new flag, is very much alive and well.

What is striking about this civilizational discourse is its staying power.

Its permanence is all the more remarkable in the light of evidence that ought to have shaken it to its very foundations. It survives despite our awareness that people have been moving, for millennia, back and forth across this semi-permeable membrane between the "civilized" and the "uncivilized" or the "not-yet-civilized." It survives despite the perennial existence of societies that occupy an intermediate position socially and culturally between the two presumed spheres. It survives despite massive evidence of cultural borrowing and exchange in both directions. And it survives despite an economic integration driven by complementarity that makes of the two spheres a single economic unit.

Much of the actual content of what it means to be "civilized," to be "Han," to be a proper "Thai" or "Burman" is exhausted by being a fully incorporated, registered, taxpaying subject of the state. Being "uncivilized" is, by contrast, often the converse: to live outside the ambit of the state. Much of this chapter is devoted to examining how state formation creates, in its wake, a barbarian frontier of "tribal peoples" to which it is the pole of comparison and, at the same time, the antidote.

Valley States, Highland Peoples: Dark Twins

Legitimating the classical state in Southeast Asia was, in modern parlance, a "hard sell." The very idea of the classical state, far from being an organic elaboration of indigenous concept of rule, was, like the modern nation-state, largely a cultural and political import. The Hinduized concept of the universal monarch provided the ideological apparatus to support a claim to ritual supremacy in a political context otherwise characterized by contending, and presumptively equal, strongmen. With the help of court Brahmins, ambitious courts from the tenth to the fourteenth century set about making large cosmological claims and incorporating local cults of their outlying provinces under an imperial ritual umbrella.[1] The effect was something like the eighteenth-century Russian court at St. Petersburg mimicking the manners, language, and rituals of the French court at Versailles. Making such a claim "stick" required not just convincing theater, as Geertz has shown, but a core population whose manpower and grain could reinforce the court's claim. And this, in turn, required coercion in the form of slaving expeditions and a system of unfree labor. The classical state, in short, was anything but self-legitimating. It was perhaps for this reason that the cosmological bluster of such states tended to compensate for their relative weakness politically and militarily.[2]

Given the fact that such states were created by an ingathering of various peoples living outside state structures, it is not surprising that the major elements representing a "civilized" existence happen to coincide with life in the padi state: living in permanent villages in the valleys, cultivating fixed fields, preferably wet rice, recognizing a social hierarchy with kings and clerics at its apex, and professing a major salvation religion—Buddhism, Islam, or, in the case of the Philippines, Christianity.[3] Nor is it surprising that each of these characteristics should be the mirror image of the surrounding societies remaining outside the sphere of the padi state: the hill peoples.

Viewed from the court center of the padi state, the thinner the air you breathe, the less civilized you are. It is no exaggeration to say that the presumptive level of civilization can, from a valley perspective, be often read as a function of altitude. Those on the mountaintops are the most backward and uncivilized; those living midslope are slightly more elevated culturally; those living in upland plateaus and growing irrigated rice are, again, more advanced, though certainly inferior to those at the core of the valley state, with the court and king at its apex, who represent the pinnacle of refinement and civilization.

"Hilliness" per se is disqualifying. Thus many of the Palaung in Burma are Theravada Buddhists, dress like Burmans, and speak fluent Burmese. They are not, however, considered civilized so long as they live in the hills. A contemporary version of this correlation was expressed by a Vietnamese ethnographer, Mac Durong, famous for his pathbreaking and sympathetic studies of minorities, many of whom, he believes, were long ago driven into the hills solely because they arrived on the scene after the Vietnamese had occupied the bottomland. The logic behind his understanding of why such groups were called *Man* (a term that has come over the centuries to mean "savage") was clear, as Patricia Pelley noted: "There *were* legitimate reasons to refer to the highland peoples as savage, and the rationale, while not explicitly stated, was apparent: civilization could be gauged by geography, and more especially, by elevation. The people in the lowlands [ethnic Vietnamese] were fully civilized; those dwelling in the midlands were partially civilized; but highlanders were still savage, and the higher the elevation the greater the degree of savagery."[4] It does not suffice to terrace land and create wet-rice padis to qualify as civilized. The Hani, along the upper reaches of the Red River in northern Vietnam, do just that and are still seen as Man.

This inversion of elevation and civilizational standing works much the same way in Thailand. As a lifelong student of the Akha (linguistically related to the Hani), the late Leo Alting von Geusau observed that the Akha, as a "mid-slope" people, are stigmatized as uncivilized, though not so uncivilized as groups living at the highest elevations. "This situation," he wrote, "is structured . . . in an inverse way to the *sakdina* [lowland Thai ranking] type of hierarchy, with the lowest class the highest up [Mon-Khmer groups such as Wa, Bulang, Khmu, Htin, and Dulong] and the socially highest situated lowest, in the valleys and plains."[5]

Linguistic usage in Burmese and Chinese reflects the way in which lowland centers of civilization are elevated symbolically. Thus to go to the capital city or to school is generally to "go up" or "climb" or "rise" (*téq*—တက်). Even if one lives on a mountaintop, one still goes "up" to Mandalay. Similarly, when one goes to rural villages or to the hills, one goes "down" or "descends" (*s'in*—ဆင်း), even if the place in question is thousands of feet above the capital in altitude. Here, as in some Western contexts, up and down have nothing to do with altitude and everything to do with cultural elevation.[6]

If living at high elevations was coded "barbarian" by the padi state, so too was physical mobility and dispersal. Here again there are strong parallels with the history of the Mediterranean world. Christian and Muslim states regarded mountain dwellers and nomadic peoples—precisely those peoples who had thus far eluded the grasp of the state—as pagan and barbarian. Muhammad himself made it abundantly clear that nomads who embraced Islam must, as a condition of their conversion, settle permanently or pledge to do so.[7] Islam was the faith of a sedentary elite, and it was assumed that one could not be a satisfactory Muslim without being settled. Bedouins were regarded as "wild men," the precise opposite of the Meccan, urban ideal. In civilizational terms, nomadism was to the Arab state what elevation was to the padi state.

In Southeast Asia as well, the idea of civilization was in large measure an agro-ecological code. Peoples who appeared to have no fixed abode, who moved constantly and unpredictably, were beyond the pale of civilization. Here the condition of remaining "legible" to the state and producing a surplus that is readily appropriable is embedded in the concept of civilization. A similar stigma has been applied in the West as in Southeast Asia to subjects, even if ethnically and religiously part of the dominant society, who have no permanent residence: variously termed vagrants, homeless, vagabonds, tramps. Aristotle thought famously that man was by nature a citizen of a city (*polis*); people who chose consciously to not belong to such a community (*apolis*) were, by definition, of no worth.[8] When whole peoples, such as pastoralists, gypsies, swidden cultivators follow, by choice, an itinerant or semi-itinerant livelihood, they are seen as a collective threat and are collectively stigmatized.

Vietnamese, however widely they may range to find work and land, think of themselves, nevertheless, as having an ancestral place to which they will, or might, return.[9] Those without an ancestral place are stigmatized as "people of the four corners of the world."[10] Hill peoples are, by extension, whole societies of vagrants, at once pitiable, dangerous, and uncivilized. The state-sponsored "Campaign to Sedentarize the Nomads" or the "Campaign for Fixed Cultivation and Fixed Residence," designed to curtail shifting cultivation and resettle highland peoples away from the frontiers and to "teach" them wet-rice cultivation, had a deep resonance among the Vietnamese population. It seemed to them and their officials that they were engaged in a magnanimous effort to bring backward and uncouth peoples into the fold of Vietnamese civilization.

Burmans, while less concerned than Vietnamese with ancestral tombs per se, have a comparable fear of and contempt for wanderers with no fixed abode. Such people are called *lu lè lu lwin* (လူ လေ လူ လွင့်), literally, "a person blown about by the wind," which could variously be rendered as vagrant, tramp, or wanderer, with the connotation of one going to waste.[11] Many of the hill peoples are seen in the same light as backward, unreliable, and without culture. For the Burmese, as for the Chinese, itinerant peoples were civilizationally suspect by definition. These stereotypes persist and plague hill peoples in Burma today. Thus a Catholic student of Padaung-Karen (both hill peoples) parentage hesitated when fleeing the military repression of the 1988 democratic movement on account of the stigma attached to taking refuge in the forest:

> I was afraid, quite simply of being branded as a jungle fugitive by my fellow countrymen. The word "jungle" [*táw*—တော] still carried pejorative overtones in the speech of urban Burmese. Anyone taking refuge with the ethnic insurgents was called a jungle child [*táw ka lé*—တော က လေး] which implied primitiveness, anarchy, violence, and disease, as well as the unpleasant proximity of wild animals which the Burmese detested. I had always been painfully sensitive about being regarded as part of a primitive tribe, and much of my ambition in Taunggyi and Mandalay had been to escape into civilization.[12]

The Qing general Ortai, who described the hill peoples of Yunnan as "barbarian nomads who were the antithesis of civilized ideals," was not only being redundant; he was expressing an equation to which all padi-state rulers might subscribe.[13]

For the Chinese, Burmese, and Siamese states, certain modes of subsistence and the agro-ecological niche in which they were practiced were irretrievably barbaric. Hunting and gathering as well as shifting cultivation were necessarily practiced in the forests.[14] This in itself was outside the pale. A seventeenth-century Chinese text describes the Lahu of Yunnan as "people of the mountains, forests and streams."[15] It claims that they eat everything raw and do not bury their dead, comparing them to apes and monkeys. Far from entertaining the possibility that, as Anthony Walker believes, they became hill swiddeners only when they fled the valleys, they were assumed to be true aboriginals. The proof of their primitive, ur- condition was precisely the list of their customs and practices—dwellings, clothes (or their absence), footwear (or its absence), diet, burial practices, and demeanor—that contravened every ideal of Confucian civilization.

Reading some of the reports of Han officials on the multitudinous and confusing hill peoples of the southwest frontier, one is left with two impressions. The first is that of an ethnographic "field guide to the birds"—the Lahu wear such-and-such colors, can be found in such-and-such a habitat, and subsist in such-and-such a manner—allowing administrators to recognize them as they "fly by," so to speak. The second impression is that they are all being placed in an evolutionary and civilizational sequence in which the ideals of Han civilization are the metric. Viewed this way, the hill tribes are ranged from very "raw" (primitive) to very cooked. Thus we get a series of the following kind: "almost Han," "on-their-way-to-being-Han," "could-eventually-become-Han-if-they-wanted-to (and if-we-wanted-them-to!)," and, finally, a category (for the "wildest" of the Lahu, for example) "uncivilizable," which meant, of course, "not-really-human."

It is a rare term for people at the periphery of state power—swiddeners, hill people, forest dwellers, or even peasants in the "deep" countryside—that does not carry stigmatizing connotations. For the Burmans, the term for villagers far from cultural centers is *táw thà* (ေတာ သား), literally, forest dweller, with the connotation of rustic, wild, and uncouth (*yaín*—ရိုင်း).[16]

The indelible association of the valley state with fixed-field grain agriculture, and hence with a quasi-permanent social order of aristocrats and commoners that represented "civilization," had ironic consequences. Those who chose to leave the realm of inequalities and taxes for the hills placed themselves, by definition, beyond the pale. Altitude could then be coded "primitive."[17] In addition, to the degree that irrigated padi cultivation massively alters the landscape, while hill agriculture appears less visually obtrusive, hill peoples came to be associated with nature as against culture. This fact enables the following false but common comparison: the civilized change the world; the barbarians live in the world without changing it.

For Thai and Burman states, the profession of Theravada Buddhism was also a necessary, but not a sufficient, condition for the inclusion of hill peoples in the charmed circle of civilization. The importance of a major salvation religion would, as with Islam in the Malay world, seem to mark off such societies sharply from Han civilization, which had no such religious test.[18] The markers for levels of civilization, even among the party ethnographers classifying the "tribes" of Guizhou and Yunnan in the 1950s, were essentially Han technologies and customs. Did they plant in irrigated fields? Did they plow and use agricultural tools? Did they live in fixed settlements? Could they speak and write Chinese? Before 1948 they would have received extra marks for erecting temples to Han-style deities—most particularly, to the God of agriculture.[19] Even today the popular Han characterizations of "minorities" codes in an identical way for "civilization."[20]

Despite many superficial differences, the religious test for civilized behavior in Thai and Burman culture was also closely linked to the technologies and customs associated with wet-rice cultivation. In strictly religious terms, adherence to Theravada Buddhism did not require (though it might provoke) momentous ritual changes; pre-Buddhist animist practices (*nat* worship and propitiation in Burma, *phi* worship and propitiation in Siam) were readily accommodated, even doctrinally, within a syncretic Buddhism. Buddhism was, however, closely associated with a shift in religious and ethnic identity. As Richard O'Connor observes in the Tai context, "Mainlanders link religion to agriculture, agriculture to ritual, and ritual to ethnic identity. When hill farmers like Karen, Lawa, or Kachin take up valley wet-rice, they find its proper cultivation requires Tai rituals. In effect, agricultural choices are bundled into ethnic wholes that function as competing agro-cultural complexes. A pragmatic shift between complexes thus begins ritual adjustments that may end as an ethnic shift."[21] O'Connor writes "ethnic shift," but he might as well have written "religious shift," inasmuch as the two are inseparable in this case. Thus we arrive at something of a civilizational paradox in this, as in the Chinese case. Conversion to Buddhism per se, when combined with attributes of "hilliness"—for example, shifting cultivation, residential mobility—is, as we saw in the case of the Palaung, not convincingly civilizing, although it is a step in the right direction. That step, however, not only makes religious conversion that much more likely but is also historically associated with becoming Tai or Burman—that is, a subject of the padi state. Thus becoming fully civilized, in the valley view, is nearly indistinguishable from becoming Han, Thai, or Burman and, in turn, by definition, being incorporated as a state subject.[22] Remaining outside the state is, as we shall see, coded "uncivilized."

The Economic Need for Barbarians

Valley states, large and small, though they looked contemptuously down on their uphill neighbors, were bound to them by powerful ties of economic dependence. Their indissoluble mutuality was underwritten by the complementarity of the agro-ecological niches each occupied. Economic partners and frequently political allies as well, valley and hill peoples, state cores and hinterlands, provided essential goods and services to each other. Together they represented a robust and mutually beneficial system of exchange. If anything, the valley centers were even more dependent on products and especially manpower from the hills than vice versa. But each was economically impoverished without its natural trading partner.

This pattern of economic mutuality has been most elaborately described in the Malay world, where it typically takes the form of exchange between upstream (*hulu*) and downstream (*hilir*) zones of a watershed. Huluhilir systems of this kind are based on the products each zone, owing to its agro-economic location, can supply the other. Many are of great antiquity. The lowland center in the Malay case is, as we have seen, typically located near the mouth of a river or at the confluence of two rivers. Its position, like that of a settlement dominating an important mountain pass on a trade route, is something of a natural monopoly, allowing it to dominate the trade along the entire watershed from this choke point. The lowland center functions as an entrepôt, exchanging lowland and overseas products for the upriver and forest products coming down the watershed.[23]

The lowland center, despite its positional advantage, did not hold the whip hand in dictating the terms of exchange. Highly mobile communities, particularly at the upper reaches of the watershed, were frequently close enough to an alternative watershed so that they could, if they chose to, shift their trade to a different entrepôt on an adjacent river system. Failing that, upstream groups were seldom so dependent on trade goods from the lowland polities that they couldn't substantially withdraw from downstream markets if they found the terms of trade too onerous politically or economically. Nor could the rulers of the entrepôt polities impose themselves militarily on a recalcitrant hinterland. The dispersal and mobility of the upstream population made them virtually immune from punitive expeditions, let alone systematic coercion. Port polities were, as a result, in competition with one another to acquire hinterland allies and the profits that trade with them made possible. Lacking the means to simply impose themselves, they were impelled to solicit loyalty by redistributing many of the gains of trade in the form of prestige goods, jewelry, and lavish gifts that upstream leaders could, in turn, redistribute to their followers to further encourage loyalty and trade.

For mainland Southeast Asian states, particularly smaller states in or near the hills, the same symbiosis between hill and valley prevailed, though it might not be so neatly mapped onto a single watershed. It is no exaggeration to say that the prosperity of such states was largely dependent on its capacity to attract to its markets the products of the surrounding hill peoples, who often outnumbered the population at the state core. Any reasonably comprehensive account of the commodities brought down (for sale, barter, debt repayment, and tribute) by hill peoples would require many pages. Here I can only suggest something of their extraordinary variety, keeping in mind that the composition of the trade shifted over time, occasionally dramatically, with changes in overland (to China) and overseas trade routes and the demand for particular commodities.

Hill people had, from at least the ninth century, been scouring the hills for commodities they knew could be traded advantageously at valley markets and at the coast. Many such products were part of an extensive international luxury trade. Among the naturally occurring forest products that could be gathered were rare and/or aromatic wood (for example, gaharu, sandalwood, sappan, and camphor woods); medicinals (rhinoceros horn, bezoar stones, dried organs of forest fauna, aloe wood); various resins (tung oil); and latexes (guta percha) from forest trees, as well as rare hornbill feathers, edible birds' nests, honey, beeswax, tea, tobacco, opium, and pepper. All these products had high values per unit weight and volume. That meant that they repaid the effort, even if they had to be carried on foot along mountainous paths to market. During the extraordinary long pepper boom from 1450 to 1650, when pepper exceeded all other commodities traded internationally in value save gold and silver, bringing a head-load of peppercorns to a coastal market could make a young man's fortune. Precious metals and gems (and, in the twentieth century, opium) provided an even more striking case of high value joined to portability. In light of the physical mobility of highland peoples, such goods could easily be carried to another market in another polity if the potential sellers were dissatisfied.

Other hill products were bulkier and less valuable. They could not be taken long distances to other markets except where water transportation was easily available. Such products included rattan, bamboo, timber, logs (all of which float), cattle, hides, cotton, and hill fruits, as well as such staples as hill (unirrigated) rice, buckwheat, maize, potatoes, and sweet potatoes (these last three from the New World). Many of these products can be left to grow or stored for long periods, allowing their sellers to withhold or sell them, depending on what price they would fetch.

Even quite large kingdoms in precolonial Southeast Asia were strikingly dependent for their prosperity on export goods from the hills. The first Thai trade mission to Beijing of Rama I (Chulalongkorn), in 1784, calculated to dazzle the Chinese, included luxury products that were almost entirely provided by the hill-dwelling Karen: elephants, eaglewood, ebony, rhinoceros horn, elephant tusks, bastard cardamom, long peppers, amber, sandalwood, peacock feathers, kingfisher feathers, rubies, sapphires, cutch, gamboges (a gum resin), sappanwood, dammar, krabao seeds, and a variety of spices.[24] Precolonial exports from Cambodia were similarly hostage to the Jarai hill people. Most of what these lowland states sold abroad "consisted of forest products from the highlands, as can be gleaned from Vietnamese and Cambodia annals and documents as well as travel accounts by Chinese and European authors."[25] The smaller Shan states were dependent on the hill peoples surrounding them both for the wealth of hill products necessary for valley life and for important export goods. One cannot see the cornucopia brought down to the five-day rotating markets in the Shan states today without appreciating how much the Shan diet, its building materials, its livestock, and its trade with the wider world—its prosperity in general—depends on abundant trade with its hinterland. With respect to the hill Kayah and the Shan, F. K. Lehman goes so far as to suggest that the main purpose of a Shan ruler is to manage this trade and profit from it.[26] Both the Shan and the Kayah had much to gain by exploiting the comparative advantage afforded by their respective ecological niches, but it seems clear that such states were at least as dependent on products from the hills as hill peoples were dependent on valley products.

Valley markets supplied hill populations with desired products unavailable in the hills. Foremost among these products were salt, dried fish, and ironware. Ceramics, pottery, and porcelain, manufactured cloth, thread and needles, wire, steel implements and weapons, blankets, matches, and kerosene were among the most important commodities eagerly sought by hill traders.[27] Under what hill peoples saw as favorable terms of exchange, a brisk

trade knitted hill and valley economies together, facilitated by a host of intermediaries—traders, peddlers, brokers, creditors, speculators—not to mention various forms of tribute. Under unfavorable circumstances, however, the
valley polities had no way of compelling the delivery of hill products. The
valley polities, especially the smaller ones, being more fixed geographically
and heavily reliant on hill trade, were more fundamentally threatened by the
defection of their hill trading partners.

A mere list of commodities, however, misses the decisive hill product
on which the valley centers absolutely depended: its population. The nucleus
of irrigated padi fields and concentrated manpower of Tai and Burman court
centers was, on a long view, forged by the assimilation, with varying proportions of compulsion and choice, of hill peoples. What the valley polities
needed most from the hills were people. Those it could not attract by the
advantages of trade and cultural opportunities, it tried to seize, as we have
seen, through slaving expeditions and wars. Thus, of all the commodities that
the hill societies could deny the valleys, their trump card was manpower. It
was the flight of hard-pressed valley subjects from the state core and the migration of hill peoples beyond the range of easy capture that was the Achilles'
heel of valley states.

Under favorable circumstances, the symbiosis of hill and valley peoples
was so durable and mutually recognized that the two "peoples" could be
thought of as an inseparable pair. The economic interdependence was often
reflected in political alliances. This pattern was strongly evident in the Malay
world, in which most trading ports, large and small, were associated with
"hilly" or seafaring, nonstate peoples who provided most of the trade goods
on which the Malay state relied. Although these people were not normally
considered "Malays"—they did not profess Islam or become direct subjects
of the Malay Raja—it is clear that much of the population of Malays had
derived historically from these groups. By the same token, commercial collecting from the hinterland and from the sea for such trading centers was also
fostered by the opportunities it presented. That is, much of the population
in the hinterland had moved there or stayed there by choice either because
of the economic advantages it offered in specialized collecting or because of
the political independence it afforded—or both. Abundant evidence suggests
human movement back and forth across these categories and indicates commercial gathering is a "secondary adaptation" (rather than some primitive
condition). We would do better, conceptually, to consider the upstream population as the "hilly" component of a composite economic and social system.[28]

And yet from the valley perspective, such people were considered essentially different, less civilized, living outside the religious pale.

Similar allied pairs were, and are, common in mainland Southeast Asia. Thus the Pwo Karen in lower Burma were allied with the Mon padi states. Living interspersed with the Mon, but generally in more forested upstream areas, they represented, as a pair with the Mon, a successful circuit of economic exchange. The Mons, judging from the chronicles, appear to have thought of them less as a sharply demarcated ethnic group than as a continuous gradient of customs and practices from pure padi planters at one pole to pure swiddeners and foragers at the other.[29] Virtually all the Tai/Shan kingdoms exhibit an analogous symbiosis between a padi core and an adjacent hill people with whom they trade, from whom they draw population, and with whom they are frequently allied. Such alliances, when solemnized by documents (invariably lowland documents), appear as tributary relations in which the hill ally is seen as the junior partner. In practice the hill peoples often held the upper hand, extracting, in effect, tribute or "protection payments" from the valley courts. Where the lowland court was dominant, as in the case of the Vietnamese and the Jarai, the hill peoples were no less essential to the court's prosperity, and their ritual role in appeasing the capricious spirits of the natural world was acknowledged.[30]

The reliance of the smaller valley states on hill trade and forest collecting was so pronounced that it acted occasionally to restrain efforts to assimilate hill peoples to lowland culture. The fear was that if, indeed, hill people took on valley religion, dress, and settlement patterns and began to cultivate wet rice, they would perforce leave off playing the valuable but stigmatized role of supplier of hill products. Cultural difference, along with the economic specialization that it fostered, was the basis of comparative advantage. Though the lowland states might poach slaves from the hills, they had every incentive to ensure that the hill-trading niche on which they depended was always occupied.[31]

The Invention of Barbarians

If semiotics has taught us anything, it is that linguistic terms are inherently relational. They can be "thought"—let alone understood—only in relation to their implicit exclusions and contrasts.[32] So it is with the terms *civilized* and *barbarian*.

The social production of "barbarians" in classical China, as Owen Lattimore has explained, was integrally tied to the rise of specialized, irrigated rice cores in the valleys and the state structures associated with them. Irrigation was "spectacularly rewarding" in the loess cores of ancient China, and this agro-political complex which concentrated production and population, and hence military might, spread farther and farther wherever the terrain was suitable. In the course of its expansion, this complex absorbed some neighboring populations and extruded others, which moved to higher ground, forests, marshlands, or jungles and maintained their less specialized, extensive, dispersed forms of subsistence. In short, the rise of irrigated-rice state cores created by definition a new demographic, ecological, and political frontier. As the padi state increasingly coded itself as "Han-Chinese" — as a unique culture, a civilization — it coded those who were not incorporated, or who refused to be incorporated, as "barbarians." Those barbarians still living within what the Chinese state saw as its frontiers were termed "inner" barbarians, and those who "detached themselves from the old matrix to become one of the components of the pastoral nomad society of the steppes" became the "outer" barbarians. By roughly the sixth century CE, "the Chinese were in the plains and in the major valleys, the barbarians in the hilly country with smaller valleys." In southwest China, in what we have called Zomia, a similar process was at work, where, to repeat Lattimore's formula, "the influence of ancient high civilizations of China and India reach[ed] far out over the lower levels where concentrated agriculture and big cities are to be found, but not up into the higher altitudes."[33]

What Lattimore calls the Chinese matrix of concentrated agriculture and state-making created, as a condition of its existence, an ecological and demographic frontier. In time this frontier became both a civilizational and an ethnic border where before there had been no sharp demarcation. The early Chinese state had ample strategic reasons to mark this new boundary with a sharply etched civilizational discourse and, in some cases, with physical barriers such as the Great Wall(s) and the Miao walls of the southwest. It is easy to forget that until roughly 1700, and later in frontier areas, the Chinese state itself faced the classical problem of Southeast Asian statecraft: sequestering a population in state space. Thus the walls and the rhetoric were calculated as much to keep a tax-shy Chinese peasantry from "going over to the barbarians" as to keep the barbarians at bay.[34]

The process by which state formation in the valleys generates a civilizational frontier which is typically, then, ethnically coded, is not confined to the Han state. Siamese, Javanese, Vietnamese, Burman, and Malay valley polities exhibit the same forms, although the cultural content is different. Writing of the Mien (Yao) of northern Thailand, Jonsson suggests that the social construction of "hill peoples" as a category is based on the hold that states established over valley agriculture and its peoples. Referring to the Indic polities of Siam, particularly Haripunyai (northern Thailand, seventh to tenth centuries CE), he notes that its cosmologically universal claims generated a barbarian periphery: "The making of polities involves the take-over of the lowland areas for intensive agriculture which, hierarchized with a court, regional towns, and farming villages constitute a universal domain. The universal domain is imagined in part by what lies beyond it: the forested wilderness, and the people who live in the latter domain are imagined by those in the former as living like animals."[35] In quite the same fashion, as cleared padi land became the basis for the elaboration of Javanese states and their cultures, so did uncleared forestland and its people become associated with an uncivilized, barbarian frontier.[36] The *orang asli* (usually translated as "aboriginal") population of Malaya came into being only as an antonym of "Melayuness." The new element, Geoffrey Benjamin and Cynthia Chou note, was Islam, and Islam created "tribals": "Previously there would have been no legal reason to define 'Malay' at all, and many of the non-Muslim populations of the time were as 'Malay' as the Muslims. . . . The post 1874 notions of Malayness, however, had the effect of converting these populations, virtually overnight, into the 'aborigines' they are considered to be today."[37]

All the classical states of Southeast Asia conjured up a barbarian hinterland just out of reach in the hills, forests, and swamps. The friction between the need—both semiotically and economically—for a barbarian frontier and, on the other hand, the impulse of universalizing cosmologies to absorb and transform that frontier is the subject to which we now turn.

The Domestication of Borrowed Finery: All the Way Down

The earliest court centers in Cambodia and Java, and later in Burma and Siam, were, ritually and cosmologically speaking, luxury imports from the Indian subcontinent. Using the ritual technology afforded them by Indian merchants and the court Brahmins who came in their wake, small lowland courts ratcheted up their ritual status vis-à-vis potential rivals. In a process Oliver Wolters has called "self-Hinduization," local rulers introduced Brahminical protocol and ritual. Sanskritized personal and place names were substituted for the vernacular. Monarchs were consecrated by magical Brahminical rites and given mythical genealogies tracing a divine origin. Indian iconography and epics were introduced, along with the complex ceremonies of South Indian court life.[38] It appears that this Sanskritization did not penetrate very deeply into lowland cultures beyond the immediate precincts of the court. According to Georges Coedès, it was a "veneer," "an aristocratic religion which was not designed for the masses."[39] Wolters, in much the same vein, calls the Sanskritic flourishes of early royal texts—and the Chinese flourishes in the Vietnamese texts—"decorative effects" intended to add an air of solemnity and erudition to otherwise vernacular practices.[40] Another interpretation, favored by M. C. Ricklefs, is that ideas about the indivisibility of the realm in fact constituted a kind of ideological makeweight—what I have earlier called cosmological bluster—against the reality that power was inevitably fragmented.[41]

Though such mimicry may have done little to improve the day-to-day power of the lowland courts, it did have an important bearing on the texture of hill-valley relations. First, it connected the lowland courts and their monarch to a universalizing, ecumenical, and charismatic center. Much as the Romans used Greek, the early French court used Latin, the Russian aristocracy and court used French, and the Vietnamese court used Chinese script and Confucianism, so the use of Sanskritic forms staked a claim to participation in a transethnic, transregional, and indeed, transhistorical civilization.[42] Even when vernacular scripts made an appearance shortly after the first millennium CE, the Sanskritic flourishes remained, and translations of the cosmopolitan classics of the Sanskritic and Pali world preceded even the translation of the Buddhist canon. Unlike the court cultures (as in southern India) that are largely elaborations and refinements of rituals and beliefs that already exist in the local vernacular tradition, the Indic courts of Southeast Asia were self-consciously modeled on an external, universalizing center.

The lowland elite, having thus vastly elevated itself via the ritual helium from south India, left its earthbound commoners and hinterland far below. As Wolters puts it, they "defined the hinterland's lowly status in the world order from the perspective of those who saw themselves at the center of a civilized 'Hindu' society."[43]

Sanskritization thus engendered the invention of barbarians by those who had, not long before, been, well . . . "barbarians" themselves. Khmer culture, originally tied to the forested uplands, now propagated, once Indic court centers were formed, "a polarity of wild and tamed, of dark, haunted bushland versus inhabited open spaces [that] runs like a leitmotiv through

Khmer cultural consciousness."[44] The cultural distance between a refined, settled court center on the one hand and a rude, uncultured zone of forests and hills outside its reach was maximized, and civilization became, as David Chandler aptly puts it, "the art of remaining outside the forest."[45]

Much the same process of symbolic hyperventilation and validation of hierarchy through external referents can be observed in the smaller realms and in the hills. Just as by 1300 every coastal plain had its miniature kingdom based on Indian conceptions of royalty, so too was the formula followed meticulously by petty chiefs who had even the slightest pretensions.[46] One could argue that such expansive ritual trappings were even more necessary in the hills than in the valleys. Largely populated by dispersed, mobile, swiddening peoples who, owing to a common property frontier, had little in the way of inherited inequalities, the hills also had little in the way of indigenous traditions that would legitimate any supravillage authority. Confederations of villages did exist for trade and warfare, but they were limited associations of nominal equals rather than permanent claims to authority. If models of supravillage authority were to be deployed at all, they would have to be borrowed from the lowland Indic courts, or, alternatively, from the Han-Chinese imperial order to the north. Claims to charismatic, personal authority were indigenous to the hills, but the universalizing, Indic, state-making formula represented an attempt to make it a permanent institution and to turn a leader with followers into a Ruler with Subjects.

The idea of the Indic or Chinese state has long had great currency in the hills. It floats up, as it were, in strange fragments from the lowlands in the form of regalia, mythical charters, kingly dress, titles, ceremony, genealogical claims, and sacred architecture. Its attractiveness derives, it seems, from at least two sources. The first and most obvious is that it provides virtually the only grounds — the only cultural format — for a successful and ambitious hill chief to transform his sway from primus inter pares into something like a petty state with a monarchy, aristocrats, and commoners. Such a move, as E. R. Leach has persuasively shown, was likely to be opposed by flight or rebellion on the part of those fearing permanent subordination. Sometimes, however, an upland chief, even a nominal one, might serve a useful purpose as an intermediary for negotiating compacts with lowland powers, organizing tribute and trade, or protecting against lowland raids for slaves. Successful diplomacy of this kind could prove decisive in the competition between hill groups as well.[47]

From a valley perspective — whether precolonial, colonial, or postcolonial — structures of stable authority in the hills were greatly to be preferred.

They provided a fulcrum for indirect rule, a negotiating partner, and someone who might be held responsible (or held hostage) if there was trouble. For
this reason, valley authorities, including colonizers, have had something of a
"hill-chief fetish." They have seen such chiefs where they did not exist, have
exaggerated their power when they did exist, and have striven to create both
tribes and chiefs, in their own image, as units of territorial rule. The state's
desire for chiefs and the ambitions of upland local strongmen coincided often
enough to create imitative state-making in the hills, though such achievement was seldom durable. Local chiefs had ample reason to seek the seals,
regalia, and titles conferred by a more powerful realm; they might overawe
rivals and confer lucrative trade and tribute monopolies. Recognition of a
lowland realm's imperial charisma was, at the same time, entirely compatible
with remaining outside its administrative reach and with a disdain for the
subject populations of these lowland realms.

   The charisma of state effects in the hills is striking. J. George Scott, on
military campaign in the Shan states in the 1890s, encountered a number of
Wa "chiefs" who had come with tribute. They urged Scott, now presumptively their ally, to join them in sacking some nearby Shan villages. Failing
that, they "clamored for some visible token that they were British subjects.
. . . I gave each of them a strip of paper with the name of the district written
across it and my signature on a half-anna stamp. . . . They were impressed
and went off to cut bamboos to store the papers. . . . They told me that
Monglem had steadily taken territory from them for the last ten or twelve
years."[48] Scott was seeking submission and tribute in the unruly hills; these
Wa "chiefs" were seeking an ally, in the service of their own political ends.
Much the same theater of tribute and alliance is reported by Leach in the
Shan hills when the area was still, in 1836, nominally under Burman administration. A Burman official was received; a ritual meal was prepared; the
solidarity of ten Kachin and Shan chiefs attending was dramatized; and the
rule of the kingdom of Ava was acknowledged. But Leach notes that several
of the chiefs attending were at war with one another. He cautions us to read
the ceremony as a state effect:

> All my example really shows is that the Burmese, the Shans, and the Kachins
> of the Hukawng Valley . . . shared a common language of ritual expression;
> they all knew how to make themselves understood in this common "language."
> It doesn't mean that what was said in this "language" was "true" in political
> reality. The statements of the ritual in question were made in terms of the sup-
> position that there existed an ideal, stable, Shan state with the *saohpa* [ruler]

of Mogaing at the head of it and with all the Kachin and Shan chiefs of the Hukawng Valley his loyal liege servants. We have no real evidence that any real *saohpa* of Mogaing ever wielded such authority, and we know for a fact that when this particular ritual took place there had been no genuine *saohpa* of Mogaing at all for nearly 80 years. At the back of the ritual there stood not the political structure of a real state, but the "as if" structure of an ideal state.[49]

The "as if" structure of an ideal state was incorporated into the architecture of actual and "would-be" states in the hills. The Shan statelets, with their own, albeit modest, wet-rice core population and professing the same Theravada Buddhism as their neighboring Siamese and Burman states, copied their architecture as well. Visiting a Shan palace [*haw* in Shan] in Pindaya, Maurice Collis noted that it was a replica, in miniature, of the Burmese royal capital: "a wooden house of two stories, with a pillared hall on the first floor, over which was a turret or *pya-that*, five little roofs piled on top of one another and ending in a gilded finial." Collis observed, "It was the style of the palace of Mandalay *in little*."[50] Mimicry of the same kind characterized monastery architecture, funeral processions, and regalia. The more negligible the kingdom, the ruder and smaller the imitation, right down to very minor Kachin chiefs (*duwa*) with pretensions to Shan-style power, whose haws were as Lilliputian as their actual power. In this connection, Leach claims that the Kachin see the Shan not so much as a different ethnic group as the bearers of a hierarchical state tradition—one that they might, under the right circumstances, emulate.[51] It is from the Shan that the Kachin borrow their state effects.

The Kayah, a Karennic people in the Shan hills, have, in the course of asserting their autonomy, copied their political system from what they conceived to be the Shan and Burman models. In this case, since the Kayah were not, by and large, Buddhists, the Theravada elements of the mimicry were omitted. All Kayah leaders, Lehman notes, whether usurpers, rebels, ordinary villagers, or millennial prophets, adhere to the state forms derived from Shan lowland courts: titles, paraphernalia, the concoction of royal genealogies, and architecture.[52] One way or another, such leaders always claimed their authority by virtue of its connection to the "as if," ideally unified, Burmese state. This symbolic subordination, while it might be compatible with actual rebellion, is a sign that such symbolism is the idiom, the singular language, of stateness—of any claim to power in the supravillage sphere. As often as not, given the very limited power of most Kayah chiefs, this language is radically at variance with the practical realities of power.

There are, however, two very different models of state authority available to hill peoples: the Indic courts to the south and the Han-Chinese court to the north. Thus a good many Kachin chiefs with aspirations model their "palaces," their ceremonies and dress, and their cosmology after the Shan pattern, which the Shan, in turn, modeled on the Chinese. In the Kachin chiefly tradition, both the symbolic spaces and the ceremonies devoted to "heavenly spirits" and to "earth spirits" bear a striking resemblance to older imperial ceremonies in Beijing.[53] The Akha, a nonstate people if there ever was one, are hardly influenced at all by Tai/Shan models of authority, but instead take their bearings from Taoist, Confucian, and Tibetan models of genealogy, authority, and cosmology—with the Buddhist elements more or less discarded.[54] Where the two state traditions were both available, they made possible quite exotic hybrids of state mimicry. In each case, however, they put the conceptual and symbolic language of a divine, universal monarch into the mouth and ritual conduct of rulers whose actual sway might not have extended beyond the borders of their own hamlets.

The Civilizing Mission

All court cultures on the periphery of Zomia developed more or less sharp distinctions between what they considered "civilized" people and "barbarians"—variously termed raw, hill people, forest people, wild people, people of streams and grottoes. The terms *civilized* and *barbarian* are, as we have seen, inseparable, mutually defining, traveling companions. Like *dark* and *light*, each can scarcely be said to have an existence at all without its contrasting twin. One can usually be inferred from the other. Thus in Han dynasty times, when the Xiongnu people were described as "having no written language, family names, and respect for the elderly," nor cities, permanent dwellings, or fixed agriculture, the list of what the Xiongnu lack is nothing but a summary of what the civilized Han have.[55] Of course, as with most binaries, those seeking to apply them in practice encounter many cases that do not admit of easy classification. Such ambiguities did not threaten the hold of binary thought in matters of civilization any more than they have in matters of race.

The standard civilizational narrative for Siamese, Burmese, Khmer, Malay, and, especially, Chinese and Vietnamese court cultures was that, over time, the barbarians were gradually assimilating to the luminous, magnetic center. Incorporation would never be total, for then the very concept of a civilizing center would cease to have any real meaning. There would always be a barbarian frontier.

Civilizing the people of the hinterland was conceptually more plausible if the barbarians were considered to be essentially "like us," only more backward and undeveloped. In the case of the Vietnamese, the Muong and Tay were literally considered to be "our living ancestors." As Keith Taylor and Patricia Pelley point out, the Muong "were popularly regarded (and are still regarded today) as the pre-Sinitic version of the Viet."[56] Muong totems, dwellings, agricultural practices, languages, and literature were minutely scoured, not so much in their own right as for the light they could shed on the origins and development of the Viet people.[57]

Recognition of the barbarians as an earlier, but not irremediably different, people led, in principle, to the assumption that they were capable of eventually becoming fully civilized. This was Confucius's belief. When asked how he could possibly consider living among barbarians, he replied, "If a gentleman lived among them, what uncouthness could there be."[58] The civilizational discourse in this case is notably singular; it is a matter of ascent to a single cultural apex. Other, different, but equally worthy civilizations are not generally recognized and hence a (civilized) biculturalism is inconceivable.

The early-nineteenth-century Vietnamese emperor Minh Mang exemplified, in his rhetoric if not in his actions, a magnanimous version of this philosophy of a civilizing mission:

> This land [of the Jarai and the Rhadé] is a distant and remote place. It is a land in which they tie knots in strings to keep records. It is a land in which people make swidden fields and harvest rice for a living and a land in which the customs are *still* archaic and simple. However, their heads have hair, their mouths have teeth, and they have been endowed with innate knowledge and ability by nature. Therefore, why should they not do virtuous things. Because of this, my illustrious ancestors brought the civilization of the Chinese to them in order to change their tribal customs.[59]

Having annexed eastern and central Cambodia, a people themselves heir to classical Khmer civilization, Minh Mang urged his officials to teach them Vietnamese customs and language, show them how to grow more rice and mulberry trees, and to raise livestock and poultry; finally, the officials were to simplify and repress any barbarous customs. "[It is] like bringing the Cambodian people out of the mud into a warm feather bed."[60]

Neither in its Chinese nor its Vietnamese guise was this vision of comfort and luxury awaiting those who chose civilization incompatible with merciless repression of those who resisted by force. Before the great mid-nineteenth-century uprisings in Guizhou, the largest of the military campaigns were those led by Han Yong (1465) and, sixty years later in 1526, by the renowned Ming scholar-general Wang Yangming to put down the great Miao-Yao uprisings. The first victory of the Ming forces in a climactic battle at Great Vine Gorge resulted in at least sixty thousand deaths, of which eight hundred were victims sent to Beijing for public beheading.[61] Later, the victorious Wang Yangming helped re-create the (in)famous *tusi* system of "ruling barbarians with barbarians" but nevertheless held to the view that the barbarians were "like unpolished gems," capable, if carefully shaped and burnished, of becoming fully civilized.[62] His explanation of why direct rule of such a rude people would create havoc is both memorable and diagnostic: "To institute direct civil administration by Han-Chinese magistrates would be like herding deer into the hall of a house and trying to tame them. In the end they merely butt over your sacrificial altars, kick over your tables, and dash about in frantic flight. In the wilderness districts, therefore, one should adapt one's methods to the character of the wilderness. . . . [Those doing so] are adapting themselves to the wild nature of these people."[63]

The pieties of civilizational discourse propagated by the imperial center are one thing. Reality was something else. These self-idealizations had little to do with life in the imperial capital and even less to do with the rough-and-tumble of the imperial frontier. In place of the *Analects* was a pandemonium of adventurers, bandits, speculators, armed traders, demobilized soldiers, poor migrants, exiles, corrupt officials, fugitives from the law, and refugees. A 1941 report from the southwest frontier identified three sorts of Han people: displaced and desperate refugees, petty artisans and traders, described as "speculators looking for lucky breaks," and finally, officials: "The higher ranks . . . lived indolently, often were overbearing opium-smokers, negligent of government orders. . . . The lower ranks indulged in petty graft and collected money from fines while illegally trafficking in opium and salt. There was not a lucrative crack into which they did not pry. These activities were bound to lead to enmity between them and the frontier tribesmen who suffered from their oppression."[64] As in any colonial or imperial setting, the experience of the subject was wildly at odds with the ideological superstructure that aimed at ennobling the whole enterprise. The pieties must, in this case, have seemed to most subjects a cruel joke.[65]

The civilizational project is alive and well in twentieth-century mainland Southeast Asia. Following a Hmong/Miao rebellion in northern Thailand in the late 1960s, General Prapas not only deployed all the counterinsurgency techniques at his disposal—including napalm and aerial bombing—but undertook to "civilize" the rebels with schools, resettlement, clinics, and sedentary agricultural techniques. The cultural campaign, Nicholas Tapp observes, was virtually a carbon copy of the Republican Chinese government's program in the 1930s in Guangdong, carried out by the "Bureau for Civilizing the Yao."[66] In contemporary China, although the stigmatizing names for minority peoples have been sanitized, the great divide remains between the Han and the many enumerated minorities. The euphemisms of "development," "progress," and "education" have replaced "raw" and "cooked," but the underlying assumption is that minority societies and cultures are "social fossils" whose days are numbered.[67]

Depending on the culture of the court center, the content of what it meant to be civilized—and reciprocally, what it meant to be stigmatized as barbarian—varied. Each represented, metaphorically, a ladder of ascent, but many of the rungs were unique and particular. In Siam and Burma, Theravada Buddhism was a key marker of civilized status.[68] In Vietnam and China literacy and, beyond that, familiarity with the classics was crucial. In the Malay world, upstream populations were, much as Wang Yangming described the Yao, "unfinished Malays." An essential rung on the way to being "finished" (the Chinese term would be *cooked*) was the profession of Islam. All these ladders, however, had at least two rungs in common, despite their cultural particularities. They stipulated, as a condition of civilization, sedentary agriculture and residence within state space.

This centripetal narrative of civilization in which nonstate peoples gradually move downhill, adopt wet-rice agriculture, and assimilate linguistically and culturally is not inherently mistaken. It describes a historical process. The Shan people—the sedentary subjects of Shan statelets—are, Leach and O'Connor agree, largely the descendants of hill peoples who have adopted valley ways.[69] Malayness was similarly confected by a process of nonstate peoples becoming subjects of the small port polities. It is similarly clear that the first Burmese kingdom at Pagan was itself an amalgam, an ingathering of many peoples.[70] This narrative is, then, not so much mistaken as radically incomplete; it records only the events that fit into the imperial self-description of court centers.

Civilization as Rule

If we examine the centripetal narrative of civilization closely, it is striking how much of the actual meaning of "being civilized" boils down to becoming a subject of the padi state. So momentous and consequential is this distinction between being a ruled subject and remaining outside the state that it is typically marked by a shift in identity—often ethnic identity. Moving to a wet-rice core, and hence into a stratified, state-structured hierarchy, meant, depending on the context, becoming Tai, becoming Burman, becoming Malay. On China's southwest frontier, it meant moving from the "raw" (*sheng*) barbarian status to "cooked" (*shu*) civilized status and, eventually, it was assumed, to Han identity itself.

A twelfth-century document from Hainan makes the association between subjecthood and being "cooked"—variously understood as being cultivated, domesticated, or, in the French idiom, *évolué*—quite clear: "Those who have submitted and are attached to the county and township administration are the cooked Li. Those who live in the mountain caves and are not punished by us or [who do not] supply corvée labor are the raw Li. These sometimes come out and engage in barter with the administered population." The "cooked" Li occupied a liminal space. They were no longer "raw" and yet were not yet assimilated Han subjects. Officials suspected them of outward conformity while "sly[ly]" cooperating with the "raw" Li to "invade governmental lands and roam about plundering travelers." Despite the fear of treachery from "cooked barbarians," they are, as a category, associated with political (state) order while the "raw" are associated with disorder. Thus the "raw Wa rob and plunder," whereas the "cooked" Wa "safeguard the road." It would be a mistake, Magnus Fiskesjö emphasizes, to believe that, for a Han administrator, *raw* was simply another word for primitive or close to nature. While all "primitives" were presumptively raw, not all developed barbarians were cooked. The key was submission to Han administration. Most of the Nuosu people (now subsumed under the Yi designation) on the Yunnan-Sichuan border, who were hierarchically organized in castelike structures and boasted a writing system, were classified as raw because they had eluded political incorporation. That small portion of the same Nuosu people which had come under Chinese rule were designated cooked. In short, "The 'raw' barbarians were those located beyond the enforceable jurisdiction of the agents of state."[71] The antiquity of this criterion may extend, if Patricia Ebrey is correct, to the Eastern Zhou period (eighth to third centuries BCE), when the distinction between those who submitted to Zhou rule and those who did not became merged with the ethnic distinction between the Chinese [*Hua* or *Xia*] and the barbarians.[72]

Returning to the eighteenth-century highland Hainan and Li barbarians, those who declared their loyalty and came under Qing administration were said "to enter the map." By doing so, they became—instantly, politically microwaved, as it were—"cooked," though their other customs and habits remained as before: "The definition of *shu* and *sheng* had mostly political and very little cultural meaning."[73] Implicit in "entering the map," in being incorporated into the bureaucratic system, was the idea that a people were being readied for a process of acculturation to the civilized norms of Han subjects—a process, it was assumed, they would eagerly embrace.[74] The first, essential step in that process, however, was the political-administrative status of being "cooked"—of being "set on the path of becoming registered, tax-paying, and corvée-delivering 'good' subjects. . . . The category of the 'barbarian' can have no permanent referent apart from being 'beyond the law.' It simply refers to those who *at any given time* are made to stand for an idea, any of the peoples living on the periphery who meet (or are cast as meeting) the minimal criteria of non-subject status, ethno-linguistic difference, and location at the periphery."[75]

It is in the light of administrative control, not culture per se, that one must understand the invention of ethnic categories at the frontier. The category Yao in fifteenth-century Guangdong was an artifact of civil status—of whether the people in question had entered the map or not. Those registered for tax and corvée, thereby also benefiting from settlement rights, became *mín* (civilian, subject), while those who did not became Yao. The "invented" Yao might be culturally indistinguishable from those who had registered, but, over time, the label became "ethnicized" by Han administrative practice.[76] Much the same could be said of the label Miao in Qing administrative practice. It came to be a portmanteau term covering dozens of distinct groups speaking often mutually unintelligible tongues. What characterized them all was their refusal to become part of the "fiscal population." Over time, an expression that initially had no coherent cultural content came to represent an ethnicized identity.[77]

Barbarism, then, is in Ming and Qing practice a political location vis-à-vis stateness—a positionality. Nonbarbarians are fully incorporated into the taxpaying population and have, presumably, adopted Han customs, dress, and language. Barbarians come in two varieties, the cooked and the raw, and these categories are also positional. The cooked are culturally distinct but now registered and governed by Han administrative norms—even if they retain their local chiefs. They have, also presumably, started their march toward cultural incorporation as Han. The raw barbarians, by contrast, are wholly outside the state population, a necessary "other," and heavily ethnicized.

Leaving the State, Going over to the Barbarians

It follows that those who move beyond the reach of the state thereby cross the conceptual boundary between civilization and barbarism. Likewise, those who leave either the regimented mín or the supervised cooked for the raw periphery enter a zone of definitive ethnicization.

Historically speaking, the process of becoming a barbarian is quite common. At certain historical moments, it has been more common than becoming civilized. It suffices only to leave state space in order to become a barbarian and, usually, an ethnicized "tribal" as well. As early as the ninth century, Chinese officials report that a people called the Shang in southwestern China originally had been Han but had, over time, gradually blended in with the "Western Barbarians."[78] And the people who later became known as the Shan Yue ethnic group and thereby barbarians (sheng) were, it appears, merely ordinary mín who had fled to avoid taxes. Early-fourteenth-century administrative reports treat them as dangerous and disorderly, but without any indication that they are distinct, racially or culturally (never mind aboriginal), from the taxpaying, administered population. But over time, living outside the reach of the state, they became the ethnic Shan Yue.[79] All those who had reason to flee state power — to escape taxes, conscription, disease, poverty, or prison, or to trade or raid — were, in a sense, tribalizing themselves. Ethnicity, once again, began where sovereignty and taxes ended. The ethnic zone was feared and stigmatized by officials precisely because it was beyond sovereignty and therefore a magnet for those who, for whatever reason, wanted to elude the state.

Much the same dynamic is at work elsewhere. In the Malay world, Benjamin writes of the "tribalization" or "re-tribalization" of previously nontribal peoples as they move beyond the jurisdiction of the Malay state or, as often happened, the Malay state itself disintegrated, creating an instant hinterland.[80] The very terms by which nonstate peoples were stigmatized encodes the absence of effective sovereignty. For example, the Meratus people in Kalimantan, by virtue of their autonomy and mobility, are stigmatized as being "not-yet-arranged/regimented" (*belum diator*).[81] A Spanish official in the Philippines in the mid-seventeenth century describes the Chico River hill population in terms that both stigmatize their statelessness and convey a hint of envy: "They were so free, so completely without God or law, without King or any person to respect, that they gave themselves freely up to their desires and their passions."[82] What passes, in the eyes of valley officials, as deplorable backwardness may, for those so stigmatized, represent a political space of self-governance, mobility, and freedom from taxes.

The civilizational series—mín, cooked barbarian, and raw barbarian—is at the same time a political series of diminishing state incorporation. It resembles in important respects the Arab-Berber civilizational series in which the *siba* is the zone outside Arab-state control and the *makhazem* the zone within Arab control. Those who live in the siba are, or become, Berbers. As with the raw and the cooked barbarians, the task of dynastic rule is to expand the circle of dynasty-supporting tribes (*guish*) and thereby expand the state's sway. The siba is, Ernest Gellner writes, best translated as "institutionalized dissidence," and its inhabitants are therefore looked down upon and coded "Berber." Tribal society, virtually by definition, exists at the edge of nontribal society as its dark reciprocal twin.[83] Unlike Southeast Asia, the "tribals" in the Middle East and North Africa share a common religion, though perhaps not its practice, with state populations. It becomes difficult to discern, under those circumstances, what "Berberdom" means except as an Arab designation for those who elude control by the state and incorporation into its hierarchy.[84]

Barbarians are, then, a state effect; they are inconceivable except as a "position" vis-à-vis the state. There is much to recommend Bennet Bronson's minimalist definition of a barbarian as "simply a member of a political unit that is in direct contact with a state but that is not itself a state." Thus understood, barbarians can be, and often have been, quite "civilized" in the sense of literacy, technological skills, and familiarity with nearby "great traditions"—say, of the Romans or the Han-Chinese. Consider, in this light, such nonstate peoples as the Irish or, in insular Southeast Asia, the Minangkabau and Batak. They may also be more powerful militarily than an adjacent state and, on that account, may raid or exact tribute from that state. Consider also, in this context, the Mongols under the Tang, the Moros, the Bedouins, the Scots, the Albanians, the Caucasians, the Pathans, and, for much of their history, the Afghans. The stronger such "barbarian" societies have been, the more likely they are to prey systematically on the nearby state spaces, with their lucrative concentration of wealth, grain, trade goods, and slaves. Bronson attributes the relative weakness of historical state formation in India and Sumatra—despite favorable agro-ecological settings—to the proximity of powerful nonstate predators.[85]

All empires, as cultural-political enterprises, are necessarily exercises in classification. Thus the Roman Empire, on a cursory reading, exhibits many of the same characteristics as those impinging on Zomia.[86] Slavery was as central to Roman statecraft as it was to Burmese, Thai, or early Han statecraft. Merchants accompanied each military campaign with a view to buying captives and reselling them closer to Rome. Many of the interbarbarian wars were fought between competitors striving to control and profit from this human trafficking. Roman culture, from province to province, as distinct from the famed uniformity of Roman citizenship, looked different depending on the various "barbarian" cultures it had absorbed.

Like their Han and mainland Southeast Asian counterparts, the Romans had a barbarian chiefdom fetish. Wherever possible they created territories, promulgated more or less arbitrary ethnic distinctions, and appointed, or recognized, a single chief who was, willy nilly, the local vector of Roman authority and answerable for the good conduct of his "people." The peoples so codified were likewise ranged along an evolutionary scale of civilization. The Celts closest to Roman power in Gaul, a stateless but culturally distinct group of peoples with fortified towns and agriculture, were comparable to cooked barbarians in the Chinese scheme. Those beyond the Rhine (the various Germanic peoples) were raw barbarians, and the mobile Huns between Rome and the Black Sea were the rawest of the raw. In the Roman province of Britain, the Picts beyond Hadrian's Wall in the north were the rawest of the raw, or "the last of the free," depending on one's perspective.[87]

Once again, positionality vis-à-vis imperial rule was a crucial marker for a people's degree of civilization. Administered (cooked) barbarians in Roman ruled provinces lost their ethnic designations as they became, like farmers, liable for taxes and conscription. All those beyond this sphere were invariably ethnicized, given chiefs, and made responsible for tribute (*obsequium*), as distinct from taxes, especially as they were seen as a non-grain-growing people. The link between direct Roman rule and barbarian status is obvious in those cases when such "provincials" rebelled against Roman rule. They were, in such cases, reethnicized (rebarbarianized!), demonstrating, in the process, that civilizational backsliding was possible and was very much a political category. Depending on the circumstances, Romans might move into barbarian territory as deserters, traders, settlers, and fugitives from the law, and "barbarians" might move into the Roman sphere, though they needed permission to do so collectively. The dividing line, despite the two-way traffic across it, was always sharply marked. Here too, "barbarians" were a state effect. "Only conquest produced real knowledge of the barbarian world, but then it ceased to be barbarian. Thus conceptually, the barbarians were forever retreating from Roman understanding."[88]

As a political location—outside the state but adjacent to it—the eth-nicized barbarians represent a permanent example of defiance of central au-thority. Semiotically necessary to the cultural idea of civilization, the bar-barians are also well nigh ineradicable, owing to their defensive advantages in terrain, in dispersal, in segmentary social organization, and in their mobile, fugitive subsistence strategies. They remain an example—and thus an option, a temptation—of a form of social organization outside state-based hierarchy and taxes. One imagines that the eighteenth-century Buddhist rebel against the Qing in Yunnan understood the appeal of "barbarian-ness" when he ex-horted people with the chant: "Api's followers need pay no taxes. They plow for themselves and eat their own produce."[89] For officials of the nearby state, the barbarians represent a refuge for criminals and rebels, and an exit for tax-shy subjects.

The actual appeal of "barbarity," of residing out of the state's reach—let alone forsaking civilization—has no logical place in the official state nar-ratives of the four major civilizations that concern us here: the Han-Chinese, the Vietnamese, the Burman, and the Siamese. All are "predicated on ir-revocable assimilation in a single direction." In the Han case, the very terms *raw* and *cooked* imply irreversibility: raw meat can be cooked but it cannot be "uncooked"—though it can spoil! No two-way traffic or backsliding is pro-vided for. Nor does it allow for the indisputable fact that the core civilizations to which assimilation is envisaged are, themselves, a cultural alloy of many diverse sources.[90]

A civilizational narrative that assumes its own cultural and social mag-netism and that depicts acculturation to its norms as a much desired ascent could hardly be expected to chronicle, let alone explain, large-scale defec-tion. And yet it is historically common. The official invisibility of defection is encoded in the narrative itself; those who move to nonstate space, who adapt to its agro-ecology, become ethnicized barbarians who were, presum-ably, always there. Before the decisive military victory of the Han forces over the Yao in the mid-fifteenth century, it appears that "Han people were to a large extent nominally turning into non-Han rather than the other way around. . . . Marginal migrants in an area under weaker government control responded to Panhu [ethnic mythology] symbols that, among other things, promised help from the Yao in the vicinity. They were the very reverse of the 'Barbarians' who went to court to pay tribute and express admiration for civilization. From the perspective of the state, the rebels betrayed civilization and attached themselves to the barbarians."[91] Barbarians bearing gifts had an honored place in the civilizational discourse. Han subjects going over to the barbarians did not! When they were mentioned at all in Qing literature, they were stigmatized as "Han-traitors" (*Hanjian*), a term that now had strong ethnic resonances.[92]

"Self-barbarianization" could occur in any number of ways. Han populations wanting to trade, to evade taxes, flee the law, or seek new land were continually moving into barbarian zones. Once there, they were likely to learn the local dialect, marry locally, and seek the protection of a barbarian chief. Remnants of disbanded rebels (most notably the Taiping in the nineteenth century) and deposed dynasts and their entourage (for example, Ming supporters in the early Qing) contributed to the influx. Occasionally, when a local barbarian kingdom was strong enough, as in the case of Nan Chao, Han populations might be captured or purchased and then absorbed. Nor was it uncommon for a Han military official appointed to rule a barbarian area to make local alliances, take a local wife, and, in time, assert his independence as a native chief. There was, finally, a kind of self-barbarianization that makes the association between coming under Han rule and being civilized crystal clear. When a district of cooked barbarians under Han rule revolted successfully, they were reclassified as raw and moved back into the "barbarian" column. What had changed was not their culture but only their subordination to Han rule.[93]

William Rowe claimed, perhaps for dramatic effect, that "going over to the barbarians" was more the norm than the exception: "The historical reality for centuries has been . . . that far more Chinese had acculturated to aboriginal life than aborigines to Chinese civilization."[94] Whatever a complete demographic account book would show, what matters in this particular context is that backsliding was common, even banal, and that it could have no legitimate place in the official narrative. In times of dynastic decline, natural disasters, wars, epidemics, and exceptional tyranny, what was a steady flow of adventurers, traders, criminals, and pioneers might become a population hemorrhage. One imagines that much of the population near the frontiers could see the positional advantage in being culturally amphibious and stepping to one side or the other depending on the circumstances. Even today, on China's southwest frontiers, there are some substantial advantages to being an ethnic minority—a barbarian. One escapes the "one-child" policy, one avoids certain taxes, and one profits from certain "affirmative action" programs benefiting minorities. Han Chinese and people of mixed ancestry in these areas are known to seek registration as Miao, Dai, Yao, Zhuang, and so on.

CHAPTER 5

Keeping the State at a Distance
The Peopling of the Hills

The pagoda is finished; the country is ruined.
—Burmese proverb

When an expanding community, in taking over new territory, expels the old occupants
(or some of them), instead of incorporating them into its own fabric, those who retreat
may become, in the new territory into which they spread, a new kind of society.
—Owen Lattimore, *The Frontier in History*

The 9/11 Commission, reporting on its investigation into the attacks on the World Trade Center in New York in 2001, called attention to the novel location of the terrorist threat. Rather than coming from a hostile nation-state, it came from what the commission called "sanctuaries" in "the least governed, most lawless," "most remote," "vast un-policed regions," in "very difficult terrain."[1] Particular sanctuaries, such as the Tora Bora and Shah-i-Kot regions along the Pakistan-Afghan border and the "hard to police" islands of the southern Philippines and Indonesia, were singled out. The commission was quite aware that it was the combination of geographical remoteness, forbidding terrain, and, above all, the relative absence of state power that made such areas recalcitrant to the exercise of power by the United States or its allies. What they failed to note was that much of the existing population in such areas of sanctuary were there precisely because these areas had historically been an area of refuge from state power.

Just as a relatively stateless, remote region provided sanctuary for Osama bin Laden and his entourage, so has the vast mountainous region of mainland Southeast Asia we have called Zomia provided an historical sanctuary for state-evading peoples. Providing that we take a long view—and by "long" I mean fifteen hundred to two thousand years—it makes best sense to see contemporary hill peoples as the descendants of a long process of *marronnage*, as runaways from state-making projects in the valleys. Their agricultural practices, their social organization, their governance structures, their legends, and their cultural organization in general bear strong traces of state-evading or state-distancing practices.

This view of the hills as peopled, until very recently, by a process of state-evading migration is in sharp contrast to an older view that is still part of the folk beliefs of valley people. This older view saw hill people as an aboriginal population that had failed, for one reason or another, to make the transition to a more civilized way of life: specifically, to settled, wet-rice agriculture, lowland religion, and membership (as subject or citizen) in a larger political community. Hill peoples, in the most stringent version of this perspective, were an unalterably alien population living in a kind of highland cultural sump, and hence unsuitable prospects for cultural advancement. On the more charitable view that currently prevails, such populations are thought to have been "left behind" culturally and materially (perhaps even "our living ancestors"), and ought, therefore, to be made the object of development efforts to integrate them into the cultural and economic life of the nation.

If, on the contrary, the population of Zomia is more accurately seen as a complex of populations that have, at one time or another, elected to move outside the easy reach of state power, then the evolutionary sequence implied by the older view is untenable. Hilliness instead becomes largely a state effect, the defining trait of a society created by those who have, for whatever reason, left the realm of direct state power. As we shall see, such a view of hill peoples as state-repelling societies—or even antistate societies—makes far more sense of agricultural practices, cultural values, and social structure in the hills.

The overarching logic of the demographic peopling of the hills, despite the murkiness and large gaps in the evidence for earlier periods, is reasonably certain. The rise of powerful valley padi states with demographic and military superiority over smaller societies led to a double process of absorption and assimilation on the one hand and extrusion and flight on the other. Those absorbed disappeared as distinctive societies, though they lent their cultural color to the amalgam that came to represent valley culture. Those extruded, or fleeing, tended to head for more remote sanctuaries in the hinterlands, often at higher altitudes. The zones of refuge to which they repaired were not by any means empty, but, over the long haul, the demographic weight of the state-evading migrants and their descendants tended to prevail. Seen from a long historical perspective, the process was characterized by fits and starts. Periods of dynastic peace and expanding commerce as well as periods of successful imperial expansion enlarged the population living under the aegis of state authority. The standard narrative of a "civilizing process," though hardly as benign or voluntary as its rosier versions imply, might be said to characterize such eras. At times of war, crop failure, famine, crushing taxation, economic contraction, or military conquest, however, the advantages of a social existence outside the reach of the valley state were far more alluring. The reflux of valley populations into those areas, often the hills, where the friction of terrain provided asylum from the state, played a major role in the peopling of Zomia and in the social construction of state-repelling societies. Migrations of this kind have been occurring on both small and large scales for the last two millennia. Each new pulse of migrations encountered those who had come earlier and those long established in the hills. The process of conflict, amalgamation, and reformulation of identities in this little-governed space accounts in large measure for the ethnic complexity of Zomia. Because it found no legitimate place in the self-representations of valley-state texts, this process was rarely chronicled. Until the twentieth century, however, it was very common. Even today, as we shall see, it continues on a smaller scale.

One state above all the others was the propulsive force setting multitudes of people in motion and absorbing others. From at least the expansion of the Han Dynasty southward to the Yangzi (202 BCE–220 CE), when the Chinese state first became a great agrarian empire, and continuing, in fits and starts, all the way to the Qing and its successors, the Republic and the People's Republic, populations seeking to evade incorporation have moved south, west, and then southwest into Zomia—Yunnan, Guizhou, Guangxi, and Southeast Asia proper. Other padi states, established later, mimicked the same process on a smaller scale and occasionally posed a strategic obstacle to Chinese expansion. The Burmese, Siamese, Trinh, and Tibetan states were the most prominent, but still minor-league states, whereas a good many even smaller padi states that played, for a time, a similar role—Nan Chao, Pyu, Lamphun/Haripunjaya, and Kengtung, to name only a few—have passed into history. As manpower machines capturing and absorbing population, they also, in the same fashion, disgorged state-fleeing populations to the hills and created their own "barbarian" frontier.

The importance of the hills as sanctuary from the many burdens imposed on state subjects has not gone unnoticed. As Jean Michaud has observed, "To some extent montagnards can be seen as refugees displaced by war and choosing to remain beyond the direct control of state authorities, who sought to control labor, tax productive resources, and secure access to populations from which they could recruit soldiers, servants, concubines, and slaves. This implies that montagnards have always been on the run."[2] Michaud's observation can, if examined in the light of the historical, agro-ecological, and ethnographic evidence, provide a powerful lens through which to understand Zomia as a vast state-resistant periphery. The purpose of this chapter and the following two is to outline in broad strokes an argument for the resolving power of this particular lens.

Other Regions of Refuge

The perspective we propose for understanding Zomia is not novel. A similar case has been made for many regions of the world, large and small, where expanding kingdoms have forced threatened populations to choose between absorption and resistance. Where the threatened population was itself organized into state forms, resistance might well take the shape of military confrontation. If defeated, the vanquished are absorbed or migrate elsewhere. Where the population under threat is stateless, its choices typically boil down to absorption or flight, the latter often accompanied by rearguard skirmishes and raids.[3]

An argument of just this kind for Latin America was made nearly thirty years ago by Gonzalo Aguirre Beltrán. Under the title *Regions of Refuge,* he argued that something like a preconquest society remained in remote, inaccessible regions far from the centers of Spanish control. Two considerations determined their location. First, they were regions of little or no economic value to the Spanish colonizers. Second, they were geographically forbidding areas where the friction of distance was particularly high. Aguirre Beltrán pointed to areas of "rugged countryside isolated from transportation routes by physical barriers, with a harsh landscape and scanty agricultural yields." Three environments that met these conditions were deserts, tropical jungles, and mountain ranges, all of which were "hostile or inaccessible to human movement."[4] In Aguirre Beltrán's formulation, the indigenous population was largely a remnant not so much pushed into, or fleeing into, such zones as left alone because it was of no economic interest to the Spanish and posed no military threat.

Aguirre Beltrán allows for the fact that some of the indigenous population was forced by Spanish land grabs to abandon the fields and retreat to the safety of those regions that were least desired by Ladino settlers.[5] Subsequent research, however, would greatly enlarge the role that flight and retreat played in this process. On a long view, it would seem that some, if not most, of the "indigenous" peoples Aguirre Beltrán discusses may actually have once been sedentary cultivators living in highly stratified societies who had been compelled by both Spanish pressure and a massive demographic collapse, owing to epidemics, to reformulate their societies in a way that emphasized adaptation and mobility. Thus Stuart Schwartz and Frank Salomon write of "downward alterations in modular group size, [less] rigidity of kinship arrangements, and [less] socio-political centralization," which transformed the inhabitants of complex riverine systems into "separately recognized village peoples." What might later be seen as a backward, even Neolithic, tribal population was more accurately seen as a historical adaptation to political threat and a radically new demographic setting.[6]

The contemporary understanding, as documented by Schwartz and Salomon, is one of massive population movements and ethnic reshuffling. In Brazil, natives fleeing from the colonial *reducciones* and the forced labor of the missions—"remnants of defeated villages, mestizos, deserters, and escaped black slaves"—often coalesced at the frontier, sometimes identified by the name of the native peoples among whom they had settled, and sometimes assuming a new identity.[7] Like Asian padi states, the Spanish and Portuguese projects of rule required the control of available manpower in state space. The net result of the flight provoked by forced settlement was to create a distinction between state zones on the one hand and state-resisting populations, geographically out of reach and often at higher altitudes, on the other. Allowing for the massive demographic collapse particular to the New World, the resonance with the Southeast Asian pattern is striking. Writing of the 1570 reducción, Schwartz and Salomon claim that the Spanish

> forced settlement in nucleated parishes, in the face of population decline and colonial labor needs. This dislocated thousands of Indians and reshuffled people all over the former Inka domains. The project to concentrate dispersed agro-pastoral settlements into uniform European style towns rarely succeeded as planned, but its consequences were somewhat regular if not uniform. They include the enduring antithesis between native outlands and high slopes, and "civilized" parish centers. . . . Population decline, tightening tribute and the regimen of forced labor quotas drove thousands from home and reshuffled whole populations.[8]

In the Andes, at least, this sharp contrast between civilized centers and "native outlands" appears to have had a pre-Conquest parallel in the distinction between Inca courts and a state-resisting population at the periphery. The altitudinal dimension, however, was reversed, with the Inca centers at higher altitudes and the periphery being the low, wet, equatorial forests whose inhabitants had long resisted Inca power. This reversal is an important reminder that the key to premodern state-building is the concentration of arable land and manpower, not altitude per se. In Southeast Asia, the larger expanses of arable padi land lie at lower elevations; in Peru, by contrast, there is actually less arable land below twenty-seven hundred meters than above, where the New World staples maize and potatoes, unlike irrigated rice, thrive.[9] Despite the reversal of altitudes in the case of Inca civilization, both the Inca and the Spanish states gave rise to a state-resisting, "barbarian" periphery. In the Spanish case, what is most striking and instructive is that much of that barbarian periphery was composed of defectors from more complex, settled societies deliberately placing themselves at a distance from the dangers and oppressions of state space. To do this often meant forsaking their permanent fields, simplifying their social structure, and splitting into smaller, more mobile bands. Ironically, they even succeeded admirably in fooling an earlier generation of ethnographers into believing that scattered peoples such as the Yanomamo, the Siriono, and the Tupo-Guarani were the surviving remnants of ur-primitive populations.

Those populations that had managed to fight free of European control for a time came to represent zones of insubordination. Such shatter zones, particularly if they held abundant subsistence resources, served as magnets, attracting individuals, small groups, and whole communities seeking sanctuary outside the reach of colonial power. Schwartz and Salomon show how the Jívaro and the neighboring Záparo, who had fought off the Europeans and come to control several tributaries of the upper Amazon, became such a magnet.[10] The inevitable consequence of the demographic influx gave rise to a characteristic feature of most regions of refuge: a patchwork of identities, ethnicities, and cultural amalgams that are bewilderingly complex.

In North America in the late seventeenth and much of the eighteenth century, the Great Lakes region became a zone of refuge and flux as Britain and France vied for supremacy through their Native American allies, most prominently the Iroquois and Algonquin. The area teemed with runaways and refugees from many areas and backgrounds. Richard White calls this zone "a world made of fragments": villages of greatly varied backgrounds living side by side and still other settlements of mixed populations thrown together by circumstances.[11] In this setting, authority, even at the level of an individual hamlet, was tenuous, and each settlement itself was radically unstable.

The crazy-quilt ethnic array in the New World zones of refuge is further complicated by runaways from a new population imported precisely to counteract the failure to enserf the remaining native population: namely African slaves. As slaves—themselves, of course, a polyglot population— fled servitude, they found themselves in zones of refuge already occupied by native peoples. In places such as Florida, Brazil, Colombia, and many parts of the Caribbean, this encounter gave rise to hybrid populations that defied simple description. Nor were slaves and native peoples the only ones tempted by the promise of life at a distance from the state. Adventurers, traders, bandits, fugitives from the law, and outcasts—the stock figures of many frontiers—also drifted into these spaces and added further to their recondite complexity.

There is something of a rough historical pattern here. State expansion, when it involves forms of forced labor, fosters (geographical conditions permitting) extrastate zones of flight and refuge. The inhabitants of such zones often constitute a composite of runaways and earlier-established peoples. European colonial expansion surely provides the best documented instances of this pattern. But the pattern is equally applicable to early modern Europe itself. The Cossack frontier created by runaways from Russian serfdom from the fifteenth century on is a case in point to which we shall return.

A second instance, that of the "outlaw corridor" in the late seventeenth and early eighteenth century between the agrarian states of Prussia and Brandenburg and the maritime powers of Venice, Genoa, and Marseille, is particularly instructive.[12] Competition among the agrarian states for conscripts led to constant sweeps for "vagrants"—virtually anyone without a fixed residence—to fulfill draconian recruitment quotas. Gypsies, the most stigmatized and scourged of the itinerant poor, were criminalized and made the object of the notorious *Zegeuner Jagt* (Gypsy hunts). To the southwest there was an equally ferocious competition between maritime states for galley slaves, who were also forcibly conscripted from among the itinerant poor. Military or galley servitude, in both zones, was a recognized alternative to the death penalty, and the raids for vagrants correlated closely with the demand for military manpower.

Between these two zones of forced servitude, however, there was a seam of relative immunity to which many of the migrant poor, particularly gypsies, fled. This no-man's land, this narrow zone of refuge, became known as the "outlaw corridor." The outlaw corridor was simply a concentration of migrants "between the Palatine and Saxony, which was too far from the Prussian-Brandenburg recruitment area as well as from the Mediterranean (in the latter case, the transportation costs were higher then the price per slave)."[13] As in the case of Aguirre Beltrán's regions of refuge and of maroon communities generally, the outlaw corridor was a state effect and, at the same time, a state-resistant social space forged in conscious response and opposition to subordination.[14]

Before we turn to Zomia proper, two examples of "hilly" refugees from state control in Southeast Asia merit brief examination. The first—the case of the Tengger highlands in East Java—is one example for which cultural and religious survival appears to loom particularly large in the motives for migration.[15] The second case appears to be a nearly limiting case—that of northern Luzon, in which the zone of refuge to which runaways repaired was virtually uninhabited.

The Tengger highlands are distinctive for being the major redoubt on Java of an explicitly non-Islamic, Hindu-Shaivite priesthood, the only such priesthood to have escaped the wave of Islamicization that followed the collapse of the last major Hindu-Buddhist kingdom (Majapahit) in the early sixteenth century. In local accounts, part of the defeated population fled to Bali, while a fraction sought refuge in the highlands. As Robert Hefner notes, "it is a curiosity that the present population of the Tengger highlands should have kept a firm attachment to a Hindu priesthood while utterly lacking Hinduism's other distinguishing features: castes, courts, and an aristocracy."[16] The highland population was periodically replenished by new waves of migrants seeking refuge from lowland states. As the valley kingdom of Mataram rose in the seventeenth century, it sent repeated expeditions into the hills to capture slaves, driving those who had evaded capture farther up the slopes to relative safety. In the 1670s a Madurese prince revolted against Mataram, now under Dutch protection, and, when the revolt was crushed, the disbanded rebels fled to the hills ahead of their Dutch pursuers. Another rebel and founder of Pasuruan, the ex-slave Surapati, was later routed in turn by the Dutch, but his descendants continued their resistance for years from their redoubts in the Tengger highlands. The case for the Tengger highlands as a product of what Hefner terms 250 years of political violence, as an accumulation of runaways—from slavery, defeat, taxes, cultural assimilation, and forced cultivation under the Dutch—is overwhelming.

By the end of the eighteenth century, much of the population had moved to the highest ground that was least accessible and most defensible, though economically precarious. The history of flight is remembered annually by the non-Islamic highlanders who throw offerings into the volcano in remembrance of their escape from Muslim armies. Their distinct tradition, despite its Hindu content, is culturally encoded in a strong tradition of household autonomy, self-reliance, and an antihierarchical impulse. The contrast with lowland patterns forcibly struck a forestry officer on his first visit: "You couldn't tell rich from poor. Everyone spoke in the same way, to everyone else too, no matter what their position. Children talked to their parents and even to the village chief using ordinary *ngoko*. No one bent down and bowed before others."[17] As Hefner observes, the overriding goal of the Tengger uplanders is to avoid "being ordered about"; an aspiration that is deliberately at odds with the elaborate hierarchies and status-coded behavior of the Javanese lowlands. Both the demography and the ethos of the Tengger highlands, then, might fairly be termed a state effect—a geographical place peopled for half a millennium by state-evading refugees from the lowlands whose egalitarian values and Hindu rites are quite self-consciously drawn up in contrast to the rank-conscious, Islamic lowlanders.[18]

A second historical case from insular Southeast Asia that structurally resembles the case I hope to make for Zomia in general is that of mountainous northern Luzon. Together with the Tengger highlands, northern Luzon can be understood as a smaller-scale Zomia, peopled largely by refugees from lowland subordination.

In his carefully documented *Ethnohistory of Northern Luzon*, Felix Keesing sets himself the task of accounting for the cultural and ethnic differences between upland and lowland peoples. He rejects accounts that begin from the premise of an essential, primordial difference between the two populations, a premise that would require us to construct separate migration histories to account for their presence on Luzon. Instead, he claims that the differences can be traced to the long Spanish period and to the "ecological and cultural dynamics operating upon an originally common population."[19] The overall picture once again is of flight going back more than five hundred years.

Even before the arrival of the Spanish in the sixteenth century, some of the island population was moving inland out of the range of Islamic slave-traders who raided along the coast. Those remaining near the coast often built watchtowers to provide ample warning in case of approaching slavers. The reasons for evading bondage, however, increased severalfold once the Spanish presence was felt. As in the padi state, the imperative of concentrating population and agricultural production in a confined space was the key to state-making.[20] The friar estates, like the Latin American reducciones, were systems of forced labor with a patina of "Christianizing civilization" as their ideological rationale. It was from these "forcing-houses" of lowland power that people fled to the hinterlands and to the hills, which were, Keesing believes, virtually unpopulated until then. The documentary evidence, he claims, "show[s] how the accessible groups faced a choice between submitting to alien control or retreating to the interior. Some retreated into the interior and others subsequently retreated to the mountains in the course of uprisings from time to time against Spanish rule. . . . Under Spanish rule, retreat into the mountains became a major theme of historical times in all nine of the sectional studies."[21]

The uplanders had, for the most part, once been lowlanders whose flight to higher altitudes had begun an elaborate and complex process of differentiation.[22] In their new ecological settings, the various groups of refugees adopted new subsistence routines. For the Ifugao, this meant elaborating a sophisticated system of terracing at higher altitudes, allowing them to continue to plant irrigated rice. For most other groups it meant moving from fixed-field agriculture to swiddening and/or foraging. Encountered much later by outsiders, such groups were held to be fundamentally different peoples who had never advanced beyond "primitive" subsistence techniques. But as Keesing warns, it makes no sense to simply assume that a people who are foragers today were, necessarily, foragers a hundred years ago; they might just as easily have been cultivators. The varied timing of the many waves of migration, their location by altitude, and their mode of subsistence account, Keesing believes, for the luxuriant diversity of the mountain ethnoscape in contrast to valley uniformity. He suggests a schematic model for how such ethnic differentiation might have come about: "The simplest theoretical picture . . . is of an original group, of which part stays in the lowlands and part goes into the mountains. Each then undergoes subsequent ethnic reformulation, so that they become different. Continuing contact, i.e., trade or even war, would affect them mutually. The upland migrating group might split and settle in different ecological settings as, say, at varying elevations, diversifying the mountain opportunities for reformulation."[23] The dichotomy between hill and valley is established by the historical fact of flight from the lowland state by a portion of its population. The cultural, linguistic, and ethnic diversity within the hills is created both by upland conflict and by the great variety of ecological settings and their relative isolation, owing to the friction of terrain, from one another.

Hill and valley lifestyles were, as in most other cases, culturally coded and charged. In Luzon the lowlands were associated with Catholicism, baptism, submission (tax and corvée), and "civilization." The hills, from the valley perspective, were associated with heathenism, apostasy, primitive wildness and ferocity, and insubordination. Baptism was for a long time seen as a public act of submission to the new rulers and flight a form of insurrection (those who fled were called *remontados*). There were, as elsewhere, distinctions made in the valley centers between "wild" (*feroces*) hill people and "tame" (*dociles*), rather like the U.S. cavalry distinguished between "friendlies" and "hostile redskins." In Luzon what was a common population riven by a basically political choice between becoming a subject of a more hierarchical valley polity or electing a relatively autonomous life in the hills was reconfigured as an essential and primordial difference between a civilized and advanced population on the one hand and a primitive, backward people on the other.

The Peopling of Zomia: The Long March

> The term savages, used by so many authors to denote all the hill tribes of Indo-China, is very inaccurate and misleading, as many of these tribes are more civilized and humane than the tax-ridden inhabitants of the plain country, and indeed merely the remains of once mighty empires.
> —Archibald Ross Colquhoun, *Amongst the Shans*, 1885

The peopling of Zomia has largely been a state effect. The nearly two millennia–deep movement of peoples from the Yangzi and Pearl river basins and from Sichuan and the Tibetan plateau defies a simple accounting, even in hands far more competent than my own. Theories and legends abound, but verifiable facts are scarce, not least because the "peoples" in question were designated by so many different and incompatible labels that one can rarely be sure just whom is being specified. There is no reason to assume, for example, that a group designated as Miao—in any case an exonym—in the fifteenth century bears any necessary relation to a group labeled Miao by a Han administrator in the eighteenth century. Nor is the confusion confined to the terminology. In the jumble of repeated migrations and cultural collisions, group after group was reshuffled and transformed so frequently that there is no reason whatever to assume any long-run genealogical or linguistic continuity to such peoples.

In the face of this truly radical uncertainty about identities, it is possible to hazard some broad generalizations about the general pattern of movement.

Table 2 Uprisings in Southwest China by Province, as recorded in the *Great Chinese Encyclopedia* to the Mid-Seventeenth Century

	722–207 BCE	206 BCE–264 CE	265–617 CE	618–959 CE	960–1279 CE	1280–1367 CE	1368–1644 CE
Sichuan	0	2	1	0	46	0	3
Hunan	5	20	18	10	112	6	16
Guangxi	0	0	0	14	51	5	218
Guangdong	0	4	3	5	23	17	52
Yunnan	1	3	3	53	0	7	2
Guizhou	0	0	0	0	0	0	91

Source: Herold J. Wiens, *China's March toward the Tropics: A Discussion of the Southward Penetration of China's Culture, Peoples, and Political Control in Relation to the Non-Han-Chinese Peoples of South China in the Perspective of Historical and Cultural Geography* (Hamden, Conn.: Shoe String, 1954), 187.

As the Han kingdoms expanded beyond their original, nonpadi heartland in the Yellow River area, they expanded into new padi state zones—that is, the Yangzi and Pearl river basins and westward along river courses and flatlands. The populations living in these zones of expansion had three choices: assimilation and absorption, rebellion, or flight (often after failed resistance). The shifting tempo of revolt by province and dynasty provides a rough geographical and historical gauge of Han state expansion. Revolts typically occurred in those zones where Han expansionary pressure was most acute. A table of uprisings sufficiently large to make it into the *Great Chinese Encyclopedia* is suggestive.

Table 2 reflects the major thrust in the early Tang Dynasty into Yunnan and the subsequent Song efforts to control Sichuan, Guangxi, and Hunan. A comparative lull, in this region at least, was followed in the late fourteenth century by a massive Ming invasion of some three hundred thousand troops and military colonists designed to rout the Yuan holdouts. Many of the invaders stayed on as settlers like the Yuan before them, and this provoked numerous uprisings, especially among the Miao and Yao in Guangxi and Guizhou.[24] Imperial aggression and armed resistance in these same areas, though not shown in the table, continued under the Manchu/Qing, whose policy of shifting from tributary rule to direct Han administration provoked further unrest and flight. Between 1700 and 1850 some three million Han settlers and soldiers entered the southwest provinces, swelling the Han proportion of the twenty million inhabitants of this zone to 60 percent.[25]

At each stage of the Han expansion, a fraction, large or small, came under Han administration and was eventually absorbed as taxpaying subjects of the kingdom. Though such groups left their mark, often indelible, on what it meant to be a "Han" in that area, that fraction disappeared as a named, self-identified ethnic group.[26] Wherever there were open lands to which those preferring to remain outside the Han state could flee, however, emigration remained an ever-present possibility. Those groups accustomed to irrigated-padi agriculture, most notably the Tai/Lao, sought out the small upland valleys where wet-rice cultivation was easiest. Other groups retreated to the more remote slopes and ravines regarded by the Han as fiscally sterile and agriculturally unpromising, where they had a sporting chance of remaining independent. This process is the dominant process by which, over centuries, it seems, the hills of Zomia were populated. As Herold Wiens, the pioneer chronicler of these vast migrations, summarizes at length,

> The effect of these invasions was the settlement of southern China by Han-Chinese in progressive stages from the Yangtzu River valley southwestward to the Yunnan frontiers, and the shifting of the tribal peoples of south China from their old stamping grounds, forcing them from the better agricultural lands. The movement of the tribes people determined to preserve their way of life were toward the sparsely settled frontier lands where the more unfavorable environment promised to deter the rapid advance of the Han-Chinese—i.e. the humid, hot, malarial regions. A second direction of movement was the vertical movement into the more unfavorable environments of the high mountain lands mostly unsuitable for rice-cultivation and undesired by the Han-Chinese agriculturalists. In the first direction moved the valley-dwelling, rice-raising, water-loving Tai tribes people. In the second direction moved the mountain-roving, fire-field or shifting agriculturalists, the Miao, the Yao, the Lolo and their related agricultural groups. Nevertheless, the vertical movements did not find sufficient room for the displaced mountain tribesmen, so that among them, also, there have been migrations to the south and southwest frontier regions and even across the frontiers into Vietnam-Laos and northern Thailand and northern Burma.[27]

The great hilly barrier to the expansion of Han state power and settlement, where the friction of distance that impedes movement is at its greatest, is in the uplands of Yunnan, Guizhou, and northern and western Guangxi. Since this rugged topography continues southward, across what have become international boundaries, into the northern sections of the mainland Southeast Asian states and northeastern India, these areas too must be considered a part of what we are calling Zomia. It is to precisely this geographical bastion against state expansion that the populations seeking to evade incorporation have been driven. Having, over time, adapted to a hilly environment and, as we shall see, developed a social structure and subsistence routines to avoid incorporation, they are now seen by their lowland neighbors as impoverished, backward, tribal populations that lacked the talent for civilization. But, as Wiens explains, "There is no doubt that the early predecessors of the present day 'hill-tribes' occupied lowland plains as well. . . . It was not until much later that there developed a strict differentiation of the Miao and Yao as hill-dwellers. This development was not so much a matter of preference as of necessity for those tribesmen wishing to escape domination or annihilation."[28]

Any attempt to craft a historically deep and accurate narrative of migration for any particular people is fraught with difficulty, in part because the groups have been reformulated so often. Wiens has, nevertheless, tried to piece together a sketchy history for the large group known, to the Han, as the Miao, a portion of whom call themselves Hmong. It appears that around the sixth century, the "Miao-Man" ("barbarians"), with their own gentry, were a major military threat to Han valleys north of the Yangzi—fomenting more than forty rebellions between 403 and 610. At a certain point they were broken up and those not absorbed were then thought to have become a dispersed, ununified people without a nobility. The term *Miao* came over time to apply rather indiscriminately to almost any acephalous people on the frontier of the Han state—virtually shorthand for "barbarian." For the past five hundred years, under the Ming and Qing, campaigns for assimilation or "suppression and extermination" were nearly constant. Suppression campaigns following insurrections in 1698, 1732, and 1794, and above all the rising in Guizhou in 1855 dispersed the Miao in many different directions throughout southwest China and mountainous mainland Southeast Asia. Wiens describes these campaigns as ones of expulsion and extermination comparable to "the American treatment of the Indians."[29]

One result of the Miao's headlong flight was their wide dispersal throughout Zomia. Although generally at higher altitudes growing opium and maize, the Miao/Hmong can be found planting wet rice, foraging, and swiddening at intermediate altitudes. Wiens explains this diversity by the timing of the Hmong appearance in a particular locality and their relative strength vis-à-vis competing groups.[30] Latecomers, if they are militarily superior, will typically seize the valley lands and force existing groups to move upward, often in a ratcheting effect.[31] If the latecomers are less powerful, they must occupy whatever niches are left, often higher up the slopes. Either way, there is a vertical stacking of "ethnicities" on each mountain or range of mountains. Thus in southwest Yunnan there are some Mon below fifteen hundred meters, Tai in upland basins up to seventeen hundred meters, Miao and Yao at even higher elevations, and finally the Akha, presumably the weakest group in this setting, who are near the crest of the mountains, up to eighteen hundred meters.

Of the cultures and peoples pushed west and southwest into the hills of Zomia, the Tai were apparently the most numerous and, today, the most prominent. The greater Tai linguistic community includes the Thai and lowland Lao, the Shan of Burma, the Zhuang of southwestern China (the largest minority in the People's Republic), and various related groups from northern Vietnam all the way to Assam. What distinguished many (but not all) of the Tai from most other Zomia peoples is that, by all accounts, they seem always to have been a state-making people. That is, they have long practiced wet-rice cultivation, they carry the social structure of autocratic rule, military prowess, and, in many cases, a world religion that facilitates state formation. "Tainess" historically may in fact more accurately be seen like "Malayness": that is, as a state-making technology borne by a thin superstratum of military elites/aristocrats into which many different peoples have, over time, been assimilated. Their greatest state-making endeavor was the kingdom of Nan Chao and its successor Dali, in Yunnan (737–1153), which fought off Tang invasions and, for a time, managed to seize Sichuan's capital, Cheng-du.[32] Before being destroyed by the Mongol invasion, this center of power had conquered the Pyu kingdom in central Burma and expended its reach into northern Thailand and Laos. The Mongol victory led to a further dispersal throughout much of highland Southeast Asia and beyond. In the hills, wherever there was a suitable rice plain, one was likely to find a small state on the Tai model. Apart from favorable settings like Chiang Mai and Kengtung, most such states were small affairs in keeping with their confined ecological limits. They were, in general, in competition with one another for population and trade routes, such that one British observer could aptly describe the hills of eastern Burma as "a bedlam of snarling Shan states."[33]

The complexities of migration, ethnic reformulation, and subsistence patterns in Zomia, or any shatter zone of long duration, are daunting. Although a group may have moved initially to the hills to escape, say, the pressure of the Han or Burmese state, innumerable subsequent moves and fragmentations might have any number of causes—for example, competition with other hill peoples, shortage of land for swiddens, intragroup friction, a run of bad luck indicating that the spirits of the place were ill-disposed, evading raids, and so forth. Any large migration, moreover, set off a chain reaction of subsidiary moves impelled by the first—rather like the sequence of invasions of steppe peoples, themselves often set in motion by others, that brought the Roman Empire to its knees or, to use a more contemporary simile, like a maniacal game of fairground bumper-cars, each adding its shock wave to the previous impacts.[34]

The Ubiquity and Causes of Flight

Many also of the Burmans and Peguans, unable any longer to bear the heavy oppressions and continual levies of men and money made upon them, *have withdrawn themselves from their native soil,* with all their families . . . and thus not merely the armies but likewise the very population of this kingdom has been of late much diminished. . . . When I first arrived in Pegu, each bend of the great river Ava [Irrawaddy] presented a long continual line of habitations, but on my return, a very few villages were to be seen along the whole course of the stream.
—Father Sangermano, c. 1800

The nearly two-millennia push—sporadic but inexorable—of the Han state and Han settlers into Zomia has surely been the single great historical process most responsible for driving people into the hills. It has not by any means, however, been the only dynamic. The waxing of other state cores, among them Pyu, Pegu, Nan Chao, Chiang Mai, and various Burmese and Thai states have themselves set people in motion and driven many of them out of range. "Ordinary" state processes, such as taxation, forced labor, warfare and revolt, religious dissent, and the ecological consequences of state building have been responsible for both a routine extrusion of beleaguered subjects and, more historically notable, moments when circumstances provoked large-scale, headlong flight.

It would be difficult to exaggerate the degree to which the cultivators of Southeast Asia—in the plains or in the hills—were footloose. Early European visitors, colonial officials, and historians of the region note the exceptional proclivity of villagers to migrate whenever they were dissatisfied with conditions or perceived opportunities in a new direction. *The Gazetteer of Upper Burma and the Shan States,* which contains a brief account of literally thousands of villages and towns, bears this out.[35] Again and again, the compilers are told that the village was founded recently or several generations back by people who had come from elsewhere, usually to escape war or oppression.[36] In other cases, settlements that were previously quite prosperous towns are either completely deserted or reduced to small hamlets of remnants. All the evidence suggests that precolonial displacement and migration was the rule rather than the exception. The startling and generalized physical mobility of Southeast Asian cultivators—including those growing irrigated rice—was completely at odds with "the enduring stereotype of the territorially rooted, peasant household." And yet, as Robert Elson explains, "mobility rather than permanency seems to have been a keynote of peasant life in this [colonial] era as well as previous ones."[37]

Much of this migration was undoubtedly a lowland affair—between one lowland kingdom and another, from the core of a kingdom to its periphery, from resource-poor areas to resource-rich ones.[38] But a good deal of this movement, as we have already seen, was movement to the hills, to higher elevations, and thus to areas more likely to be beyond the reach of a lowland state. Responding to Burmese conscription and taxes during an early-nineteenth-century Burmese invasion of Assam, the population of Möng Hkawn, a valley town in the upper Chindwin, fled to higher ground; "to avoid the oppression to which they were constantly exposed, the Shans sought an asylum in the remote glens and valleys on the banks of the Chindwin, and the Kachins among the recesses of the mountains at the eastern extremity of the valley."[39] Elaborating on this pattern, J. G. Scott wrote that the "hill-tribes" were relegated to the hills and to what he saw, mistakenly, as a far more onerous form of agriculture by virtue of defeat. "This hard work is left to mild aboriginal or other tribes, whom the Burman has long ago bullied out of the fat lowlands."[40] Elsewhere, contemplating the ethnic diversity of the hills, Scott hazarded a synoptic view of the whole of Zomia as a vast zone of refuge or "shatter zone." His formulation, echoing as it does that of Wiens noted earlier, merits quotation at length:

> Indo-China [Southeast Asia] seems to have been the common asylum for fugitive tribes from both India and China. The expansion of the Chinese Empire, which for centuries did not extend south of the Yang-tzu River, and the inroads of the Scythian tribes on the empires of Chandra-gupta and Asoka combined to turn out the aborigines both to the northeast and northwest and these met and struggled for existence in Indo-China. It is only some such theory that will account for the extraordinary variety and marked dissimilarity of races found in the sheltered valleys and the high ranges of the Shan States and the surrounding countries.[41]

Scott's view of Zomia as a region of asylum is, I believe, substantially correct. What is misleading, however, is the implicit assumption that the hill peoples the colonizers encountered were all originally "aboriginal" peoples and that their subsequent histories were those of coherent, genealogically and linguistically continuous communities. Many of the people in the hills were, in all likelihood, valley peoples who long ago had fled state space. Others, however, were "state-making" valley peoples, like many of the Tai, who lost to more powerful states and who scattered or moved together to the hills. Still others, as we shall see, were the shards of valley states: deserting conscripts, rebels, defeated armies, ruined peasants, villagers fleeing epidemics and famine, escaped serfs and slaves, royal pretenders and their entourages, and religious dissidents. It is these peoples disgorged by valley states, together with the constant mixing and reconstitution of hill peoples in their migrations, that make identities in Zomia such a legitimately bewildering puzzle.[42]

Just how decisive flight over the centuries was demographically for the peopling of the hills is difficult to judge. To gauge that would require more data than we have about hill populations a millennium or more ago. What sparse archeological evidence we do have, however, suggests that the hills were thinly populated. Paul Wheatley claimed that in insular Southeast Asia—perhaps like Keesing's mountainous Northern Luzon—the mountains were essentially unoccupied until very recently, making them "of no human significance prior to the late 19th century."[43]

The reasons why subjects of valley states might wish to, or be forced to, move away, defy easy accounting. What follows is a description of some of the most common causes. It ignores one common historical event that, as it were, placed people beyond the reach of the state without actually moving: the contraction or collapse of state power at its core.[44]

Taxes and Corvée Labor

The key to statecraft in precolonial Southeast Asia, one honored as often in the breach as in its observance, was to press the kingdom's subjects only so far so as not to provoke their wholesale departure. In areas where relatively weak kingdoms competed for manpower, the population was not, generally, hard-pressed. Indeed, under such circumstances settlers might be enticed by grain, plow animals, and implements to settle in underpopulated districts of a kingdom.

A large state lording it over a substantial wet-rice core was, as a monopolist, more inclined to press its advantage to the limit. This was especially so at the core and when the kingdom faced attack or was itself ruled by a monarch with grandiose plans of aggression or pagoda-building. Inhabiting the classical agricultural core of all precolonial Burmese kingdoms, the population of Kyauk-se was ruinously poor because of overtaxation.[45] The risk of overexploitation was aggravated by several features of precolonial governance: the use of "tax farmers," who had bid for the right to collect taxes and were determined to turn a profit, the fact that something close to half the population were captives or their descendants, and the difficulty of estimating the all-important harvest yield for any particular year, and, hence, what the traffic would bear. Corvée labor and taxes on households and land were, moreover, not the end of it. Taxes and fees were levied, in principle at least, on every conceivable activity: livestock, *nat* worship shrines, marriages, timber, fish traps, caulking pitch, saltpeter, beeswax, coconut and betel trees, and elephants, as well, of course, as innumerable tolls on markets and roads. Here it is useful to recall that the working definition of being a subject of a kingdom was not so much ethnic as the civil condition of being liable to tax and corvée.[46]

Pushed to the breaking point, the subject had several choices. The most common, perhaps, was to evade crown service, the most onerous becoming a "subject" of an individual notable or of a religious authority, all of whom competed for manpower. Failing that, movement to another adjacent lowland kingdom was an option. In the past three centuries, many thousands of Mon, Burman, and Karen have moved into the Thai orbit in just this fashion. Another option was to move outside the state's reach altogether—to the hinterland and/or the hills. All these options were generally preferred to the risks of open rebellion, an option confined largely to elites contending for the throne. As late as 1921 the response of the Mien and Hmong to intense pressure for corvée labor from the Thai state was to disappear into the forest, after which they fade from official notice. This was, presumably, precisely what they had intended.[47] Oscar Salemink reports even more contemporary instances of hill peoples moving in groups to more remote areas, often at higher elevations, to escape the impositions of Vietnamese officials and cadres.[48]

The loss of population, as noted, operated as something like a homeostatic device, sapping the power of a kingdom. It was often the first tangible sign that certain limits of endurance had been breached. A proximate sign, much noted in the chronicles, was the appearance of a "floating" population either begging or resorting to theft and banditry in their desperation. The only sure way to evade the burdens of being a subject in bad times was to move away. Such a move quite often meant moving from wet-rice agriculture to swiddening and or foraging. How common this was is impossible to tell for sure, but to judge by the number of oral histories in which hill people recount a past as padi growers in the lowlands, it is not negligible.[49]

War and Rebellion

We are like ants, traveling away from our trouble to a safe place. We left everything behind to be safe.
—Mon villager fleeing to Thailand, 1995

Constant rebellions and wars between the Peguans and Burmese and Shans . . . afflicted the country for 500 years. All those who were not killed were driven away from their former homes by ruthless invaders or were drafted off to fight for the king. . . . Thus in some cases the proprietors [cultivators] were killed out, in others they left for districts so remote that it was impossible to retain a hold on the ancestral property, however great their attachment to it.
—J. G. Scott [Shway Yoe], *The Burman*

The expression "states make wars and wars make states," coined by Charles Tilly, is no less true for Southeast Asia as it was for early modern Europe.[50] For our purposes, the corollary of Tilly's adage might be: "States make wars and wars—massively—make migrants." Southeast Asia wars in the same period were at least as disruptive. Military campaigns mobilized more of the adult population than their European counterparts, and they were at least as likely to spawn epidemics (cholera and typhus, in particular), famine, and the devastation and depopulation of the defeated kingdom. The demographic impact of the two successful Burmese invasions of Siam (1549–69 and the 1760s) was enormous. The core population around the defeated capital vanished; a small fraction was captured and returned to the Burmese core, and most of the rest dispersed to areas of greater safety. By 1920 the population of the Siamese core region had only just recovered to its preinvasion level.[51] The hardships even a successful war was likely to inflict on the staging area of the campaign were often no less devastating than those inflicted on the enemy. Having sacked the Siamese capital, Burmese King Bayin-naung's mobilization had exhausted the food and population surpluses of the delta area around Pegu. After his death in 1581, subsequent wars between Arakan, Ayutthaya, and the Burmese court at Taung-ngu turned the territory near Pegu into a "depopulated desert."[52]

Warfare for civilian noncombatants, especially those on the route of march, was, if anything, more devastating than for conscripts. If a late-seventeenth-century European army of sixty thousand troops required forty thousand horses, more than one hundred carts of provisions, and almost a million pounds of food per day, one can appreciate the wide swath of pillage and ruin a Southeast Asian army left in its wake.[53] For this reason the invasion routes were seldom the most direct, as-the-crow-flies trajectory but rather traced routes calculated and timed to maximize the manpower, grain, carts, draft animals, and forage—not to mention the private looting—that a large army required. A simple calculation can help convey the extent of the devastation. If we assume, as John A. Lynn does, that an army forages 8 kilometers on either side of its line of march and marches 16 kilometers a day, it would then scour 260 square kilometers of countryside for each day of the campaign. A ten-day march by the same army might then affect 26 thousand square kilometers.[54] The major threat from incessant wars was, in manpower-starved kingdoms, not so much that of being killed; a lucky combatant in this form of military "booty-capitalism" might actually aspire to capture people himself and sell them as slaves for a profit. The danger, rather, was the utter devastation visited on those who lay athwart the line of march—the danger of being captured or else having to flee and abandon everything to the army. It mattered little whether the army in question was "one's own" or that of a neighboring kingdom, the quartermaster's requirements were the same, and so, largely, was the treatment of civilians and property. A striking example comes from the Burmese-Manipur War(s), which continued sporadically from the sixteenth century into the eighteenth. The repeated devastation drove the Chin-Mizo plains-dwellers from the Kabe-Kabaw Valley up into the hills, where, subsequently, they became known as a "hill people"—presumably "always there."

The late-eighteenth-century mobilizations of Burmese King Bò-daw-hpaya (r. 1782–1819) in the service of his extravagant dreams of conquest and ceremonial building were ruinous to the kingdom as a whole. First, a failed invasion of Siam in 1785–86 in which half the army of perhaps three hundred thousand disappeared, then a massive labor requisition to build what would have been the largest pagoda in the world, followed by mobilizations to repel the Thai counterthrust and to extend the Meiktila irrigation system, and, finally, another general mobilization for a last, and disastrous, invasion of Thailand from Tavoy sent the population of the kingdom reeling. An English observer noted that the population of lower Burma was fleeing "to other countries" in fear of conscription and the predations of armies. Banditry and rebellion were widespread, but the typical response was to flee to areas farther from the state core and from the king's own marauding army. Rumors of its approach would send subjects across the horizon in dread and mortal fear, for their own troops "bore every appearance of the march of a hostile army."[55] And for every major war there were probably scores of smaller campaigns between petty kingdoms, or, for that matter, civil wars between claimants to the throne, like the one in 1886 in Hsum-Hsai, a petty principality in the modest Shan kingdom of Hsi-paw, that left the district largely deserted. The prolonged civil war in the late nineteenth century for control of another Shan state, Hsen-wi, was so devastating that finally "the greatest of the modern Shan capitals would hardly form a bazaar suburb to one of the older walled cities."[56]

The first aim of a civilian was to avoid conscription. In a time of mobilization, conscription quotas were set for every district. Sure indications of evasion were the frequent successions of increasingly draconian quotas (for example, first, one of every two hundred households, then one of fifty, then one of ten, and finally a general mobilization). The quotas were rarely reached, and tattooing was used to mark recruits so that they could be identified later. It was also possible in the late Kon-baung period, and probably earlier as well, for those of some means to bribe their way out of conscription. But the surest way of avoiding the military draft was to move out of the padi state core and away from the army's route of march. It was the misfortune of the Sgaw and especially the Pwo Karen to inhabit the invasion (and retreat!) routes in the Burmo-Siamese wars of the late eighteenth century. Ronald Renard claims that it was precisely in this period that they dispersed to the mountains along the Salween River and took to living in more easily defended longhouses along the ridges. Even those who much later placed themselves under Thai protection refused to establish permanent settlements since they "still preferred the wandering, swiddening life which, they claimed, freed them from the vulnerability of being attached to specific lands."[57]

Once an army was conscripted, heroic efforts were necessary to hold it together throughout an arduous campaign. A late-sixteenth-century European voyager noted the pillaging and burning characteristic of Burmese-Siamese warfare and then added, "but in the end they never return home without leaving half of their people."[58] Since we know that such wars were not particularly sanguinary, it is most likely that the bulk of the losses were to desertion. Evidence from the *Glass Palace Chronicle* account of a failed Burmese siege confirms this suspicion. After a five-month siege, the attackers were short of provisions and an epidemic broke out. The army, which began with 250,000 troops, according to the chronicle, disintegrated totally, and after a disastrous retreat, "the King reached his capital with a small escort."[59] The vast majority, one imagines, deserted once the siege faltered and the epidemic began, making their way back or beginning new lives in a safer place. In a late-nineteenth-century Burmese military expedition against the Shan, J. G. Scott reported, the minister in charge of the troops "effected nothing warlike, and rumor said he was so fully occupied keeping the troops from dispersing, that he had no time to fight."[60] We know that rates of desertion, as in virtually all premodern armies, were high, especially in a failed campaign.[61] How many of the deserters—or displaced civilians, for that matter—ended up in the hills and other faraway places is impossible to judge. But the fact that many of the troops were either "press-ganged" or slaves and their descendants and that, owing to the warfare itself, many of them had nothing to return to suggests that many of the deserters began new lives elsewhere.[62]

There are some shards of evidence that the dangers and displacement of warfare pushed many onetime padi cultivators to the hinterlands and to higher elevations, and hence to new subsistence routines. The Ganan, for example, are today an apparently minority people, some eight thousand strong, living in the headwaters of the Mu River (Sagaing Division, Burma) among three thousand–foot peaks cleaved by deep ravines.[63] They were, or had become, it seems, a lowland people and an integral part of the Pyu padi state until its centers were sacked and destroyed by Mon, Burman, and Nan Chao forces between the ninth and fourteenth centuries. They fled up the Mu River watershed because it was "away from the battlefields"; there they became, and remain, swiddeners and foragers. They have no written language, and they practice a heterodox variant of Buddhism. Their account accords, as we shall see, with that of many contemporary hill people who claim a lowland past.

Here and there, one encounters more contemporary evidence of flight to the hills to evade capture or the predations of warfare. J. G. Scott believed that the present hill groups around Kengtung/Chaing-tung, in Burma east of the Salween, were once settled on the plain around Kengtung and were driven by Thai invasions into the hills where they now swidden.[64] And Charles Keyes cites a nineteenth-century missionary account of an isolated Karen group which had fled the Siamese to a nearly inaccessible mountain gorge between Saraburi and Khorat from a previously more lowland setting.[65] The northern Chin, for their part, fled to more remote hills to escape Shan-Burmese warfare in the eighteenth and nineteenth centuries, occasionally providing refuge in turn to rebel Burmese princes fleeing the king's troops.[66]

In the context of warfare, it is important to note that the devastation of a state's padi core has the effect of nullifying state space in terms of both political power and ecology. Even allowing for hyperbole, the following description of Chiang Mai after the Burmese invasion is instructive: "Cities became jungles, rice fields became grasslands, land for elephants, forests for tigers, where it was impossible to build a country."[67] It would be tempting to believe that plainsmen, now free of their burdens as state subjects, could remain in place. The problem, however, was that the defeat of a kingdom provoked a competitive scouring of the remnant population by neighboring states and slave-raiders. Shifting from the plains to a location far less accessible to armies and slavers offered a reasonable chance of autonomy and independence. This is exactly the option, Leo Alting von Geusau claims, that was taken by the Akha and many other groups today viewed as hill people "from time immemorial":

> Over many centuries, therefore, the more inaccessible parts of mountainous Yunnan and neighboring Vietnam, Laos, and Burma became the zones of refuge for tribal groups marginalized by the smaller vassal states which occupied the lower land areas. In this process of marginalization, tribal groups such as the Hani and Akha also selected and constructed their habitats—in terms of altitude and surrounding forestation—in such a way that they would not easily be accessible to soldiers, bandits, and tax collectors. Such processes have been termed "encapsulation."[68]

Raiding and Slaving

Raiding is our agriculture.
—Berber saying

Concentrated population and grain production was, as we have seen, normally a necessary condition for state formation. Precisely because such areas offered a potential surplus for state-building rulers, so also did they represent an irresistible target for raiders. For all but the largest court centers, the threat of raids by slavers and/or bandits was a real and present danger. Fear of Malay slave raiders in the early colonial period had depopulated many of the coastal areas of Burma and Siam; the Karen on this account avoided roads and exposed beaches. Prolonged vulnerability was likely to be turned into a system of subordination and predation. A situation of this kind prevailed in the upper Chindwin Kubo Valley, where the hill-dwelling Chins had made themselves masters of the valley Shans, carrying many of them off as slaves.[69] A substantial town of five hundred households and thirty-seven monasteries in 1960 was reduced, in this way, to only twenty-eight houses.

It was generally in the interest of hill people, where they did dominate the adjacent valley, to defend valley settlements with which they could trade and from which they could extract a regular tribute. Under stable conditions, a kind of protection racket–cum–blackmail relationship developed. On occasion, hill groups such as the Kachin found it in their interest actually to establish settlements "in the plains or on the rivers at the foot of the hills." Much as the Berbers talked about tribute from sedentary communities as "our farming," so, in the Bhamo area along the upper Irrawaddy, did the Kachin appoint Burmese and Shan headmen. "It appears that there was hardly a village in the whole Bhamo district which was thus not protected and the Kachins were really masters of the country."[70] At its most placid and routinized, this arrangement comes close to resembling the successful premodern state: namely, a monopolistic protection racket that keeps the peace and fosters production and trade while extracting no more rents than the traffic will bear.

And yet again and again, hill people in such zones raided valley settlements to the point where they "killed the goose that laid the golden egg," leaving a devastated and uninhabited plain.[71] Why? The answer, I believe, is to be found in the political structure of the hills, characterized by many small competing polities. Each of these hill polities might have "associated" valley settlements that they were protecting. In the simplest, most schematic terms, it would look roughly like figure 2.

Because Kachin group A might live three or four days from a village it protected, Kachin group B might be able to raid the village protected by A and get away. When the raid became known, Kachin group A might then retaliate by raiding another lowland settlement protected by offending group B. This might, of course, spark a highland feud unless some accommodation was reached.[72]

There are several consequences of this pattern that bear on the general argument I am making. The first is that what looks, especially to valley peoples(!), as generalized raiding by hill "tribes" is, in fact, a fairly finely articulated expression of hill politics. Second, if this pattern is widespread, it leads to the depopulation of large areas and a withdrawal of vulnerable lowlanders to, in this case, places farther from the hills and nearer the river where flight was easiest. Finally, and perhaps most important, the primary objective of these raids was the taking of slaves, many of whom would be kept by the

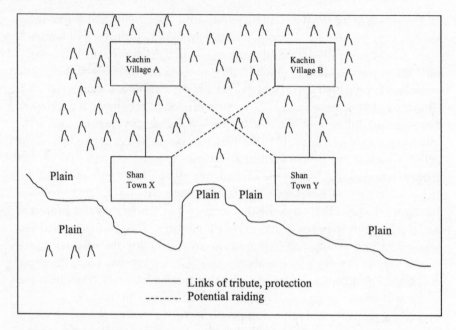

2. Schema of hill-valley raiding and tribute relations

Kachin or sold to other hill peoples or slave-traders. To the degree that such raiding was successful, it represented a net demographic transfer of population to the hills. It was yet another process by which valley people became hill people and by which the hills were made more cosmopolitan culturally.

Certain hill peoples became known, and even notorious, as slave-raiders. In the Shan states generally, the Karenni (Red Karen) were particularly feared. Postharvest raiding for slaves became, in certain areas, routine.[73] "Thus, in most of the Karenni villages are to be found Shan-yangs of the Karen tribes, Yondalines, Padaungs, and Let-htas of the mountain ranges to the northwest, all doomed to a hopeless state of slavery. . . . They are sold to the Yons (Chiang Mai Shan) by whom they are resold to the Siamese."[74] The list of Karenni captives is indicative, for it contains the names of hill peoples as well as valley populations. Slave-raiding peoples like the Karenni, specializing in the most valuable trade good, people, not only abducted valley dwellers to incorporate them into hill society or to resell them in valley markets; they also abducted vulnerable hill people and enslaved them or resold them. They were, in a sense, a reversible conveyor belt of manpower, now supplying the raw material for state-making in the valley, now looting vulnerable valley settlements for their own manpower needs. In any event, the pattern helps explain why plainsmen were wary of raiders and why weaker hill peoples retreated to inaccessible locations, often in fortified and concealed ridgetop stockades, to minimize their exposure.[75]

Rebels and Schismatics to the Hills

Rebellions and civil wars in the lowlands hold many of the same terrors for villagers as do wars of conquest or invasions. They provoke similar patterns of flight as people frantically move to locations where they imagine they will be safer. What is notable, however, is that these repertoires of flight have logic to them, and that logic depends heavily on class, or, more precisely, on the degree to which one's status, property, and life are guaranteed by the routines of state power. The logic is evident even in the fracture lines of flight during the early years of the Vietnam War in the south from 1954 to 1965. Landlords, elites, and officials, fearing for their safety, increasingly gravitated away from the countryside and toward provincial capitals and eventually, as the conflict escalated, to Saigon itself. The closer to the state core, their movements seemed to say, the safer they were. Many ordinary peasants, by contrast, shifted from a more sedentary life in large villages to more remote, mobile settlements outside the state's easy reach. It is as if the tenuous, social compact of state-based society had come undone: elites heading for the center, where the coercive power of the state was most felt, and vulnerable nonelites heading for the periphery, where the coercive power of the state was least felt.

Rebels, of course, unless they are very powerful, have even more compelling reasons to head for the hills. The earlier stages of the war in Indochina (1946–54) caused, as Hardy explains, "the movement of large numbers of Viêt people from the Red River Delta into the remotest parts of the northern highlands. Forests provided cover for the revolution all the way to the valley of Dien Bien Phu, near the border with Laos."[76] The pattern is historically deep in Vietnam and elsewhere. It can be traced, at least, to the massive Tay Son rebellion (1771–1802), which began when three brothers from Tay Son village fled to the nearby hills for safety and to recruit followers. It continued through the Can Vuong movement in early colonial Vietnam, to the Nghe-Tinh uprisings of 1930, and, finally, to the Vietminh base area in the hills among the minority Tho people.[77] State evasion by threatened rebels and noncombatants alike often entails migration to new ecological settings and the adoption of novel subsistence routines. Such routines are not only more suited to the new location but are also typically more diverse and mobile, thus making their practitioners less legible to the state.

Defeated rebellions, like war in general, drove the vanquished to the margins. The larger the rebellion, the greater the population displaced. In this respect, the second half of the nineteenth century in China was a time of enormous upheavals, which put hundreds of thousands to rout, many of whom then sought refuge farther away from Han power. The greatest of these upheavals resulted from the Taiping Rebellion from 1851 to 1864, certainly the largest peasant rebellion in world history. The second upheavals, in Guizhou and Yunnan, sometimes called the Panthay Rebellion, were massive uprisings lasting from 1854 to 1873 and involving "renegade" Han and Miao/Hmong hill people, as well as Hui-Chinese Muslims. Although the so-called Miao Rebellion never reached the amplitude of the Taiping rising—which cost the lives of some twenty million people—it nevertheless persisted for nearly two decades before its suppression. Defeated rebels, their families, and whole communities in headlong flight retreated into Zomia in the case of the Taiping Rebellion and, in the case of the Miao Rebellion, deeper and farther south within Zomia. In flight from Han power, these migrations not only led to widespread looting, banditry, and destruction but they also further complicated the already diverse ethnoscape of the hills. In a ratchet effect, fleeing groups often drove others before them. Thongchai Winichakul claims that many of the Chinese entering northern Siam in the late nineteenth century were remnants of the Taiping forces.[78] The defeated remnants of the Miao Rebellion pushed south and many Lahu and Akha groups, not involved in the rebellion itself, moved south with them or ahead of them to stay out of harm's way.[79] In the twentieth century, a successful rebellion—the Communist Revolution in China—produced a new stream of migrants: defeated Republican-Kuomintang troops. Settling in the area that is today known as the Golden Triangle, where Laos, Burma, China, and Thailand (nearly) meet, they have with their hill allies come to control much of the opium trade. Thanks to the friction of terrain that their remote location in the hills affords, they also take political advantage of being situated along the seam of four nearly contiguous national jurisdictions.[80] They are hardly the most recent migrants into Zomia's region of refuge. In 1958, under pressure from Chinese party cadres and soldiers, fully one third of the Wa population crossed the border from the People's Republic into Burma seeking refuge.[81] During the Cultural Revolution, another pulse of migration followed.

The retreat of Kuomintang forces to the Golden Triangle serves to remind us that the hills and Zomia in particular have long been a destination of retreat (and renewed military preparations) for officials of a defeated dynasty, princely pretenders, and losing factions in court politics. Thus at the beginning of the Manchu Dynasty, fleeing Ming princes and their entourages retreated to safety in Guizhou and beyond. In Burma the Shan and Chin Hills were host in precolonial and early colonial times to princely rebels and fugitive claimants to the throne of Burma (*mín laún*).

Political dissent and religious heresy or apostasy are, especially before the nineteenth century, difficult to distinguish from each other, so frequently are they alloyed. Nevertheless, it merits emphasis that the hills are associated as much with religious heterodoxy vis-à-vis the lowlands as they are with rebellion and political dissent.[82] That this should be the case is not surprising. Given the influence of the clergy (*sangha*) in Theravada countries like Burma and Siam and a cosmology that potentially made the ruler into a Hindu-Buddhist god-king, it was at least as vital for the crown to control the abbots of the realm as it was to control its princes—and at least as difficult. The crown's ability to impose its religious writ at a distance was about as extensive as its ability to impose its political writ and its taxes. This distance varied not only with the topography but also temporally, with the power and cohesion of the court. The religious "frontier" beyond which orthodoxy could not easily be imposed was therefore not so much a place or defined border as it was a relation to power—that varying margin at which state power faded appreciably.

The wet-rice valleys and the level plains of the typical valley state are not merely topographically flat; they can also be thought of as having been culturally, linguistically, and religiously flattened. The first thing that strikes any observer is the relative uniformity of valley culture compared to the luxuriant diversity of dress, speech, ritual, cultivation, and religious practice to be found in the hills. This relative uniformity is, to be sure, a state effect. Theravada Buddhism, as a would-be universal creed, was very much the religion of a centralizing state compared with the local deities (*nat, phi*) that predated its spread. Despite their syncretism and incorporation of animist practice, Theravada monarchs, when they could, proscribed heterodox monks and monasteries, outlawed many Hindu-animist rites (many of them dominated by females and transvestites), and propagated what they took to be "pure," uncorrupted texts.[83] The flattening of religious practice was, then, a project of the padi state to ensure that the only other kingdomwide institution of elites besides the crown's own establishment was firmly under its control. A certain uniformity was also achieved because the larger abbeys were, after all, run by a surplus-appropriating elite that, like the crown itself, thrived best on the rich production and concentrated manpower available at the state core.

Centralized power helps explain a certain level of religious orthodoxy at the core, but it doesn't fully account for the enormous religious diversity in the hills. The heterodoxy of the hills was itself a kind of state effect. Aside from being beyond the easy reach of the state, the hill populations were more scattered, diverse, and more often isolated. Where there was a Buddhist clergy, it was more dispersed and more decentralized, poorer, and, because it lacked royal patronage or supervision, more dependent on the favor of the local population. If that population was heterodox, as it often was, so too was its clergy.[84] Schismatic sects were therefore quite likely to spring up in the hills. If and when they did, they were difficult to repress, being at the margins of state power. Two other factors, however, are decisive. The first is that the combination of scriptural Buddhism and the Jataka stories of the previous lives of the Buddha, not to mention the cosmology of Mount Meru around which palace architecture was organized, provided a strong warrant for withdrawal. Hermits, wandering monks, and forest orders all partook of the charisma and spiritual knowledge that came from a position outside society.[85] The second decisive factor is that heterodox sects, proscribed in the valleys, typically moved out of danger and into the hills. Hill demography and geography not only facilitated religious heterodoxy, they also served as a zone of refuge for persecuted sects in the valleys.

The Shan Hills of Burma, an upland area of petty valley states created by a Buddhist, rice-planting people, present a striking case in point. Michael Mendelson, in his major study of the *sangha* in Burma, writes of the *Zawti* (light, radiance) reformist sect that appears to have been "chased out of Burma proper" in the late nineteenth century and to have settled in the Shan Hills.[86] It adopted some distinctive Shan Buddhist customs along with Shan texts and iconography. At the same time, the sect followed some of the heretical practices of the Paramats (a sect favored briefly by King Bò-daw-hpaya at the beginning of the nineteenth century). Mendelson closes his brief account of the sect with a hunch that accords with the "zone of refuge" perspective: "An important lead that should be followed up by scholars is the possibility that the Shan States provided a refuge for many centuries to sects chased out of Burma proper for 'heretical beliefs.'"[87] The Shans became Buddhists only late in the sixteenth century and it may be that the exodus of banned sects from the Burmese core played a role in their conversion. In this vein, while

Edmund Leach notes that all Shans are Buddhists—virtually a condition of Shanness—he hastens to add, "The majority, it is true, are not very devout, and Shan Buddhism includes a number of decidedly heretical sects."[88] Much earlier, in his *Gazetteer,* Scott describes monks in the Shan states who are armed traders with fortified positions, who smoke and wear skullcaps. He then quotes a Dr. Cushing to the effect that the degree of heterodoxy increases with the distance from the center of Burmese power.[89] A journalist traveling clandestinely through the Shan states in the 1980s mentions Buddhist monks near the Chinese border who slept with women, smoked opium, and lived in fortified monasteries.[90] It seems probable from such fragmentary evidence that Shan Buddhist may represent something of a living historical archeology of dissident Buddhist sects suppressed and expelled from the Burmese heartland over the past few centuries.

As Zomia became a place of refuge for lowland rebels and defeated armies, so also it became an asylum for banned religious sects. Projecting this process back over many centuries, one can see how Zomia came to resemble something of a shadow society, a mirror image of the great padi states—albeit using much of the same cosmological raw material. It was a catchment area for those ideas and people who were the casualties of state-making, the collateral damage of dynastic schemes. The pluralism expelled from the valleys can be found in profusion in the hills—shards that tell us what the lowland kingdoms drummed out of the valley and therefore what they might, in other circumstances, have become.

The frequency with which peripheries—mountains, deserts, dense forests—have been strongly associated with religious dissent is too common to be overlooked. The Cossack frontier of tsarist Russia was notable not only for its egalitarian social structure but also for being a bastion of Old Believers whose doctrines played an important role in both the massive Razin and Pugachev peasant revolts. Switzerland was long marked by egalitarianism and by religious heterodoxy. The Alps generally were seen by the Vatican as a cradle of heresy. The Waldensians found refuge there, and, when threatened with forced conversion by the duke of Savoy in the mid-seventeenth century, they moved to the highest valleys. The Reformation itself swept the Alpine region, though, owing to its geographical fragmentation, it splintered regionally, with Geneva becoming Calvinist and Basel Zwinglian.[91]

Hill heterodoxy could be seen as a fairly simple reflection of political and geographical marginality, a zone of resistance to which persecuted minorities can, in a pinch, repair. This view, however, would not begin to do justice to the dialogical nature of hill difference as a cultural choice embraced as an expression of distinctness and opposition. The mountain Berbers, it has been noted, have often reformulated their religious dissent in implicit contention with nearby rulers: "When the Romans who controlled the province of Ifriqiya [Africa] became Christianized, the highland Berbers (whom they never fully subjugated) also became Christians—but Donatist and Arian heretics, so as to remain distinct from the church of Rome. When Islam swept the area the Berbers became Muslims, but soon expressed their dissent from the inequalities of Arab Muslim rule by becoming Kharijite heretics." Robert LeRoy Canfield has carefully traced a comparable pattern of finely calculated Islamic religious dissent in the Hindu Kush Mountains of Afghanistan.[92] Where the major agrarian valley centers are Sunni dominated, the adjacent hill people adhere largely to the Imami sect (a variant of Shi'a), and the more remote, inaccessible hill peoples follow Ismaili beliefs. Such affiliations follow ecological contours and often span both linguistic and ethnic boundaries. Both forms of dissent powerfully connote populations that have not submitted to a state that defines itself in terms of Sunni orthodoxy. Religious identity in this case is a self-selected boundary-making device designed to emphasize political and social difference. We shall see the same process at work in mainland Southeast Asia when we examine millenarian beliefs in the hills in Chapter 8.

Crowding, Health, and the Ecology of State Space

Farmers [as opposed to hunter-gatherers] tend to breathe out nastier germs, to own better weapons and armor, to own more powerful technology in general, and to live under centralized governments better able to wage wars of conquest.
—Jared Diamond, *Guns, Germs, and Steel*

Sedentary grain cultivation and the rearing of domestic livestock (pigs, chickens, geese, ducks, cattle, sheep, horses, and so on) constituted, it is clear, a great leap forward for infectious diseases. Most of the deadly epidemic diseases from which we suffer—smallpox, flu, tuberculosis, plague, measles, and cholera—are zoonotic diseases that have evolved from domesticated animals. Crowding is crucial. And crowding means the concentration not only of people but also of domestic animals and the "obligate" pests that inevitably accompany them: rats, mice, ticks, mosquitoes, fleas, mites, and so on. So far as the diseases in question are spread by proximity (coughing, touch, shared water sources) or through the obligate pests, the density of hosts per se represents an ideal environment for rapidly spreading epidemic diseases. Rates of mortality in early modern European cities exceeded the natural rate of increase until roughly the mid-nineteenth century, when sanitation measures and clean water supplies cut the death rate appreciably. There is no reason to believe that Southeast Asian cities were any more salubrious. The great majority of these diseases might appropriately be called "diseases of civilization"; they appear in the historical record along with grain-growing cores and the concentration of flora, fauna, and insects they presuppose.[93]

The chronicles of padi states and the testimony of early European witnesses attest to the frequency of devastating epidemics in the larger cities of premodern Southeast Asia.[94] In a comprehensive and meticulous study of north and central Sulawesi, David Henley argues that epidemic diseases, particularly smallpox, represented a major obstacle to population growth. Perhaps reflecting the effects of crowding and the proximity to trade routes, the coastal population seemed less fit than "the populations of the upland areas," who "made a healthier and stronger impression."[95]

It appears that virtually everyone understood that in the case of epidemics the safest course was to leave the city immediately and disperse to the countryside or to the hills. While people were not generally aware of the actual disease vector, they implicitly knew that dispersal and isolation retarded the spread of the disease. For hill peoples in general, the lowlands are thought to be unhealthy. Such an association might, for peoples living above one thousand meters, be related to the prevalence of malaria at lower altitudes, or it could reflect the fear of urban epidemics and the risk of shipborne diseases brought by traders. In Luzon the Igorot living at lower elevations knew, the moment an epidemic broke out, that they must return to the hills, scatter, and close off the passes if they wanted to remain safe from its ravages.[96] How demographically important the flight to the hills was in response to epidemics, or what proportion of those fleeing returned when the danger was past, is impossible to tell. But when flight provoked by drought and famine is added to the equation, its demographic impact may well have been substantial.

All agriculture is a risky proposition. But on balance, padi-core agriculture was more risk prone in most respects — with one major exception — than upland agriculture, let alone foraging. The major single advantage of irrigated wet rice when the water comes from perennial streams is that it is, for a time anyway, drought resistant.[97] On the other hand, the great diversity of upland swiddening and foraging provides so many sources of nutrition that the failure of one or two crops, while bringing hardship, is less often catastrophic. Perhaps most important, the epidemiological consequences of the crowding of a species of cultivar had many of the same drawbacks as the crowding of

Homo sapiens. The relatively narrow genetic base of grain production provides an ideal epidemiological habitat for the insects, fungi, rusts, and other crop pests specialized, say, to the padi plant. The buildup of such pests could, in an irrigated plain largely planted to rice, quickly become catastrophic.

When the rains fail or when visible pests attack the crop, the cause of crop failure is reasonably obvious, although drought-stricken crops can then succumb to another pathogen the way a patient in compromised health can be vulnerable to any opportunistic infection. A plague of rats in the late sixteenth century devastated Hanthawaddy in lower Burma, devouring most of its stores of grain.[98] As the food ran out, people fled. It is clear, however, that the plague of rats itself was caused, or at least sustained, by the presence of substantial stores of grain. The causes, by contrast, of the great crop failure and famine that struck upper Burma between 1805 and 1813 are obscure. Drought appears to have played a role, as did, according to Thant Myint-U, Malthusian population pressures on a limited agricultural heartland.[99] Whatever the precise cause, it greatly accelerated the exodus of population. In particular, it prompted a huge "movement to shifting cultivation," and so much padi land was empty that Kon-baung tax administrators had to invent a new cadastral category to account for it. Whether or not these absconding subjects moved far into the hills is obscure, but one thing is clear: they abandoned the padi core in droves.[100]

The suggestion of Malthusian pressure at the core raises the intriguing possibility that the padi core may have been ecologically, as well as fiscally, self-limiting. This is precisely what Charles Keeton has argued.[101] In his view, the massive deforestation around the dry zone under King Mindon had resulted in increased runoff and the siltation of irrigation tanks and canals. Many of the canals were abandoned. A slight downward fluctuation in rainfall—in an area with very low precipitation (fifty to sixty-five centimeters annually) to begin with—could touch off a drought and exodus. On this view, the dry zone had become a degraded and fragile ecological setting, prone to crop failure. Some of those fleeing the famine may have gone to the hills; the majority, at the end of the nineteenth century, headed for the booming, open frontier of the Irrawaddy Delta. In any case, they too left the padi core.

Against the Grain

The dynastic self-portraits of precolonial padi states in Southeast Asia and of the Ming and Qing dynasties are, in the official sources, represented in rosy colors as a rather benign ingathering of peoples. Wise administrators shepherd rude peoples toward a literate, Buddhist or Confucian court center in which sedentary wet-rice cultivation and becoming a full subject of the realm stand as the marks of civilizational achievement. Like all ideological self-representations, the Hegelian ideal they depict seems, like the use of the term *pacification* in the Vietnam War, a cruel parody of lived experience, especially at the frontier.

Ignoring for the moment the larger question of what "civilization" might be understood to represent, the self-portrait is radically wrong in at least two respects. First, the process of ingathering was, typically, anything but a benign, voluntary journey toward civilization. Much of the population at the center was a captive population—taken en masse as prizes of war and driven back to the core or purchased, retail, as it were, from slaving expeditions selling the state what it most needed. In 1650 the proportion of hereditary *ahmudan* (service regiments mostly made up of slaves and their descendants) within a two hundred–kilometer radius of the capital at Ava was 40 percent. A massive deportation of war captives from Manipur, the Shan Hills, and lower Burma from 1760 to 1780 was intended to further increase the by now depleted ahmudan ranks. Siam was an even more striking example of a kingdom of captives. In the late seventeenth century, according to one observer, one-third of the population of central Siam consisted of "foreigners descended chiefly from Lao and Mon war captives." Its population depleted by Burmese invasions, Siam launched a massive campaign of military capture in the early nineteenth century to the point where "All told, Laos, Mons, Khmers, Burmese, and Malays may have equaled the number of self-identified Siamese in the central basin."[102] All of this is not to deny that outlying peoples in substantial numbers gravitated toward the opportunities and advantages at the court center in good times. It is, however, to deny that such state-making, in these demographic circumstances, was even conceivable without capture and bondage.

The second and more egregious omission of this self-portrait is the overwhelming evidence for flight from the state core. To recognize it, of course, would be to manifestly contradict the civilizational discourse; why on earth would anyone choose to leave the padi core and "go over to the barbarians"? Observers with a myopic historical perspective might be forgiven this error, inasmuch as the past sixty years or so *have* been characterized by a massive increase in the urban, core population and a growing control over the hills by the modern state. For well more than a millennium before that, however, it is abundantly clear that it was at least as common for people to flee the state as to approach it. The process was anything but regular, with wild oscillations between a virtual emptying out of the padi core to its full demographic occupation.

The motives for flight from the state core are numerous, but they can be roughly catalogued. Contrary to the civilizational discourse which implicitly assumes that anyone would prefer to plant padi in the lowlands were it not for predatory states, there were positive reasons for preferring hill swiddening or foraging to wet-rice cultivation. So long as there was plenty of open land, as was the case until fairly recently, swiddening was generally more efficient in terms of return to labor than irrigated rice. It offered more nutritional variety in settings that were generally healthier. Finally, when combined with foraging and hunting for goods highly valued in the lowlands and in international commerce, it could provide high returns for relatively little effort. One could combine social autonomy with the advantages of commercial exchange. Going to the hills, or remaining in the hills if you were already there, was not, in most circumstances, a choice of freedom at the cost of material deprivation.

After a demographic collapse following a famine, epidemic, or war—if one were lucky enough to have survived—swiddening might become the norm, right there on the padi plain. State-resistant space was therefore not a place on the map but a position vis-à-vis power; it could be created by successful acts of defiance, by shifts in farming techniques, or by unanticipated acts of god. The same spot could oscillate between being heavily ruled or being relatively independent, depending on the reach of the padi state and the resistance of its would-be subjects.

With respect to actual flight, we might usefully distinguish between the slow, grinding, routines that extruded people year by year and the larger events that produced a mass exodus. In the former category, the growing burdens of taxes and corvée in an ambitious reign might provoke a steady stream of ruined subjects who moved beyond the state's power. Religious dissidents, the losers in factional struggles, village outcasts, criminals, and adventurers might, as well, move to the frontier. Emigrés of this kind, as we shall see, were readily absorbed into the existing hill societies.

Whether, in the long run, the steady, cumulative departure of subjects or the crises that produced mass exoduses contributed most to the loss of core populations is hard to gauge. The former, precisely because it was unspectacular, is more likely to be found in the tax-receipt records than in the chronicles. War, famine, fire, and epidemics are more newsworthy and therefore more apparent in the chronicles and archives. These four, along with tyranny, constitute the five famous scourges of Burmese folk sayings.[103] They are primarily responsible for the large-scale shuffling of populations from one state to another, migration from the padi core to the margins of state power, and, in the hills themselves, a repositioning of populations.

There is no way of predicting the catastrophe represented by, say, war, famine, or epidemics, and no way of knowing in advance their duration or severity. By their nature such events set in motion tumultuous, headlong panic and flight. And yet such disasters were so much a part of the precolonial Southeast Asian landscapes that one imagines that many populations had "routines of disaster," much as peasants in time of food shortage have a knowledge of famine foods they can eat to tide them over. Dispersal, routes of escape, and alternative subsistence routines must have been part of the crisis repertoire of much of the core peasantry.[104]

Mass exodus, often coupled with rebellion and banditry, punctuated the precolonial history of most Southeast Asian states. We might distinguish here between the catastrophes that drove the core population to seek safety—in another state, at the margins of power, and in the hills—from the resistance and flight of populations who were, for the first time, being forcibly incorporated into the state by an ambitious dynasty. Both were in evidence in Northern Vietnam from the fourteenth century to the sixteenth. Drought, rebellions, and invasions from 1340 to 1400 led to a collapse of the padi-growing population in the Red River Delta. It plummeted by 800,000 to perhaps 1.6 million, with many of the refugees apparently moving into the hills. In the early sixteenth century a demographically recovered heartland attempted to extend its power to the "hilly Vietnamese districts west, north, and northeast of the capital." A series of rebellions, led in part by miracle-working Buddhist and Taoist adepts, offered determined resistance and put many thousands to flight, many of them, presumably, farther into the hills. The early-nineteenth-century Siamese court encountered similarly ferocious resistance when it tried to extend its control to the southern Lao area, tattooing taxpayers (the "red-iron" policy), raising corvée demands, "and countenancing or promoting wholesale enslavement of upland and tribal peoples."[105] When the rebellions were crushed, it is plausible to assume that those wishing to escape incorporation would head for the hills, and those menaced by slaving expeditions would retreat even farther into the hills to remain out of range. From the Mongol invasions of the thirteenth century through much of the fifteenth century, upper Burma experienced chaos and famine, during which, Michael Aung-Thwin reports, "large segments of the population moved away from traditionally secure areas to enclaves of safety."[106] Exactly where these refugees went is unclear, but a substantial portion must have scattered to the nearest periphery of dynastic power, which would have been, in most cases, uphill. Only in the nineteenth century did the delta of lower Burma, itself initially a place of refuge, become the standard destination for those fleeing the core of Burmese power.

Fragmentary as the evidence is, we can venture a guess or two about the patterns of oscillation in the state-administered populations at the center of the padi state and those beyond its grasp. In terms of distance from dynastic power, we can imagine something of a continuum between a heavily administered, rice-growing population at the center on the one hand and ridgeline-dwelling, stockade builders who are quite beyond the state's reach on the other. Those at the edge of the core population and those in the nearby hilly hinterland would occupy an intermediary position relative to state power. Schematically, and speculatively, it makes some sense to think that, when beleaguered, a population would move as a first step to the next safest adjacent zone. Thus those at the center, faced with a war or famine, would move toward the core's edge. Those at the core's edge might first try to seal themselves off from the disruptions at the center by fiscally seceding and defending themselves.[107] Should this strategy fail, they in turn would head for the nearby hinterland and the hills. Those in the hinterland and hills, faced with an extension of state power in the form of direct administration or slave raids, could rebel or flee—or rebel and *then* flee, perhaps deeper or higher into the hills.[108] Each segment, then, when endangered, would presumably move along the continuum to the next position farther from state power. Under more favorable conditions at the core, this process would work in reverse, as many moved closer to the core to take advantage of the trade and status opportunities there.

Where Oliver Wolters writes of a "concertina" mandala state in Southeast Asia, we might extend the simile to the mandala's population, now approaching, now moving just out of reach, depending on the balance of danger and reward. The population on this view ought to be viewed as politically amphibious. The capacity to cycle back and forth, over time, between relative stateness and statelessness depended on a large open frontier and on having handy the repertoires of social structure and subsistence that would serve them in a new niche. But was it, after all, an entirely new niche? Once we recall that such a large proportion of the population were captives or descendants of captives—a great many of them culled from the hills—then, perhaps, for some of them, the journey away from the state was something like a homecoming.

The Friction of Distance: States and Culture

Nothing is more difficult than to conquer a people [the Igorots] who have no needs and whose ramparts are the forests, mountains, impenetrable wildernesses, and high precipices.
—Spanish official, eighteenth-century Philippines

Precolonial and colonial officials both understood that the military obstacles to the conquest of remote mountainous areas were formidable. The combination of a mobile and generally hostile population and a rugged topography meant that even punitive expeditions, let along military occupation, were risky enterprises. As the Glass Palace Chronicle notes of one such campaign, "The Mahaupayaza and the king of Ava who had been ordered to go in pursuit of the Sawbwa of Mogaung were recalled, as it was found impossible for the pursuers to proceed without very great hardship in a mountainous country where the passes were blocked with snow drifts and mists and fogs did not lift until noon."[109] Scott, leading a better-armed military campaign of "pacification" in northern Burma at the end of the nineteenth century, noted the relationship of the difficulty of troop movement to the length of time it took to subdue a district: "Where wide tracts of uncultivated forest, miles of waterlogged country, reeking with malaria, or confused tangles of scrub jungle and ravines afforded the dacoits safe-retreats [such districts] were not reduced to order for a year or two longer."[110] For the French in Vietnam, it was no different. A 1901 report warned of the obstacles to controlling dissent and trouble in the hills protected by "the shelter of steep mountains and almost impenetrable forest."[111]

The above is, of course, the view from the valley state. From the perspective of those retreating to the hills, it was a natural advantage they could exploit. They could, as the Igorot did, cut off the mountain passes and, when necessary, retreat deeper and deeper into the hills. The mountains favored defensive warfare in general and provided innumerable places where a small group could hold off a much larger force. The deepest recesses of a mountainous zone, where the cumulative friction of travel from the nearest lowland center is greatest, are the least accessible to direct state control. In such places the term *mountain fastness* takes on a literal meaning. For the British, the "wild" Wa, located between Thailand, China, and the eastern Shan states of Burma, lived in such a zone. Turn-of-the-century maps could not begin to depict, according to a colonial officer, the actual difficulty of the terrain in which main ridges "were crises-crossed with sharp angled hills."[112] Even today, the Wa—perhaps two million strong—"live in what is undoubtedly one of the last great mountain wildernesses in the modern world."[113]

The degree of friction represented by a landscape cannot simply be read off the topography. It is, to a considerable degree, socially engineered and manipulated to amplify or minimize that friction. To follow the British progress in projecting their power into the hills is, to a great extent, to follow the progress of their distance-demolishing technologies: bridges, all-weather roads, forest-felling, accurate maps, and the telegraph. The advanced techniques of defoliation, helicopters, airplanes, and modern satellite photography further diminish that friction. Friction is thus not simply "there" in some mechanical way; it is constantly being sculpted for one purpose or another. For those wishing to maximize the friction of distance, a host of countervailing strategies are available: destroying bridges, ambushing or booby-trapping passes and defiles, felling trees along roads, cutting telephone and telegraph wires, and so forth. A great part of the literature on guerrilla warfare (that part that is not about techniques for gaining intelligence) is about efforts to manage the landscape to one's advantage.

The military logic that governs the friction of distance operates as well to shape social and cultural influence. Working out its consequences schematically helps to illuminate some of the social differences between hill societies and padi states. Many of the major cultural influences in Southeast Asia have been exogenous—brought by seaborne traders. Brahminical Hinduism, Buddhism, and, later, Islam arrived in this fashion. From the seacoast, where they landed, these influences tended to spread along the major arteries of human commerce and movement—plains, river basins—carried along by the trajectories of movement of this lowland population. One might think of a time-lapse photographic series in which the influence of these cultural ideas is spread most readily over areas with the least friction of terrain and the largest volume of human traffic.

Notice, in this connection, how locations of very high friction—swamps, marshes, ravines, rugged mountains, heaths, deserts—even though they may be quite close to the state core as the crow flies, are likely to remain relatively inaccessible, and thus zones of political and cultural difference. If we add a vertical or altitudinal dimension, in the case of large mountain ranges, to a long-run temporal or time-lapse dimension, it is easy to see how certain kinds of cultural stratification might develop. A cultural complex, say Hindu-Shaivite cultism, moves from the coast, with state power and commercial exchange along the watercourses and across arable plains. Those, say animists, who, for one reason or another, choose not to adapt to this complex, move or are driven farther up the watershed, farther into the interior and out of range. Let's then imagine that another cultural complex, say Buddhism, or Islam, succeeds the first. This new pulse, perhaps also state-assisted, might push those Hindu-Shaivite populations not wishing to assimilate, farther up the watershed, in turn driving the earlier animist refugees to still higher elevations and/or deeper into the interior. It is easy to see how one might get, in these circumstances, something like the Tengger Highlands described earlier: a kind of vertical sedimentation of cultural pulses from afar—the oldest (deepest) now highest in elevation and the newest (most shallow) in the lowland plains. In practice, of course, the patterns of migration are far more complex, and in the twentieth century Christian missionaries in mainland Southeast Asia have "skipped," as it were, directly to the highlands. What this crude schema does help us understand, however, is why those living in higher and more remote locations less accessible to the state may also be culturally distinct and, in a sense, historically stratified as well.[114]

Mini-Zomias, Dry and Wet

Our focus has been on the vast, contiguous hilly area we have chosen to call Zomia. But the principles of the friction of distance, regions of refuge, and state-resistant topographies work elsewhere on a smaller scale. One historically important case is that of the Pegu Yoma in Burma, a four hundred–kilometer–long, forested mountain tract, some sixty-five to two hundred kilometers in width running through the heart of Burma between the Irrawaddy and Sittang rivers.

As the closest state-resistant space to the rich plains, the Pegu Yoma was long a redoubt for runaways, rebels, and bandits. Its dense forest, its hidden valleys, and, above all, its proximity to prosperous rice-growing villages was such that Sir Charles Crosthwaite wrote, "No dacoit could have wished for better conditions."[115] However, as the location of one of the last great stands of teak, the key revenue-producing commodity in early-twentieth-century colonial Burma, it became a valuable prize. Despite the resources de-

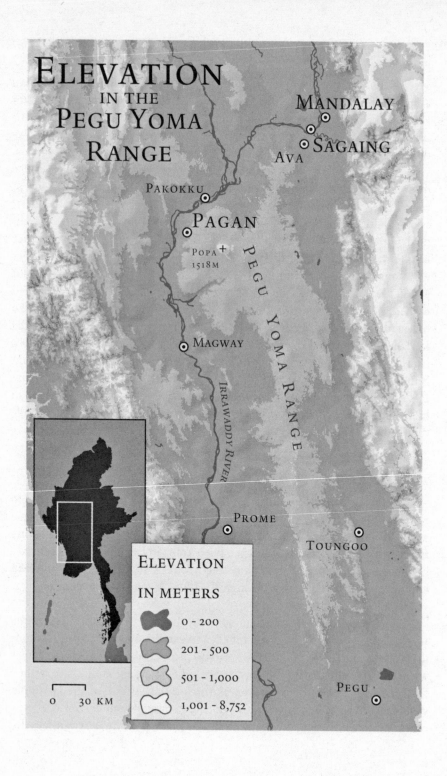

ELEVATION
IN THE
PEGU YOMA
RANGE

MANDALAY

SAGAING

AVA

PAKOKKU

PAGAN

POPA + 1518M

MAGWAY

PEGU YOMA RANGE

IRRAWADDY RIVER

PROME

TOUNGOO

ELEVATION
IN METERS

0 – 200

201 – 500

501 – 1,000

1,001 – 8,752

0   30 KM

PEGU

voted to its control, the Pegu Yoma slipped from British hands in the Second Anglo-Burmese War (1885–87), again during the great Hsaya San Uprising (1930–32), and, finally and definitively, on the outbreak of World War II. After the war, and for nearly thirty years until 1975, it was the major base area for communist rebels in the north and Karen rebels in the south, who nearly brought down the government in Rangoon. So secure was this rebel base area that the Communist Party Burma (CPB) thought of it as its own Yennan and named the Central Marxism-Leninism School in its mountain fastness "The Golden City of Beijing."[116] When it was finally cleared in 1975, both the CPB and the Karen National United Party (KNUP) lost their last base within striking distance of the central plain and the central government. Although it was sparsely populated, the Pegu Yoma merits its own chapter in any account of state-resistant spaces in Burma.[117]

Poppa Hill, or Mount Poppa, at the northern extremity of the Pegu Yoma, today an important Buddhist shrine and pilgrimage site, was until fairly recently a renowned state-resistant space. Located southwest of Mandalay, between Meiktila and Chauk, this abrupt fifteen hundred–meter peak is surrounded by spurs with ravines and scrub jungle. Though not extensive enough to serve as a major zone of refuge or revolutionary base area, it was close enough to trade routes and valley populations to serve as a hideout for bandit gangs and cattle thieves. One such band held out for a full ten years after the British annexation.[118] Poppa was just one of literally hundreds of what the British termed fastnesses that proved hard to conquer and to hold. They might harbor kingly pretenders, heterodox forest sects, rebels, and bandits. Each locale had its own particular history as a state-resistant place, and those wishing for whatever reason to distance themselves from the state knew it as a possible sanctuary. What they all had in common was a bewildering geography that favored defense and retreat, as well as a sparse and mobile population with a tradition of statelessness.

A complete accounting of state-resistant places would have as many pages devoted to low, wet places—marshes, swamps, fens, bogs, moors, deltas, mangrove coasts, and complex waterways and archipelagoes—as to high mountain redoubts. Because such difficult-to-govern places were more likely to be located near rich padi-growing areas, at low elevation, they posed an equal or greater threat to lowland political order. Jiaxing, just south of the Yangzi Delta, was, in the early seventeenth century, just such a disorderly

Map 7. Elevation in the Pegu-Yoma range

place. The maze of creeks and waterways represented nearly intractable problems of political order. A prefect charged with controlling it wrote, "These larger streams are removed by lakes, wetlands, inlets and broads which form a vast expanse, reaching for innumerable kilometers. These are the refuges where bandits from every corner come together, and from which they emerge and into which they disappear."[119]

Just as wetlands can provide a kind of natural defensive perimeter for state cores, as they did for Venice and Amsterdam, they can by the same token serve as a sanctuary for rebels, bandits, and their water-borne equivalents, pirates. The great thirteenth-century Chinese classic *Water Margin* is a swashbuckling account of disgraced or betrayed officials and their huge bandit following in the marshlands.[120] A great marsh with an even longer (three millennia or more) storied history is the Mesopotamian Marsh between the Tigris and Euphrates (today on the Iraq-Iran border). This fifteen thousand–square–kilometer marsh that shifts shape season by season was, until recently, home to a sizable population living on floating islands well away from any state presence. Wilfred Thesiger, an adventurer whose account *The Marsh Arabs* first brought this world to the attention of the English-speaking world, noted that the marshes, "with their baffling maze of reed-beds where men could move only by boat, must have afforded a refuge to remnants of a defeated people and been a centre for lawlessness and rebellion since the earliest times."[121] The combination of a labyrinth of indistinguishable (to the untrained eye of the outsider!) waterways subject to seasonal change gave a decisive advantage to its mobile inhabitants over any official intruder. The draconian remedy, in this as in other cases of a marshy resistant zone, was to drain the marsh and destroy the habitat once and for all. This great project in extending state space was finally accomplished by Saddam Hussein after the massive losses of the Iran-Iraq War fought in this same area. The draining of large marshes and swamplands, a final solution not available to rulers confronting mountain sanctuaries, has always been, whatever its other rationales, an exercise in obliterating potential sites of resistance and rebellion.[122]

In white-settler-ruled North America, swamps, quite as much as mountains and the frontier, were sanctuaries of rebellion and escape. The Seminoles, under Chief Osceola, together with their runaway slave allies, fought a seven-year rear-guard action against federal troops bent on enforcing Andrew Jackson's policy of Indian removal.[123] The Great Dismal Swamp on the eastern Virginia–North Carolina border was home to thousands of escaped slaves for several generations, "right in the midst of the strongest slave-holding communities in the South."[124] They joined renegade whites, southerners avoiding conscription, deserters, those fleeing the law, moonshine distillers, hunters, shingle-cutters, and trappers. The "Great Dismal," like the swamp in the *Water Margin,* also had a literary presence, thanks to Longfellow's poem "A Slave in the Dismal Swamp" and Harriet Beecher Stowe's *Dred: A Tale of the Dismal Swamp* (1856). As with the sanctuary of the Marsh Arabs, there were repeated calls to have the Great Dismal drained because it allowed the "lowest sort" of people to find freedom and independence.[125]

Coastal environments, particularly in Southeast Asia, have also provided cover for rebels and those who would evade the state. The shifting deltas of the major rivers of mainland Southeast Asia (the Mekong, Chao Praya, and Irrawaddy), indented with countless tidal creeks and estuaries, were nearly impossible to police and administer. The authorities, even in force, were no match for a fugitive population that knew its watery terrain intimately and could disappear at a moment's notice. Worried about geographical settings that would favor revolutionaries, the French and the U.S.-backed Saigon government both pointed to the mountains and the wetlands as places to watch. "The Central Highlands and the marshy plains of the western Mekong Delta [the Trans-Bassac] were the two main strategic regions highlighted as vulnerable to communist infiltration."[126] Karen rebels against the Burmese government also took full advantage of the "impenetrable region of great mangrove swamp, forest reserves, muddy rivers, and hidden creeks, where government forces have always had to move slowly."[127]

The mangrove habitat, with its impossibly tortuous passages, recondite to anyone except those with long experience, perhaps represents something of an ideal setting for evasion. As protective cover it probably has no equal. "Winding channels and creeks, obstructed by mud and sand banks, here vanish from sight behind a concealing wall of vegetation, the narrow lane of the mangrove labyrinth being crowded over with branches or the long fronds of the *nipah* [palm]. Here, in a moment of anticipated danger, the water-borne people of the locality familiar with its intricate geography can successfully escape detection."[128]

A geography that was favorable to hiding and escape was, by the same token, favorable to raiders. The mangroves were close to the shipping lanes just as the Pegu Yoma was close to the prosperous lowlands. Raiders could dart out and back, plundering ships, raiding coastal settlements, and taking slaves. Like the Vikings, the sea gypsies had an amphibious existence as traders and raiders. Like the Vikings, the sea gypsies had fast, shallow-draft *perahu,* enabling them to escape up small creeks where larger vessels could not go and to raid settlements at night from the often unprotected, upstream side. Using the mangroves to their advantage, they posed for a time a major threat to Dutch and British maritime trade in Southeast Asia. Even today, their highly armed, motorized, lineal descendants bedevil the great tankers plying the Straits of Melaka.[129]

Like the hills, the swamps, marshes, and mangroves are places to repair to and potentially places from which to raid. But above all, they are places of low-stateness, where populations that would for whatever reason evade the writ of the state can find refuge.

Going over to the Barbarians

We know that some of the border Chinese began to follow the same line of divergent evolution [pastoral nomadism] and that it was to retain the Chinese within China as well as to keep the new style barbarians out of China that the Great Wall was built.
—Owen Lattimore, "The Frontier in History"

Older narratives and lowland folk versions of who the minorities are and how they got there typically treat them as an original, indigenous people from whom valley populations descended. Current narratives by historians and ethnographers of the minorities now living in Zomia often portray them as migrants trailing a saga of defeat, persecution, marginalization. The tale is generally one of unjust victimization. Two implicit assumptions help sustain this narrative. The first is that all hill peoples would prefer to be valley cultivators, that many of them were once lowland people, and that they were driven into the hills, reluctantly, by virtue of force majeure. The second assumption is that they would naturally want to avoid the stigma of "barbarity" and backwardness that attaches to them—that barbarity is the logical outcome of their flight. Since, by lowland standards, civilized people are wet-rice growing, taxpaying subjects of a state, to leave that condition, to move out of the state's orbit and adopt new subsistence routines is, ipso facto, to place oneself beyond the pale.

To leave the story here is to miss the important intentionality—the agency—of these migrations. Where there is an open-land frontier and trade with lowland settlements, hill dwellers can enjoy a relatively prosperous life with less labor, not to mention avoiding taxes and corvée. Just as Lattimore noted that many of the pastoralists on the northern and western frontiers of China were cultivators of various backgrounds "who decided to break away from poverty-stricken farming to a more secure life as herdsmen," so has the move to upland swiddening and foraging often been a voluntary move in terms of narrow economic self-interest.[130] And when to that self-interest we add the advantage of keeping more of one's crop and disposing of more of one's own labor, the positive reasons for distancing oneself from state power might be convincing in material terms alone.

Because the shift to hill livelihoods was, in valley terms, always associated with a decline in status, it was inconceivable that it could have occurred voluntarily. Hill populations, by valley accounts, were either an aboriginal population that had never been civilized or, more sympathetically, a population driven from the lowlands by force. Constantly aware of the contempt in which they were held, many of the tribal peoples in their oral histories explain their current location and status by some combination of victimization, treachery, and negligence. Nevertheless, it is abundantly clear that all hill groups have incorporated large numbers of "defectors" from civilization by working them into their genealogies. A great many of these defectors were Han Chinese who found it convenient to leave civilization for the hills. As we have seen, there was no logical place for such counternarratives in the self-portrait of Han-Confucian statecraft. Thus the Great Wall(s) and the anti-Miao walls of Hunan were seen officially as a barrier to barbarians, whereas, in fact, they were built just as surely to hold a taxpaying, sedentary, cultivating population within the ambit of state power. As Magnus Fiskesjö shows, "many of the imagined barbarians of the past and many so-called 'Miao rebels' [of the mid-nineteenth century] were actually majority Chinese on the run from tax obligations or criminal liabilities in mainstream society."[131] Trade, the search for land, and marriage were other reasons why Han and other migrants to the hills might find it advantageous to join hill society. Self-marginalization, or "self-barbarization" in valley terms, might have been, at times, quite common. Civilizational discourse, however, made such conduct unthinkable.[132]

If, in fact, groups choose not to be assimilated to the culture and routines of the valley state, if they choose instead, deliberately, to place themselves at a physical and cultural distance from that civilization, then we need a way to describe this process that treats it as more than a loss or a fall from grace. Geoffrey Benjamin, in trying to capture the way in which hill peoples in peninsular Malaya positioned themselves—ecologically, economically, and culturally—vis-à-vis the Malay state, has coined the term *dissimilation*.[133] Dissim*i*lation—not to be confused with dissim*u*lation—refers to the more or less purposeful creation of cultural distance between societies. It may involve the adoption and maintenance of linguistic differences, of distinctive histories, of differences in attire, burial and marriage rites, housing styles, forms of cultivation, and altitude. And since all such cultural markers are meant to distinguish a group from one or more others, they are necessarily relational. Dissimilation can have the effect of staking a claim to a particular niche in the overall hill-valley economy—for example, "We are foragers in the forest; we do not touch the plough." Pursued over time and elaborated, such dissimilation, of course, leads to ethnogenesis, a subject we shall explore in Chapter 7.

In the context of the history of migration away from state cores, however, we want in this final section to emphasize the most important aspect of dissimilation for many hill peoples. The key act of dissimilation is the assertion "We are a nonstate people. We are in the hills swiddening and foraging because we have placed ourselves at a distance from the valley state."

Autonomy as Identity, State-Evading Peoples

For many hill peoples, dissimilation, the staking out of the difference and distance between one society and another, meant putting a literal distance between themselves and lowland states. In a sense, the process was overdetermined, even tautological. Consider, for example, the long process of migration itself. A smaller or militarily weaker people in the lowlands, say, finds itself facing defeat and subjugation or, more likely, both. Some fraction of this beleaguered group stays put, is subjugated, and, over time, assimilated. Another fraction, say, withdraws and moves to the hinterland or hills, to maintain its autonomy while perhaps having to change its subsistence routines. Assume, further, that the group is named; let's call them the Meadowlarks. The Meadowlarks who remain in place will be absorbed into the prevailing lowland culture while leaving their own distinctive mark upon it; they will no longer, however, be "Meadowlarks," but "Chinese," "Burmese," "Siamese," "Tai." Those who leave in substantial numbers, although they change as well (perhaps even more!), will still be known as the Meadowlarks and, what is more, one major aspect of their history will have become their migration away from the valley state. From the valley perspective as well, "Meadowlarks" will be marked by flight and state evasion. If the process is repeated several times, the aspect of state evasion may come to represent the essential character of a people.

The process is schematically what several ethnographers and historians describe as typifying the experience of the Miao/Hmong over, especially, the past three centuries of rebellion and flight. Nicholas Tapp describes the process of bifurcation. On the one hand, there were the "cooked" (*shu*) Miao, or "Chinese-Miao," who accepted Chinese sovereignty, Chinese names, and permanent-field agriculture, most of whom over time were absorbed into Han culture. On the other hand were the "raw" (*sheng*) Miao, or "Miao-Miao," who moved (or remained) higher in the hills, swiddening and raiding, and at a distance from the Chinese state.[134] Another student of Miao/Hmong history believes that "when the Hmong suffered from land scarcity, lack of forest, excessive or unjust tax levies, and various official or landlord abuses, the majority tried to adapt to the new situation. Some rose up and were ready to fight, while others chose to move to a new administrative area or to another country. These migrations only concerned part of the Hmong population, the vast majority choosing to stay put and adjust."[135] On this account, the fugitive, stateless Hmong, marked indelibly by their flight and their refusal to "enter the map," are a remnant. Most of those who had historically been known as Hmong would have been absorbed as subjects of the Han state and hence disappeared as a distinguishable group. If we also allow for the fact that others who rebelled or fled along with them were absorbed into the ranks of the Hmong, then this remnant may have little in the way of genealogical, let alone genetic, continuity. The continuity — the meaning — of Hmongness may lie more powerfully in a shared history of rebellion and flight than in any presumed claim to ancestral blood ties.

A comparable story might apply to a great many (but not all) hill peoples of Zomia. The Wa, Akha, Lahu, Lisu, Khamu, Palaung, Padaung, Lamet, and some Karen seem to share a history in which, often after rebellion, some remained behind while others fled out of range while absorbing, along the way, other migrants. Shanshan Du believes that in the past three centuries the Lahu have been involved in some twenty revolts, after which many "stayed in areas of Han imperial control while others migrated south to the more marginal and mountainous regions after major suppressions."[136] The complex history of the Karen, especially the Pwo Karen, has many of the same elements. Allied with the Mon and, after the fall of Pegu in the mid-eighteenth century, with the Siamese, the Karen appeared in many cases to have been absorbed by the Mon, Siamese, Shan, and Burmese polities. Many whom we today know as the Karen are those who choose to flee or to remain in the hills as a stateless, if vulnerable, autonomous people.[137] Most of those who have ever been Karen, Lahu, and Hmong have, as a historical matter, been assimilated into the composite lowland as state subjects while their absconding remnant has retained its distinct identity, compiling thereby a history of flight and statelessness.[138]

The most carefully elaborated case of what might be called "flight from the state as identity" is that of the Akha described in the work of the late Leo Alting von Geusau. Some 2.5 million strong, including the Hani (Ha Nhi) in northern Vietnam, the Akha speak a Tibeto-Burman tongue and were in the past considered to be among the "black-bone" (raw, sheng) non-Sinicizing Yi-Lolo. Today they are located in southern Yunnan (Sip Song Phan Na) and in adjacent areas of Laos, Burma, and Thailand. Over the past two centuries they have been driven farther south by war, slavery, and the search for new swiddens. The two lowland kingdoms with which they have been in touch are the Han and the Tai, although the Han has left a far deeper impression on their cultural practices and beliefs.

Most important for our purposes is that the Akha keep elaborate (if un-reliable) genealogies and tell their own history through their bards, or *phima*. Some of this history can, it seems, be documented. But documented or not, this oral history is diagnostic of a people for whom flight and statelessness are defining characteristics. They were, they believe, originally an upland people who gradually moved to the lowlands and to rice planting, though apparently not subjects of a state. Then, in southern Yunnan, Tai warrior groups arrived as state bearers, absorbing some of the Akha while driving the rest up into the hills, along with the Palaung and others. Von Geusau claims that this accords with the establishment of the first city-state (muang) by the Tai-Lue warrior Ba Zhen in the late twelfth century, driving many of the original inhabi-tants away. This was followed by the Mongol invasions, the Yuan Dynasty in the mid-thirteenth century, and the expansion of state power in this region. From this point on, the Akha have seen themselves as a state-evading people, selecting their location and their livelihood routines so as "not to be easily accessible to soldiers, bandits and tax-collectors."[139] They have not, despite their flight, remained genetically isolated. Using pliable rules of adoption and creative genealogies, they have, on von Geusau's reckoning, absorbed Tai and Han Chinese as well as other mountain peoples, such as the Lahu, Palaung, Khamu, and Wa.

Akha flight and statelessness is normatively coded in their history and cosmology. A key figure in their legends is the would-be Akha king of the thirteenth century, Dzjawbang, who instituted a census (the iconic tax and state-making move!) and was slain by his own people. His son Bang Dzjui is an Icarus figure whose shamanic horse with wings mended with beeswax flies too close to the sun and is killed. Both stories are cautionary tales about hierarchy and state formation. The standard shamanic curing rituals intended to restore a wandering soul to its body carry the same state-evading moral: "A journey to this [spirit] world with nine layers is described as a descent from the mountains to the lowlands, where the person's soul has been captured in the 'labyrinth of the dragon' and condemned to perform corvée or slave labor for life. In order to recover a person's soul, they have to offer a pig or other large animal, such as a buffalo . . . in exactly the manner that was usual in the slave trade."[140] When it comes to what one might call religion, the same principle prevails. Beyond a respect for specialists, for those with long genealogies, and for blacksmiths, the Akha insist that they believe in no higher god and that, literally, they do not bow their head to anyone. It would be hard to imagine a people whose oral history, practices, and cosmology represented a more comprehensive rejection of states and permanent hierarchies.

CHAPTER 6

State Evasion, State Prevention
The Culture and Agriculture of Escape

I magine, once again, that you are a Southeast Asian counterpart to Jean-Baptiste Colbert. This time, however, your task is not to design an ideal state space of appropriation but, rather, the precise opposite. How would you go about designing a topography, a subsistence strategy, and a social structure that was as resistant to state formation and appropriation as possible?

Much of what you would design, I believe, would be an inversion of how the padi state was sculpted. In place of a flat, relatively frictionless alluvial plain, you would conjure up a rugged landscape where the "friction of terrain" was forbiddingly high. In place of concentrated grain crops that ripen simultaneously, you would prefer shifting, diverse, dispersed, root crops of uneven maturation. In place of permanent settlement and fixed political authority, you would devise a scattered, mobile pattern of residence and a fluid, acephalous social structure capable of easy fissioning and recombination.

In broad strokes, this is what one finds throughout much of Zomia, a pattern of settlement, agriculture, and social structure that is "state repelling." That is to say, it represents an agro-ecological setting singularly unfavorable to manpower- and grain-amassing strategies of states. The pattern is state repelling in two distinct ways. The first and most obvious is that an existing state will hesitate to incorporate such areas, inasmuch as the return, in manpower and grain, is likely to be less than the administrative and military costs of appropriating it. Tributary status might be plausible, but not direct rule. The second state-repelling feature of this social landscape is that it makes the rise of an indigenous state in this space exceedingly unlikely. The critical mass of concentrated manpower, wealth, and grain on which a state must rest is essentially lacking. Furthermore, demography and agronomy unfavorable to state appropriation are, it turns out, proof against other forms of appropriation as well: in particular, raiding. Slave-raiding expeditions, marauding armies, bandits, starving would-be pillagers of foodstuffs will, like states, find "state spaces" more lucrative for raiding than the slim pickings in sparse, mobile, root crop–growing societies with no permanent structure of authority. Such hill societies are, in this sense, not simply state repelling but appropriation resistant in general.

I have used the device of a Colbertian strategist and the idea of "design" quite deliberately. Much of the history and ethnography of the hill peoples in mainland Southeast Asia tends, implicitly or explicitly, to naturalize their location, their settlement pattern, their agriculture, and their social structure, to treat these as givens, dictated, as it were, by traditional and ecological constraints. Without gainsaying the existence of some constraints, I wish to emphasize the element of historical and strategic choice. What is striking, on any long historical view, is the great flux and variety in patterns of hill and valley residence, in social structure, in forms of agriculture, and in ethnic identity. Patterns that may appear static, even timeless, at first sight, display a remarkable plasticity if one steps back and widens the historical lens to a span of a few generations, let alone a few hundred years or a millennium. The evidence, I think, requires that we interpret hill societies—their location, their residence pattern, their agricultural techniques, their kinship practices, and their political organization—largely as social and historical choices designed to position themselves vis-à-vis the valley states and the other hill peoples among whom they live.

An Extreme Case: Karen "Hiding Villages"

A limiting case can often, by its very starkness, illustrate the basic dynamics of a social process. The draconian counterinsurgency strategy of Burma's military rulers in largely Karen areas is a case in point. Here, the "state space" around the military base is less a mere zone of appropriation than a full-fledged concentration camp. "Nonstate space," by contrast, is not so much an area outside the effective realm of the taxman as a refuge to which people run for their lives.[1]

In the Orwellian euphemism of the Burmese army, the civilian zones that they control in Karen areas are called peace villages, while the zones sheltering those who have escaped beyond their reach are called hiding villages. The official description represents "peace villages" as ones whose headmen have agreed not to assist the insurgents and to provide free labor to the military camp on a rotating basis, in return for which the villagers will not have their houses burned or be forcibly relocated. Peace villages are, in fact, frequently relocated by force to the border of the military camp itself, where they provide a ready pool of laborers and hostages. Their inhabitants are registered and given identity cards. Their agricultural land, betel nut trees, and cardamom bushes are assessed for the purpose of military taxation and requisitions. In a miniature—and militarized—version of the padi-state cores we examined in Chapter 3, the base commanders tend, in fact, to extract most of the labor, cash, and food they require from the peace villages closest to headquarters. The villagers implicitly understand the connection between the concentration of population and forced labor. In one of the many cases documented, seven villages had been forcibly consolidated into two, Kler Lah and Thay Kaw Der, nearby the barracks. As one resident said, "When they can't find people to be porters, they take all the villagers from Kler Lah and Thay Kaw Der. They don't mind if they are male or female, they take them. . . . The SPDC [government] forced them to relocate there in 1998. That is why it is very easy to force them to do forced labor or porter [since they are in one place]."[2] In a comparable relocation area, a villager also noted how concentration near the military base exposed them to exploitation. "In my opinion, they asked the villagers to move to these places so they could make them work. . . . If the villagers stay in one place, then it is easy for the Burmese to make them work."[3]

Forced to provision themselves from local sources, and with a tradition of corruption and plunder, military units have transformed relocation areas into zones of hyperappropriation. The "ideal type" of military space is a flat, open terrain (no ambushes!) along a major road, surrounded by a registered, relocated civilian population growing crops in easily monitored fields, who serve as trip wires and hostages, as well as a source of labor, cash, and foodstuffs. In an amplified version of the padi state, the Burmese army presses so severely on the manpower and resources of its captive population that a large proportion of them eventually flee in desperation.[4]

Just as the villagers sequestered around a military base represent a virtual parody of state space, so are the state-repelling techniques of those who flee its burdens an exaggeration of the strategies to be examined in this chapter. Briefly put, such strategies include fleeing to inaccessible areas, scattering and breaking up into smaller and smaller groups, and pursuing subsistence techniques that are invisible or unobtrusive.

The quickest available refuge lies, generally, farther up the water courses and higher in the hills. "If we have to run, we will run up into the hills," reports a Karen village elder. If they are pursued, they retreat still farther upstream to higher altitudes. "Then they came and looked for us so we fled upstream." And: "The third time they came we fled up here."[5] The advantage of such refuges is that they are not very far, as the crow flies, from one's village and fields but are nevertheless far from any road and virtually inaccessible. As the degree of military pressure increases, such so-called hiding villages (*ywa poun*—ရွာ ပုန်း) split into smaller units. Whereas the small villages from which they come may have fifteen to twenty-five households, hiding villages seldom comprise more than seven households and, if still endangered, split up into small family groups. The greater the degree of disaggregation, the less visible any particular group is, and the less likely to be pursued and captured or killed. In the final analysis, in this case, villagers may hazard the trek to the Thai border and to the refugee camps there—altogether outside the jurisdiction of the Burmese state.

Those who choose to remain in the hills adopt subsistence strategies designed to escape detection and maximize their physical mobility should they be forced to flee again at a moment's notice. Foraging for forest foods is the ultimate in unobtrusive subsistence; it leaves no trace except for the passage of the forager. But pure foraging is rarely sufficient.[6] As one villager concealed in the hills explained, "The people in the village have to eat roots and leaves just like I was eating in the forest. I had to live on roots and leaves for four or five days at a time. . . . For one year I've lived in the forest in a hut because I was too afraid to stay in the village. I planted banana trees and ate roots and some vegetables."[7] Many who fled to the forest brought as much rice as they could carry, which they hid in small lots. But those who stayed any length of time cleared very small plots to grow maize, cassava, sweet potatoes, and a few cardamom bushes. The pattern was to open many small, scattered, unobtrusive plots; the same principles of dispersal and invisibility governing the behavior of human refugees also governed their agricultural choices. Where possible, they chose crops needing little care, crops that matured quickly, root crops that could not easily be destroyed or confiscated and which could be harvested at leisure. People, fields, and crops were each deployed to evade capture. Villagers were well aware of what they were sacrificing in the interest of bare survival. Village rituals, schooling, sports, trade, and religious observances were all curtailed if not eliminated solely to avoid what amounted to military serfdom in hyperstate space.

The techniques of evasion practiced by desperate Karen villagers represent an extreme instance of strategies that characterize much of the history and social organization of Zomia as a whole. A good deal of what we have come to consider "hill" agriculture, "hill" social structure, and "hill" location itself is, I would argue, largely defined by patterns of state evasion (and prevention). Such strategies have been devised and elaborated over many centuries in constant "dialogue" with lowland padi states, including the colonial regime.[8] This dialogue is, in important respects, constitutive of both hill societies and their padi-state interlocutors. Each represents an alternative pattern of subsistence, social organization, and power; each "shadows" the other in a complex relationship of mimicry and contradiction. Hill societies operate in the shadow of lowland states. By the same token, the lowland states of Southeast Asia have been surrounded, for the whole of their existence, by relatively free communities in the hills, swamps, and labyrinthine waterways that represent, simultaneously, a threat, a zone of "barbarism," a temptation, a refuge, and a source of valuable products.

Location, Location, Location, and Mobility

Inaccessibility and dispersal are the enemies of appropriation. And for an army on the march, as for a state, appropriation is the key to survival. "The whole army continued the pursuit of the flying [sic] king, but, as the marches were rather forced and the villages few and far between in a tract scarcely populated, sufficient provisions to feed this army of men and animals could not be obtained, with the result that they were not only fatigued with continual marching but half starved from want of regular meals. Many died of disease, starvation, and exhaustion from want of food, but the pursuit was still persisted in."[9]

The first principle of evasion is location. Owing to the friction of terrain, there are locations that are virtually inaccessible even to a nearby (as the crow flies) state. One could, in fact, calculate something of a gradient of relative inaccessibility for different locations from any particular padi state. Such a gradient is implicit in Clifford Geertz's description of the reach of what he terms the "theatre-state" in Bali. He notes that "upland lords," because they were located in more rugged country "had a natural advantage in resisting military pressure."[10] Even farther uphill, "at the highest altitudes, a few usually dry-farming communities existed beyond the effective reach of any lords at all." Within Zomia itself, most of the southwest province of Guizhou was perhaps the most forbidding, inaccessible area in purely geographical terms. A standard saying about Guizhou had it that "no three successive days are clear, no three square feet are level, and no one has more than three cents in his pocket." One late-nineteenth-century traveler noted that he had not seen even a single cart during his whole time in Guizhou—trade, "such as it is, being conducted on the backs of bipeds and quadrupeds." Many places, reputed to be accessible only to monkeys, were in fact zones of refuge for bandits and rebels.[11] Location, in this context, is but one of many possible forms by which marginality to state power finds expression. As we shall see, physical mobility, subsistence practices, social organization, and settlement patterns can also be deployed, often in combination, to place distance between a community and state appropriation.

On any long historical view, location at the periphery of state power must be treated as a social choice, not a cultural or ecological given. Location, just like subsistence routines and social organization, is variable. Over time such shifts have been observed and documented. Most frequently they represent a "positionality" vis-à-vis forms of state power.

Recent scholarly research has served, for example, to undermine naturalized understandings of such "nonstate" peoples as the so-called *orang asli* ("original people") of Malaysia. They were previously understood to be the descendants of earlier waves of migration, less technically developed than the Austronesian populations which succeeded and dominated them on the peninsula. Genetic evidence, however, does not support the theory of separate waves of migrating peoples. The orang asli (for example, Semang, Temuan, Jakun, Orang Laut) on the one hand and the Malays on the other are best viewed not as an evolutionary series but as a political series. Such a view has been most convincingly elaborated by Geoffrey Benjamin.[12] For Benjamin, *tribality* in this context is simply a term applied to a strategy of state evasion; its polar opposite is *peasantry*, understood as a system of cultivation incorporated into the state. On his reading, most of the "tribal" orang asli are nothing more and nothing less than that fraction of the peninsular population that has refused the state. Each "tribe"—Semang, Senoi, and Malayic (Temuan, Orang Laut, Jakun)—represents a slightly different state-evading strategy, and anyone adopting one such strategy in effect thereby becomes Semang, Senoi, or whatever. Similarly, such nonstate peoples have always had, even before Islam, the option of becoming Malay. Many have in fact done so, and

Malayness bears traces of this absorption. At the same time, all orang asli are, and have always been, linked to lowland markets by exchange and trade as well.

For our purposes what is significant is that a peripheral location with respect to the state is a political strategy. As Benjamin puts it,

> First, . . . tribality has resulted largely from choice and, second, . . . the presence of state-based civilization (both modern and pre-modern) has figured largely in that choice. . . .
>
> All the more reason, then, for us to remember that many tribal populations have been living in geographically remote regions out of choice, as part of a strategy to keep the state off their backs.[13]

The second principle of evasion is mobility: the ability to change location. The inaccessibility of a society is amplified if, in addition to being located at the periphery of power, it can easily shift to a more remote and advantageous site. Just as there is a gradient of remoteness from state centers, so also might we imagine a gradient of mobility from a relatively frictionless ability to shift location to a relative immobility. The classic example of physical mobility is, of course, pastoral nomadism. Moving with their flocks and herds for much of the year, such nomads are constrained by the need for pasture but are unmatched in their ability to move quickly and over large distances. Their mobility is at the same time admirably suited to the raiding of states and of sedentary peoples. And indeed, pastoral nomads aggregated into "tribal" confederations have often posed the most serious military threat to sedentary grain-producing states.[14] For our purposes, however, what is important are the evasive strategies vis-à-vis state power that nomadism makes possible. Thus, for example, Yomut Turkmen, located on the periphery of Persian state power, have used their nomadic mobility both to raid grain-growing communities and to escape the taxes and conscription of the Persian authorities. When large military expeditions were sent against them, they would retreat to the steppe-desert, beyond reach, with their livestock and families. "Thus, mobility provided their ultimate defense against effective control over their political affairs by the Persian government."[15] In a setting where other forms of subsistence were readily available, they chose to retain their nomadism for its strategic advantages: political autonomy, raiding, and the avoidance of the taxman and the military press-gang.

Highland Southeast Asia has, for ecological reasons, no substantial groups of herding peoples. The nearest equivalent, in terms of ease of movement, are nomadic foragers. Most hill people pursue livelihoods that incorporate a certain amount of foraging and hunting and can, when pressed, rely heavily upon it. But those groups specialized to foraging both are located in areas far from state power and have a mode of subsistence that requires physical mobility—a habit that serves them well when they are threatened. Such people have been typically understood by historians and lowland populations alike as remnants of distinct and, in evolutionary terms, more primitive "tribes." Contemporary scholarship has overturned this judgment. Far from a response to having been left behind, foraging in the modern era is seen as a largely political choice or adaptation to evade capture by the state. Terry Rambo, writing about the foraging Semang of the Malay Peninsula, clearly states the new consensus: "Thus the Semang appear to be very primitive not because they represent a surviving Paleolithic stratum that has been pushed into an isolated, marginal refuge area, but rather because a nomadic, foraging adaptation is both the most profitable and safest strategy for a defensively weak minority ethnic group living close to military-dominant, and often hostile, agriculturalists. . . . From the standpoint of security, the adaptation also makes sense because nomads are much harder to catch than settled farmers."[16]

It does not follow, however, that the extreme forms of dispersal are the safest. To the contrary, there is a small minimum group size below which new dangers and disadvantages loom. There is first the need to defend against raiding, especially slave-raiding, which requires a small community. A single isolated swidden field is also far more exposed to pests, birds, and other wild animals than a group of swiddens ripening together. Pooling the risks of illness, accident, death, and food shortages also argues for a minimum group size. Thus the atomization of Karen refugees fleeing the Burmese military is a limiting case, sustainable only for a short period. Even for fugitive peoples, then, long-run self-protection requires groups of at least several families.

Once we view subsistence strategies more as political options from among a range of livelihood alternatives, the mobility that any particular form of subsistence provides must enter the calculation. Foraging, along with nomadic pastoralism, affords the greatest mobility for groups wanting to give the state a wide berth. Shifting cultivation (swiddening) affords less mobility than foraging but much more mobility than fixed-field farming, let alone irrigated rice padis. For the architects of state space, any substantial move from wet rice at the core toward foraging at the remote periphery is a threat to the manpower and foodstuffs underwriting state power.

There is no reason, then, to assume that hill swiddeners and foragers are isolated in the hills by default or by virtue of their backwardness. On the contrary, there is ample reason to assume that they are where they are and do what they do intentionally. This is, in effect, the historic choice made by many former plains-dwellers who fled to the hills when oppressed by ruinous taxation or threatened with servitude by a more powerful people. Their intentions are inscribed in their practice, in the sense that they have not chosen, as have others, to assimilate into lowland societies. One of their intentions, it appears, is to avoid capture, as slaves or subjects, by states and their agents. As early as the ninth century a Chinese official in southwest China observed that it was impossible to resettle "barbarians" around centers of Han power because they were scattered in forests and ravines and "therefore managed to evade capture."[17] Nor should we overlook the attraction of the autonomy and the relatively egalitarian social relations prevailing in the hills, as important a goal as evading corvée and taxes.

Neither does the desire for autonomy exhaust the positive reasons why hill peoples might prefer their situation to the alternatives. We know from both contemporary and archeological data that foragers, in all but the most severe environments, are more robust, healthier, and freer from illnesses, particularly epidemic zoonotic diseases, than the population of more concentrated sedentary communities. All in all, it seems that the appearance of agriculture initially did more to depress standards of human welfare than to raise them.[18] By extension, shifting agriculture, by virtue of its diversity and dispersal of population, is likely to favor a healthier population so long as sufficient land is available. Hill livelihoods, then, may be preferred for reasons of health and leisure. Mark Elvin's account of the early Chinese state prohibiting its subjects from foraging and swiddening may reflect this preference, as does the widespread belief of hill peoples that the lowlands are unhealthy. This last belief may rest on more than the fact that malaria-bearing mosquitoes historically have rarely been found above nine hundred meters.

Premodern populations, despite their ignorance of the means and vectors of disease transmission, always understood that their chances of survival were improved by dispersal. In his *Journal of the Plague Year*, Daniel Defoe recounts that those with the means left London for the countryside at the first sign of the black plague. Oxford and Cambridge universities dispersed their students to sanctuaries in the countryside when the plague struck. For much the same reason, William Henry Scott reports, in Northern Luzon both lowlanders and "submitted" Igorots went to the hills and scattered to escape epidemics. Igorots already in the hills knew that they should disperse and close off the passes to the hills to avoid the contagion.[19] There is, then, every reason to believe that the threat posed by the lowland state was not confined to slavers and tribute-takers but extended to invisible microbes as well. This would represent, by itself, another powerful reason to choose to live beyond the range of the padi state.

Escape Agriculture

Do not cultivate the vineyard; you'll be bound
Do not cultivate grains; you'll be ground
Pull the camel, herd the sheep
A day will come, you'll be crowned.
—Nomad poem

New World Perspectives

Any effort to examine the history of social structure and subsistence routines as part of a deliberate political choice runs smack against a powerful civilizational narrative. That narrative consists of a historical series arranged as an account of economic, social, and cultural progress. With respect to livelihood strategies, the series, from most primitive to most advanced, might be: foraging/hunting-gathering, pastoral nomadism, horticulture/shifting cultivation, sedentary fixed-field agriculture, irrigated plow agriculture, industrial agriculture. With respect to social structure, again from the most primitive to most advanced, the series might read: small bands in the forest or savannah, hamlets, villages, towns, cities, metropolises. These two series are, of course, essentially the same; they chart a growing concentration of agricultural production (yield per unit of land) and a growing concentration of population in larger agglomerations. First elaborated by Giovanni Battista Vico at the beginning of the eighteenth century, the narrative derives its hegemonic status not only from its affinity with social Darwinism but from the fact that it maps nicely on the stories most states and civilizations tell about themselves. The schema assumes movement in a single direction toward concentrated populations and intensive grain production; no back-sliding is envisioned; each step is irreversible progress.

As an empirical description of demographic and agricultural trends in the now-industrialized world for the past two centuries (and the past half-century in poorer nations), this schema has much to be said for it. Europe's nonstate ("tribal") populations had, for all practical purposes, disappeared by the eighteenth century, and the nonstate population of poorer countries is diminishing and beleaguered.

As an empirical description of premodern Europe or of most poor nations until the twentieth century, and as an empirical description of the hilly areas of mainland Southeast Asia (Zomia), however, this narrative is profoundly misleading. What the schema portrays is not simply a self-satisfied normative account of progress but a gradient of successive stages of incorporation into state structures. Its stages of civilization are, at the same time, an index of diminishing autonomy and freedom. Until quite recently, many societies and groups have abandoned fixed cultivation to take up shifting agriculture and foraging. They have, by the same token, altered their kinship systems and social structure and dispersed into smaller and smaller settlements. The actual archeological record in peninsular Southeast Asia reveals a long-term oscillation between foraging and farming depending, it would seem, on the conditions.[20] What to Vico would have seemed to be lamentable back-sliding and decay was for them a strategic option to circumvent the many inconveniences of state power.

We have come to appreciate only very recently the degree to which many apparently more primitive peoples have deliberately abandoned settled agriculture and political subordination for a more autonomous existence. Many of the orang asli of Malaysia provide, as we have noted, a case in point. It is in the post-Conquest New World, however, that some of the more striking cases have been documented. The French anthropologist Pierre Clastres was the first to argue that many of the hunting-and-gathering "tribes" of South America, far from being left behind, had previously lived in state formations and practiced fixed-field agriculture. They had purposely given it up to evade subordination.[21] They were, he argued, quite capable of producing a larger economic surplus and a larger-scale political order, but they had chosen not to so as to remain outside state structures. Termed disparagingly by the Spaniards as peoples "without God, law and king" (unlike the Inca, Maya, and Aztecs), they were, Clastres saw, rather peoples who had elected to live in a relatively egalitarian social order with chiefs who had little or no power over them.

The precise reasons why such groups would have taken to foraging in small bands is a matter of some dispute. Several factors, however, played a role. First and foremost was the catastrophic demographic collapse—as great as 90 percent mortality in many areas—due to European-borne diseases. This not only meant that established social structures were devastated but that the land available to the survivors for foraging or shifting agriculture was vastly expanded.[22] At the same time, many were fleeing the Spaniards' infamous *reducciones,* designed to turn them into indentured laborers, as well as the epidemics that characterized such concentrations of population.

A paradigmatic case is that of the Siriono, of Eastern Bolivia, described initially by Allan Holmberg in his anthropological classic *Nomads of the Long-bow.* Apparently lacking the ability to make fire or cloth, living in rude shelters, innumerate, having no domestic animals or developed cosmology, they were, Holmberg wrote, Paleolithic survivors living in a veritable state of nature.[23] We now know beyond all reasonable doubt that the Siriono had been crop-growing villagers until roughly 1920, when influenza and smallpox swept through their villages, killing many of them. Attacked by numerically superior peoples and fleeing potential slavery, the Siriono apparently abandoned their crops, which, in any event, they did not have the numbers to defend. Their independence and survival in this case required then to divide into smaller bands, foraging and moving whenever threatened. They would occasionally raid a settlement to take axes, hatchets, and machetes, but at the same time they dreaded the illnesses that the raiders often brought back with them. They had become nonsedentary by choice—to avoid both disease and capture.[24]

Clastres examines many such instances of previously sedentary peoples who, threatened by slavery, forced labor, and epidemics, adopted nomadic subsistence strategies to stay out of harm's way. The Tupo-Guarani groups in particular were, it is clear, populous agricultural peoples who in the seventeenth century, by the tens of thousands, fled the triple threat of Jesuit reducciones, Portuguese and mestizo slave-raiders intent on sending them to plantations at the coast, and epidemics.[25] They appeared to the ahistorical eye, much later, as a backward, technologically simple people—an aboriginal remnant. In reality, they had adapted to a more mobile life as a means of escaping the servitude and disease that civilization had to offer.

There is still another New World case of escape agriculture closer to hand. That is the study of maroon communities—of African slaves who had escaped and established communities outside the easy reach of slavers. These communities ranged in size from Palmares in Brazil, with perhaps twenty thousand inhabitants, and Dutch Guiana (Surinam), with that many or more, to smaller settlements of escapees throughout the Caribbean (Jamaica, Cuba, Mexico, Saint-Domingue), as well as in Florida and on the Virginia–North

Carolina border in the Great Dismal Swamp. I shall elaborate a theory of "escape agriculture," but here we may simply note the overall pattern of the agricultural strategies employed in maroon communities.[26] We shall, in the context of describing upland peoples in Southeast Asia, encounter practices that bear a strong family resemblance to those of the maroons.

Runaway slaves clustered in precisely those out-of-the-way places where they could not easily be found: swamps, rough mountain country, deep forests, trackless wastes. They chose, when possible, defensible locations accessible by only a single pass or trail that could be blocked with thorns and traps and observed easily. Like bandits, they prepared escape routes in case they were found and their defenses failed. Shifting cultivation, supplemented by foraging, trade, and theft, was the commonest maroon practice. They preferred to plant root crops (for example, manioc/cassava, yams, and sweet potatoes), which were unobtrusive and could be left in the ground to be harvested at leisure. Depending on how secure the site was, they might plant more permanent crops, such as bananas, plantains, dry rice, maize, groundnuts, squash, and vegetables, but such crops could more easily be seized or destroyed. Some of these communities were short-lived, others survived for generations. Outside the law by definition, many maroon communities lived in part by raiding nearby settlements and plantations. None, it seems, were self-sufficient. Occupying a distinctive agro-ecological zone with valued products, many maroon settlements were closely integrated into the larger economy by clandestine and open trade.

Shifting Agriculture as "Escape-Agriculture"

Rather than being dictated by necessity, then, the adoption of shifting agriculture
may have been part of a distinctive politics.
—Ajay Skaria, *Hybrid Histories*, 1999

Shifting cultivation is the most common agricultural practice in the hills of mainland Southeast Asia. Those who practice it are rarely understood to have made a choice, let alone a political choice. Rather, the technique is seen by lowland officials, including those in charge of development programs in the hills, as both primitive and environmentally destructive. By extension, those who farm this way are also coded as backward. The implicit assumption is that, given the skills and opportunity, they would abandon this technique and take to permanent settlement and fixed-field (preferably irrigated rice) farming. Again, movement from swiddening to wet rice was seen as unidirectional and evolutionary.

Contrary to this view, my claim is that the choice of shifting cultivation is preeminently a political choice. This claim hardly originates with me, and, in the argument that follows, I shall rely on the judgment of many historians and ethnographers who have examined the issue closely. The foremost Chinese specialist on swiddening techniques and swiddening peoples in Yunnan rejects outright the claim that it is an earlier or more primitive technique form of cultivation, bound to be abandoned once its practitioners master irrigation techniques: "But it must be stressed here that it is incorrect to take Yunnan swidden agriculture as a representative of such a primitive 'stage' of agricultural history. In Yunnan, swiddening, knives and axes, coexist with hoes and plows, and have their different uses and functions. It is difficult to say which came earlier and which later. . . . But the crux of the matter is that there is no basis for taking our 'pure' swidden agriculture as the original state of affairs."[27]

To choose swiddening or, for that matter, foraging or nomadic pastoralism is to choose to remain outside state space. This choice has historically been the bedrock of freedom enjoyed by Southeast Asian commoners. The subjects of the small Tai statelets (muang) in the hills, Richard O'Connor points out, always had two alternatives. One alternative was to shift residence and affiliation to another muang where conditions were more advantageous. "Yet another escape was to farm the hills rather than paddy land." O'Connor points out: "A hill farmer had no corvée obligations."[28] More generally, swiddening facilitated physical mobility and, on that account alone, according to Jean Michaud, could also "be used as an escape or survival strategy by groups needing to move such as the Hmong or Lolo from China. . . . These once sedentarized groups were set in motion by adversity, wars, climatic change, or untenable demographic pressure in their homelands."[29] Shifting cultivation was understood to be outside the fiscal and manpower apparatus of even the smallest states. It is for precisely this reason that the representatives of historical states in mainland Southeast Asia have spoken unanimously in discouraging or condemning swidden cultivation. Shifting cultivation was a fiscally sterile form of agriculture: diverse, dispersed, hard to monitor, hard to tax or confiscate. Swiddeners were themselves dispersed, hard to monitor, hard to collect for corvée labor or conscription. The features that made swiddening anathema to states were exactly what made it attractive to state-evading peoples.[30]

Irrigated rice and shifting cultivation are not a temporal, evolutionary sequence, nor are they mutually exclusive alternatives.[31] Many hill populations practice both irrigated-rice cultivation and shifting cultivation simultaneously, adjusting the balance according to political and economic advantage. By the same token, valley populations have in the past replaced irrigated rice with swiddening, especially when epidemics or migrations suddenly made more land available. In a great many geographical settings, shifting, dry cultivation, or irrigated rice is possible. With terracing and the availability of reliable springs or streams, irrigated rice can be grown at relatively high altitudes and in steep terrain. The sophisticated rice terraces of the Hani in the upper reaches of the Red River in Vietnam and of the Ifugao in Northern Luzon are cases in point. Spring- and stream-fed, terraced rice fields are also found among the Karen and Akha. The earliest archeological remains of rice cultivation in Java and Bali come not from the lowlands but from the midslope uplands skirting mountains and volcanoes, where perennial springs and a pronounced dry season made it practical.[32]

Lowland officials, both colonial and contemporary, have seen shifting cultivation not simply as primitive but as inefficient in the strict sense of neoclassical economics. To some degree this is an unwarranted deduction from the apparent disorder and variety of a swidden as compared to a monocropped rice padi. At a deeper level, it represents a misunderstanding of the concept of efficiency. Wet rice is, to be sure, more productive per unit of land than shifting cultivation. It is, however, typically less productive per unit of labor. Which of the two systems is the more efficient depends mainly on whether land or labor represents the scarcer factor of production. Where land is comparatively plentiful and labor scarce, as has been the case historically in most of mainland Southeast Asia, shifting cultivation was more labor saving per unit of output and hence more efficient. The importance of slavery in state-making is evidence that coercion was required to capture shifting cultivators and move them to the labor-intensive padi fields, where they could be taxed.

The relative efficiencies of each agricultural technique varied not only with the demography but also with agro-ecological conditions. In areas where annual river flooding deposited fertile silt that could be easily worked, flood-retreat farming of irrigated rice was far less labor intensive than where elaborate irrigation works or ponds (tanks) were required. Where, on the contrary, the terrain was steep and the water supply unreliable, the labor cost of irrigated rice would be nearly prohibitive. Such evaluations of relative efficiency in terms of factor costs, however, entirely miss the determining political context. Despite the enormous amounts of labor involved in their construction and maintenance, elaborate irrigated rice terraces have been created in the hills against any plausible neoclassical logic. The reason, it appears, is largely political. Edmund Leach wondered about terracing in the Kachin hills and concluded that it took place for military reasons: to protect a key pass and to control its trade and tolls, which required a concentrated and self-provisioning military garrison.[33] Such an enterprise was, in effect, an effort to sculpt a miniature agro-ecological space in the hills that might support a statelet. In other instances it seems that terracing, like the fortified ridge settlements reported by early colonial travelers, were necessary for defense against raiding by lowland states and the slaving expeditions that fed their manpower needs. Here again, the logic was political, not economic. A successful defense against slave raids required both a relatively inaccessible location and a critical mass of concentrated defenders who could prevail against any but the largest and most determined foes.[34] Michaud suggests that the highland wet-rice terraces of the Hani in northern Vietnam are the work of a people who wish to be sedentary and at the same time well away from state centers.[35]

Under most conditions, however, shifting cultivation was the most common agropolitical strategy against raiding, state-making, and state appropriation. If it makes sense to think of rugged terrain as representing a friction of distance, then it may make just as much sense to think of shifting cultivation as representing, strategically, the friction of appropriation. The decisive advantage of swiddening is its inherent resistance to appropriation, a political advantage that, in turn, pays economic dividends.

To illustrate this political advantage, let us imagine a demographic and agro-ecological setting in which either swiddening or wet rice is possible and in which neither technique is markedly superior to the other in terms of efficiency. The choice in this case becomes a political and sociocultural one. The great political advantage of swiddening is population dispersal (favoring escape rather than defense), poly-cropping, staggered maturities of crops, and an emphasis on root crops that can remain in the ground for some time until harvested. For the state or a raiding party, it represents an agricultural surplus and population that is difficult to assess, let alone seize.[36] It is an agricultural technique that, short of foraging, maximizes the friction of appropriation. If, on the other hand, the population chooses to grow padi rice, they represent an easy target for a state (or raiders), who know where to find them and their crops, carts, plow animals, and possessions. The likelihood of having oneself and one's crops confiscated or destroyed is greatly increased; the friction of appropriation is reduced.

Thus even a purely economic evaluation of shifting cultivation must allow for the political advantage it offers in evading taxes and corvée and in making raiding less lucrative. If the gross return from padi farming were more or less equivalent to the return to shifting cultivation, its net return would still be inferior because, with padi farming, the farmer must surrender "rents" in the form of labor and grain. There are, then, two advantages to swiddening: it offers relative autonomy and freedom (though not without its own dangers), and it allows the farmers to dispose of their own labor and of the fruits of their labor. Both are essentially political advantages.

To practice hill farming is to choose a social and political life outside the framework of the state.[37] The element of deliberate political choice is emphasized most eloquently by Michael Dove in his analysis of Javanese states and agriculture: "Just as cleared land became associated with the rise of Javanese states and their cultures, so did the forest become associated with uncivilized, uncontrollable, and fearful forces. . . . The historical basis for this fear was empirical, since the swidden cultivators of ancient Java were neither part of a reigning court culture nor—and this is most important—under its control."[38] It is but a small step to suggest, as Hjorleifur Jonsson has in his study of the Yao/Mien on the Thai-Chinese border, that swiddening is practiced in large part because it is beyond the reach of the state. It is the state's identification with wet rice, he suggests, that gives rise to the political meaning of what might otherwise be a more politically neutral choice among agricultural techniques. "The two agricultural methods may historically have been practiced in conjunction, but the state's issue of control forces people to stand with the state as wet-rice farmers, craftspeople, soldiers or whatever, or they stand without, as swidden farmers."[39]

The Hmong/Miao provide an instructive case. They are typically considered an emblematic highland ethnic group living above nine hundred meters by swidden farming of opium, maize, millet, root crops, buckwheat, and other highland cultivars. But in fact, Hmong can be found practicing a great variety of agricultural techniques. As one farmer put it, "We, Hmong, some of us only cultivate [dry] fields, some of us only cultivate wet rice, and some of us do both."[40] What appears to be operating here is a political judgment about how much distance a community should put between itself and the state. Where the state is not a clear and present danger—or, more rarely, an irresistible temptation—the choice is not so politically freighted. But where the state looms over the choice both culturally and politically, agricultural technique comes to represent a decision between being a state subject or a "hill tribe"—or, still more precarious, straddling the divide. Of the subsistence alternatives available to cultivators, shifting agriculture, by virtue of the obstacles (friction) it places in the way of appropriation, is the most common state-repelling option.

Crop Choice as Escape Agriculture

The logic of escape agriculture and the friction of appropriation apply not only to a technical complex as a whole, such as shifting cultivation, but to particular crops as well. Of course, the overall resistance of swiddening to state appropriation lies both in its hilly location and dispersal and in the very botanical diversity it represents. It is not uncommon for shifting cultivators to plant, tend, and encourage as many as sixty or more cultivars. Imagine the bewildering task facing even the most energetic tax collector attempting to catalogue, let alone assess and collect taxes, in such a setting.[41] It is for this reason that J. G. Scott noted that the hill peoples were "of no account whatever in the state" and that "it would be a sheer waste of energy in the eyes of an official to attempt to number the houses or even the villages of these people."[42] Add to this the fact that nearly all swidden cultivators also hunt, fish, and forage in nearby forests. By pursuing such a broad portfolio of subsistence strategies they spread their risks, they ensure themselves a diverse and nutritious diet, and they present a nearly intractable hieroglyphic to any state that might want to corral them.[43] This is a major reason why most Southeast Asian states were reduced to capturing the swiddeners themselves and removing them forcibly to an already established, state space.[44]

Particular crops have characteristics that make them more or less resistant to appropriation. Cultivars that cannot be stored long without spoiling, such as fresh fruits and vegetables, or that have low value per unit weight and volume, such as most gourds, rootcrops, and tubers, will not repay the efforts of a tax gatherer.

In general, roots and tubers such as yams, sweet potatoes, potatoes, and cassava/manioc/yucca are nearly appropriation-proof. After they ripen, they can be safely left in the ground for up to two years and dug up piecemeal as needed. There is thus no granary to plunder. If the army or the taxmen wants your potatoes, for example, they will have to dig them up one by one. Plagued by crop failures and confiscatory procurement prices for the cultivars recommended by the Burmese military government in the 1980s, many peasants secretly planted sweet potatoes, a crop specifically prohibited. They shifted to sweet potatoes because the crop was easier to conceal and nearly impossible to appropriate.[45] The Irish in the early nineteenth century grew potatoes not only because they provided many calories from the small plots to which farmers were confined but also because they could not be confiscated or burned and, because they were grown in small mounds, an [English!] horseman risked breaking his mount's leg galloping through the field. Alas for the Irish, they had only a minuscule selection of the genetic diversity of New World potatoes and had come to rely almost exclusively on potatoes and milk for subsistence.

A reliance on root crops, and in particular the potato, can insulate states as well as stateless peoples against the predations of war and appropriation. William McNeill credits the early-eighteenth-century rise of Prussia to the potato. Enemy armies might seize or destroy grain fields, livestock, and aboveground fodder crops, but they were powerless against the lowly potato, a cultivar which Frederick William and Frederick II after him had vigorously promoted. It was the potato that gave Prussia its unique invulnerability to foreign invasion. While a grain-growing population whose granaries and crops were confiscated or destroyed had no choice but to scatter or starve, a tuber-growing peasantry could move back immediately after the military danger had passed and dig up their staple, a meal at a time.[46]

Other things equal, crops that will grow on marginal land and at high altitudes (for example, maize) favor escape because they allow their cultivators more space to disperse in or flee to. Cultivars that require little attention and/or that mature quickly are also state repelling inasmuch as they afford more mobility than labor-intensive, long-maturation crops.[47] Unobtrusive crops of low stature that mimic much of the natural vegetation around them thwart appropriation by being easy to overlook.[48] The greater the dispersal of the crops, the more difficult they are to collect, in the same way that a dispersed population is more difficult to grab. To the degree that such crops are part of the swiddener's portfolio, to that degree will they prove fiscally sterile to states and raiders and be deemed "not worth the trouble" or, in other words, a nonstate space.

Southeast Asian Swiddening as Escape

Once we have shed the erroneous idea that shifting cultivation is necessarily historically prior to, more primitive than, and less efficient than fixed-field cultivation, there remains one further illusion to shed. That illusion is that it is a relatively static technique that has not changed much in the past millennium. On the contrary, one could argue that swiddening and, for that matter, foraging have undergone far more transformation in that period than has wet-rice cultivation. Some scholars claim that the shifting cultivation with which we are familiar was essentially a product of iron and, later, steel blades, which massively reduced the labor required to clear swiddens.[49] What is certain, however, is that the steel axe made escape through shifting agriculture both possible in previously hard-to-clear areas and less onerous generally.

At least two other historical factors worked to transform swiddening. The first was international trade in high-value goods that had, at least since the eighth century, linked both swiddeners and foragers to international markets. Pepper, which was the most valuable commodity in world trade between 1450 and 1650, save gold and perhaps slaves, is the most striking example. Before that medicinal herbs, resins, animal organs, feathers, ivory, and aromatic woods were much sought after in the China trade. One Bornean specialist goes so far as to argue that the very purpose of shifting cultivation was to sustain a population of traders scouring the forest for valuable trade goods.[50] The final factor transforming shifting cultivation was the arrival of an entire suite of New World plants from the sixteenth century on that vastly extended the scope and ease of swiddening. Quite apart from its margin of political autonomy, then, the comparative economic advantage of swiddening vis-à-vis irrigated rice would only have improved from the sixteenth century to the nineteenth, while affording, as it always had, access to international trade goods.

How decisive such factors were in the massive flight and movement to shifting cultivation by Burmese living in the state core region in the early years of the nineteenth century is difficult to gauge. Nevertheless, the event is diagnostic for our purposes. Swiddening is typically seen as a practice confined to ethnic minorities. Here, however, we have a case of a putatively Burman padi-state population turning to it. The circumstances of their departure from the core approximate a limiting case of crushing taxes and corvée. As noted in Chapter 5, King Bò-daw-hpaya's early-nineteenth-century ambitions for conquest, pagoda building, and public works caused massive destitution among his subjects. The response was rebellion, banditry, and above all, headlong flight. Core land was abandoned by cultivators to such an extent that officials began to record large tracts of abandoned farmland. "In the face of these exactions, many families decamped to less accessible rural locales." This prompted, as William Koenig notes, a wholesale "movement to shifting cultivation."[51] A massive reapportionment of population ensued, with the king's subjects fleeing out of range and/or practicing a form of agriculture far more impervious to seizure.

There are also good reasons to believe that much of the Mon population, previously sedentary, Theravada, wet-rice cultivators, abandoned their padi fields as a consequence of a series of wars, punctuated with revolts, against the Burman court at Ava in the mid-eighteenth century. Their flight, along with many of their Karen allies, from the chaos and defeat appears to have been accompanied by a retreat to shifting agriculture to protect their food supply as well.[52]

Flight and shifting cultivation were not uncommon as a response to the colonial state when its claims, too, became intolerable. Georges Condominas notes that French colonial officials in Laos complained frequently of "seeing whole villages move when their responsibilities became too burdensome; for example, their village was situated near a road which they were constantly expected to maintain."[53] Such movement was typically associated with swiddening since the Laotian, Thai, and Vietnamese peasantry knew that their swiddens were illegible and hence likely to evade appropriation.

The resort to shifting cultivation and foraging as a means of escape from the deadly perils of warfare is not merely of antiquarian interest. During World War II and the subsequent counterinsurgency warfare in Southeast Asia, retreat up the watershed and out of harm's way was often an option. The Punan Lusong in Sarawak had begin to grow rice before 1940, but with the Japanese invasion they returned to the forest as foragers and swiddeners and did not return to fixed cultivation until 1961. In this they were not unlike neighboring Kenyah and Sebop farmers, who may leave their fields to range the forests for two or three years at a time, subsisting on sago palm and game. Nor did this adaptation necessarily signal penury, although during the war the usual trade outlets were closed, since sago palm has at least double the caloric return to labor as hill-rice swiddening.[54] On the peninsula in Western Malaysia, the Jakun (Orang Malayu Asli) fled to the upper reaches of the Sungei Linggui (Linggui River) to avoid contact with or capture by the Japanese forces. Prized for their knowledge of the forest, they were liable to be pressed into service as guides and porters by the Japanese and, afterward, during the Emergency, by British forces or Communist rebels. They lived on the run on cassava, sweet potatoes, bananas, some vegetables, and a small amount of rice for the old people and children. They ate their noisy roosters lest the crowing betray their whereabouts.[55]

Southeast Asian Escape Crops

"Escape crops" may have one or more of several characteristics that facilitate evasion of raiding either by states or by freebooters. In many cases they simply qualify by being well adapted to environmental niches that are difficult to map and control: high, rugged mountains, swamps, deltas, mangrove coasts, and so on. If, in addition, they are of staggered maturity, fast growing, and easily hidden, if they require little care, are of little value per unit weight and volume, and grow below ground, they acquire greater escape value. Many such cultivars are ideally adapted to swiddening routines, in which case their escape value is still further enhanced.[56]

Before the introduction of New World crops, a few high-altitude grains offered those seeking autonomy from the state a certain amount of running room. Oats, barley, fast-growing millets, and buckwheat were tolerant of poor soils, high altitudes, and short growing seasons, as were cabbage and turnips, and allowed people to settle at higher altitudes than hill rice would permit. Old World roots and tubers, taro and yams, as well as the sago palm, were also favored by nonstate peoples.[57] Taro could be grown at relatively high elevations, though it required wet, fertile soils. It could be planted anytime; it ripened quickly; it required little care or preparation before eating; and once ripe it could be left in the ground and dug up as needed. Yams, which also grew wild, had many of the same advantages, and then some. Though yams required more labor and had to be planted at the end of the rainy season, they were less susceptible to insect and fungal attack, would grow under a greater variety of conditions, and could be sold as a cash crop in markets. Until both were overtaken by New World cultivars, yams tended to replace taro because, Peter Boomgaard believes, much of the land suitable for taro was increasingly planted to irrigated rice, while yams were more suited to the drier hillsides. The sago palm (not a true palm) and the powdery starch derived from splitting its trunk, crushing, kneading, washing, and grating its pith also qualifies as an escape food. It is naturally occurring and fast growing, involves less work than hill rice or perhaps even cassava, and will thrive in swampy environments. Its starchy powder can be sold or bartered, as can yams, but it will not grow at altitudes above nine hundred meters.[58] All these foods were known as "famine" foods. Even wet-rice growers often depended on them during that hungry time before the new rice crop was gathered. For others, however, they were the basis of a diet that could be shielded from state appropriation.

Escape agriculture was radically transformed beginning in the sixteenth century with the introduction of New World plants. Maize and cassava played such a decisive role in this transformation that each merits its own discussion. Some of the generic characteristics of New World crops, however, stand out. Above all, like many "exotics" taken to completely new ecological settings, they initially had no natural pests and diseases, as they had at home. Hence they tended to thrive in the new environment. This advantage, as much as any, explains why they were adopted with great alacrity in much of Southeast Asia, especially by those who wished to live beyond the reach of the state. The sweet potato was a striking example. Georg Eberhard Rumphius, the great Dutch botanist and illustrator, was amazed to discover how swiftly its cultivation had spread throughout the Dutch East Indies by 1670. Among its advantages were high yields, disease resistance, nutritional value, and tastiness. Its value as an escape crop, however, rested on three characteristics: it matured quickly, it had a higher caloric yield for the labor than indigenous edible roots and tubers, and, perhaps most decisive, it could be grown successfully at higher elevations than yams or taro. Boomgaard implies that the sweet potato may have aided flight by raising the population of highland areas where it was often (as in New Guinea) combined with pig husbandry. Its cultivation had also spread to nomadic and semisedentary populations in such inaccessible places as the island of Buru.[59] The sweet potato's status as an escape crop was even more evident in the Philippines, where the Spaniards blamed it for the nomadism of the Igorot, whom they could neither count nor settle: "[They move] from one place to another on the least occasion for there is nothing to stop them since their houses, which are what would cause them concern, they make any place with a bundle of hay; they pass from one place to another with their crops of yames and camotes [sweet potato] off of which they live without much trouble, pulling them up by the roots, since they can stick them in wherever they wish to take root."[60] Any crop that allowed people to move to hitherto inaccessible areas and to provision themselves successfully there was, by definition, a crop stigmatized by the state.

Amid our discussion of food-crops, it is important to recall that no matter how isolated a hill people or maroon community was, they were never entirely self-sufficient. Virtually all such groups grew, hunted, or foraged for valuable trade goods that could be bartered or sold in lowland markets. They aimed to have the advantages of trade and exchange while remaining politically autonomous. Historically such trade crops included cotton, coffee, tobacco, tea, and, above all, opium. These crops required more labor and had sedentarizing features, but if the communities that grew them were beyond the state's range, they were compatible with political independence.

For any particular crop, it is possible to estimate roughly how suitable it is for the purpose of state evasion. Table 3 is confined, with the exception of opium and cotton, to a comparison of food crops along these dimensions.[61] An ordinal scale of "escapability" is unrealistic inasmuch as considerations of labor intensivity, hardiness, and storability admit of no comprehensive metric. Given a specified agro-ecological niche, however, nominal comparisons are plausible. The examination of how two such crops, maize and cassava (also known as manioc or yucca), both New World cultivars, came to be valued for their escape characteristics will provide the historical context that the more global comparisons in the table necessarily lack.

MAIZE

Brought by the Portuguese to Southeast Asia in the fifteenth century, maize spread rapidly.[62] It was firmly established throughout maritime Southeast Asia by the late seventeenth century, and by the 1930s it counted for roughly a quarter of smallholder cropping. So firmly had it become established and worked into local cosmologies that, along with the chili pepper, another New World cultivar, it was considered an indigenous crop by most Southeast Asians.

If one were designing an escape grain, one could hardly do better. Maize had many advantages over hill rice. Not only did it have higher caloric yields per unit labor and per unit land than hill rice, but its yields were more reliable; it could survive more erratic weather. Maize could easily be intercropped with other cultivars; it matured quickly; it could be used as fodder; it stored well if dried; and it was nutritionally superior to hill rice. For our purposes, however, what mattered most is that it "could be grown in areas that were too high, too steep, too dry, and too infertile for hill rice."[63] These virtues allowed both hill peoples and valley peoples to colonize new zones that had previously been forbidding. They could settle farther up a watershed, at an elevation of twelve hundred meters or more, and still have a reliable staple. They could, in steep, inaccessible places where the friction of distance provided some security, establish a quasi-sedentary existence outside the ambit of the state. In upland plateaus where irrigated rice had been grown for a long time, it allowed communities to colonize the nearby hills outside the padi core.

With maize, an autonomous existence outside the padi state suddenly

Table 3 Escape Characteristics of Crops

Crop	Storability	Labor Intensivity	Climate/Soil (Wet/Dry)	Disease Prone	Elevation Bandwidth	Value Per Unit Weight and Volume (Assuming a Cash Economy)	Possible to Store in the Ground?
Taro	Low	Moderate to high, depending on irrigation use	Warm and wet	In 20th century	Grown at low and moderate elevations (0–1,800 meters)	Low	For a short period
Cassava	Low, but can be dried	Low	Hot climate; tolerant of dry soils	In 20th century	Grown at low and moderate elevations (0–2,000 meters)	Low	Yes
Opium	High when processed	High	Tolerant	Yes	Usually grown at high elevations	Very high when processed	No
Maize	Moderate	Moderate	Hot and humid	In 20th century	Grown at very wide range of elevations (0–3,600 meters)	Low	No
Yams	High	Moderate to high	Very wet and hot	No	Grown at low elevations (0–900 meters)	Low	Yes
Sweet potatoes	Moderate (six months at optimal humidity)	Low	Prefers wet	Yes	Grown at low elevations (0–1,000 meters in tropics)	Low	Yes

Oats	High	Moderate to high	Wet temperate	Yes	Grown at low and moderate elevations	Low	No
Sorghum	High	Moderate to high	Many varieties, but best suited for hot and dry climates	No	Grown at low and high elevations but prefers low	Low	No
White potatoes	Moderate	Low	Extremely adaptable; best in climates with cool nights	In 19th and 20th centuries	Grown at very wide range of elevations (0–4,200 meters)	Low	Yes
Jacob's/Job's Tears	High	Moderate to high	Very wide range of climates	No	Grown at low and moderate elevations	Low	No
Barley	High	Moderate to high	Wider ecological range than any other cereal grain, especially in cold climates	In 20th century	Grown at high and low elevations	Moderate to low	No
Cotton	High	High	Hot climates	Yes	Low elevations	Moderate	No
Buckwheat	Low (moderate as animal feed)	Moderate to high	Tolerant of marginal soils, prefers cold climates	No	Tolerant of high elevations	Low	No
Pearl millet	High	Moderate to high	The most drought- and heat-tolerant of cereals	No	Grown at low and moderate elevations	Low	No

continued

Table 3 Continued

Crop	Storability	Labor Intensivity	Climate/Soil (Wet/Dry)	Disease Prone	Elevation Bandwidth	Value Per Unit Weight and Volume (Assuming a Cash Economy)	Possible to Store in the Ground?
Peanuts	High	Low to moderate (generally the same as the dominant crop on a given farm)	Tropical or sub-tropical climates	In 20th century	Low elevations (0–1,500 meters)	Moderate	No
Bananas	Moderate	Low as subsistence crop, moderate to high as export crop	Tropical	Yes	Low and moderate elevations (0–1,800 meters)	Low as subsistence crop, moderate as export crop	No

Sources:

D. E. Briggs, *Barley* (London: Chapman and Hall, 1978).

D. G. Coursey, *Yams: An Account of the Nature, Origins, Cultivation, and Utilisation of the Useful Members of the Dioscoreaceae* (London: Longman's, 1967).

Henry Hobhouse, *Seeds of Change: Five Plants That Transformed Mankind* (New York: Harper and Row, 1965).

L. D. Kapoor, *Opium Poppy: Botany, Chemistry, and Pharmacology* (New York: Haworth, 1995).

Franklin W. Martin, ed., *CRC Handbook of Tropical Food Crops* (Boca Raton: CRC Press, 1984).

A. N. Prentice, *Cotton, with Special Reference to Africa* (London: Longman's, 1970).

Purdue University, New Crop Online Research Program, http://www.hort.purdue.edu/newcrop/default.html.

Jonathan D. Sauer, *Historical Geography of Crop Plants: A Select Roster* (New York: Lewis, 1993).

W. Simmonds, *Bananas* (London: Longman's, 1959).

United Nations Food and Agriculture Organization. *The World Cassava Economy: Facts, Trends, and Outlook* (New York: UNFAO, 2000).

became far easier and more tempting. The opportunity was seized by so many people that it prompted a significant redistribution of population. As Boomgaard puts it, "Maize, then, may have enabled groups or individuals, who, for political, religious, economic, or health reasons, wanted to leave the population centers in the lowlands or the upland villages to survive and even flourish in hitherto sparsely populated mountain areas."[64] A stronger claim has been made that the availability of maize was instrumental in the constitution of upland, nonstate societies. In the case of the Hindu-Javanese living in the Tengger uplands of East Java, Robert Hefner believes that maize may well "have played a role in facilitating the slow retreat of the Hindu farmers upslope into the less accessible terrains of the Tengger highlands in the aftermath of the Muslim conquest of Hindu Majapahit."[65] Elsewhere, it appears that maize and other upland crops (potatoes, cassava) were often critical in the creation of upland populations and in codifying their political and cultural distinctiveness from the lowland state. The reasons for moving away from state space could vary dramatically — religious division, war, corvée, forced cultivation under colonial schemes, epidemics, flight from bondage — but the availability of maize was a new and valuable tool for potential runaways.[66]

The highland Hmong living in or near Thailand and Laos have, for the past two centuries, been fleeing both from Han military pressure and from the aftermath of failed rebellions against the Han and, later, the French in Tonkin. Living at altitudes generally above one thousand meters and growing maize, pulses, root crops, gourds, and the opium poppy, they are very much a nonstate people. It is maize, in particular, that has been instrumental in making good their escape. Hill rice will generally not grow above one thousand meters; the opium poppy, on the other hand, thrives only above nine hundred meters. If the Hmong were to rely on hill rice and opium as their main crops, they would be confined to the narrow band between nine hundred and one thousand meters. With maize, however, they can range another three hundred meters higher, where both maize and the opium poppy thrive and where they are even less likely to attract the attention of the state.

CASSAVA/MANIOC/YUCCA

The champion New World escape crop was, without question, cassava.[67] Like maize, it spread quickly throughout both maritime and mainland Southeast Asia. It could be grown almost anywhere under an amazing variety of conditions. So hardy and self-sufficient is this large root plant that preventing it from growing seems almost more difficult than cultivating it.[68]

It is ideal for opening new land; it is drought resistant; it will tolerate soils in which virtually nothing else can be grown; it, like other transplanted New World cultivars, has few natural enemies; and, compared with taro and the sweet potato, it is less attractive to wild pigs.[69] If it has one drawback, it is that it does not flourish at the highest altitudes like maize and the potato, but otherwise, it places few restrictions on where one can settle or roam.

Cassava shares escape features with other roots and tubers. Although it does not mature as fast as, say, the sweet potato, it can be allowed to ripen and left in the ground until needed. The combination of its versatility and hardiness, together with the fact that only the aboveground foliage can be destroyed by fire, earned it the name *farina de guerra*—roughly, staple or flour of war—in the Spanish-speaking world. Guerrillas represent, after all, something of a limiting case of state-evading, mobile peoples. A further advantage of cassava is that, once harvested, it can be made into a kind of flour (tapioca) which can then be stored for some time. Both the root and the flour can be sold in the market.

Perhaps the most striking advantage of cassava, however, is its undisputed status as the crop requiring the least labor for the greatest return. For that reason, it was much favored by nomadic peoples who could plant it, leave, and then return virtually anytime in the second and third years to dig it up. In the meantime, its leaves can be eaten. Cassava allows its planters to occupy virtually any ecological niche, roam more or less at will, and avoid a great deal of drudgery. On the basis of its striking advantages, it became the most common root crop, displacing the sweet potato, which had, in turn, displaced the yam.

To the padi state, whether precolonial or colonial, such easily accessible and labor-saving subsistence crops, though valued in a pinch as famine foods, were a threat to state-making. The state's interests were best served by maximizing padi land or, failing that, other important cash, export crops such as cotton, indigo, sugar cane, and rubber, often using servile labor. Access to New World escape crops made the economics of escape as tempting as its politics. Colonial officials tended to stigmatize cassava and maize as crops of lazy natives whose main aim was to shirk work. In the New World, too, those whose job it was to drive the population into wage labor or onto the plantations deplored crops that allowed a free peasantry to maintain its autonomy. Hacienda owners in Central America claimed that with cassava, all a peasant needed was a shotgun and a fishhook and he would cease to work regularly for wages.[70]

Cassava, like many root crops, has a large impact on social structure that, in turn, bears on state evasion. This impact makes for an illuminating contrast with grain cultures generally, and with wet-rice cultures in particular.[71] Wet-rice communities live by a single rhythm. Planting, transplanting, and harvesting, and their associated rituals, are closely coordinated, as is water control. Cooperation in water management, crop watching, and labor exchange is rewarded if not mandated. Not so with root crops like sweet potatoes and cassava. Planting and harvesting take place more or less continuously according to the choices and needs of the family unit. Little or no cooperation is required by the agronomic characteristics of the crop itself. A society that cultivates roots and tubers can disperse more widely and cooperate less than grain growers, thereby encouraging a social structure more resistant to incorporation, and perhaps to hierarchy and subordination.

Social Structures of Escape

The padi state requires and fosters a legible landscape of irrigated rice and the concentrated population associated with it. This accessible economy and demography might be termed an appropriable landscape. Just as there are economic landscapes that lend themselves to monitoring and appropriation, so too are there social structures that lend themselves to control, appropriation, and subordination. The contrary is also true. There are, as we have seen, agricultural techniques and crop regimens that are resistant to appropriation, and hence are state repelling. By the same token, there are patterns of social and political organization that are resistant to monitoring and subordination. Just as shifting cultivation and cassava planting represent a "positionality" vis-à-vis the state, so, too, do various forms of social organization represent a strategic position with respect to the state. Social structure, like agricultural technique, is not a given; it is substantially, especially over time, a choice. Much of that choice is in a broad sense political. Here a dialectical view of social organization is necessary. Peripheral political structures in mainland Southeast Asia are always adjusting to the state systems that make up their immediate environment. Under some circumstances they, or rather the human actors who animate them, may adjust that structure so as to facilitate alliances with or incorporation into a nearby state. At other times, they may pattern themselves so as to break loose from ties of tribute or incorporation.

Social structure, in this view, ought to be seen not as a permanent social trait of a particular community but rather as a variable, one of the purposes of which is to regulate relations with the surrounding field of power. Nowhere has this position been more articulately stated than by F. K. Lehman (aka Chit Hlaing) in his study of the Kayah in eastern Burma. After noting, as had Leach before him, the oscillation of social organization over time, he directed attention to the rules of transformation by which this oscillation might be understood: "Indeed, it seems impossible to make sense of the Kayah, or any other category of Southeast Asian hill people, without thinking of the social system in approximately the foregoing terms. It appears to be an ineluctable premise of these societies that one changes one's social structure, sometimes even one's 'ethnic' identity, in response to periodic changes in ongoing relations with neighboring civilizations."[72]

Broadly speaking, whenever a society or part of a society elects to evade incorporation or appropriation, it moves toward simpler, smaller, and more dispersed social units—toward what we have earlier termed the elementary forms of social organization. The most appropriation-resistant social structures—though they also impede collective action of any kind—are acephalous ("headless") small aggregates of households. Such forms of social organization, along with appropriation-resistant forms of agriculture and residence, are invariably coded "barbarian," "primitive," and "backward" by the lowland padi "civilizations." It is no coincidence that this metric of more or less civilized agriculture and social organization should so perfectly map onto their suitability for appropriation and subordination, respectively.

"Tribality"

The state's relation with tribes, though it preoccupied Rome and its legions, has long since disappeared from European historiography. One by one, Europe's last independent, tribal peoples—the Swiss, the Welsh, the Scots, the Irish, the Montenegrins, and nomads of the south Russian steppe—were absorbed into more powerful states and their dominant religions and cultures. The issue of tribes and states, however, is still very much alive in the Middle East. Thus it is from the ethnographers and historians of tribal-state relations there that we can begin to take our bearings.

Tribes and states, they agree, are mutually constituting entities. There is no evolutionary sequence; tribes are not prior to states. Tribes are, rather, a social formation defined by its relation to the state. "If rulers of the Middle East have been preoccupied by a 'tribal problem,' . . . tribes could be said to have had a perennial 'state-problem.'"[73]

One reason why tribes often appear to be stable, enduring, genealogically and culturally coherent units is that the state typically desires such units and sets out, over time, to fashion them. A tribe may spring into existence on the basis of political entrepreneurship or through the political identities and "traffic patterns" that a state can impose by structuring rewards and penalties. The tribe's existence, in either case, depends on a particular relationship to the state. Rulers and state institutions require a stable, reliable, hierarchical, "graspable" social structure through which to negotiate or rule. They need an interlocutor, a partner, with whom to parlay, whose allegiance can be solicited, through whom instructions can be conveyed, who can be held responsible for political order, and who can deliver grain and tribute. Since tribal peoples are, by definition, outside the direct administration of the state, they must, if they are to be governed at all, be governed through leaders who can speak for them and, if necessary, be held hostage. The entities represented as "tribes" seldom exist with anything like the substantiality of state imaginings. This misrepresentation is due not only to the official identities cooked up by the state but also to the need of ethnographers and historians for social identities that can serve as a coherent object of description and analysis. It is hard to produce an account of, let alone govern, a social organism that is continually going in and out of focus.

When nonstate peoples (aka tribes) face pressures for political and social incorporation into a state system, a variety of responses is possible. They, or a section of them, may be incorporated loosely or tightly as a tributary society with a designated leader (indirect rule). They may, of course, fight to defend their autonomy—particularly if they are militarized pastoralists. They may move out of the way. Finally, they may, by fissioning, scattering, and/or changing their livelihood strategy, make themselves invisible or unattractive as objects of appropriation.

The last three strategies are options of resistance and evasion. The military option has, with a few exceptions, rarely been available to nonstate peoples in Southeast Asia.[74] Moving out of the way, inasmuch as it often involves adoption of shifting cultivation or foraging, has already been examined. What remains to be explored is the final strategy of social reorganization. It involves social disaggregation into minimal units, often households, and is often accompanied by the adoption of subsistence strategies that favor small, scattered bands. Ernest Gellner describes this deliberate choice among the Berbers with the slogan "Divide that ye be not ruled." It is a brilliant aphorism, for it shows that the Roman slogan "Divide and rule" does not work past a certain point of atomization. Malcolm Yapp's term for the same strategy, *jellyfish tribes,* is just as apt, for it points to the fact that such disaggregation leaves a potential ruler facing an amorphous, unstructured population with no point of entry or leverage.[75] The Ottomans, in the same vein, found it far easier to deal with structured communities, even if they were Christians and Jews, than with heterodox sects that were acephalous and organizationally diffuse. Most feared were such forms of autonomy and dissent as, for example, the mystical Dervish orders, which deliberately, it seems, avoided any collective settlement or identifiable leadership precisely to fly, as it were, beneath the Ottoman police radar.[76] Faced with situations of this kind, a state often tries to find a collaborator and create a chiefdom. While it is usually in someone's interest to seize this chance, nothing, as we shall see, prevents his would-be subjects from ignoring him.

The elementary units of the tribal structure were like bricks; they could lie scattered or in heaps without discernible structure, or they could be joined together to build large, sometimes massive, tribal confederations. As Lois Beck, who has examined this process in exquisite detail for the Qashqa'i of Iran, describes it, "Tribal groups expanded and contracted. Some tribal groups joined larger ones when, for example, the state attempted to restrict access to resources or a foreign power sent troops to attack them. Large tribal groups divided into small groups to be less visible to the state and escaped its reach. Intertribal mobility [shifting ethnic identity] was a common pattern and was part of the process of tribal formation and dissolution." In a Middle Eastern version of Pierre Clastres's argument for Latin America, Beck points to agriculturalists who shifted to nomadism and sees both social organization and subsistence strategies as political options, sometimes deployed in the service of illegibility. "The forms that many people identify as primitive and traditional were often creations responding to, and sometimes mirroring, more complex systems." Beck adds: "Such local systems adapted to and challenged, or distanced themselves from, the systems of those who sought to dominate them."[77] Social structure, in other words, is, in large measure, both a state effect and a choice; and one possible choice is a social structure that is invisible and/or illegible to state-makers.

This theme of social shape-shifting is articulated in accounts of nomadic and foraging peoples. The amorphous nature of Mongolian social structure and its lack of "nerve centers" were credited by Owen Lattimore as preventing Chinese colonization.[78] Richard White's meticulous analysis of Indian politics in colonial North America emphasizes the radical instability of tribal structure and identity, the autonomy of local groups, and the capacity to shift to new territory and alternate subsistence strategies quickly.[79] In the ethnic, migrant shatter zones that White examines, and which characterize much of Zomia, identities are genuinely plural. Such populations do not so much change identities as emphasize one aspect of a cultural and linguistic portfolio that encompasses several potential identities. The vagueness, plurality, and fungibility of identities and social units have certain political advantages; they represent a repertoire of engagement and disengagement with states and with other peoples.[80] Studies of pastoral nomadic groups such as the Turkmen on the Iranian-Russian border or the Kalmyk in Russia emphasize the capacity of such groups to divide or segment into small independent units whenever it was advantageous.[81] A historian of the Kalmyk quotes Marshall Sahlins's general description of tribesmen: "The body politic may then retain features of a primitive organism, covered by a protective exo-skeleton of chiefly authority, but fundamentally uncomplicated and segmented underneath."[82]

Several features of such societies appear to foster, and in some cases may require, a social structure that can be both disaggregated and reassembled. The existence of such common property resources as pasture, hunting grounds, and potential swiddens allows groups to strike out on their own and, at the same time, impede the development of large, permanent distinctions in wealth and status characteristic of inheritable private property. Equally important is a mixed portfolio of subsistence strategies — foraging, shifting cultivation, hunting, trade, livestock raising, and sedentary agriculture. Each form of livelihood is associated with its own forms of cooperation, group size, and settlement pattern. Together, they provide a kind of practical experience, or praxis, in several forms of social organization. A mixed portfolio of subsistence techniques yields a mixed portfolio of social structures that can easily be invoked for political as well as economic advantage.[83]

Evading Stateness and Permanent Hierarchy

Every state with ambitions to control parts of Zomia — Han administrators in Yunnan and Guizhou, the Thai court in Ayutthaya, the Burmese court in Ava, Shan chiefs (Sawbwa), the British colonial state, and independent national governments — has sought to discover, or, failing that, to create chiefdoms with which they could deal. The British in Burma, Leach noted, everywhere preferred autocratic "tribal" regimes in compact geographical concentrations with which they could negotiate; conversely, they had a distaste for anarchic, egalitarian peoples who had no discernible spokesman. "In the Kachin Hills area . . . and also in many other areas of low population density, there is a large preponderance of very small independent villages; the headman of every village claims to be an independent chief of full *du baw* status. . . . This fact has been noted repeatedly and is the more remarkable in that the British administration was consistently opposed to such fragmented settlement."[84] Another turn-of-the-century British official warned observers not to take the apparent subordination of petty Kachin chiefs seriously. "Beyond this nominal subordination, each village claims to be independent and only acknowledges its own chief." This independence, he emphasizes, anticipating Leach, characterizes even the smallest social units; it "extends down even to the household and each house owner, if he disagrees with his chief, can leave the village and set up his own house elsewhere as his own sawbwa."[85] Accordingly, the British, like other states, tended to label the democratic, anarchic peoples as "wild," "raw," "crude" (*yain*— ၍င်း) vis-à-vis their more "tame," "cooked," "cultured," and autocratic neighbors, even if those neighbors shared the same language and culture. Stable, indirect rule of anarchic "jellyfish" tribes was well nigh impossible. Even pacifying them was both difficult and impermanent. The British chief commissioner from 1887 to 1890 noted that the conquest of the Kachin and Palaung areas had to be accomplished "hill by hill" inasmuch as these peoples "had never submitted to any central control." The Chins were, in his view, at least as frustrating. "Their only system of government was that of headmen of villages or at the most a small group of villages, and, consequently, negotiation with the Chin as a people was impossible."[86]

Daunted by the recalcitrant and slippery Chin, the British set about creating a chief in the "democratic" Chin area and enforcing his writ. Colonial support allowed the chief to sponsor lavish community feasts, which in a "feasting society" enhanced his relative status vis-à-vis commoners. In reaction, a new syncretic cult arose that repudiated community feasts while continuing the tradition of individual feasts that served to increase personal, not chiefly, status. This Pau Chin Hau cult was in short order adopted by the entire Zanniat (a democratic tribal area) and more than a quarter of the Chin population in that administrative division.[87] In this, as in many instances, it appears that independent status—taking one's distance from the state and statelike formations—"was more highly valued than economic prosperity."[88]

The Wa, seen as perhaps the fiercest of the hill peoples, with a reputation for taking heads, are, like the "democratic" Chin and the gumlao Kachin, strongly egalitarian. They emphasize the equality of access to feasting and status competition, refusing to allow those who were already prominent or too wealthy to conduct further sacrifices lest they aspire to chiefdom status. This egalitarianism is, as Magnus Fiskesjö points out, constructed as a state repelling strategy: "The Wa egalitarianism, mistakenly construed as a 'primitive' society in Chinese or other evolutionisms, can also be understood as a way of avoiding the collapse of autonomy in the face of threats from the greater powers that loom on the horizon: the state(s) waiting to exact tribute or to enforce taxation, as they were already doing in the intermediary buffer zone (which here, in a sense, served the role of an 'anti-barbarian' defensive wall system we see elsewhere in China)."[89]

Another response to the pressure to create a political structure through which the state can act is to dissimulate—to comply by producing a simulacrum of chiefly authority without its substance. The Lisu of northern Thailand, it seems, do just that. To please lowland authorities, they name a headman. The Potemkin nature of the headman is apparent from the fact that someone without any real power in the village is invariably named rather than a respected older male with wealth and ability.[90] An identical pattern has been reported for hill villages in colonial Laos, where bogus local officials and notables were produced on demand while respected local figures continued to guide local affairs, including the performance of the bogus officials![91] Here "escape social structure" is not so much a social invention for state evasion as it is an egalitarian, existing social structure that is protected by an elaborate staged performance of hierarchy.

The most celebrated ethnography of hill peoples anywhere in Zomia is Edmund Leach's study of the Kachin, *Political Systems of Highland Burma*. Leach's analysis has been the subject of a nearly unprecedented volume of scrutiny and criticism by nearly two generations of scholars. It is clear that Leach deliberately disregarded the larger political and economic changes (British imperial rule and the opium economy in particular) impinging on Kachin social organization in favor of his structuralist idea of an oscillating equilibrium.[92] He also appears to have seriously misconstrued the vernacular terms for Kachin marriage-alliance systems and their effect on the permanence of social ranking by lineage. A thorough critical examination of his contribution by contemporary ethnographers appears in a volume recently edited François Robinne and Mandy Sadan.[93]

Nothing in this distinguished critical literature, however, questions the

fact that there are important differences in the relative openness and egalitarianism of various Kachin social systems or that there was, near the close of
the past century, something like a movement to assassinate, depose, or desert
the more autocratic chiefs. At its core, Leach's ethnography is an analysis of
escape social structure—a form of social organization designed to thwart capture and appropriation either by Shan statelets or by the petty Kachin chiefs
(*duwa*) who attempt to mimic Shan power and hierarchy. Leach argues, to
put it very briefly and schematically, that there are three models of political
organization in the Kachin area: Shan, *gumsa,* and *gumlao.* The Shan model
is a statelike structure of property and hierarchy marked by a hereditary (in
principle) chief and systematic taxes and corvée. At the other extreme is the
gumlao model, a model that repudiates all hereditary authority and class difference—though not individual differences in status. Gumlao villages, which
were unrecognized by the British, are independent and typically have a ritual
organization and tutelary deities that reinforce equality and autonomy. The
Shan and gumlao forms, Leach argues, are relatively stable. Here it is crucial to underline that these are not ethnic distinctions as understood phe-
nomenologically by Leach's subjects. To move in a "Shan" direction is to be
associated more closely with the hierarchy, ritual, and opportunities of this
statelike social formation. To move in a gumlao direction is precisely to take
one's distance from the Shan state and its practices. Historically, people have
moved back and forth between these models and codes.

The third model, the gumsa form, is an intermediate model of theoreti-
cally rigid and stratified lineages where wife-taking lineages are socially and
ritually superior to wife-giving lineages, leading to a division between commoners and aristocrats.[94] This model, Leach claims, is particularly unstable.[95]
The head of a top-ranked lineage in the gumsa system is well on the way to
transforming himself into a petty Shan ruler.[96] At the same time, his effort to
make his status permanent and to turn lower-ranked lineages into his serfs
threatens to provoke a rebellion or flight, and hence a move toward gumlao
equality.[97]

For our purposes, Leach's Kachin ethnography illustrates a model of
egalitarian social organization readily at hand to prevent or evade state formation. Leach writes of the oscillation between these three models as if it
were a permanent feature of Kachin society. And yet the gumlao form was
also, in part, the result of a specific historical revolution. The *Gazetteer of
Upper Burma* reports that the gumlao "revolt" began when two suitors for
the daughter of a chief (duwa) were refused (an acceptance would have raised

their status and that of their kin group).[98] They killed that duwa and the man to whom the daughter had been given. They went on, with followers, to depose many duwa, some of whom escaped death or exile by giving up their titles and privileges. This story is in keeping with the view, expressed by Leach, that the gumsa structure, by its stratified rankings, is likely to block the status aspirations of men from lower-ranked lineages, typically expressed through competitive feasting.[99] Leach's own account of the proximate cause of the revolt is far more nuanced and elaborate, but at its center is the refusal to provide corvée labor, which, along with the thigh of slaughtered animals, was the prerogative of a chief.[100]

Gumlao villages come about in either of two ways. First, as just described, they are the result of small-scale leveling revolutions that establish small, commoner republics. The second and perhaps more common origin is the migration of families and lineages from more stratified villages to found new, more egalitarian villages. The origin myths of gumlao villages emphasize one or the other. At this point, Leach proposes that the gumlao itself is unstable, since, as inequalities develop, those advantaged will strive to legitimate and codify those advantages with gumsa trappings. But another interpretation is possible: that gumlao communities are typically reproduced by fission, by small groups of families of equal status striking out on their own when they find that the inequalities have become stifling. Fission, as well as small-scale revolution, was greatly conditioned by demography and developments in the larger world. Inequalities might prove far more stifling where British pressure had diminished caravan revenue and slaving. The attractions of the frontier might prove more alluring in a booming opium market. Where there was less demographic pressure and hence plenty of available swidden land, fission was probably far more likely than revolt.[101]

Gumlao areas were anathema to the state. An early British account of the Kachin areas contrasted the ease of marching through the villages of a well-disposed hereditary chief with the difficulty of traversing "a gumlao village which is practically a small republic, the headman, however well-meaning he may be, is quite unable to control the actions of any badly-disposed villager."[102] Gumlao social organization was state repelling in a number of ways. Its ideology discouraged, or killed, would-be hereditary chiefs with feudal pretensions. It was resistant to tribute or control by the neighboring Shan principalities. Finally, it presented a relatively intractable anarchy of egalitarian, Lilliputian republics that were hard to pacify, let alone govern.

I have devoted some considerable space to gumlao villages as escape social structure not simply because it is well documented, thanks to Leach. There is more than a little evidence that many, if not most, hill peoples have bifurcated or even tripartite models of social organization: one approximating the egalitarian gumlao Kachin model, one approximating the more stratified gumsa model, and, occasionally, another approximating a petty Shan kingdom. Leach notes that "contrasted theories of government of this kind are current throughout the Burma Assam frontier area" and cites studies of the Chin, Sema, Konyak, and Nagas.[103] To Leach's list, we can add more recent studies of the Karen and the Wa.[104] It would seem that just as hill peoples in mainland Southeast Asia are likely to have escape crops and escape agriculture in their economic repertoire, so too are they likely to have state-thwarting social models in their political repertoire.

In the Shadow of the State, in the Shadow of the Hills

Shortly before Burmese independence, an inquiry was held, to which tribal representatives were summoned. The chief of Mongmon, in the remote Northern Wa State, was asked what kind of administration he would favor. He replied, reasonably enough, "We have not thought about that because we are a wild people."[105] The point about being a Wa, he understood better than the officials questioning him, was precisely not to be administered at all.

This diagnostic misunderstanding underlines the key fact that most hill societies are "shadow" or "mirror" societies. I mean by this that they are structures of political, cultural, economic, and often religious positioning, often self-consciously contradicting the forms and values of their more state-like neighbors. This defiance may come at some economic cost, according to Leach. He concludes that "the Kachins often value independence more highly than economic advantage."[106] At the same time, those who migrate to lowland states and assimilate—and historically there have been a great many—enter valley society at its lowest rungs. In short-run status terms, as Lehman explains, a Chin entering Burman society has a choice between being a defective Burman or a successful Chin.[107]

Identity in the hills is an implicit dialogue and debate about how to live. The interlocutors are the contrasting civilizations closest at hand. For peoples such as the Miao/Hmong, whose oral history records a long running battle with the Chinese/Han state, it is that dialogue which looms largest. The story the Hmong tell about themselves is thus something of a posture, a defense, a positioning in a debate with the Han and their state. Some Hmong debating points: they have emperors and we are all (notionally) equal; they pay taxes to overlords and we pay none; they have writing and books and we lost ours while fleeing; they live crowded in lowland centers and we live free, scattered in the hills; they are servile and we are free.[108]

One might be tempted to conclude from this way of putting it that hill "ideology" was entirely derivative of valley ideologies. That would be mistaken for two reasons. First, hill ideology is in dialogue not only with valley societies but with other adjacent hill peoples and has other weighty matters like genealogy, the propitiation of the spirits, and the origin of man to deal with—matters that are somewhat less inflected by the debate with the valley centers. Second, and perhaps more important, if hill ideologies can be said to be deeply influenced by lowland states, it is equally the case that the lowland states, themselves historical aggregates of ingathered peoples, are preoccupied in explaining the superiority of their "civilization" vis-à-vis their "ruder" neighbors.

At least three themes in this connection appear again and again in the narratives and positional self-understandings of hill peoples. They might be termed equality, autonomy, and mobility, all understood relatively. As a matter of practice, of course, all three are encoded in material life in the hills—in location well away from lowland states, in dispersal, in common property, in shifting cultivation, and in the choice of crops. By choice, as Lehman has pointed out, hill peoples have "practiced an economy that the Burman [state] institutions were not adapted to exploit and, therefore, never thought of as part of the Burman kingdom."[109] Just as "wet-rice cultivation implied a subject relationship to the polity, so to engage in swiddening was to some degree a statement of political positioning within a bifurcated regional culture of universalizing polities and forested hinterlands."[110]

The gumlao Kachin, as we have seen, have a history of enforcing egalitarian social relations by deposing or assassinating overreaching chiefs. One imagines that this history and the narratives that accompany it operate as a chilling cautionary tale for lineage chiefs with autocratic ambitions. Whole districts in Karen, Kayah, and Kachin areas are known for their traditions of revolt.[111] Where the Kachin had chiefs, they were frequently ignored and shown no special respect. Other peoples have analogous traditions. The Lisu "loathe assertive and autocratic headmen," and the "stories Lisu tell of murdered headmen are legion."[112] The strict veracity of these stories matters less than the announcement it makes about norms of power relations.[113] Similar stories circulate among the Lahu. Their society is described as "extremely egalitarian" by one ethnographer, and another claims that they are, in gender terms, as egalitarian as any people in the world.[114] The Akha, for their part, reinforce their egalitarian practices with a mythic charter in which a chief and his son, who has a shamanic horse with wings mended with beeswax, flies too high. As with Icarus, his wings melt and he falls to his death. The "'flowery' exaggerated way" the story is told, "clearly shows an aversion to hierarchical chiefdom and state-formation."[115]

The autonomy of hill peoples from permanent internal hierarchy and from state formation has depended absolutely on physical mobility. In this respect, the gumlao revolt is the exception that proves the rule. Flight, not rebellion, has been the basis of freedom in the hills; far more egalitarian settlements were founded by runaways than by revolutionaries. As Leach notes, "In the Shan case the villagers are tied to their [padi] land; the rice fields represent a capital investment. Kachins have no investment in the taungya [swidden—literally "hill cultivation"]. If a Kachin doesn't like his chief he can go somewhere else."[116] It is the ability and, indeed, the practice of hill peoples to move at the drop of a hat and on the slightest pretext that bedeviled both the colonial regimes and the independent states of Southeast Asia. Although much of Zomia could be aptly described as a vast zone of refuge from state-making, movement was constantly taking place within Zomia from more stratified, statelike places to more egalitarian frontiers.

The hill Karen provide a case in point. Part or all of their small settlements would move to a new location, not simply to clear a new swidden but for many nonagricultural reasons as well. An inauspicious sign, a series of illnesses or death, a factional split, pressure for tribute, an overreaching headman, a dream, the call of a respected religious figure—any of these might be enough to prompt a move. Various state efforts to sedentarize the Karen and make use of them were frustrated by the constant fissioning and mobility of their settlements. In the mid-nineteenth century, when many Karen had, along with their Mon allies, fled Burma and accepted Thai authority, they would not permanently settle, as the Thai officials desired.[117] For their part, the British tried to settle the Karen in subsidized "forest villages" in the Pegu Yoma, where they would practice a restricted swiddening regime and, not incidentally, become the guardians of valuable stands of teak. The scheme was resisted and the Karen moved away.[118] Everything we know about the hill Karen—their historical fear of slavery, their self-image as an orphaned and persecuted people—suggests that their social structure and swiddening were designed to keep them at a safe distance from captivity. Safety also meant adopting pliable social structures. The hill Karen are commonly described as having an autonomous and loosely structured society—one that splits easily over economic, social, political, or religious issues.[119]

The utter plasticity of social structure among the more democratic, stateless, hill peoples can hardly be exaggerated. Shape-shifting, fissioning, disaggregation, physical mobility, reconstitution, shifts in subsistence routines are often so dizzying that the very existence of the units beloved of anthropologists—the village, the lineage, the tribe, the hamlet—are called into question. On what unit the historian, the anthropologist, or, for that matter, the administrator should fix his gaze becomes an almost metaphysical issue. The lowest-status hill peoples, it appears, are especially polymorphous. They deploy a wider range of languages and cultural practices that allow them to adapt quickly to a broad range of situations.[120] Anthony Walker, ethnographer of the Lahu Nyi (Red Lahu), writes of villages that divide up, move, evaporate altogether, scatter to other settlements, and absorb newcomers, and he writes of new settlements suddenly appearing.[121] Nothing appears to remain in place long enough to sit for its portrait. The elementary unit of Red Lahu society is not the village in any meaningful sense. "A Lahu Nyi village community is essentially a group of households whose members, for the time being, find it convenient to share a common locale under a common headman more or less acceptable to them." The headman, Walker writes, is headman of a "collection of jealously independent households."[122]

Here we are dealing not merely with "jellyfish" tribes but with "jellyfish" lineages, villages, chiefdoms, and, at the limit, jellyfish households. Along with shifting agriculture, this polymorphism is admirably suited to the purpose of evading incorporation in state structures. Such hill societies rarely challenge the state itself, but neither do they allow the state an easy point of entry or leverage. When threatened, they retreat, disperse, disaggregate like quicksilver—as if their motto was indeed "Divide that ye be not ruled."

CHAPTER 6½

Orality, Writing, and Texts

Poetry is the mother tongue of the human race as gardening is older than the field, painting than writing, singing than declaiming, parables than inferences, bartering than commerce . . .
—Bruce Chatwin, *Songlines,* quoting J. G. Hamann

For, in its severity, the law is at the same time writing. Writing is on the side of the law; the law lives in writing; and knowing that the one means that unfamiliarity with the other is no longer possible . . . writing directly bespeaks the power of the law, be it engraved in stone, painted on animal skins, or drawn on papyrus.
—Pierre Clastres, *Society against the State*

A diagnostic feature of the condition of barbarism is, for lowland elites, nonliteracy. Of all the civilizational stigmas that hill peoples bear, the general ignorance of writing and texts is the most prominent. Bringing preliterate peoples into the world of letters and formal schooling is, of course, a raison d'être of the developmental state.

But what if many peoples, on a long view, are not *pre*literate, but, to use Leo Alting von Geusau's term, *post*literate?[1] What if, as a consequence of flight, of changes in social structure and subsistence routines, they left texts and writing behind? And what if, to raise the most radical possibility, there was an active or strategic dimension to this abandonment of the world of texts and literacy? The evidence for this last possibility is almost entirely circumstantial. For this reason, and perhaps due to a failure of nerve on my part, I have bracketed this discussion from the foregoing account of escape agriculture and escape social structure. The case for the "strategic" maintenance (if not creation) of nonliteracy, however, is cut from the same cloth. If swiddening and dispersal are subsistence strategies that impede appropriation; if social fragmentation and acephaly hinder state incorporation; then, by the same token, the absence of writing and texts provides a freedom of maneuver in history, genealogy, and legibility that frustrates state routines. If swiddening and egalitarian, mobile settlement represent elusive "jellyfish" economic and social forms, orality may be seen as a similarly fugitive jellyfish variant of culture. On this reading, orality may in many cases be a "positionality" vis-

à-vis state formation and state power. Just as agriculture and residence practices may oscillate over long periods to reflect a strategic positioning, so may
literacy and texts be taken up, then set aside, then taken up again for similar
reasons.

I have chosen to use the term *nonliteracy* or *orality*, in preference to
illiteracy, to call attention to orality as a different and potentially positive
medium of cultural life as opposed to a mere deficiency. The sort of "orality"
we are speaking of is also to be distinguished from what some have called
primary illiteracy: a situation in which a social field confronts literacy for
the first time. Nonliterate peoples in the Southeast Asian massif, by contrast,
have for more than two thousand years lived in contact with one or more
states with small literate minorities, texts, and written records. They have
had to position themselves vis-à-vis such states. Finally, it should go without
saying that until very recently the literate elite of the valley states were a tiny
minority of the total subject population. Even in the valley states, the vast
majority of the population lived in an oral culture, inflected though it was by
writing and texts.

Oral Histories of Writing

Knowing the stigma historically attached to their nonliteracy by lowland
states and colonizers, most hill peoples have oral legends that "account for"
why they do not write. What is rather surprising is the remarkable similarity
of many of these legends, which are not confined to mainland Southeast Asia
but may be found in the Malay world and, for that matter, in Europe. These
stories converge around one theme: the people in question once did have
writing but lost it through their own improvidence, or would have had it had
they not been cheated of it by treachery. Such legends are, like ethnic identity
itself, a strategic positioning vis-à-vis other groups. We have every reason to
imagine that such legends, like ethnic identity, will be adjusted if the circumstances shift appreciably. That these legends often bear a family resemblance
to one another is perhaps attributable more to the common strategic location
of most stateless hill peoples in relation to the large valley kingdoms than to
any cultural inertia.

One common account of how the Akha "lost" writing is fairly typical
of the genre. Long ago they were, they claim, a valley-dwelling, rice-planting
people incorporated in states. Having to flee the valleys owing, by most accounts, to Tai military superiority, they scattered in several directions. Along

the route of flight "they ate their books of buffalo-hide when they were hungry, and so lost their script."[2] The Lahu, hill neighbors of the Akha along the Burma, Thai, and China border, tell of having lost their script when they ate the cakes on which their deity Gui-sha had inscribed their letters.[3] The Wa tell a similar story. They also claim to have had writing, which was inscribed on an oxhide. When they became famished and had nothing else to eat, they devoured the oxhide and so lost their script. Another Wa story relates that, as the original people, they had a trickster genius, Glieh Neh, who sent all the men off to war while he stayed back and made love to all the women. Caught and condemned, Glieh Neh asked to be drowned in a coffin with all his musical instruments. Cast adrift, he played so beguilingly that all the downriver creatures helped set him free. In turn, he taught the lowlanders all his skills, including that of writing, and the Wa were left illiterate. Writing is, for the Wa, associated with the trickster figure; the word for writing is the same as the word for trading and implies deception and cheating.[4] The Karen provide many variants of a legend claiming that three brothers (Karen, Burman, and Han or European) were each given scripts. While the Burman and the Han kept theirs, the Karen brother left his, written on a hide, atop a stump while swiddening, and it was eaten by wild (or domesticated) animals. Stories of this genre could be multiplied almost indefinitely; a fairly comprehensive survey of the variations on this theme for the Karenni groups alone is found in Jean-Marc Rastdorfer's work on Kayah and Kayan identity.[5] The Lahu, for their part, speak of once having known how to write their language and refer to a lost book. They, in fact, have been known to carry papers with hieroglyphic marks which they cannot read.[6] The impression that such accounts are powerfully influenced by an implicit dialogue with more powerful groups associated with states and writing is reinforced by its occurrence outside the region as well.[7]

Stories of treachery are as common as those of carelessness. A single ethnic group may have both genres in its repertoire. Perhaps each variant is appropriate to particular audiences and situations. One Karen account of lost literacy blames the Burmese kings, who are said to have found and executed every literate Karen until there was no one left to teach the others. A Khmu (Lamet) legend in Laos associates the loss of writing with a fall into political subordination. Seven villages came together to swidden on the same mountain and swore to jointly oppose their Tai overlord. The oath was written on a buffalo rib, which was then solemnly buried on the mountaintop. Later, however, the rib was dug up and stolen, and "that day we lost the knowledge of writing and we have since then suffered from the power of the *lam* [Tai over-lord]."[8] A Chin story, collected at the turn of the century, blames Burmese deceit for the group's illiteracy. The Chin were, like other races, born from 101 eggs. As the last born, the Chin were most loved, but the earth was already apportioned, and they were given the remaining mountains and its animals. The Burmese guardian appointed over them cheated them of elephants (a royal symbol) and showed them the blank back side of a writing slate so that they never learned even a single letter.[9] The White Hmong's portfolio of literacy stories allows for both carelessness and treachery. In one account, the Hmong, in their flight from the Han, fell asleep and their horses ate up their texts, or they were mistakenly put in a stew and eaten. A second and more ominous account claims that the Han, in the course of driving the Hmong out of the valleys, took their texts and burned them all. The educated ones went to the mountains, and when they died, there was no more writing.[10]

For some groups, like the Hmong and Mien, the loss of writing seems closely associated with a general claim to a history as a lowland, state-bearing people. Before we were driven out of the lowlands, their story implicitly claims, we had kings, we planted irrigated rice, and we had writing; we had all those things we are now stigmatized for not having. The arrival of literacy and written scripts, by these lights, is nothing new; it is the recapturing of something lost or stolen. Little wonder that the arrival of missionaries with their bibles and scripts for vernacular tongues often seemed like a restoration of lost cultural property, all the more welcome because it was not Burmese or Han.

What are we to make of these legends of lost literacy? It is conceivable, providing once again that we take a very long historical view, that these legends embody a germ of historical truth. Tai, Hmong/Miao, and Yao/Mien, from what we can reconstruct of their migration histories, came from lowland settings and may well have once been padi-state peoples—even, in the case of many Tai groups, state-makers themselves.[11] Many other hill peoples were, in the distant and not so distant past, closely associated with, if not incorporated in, valley kingdoms with literate elites. Those who moved from such valleys to hill settings would, on this assumption, have plausibly included at least a small literate minority. The Hmong legend of the literate minority dying out might, then, contain a grain of truth, though it does not explain why this knowledge was not passed on. The Karen have been at one time or another closely associated with several literate padi-state traditions—Mon-Pegu, Tai–Nan Chao, Burman, and Thai: an association that would almost certainly have fostered a small literate class. The Ganan, a now nonliterate people along the upper reaches of the Mu River, were almost surely part of the literate Pyu kingdom(s) before they fled to their redoubt in the hills. Like a great many other hill peoples, the Ganan and Hmong retain many of the cultural practices and beliefs of the lowland peoples with whom they were once associated. If, as I have argued, many, if not most, contemporary hill peoples have a "valley" past, then such cultural continuities should occasion no surprise. Why, then, in most cases, did they not also bring literacy and texts along with them?

The Narrowness of Literacy and Some Precedents for Its Loss

There is no place in any of the standard civilizational narratives for the loss or abandonment of literacy. The acquisition of literacy is envisaged as a one-way trip in just the same fashion as is the transition from shifting agriculture to wet-rice cultivation and from forest bands to villages, towns, and cities. And yet literacy in premodern societies was, under the best of circumstances, confined to a very small portion of the population. It was the social property of scribes, accomplished religious figures, and a very thin stratum of scholar gentry in the case of the Han. To assert, in this context, that a whole society or people is literate is incorrect; in all premodern societies the vast majority of the population was illiterate and lived in an oral culture, inflected though it was by texts. To say that, demographically speaking, literacy hung by a thread would in many cases be no exaggeration. Not only was it confined to a tiny elite, but the social value of literacy, in turn, depended on a state bureaucracy, an organized clergy, and a social pyramid where literacy was a means of advancement and a mark of status. Any event that threatened these institutional structures threatened literacy itself.

Something very much like this institutional collapse seems to lie behind the four-century-long "Greek Dark Age," lasting roughly from 1100 BCE (the time of the Trojan War) until 700. Before that Mycenaean Greeks, a small number of them at any rate, kept records in a difficult-to-learn syllabary script (Linear B) borrowed from the Minoans and used primarily for keeping palace administrative transactions and tax records. For reasons that are still not entirely clear—a Dorian invasion from the north, internal civil war, ecological crisis, famine—the palaces and towns of the Peloponnese were sacked, burned, and abandoned, leading to a collapse of long-distance trade, refugee movements, and a general diaspora. The epoch is termed the Dark Age precisely because no written records survive, apparently because the knowledge of the Linear B script was abandoned in the chaos and dispersal of the time. The Homeric epics of the Iliad and the Odyssey, oral tales passed from bard to bard and only later written down, are the only cultural artifacts to have survived the Dark Age. Around 750 BCE, under more peaceful conditions, the Greeks regained literacy, this time borrowing from the Phoenicians a genuine alphabet that allowed a graphic representation of the sounds made by actual speech. This episode is one of the clearest examples we have of literacy apparently lost and later regained.[12]

Another instance in which literacy appears to have been largely but not entirely lost is in the period following the collapse of the tattered vestiges of the Roman Empire around 600 CE. Literacy in Latin, which had previously been both expensive and necessary to a nonmilitary career in the Empire, was now of no particular value except perhaps as an ornament. The path to security and power for local elites now lay in military service to the local king. Literacy receded to the point that it was largely confined to the clergy even in areas of Gaul that had been quite Romanized previously. In distant Britain the veneer of a Roman culture and education evaporated altogether. It had been the Roman state, and its institutions that had maintained the context in which literacy was "an essential component of 'eliteness,'" just as the Mycenaean social order had upheld the more restricted Linear B literacy in ancient Greece. When that institutional nexus crumbled, so did the social foundations of literacy.[13]

Assuming that many of the contemporary hill peoples were, at one time or another, living near or in lowland states with some degree of literacy, and assuming further, as seems reasonable, that a small fraction of their own elites became literate, say in Chinese, how might we account for a subsequent loss of literacy? Here again, the first thing to bear in mind is how very thin this literate stratum was in Han society, let alone among the peoples the Han state encountered as it expanded its reach. We may be talking about a mere handful of people. Second, those who were literate in the script of the lowland state would have almost certainly have been elites whose bicultural skills fitted them best to become allies and administrators of the lowland state and, if they so chose, to take the path of assimilation. If, then, as most historians suppose, large fractions of today's minority peoples in the hills were earlier absorbed in the process of Han expansion, one would suppose that this literate minority would be more likely to stay behind and assimilate, inasmuch as they had the most to gain by doing so. A people migrating or fleeing lowland centers of power would, on this assumption, have left most, perhaps all, of its literate minority behind. Speculating further, the few literates who migrated with those resisting and fleeing must have had an ambiguous status among their compatriots; skilled in the script of the state they were fleeing, they might be seen as helpful or, perhaps, as a potential fifth column. In the latter case, they may have elected to let their literacy lapse and not to instruct others.

Another potential explanation for the loss of literacy is that it was merely a logical consequence of the fragmentation, mobility, and dispersal of social structure entailed by migration to the hills. Leaving behind the lowland centers meant stripping down the complexity of social structure in the interest of mobility. In this context, literacy and texts were of no further use and died out as a practice, though not as a memory.[14] As in the Roman case, so much of the practice of literacy was directly dependent on the existence of a particular state and its bureaucratic routines: knowledge of state documents, law codes, chronicles, record keeping in general, taxes and economic transactions, and, above all, the structure of officeholding and hierarchy linked to that state made literacy a sought-after prestige good. Once this structure was left behind, the social incentives driving the acquisition and transmission of literacy would have diminished precipitously.

On the Disadvantages of Writing and the Advantages of Orality

The argument thus far for the loss of literacy has hinged on the loss of literates and of the contexts that made their services valuable. A stronger case, I think, can be made for the positive advantages of moving to an oral culture. Such an argument rests essentially on the manifest advantages of flexibility and adaptation that an oral tradition has over a written tradition.

For the sake of this argument, I bracket those cases in which secret scripts and inscriptions are used for their magical efficacy.[15] Magical writing is common throughout the region. Scripts and signs are deployed in much the same way as magic spells or incantations and are expected to "act on the world" as signs. Carried as talismans, tattooed on the body, and perhaps blessed by monks and shamans who vouch for their power to protect their bearer, such writings operate as powerful fetish objects. While they testify to the symbolic power of writing and merit analysis in their own right, they do not constitute literacy in the sense understood here. I also exclude those scripts found in the region which seem to be totally confined to their role as aide-mémoire in the service of the oral culture. Thus the Yao/Mien in southern Hunan province are said to have had, from pre-Han times, a simple script designed to help them memorize laments that could then be embroidered on cloth. This sort of restricted literacy without permanent texts, literature, or documents, however fascinating as an appropriation of literacy in an essentially oral culture (as if Homer had a script to help him memorize and then recite difficult passages in the *Odyssey*), will also be bracketed in this discussion.[16]

The existence of special, restricted forms of writing is a salutary reminder that texts, in the broad sense of the term, can take many forms, of which books and documents are but two. All hierarchies, I would venture, that aspire to intergenerational durability produce, as a matter of course, "texts" that assert claims to authority and power. Such texts, before the advent of writing, might take the form of material objects: crowns, coats of arms, trophies, cloaks, headdresses, royal colors, fetish objects, heirlooms, steles, monuments, and so on. The state, as the most ambitious claimant of this kind, multiplies such texts as assertions of permanence. Early states combined the permanence of stone tablets with writing or pictograms as claims to lasting power.

The key disadvantage of monuments and written texts is precisely their relative permanence. Contingent though they are, they become, once erected or written down, a sort of social fossil that can be "dug up" at any time, unchanged. Any written text makes a certain kind of orthodoxy possible— whether that text is a legend of origin, an account of migrations, a genealogy, or a religious text such as the Bible or the Koran.[17] No text, of course, has a perfectly transparent meaning, and if there are multiple contending texts, the room for interpretive maneuver is that much larger. Nonetheless, the text itself is a fixed point of departure; it makes some readings implausible if not impossible. Once there is a text as an indisputable point of reference, it provides the kind of yardstick from which deviations from the original can roughly be judged.[18] This process is most striking when the text in question has been deemed authoritative. Let's say a text asserts that X people originated from a particular place, fled from unjust taxes of a particular lowland king, followed a certain itinerary, worship particular tutelary spirits, and bury their dead in a certain way. The very existence of such texts has powerful consequences; it facilitates the development of an orthodox, standard account. That standard account can be learned directly from the text, and this fact privileges that class of literate scribes who can read the texts. Any subsequent account, depending on its fit with that standard account, allows various degrees of heterodoxy to be inferred. By contrast, debates in oral cultures about whether such-and-such a spoken account is credible cannot be referred back to an authoritative, written text.

Such documents, furthermore, are, like all such documents, created in a particular historical context and reflect that context. They are "interested," historically positioned texts. When they were created, they may well have served as a charter for an advantageous account of a group's history. What happens when the situation changes substantially and the textual account becomes inconvenient? What if yesterday's enemies have become today's allies and vice versa? If the text is sufficiently polysemic, it can be reinterpreted to bring it into line. If not, it can be burned or abandoned, though in the case of monuments it might involve chiseling off certain names and recorded events![19] It is easy to see that, over time, a fixed account can become as much of a trap and impediment as an instrument of successful diplomacy.[20]

For hill peoples and for stateless peoples generally, the world of writing and texts is also indelibly associated with states. Lowland padi states were centers of literacy not merely because they were cult centers for world religions but also because writing is a crucial technology of administration and statecraft. It is hard to conceive of a padi state without cadastral maps of taxable land, registration lists for corvée labor, receipts, record keeping, royal decrees, legal codes, specific agreements and contracts, and lists, lists, lists—in short, without writing.[21] The elementary form of statecraft is the population list and household census: the basis for taxation and conscription. Of all the written texts recovered from the early Mesopotamian kingdom of Uruk, fully 85 percent were economic records.[22] As Claude Lévi-Strauss notes, "Writing appears to be necessary for the centralized, stratified state to reproduce itself. Writing is a strange thing. . . . The one phenomenon which has invariably accompanied it is the formation of cities and empires: the integration into a political system, that is to say, of a considerable number of individuals into a hierarchy of castes and slaves. . . . It seems rather to favor the exploitation than the enlightenment of mankind."[23]

In a common Akha account of their wanderings ("roads") as a people, they are described as having once been a rice-growing valley people who were sorely oppressed by Yi-Lolo rulers. The key figure in this part of the narrative is a King Jabiolang, whose great crime in their eyes was to have initiated a yearly census.[24] The idea of a census (*jajitjieu*) stands symbolically for the entire apparatus of state power. Early colonial history is rife with indigenous resistance to the first colonial census; peasants and tribesmen alike understood perfectly well that a census was the necessary prelude to taxes and corvée labor.

A similar attitude toward writing and record keeping permeates the history of colonial peasant rebellions against the state. The first target of peasant wrath was often not so much the colonial officials themselves as the paper documents—land titles, tax lists, population records—through which the officials seemed to rule. Implicitly, it seemed to the insurgents that burning down the public records office promised, by itself, a kind of emancipation. Nor was the association of writing with state oppression confined to the colonial world. The radical wing in the English Civil War, exemplified by the Diggers and Levelers, regarded the Latin of the law and of the clergy as a deliberately mystifying technology designed to fleece them. Knowledge of letters was itself prima facie cause for suspicion.[25]

Much of early state-making seems to have been a process of naming units that were once fluid or unnamed: villages, districts, lineages, tribes, chiefs, families, and fields. The process of naming, when joined to the administrative power of the state, can create entities that did not previously exist. For Han officials, one distinguishing characteristic of "barbarians" was that they did not have patronyms. Such stable names were, among the Han themselves, the result of a much earlier exercise in state-making. In this sense, the very units of identity and place, which then acquire a distinctive genealogy and history, are, in their official, stable form, a state effect linked to writing.

For many stateless, preliterate or postliterate peoples, the world of literacy and writing is not simply a reminder of their lack of power and knowledge and the stigma attached to it. It is, at the same time, a clear and present danger. The acquisition of writing, associated as it is with state power, could as easily be an avenue for disempowerment as for empowerment. To refuse or to abandon writing and literacy is one strategy among many for remaining out of reach of the state. It might seem far more prudent to rely instead upon "knowledges that resist bureaucratic codification."[26]

For stateless peoples wedged between powerful lowland states and for whom adaptability, mimicry, reinvention, and accommodation are therefore important survival skills, an oral, vernacular culture holds substantial attractions. In an oral culture, there cannot be a single authoritative genealogy or history that can serve as the gold standard of orthodoxy. In the case of two or more renditions, which one is given credence depends largely on the standing of the "bard" in question and on how closely the account conforms to the interests and tastes of the audience.

An oral tradition is, in most respects, inherently more democratic than a written tradition for at least two reasons. First, the ability to read and write is typically less broadly distributed than the ability to tell stories.[27] Second, there is rarely any simple way to "adjudicate" among variant tellings of oral history; certainly there is no fixed, written text to which the variants can be compared for veracity. Oral communication, even by "official" bards, is by definition limited to the size of the face-to-face audience assembled to hear it. The spoken word, like language itself, is a collectivist activity inasmuch as "its conventions have to be shared by whole groups of societies of varying size before any of its 'meanings' become available to individuals within the society" at the moment of transmission.[28] From the moment a spoken text (a particular performance) is frozen in writing as preserved speech, it effaces most of the particularity of its origin—cadence, tone, pauses, accompanying music and dance, audience reaction, bodily and facial expression—any one of which might be essential to its original meaning.[29]

In fact, in the case of oral histories and narratives, the concept of "the original" simply does not make any sense.[30] Oral culture exists and is sustained only through each unique performance at a particular time and place for an interested audience. These performances are, of course, far more than the transcript of the words spoken; each includes the setting, the gestures, and the expression of the performer(s), the audience reaction, and the nature of the occasion itself. Oral culture has therefore an inalterable presentness— if it was of no interest, if it served no purpose for its contemporary audience, it would cease to exist. A written record, in radical contrast, can persist more or less invisibly for a millennium and suddenly be dug up and consulted as an authority.

Thus oral traditions are to written traditions more or less what swidden agriculture is to irrigated wet-rice agriculture or what small, dispersed kin groups are to settled, concentrated societies. They are the "jellyfish," shape-shifting, pliable form of custom, history, and law. They permit a certain "drift" in content and emphasis over time—a strategic and interested re-adjustment of, say, a group history in which certain events are now omitted and others given stronger emphasis, and still others "remembered." Should a group with a common background split into two or more subgroups, each of which finds itself in a materially different setting, one imagines that their oral histories will diverge accordingly. As the different oral traditions drift imperceptibly apart, there can be no reference point—which a shared written text would provide—by which to gauge how far and in what ways each tradition had diverged from the once common account. Because oral traditions survive only through retelling, they accumulate interpretations as they are transmitted. Each telling forcibly reflects current interests, current power relations, and current views of neighboring societies and kin groups. Barbara Andaya, writing of oral traditions in Sumatra (Jambi and Palembang), captures the process of adjustment and modification. "With the community's implicit agreement, details extraneous to the present slipped away from legend to be replaced by newly relevant elements that were incorporated as ancestral lore, thus rendering the past continually meaningful."[31]

Oral traditions are capable of impressive feats of faithful transmission over many generations if the group bearing the tradition so desires. We know enough about the bardic tradition through the pathbreaking studies of Serbian oral epics and, by extension, the Homeric epics to understand that rhyme, meter, and long apprenticeship can provide high fidelity in the oral transmission of very long passages.[32] Among the Akha, a special caste of *phima*, teachers and reciters, has preserved quite elaborate recitations of long genealogies, the major events in Akha history, and customary law, which they sing on ceremonial occasions. The fact that widely separated groups of Akha with quite different dialects have preserved nearly identical oral texts is testimony to the efficacy of such techniques. More impressive still is the fact that the Akha and Hani, who split more than eight hundred years ago, have preserved oral texts with a high degree of mutual intelligibility.[33]

I encountered an impressive contemporary example of detailed oral history in a PaO village two days' walk east of Kalaw in the Burmese Shan states. At the end of the evening meal, a few villagers asked an elderly man to chant the story of U Aung Tha, perhaps the most famous PaO politician after World War II. U Aung Tha was murdered near Taunggyi in 1948 by unknown assailants. The recitation, which I tape-recorded, lasted more than two hours. Far from being the heroic, swashbuckling epic that I had anticipated, it proved, on translation, to be a far more mundane and exceptionally detailed account of the last days of U Aung Tha. It resembled nothing so much as a meticulous police report detailing when Aung Tha arrived in the village, his companions and what they were wearing, the color of his jeep, whom he spoke to, when he bathed, when several men arrived to ask where they could find him, how they were dressed, the jeep they drove, what they said to Aung Tha's wife, where Aung Tha's body was found, what he was wearing, the identifying ring on his finger, the autopsy findings, and so on. At the end of the recitation, the singer admonished his listeners "to take the example of this true story in order to prevent loss or defect in everything." It was as if every effort had been made, by scrupulously careful oral transmission over half a century, to preserve all the evidence and material facts intact in case a serious police investigation ever took place! I was also surprised to learn that this singer and others throughout PaO areas were paid to chant this story of U Aung Tha's murder at weddings and feasts. Despite being short on histrionics and long on factual detail, it was a popular and revered story.[34]

Oral traditions, then, appear to provide, under certain circumstances, something of the word-for-word constancy of a fixed, written text, together with the potential flexibility of strategic adjustment and change. They can, as it were, have it both ways; they can claim to be precise ur-texts while in fact being substantially novel—and there is no easy way of evaluating this claim.

The reasons for strategic and opportunistic adaptation of oral traditions are manifold. Once it is fully appreciated that any account of custom, genealogy, or history is a situated, interested account, variation over time is the presumed norm. Among the Kachin, where the telling of tales is a matter for professional priests and bards, "every professional tale will occur in several different versions, each tending to uphold the claims of a different vested interest." In the jostling among different Kachin lineages over relative ranking and competing aristocratic claims, each story of the origin of the Kachin, their history, and the spirits they worship takes on a coloring that is designed to promote the interests of a particular lineage. And, as Edmund Leach warns, "There is no 'authentic version' of Kachin tradition, there are merely a number of stories which concern more or less the same set of mythological characters and which make use of the same kinds of structural symbolism . . . but which differ from one another in crucial details according to who is telling the tale."[35] What applies to the kin group or the lineage applies also to larger social units such as an ethnic group. As its situation changes over time, so do its interests, and thus so does its account of its history, customs, and even deities. One would expect that Karen groups living in different settings—adjacent now to the Mon, now to the Thai, now to the Burman or Shan—would develop oral traditions inflected by each of the settings in which they found themselves. To the extent that their precarious political position is subject to sudden and radical change, the pliability of an oral tradition would be a positive advantage. If, as Ronald Renard maintains, Karen culture can "turn on a dime" and is superbly adapted to travel and change, their oral traditions may be at least as useful to this end as shifting cultivation and physical mobility.[36]

Far from being cynically manipulated, let alone manufactured out of whole cloth, the drift of oral traditions is likely to occur by imperceptible degrees, by bards who do not see themselves as embroiderers of the truth. The drift is a case of selective emphasis and omission, as certain accounts seem more important or relevant to current conditions. Here the term *bricolage* applies, inasmuch as variant oral traditions often share the same basic elements, but their arrangement, the emphasis placed on one or another element, and their moral loading convey different meanings.[37] The recitation of genealogical histories by which many hill peoples establish links of alliance or enmity with others is a case in point. Any number of genealogical linkages could be made, so numerous are one's ancestors. A mere eight generations back, patrilineal reckoning yields 255 direct ancestors. Bilateral reckoning would double that to 510. Which of these lines of ancestry to omit, to trace, to emphasize is, in one sense, arbitrary. By one or another tracing, most Americans have Abraham Lincoln as an ancestor. They are just as likely to have John Wilkes Booth in their lineages but are less likely to seek out and emphasize that connection! Simply by strategic selection and emphasis of particular ancestors, it is possible to establish an actual genealogical connection that might help legitimate current alliances. Elaborate genealogies are, in this respect, a vast portfolio of possible connections, most of which remain in the shadows but could, if necessary, be summoned. The more turbulent the social environment, the more frequently groups fission and recombine, the greater the likelihood that more of the portfolio of shadow ancestors will come into play. The Berbers are said to be able to construct a genealogical warrant for virtually any alliance of convenience necessary to politics, grazing rights, or war.[38]

A written genealogy, by contrast, freezes one variant of an evolving oral flux and, as it were, removes it from time, making it available in that form to future generations. The first written political record in Japan (712 CE) is a genealogical history of the great families that was pruned of "untruths," memorized, and then written out as the founding document of an official tradition. Its purpose was precisely to codify a selective and self-interested confection of many oral traditions and to decree it as a permanent sacred history.[39] Henceforth other variants would be considered heterodox. The creation of an official, dynastic genealogy has elsewhere been linked directly to the moment of political centralization. The rise to hegemony of one of the many petty kingdoms of Makassar was, in effect, solidified by the promulgation of a written genealogy "documenting" the quasi-divinity of the victorious ruling family.[40] Early written genealogies are nearly always devised to stabilize a claim to power that eluded such stabilization when it was asserted only orally. Examining the first written genealogies in early historic Scotland, Margaret Nieke captures the difference between oral and written forms:

> Within the traditions of an oral society . . . suitable genealogies could be created with relative ease by deliberate manipulation of the evidence, since there was little in the way of externally validating whatever claims were made. . . . Once recorded in documentary form, a genealogy could establish certain individuals and families as office bearers much more firmly than had ever been the case before. The fabrication of claims to challenge power and position of such individuals would then have necessitated access to those lists which did exist, as well as to the technology whereby alternative versions could be produced.[41]

One could say much the same about the portfolio of possible histories at a group's disposal as about their genealogical options. The possibilities for selection, emphasis, and omission are legion. Take, as a fairly banal example, U.S. relations with Great Britain. The fact that Americans fought two wars with Great Britain (the Revolutionary War and the War of 1812) is generally softpedaled in view of more recent alliances in the twentieth century's world wars and the cold war. Were the United States currently an enemy of the United Kingdom, one imagines that a different historical account would prevail.

The possibilities are, to be sure, as rich for written histories and genealogies as they are for oral histories and genealogies. The difference is that the selective forgetting and remembering is more unobtrusive and smooth in the case of an oral tradition. Within an oral tradition there is simply less friction to impede innovation, and what is in fact quite novel can pass itself off as the voice of tradition without much fear of contradiction.

The Advantage of Not Having a History

If an oral history and genealogy provide more room for maneuver than a written history and genealogy, then perhaps the most radical step of all is to claim virtually no history or genealogy at all. Hjorleifur Jonsson contrasts the Lisu, in this respect, with the Lua' and the Mien. The Lisu, aside from insisting that they kill assertive chiefs, have a radically abbreviated oral history. "Lisu forgetting," Jonsson claims, "is as active as Lua' and Mien remembrance." He implies that the Lisu chose to have virtually no history and that the effect of this choice was to "leave no space for the active role of supra-household structures, such as villages or village clusters in ritual life, social organization, or in the mobilization of people's attention, labor, or resources."[42]

The Lisu strategy radically extends their room for maneuver in two ways. First, any history, any genealogy, even in oral form, represents a strategic positioning vis-à-vis other groups: it is only one of many such possible positionings. A particular choice might prove inconvenient. Adjusting that positioning, even in oral accounts, is not instantaneous. The Lisu, by refusing to pin themselves down to any account of their past — except for their tradition of autonomy — have no position to modify. Their room for maneuver is virtually limitless. But Lisu historylessness is profoundly radical in a second sense. It all but denies "Lisuness" as a category of identity — except perhaps for outsiders. By denying their history — by not carrying the shared history and genealogy that define group identity — the Lisu negate virtually any unit of cultural identity beyond the individual household. The Lisu, one might say, have devised the ultimate "jellyfish" culture and identity by not positioning themselves at all! This option would appear to curtail the possibilities of collective resistance while maximizing their capacity to adapt to a tumultuous environment.

Relatively powerless hill peoples, I have argued, may well find it to their advantage to avoid written traditions and fixed texts, or even to abandon them altogether, in order to maximize their room for cultural maneuver. The shorter their genealogies and histories the less they have to explain and the more they can invent on the spot. In Europe, the case of the Gypsies may be instructive. Widely persecuted, they have no fixed written language but a rich oral tradition in which storytellers are highly revered. They have no fixed history. They have no story they tell about their origins or about a promised land toward which they are headed. They have no shrines, no anthems, no ruins, no monuments. If there were ever a people who needed to be cagey about who they are and where they came from, it is the Gypsies. Shuttling between many countries and scourged in most, the Gypsies have constantly had to adjust their histories and identities in the interest of survival. They are the ultimate bobbing and weaving people.

How much "history" does a people need or want? This brief examination of oral and written histories raises the larger question of what, after all, is the history-bearing social unit, whether that history be oral or written?

Given the existence of a centralized government and a ruling dynasty, it seems apparent that rulers would want to craft claims (even if fabricated) for their legitimacy and ancientness by genealogies, court legends, poetry, epics, and hymns of praise. It is hard to imagine any institutional claim to naturalness and inevitability that does not rely in large part on history, oral or written. A similar case can be made for virtually any social ranking. The claim that one particular lineage should be ranked above another or that a particular town ought to be privileged over another, if it is not to seem arbitrary, or based on raw power, will be justified by reference to history and legends. One might even say that assertions of superior rank or inequalities beyond a single generation necessarily require a historical warrant. Such claims need not be written or oral; they may rest, as they often do in the hills, on the possession of valued regalia, gongs, drums, seals, heirlooms, even heads, the display of which on ceremonial occasions represents such a claim. Sedentary communities, even if they are not strongly ranked, are likely not only to have a story about their founding and past but to historicize their claim to their fields and house lots to the extent that those have become valuable property.

What, however, of people living at the margins of the state, in unranked lineages, and moving their fields frequently, as swiddeners typically do? Does it not follow that such peoples might not only prefer an oral history for its plasticity but might need less history altogether? First, the "history-bearing unit" itself, including lineages, may be shifting and problematic. Second, whatever the history-bearing unit might be, it is for swiddeners likely to have little in the way of entrenched historical privileges to defend and many strategic reasons to leave their history open to improvisation.

In his classic book on oral history, Jan Vansina makes a persuasive case along these lines in contrasting the oral traditions of neighboring Burundi and Rwanda. They have much in common, but Burundi is far less hierarchical and centralized and has, as a result, Vansina claims, far less oral history than centralized Rwanda. Burundi, unlike Rwanda, had no royal genealogy, no court songs, no dynastic poetry.

> The fluidity of the whole political system is striking. There was nothing to favor the rise of detailed oral traditions: no provincial history because provinces were unstable, no histories of important families because besides the royal family [a usurper with little authority] there were none, and no centralized government hence no official historians. . . . It was in everyone's interest to forget the past. The former senior regent of the country told me that history was of no interest at court so there were practically no historical accounts. The political system shows why.[43]

Written and oral cultures are not mutually exclusive; no oral culture is untouched by texts, and no text-based society lacks a parallel and sometimes resistant oral tradition. As with wet-rice agriculture and swiddening, or with hierarchical and relatively egalitarian social forms, it may be more useful to speak of oscillation. As the advantages of text-based states grew, stateless societies may have moved toward literacy and writing; as these advantages diminished, stateless peoples may have remained or moved toward more exclusively oral traditions.

The relationship of a people, a kinship group, and a community to its history is diagnostic of its relationship to stateness. All groups have some kind of history, some story they tell themselves about who they are and how they came to be situated where they are. After this common ground, the similarity ends. Peripheral, acephalous groups are likely to emphasize itineraries, defeats, migrations, landscapes. Rank, heroic origins, and claims to territory are, by contrast, the stuff of centralization and (would-be) state formation. The form traditions take also varies. Written traditions are of enormous instrumental value to the process of permanent political centralization and administration. Oral traditions, on the other hand, have substantial advantages for peoples whose welfare and survival depend on a fleet-footed adjustment to a capricious and menacing political environment. Finally, there would seem to be something of a difference in how much history a people choose to have. The Lisu and Karen, for example, seem to prefer to travel lightly and to bring along as little excess historical baggage as possible. Like skippers of tramp steamers, they know from experience that they cannot be sure what their next port of call might be.

Stateless peoples are typically stigmatized by neighboring cultures as "peoples without history," as lacking the fundamental characteristic of civilization, namely historicity.[44] The charges are wrong on two counts. First, the stigmatization presupposes that only written history counts as a narrative of identity and a common past. Second, and more important, how much history a people have, far from indicating their low stage of evolution, is always an active choice, one that positions them vis-à-vis their powerful text-based neighbors.

CHAPTER 7

Ethnogenesis
A Radical Constructionist Case

Ernest Renan was right when he wrote over a century ago: "Forgetting, and I would even say historical error, are an essential factor in the creation of a nation, and so it is that progress in historical studies is often a danger to nationality." That is, I believe, a fine task for historians: to be a danger to national myths.
—Eric Hobsbawm, *Nations and Nationalism since 1780*

There is nothing more universally modern than purveyors of ancient identities.
—Charles King

The Tribes are by no means to be found together in separate colonies, but are mixed up quite indiscriminately. Moreover, among their [Kachin] villages are also to be found Palaung, "La," Wa, Chinese, and a few Shans.
—J. G. Scott, *Gazetteer of Upper Burma and the Shan States*

The Incoherence of Tribe and Ethnicity

L ike any heir who had come into a large estate, the British proceeded, as elsewhere, to take inventory of their new possessions in Burma. If the cadastral survey was the instrument for inventorying the real estate, the census was the instrument for enumerating the peoples inherited through conquest.

Once they came to the hills, the administrators in charge of the 1911 and subsequent censuses were faced with a baroque complexity that all but defeated their mania for classificatory order. How to proceed when most of the "tribal" designations were exonyms applied by outsiders and not used at all by the people so designated? Different outsiders seldom agreed on a common term. Furthermore, such exonyms were either derogatory ("slaves," "dog-eaters") or generic in a geographical sense ("hill people," "upstream people"). Take, for example, the Marus along the border with China in the Northern Shan states described by J. G. Scott in the *Gazetteer of Upper Burma*. They did not call themselves Kachin, nor did the "authorities," but their neighbors insisted that they were indeed "Kachin." "They dress and intermarry with 'Kachin' [Jingpo] but their language is closer to Burmese than Jingpo."[1] What should they be called in the census?

The operationalization of "race" in the 1911 and 1931 censuses was, in fact, language. According to the linguistic theories of the time, it was "accepted as dogma that those who speak a particular language form a unique, definable unit and that this unit had a particular culture and a particular history."[2] With the equation of "tribe" or "race" (the two were used interchangeably in the census) and "mother tongue," the fun had just begun. The trainers of the enumerators had to point out very carefully that the "mother tongue" was the language "spoken from the cradle" and might "not be the language spoken ordinarily in the home"; this last was to be recorded as a subsidiary language. Except for Burmans at the padi-state core who were generally monolingual, bilingualism among minority hill peoples was the rule rather than the exception. Those with Karen, Shan, or other (non-Burman) Tibeto-Burman languages as their mother tongues were typically bilingual, and often trilingual.[3] Nor did the complexity dissolve at the microcosmic level of a single village. In a single "Kachin" village of a mere 130 households were found no fewer than six "mother tongues," though the villagers used Jingpaw as a lingua franca on the order of Malay or Swahili.[4]

The equation of mother tongue with tribe and history assumes implicitly that the spoken language is the constant, steady thread that knits together a people. And yet the authors of the census go out of their way to note the "extreme instability of language and racial distinctions in Burma." In an exasperated and instructive, not to say entertaining, appendix to the census titled "A Note on Indigenous Races in Burma," J. H. Green goes further:

> Some of the races or "tribes" in Burma change their language almost as often as they change their clothes. Languages are changed by conquest, by absorption, by isolation, and by the general tendency to adopt the language of a neighbor who is considered to belong to a more powerful, more numerous, or more advanced tribe or race. . . . Races are becoming more and more mixed, and the threads are more and more difficult to untangle.
>
> The unreliability of the language test for race has again become apparent in this census.[5]

The conclusion, obvious to Edmund Leach if not to the designers of the census, is that language groups were not established by heredity, nor were they stable over time. This use of language to infer history was therefore "nonsense." It is a conclusion shared by most who have considered the issue closely.[6]

Again and again one encounters the frustration of those taking the inventory of peoples but, to their dismay, confronting an apparent mess. A tidy, objective, and systematic classification of tribes would require, they believed, a stable trait, or traits, that all members of a tribe shared and that were not to be found outside that tribe. If mother tongue would not serve this purpose, neither would, it turned out, most other traits. It was clear enough that there were "Kachin," and Karen, and Chin; what was not clear was where one began and another ended, and whether they had been Kachin, Karen, and Chin in the previous generation or whether they would remain so in the next.

The large group (7.5 million in China alone) known as Miao and the related Hmong in Thailand and Laos present a case in point. They speak three major languages, and within each of those languages there are dialects that are mutually unintelligible. Beyond that, most Miao men and many Miao women can speak three languages or more. There are self-identified Miao groups who dwell in valleys growing irrigated rice, and others at higher altitudes swiddening (opium, maize, buckwheat, oats, potatoes), foraging, and hunting. There are Miao who have largely adopted Chinese dress, rituals, and language and others in remote, isolated locations, who, while still bearing often archaic features of Sinitic culture, have held themselves apart from lowland practices. At the micro level of an individual village, the same cultural "sprawl" is evident. Intermarriage between Miao and other groups (Khmu, Lisu, Chinese, Tai, Karen, Yao, and so on) is extremely common, as is adoption from other groups.[7] Even those characteristics that many Miao believe distinguish them culturally, such as cattle sacrifices and reed organ pipes, are in fact shared with others. Not a little of this sprawl derives from the fact that in parts of China, Han officials used the term *Miao* to designate any groups that were rebellious and refused to submit to Han administration. Over time, this appellation, reinforced by state routines of administration, has stuck; the "Miao" are often those people called Miao by powerful others—by those, that is, who can to a great extent impose their categories.

The diversity of the Karen is no less daunting. No single trait such as religion, clothing, burial rituals, or even a shared intelligible language applies to all of them. Each of the subdivisions of the Karen also displays an amazing variety. As Martin Smith notes, "the term 'Sgaw Karen' could today apply equally to a Burmese-speaking, University of Rangoon graduate, born and brought up in Bassein in the Delta, and an illiterate, animist, hill-tribesman in the Dawna Range [near the Thai border] who has never even met an ethnic Burman."[8] The Karen practices of adoption and intermarriage across ethnic groups, though perhaps less widespread than among the Miao or Yao, are nevertheless quite common. Nor does it appear that "Karenness" is necessarily an exclusive ethnic identity. In Thailand, at least, according to Charles Keyes, it is possible for someone to be "Karen" in a domestic, village, and church setting and to be "Thai at the market, in politics, and in interaction with Thais. Much the same is true, he believes, for the routinely frictionless movement between Thai and Chinese identities, between Thai and Khmer, Thai and Lao. Karen and many other minorities often appear to be ethnic amphibians, able to pass between such identities without a sense of conflict. Living in close symbiosis with another cultural complex, ethnic amphibians learn, often consummately, the performance required in each setting. Keyes points also to the Lua/Lawa, swiddeners and animists, who speak a Mon-Khmer tongue at home but who are so versed in the Thai language, lowland cultivation techniques, and Buddhism that they can become Thais virtually overnight when they move to the valley. Faced with the cultural plenitude of Karenness, Keyes takes the next logical step of minimizing the importance of shared cultural traits and declares that ethnicity is a self-making project. As he puts it, "ethnic identity itself [that is, its assertion] provides the defining cultural characteristic of ethnic groups." Those who adopt this identity—assuming that other Karens accept it—become ipso facto Karen.[9]

What is clear beyond any reasonable doubt is that the trait-based desiderata of ethnicity find little traction in highland Southeast Asia. Even the desideratum of hilliness per se and the swiddening and dispersal that go with it are not completely satisfactory. Most of the Kachin, the Miao, and the Karen, it is true, are associated with hill residence and swiddening. Many of their rituals derive from "fire-field farming" and from hunting and foraging. But at the same time, a considerable number of self-identified Kachin, Miao, and Karen have come to occupy different subsistence niches, including fixed-field, irrigated padi cultivation, and have adopted other features of lowland residence, including the language of the padi core.

A major reason why trait-based designations of ethnic or tribal identity fail utterly to make sense of actual affiliations is precisely that hill groups themselves, as manpower systems, absorbed whomever they could. This absorptive capacity led to great cultural diversity within hill societies. The adoption of newcomers, rapid social mobility for captives, and genealogical sleight of hand fostered hill systems that were culturally accommodating. Even the presumably distinctive ranked segmentary lineage system of the Kachin, far from being rigid, was deployed to incorporate neighboring Lisu and Chinese. It was, as François Robinne has argued, a striking example of pluriethnic inclusiveness.[10]

The failure of any trait or complex of traits to draw a bright boundary around a "tribe" is reflected in the bewilderment of those whose job it was to create a Linnaean classification of peoples. Thus one could write of the struggle of colonial officials, confronted with the diversity of the Naga Hills (now on the Burma-India border), "to make sense of the ethnographic chaos they perceived around them: hundreds, if not thousands, of small villages seemed to be somewhat similar to each other but also very different, by no means always sharing their customs, political system, art or even language."[11] The confusion was genuine and four-barreled. First, any particular trait was likely to be a gradient and occasionally a seamless continuum from one village or group to another. Lacking sharp, discontinuous changes in ritual, dress, building styles, or even language, any line of demarcation was arbitrary. Second, if one did in fact meticulously chart small variations and then try, conscientiously, to justify a particular trait boundary, another nearly insurmountable problem arose. The boundaries for trait A, B, and C did not map onto one another; each yielded a different line of demarcation, a different classification of "ethnicities." The third and fatal difficulty was that any such trait-mapped ethnicities were unlikely to coincide with the phenomenological understandings of the tribal people whose life-world was being mapped. The colonial ethnographers' map said they were A, but they said they were B and had always been. How could that not matter? And if the classification exercise somehow survived these blows, a fourth difficulty, time, would surely be the coup de grâce. Those with some sense of historical change understood that in terms of traits or in terms of self-identification, the A had, not so long ago, been B and seemed, alarmingly, now on their way to becoming C. How could an ethnic group, a tribe, be so radically unstable over time and still be a people?

The radical flux of identity should, in one respect, occasion little surprise. Zomia is and has been what might be called a "fracture zone" of state-making, much like the Caucasus and the Balkans. It has been peopled for two millennia at least by wave after wave of people in retreat and flight from state cores—from invasion, slave raids, epidemics, and corvée. There, in this zone of refuge, they joined a hill population located in a geographical setting of such ruggedness and relative isolation that it encouraged the drift of dialects, customs, and identity. The great variety of subsistence techniques, keyed in large part to altitude, only encouraged this diversity. Add to this the exchange of populations within the hills by slaving, raiding, intermarriage, and adoption, and the complexity of identities is compounded, helping to explain the crazy-quilt pattern encountered by the colonizers. The conclusion reached by Geoffrey Benjamin and Cynthia Chou, contemplating an analogous flux in the Malay Peninsula, applies equally to Zomia: "The interflow of genes, ideas, and languages has been so intensive and multidirectional as to render futile any attempt to delineate the various 'peoples' in terms of completely distinct bundles of geographical, linguistic, biological, or cultural-historical features."[12] This radical undermining would seem to leave us at an impasse. There is, clearly, no such thing as a "tribe" in the strong sense of the word— no objective genealogical, genetic, linguistic, or cultural formula that will unambiguously distinguish one "tribe" from another. But, we might well ask, who is confused? The historian and the colonial ethnographer might be mystified. The mixed villages in northern Burma were "anathema to the tidy bureaucratic officials" who, until, the last moment of imperial rule, were still trying in vain to draw administrative lines between the Kachins and Shans.[13] But hill people were not confused; they were in no doubt who they were and who they were not! Not sharing the researcher's or administrator's mania for mutually exclusive and exhaustive categories, hill people were not paralyzed by identities that were plural and variable over time. On the contrary, as we shall see, the ambiguity and porosity of identities was and is, for them, a political resource.

There are, of course, "tribes" in the lived experience of hill peoples. Self-identified Karen, Kachin, Hmong, and others have fought and died for identities that many believe have a deep and continuous history, a belief that would probably not stand up to critical scrutiny. Such powerful identities are, in this respect, no less fictitious and constructed than most national identities in the modern world.

The only viable analytical alternative is to take such self-identifications as our point of departure. As was proposed nearly forty years ago, we must treat tribal divisions as "essentially political in origin." Ethnic identity on this reading is a political project. When, as Michael Moerman noted, hill peoples in Thailand such as Karen, Tai, Lawa, Palaung, and T'in are in an ecological situation that allows a choice "among major bases and symbols of ethnicity [such] as religion and type of farming, as well as among such emblems as dialect, diet, and dress," the key question becomes what calculations govern that choice.[14]

The perspective adopted and elaborated here is a radical constructionist one: that ethnic identities in the hills are politically crafted and designed to position a group vis-à-vis others in competition for power and resources. In a world crowded with other actors, most of whom, like modern states, are more powerful than they, their freedom of invention is severely constricted. They craft identities, but not in circumstances of their own choosing, to paraphrase Marx. The positioning in question is above all a positioning vis-à-vis the lowland state and other hill peoples. That is the function of hill identities. Those who, over many centuries, migrated into Zomia were, in effect, refusing assimilation into the lowland states as peasants. In coming to the hills, they joined a population that had never been incorporated in a lowland state or one that had left it a long time ago. The basic choice was between statelessness and incorporation. Within each of these choices there were, of course, several possible calibrated variations. This perspective has been persuasively articulated by Hjorleifur Jonsson, who, in his important study of the Mien in northern Thailand, relates "how people have moved among the categories of state-subjects and non-subject clients in the forest, as well as from being autonomous uplanders dividing into two social directions, some becoming state clients and others abandoning village life for foraging in small bands. This relates back to the general case of a shifting social landscape, and how people move among structural categories, in and out of particular relationships, repeatedly reformulating the parameters of their identities, communities, and histories."[15] On this view, what imperial administrators and census takers saw as an exasperating confusion could more appropriately be seen as evidence of how subsistence routines, social structures, and identities could be deployed to express a "positionality" vis-à-vis the major lowland states.

Ethnic and "tribal" identity, in the nineteenth century and much of the twentieth, has been associated with nationalism and the aspiration, often thwarted, to statehood. And today, the utter institutional hegemony of the nation-state as a political unit has encouraged many ethnic groups in Zomia to aspire to their own nation-statehood. But what is novel and noteworthy for most of this long history in the hills is that ethnic and tribal identities have been put to the service not merely of autonomy but of statelessness. The paradox of "antistate nationalism," if it might be called that, is typically overlooked. But it must have been a very common, perhaps the most common, basis for identity until, say, the nineteenth century, when, for the first time, a life outside the state came to seem hopelessly utopian. E. J. Hobsbawm, in his perceptive study of nationalism, took note of these important exceptions: "One might even argue that the peoples with the most powerful and lasting sense of what might be called 'tribal' ethnicity not merely resisted the imposition of the modern state, national or otherwise, but very commonly any state: as witness the Pushtun-speakers in and around Afghanistan, the pre-1745 Scots highlanders, the Atlas Berbers, and others who will come readily to mind."[16]

The most significant others who ought to come readily to mind are, of course, the innumerable hill peoples of Zomia who have been avoiding states for more than a millennium. It is perhaps because they have fought and fled under so many names, in so many locations, and against so many states, traditional, colonial, and modern, that their struggle lacked the single banner that would have easily identified it.

State-Making as a Cosmopolitan Ingathering

The founders of the early padi state had to assemble their subjects from among hitherto stateless populations. And when, as so often happened, a state disintegrated, subsequent state-makers had to reassemble subjects from among the shards available by raiding other states or incorporating stateless hill peoples. Earlier "wave" theories of migration supposed that large numbers of Burmans and Tais swept down from the north into the alluvial plateaus suitable for irrigated rice and defeated or chased off the earlier inhabitants. This view, now discredited for lack of evidence, implicitly assumed that the Burmans and Tais came as whole societies, rulers and subjects, to establish themselves as conquerors. It now appears far more plausible that the Burmans and Tai who appeared were a kind of militarily and politically adept pioneer elite with the skills to organize and dominate a padi core. Their subjects, on this reading, were gathered in from the surrounding stateless hills and confected into the node of power we have called the padi state. Providing that we take the long view, then, most of the people today known as Shan are ex–hill people who have, over time, been completely incorporated into the Shan valley polity. Most of those who appear today as Burman are the descendants—recent or long ago—of non-Burman populations from both hill and valley (Shan, Kachin, Mon, Khmer, Pyu, Chin, Karen, and so on). Most Thai are, in the same fashion, ex–hill people, and, on the longest view, the creation of "Hanness" itself should be seen as the most successful, long-term, state-based ingathering of all time. The early need for manpower was such that none of these states could afford to be too particular about where its subjects came from.

The most carefully observed and elaborated model of such ingathering comes to us from the studies of the Malay maritime trading center—the *negeri*—largely because Europeans have been describing it since before the sixteenth century. Designed as an "interstitial" polity to mediate between hill collectors and international trade, and to defend its strategic location, the negeri amassed manpower both by force and by the attraction of commercial gain. Its water-borne slaving expeditions cast a wide net, and the captives thus assembled were incorporated into the negeri. The formula for full incorporation was minimal: becoming a retainer of a Malay chief, professing Islam, and speaking Malay, the lingua franca of trade in the archipelago. A negeri was less an ethnicity than a political formula for membership in the polity. As a result of the vagaries of trading and raiding, each Malay trading negeri took on a different cultural complexion depending on the mix of peoples it had incorporated over time: Minangkabau, Batak, Bugis, Acehnese, Javanese, Indian, and Arab traders and so on. At its most successful, a negeri such as Melaka would become a magnet for traders from far away, rivaling Venice. Its radical dependence on fluctuating overseas trade, however, made the negeri a very fragile affair.

The small Tai or Shan *muang* (polity), though somewhat less vulnerable to radical oscillations in trading fortunes, resembled the negeri in many respects.[17] It was in constant competition with its neighbors and larger states for manpower. It too captured or admitted its subjects without regard to their background. It too was highly stratified but open to rapid social mobility. The terms of full membership were the profession of Theravada Buddhism—another universal religion—padi cultivation, fealty to a Tai lord, and the ability to speak the local Tai language.

The small Tai and Shan statelets spread all the way from northern Vietnam across Zomia to northeastern India. Because they were so numerous and so small, they represent a much-observed laboratory for many padi-state processes that have also operated historically on the Burmese, Thai (the most successful of the Tai states!), and even Han states.

It is a rare historian or ethnographer who has not remarked on the degree to which many—in some cases most—Tai and Shan commoners were, as Leach puts it, "descendants of hill tribesmen who have in the recent past been assimilated into the sophisticated ways of Buddhist-Shan culture."[18]

Georges Condominas much later echoed the view that "especially in the Shan states and other Tay [Tai] principalities, the bulk of the population remained composed of non-Tay."[19] In keeping with the openness of the muang, the non-Tai who lived there could use their own language as well as Tai and follow their own customs.

The combination of slavery and fluid social mobility—and the alchemy with which ex–hill people became valley Shan or Tai (or Burman or Thai)—was such that historians have been careful to distinguish these forms of bondage from those of their New World counterparts.[20] Leach describes a typical process of entry through bondage. Kachins, as individuals or as groups, enter the service of Shans as laborers or soldiers and, in recompense, acquire Shan wives. By settling in the valley and adopting the rituals of the new place (his Shan wife's local spirit guardians or nats), he severs his link to his Kachin kinsmen and enters the Shan system of stratification at the bottom. Shan terms for Kachin in general incorporated a prefix (*kha*) meaning serf, and Leach estimates that "nearly all low class Shans" in the Kachin Hills area were "of slave [captive] or commoner Kachin origin."[21] Observing over a slightly longer time frame, Condominas shows that ex–hill people entering the Tai system as slaves became, before long, commoners with other Tai. And if, in the course of a power struggle, one of them managed to seize power, he was given a noble Tai name and his genealogy was reworked to bring his origin into line with his power.[22] So despite a Tai saying declaring that "a Kha [serf] is as different from a monkey as a Tai is from a Kha," the formulas for citizenship in this intensively competitive polity avoided practices that would drive its population away.

But the generalized practice of raiding and slavery could lead to a more rapid transformation of a polity. A visitor to Chiang Mai in 1836 described a Shan chief who had twenty-eight wives, all taken as captives, while his subordinates had themselves seized women as well. With the majority of wives of alien origin, J. G. Scott reports that "the physical features of the inhabitants of a locality might completely change in a couple of generations, and the language as well, for the mothers teach the children." He adds that for years it had been the Shan custom for Shan chiefs to have "Chinese, Burmese, Karen, and Kachin wives, sometimes captured, sometimes bought, sometimes received as presents. Occasionally, the issue of such unions took power, with the result that often a Sawbwa is of a different race than the bulk of his subjects."[23]

Another route to "Shanness" or "Tainess," which is to say to hierarchy and stateness, had a more wholesale quality to it. This was for a successful Kachin chief to transform his more "open-rank" egalitarian realm into a petty Shan-style kingdom. Much of Leach's classical work is devoted to this theme. Typically, the strategy involved a powerful Kachin chief taking a wife from an aristocratic Shan lineage. This marriage, while it transformed the Kachin chief overnight into a Shan prince, at the same time barred him from continuing to give wives to Kachin lineages without prejudicing his status as a Shan prince. The effect was to prevent his compatriot Kachin lineages from achieving status by contracting marriages with his (chiefly) lineage. His Kachin followers then had a choice between acquiescing in the transformation and, in effect, becoming Shan commoners; revolting and killing or driving off the chief; or leaving and founding a new community. It is this logic that Leach traces out so brilliantly.[24] Wherever a Kachin chief found himself in a position to collect tribute regularly from traders and lowlanders, he inevitably tried to set himself up as a petty Shan Sawbwa, not always successfully.

This process of petty state-making, of turning hill people into valley people, could, it seems clear, just as easily be reversed. The Tai/Shan statelets were at least as vulnerable as the larger padi states to the decomposing forces of invasion, famine, tyrannical rule, raids, and civil wars of succession. What became of the dispersed population of a collapsed Shan statelet? Many, it seems from the evidence, may have moved to more hospitable Shan states within striking distance. Many others, perhaps especially the "recently" ex-Kachin and ex-Lisu, must have returned to the hills, resumed swiddening, and readopted their prior identities. This would have been a relatively easy and familiar option and would not have prevented them from returning to the padi core when it became safe to do so. It makes sense to see this ethnic transformation, before the twentieth century at least, as a two-way street and ethnic identities as dual or amphibious.

For a great many hill people in Southeast Asia, the lowland state identity closest at hand was the Tai muang, a "low church" version of the more distant, "high" models available from the Han, Burman, and Thai courts. A successful valley state would attract Kachin, Lisu, Akha, Wa, Khmu, Lue, Mien, and many other hill peoples to a new identity that was, one suspects, less definitive or permanent than becoming a subject of a much larger kingdom. For some ethnic groups, located in the interstices of two or more padi states, there were more risks and more choices. This seems to have been the situation of the Karen, especially the Pwo Karen, located between the Mon, Burman, and Thai padi states. Much of the Burman population of lower

Burma was undoubtedly of Mon or Karen origin, and a convincing case has been made that the Karen are culturally, and strategically, medially positioned between these three valley states, able, with little friction, to move between one identity and another.[25] The Karen have both exploited this medial position and suffered grievously from it. While they have boasted of their role as agents and representatives of the Thai court in exacting tribute from other hill peoples in elegiac terms—"Our administration was so oppressive and the taxes so heavy that the tumplines of the carrying baskets rang like guitar strings when the people were bringing in their tribute"—they were the first to pay a heavy price as a suspected Thai "fifth column" during the devastating Burmese invasions of Siam.[26]

If, as seems evident, group boundaries are porous and identities flexible, then we would expect that they would shift over time as one identity became increasingly advantageous and another less so. Such seems clearly to have been the case recently with the Zhuang, a Tai language–speaking group and, today, one of the largest official minority groups in China. Perhaps driven, like other groups, into hilly southwest China by Han expansion, the Zhuang considered themselves a valley people like other Tai. They settled at generally lower altitudes below the swiddening Yi, Miao, and Yao. They came to occupy—or better stated, to create—a cultural niche intermediate between the Han and the highlanders above them. The saying was: "The Miao live at the head of the mountain; the Zhuang at the head of the river, and the Han at the head of the street."[27] Over time, the hitherto stigmatized Zhuang invented a mythical Han origin for themselves and, in effect, "played Han" to the minorities above them. The revolutionary government's new delineation of nationalities according to Stalinist criteria, however, identified them, mostly on the grounds of language, as "Zhuang." This seemed at first a new stigmatization, and most putative Zhuang resisted the classification, claiming instead that they were "Han who can speak the Zhuang language." In the 1953 census most Zhuang-speakers did not self-identify as Zhuang. The party created Zhuang administrative districts despite vernacular, folk understandings at variance with their categories.

Under the new minority policy, however, there were substantial new advantages to a "Zhuang" identity: new political and administrative posts, preferential access to technical schools and higher education, and exemption from the "one-child" policy. Suddenly, the cash value of an official Zhuang identity skyrocketed to a point where it more than compensated for the possible stigma, and the new identity took hold. The "Zhuang-Han," of course, were still, in a vernacular sense, Zhuang-and-Han, but one side of their Janus-faced identity, the official side, had become more valuable. The new dispensation reversed what had apparently been a process of gradual Sinicization of the "Zhuang."

To see the growth of the valley states as the product of certain techniques of cosmopolitan ingathering, some more coercive and some less so, is decentering. It serves to correct the more ethnic understanding of statemaking that characterized both early historiography and modern nationalist histories. Shan culture, Leach concluded, "is not to be regarded as a complex imported into the area ready-made from somewhere outside, as most authorities seem to have supposed. It is an indigenous growth resulting from the economic interaction of small scale military colonies with an indigenous hill population over a long period."[28] Much the same could be said for the Burmese and Siamese precolonial states at their most successful. Each was an effective political formula for the gathering and holding of populations from various linguistic and cultural origins at the padi core—for creating a concentrated, productive force suitable for state-building. As suggested earlier, the Burmese and Siamese were to the numerous and varied populations they incorporated as the two thousand conquering Norman families were to the indigenous peoples of Britain.

Burmese and Thai polities are, then, best seen as recipes for statemaking rather than as ethnic projects. First, there were, it appears, no massive wholesale invasions from the north eliminating or replacing the previous inhabitants. Second, if we squint a bit at the cultural foundations of the precolonial padi state, they make best sense as frameworks for state space rather than as ethnicized markers. The keystone, of course, is the technique of irrigated rice cultivation that makes possible a padi core in the first place. It was not, however, a technique exclusive to the Burmese and Tai, inasmuch as it had been the basis of the Khmer, Pyu, and Mon courts earlier. The cosmology and architecture of the Indic court center is, as it were, the ideological superstructure of the divine monarchy and was adapted for that purpose. Theravada Buddhism, another import, served as a universal domain, to assemble "ethnic deities and spirits" under a new hegemon, much as the padi state's subjects were gathered around the court. Local spirits (nat, phi) were accommodated as subsidiary deities much as Catholicism accommodated pagan deities under the rubric of the saints. Even the languages of the state-builders, Burmese and Thai, were, in their written form (from Sanskrit via Pali), linked to the legitimating cosmology of Buddhism and the Indic state. Much of what passes as the ethnic particularity and distinctiveness of the Shan, Burmese, and Thai cultures is closely tied to the basic devices for state-building. Put another way, "stateness" is built into the foundations of ethnicity. Reciprocally, in the Shan, Burmese, and Thai view, much of the ethnicity of those populations in the hills, those not-yet-gathered-in, consists precisely in their statelessness.

Valleys Flatten

The great distinction, culturally, between the valley kingdoms and the hills is the striking uniformity of valley society religiously, linguistically, and, over time, ethnically as well. While the historical process of ingathering was a cosmopolitan enterprise, the population thus assembled came to share a set of common cultural practices and institutions. One could travel hundreds of miles within the padi state and still encounter religious practices, architecture, class structures, forms of governance, dress, language, and ritual that were strikingly similar from one end to the other. By contrast, traveling even a short distance in the hills would expose one to a crazy-quilt of languages, rituals, and identities. Valley systems, in the words of Hjorleifur Jonsson, are centripetal, while hill systems are centrifugal. This "sharp contrast between the rather uniform lowland areas and a bewildering variety of the upland areas" is not, he insists, the result of different migrations but rather the systematically different social outcomes of the centripetal tendencies of closed-rank systems, on the one hand, and the centrifugal tendencies of open-rank systems on the other.[29]

This cultural distinction not only marks off the hills from the great valley kingdoms of the Burmese, Thai, Han, and Vietnamese; it is just as notable in the contrast between the Shan statelets and their hilly neighbors. Leach highlighted this discrepancy a half-century earlier and pointed to the probable cause:

> The hill people who are neighbors to the Shans are astonishingly varied in their culture; the Shans, considering their wide dispersal and their scattered form of settlement, are astonishingly uniform. My argument is that this uniformity of Shan culture is correlated with a uniformity of Shan political organization which is in turn largely determined by the special economic facts of the Shan situation. My historical assumption is that the valley Shans have everywhere, for centuries past, been assimilating their hill neighbors, but the unchanging economic factors in the situation have meant that the pattern of assimilation has everywhere been very similar. Shan culture itself has been modified relatively little.[30]

The uniformity of the petty Shan kingdoms lies, as Leach implies, in the fact that they are miniature state spaces geographically, economically, and politically.

Each of the Shan states lies between six hundred and nine hundred meters in a valley or plain, "some long and narrow, some rounded like a cup, some flattened like a saucer, some extensive enough to suggest the Irrawaddy Valley on a miniature scale."[31] As in the larger valleys, each of these areas was suitable for wet-rice cultivation, and Shanness became synonymous with padi planting. The compacting of people and grain in the small core area made possible state formation on a correspondingly small scale. Padi planting, however, had other decisive social effects. Strong reliance on a single crop, as in the larger valleys, comes to dominate the work routines and social organization of much of the population. Each household planted, transplanted, weeded, and harvested the same crop at virtually the same time, and in much the same way. Coordination of water use required a certain level of institutionalized cooperation and dispute settlement. Agricultural uniformity, in turn, facilitated ritual uniformity around the padi plant itself, its harvest rituals and the control of water. A padi-planting society also shaped a common material culture—diet, cuisine, farm implements, plow animals, household architecture, and so on.[32]

Permanent padi-field cultivation also leads to systems of landed property and inheritance and the social class distinctions they foster. Inequalities per se do not distinguish the valleys from the hills. Status differences and inequalities abound in the hills, but in contrast to inequality in the padi state, they are not underwritten by inherited inequalities of property enforced, if need be, by the coercive power of a rudimentary state. The homogenizing effects of a common agrarian regime and a class system were frequently punctuated by rebellion, which typically reproduced the previous social order under new management. The only structural alternative was flight to the common-property regime and the open-ranked systems of the hills.

Social and cultural homogeneity in the valley state was also an artifact of the political sway possible over a padi zone in which the friction of terrain was low. It permitted the creation and maintenance of a common institutional order, as well as the density of trade and exchange that fostered cultural integration. Power could be projected far more easily across this geographical space than across the heterogeneous hills. Precisely because it exercised many of the same functions, albeit on a miniature scale, as the great valley states, the Shan realm's palace, ritual, and cosmology constituted a provincial imitation of the palace, ritual, and cosmology at Ava, Amarapura, and Mandalay.

The process of valley homogenization throughout Southeast Asia, Victor Lieberman claims, was much advanced by increasing state centralization between 1600 and 1840. A combination of imitative state-building modeled on the West and enlarged revenues from international trade allowed the mainland state to stamp out religious heterodoxy, create a more uniform and efficient tax regime and administration, and promote kingdomwide economic integration and militarization.[33] Advances in firearms, military organization, land surveying, record keeping, and the dissemination of texts had, on a modest scale, the same distance-demolishing effects as railroads, steam power, and the telegraph were to have later in the nineteenth century. While the valley states were busy fabricating more uniform Burmese, Siamese, Vietnamese, and Shan, the hills continued to fabricate further differences, heterogeneity, and new identities.

Identities: Porosity, Plurality, Flux

Most hill people in mainland Southeast Asia, before the colonial state insisted on classifying them, did not have what we might consider "proper" ethnic identities. They often identified themselves by a place name—the people of X valley, the people of Y watershed—or by kin group or lineage. And to be sure, their identity would vary depending on whom they were addressing. Many names were implicitly relational—the "uphill" people, the people of the "west ridge"—and their designation made sense only as one element in a relational set. Still other names were exonyms used by outsiders—as was often the case for the Miao—having no further meaning except in that context. Identities were, to complicate matters further, plural; most hill people had a repertoire of identities they could deploy in different contexts. And such identities as there were, were subject to change: "Ethnic identity and language differences have tended to be fluid in mainland Southeast Asia. A group could change *both* in a relatively short period of time as a result of being in close contact with other peoples."[34] A certain plasticity of identity was built into precolonial power relations. Many valley peoples, as well as hill peoples, found themselves located between two or more power centers whose waxing and waning influence shaped their world. Before the advent of modern statecraft, with its practices of territorial administration and mutually exclusive sovereignties and ethnicities, such ambiguities were common.

Flexible identities also characterized systems of social stratification in which those of lower status sought to emulate, or at least to defer to, powerful others of higher status. In his analysis of a Tai area of northern Vietnam, Grant Evans notes the duality of identities and how they are deployed.[35] Thus a low-status group, the Sing Moon, considered serfs by the Black-Tai, speak Tai in addition to their own language, have a Tai name as well as their own "ethnic" name, and generally emulate the Tai. The Black-Tai, for their part, in the past emulated Vietnamese mandarin dress and incorporated Vietnamese vocabulary, while the higher-status White-Tai went so far as to adopt Vietnamese funeral ritual and to assimilate into Vietnamese society through intermarriage. Tai elites in general, Evans shows, are culturally amphibious; they deploy the strongly Tai side of their identity when exercising power over their nominally Tai equals and inferiors and the Vietnamese side when dealing with those above them. His point is that identities are plural and that they are systematically structured by relations of power and prestige. This general theme is elaborated with great subtlety by Jonsson in his analysis of the Mien (Yao) of northern Thailand, who embody several registers of self-representation, each of which can be strategically enacted, depending on the context.[36]

Quite apart from the confusion of colonial officials and census takers, later ethnographers and historians of Burma have only confirmed Leach's earlier judgment that ethnic boundaries are labile, porous, and largely artificial. Thus, for example, different observers could classify the same group of people as "Karen," "Lawa," or "Thai" depending on the criteria used and the purposes of the classification. Where different peoples had long lived in close proximity, they often merged seamlessly into one another so that demarcating a boundary between them seemed both arbitrary and futile.[37] And, as we noted earlier, the Lua/Lawa, a swiddening, Mon-Khmer-speaking animist people, are so intimately familiar with the Thai language, padi cultivation, and Buddhism that it is no exaggeration to say that they can be a convincing Lua on Monday and a convincing Thai on Tuesday. To relegate them to a single ethnic category makes little sense. A better description might be to say that X had a bandwidth of traits or identities that could be deployed or performed as the situation required. A person's ethnic identity in this sense would be the repertoire of possible performances and the contexts in which they are exhibited.[38]

Another way of recognizing the bandwidth or repertoire of identities available to many actors is to recognize, as Leach did, that they have, as it were, status positions in several different social systems at the same time. So common was this that F. K. Lehman believed that throughout much of the region ethnicity, far from being an ascriptive "given," was a choice. "Whole communities might be faced with a conscious choice about what group to belong to."[39] This seems a useful way to conceive of such plural identities, providing that we keep three qualifications in mind. The first is that powerful outsiders, especially states, constrain the identity choices of most actors. Second, movement toward one of an array of identities does not exclude the possibility that, should circumstances change, that movement might be reversed. Finally, and surely most important, we must never confuse what an outsider might perceive as a momentous shift in identity with the lived experience of the actors involved. Leach points out in this context that "Kachin" communities, whether egalitarian or stratified, and Shan communities share much of the same ritual language, although they interpret it differently. When an economically well-situated small Kachin polity becomes part of a Shan muang, it will appear to an external observer that the Kachin have become Shan. This is true enough, but to the actor, "this change may be hardly noticeable. In becoming 'sophisticated,' the individual merely begins to attach Shan values to the ritual acts which previously had only a Kachin significance." It is only the external observer "who tends to suppose that shifts in the culture and social organization of a group must be of shattering significance."[40]

There is surely something defective about any analytical understanding of identity change that is so radically at variance with the experience of real actors. Ethnic change can, I believe, be differently formulated so as to accommodate better the vernacular understandings of local actors. If we assume, for many hill people, a plurality of identity repertoires, then it follows, as we have seen, that various portions of that repertoire will be elicited by a particular social context of action. Performed identity will, in other words, be situationally cued. Someone with, say, a broad Karen-Thai repertoire will dress, speak, and behave differently in the Thai marketplace than in the context of the Karen village festival. There is, of course, no reason at all to suppose one part of the repertoire is more authentic or "real" than any other. To a great extent, then, the expressed or enacted identity is a function of the relative frequency of the social context in which it is appropriate. If, say, the Karen-Thai in question moves into a predominantly Thai, lowland settling and plants irrigated rice, then the frequency of the Thai social and cultural context will prevail, and with it the Thai portion of the enacted repertoire. What looks to an outside observer like a change in ethnic identity is no more and no less than a shift in the relative frequency with which the Thai-coded part of the repertoire is performed. This could occur gradually and, in any event, if conceived in this fashion need not imply any momentous subjective sense of displacement or loss.

The historical relationship between the Mon and the Burmans, both lowland padi-planting peoples, not only provides an illustration of identities as plural and performed but also suggests the strategic value of having a range of identities at one's disposal. At the start of the eighteenth century, both Mons, who slightly predominated, and Burmans shared the Irrawaddy Delta. The main differences between them had to do with body markings (Burmans tattooed below the waist), hair style (Mons cut their hair round in front, while Burmans had long hair gathered in a top knot), clothing, and language. A change in identity was a matter of substituting these codes, and in those sections of the Delta where Mons and Burmans lived adjacent to each other and were bilingual, this was a comparatively simple matter. As Ava's power waxed, so did the proportion of the population adopting Burman cultural codes—speaking Burmese and tattooing their thighs. As Pegu's power waxed, Burmans in its orbit cut their top knot and spoke Mon. Independent municipalities, nominally tributary to Ava or Pegu, switched their loyalties. Although it seemed clear that the conflict itself served to crystallize and politicize certain cultural markers that later came to be seen as ethnic, the origin of the conflict was by no means ethnic.

One sees in this context the adaptive value of certain identities.[41] Being able to represent oneself, as the circumstances dictate, as Burman or Mon must have been the salvation of many a bystander or captured combatant in these wars between Pegu and Ava. It is tempting to see this command of a "mixed portfolio" of identities as a cultural insurance policy, an escape social structure. Like a chameleon's color adapting to the background, a vague and shape-shifting identity has great protective value and may, on that account, be actively cultivated by groups for whom a definite, fixed identity might prove fatal. Like the "jellyfish" tribes described earlier, such plasticity affords outsiders no easy institutional access.

Radical Constructionism: The Tribe Is Dead, Long Live the Tribe

"Tribes" in the strong sense of the word have never existed. By "strong sense," I mean tribes as conceived as distinct, bounded, total social units. If the test of "tribeness" is that the group in question be a genealogically and genetically coherent breeding population, a distinct linguistic community, a unified and bounded political unit, and a culturally distinct and coherent entity, then virtually all "tribes" fail the test.[42] As noted earlier, the actual disposition of cultural practices, social integration, languages, and ecological zones rarely offers a sharp break, and when it does, one such break almost never maps on another. Nor is "tribe," as it was once imagined, part of an evolutionary series of some kind—for example, band-tribe-chiefdom-state, or, alternatively, tribe-slavery-feudalism-capitalism.

States and empires have been founded by peoples conventionally understood as tribes—Jinggis Khan, Charlemagne, Osman, the Manchu. And yet, it would be far more correct to say that states make tribes, than to say tribes make states.

Tribes are what have been called a "secondary form," created in two ways and only in the context of a state or empire. The antonym or binary to "tribe" is "peasantry." The difference, of course, is that the peasant is a cultivator already incorporated fully as a subject of a state. Tribes or tribals, on the other hand, are those peripheral subjects not (yet?) brought fully under state rule and/or those who have chosen to avoid the state. Colonial empires and the modern state have been most prolific at creating tribes, but the designation of a tribal periphery was just as common for such earlier empires as the Roman, Tang China, and even the small Malay trading state.

The "tribe" might be called a "module of rule." Designating tribes was a technique for classifying and, if possible, administering the non- or not-yet-peasants. Once a tribe and its tribal area had been marked off, it might be used as a unit for tribute in goods and men, as a unit over which a recognized chief could be appointed and made responsible for its conduct, and as a military zone of pacification. At the very least, it created, however arbitrarily, a named people and their supposed location for purposes of bureaucratic order where an otherwise indistinguishable mass of settlements and peoples without structure had often prevailed.

States and empires create tribes precisely to cut through the flux and formlessness that characterize vernacular social relations. It is true that vernacular distinctions were made between, say, swiddeners and foragers, between maritime and inland populations, between grain growers and horticulturalists. Such distinctions, however, crisscrossed many other distinctions of language, ritual, and history; they were typically gradients rather than sharp discontinuities and rarely became the basis for political authority. At some level, it simply did not matter how arbitrary the invented tribes were; the point was to put an administrative end to the flux by instituting units of governance and negotiation. Thus the Romans insisted on the territorialization of named barbarians under chiefs who, in principle, could be held responsible for their conduct. The bureaucratic grid was necessary "because there was so much fluidity in social bonds and internal barbarian politics."[43] Whether the designations made vernacular sense to the natives was largely beside the point. In late imperial and Republican China, on the southwest frontier, the names for the subdivision of the troublesome "Miao" were arbitrary designations based loosely on women's dress and bore no relation to the vernacular terms of self-identification.[44]

Colonial rulers faced much the same "anarchy" of vernacular identifications and resolved it by decreeing administrative tribes that were no less arbitrary. Armed with ethnographers and deterministic theories of social evolution, the French in Vietnam not only drew boundaries around the tribes they dimly discerned and appointed chiefs through whom they intended to rule but placed the peoples so designated on a scale of social evolution.[45] The Dutch accomplished much the same administrative alchemy in Indonesia by identifying separate indigenous customary law (adat) traditions which they proceeded to codify and use as a basis for indirect rule through appointed chiefs. As Tanya Li puts it, "The concept of 'adat community' assumed, as it simultaneously sought to engineer, a rural population separated into named ethnic groups with 'traditions' stable enough . . . to serve as definitions of group identity and centralized political structures with recognized leaders."[46]

This technology of rule, at a single stroke, not only proposed new and sharp identities but assumed a kind of universal, hierarchical, chiefly order. Acephalous, egalitarian peoples without chiefs or any permanent political order beyond the hamlet or lineage had no place in the new dispensation.[47] They were hustled willy-nilly into a world of chiefs by fiat whether they liked it or not. Peoples whose vernacular order was egalitarian lacked the institutional handles by which they could be governed. Those institutions would have to be provided, if necessary, by force. In what became known as the Shan states of eastern Burma, the British were confronted with a population roughly half of whom were acephalous and egalitarian (gumlao Kachin, Lahu, PaO, Padaung, Kayah). Seeking the hierarchical institutions that would provide a political entry point for indirect rule, the British naturally chose to rely instead on some forty or so Shan sawbwas who, more often in theory than in practice, laid claim to rule their local domains. Though this choice sparked resistance then and later, it was the only institutional transmission belt available to the British.

Once invented, however, the tribe took on a life of its own. A unit created as a political structure of rule became the idiom of political contestation and competitive self-assertion. It became the recognized way to assert a claim to autonomy, resources, land, trade routes, and any other valuable that required a statelike claim to sovereignty. The recognized idiom for making a claim within a state was an appeal to class or to estate—the peasantry, the merchants, the clergy. The recognized idiom for claims outside state space was an appeal to tribal identities and entitlements. Nowhere was this more apparent than in the white settler colony of North America. As Alfred Kroeber aptly writes, "The more we view aboriginal America, the less certain does any consistently recurring phenomenon become that matches with our conventional concept of tribe; and the more largely does this concept appear to be a White Man's creation of convenience for talking about Indians, negotiating with them, administering them—and finally impressed upon their own thinking by our sheer weight . . . the time may have come to examine whether it is not overwhelmingly such a construct."[48]

In this secondary sense, named tribes with self-consciousness of their identities do most certainly exist. Rather than existing in nature, they are a creative human construction—a political project—in dialogue and competition with other "tribes" and states. The lines of demarcation are essentially arbitrary at the outset, given the great variety of ethnographic difference. The political entrepreneurs—officials or not—who endeavor to mark out an identity based on supposed cultural differences are not so much discovering a social boundary as selecting one of innumerable cultural differences on which to base group distinctions. Whichever of these differences is emphasized (dialect, dress, diet, mode of subsistence, presumed descent) leads to the stipulation of a different cultural and ethnographic boundary distinguishing an "us" from a "them." This is why the invention of the tribe is best understood as a political project.[49] The chosen boundary is a strategic choice because it organizes differences in one way rather than another, and because it is a political device for group formation. The only defensible point of departure for deciding who is an X and who is a Y is to accept the self-designations of the actors themselves.

Tribe-Making

States fabricate tribes in several ways. The most obvious is to create them as a template for administrative order and political control. But it is striking how often a tribal or ethnic identity is generated at the periphery almost entirely for the purpose of making a political claim to autonomy and/or resources.

The creation of the Cossacks as a self-conscious ethnicity, conjured up out of thin air, so far as origins are concerned, is particularly instructive for understanding ethnogenesis in Southeast Asia. The people who became the Cossacks were runaway serfs and fugitives from all over European Russia. Most of them fled in the sixteenth century to the Don River steppelands "to escape or avoid the social and political ills of Muscovite Russia."[50] They had nothing in common but servitude and flight. On the vast Russian hinterland, they were geographically fragmented into as many as twenty-two Cossack "hosts" all the way from Siberia and the Amur River to the Don River basin and the Azov Sea.

They became a "people" at the frontier for reasons having largely to do with their new ecological setting and subsistence routines. Depending on their location, they settled among the Tatars, Circassians (whose dress they adopted), and Kalmyks, whose horseback habits and settlement patterns they copied. The abundant land available for both pasture and agriculture meant that these pioneer settlers lived in a common property land regime where each family had its own independent access to the means of subsistence and complete freedom of movement and residence. An ethos of independence and egalitarianism, desired by a people who had known servitude, was underwritten by the political economy of frontier ecology.

Cossack society was, at this stage, something of a mirror image of tsarist Russian servitude and hierarchy. All three of the great peasant uprisings that threatened the empire began in the Cossack lands. Here, as in Zomia, the stateless frontier also attracted religious dissidents, most prominently the so-called Old Believers, who associated religious reforms with servitude.[51] After the defeat of the Bulavin uprising (1707–8), the autonomy of the Cossacks was made contingent on supplying fully equipped cavalry units to the tsar's forces. And after the ruthless military campaign of suppression against those Cossacks most closely associated with the Pugachev rebellion (1773–74), the rudimentary local democratic assemblies of the Cossacks were supplanted by a titled, landholding Cossack nobility with its own serfs—mostly from the Ukraine.

Not by any stretch of the imagination a coherent "people" at the outset, the Cossacks are today perhaps the most solidaristic "ethnic" minority in Russia. To be sure, their use as a "martial minority"—like the Karen, Kachin, Chin, and Gurkha levies in South and Southeast Asia—contributed to this process of ethnogenesis.[52] It did not, however, initiate it. As an invented ethnicity, Cossackdom is striking, but it is not unique. Cases of essentially maroon communities that became distinctive, self-conscious, ethnic formations are reasonably common. In place of the Cossacks, the case of the maroons of Surinam—who developed into no fewer than six different "tribes," each with its own dialect, diet, residence, and marriage patterns—would have served just as well.[53] The Seminoles of North America or Europe's Gypsies/ Roma are also cases of ethnicities that were fused from unpromising, disparate beginnings, by a common ecological and economic niche as well as by persecution.

All ethnicities and tribal identities are necessarily relational. Because each asserts a boundary, it is exclusionary and implicitly expresses a position, or a location, vis-à-vis one or more other groups falling outside the stipulated ethnic boundary. Many such ethnicities can be understood as asserted structural oppositions between binary pairs: serf–versus–free Cossack, civilized–versus–barbarian, hill–versus–valley, upstream (*hulu*)–versus–downstream (*hilir*), nomadic–versus–sedentary, pastoralist–versus–grain producer, wetland–versus–dryland, producer–versus–trader, hierarchical (Shan, *gumsa*)–versus–egalitarian (Kachin, *gumlao*).

The importance of "positionality," and often agro-economic niche, is so common in the creation of ethnic boundaries that what begins as the term for a location or a subsistence pattern comes to represent ethnicity. For Zomia and the Malay world it is striking how frequently a term merely designating residence in the hills of, for example, Padaung, Taungthu, Buikitan, Orang Bukit, Orang Hulu, Mizo, Tai Loi, has become the actual name for a tribe. Many such names surely began as exonyms applied by valley states to the hill people with whom they traded, and connoted rudeness or savagery. Over time, such names have often taken hold as autonyms carried with pride. The frequent coincidence of ecological and occupational niches and ethnic boundaries has often been noted by anthropologists, and Michael Hannan has gone so far as to claim that "in equilibrium, ethnic group boundaries coincide with niche boundaries."[54]

The most essentialized distinction of this kind is perhaps that between the barbarians and the grain-growing Han people. As the early Han state grew, those remaining in, or fleeing to, "the blocks of hilly land, marsh, jungle, or forest" within the empire became known by various terms but were, as we have seen, collectively called "the inner barbarians." Those extruded to the steppe fringe, where sedentary agriculture was impossible or unrewarding, were "the outer barbarians." In each case, the effective boundary between different peoples was ecological. Baron von Richtofen in the 1870s vividly described the abruptness of the boundary between geologies and peoples:

"It is surprising, after having crossed over several [patches of loess soil], to see, on arriving on the summit of the last, suddenly a vast, grassy plain with undulating surface. . . . On the boundary stands the last Chinese village; then follows the 'Tsauti' [grassland] with Mongol tents."[55] Having shown that "the Mongols" were not some ur-population, but instead enormously diverse, including many ex-Han, Lattimore saw the hegemony of ecology: "The frontiers between different types of soil, between farming and herding, and between Chinese and Mongols coincided exactly."[56]

Ecological niche, because it marks off different subsistence routines, rituals, and material culture, is one distinction around which ethnogenesis can occur. But it is neither a necessary nor a sufficient condition for ethnic or tribal formation. Inasmuch as the creation of such markers is a political project, it follows that they can also be attached to distinctions of no intrinsic importance in order, for example, to stake a claim to a valuable resource. The invention of the Kayah/Karenni "tribe" as a people distinct from other nearby Karennic people seems a clear case of this kind.[57]

The birth of the Karenni in the early nineteenth century is recent enough to allow us some grounded speculation about the origin of the "tribe." It appears to be associated with the arrival of Karen millenarian pretenders claiming to be princes on the Shan model among this otherwise egalitarian, non-Buddhist community in the 1820s. As we shall see in the next chapter, millenarian movements have played a disproportionate role in the genesis of new communities in the hills. The creation of a Shan-style kingdom with its own Sawbwa "succeeded in transforming one of a mere congeries of central Karen dialects into a very distinctive Kayah social and cultural system."[58] Imitative state-making of this kind is not so unusual. What is unusual is its success both politically and culturally. That success, in turn, was contingent on the happy fact that the newly minted Karenni statelet was home to the most valuable stands of teak in the country.

The assertion of a new tribal identity outfitted with a small-scale state apparatus had the effect of establishing a local monopoly over the trade in teak. Charismatic leadership served to fuse these loosely related Karennic communities into something like a joint stock company "in order to wrest control of the increasingly lucrative teak trade from the Shan for whom they had been working."[59] The Karenni ethnic entrepreneurs borrowed the statecraft model closest at hand: that of the Shan padi state, itself borrowed in turn from the Burmese monarchy, which would serve to make a sovereign claim to the teak and defend it. As an identity-creating and resource-controlling strategy, it succeeded admirably.

Many identities are crafted, it is clear, with similar purposes in mind: to defend a strategic trade route location, to assert an exclusive claim to water, minerals, or valuable land, to claim ownership of a particular commodity, to defend fishing or hunting rights against competition, to guard entry into a lucrative occupation, or to claim ritual privileges. The creation of tribes and ethnicities in this sense might be termed the standard mode of claim-making by stateless people who interact with states. It serves, for such societies, essentially the same purpose that the formation of a trade union, a corporation, or a craft guild would serve in a more contemporary society.[60] Those who successfully stake a claim to resources on this basis acquire a powerful reason for embracing the new identity. By the same token, they exclude others from access to these same resources. Those thereby excluded and forced into a less desirable niche are often reciprocally ethnicized.[61]

The demarcation of tribes in Africa was, as in all colonies, an official imperial project as well. A small army of specialists was busy drawing ethnic boundaries, codifying customs, assigning territories and appointing chiefs to create manageable units of imperial rule, often over stateless peoples. Some grid of classification had to be imposed on a bewildering cultural variety so as to yield named units of tribute, taxes, and administration. Driving the enterprise, Wilmsen writes, was "that self-fulfilling prophecy that foretold the existence of tribes and, through administrative order, created what it could not discover." The tribe, once established as the only social form proper to the representation of stateless peoples, became quickly hegemonic. Arbitrary or fictitious as it might be, "natives understood that they must draw themselves up into tribes" in order to function within the colonial framework.[62] The enterprise of dividing up the natives into mutually exclusive, territorially delimited tribes was not an administrative mania peculiar to Cartesian Enlightenment thinking or, for that matter, Anglo-Saxon, Calvinist tidiness. And one need only read Caesar's *Gallic Wars* to notice a tribal order of the same kind which, however confounded it might have been by facts on the ground, was a gleam in the eye of every Roman governor. The Han-Chinese imperial project, with its appointed tributary chiefs (*tusi*) and named barbarians, bears the marks of a comparable administrative exercise. The tusi system (ruling barbarians with barbarians) was devised in the Yuan Dynasty (1271–1368) and flourished until the eighteenth century in those areas of the empire where direct control was either impossible or fiscally unprofitable.[63]

Underneath the arbitrary exercises of classification elaborated by states lies the ever-changing tumult of local struggles over resources, prestige, and power. These struggles constantly produce new social and cultural cleavages—quarrels over ritual, factions striving to control the best land, lineages vying for marriage alliances, succession struggles for local leadership. The potential basis of new and competitive social units, in other words, is being reproduced daily.

Following Max Gluckman's original insight, we can roughly distinguish between centripetal and centrifugal conflict.[64] When factions battle over a chieftainship, implicitly agreeing on what the prize is and so reaffirming the importance of the unit itself, their conflict is centralizing. When a faction splits off or secedes to found another unit, such conflict is decentralizing or centrifugal. The demographic and geographic setting of Zomia, in this context, promoted centrifugal conflict. It was a relatively simple matter, say, for the losing faction in a leadership dispute to hive off, open new swiddens, and found a new settlement. It was a relatively egalitarian alternative to what otherwise might have become subordination and permanent hierarchy. The friction of distance also meant that separate communities often remained in relative isolation, especially as compared with valley society. Just as rugged topography and relative isolation, given time to percolate, promote growing differences in speech dialects—a kind of linguistic speciation—so, too, the conditions of Zomia encourage the multiplication and solidification of cultural difference. These processes of cultural drift and differentiation are often the raw material for "tribal" distinctions. But we must not confuse cultural difference with tribal or ethnic group identity. The creation of named tribes or ethnic groups is a political project that sometimes makes use of cultural differences. Many striking cultural differences, on the other hand, are never politicized, and by the same token, striking cultural differences are frequently accommodated within the same tribal polity.

Once launched, the "tribe" as a politicized entity can set in motion social processes that reproduce and intensify cultural difference. They can, as it were, create the rationale for their own existence. Political institutionalization of identities, if successful, produces this effect by reworking the pattern of social life. The concept of "traffic patterns" used by Benedict Anderson to describe the creation by the Dutch colonial regime in Indonesia, virtually from thin air, of a "Chinese" ethnic group, best captures this process.[65] In Batavia, the Dutch discerned, according to their preconception, a Chinese minority. This mixed group did not consider itself Chinese; its boundaries merged seamlessly with those of other Batavians, with whom they freely intermarried. Once the Dutch discerned this ethnicity, however, they institutionalized their administrative fiction. They set about territorializing the "Chinese" quarter, selected "Chinese" officials, set up local courts for customary Chinese law as they saw it, instituted Chinese schools, and in general made sure that all those falling within this classification approached the colonial regime as Batavian "Chinese." What began as something of a figment of the Dutch imperial imagination took on real sociological substance through the traffic patterns of institutions. And voilà!—after sixty years or so there was indeed a self-conscious Chinese community. The Dutch had, to paraphrase Wilmsen, through an administrative order, manufactured what they could not discover.

Once a "tribe" is institutionalized as a political identity—as a unit of representation with, say, rights, land, and local leaders—the maintenance and reinforcement of that identity becomes important to many of its members. Geoffrey Benjamin has shown that highland groups such as the Senoi and Semang responded to the lure and danger of the colonial and Malay state by becoming more "tribal," by instituting a set of marriage practices that promoted dispersal and foraging. A cultural taboo against the use of the plow further discouraged sedentism.[66] The more successful the identity is in winning resources and prestige, the more its members will have an interest in patrolling its borders and the sharper those borders are likely to become.[67] The point is that once created, an institutional identity acquires its own history. The longer and deeper this history is, the more it will resemble the mythmaking and forgetting of nationalism. Over time such an identity, however fabricated its origin, will take on essentialist features and may well inspire passionate loyalty.

Genealogical Face Saving

In the egalitarian societies usually designated tribal, I would argue that the most prevalent mode of reckoning descent is by stipulation.
—Morton Fried, *The Notion of Tribe*

Early colonial officials could, in a sense, be forgiven for "finding" tribes in the hills.[68] Not only was it their expectation, but the self-representation of many hill peoples reinforced that expectation. Where there were no states to speak of, the principles of social cohesion were formally ordered by kinship, genealogy, and lineage. These principles were, of course, exactly what the colonizers expected to find in the tribal zone. While the political realities of competition, usurpation, rebellion, migration, social fission, and fluctuating, plural identities were dizzyingly complex and in constant motion, what Marxists would call the ideological superstructure maintained the appearance of a well-ordered, historically coherent descent group. The formal roles of succession, descent, and precedence were saved by a kind of genealogical and historical legerdemain. If a sense of continuity and symbolic order are important for a given state of affairs, then this process makes eminent sense. After all, contingencies of a fragmented and tumultuous hill politics could not be foreseen, let alone ordered. It was far easier to adjust and interpret the outcome of, say, a successful usurpation or an anomalous marriage in a way that artfully demonstrated that, after all, the rules had been satisfied and were still intact.

All hill peoples, without exception, as nearly as I can tell, have had long experience in reworking their genealogies to absorb strangers. Hill societies were also manpower systems and sought to augment their numbers by absorbing new migrants, by adoption, by marrying and incorporating outsiders, by purchase, and by slave-raiding expeditions. The new manpower was welcome not only for opening new swiddens but also to improve the political and military weight of the receiving group. Valley societies, seeking manpower as well, readily absorbed its newcomers into a class order, typically at the bottom. Hill societies, by contrast, attached newcomers to descent groups or kindreds, often the most powerful ones.

The Karen have something of a reputation as less likely to intermarry than many other hill peoples, but, living in the interstices of many more powerful neighbors, they are in fact prodigious at incorporating new members. A partial list of those absorbed would include Chinese, Shan, Lamet, Lisu, Lahu, Akha, Burmans, Mon, Lao, and Lue.[69] The Akha, also an "in-between" people in the sense of being a midslope society with valley peoples below them and other hill peoples above them, have a long-established system of assimilating people. A man marrying into this society, known for its exceptionally long oral genealogies, is accepted as the founder of a new (junior) lineage so long as he practices ancestor service, has a son, and speaks Akha. Many of the lineages with comparatively short genealogies (a mere fifteen or twenty generations) actually recall their ancestors' previous identity: Yunnan-Chinese, Wa, Tai. A captured slave is incorporated into his master's lineage or one genealogically close to it. According to Leo Alting von Geusau, the repertoires of incorporation are so long-standing and routine that it is clear, over time, that the Akha, while remaining the Akha, have been massively replenished, in a genetic sense, by infusions of newcomers.[70] Genealogically speaking, however, the tumult disappears inasmuch as all of the immigrants are in short order "naturalized" by being worked into the warp and woof of existing descent patterns.

The same genealogical sleight of hand operates to devise chiefly lineages that reconcile the facts of power with the ideology of descent. A chiefly Kachin lineage can produce a genealogy forty or more generations deep. Leach regards these genealogies as "fictional" and "of no value as evidence of historical fact." Once a lineage has become influential, it in turn inspires commoner lineages to rewrite their own genealogies in order to stress, to their advantage, their closeness to the powerful lineage. Actual power in the Kachin lineage system turns on lavish feasting while meeting ritual obligations, thereby establishing a claim to the loyalty and labor (manpower) of all those in the sponsor's debt. Anyone who successfully fulfills what are seen as the obligations of an aristocrat will be accepted as an aristocrat, virtually no matter what the facts of descent may be.[71] Leach makes it abundantly clear that a genealogy can be devised to throw a mantle of legitimacy over virtually any set of actual power relations: "Social climbing then is the product of a dual process. Prestige is first acquired by an individual by lavishness in following ritual obligations. This prestige is then converted into recognized status by validating retrospectively the rank of the individual's lineage. This last is largely a matter of manipulating the genealogical tradition. The complicated nature of Kachin rules of succession makes such manipulation particularly easy." Furthermore, "Any influential aristocrat" can "reconstruct remote sections of his genealogy in his own favor." Despite the fact that in principle "a man's rank is . . . precisely defined by his birth, there is almost infinite flexibility in the system as actually applied."[72]

The "tribality" of the hills was thus abetted by elaborate genealogical myths reconstituted as necessary so as to legitimate, by descent, the actual distribution of power in society. Saga tellers were the specialists whose job it was to bring the myths in line with the facts. Driven by some combination of myopia and administrative convenience, colonial officials sought out hierarchy and tribality, and the elaborate myths of descent in the hills were there to encourage them. They established a Shan state in an area where less stratified people were just as numerous. Among the Kachin, they much preferred the aristocratic, chiefly, autocratic variety and showed great distaste for the "anarchic," democratic, gumlao Kachin.[73]

For the Karenni as well, recruitment to leadership depends largely on charisma, feasting, and political and military skills. The importance of heredity and genealogical standing lies in the way in which political success must be reconciled with the ideological rule of rightful descent. "Even a usurper," Lehman explains, "upon seizing power, attempted to show that one or more of his ancestors was of the 'royal bone' even though the usurper may have been an ordinary villager." Inasmuch as the Karenni, and Karen society in general, follow cognatic kinship, in which male and female lines are reckoned, finding the requisite connection was even easier than with the Kachin. If, then, the colonizers were looking for tribes constituted by orderly rules of descent and long histories, the uplanders they encountered were only too happy to oblige them with retrospective genealogical order in which they themselves clothed their turbulent politics.[74]

The tribe, as a formal social institution, appears, in other regions as well, to be more in evidence as a kind of ideological exoskeleton than as a useful guide to political realities. One of the most famous tribes in history—that of Osman, founder of the Ottoman Empire—was in fact a motley collection of different peoples and religions collaborating for political purposes. This was not an exception. Surveying the evidence, Rudi Paul Lindner claims that "Modern anthropologists' field studies [in the Middle East] show that tribal, clan, and even camp membership are more open than the tribal idiom or ideology might indicate."[75] The tribe was, in Osman's case, a useful vehicle to bring together Turkish pastoralists and Byzantine settlers. And if blood ties were deemed desirable in keeping with the idea of the tribe as consanguines, then clan genealogies could be recalled to forge distant relationships. The segmentary lineage model is, without doubt, a common tribal ideology, but it is not common tribal practice except insofar as it is necessary to keep up appearances.[76]

The hegemony of blood ties and rules of genealogical descent, as the only legitimate foundation for social cohesion, though at variance with the facts, was so powerful as to dominate self-representations. It was, for hill people, the only way to justify actual power. Like Charles Dickens's couple the Veneerings, who were quite as determined to keep up appearances to themselves as to their neighbors, the mimicry is not a cynical ploy but a mode of reasoning about social relations. One can even think of it as a democratic mechanism in which the members of a community confer retrospective legitimacy on leaders who observe the obligations of ritual and generosity incumbent on chiefs. Tribal thinking in this special sense was as deeply embedded in highland ideology as it was in the imagination of the colonizers.

Given what we know of the ambiguity of ethnic identities, the porosity of their boundaries, the creation and demise of different identities, and the constant "power politics" taking place beneath the comparatively placid surface of genealogical continuity, a radical constructionist position on upland identities seems inescapable. At the very least, as Leach has shown for the Kachin, any hill population will have a range of social forms it can assume. Much of the determinate form applied to this flux was, as we have seen, an artifact of the imperial imagination. Thomas Kirsch, following Leach's lead, directed attention to the flux of social organization itself as an important phenomenon to be explained. He argued that "none of these various upland peoples enshrined in the ethnographic tradition of Southeast Asia has (or had) any permanent or immutable ethnographic status. Rather they are all undergoing a continuous process of change."[77]

The very indeterminacy of social forms in the hills, the pliability of histories and genealogies, the baroque complexity of languages and populations is not just a puzzle for rulers, ethnographers, and historians; it is a constitutive feature of hill societies. First, it is what one might expect in a zone of refuge, peopled, as in parts of Latin America, by a multitude of migrants, deserters, ruined peasants, rebels, and a preexisting, variegated hill society. The topography itself conspired to promote and preserve the cultural and linguistic pluralism of the hills. But it also seems reasonable to see this indeterminacy as an adaptive response to a context subject to radical, sudden, and unpredictable change. Noting how the Karen are spread throughout many ecological zones and adjacent to several more powerful valley kingdoms, Renard believes that the remarkable suppleness of their social structures, their oral histories, kinship patterns, subsistence techniques, cuisine and architecture is adapted for travel and change. If necessary, most Karen groups can turn on a dime. It is a quality that has great adaptive advantages and has served them well.[78]

Never quite knowing what role they will be called on to play, what situations they will have to adapt to, hill peoples find it in their interest to develop the widest cultural repertoire possible. Jonsson refers to much of this repertoire as "tribal identity formation" and notes in particular that "tribality," being virtually the only idiom for extravillage action, was one element of that repertoire. He convincingly places the range of social and economic practices at the disposal of hill peoples at the center of his analysis: "People have moved among the categories of state subjects and non-subject clients in the forests, as well as from being autonomous uplanders, dividing in two social directions, some becoming state clients and others abandoning village life for

foraging in small bands. This relates back to the general case of a shifting social landscape, and how people move among structural categories, in and out
of particular relationships, repeatedly reformulating the parameters of their
identities, communities and histories."[79]

We can, I think, discern two axes along which these options are arrayed;
they are all but explicit in Jonsson's analysis. One axis is that of equality-
versus-hierarchy and the second is statelessness-versus-"stateness," or state
subjecthood. The foraging option is both egalitarian and stateless, while absorption into valley states represents hierarchy and subjecthood. In between
are open-ranked societies with or without chiefs and hierarchical chiefly systems sometimes tributary to states. None of these quasi-arbitrarily defined
locations along these axes is either stable or permanent. Each represents,
along with others, one possible adaptation to be embraced or abandoned
as the circumstances require. We now turn finally to the structure of these
choices.

Positionality

In puzzling through how the Karenni/Kayah came into being as an identity
and a petty state, Chit Hlaing [F. K. Lehman] concluded that they could be
understood only as a position or strategic relationship within the larger constellation of other Karennic-speaking groups and the adjacent padi states,
especially the Shan and Burman. It followed that when that constellation was
transformed or disrupted, it would prompt the Karenni to adjust their social
structure or even their very identity accordingly.[80]

If we then think metaphorically of the system Lehman points to as a
solar system, we can talk broadly of the mass of different bodies that make it
up, the relative distances between them, and the gravitational pull each exerts
on the others. The largest planets in these systems are, to pursue the metaphor, the padi states. They wax and wane, they may, by their rivalry, limit one
another, and the smallest of them may be hostage to its hilly neighbors, but
by and large their concentration of manpower, material culture, and symbolic
centrality make them centers of gravity.

Here, however, the metaphor breaks down, inasmuch as the padi state
can be a repelling force as well as an attractive one, and it exerts several different kinds of influence. Its cultural charisma, its symbolic reach, is greater
than any other force it exerts. Even in the most remote hill settlements one
encounters symbols of authority and tokens of power that seem to float up in

fragments from the valley states: robes, hats, ceremonial staffs, scrolls, copies of court architecture, verbal formulas, bits of court ritual. There is hardly any claim to extravillage authority in the hills that does not deploy some cosmopolitan trapping to enhance its assertion of authenticity. In the hills where Han and Theravada symbolic penumbras overlap, fragments from both lowland systems mingle promiscuously. These feather-light symbolic shards travel easily to the hills because they are largely ornamental—a form of cosmological bluster. They recapitulate, in miniature, the journey made by the ideas and symbolic technology of divine kingship from South India to the classical courts of Southeast Asia.

Economically, the gravitational attraction of the padi-state core is nearly as broad. The lowland court centers in the mainland, as in the Malay world, were the outlets, for more than a millennium, for an international luxury trade in which hill products were the most valuable commodities. As explored earlier, the hills and valleys, as different ecological zones, were locked in mutual economic dependence. This trade could not, by and large, be coerced. Even in the case of tribute-based exchange, the hill tributary, though nominally inferior according to valley documents, often had the upper hand, and tribute relations were welcomed as opportunities for mutually advantageous exchange. The economic integration of hill and valley was extensive because it was uncoerced and mutually beneficial.

The reach of the Southeast Asia padi state was quite modest, however, when it came to direct, political-administrative control. Topography, military technology, low population, and an open frontier conspired to limit the successful application of coercion to a relatively small core area. Where coercion did come into play was in slaving expeditions (via war and intermediary slave-raiders) designed to capture and settle a large population within this narrow sphere of control. Flight could negate that achievement.

Given these sharp limitations, almost every valley state had a working alliance—sometimes formalized—with one or more adjacent hill populations. It was in the interest of some hill groups to settle close by the valley core to take advantage of the often rich ecotone zone between hill and valley in an attempt to dominate, as intermediaries, the trade between them. In the case of the Yao/Mien with the Chinese court and the Lawa with the courts of Chiang Mai and Jengtung, the alliance apparently took the form of a written decree or code.[81] In essence, the "contract" depicts a kind of bargain. In return for tribute and good behavior (no rebellions!), the hill people, in the case of the Yao, are given leave to "cross the mountains" to find new swiddens, are exempt from taxes, corvée, and tolls, and will not be required to kneel before lords and officials. The documents are filled with civilizational discourse placing the Yao and Lawa well outside the magic circle of civilized life. As Jonsson astutely points out, they also have the effect of naming and perhaps stabilizing an identity in flux, implicitly abrogating to the court center the right to confer land and mobility rights, and go far toward demarcating a "tribal territory" and assuming that it will have accountable chiefs. The document could be considered, in Han terms at least, a formula for "cooking barbarians."

Such valley charters for hill peoples can as well, I think, be read against the grain. It was vitally important for the valley courts to have nearby hill allies. They constituted a crucial buffer and early warning system between the valley core and its valley-state enemies across the mountains.[82] The hill allies could guard vital trade routes and mediate trade and diplomatic relations with other hill peoples. Finally, they could become slave raiders themselves, helping to replenish the unstable core population. Though such arrangements might look like deference and submission to a valley official, they could as easily be seen as a hill achievement, insisting on their terms for an alliance, including not having to bow and scrape before valley officials. Truly "cooked" barbarians would, presumably, bow. The way in which the Yao/Mien is known to flourish the document to valley officials and outsiders suggests that it might be construed this way.[83]

Such arrangements are legion. Located in the interstices of several lowland kingdoms, groups of Karen became, at one time or another, allies of each. They were integral to the initial victory of Mon-Pegu over Ava in the mid-eighteenth century, contributing three thousand troops under a pretender who may have been Karen or Mon-Karen. The Pwo Karen in this area were known as the Mon-Karen (Talaing-Kariang), as distinct from the more northerly Sgaw Karen, sometimes known as the Burman-Karen. When the Pegu kingdom was crushed and much of its population dispersed, the Karen fled with the Mon, seeking Thai protection. The Thai "planted" Karen on the frontier as an early-warning system and—in Burmese eyes—a fifth column. To the Tai kingdom of Chiang Mai, Karen were considered "keepers of the forest," ritually important as first-comers to the land and valuable allies and trading partners. The identity of different Karen groups was thus marked in each location and period by the lowland society with which it was affiliated.[84]

Every "civilized" lowland padi state required one or more hill-dwelling barbarian allies in a relationship that was often mutually advantageous. The Akha have been paired to the Tai states of Kengtung and Sipsongpanna, the Chin to the Burmese court, the Lawa to the Tai Yuan at Chiang Mai, the Wa to various Shan/Tai states, the Pwo-Karen to the Mon, the Lawa to La Na and earlier to Lamphun, the Jarai to the Kinh, the Palaung to the Shan, upland Tai to the Lao, Kachin to Shan; and in the northwest, the Naga are said to have been a kind of highland auxiliary to the Manipuri court.[85] In each case there grew up a kind of cultural symbiosis in which the hill allies, or some of them, came more closely to resemble their valley partners.

This does sound very much like a formula for "cooking" barbarians. More than that, it was a formula for absorption and assimilation. If, as has been argued, the Thai and Burmans came in small numbers as military colonists, then these and other valley populations may well have been constituted in just this fashion.[86] Close hill allies were increasingly likely to be governed by chiefs with valley connections and to be increasingly hierarchical. They would then correspond in the Han scheme to "cooked barbarians." The Han civilization series—raw barbarians, cooked barbarians, full subjects/"entered the map"—is structurally similar to the Shan civilizational series outlined by Leach: egalitarian/gumlao, stratified gumsa, Shan.[87] Leach portrays ethnic succession in what might be termed a gradient. Such succession is to be found in much the same form stretching between all padi states and their adjacent hill allies. This is, after all, the social and cultural route by which hill people become valley subjects: physical proximity, exchange and contact, linguistic integration, ritual appropriation and, in the classical case, wet-rice cultivation. It is to be stressed that this route is a gradient, not a series of abrupt, wrenching changes; it may not even be perceived at all in terms of ethnic succession!

If we can imagine this ethnic succession as a relatively seamless affair, then it follows that it could be just as seamless when the direction is reversed. The route to lowland "civilization" is also the route to highland autonomy, with innumerable way stations in between. In the case of wars or epidemics, the transition might be abrupt (though perhaps familiar), but it might just as often have been a gradual and imperceptible process as the padi state decayed, as trade routes shifted, or as taxes became more onerous. The way to the valley state was a two-way street and leaving need be no more jarring or traumatic than entering.

Egalitarianism: The Prevention of States

Blow us all up with cannons or make us all eighteen thousand of us Nawabs.
—Pashtun elders to British

The Lamet simply could not understand the concept "chief."
—Karl Gustav Izikowitz, *Lamet*

Because of their savagery, the Bedouins are the least willing of all nations to subordinate themselves to each other as they are rude, proud, ambitious and eager to be leaders.
—Ibn Khaldun

A major reason why Leach's *Political Systems of Highland Burma* is such a durable classic is that the opposition between what he calls the autocratic factions and democratic-egalitarian factions he finds among the Kachin travels well outside its immediate ethnographic context. For stateless peoples living on the margins of states, it seems to represent a fundamental choice about positioning. In canvassing the literature of his time, especially works on the Assam-Burma border region, Leach found many other examples of the contrast between democratic-egalitarian forms and autocratic-monarchical forms within indigenous groups. He cites work on the Chins, the Sema, the Konyak, and the Naga.[88] To these examples we could add the Karen, the Lahu, the Wa, the Karenni, and perhaps a good many more if one conducted a comprehensive search of the literature.[89]

The British-led "pacification" forces were struck by the resistance they met in egalitarian Kachin areas. "Our opponents here, were the Kumlao Kachins, whose principal characteristic is that they do not own the authority of any chief, even in single villages."[90] They had, it was noted, "no form of salutation or obeisance." Acephalous communities like the gumlao were subversive to British—or any other—administration; they provided no institutional levers or handles with which to enter the community, negotiate with it, or govern it. The colonial administration accordingly would only recognize "properly constituted tracts under a Duwa" and cautioned officers, even in these villages, to be alert to "this spirit of independence" and to suppress it without delay.[91] Thus the compiler of the *Gazetteer*, proud heir to a democratic tradition himself, can write without a trace of irony, "Such republican or democratic communities are no longer permitted within the Burma administrative boundary."[92]

In the case of the Kayah, as Lehman demonstrates, the democratic and autocratic principles are embedded in "two simultaneous ritual cycles and sets of personnel."[93] What one might call the aristocratic cult makes symbolic gestures beyond the locality and, in particular, adopts the trappings and symbols of the Shan kingdoms and the Burmese royal capital at Mandalay. Its ritual center is the center of the village where tall teak poles—a diagnostic feature of Kayah villages—which are equated with the flagstaff found in most Shan and Burmese pagodas (symbolizing the submission of local spirits to the Buddha) and are topped with an umbrella-form (*hti*) finial which decorates most Buddhist architecture. The hereditary priesthood devoted to this cult makes offerings to a high god whose name is derived from the Shan term for lord, as is the term *sawbwa*. The priesthood may not mix with, intermarry with, or accept offerings from the other cult's priests, who are devoted to the local spirits (*nat*) of the countryside, especially the forest.

What seems important for our purposes is that the ritual complex of the Kayah appears thoroughly amphibious. Both democratic and autocratic components are present but are ritually segregated. One complex seems, by copying lowland forms, to contribute to the ideological superstructure of the sawbwas and state formation in general, while the alternative cult is purely local and makes no reference to chiefly authority. If fluidity of identity—being able to "turn on a dime"—involves shifts from hierarchical to non-hierarchical forms, then the Kayah seem fully equipped, ritually, for either eventuality.

A final comparison of egalitarian and hierarchical social formations points to some of the cultural practices that work to hinder the development of permanent hierarchies of state and power. The Lua/Lawa, a relatively stratified hill society, and the Lisu, a relatively egalitarian group, are illustrative. Among the Lua there is strong emphasis on the ritual and feasting superiority of elite (*samang*) lineages, which, at the same time, control access to land.[94] The ruling lineages have elaborate and deep genealogies emphasizing their status and their connection with powerful lowland courts—Chiang Mai, in particular. Prominent in that connection is a "charter" somewhat like that of the Mien, exempting them from corvée, conscription, and supplying fodder for elephants and horses, and confirming their right to swidden. The Lisu, on the other hand, emphasize equal access of all lineages to competitive feasting, open access to land, and the lack of essential differences in rank or status.

For our purposes, however, two features of the egalitarian Lisu are notable. First, they have short and truncated genealogies, in what amounts to a refusal of history. The purpose, after all, of most lineage histories, oral or written, is to establish a claim to distinction and rank—to establish a "lineage" for those claims. If, then, lineage histories are abbreviated or ignored altogether, it amounts to something of a cultural discouragement, if not prohibition, of historical claims to superiority. To have little or no history is, implicitly, to put every kin group on roughly the same footing. We have seen at some length how the absence of a written textual history and written genealogies may have the same strategic and adaptive advantages for subaltern groups. Oral genealogies, however contrived and invented, are also claims of the same genre, and to repudiate them is also an egalitarian move. It is often and correctly noted that text-based civilizations have consistently seen the stateless people outside their grasp as peoples without history.[95] But what we encounter here is the practice of disavowing status-building histories in the name of preventing hierarchy and its frequent companion, state formation. The Lisu are without history not because they are incapable of history but because they choose to avoid its inconveniences.

The absence of history in this sense contributes to the fact that in egalitarian groups, each lineage—or, for that matter, each family—has its own particular customs and usages. There is, however, one "tradition" to which most Lisu proudly point: namely, the tradition of murdering headmen who become too autocratic. As Paul Durrenberger puts it, "The Lisu loathe . . . assertive and autocratic headmen," and the "stories Lisu tell of murdered headmen are legion."[96] Such traditions can also be found among a good many egalitarian hill peoples. How frequently these traditions are acted upon is hard to establish, although the original gumlao revolt against Kachin headmen reported in the sources appears to have been a case in which they sustained something of a political movement. Such cautionary tales are, in any event, a kind of egalitarian, structural prophylactic warning of the possible consequences to any would-be autocratic headman bent on cementing his lineage's power.

Among the hierarchical Lua, lineages are ranked; they jockey for status; and part of the jockeying rests on claims to superiority based on different, and fabricated, origin myths and genealogies. The Lisu, like the gumlao Kachin, deny lineage ranking and ranked feasting, deny history, and, more directly, thwart the emergence of ambitious headmen who might take them in that direction. The egalitarian Lisu have, in effect, created a culture that is a fairly comprehensive program of state prevention.

The incorporation of egalitarian and hierarchical models of social organization within a recognizably single culture is by no means confined to the

Kachin-Shan context. It is found throughout much of Southeast Asia.[97] More speculatively, there is some reason to suppose that it is a structural regularity of many stateless peoples living on the borders of states. Thus Robert Montagne's classic thesis on Berber society in Morocco proposed that "Berber society oscillates between two rival and opposed social forms, between, on the one hand, democratic or oligarchic tribal republics ruled by assemblies or hierarchies of assemblies, and, on the other hand, ephemeral tribal tyrannies, exemplified in modern times by the great Caids of the South."[98] As was the case with the Kachin, the Berbers had no indigenous model of state-making, and their form, when states did first arise among them, was based on the Hellenic model of the states they abutted. To mention just one of many parallel cases, Michael Khodarkovsky's study of the Kalmyk nomads and the Russian state posits the same oscillation. The nominally ruling lineage, along with the clergy, was devoted to creating a dynasty by hereditary succession and centralized power. Other tribal leaders favored decentralization and "indeterminacy" of succession rules: that is, open ranks. "Two structurally antagonistic tendencies, one propelling the top of the society toward increasing centralization, the other consolidating a separatist tendency, may explain the endless cycles of civil wars so often associated with nomadic society."[99] What Khodarkovsky makes clear, however, is that the centralizing tendency was closely associated with accommodation to the adjacent state. Thus the tsarist regime promoted Kalmyk khans as a form of institutional linkage and control. As it was for the British and imperial China, tribal anarchy was anathema to the tsars. Centralization and autocracy depended on a combination of the power of the tsarist state—including the benefits it could bestow—and the political ambitions of Kalmyk khans.

Egalitarian, acephalous peoples on the fringes of states are hard to control. They are ungraspable. To the command "Take me to your leader" there is no straightforward answer. The conquest or co-optation of such peoples is a piecemeal operation—one village at a time and, perhaps, one household at a time—and one that is inherently unstable. No one can answer for anyone else. Acephaly is therefore, like the "jellyfish tribes" of the Middle East described earlier, itself something of an escape social structure. The logical corollary of acephaly is typically the inability to unite except under very special circumstances (for example, charismatic religious leadership and brief military confederacies). A social structure that thwarts incorporation by an outside state also inhibits crystallization of any internal statelike structure.

What are the material conditions that underwrite such egalitarian social structures? The circumstances of the gumlao Kachin, Lisu, Berbers, and Kalmyks are suggestive in this respect. An open common property frontier seems particularly vital. Just as fixed, inheritable property in land facilitates permanent class formation, a common property frontier equalizes access to subsistence resources and permits the frequent fission of villages and lineages that seems central to the maintenance of egalitarianism. The farther away, in terms of friction of terrain, such peoples live from state centers and the more mobile their subsistence routines—foraging, pastoralism, shifting cultivation—the more likely they are to maintain the egalitarian, stateless option. Enclosure of the commons and encroachment by the state are everywhere a threat to such arrangements.

Much of the logic behind the exceptionally complex checkerboard identities in the uplands and the movement between them is best understood as a strategic choice of position vis-à-vis lowland states. Relative altitude and agro-economic niche are often indicative of such positioning. This perspective is most obvious with identities invented by lowland states to suit their own administrative purposes. Following the mid-Ming dynasty "Yao wars," those who collaborated and settled under imperial rule became "mín," or subjects, and those who did not became, by definition, "Yao."[100] The ethnic term meant nothing beyond non-taxpaying hill people; it had, initially, no cultural or linguistic coherence. The term *Miao*, as we have seen, was similarly often applied comprehensively to all those in an area who were still defiantly beyond the state's grasp. And, of course, the terms *raw* and *cooked*, *wild* and *tame*, *jungle* and *house* (as applied to the Karen) can be understood as references only to the degree of political submission.

Quite apart from state-applied exonyms, ethnic identities, subdivisions, and even villages—as in gumlao and gumsa Kachin—came to acquire reputations for relative degrees of hierarchy and linkage to states. The highland Akha, according to von Geusau, chose subsistence routines that maximized their autonomy and specifically chose locations that put them beyond easy reach of states and slave-raiders.[101]

We should distinguish here between state-repelling characteristics and state-preventing ones. They are related but not identical. State-repelling traits are those that make it difficult for a state to capture or incorporate a group and rule it, or to systematically appropriate its material production. State-preventing traits, on the other hand, are those that make it unlikely that a group will develop internally durable, hierarchical, statelike structures.

The state-repelling features we have repeatedly encountered in the foregoing analysis can be summarized in general terms. First, a society that is physically mobile, widely dispersed, and likely to fission into new and smaller units is relatively impervious to state capture for obvious reasons.[102] These features are, in turn, highly correlated, not to say mandated, by the choice of subsistence routines. Foraging, hunting, and gathering (land-based or maritime) encourage mobility, dispersal, and fission. One can easily stipulate a series or gradient of declining mobility, dispersal, and fission that moves from foraging to swiddening and then to fixed-field crops and irrigated rice. For crop-planting societies, as we saw in Chapter 6, versatile, unobtrusive root crops of staggered maturity are far more state repelling than aboveground grain crops of synchronous maturity. Outside Southeast Asia, the series would also include nomadic pastoralism, with its great advantages in mobility and dispersal.

A third state-repelling feature is a highly egalitarian social structure that makes it difficult for a state to extend its rule through local chiefs and headmen. One of the key material conditions of egalitarian structure—necessary but not sufficient—is open and equal access to subsistence resources. Common-property land tenure and an open frontier are, in this respect, the material conditions that underwrite egalitarianism. In fact, the two major state-repelling subsistence routines, foraging and swiddening, both of which promote mobility and dispersal, are virtually unthinkable without an open, common-property frontier. Its disappearance is a mortal blow to autonomy.

A final state-thwarting strategy is distance from state centers or, in our terms, friction-of-terrain remoteness. Until nearly the twentieth century, remoteness alone sufficed to put some groups definitively outside the reach of the state. As a distance-making strategy, remoteness could, in fact, substitute for other state-repelling strategies. The Hani and Ifugao could safely grow irrigated rice in their remote highland terraces precisely because they were at such a great remove from state centers.

Certain peoples have for so long manifested these state-repelling characteristics that the invocation of their very name conjures up statelessness—often glossed by nearby states as "wildness" or "rawness" or "barbarity." The Lahu, Lisu, gumlao Kachin, Akha, Wa, Khmu, and Hmong, to mention a few, largely fit this description. Providing that one allows for variation over time and the various subdivisions of many ethnic groups, one could, if so inclined, devise something of a nominal scale of state-repelling characteristics along which any particular group might be ranked.

The other pole of the scale would be anchored by what might be called "state-adapted" characteristics: densely settled, sedentary, grain-growing societies marked by property in land and the disparity of power and wealth that it promotes. Such characteristics are, of course, socially engineered into state space. The peoples manifesting these state-adapted features and therefore indelibly marked by their "stateness" are the Shans, Burmans, Thais, Mons, Pyus, Khmer, and Kinh/Viet. To paraphrase Fernand Braudel, not all the human traffic in the world moving back and forth between these poles is likely to erase these indelible associations. At the stateless extreme we get dispersed, mobile foragers or small clusters of people along remote ridges far from any state center; at the other, taxpaying, padi-planting peasants near the state core.

What is surely most important in this ethnic positioning vis-à-vis the state is the constant movement of individuals between these positions and, indeed, the shift over time in what, say, the position "Karenni," "Lahu-nyi," or "Kachin" might mean. At any one place and time, historically, the ethnic identities on offer might be seen as a bandwidth of possibilities for adjusting one's relationship with the state—a gradient of identifications which may be, over time, fitted to the prevailing economic and political conditions. To be sure, it makes eminent economic sense for padi planters to drop everything and take up foraging when the price of resins, medicinal plants, or edible birds' nests shoots up. But the move to foraging can as easily occur because it is a state-evading strategy. Similarly, the choice between padi planting and swiddening is more likely to be a political choice than a mere comparative calculation of calories per unit of labor. Insofar as the choice of subsistence routines, altitude, and social structure are associated with particular cultural identities and a "positionality" vis-à-vis the lowland state, then a change in ethnic identity may represent, first and foremost, a political choice that just happens to carry with it implications for cultural identity.[103]

Some Lahu, for example, have moved to remote mountains and to foraging and, on other occasions, to settled village life and cultivation. As recently as 1973 many Lahu left Kengtung, Burma, for the hills, following a failed revolt against taxation and corvée imposed by the Burmese regime.[104] The Khamu have a comparable, though less rebellious, history; some have abandoned village life for foraging at times, and some have moved to the valleys to become Buddhist padi planters.[105] And of course, as Leach discovered, many Kachin had been moving between different social forms, each of which expressed more of a positioning vis-à-vis the Shan valley state and hierarchy than it did any momentous cultural shift. To reiterate what should now be obvious, swiddening and foraging as practiced for the past few centuries in Southeast Asia are not prior to padi planting in some scheme of social evolution; they are, instead, "secondary adaptations," indicative of a largely political choice.[106]

Jonsson has noted astutely that "ethnic distinctions may primarily have to do with lowland affiliations." In this respect, he claims that "Ethnic groups do not have a [determinate] social organization," by which he means to imply that a particular named identity can, in terms of subsistence, cultural affiliations, internal hierarchy, and above all its relationship to lowland states, vary widely.[107] In other words, not only are individuals and groups moving between ethnic identities as a consequence of positioning themselves, but these identities themselves are labile, as the aggregate of decisions their bearers take has the effect of repositioning the very meaning of that ethnic identity.

If hill peoples have at hand a bandwidth of identities that they can take up, and if each of these identities calibrates a different relationship to lowland states, what can one say about historical trends? Here the shift in the past half-century has been momentous. Until then, as we have seen, Zomia was largely a zone of refuge for societies and fragments of societies fleeing or choosing to place themselves beyond the grasp of valley states. The mosaic of named ethnic identities is testimony to a long and complex history of migrations and remigrations marked by rebellions, war, and cultural reformulations. Originally, much of Zomia's population came from the lowlands, particularly from China, and, however they came by their ethnic name, they kept it largely because they had left the realm of state power. Those who stayed—perhaps a majority—became part of the lowland cultural amalgam and were no longer called Miao, Yao, or Tai. This history, together with the exceptional ecological diversity and the geographical isolation of the region, has produced perhaps the largest mosaic of relatively stateless peoples in the world.

For the past half-century, however, the gradient of available identities has, as it were, been radically tilted in favor of various degrees of state control. The classical narrative of "raw" barbarian peoples being brought to civilization has been replicated by a narrative of development and nation-building. While the older narrative was, owing to the limitations of state power, more an aspiration than reality, the new narrative is more imposing. At least three factors account for this. First, the modern idea of full sovereignty within a nation-state and the administrative and military wherewithal to effect it means that little effort is spared to project the nation-state's writ to the borders of adjacent states. Zones of overlapping, ambiguous, or no sovereignty—once virtually all of Zomia—are increasingly rare. Second, the material basis of egalitarian, acephalous societies—common property in land—is increasingly replaced by state allocation of land rights or individual freehold tenure. And finally, the massive growth of lowland populations has prompted a massive, growing, state-sponsored or abetted colonization of the hills. The colonists bring with them their crops, their social organization, and, this time, their state. The result is the world's last great enclosure.

CHAPTER 8

Prophets of Renewal

And since it would be good to give a name to this seeker of salvation in Burmese
Buddhism, however unclassifiable he may be, why not—inspired once again by the
Weberian expression—simply call him *the enchanter of the world.*
—Guillaume Rozenberg, *Renoncement et puissance*

But it is a world permanently in quest of opportunities for enchantment, and often ready
to identify and respond to the most fugitive of cues: not just the youth, energy, and the
determination of Tony Blair but the cinematic vigor of Arnold Schwarzenegger or the
entrepreneurial momentum of Silvio Berlusconi.
—John Dunn, *Setting the People Free*

T he mere enumeration of the hundreds, nay thousands, of rebellions mounted by hill people against encroaching states over the
past two millennia defies easy accounting. Cataloguing them
in some tidy Linnaean classification scheme seems even more
daunting.

These uprisings, usually led by people styling themselves (and/or taken
to be) wonder-working prophets, shoulder their way to the front of the historical record by virtue of how large they loom in the archives. Precisely because they menaced the routines of administration and tributary relations and
because they contradicted the civilizational narrative of a peaceful ingathering of peoples, they have demanded attention. Each uprising provoked its
own particular blizzard of military and police reports, finger-pointing, trials
and executions, commissions of inquiry, policy changes, and administrative
reforms. Thus it is that most uplanders appear in the archives of Han, Viet,
Siamese, and Burman states either as contributors to the routine statistics on
tribute, corvée labor, and taxation or as barbarians in open rebellion against
the state. The sheer volume of the paper trail dealing with uprisings makes it
possible for an unwary scholar to write a history of many a hill people as if it
consisted largely of rebellions—and, of course, to narrate that history largely
from the perspective of those charged with suppressing them.

The study of rebellion in Zomia has, as we shall see, much to teach us about resistance to the lowland states. But to focus largely on these flash points is to overlook processes equally as important to the evolution of hill society but far less dramatic. It is to overlook, for example, the deep history of migration and flight, sometimes in the aftermath of rebellion but, just as often, as an alternative to a military confrontation. It is to overlook the equally important processes of accommodation with and assimilation into lowland states and peoples. Those taking this path, of course, typically become, over time, Thai, Mon, Han, Burman, and Kinh and therefore disappear from the historical record as Karen, Hmong, Mien, Shan, and so on. But we have no reason to assume that they were any less numerous than those who remained identified with hill societies. And finally, to dwell on rebellions is to overlook the hill allies, auxiliaries, and mercenaries of the valley states who took part in the suppression of the rebellions. Providing that we are not mesmerized by the paper trail into thinking that the hills were in permanent rebellion, then the prophesies and ideas animating the hill risings against lowland states provide a powerful instance of the fractious dialogue between states and peripheral peoples.

A Vocation for Prophecy and Rebellion: Hmong, Karen, and Lahu

Some peoples in the massif seem to have a vocation for prophets and rebellion. To judge by the literature, the Miao/Hmong, the Karen, and the Lahu fall into this category. Their rebellions are also the best documented. For the Miao/Hmong, who number nearly 9 million, and the Karen, who number more than 4 million, this may be in part an artifact of their size vis-à-vis other minorities, such as the Lahu (population about 650,000) or the Khmu (568,000), who seem similarly inclined but less numerous.

Hmong

The deepest historical record of rebellion surely belongs to the Miao/Hmong.[1] They, for their part, trace the origin of their conflicts with the Han to the legendary defeat of their king Chi-You by the equally legendary Yellow Emperor of the Han, Huang Di, in the third millennium BCE! In the two centuries after 400 CE, Herold Wiens has calculated, there were more than forty Miao rebellions, as the Miao contested with the Han for control of the lowlands between the Yellow and Yangzi river basins. Other rebellions followed, and most authorities agree that the past two thousand years of Miao history has been one long skein of rebellion, defeat, migration, and flight.[2] Until the mid-fourteenth century, Miao history involves a lot of guesswork, inasmuch as *Miao* was often used as a portmanteau term to label many stateless peoples who resisted Han administration. In addition, in this period, the Miao and the Yao/Mien were not sharply distinguished.[3]

The staccato of rebellion, repression, and flight from 1413 on, when the Ming authorities sought to enlarge their control and promote large-scale military settlement in Guizhou, is, however, not in dispute. During the Ming and Qing dynasties (1368–1911) there was "hardly any time . . . when suppression or pacification campaigns were not being undertaken against the Miao and Yao."[4] Two historians of this period, not given to hyperbole, characterize these as campaigns of "extermination."[5] There were large-scale uprisings in 1698, 1733–37, 1795–1803, and, finally, the massive "Miao Rebellion," which swept Guizhou from 1854 to 1873, overlapping with the largest peasant revolt in history in central China, the great Taiping Rebellion. The Miao Rebellion was crushed only with great difficulty, some areas remaining under rebel control for more than a decade. Its defeat, in turn, set in motion a large-scale exodus of Hmong and Taiping remnants moving into the hills of northern Vietnam, Laos, and Thailand.

Having fled forced assimilation and sought autonomy across China's southern borders, the Hmong found themselves similarly threatened by the French in Indochina and the Siamese in northern Thailand. There followed a long series of rebellions against the French in 1904, 1911, 1917–18, 1925, 1936, and 1943, and against the Siamese authorities in 1901–2 and 1921.[6] Two features of virtually all these rebellions, as well as those of the Lahu and Karen, which we shall explore later, bear emphasis: they were led by prophetic figures appealing to millenarian expectations, and they tended to appeal, as well, to other, neighboring upland peoples.

Karen

The Karen have an equally impressive, if less well-documented, history of rebellion and prophetism. Their history serves to illuminate the pervasiveness of a culture of liberation and dignity fashioned, for the most part, from the cosmology of the lowland states. Located along the Burmese-Thai border, the Karen number roughly 4.5 million and represent the most numerous highland minority in both countries. Some Karen are Buddhists, some animist, and some Christian. Indeed, the cultural diversity among the Karennic groups is so great that many studies of them begin by pointing out that there is no single trait that all of them share. The Baptist missionary D. L. Brayton, however, disagreed: "It is a trait in the national character of the Karen to have prophets rising up among them."[7] No matter what their religious convictions, the Karen have shown, again and again, a devotion to wonder-working, charismatic, heterodox healers, prophets, and would-be kings. As Jonathan Falla, who worked as a nurse in a Karen rebel camp in the late 1980s, noted, the tradition is still very much alive: "They are millenarians, forever generating warrior leaders, sects, 'white monks' and prophets, all persuading themselves that the Karen kingdom is, once again, at hand. Animists talk of the coming of Y'wa, Baptists of the coming of Christ, and the Buddhists of the Arrimettaya, the future Buddha. Somebody is imminent, Toh Meh Pah is coming, something will happen. 'Remember the Israelites in Egypt, Jo. Forty years in the wilderness, and then the Promised Land. The same will happen for the Karen, when forty years have passed.'"[8]

It was the good fortune of the Baptist missionaries to have brought the Bible to a people who had long believed in messiahs. It was their mistake to imagine that the Baptist messiah was the last messiah the Karens, in their impatience, would be needing.

Each of the prophetic traditions embraced with such enthusiasm by the Karen envisions a new mundane order in preparation for the divine coming. Frequently, a holy man — whether a healer, a priest, a hermit (yà thè — ရ သေ), or a monk — will be the herald of the coming order and be seen as the "field of merit" around whom the faithful gather.[9] What is heralded might, depending on the circumstances, be the imminent king (mín laún — မင်း လောင်း) or embryo-Buddha, the Ariya Mattreya (cakkavatti) or a Karen king/savior figure such as Toh Meh Pah, Y'wa, Duai Gaw/Gwae Gaw (a former rebel leader), or another. Virtually all of these cosmologies of charisma have lowland analogues. Mín laún rebellions in Burma and phu mi bun "holy man" rebellions in Siam bear a close resemblance and might fairly be said to constitute the "once-and-future-king" traditions of the Burmese and the Siamese. The Karen kingdom invokes a silver city and a gold palace to which the righteous shall go when the millennium arrives. Verses from the Karen prophetic tradition recorded by missionaries in the mid-nineteenth century capture the spirit of these aspirations:

That a Karen King would yet appear
The Talain [Mon] Kings have had their season
The Burmese Kings have had their season
And the foreign Kings will have their season
But the Karen King will yet appear
When the Karen King arrives
There will only be one monarch
When the Karen King arrives
There will be neither rich nor poor
When the Karen King arrives
Every thing [creature] will be happy
Lions and leopards will lose their savageness.[10]

The pervasive idea of a reversal of fortunes, of a world turned upside down, of the conviction that it is the Karen's turn to have power and the wealth, palaces, and cities to go along with it, animates a long tradition of rebellions.

The locus classicus for mín laún rebellions among the Karen appears to lie in the mid-eighteenth century, amid the wars between the largely Mon kingdom of Pegu/Bago in southern Burma and Ava, the largely Burman kingdom in the north.[11] A mín laún from a Karen village north of Pegu appeared in 1740; his name was Tha Hla, though he was called Gwe Mín.[12] He may or may not have been Karen, but there is no doubt that he had a strong Karen following.[13] What began as a revolt against the high taxes imposed on Peguans by the Burmese governor ended with Gwe Mín being proclaimed king of Hanthawaddy (Pegu region) and taking the official title S'mín Dhaw Buddahekheti dammaraja: Buddha field of merit. His tenure was brief but he was "their" king. His reign lasted until he was deposed by his first minister in 1747, amid the Ava-Pegu Wars, culminating in the comprehensive defeat of Pegu by the new Burman king Alaunghpaya in 1757. The devastation of this period is known in Karen oral tradition as the "Alaunghpaya Hunger." Many thousands of Mon and Karen fled persecution by withdrawing to remote hills to the east or by placing themselves under the protection of the Siamese.

From then on, the mín laún and rebellions came thick and fast. Another mín laún, perhaps nearly contemporaneous with Gwe Mín, called Saw Quai Ren was the first in a line of at least ten mín laún said to constitute a dynasty.[14] Subsequent mín laún and their followers expected Saw Quai Ren to reappear with an army. In 1825–26, a Karen prophet proclaimed the imminent return of Y'wa and, taking advantage of the Burmese defeat in the first of three

Anglo-Burmese Wars, threw off Burmese rule for four years before finally being defeated. In 1833 Adoniram Judson, an early missionary and founder of what later became the Rangoon University, met a Sgaw Karen prophet with a large following, Areemaday. The prophet expected a great war after which a king would restore a Buddhist peace. Resisting the importuning of Christian missionaries, the prophet and his entourage established a small zone of religious order and later allied with a Kayah prince to fight a Burmese force in 1844–46. Areemaday, who had declared himself mín laún, was killed in the battle along with many of his followers. In 1856 another Karen imminent king in the Salween Hill tracts gathered Shan and Karenni recruits and refused to pay taxes to the Burman official of the young British colony.[15] In 1867, in the mountains near Papun, a self-proclaimed mín laún rose among the Karen, although he was stigmatized by the colonial authorities as a bandit. A mín laún typically declared himself by inaugurating a pagoda and hoisting the finial (t'í—ဆ:) of its spire into place, a monarchical privilege.

One imagines that many smaller-scale prophets, because they were politically passive or never attracted enough followers to qualify for a place in the colonial archives, were active among Buddhist Karen but escaped notice. They are also a religious fixture of twentieth-century Karen Buddhist society. Shortly before the Japanese invasion, a Karen calling himself Phu Gwe Gou founded a millenarian movement in the Salween area. He was assassinated by the British-organized Force 136 in the course of the war.

Among Karen in the Burmese-Thai border area, Mikael Gravers identifies two distinctive millenarian cosmologies. Adherents of one, calling themselves Pwo Karen of the Yellow Thread Movement, are followers of a hermit who prescribed their rites and practices. They are enjoined, among other things, to cease raising pigs and drinking alcohol, to wear a seven-threaded yellow wristband, to erect a pagoda with the pole in front dedicated to the Earth Goddess (Hsong Th' Rwi), who protects Buddhist merit-making before the arrival of the Ariya. This tradition, called Lu Baung, is locally led by the hermit's disciple who, under certain conditions, might proclaim himself the mín laún and touch off a rebellion. As late as the year 2000, a clash between Lu Baung Karen villagers and the Thai border police patrol led to the murder of five policemen.[16]

A second millenarian Buddhist cosmology that circulates among the Karen is represented by the Telakhoung tradition. While it shares many features with the Lu Baung, it is distinctive in its "dynastic" descent line from the original hermit-prophet, Saw Yoh, and in the exclusion of women from its rituals. Gravers regards the Telakhoung as a more hierarchical, "valley" version of the Lu Baung, with its statelike structures and a vision of the future in which all religions will combine. It appears that just as hill peoples often have a dualistic social structure—some variants more egalitarian and others more hierarchical—so do their prophetic movements share an analogous duality.

Lahu

The Lahu, speakers of a Tibeto-Burman tongue related to Akha, Hani, Lisu, and Lolo (Yi), are a highland swiddening people whose "heartland" is in the southwestern corner of Yunnan. Ninety percent of the Lahu population of roughly 650,000 is to be found in western Burma and Yunnan between the upper reaches of the Salween (Nu) and Red rivers. They are, even by hill standards, an exceptionally egalitarian society with little or no political unity beyond the hamlet level, and, to judge from the ethnographer most familiar with them, very little effective authority even within the hamlet.[17] What they do have in abundance, however, are prophets and a deep prophetic tradition. They have deployed this prophetic tradition with its Mahayana, animist, and, now, Christian elements to assert themselves against a variety of lowland foes: Han, Thai, the British, and the Burmans.

This brief account of Lahu prophetism is meant to serve three purposes. First, it puts a necessary, though abbreviated, historical and ethnographic footing under the religious cosmology that animates Lahu prophets and their followers. Second, it illuminates how a confection of syncretic religious ideas, many of them from state centers, and a mimicry of lowland-state institutional forms can be reshaped so as to oppose lowland agendas. Finally, it illustrates how such ideas and their carriers can, on occasion, provide the social cohesion necessary for collective action, not only among the otherwise atomistic Lahu but also between them and other hill societies such as the Wa, Karen, Lisu, Akha, and even Tai.

The movements of the Lahu southward and to higher ground over the past four centuries, largely in response to pressure from Han authorities and settlers, are reasonably well established. Before then, during the early Ming Dynasty (1368–1644), it appears that at least one branch of the Lahu (the Lahu Na) contended with the Tai for control of the fertile bottom land along the Lincang River in southwestern Yunnan. The Tai prevailed and the Lahu were driven into the hills, where many became tributaries to the larger Tai polities. Thus, like quite a few other hill peoples, the Lahu, who now appear as ur-swiddeners and opium cultivators, may have become swiddeners only following a defeat and perhaps to avoid being absorbed by the Tai as serfs.

The larger and more threatening presence looming over the Lahu was the aggressively expansionist early Qing Dynasty. An early Qing account of the Lahu, quoting even earlier sources, makes it clear the degree of contempt in which they were held by Han officials: "They are black, ugly, and foolish. They eat buckwheat as well as tree bark, wild vegetables, vines, snakes, insects, wasps, ants, cicadas, rats and wild birds. They do not know how to build houses but live in rock caves. They are of the same kind as the *ye ren* [wild men]."[18] It was also common lore among the Han that the Lahu were born with tails, which dropped off after a month.

Under the Ming policy of "ruling barbarians with barbarians," the Lahu were ruled fairly lightly by Tai chiefs appointed over them. This practice changed dramatically when the Qing began to apply their new policy of direct administration by Han civil magistrates in Lahu areas. To implement direct rule, the Han authorities dismissed Tai officials, conducted a cadastral survey of cultivated lands by soil fertility, and began registering households with a view toward imposing a systematic tax regime. This policy, applied first in 1725, touched off a series of major rebellions beginning in 1728 and lasting six years. They all involved interethnic coalitions of Lahu, Tai, Hani, Lopang, and Yi opposed to the new taxes and the encroaching Han settlers, as well as the imperial monopoly on tea. In the later phases of these rebellions, the Lahu were led by a Tai monk "who claimed supernatural ability to deliver them from oppression."[19]

The central role of wonder-working monks or what have been called Lahu "god-men" becomes unmistakably clear at the turn of the century in a series of uprisings (1796–1807) by Lahu, Wa, and Bulang, this time against the taxes and corvée exacted by their remaining Tai overlords. A revered Mahayana monk of Han ethnicity, known locally as the "Copper and Gold Monk," was instrumental in rallying the Lahu to the rebels' cause. The crushing of this rebellion by imperial troops appears to have set off a large-scale migration southward into Burma's Shan states. Those Lahu who remained in the area of the uprisings have subsequently become increasingly Sinicized.

By 1800 a kind of cultural template had been established for Lahu rebellions, which were innumerable. They were almost always led by holy men seen by the Lahu as god-kings who could cure illnesses, purify the community, and constitute a Buddhist "field of merit." Thanks to the careful reconstruction of this cultural complex by Anthony Walker, we can identify the key elements of Lahu cosmology that make up this amalgam.

Like many of their neighboring hill societies—the Kachin, Lisu, Akha—the Lahu have a legendary creator-god, a dualistic male-female figure who formed the heaven and the earth.[20] This pre-Buddhist tradition became, by the mid-nineteenth century at the latest, thoroughly fused with Mahayana Buddhism (not the Theravada of the Tai), to which the Lahu were converted by a succession of charismatic monks who established temples (*fofang*) in the Lahu hills. The second of these monks, A-sha, and his sister were also credited by legend with defeating the Wa, converting them to Mahayana practices, and subordinating them to the Lahu. Mahayana brought with it the Golden Land tradition of a new world of equality, peace, material abundance, and autonomy from outside rule. Above and beyond bringing millenarian beliefs, Mahayana monastic structure provided something of a pan-Lahu organizing grid that served both as a social mechanism for dispute settlement and, at the same time, a supravillage network for rebellion. The teacher-disciple relationship so central to Mahayana and Tantric Buddhism led to "daughter" temples linked in discipleship and doctrine to the fofang of the most revered founding monks.

Lahu prophets subsequently were virtually all charismatic monks who saw themselves, and were seen, as the incarnation of the Lahu creator-spirit, Gui-sha, and simultaneously the Buddha Sakyamuni (Burmese *s'eq k'yà mín*—သိကြား မင်း) come to restore an ethical, peaceful world. The two figures become one and the same: an imminent divinity representing both the Lahu ancestral spirit and the conquering, wheel-turning, imminent Buddha. As Walker understands it, "A recurrent phenomenon of the Lahu experience, often disturbing the ritual routine . . . is that of a holy man who, invoking his oneness with Guisha's divinity, seek[s] to surmount the limitation of a village-based social organization in order to challenge the hegemony of externally imposed political control."[21] As in the case of the Karen prophets, Lahu prophets arise both to restore traditional ethical principles and to resist subordination to valley states—in this case, Han or Tai.

The frequency of Lahu prophetic movements allows us to identify something of a "career trajectory," even for an activity so decidedly unroutine as becoming a god-man. A local village priest has a mystical experience—perhaps as the result of an illness—and claims healing powers through the use of trance or possession. If his claim is accepted and he gains a substantial extravillage following for his curing powers, he may claim (or his followers may claim) that he has Gui-sha's divine nature. He is then likely to insist on ritual and doctrinal reforms (diet, prayer, taboos) to cleanse the community and prepare for a new order. A final step, one that will invariably catapult him into the archives of his lowland neighbors and perhaps sign his death warrant, is when, as god-man, he proclaims a new order and unites his followers in defiance of the lowland state.

Walker provides accounts of those twentieth-century god-men who made it into the archives. The Chinese records describe a Lahu prophet–led uprising in 1903 preceded by a monthlong assembly with gourd-pipe dancing and chanting. Its prophet was killed in the subsequent fighting. A Karen assistant to Harold Young, an American Baptist missionary, reported meeting a Lahu man north of Kengtung "who claimed to be a messianic king" and whose following included Akha and Shan as well as Lahu. In 1918 Lahu rebels attacked a Chinese magistrate's office (*yamen*), some of them carrying paper portraits of the Maitreya Buddha. By the 1920s, as Christianity began to make inroads among the Lahu, an American missionary reported that a Yunnanese convert with a reputation for prophecy and healing had attracted a huge following, for whom he had prescribed new dietary laws. Although the account is fragmentary, this Christian god-man appears to have followed much the same script as had Lahu Buddhist prophets before him.

In 1929 a Lahu healer near Kengtung with a large multiethnic following suddenly fortified his village, refused to pay taxes, and prepared to attack and seize the small Tai statelet of Muang Hsat for the Lahu. British colonial troops intervened at this point to destroy his fort and disperse his armed followers. Another Lahu prophet, active from 1930 to 1932, attacked a local Wa chief and then retreated into the inaccessible Awng Lawng mountains, along with his numerous followers. There, he ruled a partly independent kingdom.

Although the archives, written from a state perspective, often describe rebels and uprisings as essentially irrational, it is not hard to reconstruct more plausible precipitating factors, such as the desire to defend autonomy against valley-state incursions. This was surely the case in the massive and comparatively recent clashes in 1973 between Burma's military government and the Lahu near Kengtung.[22] The spiritual and secular leader of the Lahu, revered for the past sixty years as endowed with Gui-sha's divinity and hence the guardian of the Lahu moral order, was Maw Na Pau Khu. The proximate reasons for the clash were the campaign by Burma's army to disarm the Lahu, take over the opium trade, and impose taxes on households, livestock, and the slaughter of animals for market. For Burmese authorities, the prophet represented an intolerable zone of autonomous power they were determined to break. After two Lahu traders were arrested, the fighting began. Thousands of Lahu were involved; hundreds were killed, in part owing to their initial belief in their invulnerability. The Burmese losses in the more than fifty engagements that ensued were also considerable. There even appears to be a direct link between this particular rebellion and a subsequent anti-Han prophetic movement in Yunnan in 1976.[23]

That Christians, particularly Baptists, should have made many converts among the Lahu is not surprising. Generally receptive to prophetism, many Lahu saw in Baptism a way to general health ("everlasting life") and a powerful ally in their age-old attempts to free themselves from Han and Tai domination. The opening of schools and the acquisition of a prophetic book promised to put them on an equal footing with valley societies that stigmatized them for their backwardness. And in fact, many early Lahu converts who heard William Young's sermons understood him to be another wonder-working divinity calling, as had other prophets they followed in the past, for a return to ethical conduct (giving up alcohol, opium, gambling) in preparation for a new dispensation. In other words, the Lahu who converted could retain virtually all their cosmology and prophetic expectations with little adjustment. That the promise of being delivered from subordination to their Tai and Han overlords was paramount was astutely registered by two Presbyterian observers of Young's success: "We mention first [the political phase of the movement] because in our judgment political considerations such as exemption from taxes, mitigation of forced labor and relief from the necessity of bringing gifts to their [Tai] rulers were the most prominent considerations in the minds of most of the Lahu State who have been baptized."[24]

Theodicy of the Marginal and Dispossessed

In a world with the odds stacked so massively against them, surely the astounding fact about marginal hill peoples and many of the world's dispossessed is that they should so often believe and act as though their deliverance were at hand. Though it so often ends tragically, this radical bias for hope, the conviction that the world is headed their way, is worthy of our careful attention and perhaps even our admiration. It is hard to imagine what the world would be like if the dispossessed, knowing the long odds, were all hard-headed realists. Marx, even in the context of his critique of religion, was not above a certain admiration. In a passage of which only the very last phrase is generally quoted, he wrote, "But man is no abstract being squatting outside the world. Man is the world of man — state, society. This state and this society produce religion, which is an inverted consciousness of the world; because they are in an inverted world. . . . Religious suffering is, at one and the same time, the expression of real suffering and a protest against real suffering. Religion is the sigh of the oppressed creature, the heart of a heartless world, and the soul of soulless conditions. It is the opium of the people."[25] The repeated insistence among so many hill peoples on reading the world in their favor, on believing in their imminent emancipation, bears an unmistakable family resemblance to the expectations of other dispossessed and stigmatized peoples: the Anabaptists of the Reformation civil wars, the cargo cults of Melanesia, the belief of Russian serfs that the tsar had issued a decree freeing them, the conviction among New World slaves that a redeemer was at hand, and hundreds of other millenarian expectations of a coming (or returning) king or god, by no means confined to Judeo-Christian settings. Ironically, these misreadings of the world were occasionally so widespread and massive that they touched off rebellions that in fact changed the odds.

Given their elements of divine intervention and of magic, it is all too easy to exoticize prophetic movements cast in religious garb. This is a temptation that should be resisted. It should be resisted because virtually all popular struggles for power that today would qualify as "revolutionary" were, before the last quarter of the eighteenth century, generally understood in a religious idiom. Popular mass politics was religion, and religion was political. To paraphrase Marc Bloch, millennial revolt was as natural to the seigneurial (feudal) world as strikes, let us say, are to large-scale capitalism.[26] Before the first two avowedly secular revolutions in North America and France in 1776 and 1789, virtually all mass political movements expressed their aspirations in religious terms. Ideas of justice and of rights and, indeed, what we might today call "class consciousness" were religiously phrased. If, then, we are interested in popular aspirations and subaltern politics, we will rarely find them dressed in completely secular clothing. That such aspirations should take an extramundane form is not trivial, as we shall see. But when is politics not, at some level, a theological debate about moral order?

The strong and continuing animist substratum of popular religion, not excluding the salvation religions of Buddhism, Christianity, and Islam, also ensures that "real-existing" practical religion does not ignore mundane concerns. Animist religious practices, after all, are largely about influencing worldly affairs: ensuring good crops, curing disease, influencing the hunt, succeeding in love and war, thwarting enemies of all kinds, succeeding in exams, ensuring human fertility. Most of the actual practice of the salvation religions, as opposed to the high doctrine, reflects this animist preoccupation with worldly results. The cult of the *nats* and the *phi* in Burmese and Siamese Theravada practice, respectively, is so deeply embedded that ordinary practitioners rarely experience a tension between this popular animism and canonical Buddhism.[27]

Prophets Are a Dime a Dozen

A prophetic rebellion is often named, reasonably enough, after the prophet who appears as its central, charismatic figure (for example, the Saya San Rebellion in lower Burma, 1930–31). This practice seems to me an unfortunate misplacing of emphasis. First, while most prophetic movements do revolve around single charismatic figures, on many occasions a generalized millenarian activity lacks a single leader, or has a series of figures, none of whom appears to play a decisive role.

A second and far more important objection is that prophets seem rarely to be in short supply. Only those whose activities reach a level that catapults them into the archives, newspapers, and police and court records commend our attention. As Guillaume Rozenberg notes in the case of Burmese hermit monks, "We haven't even considered the innumerable failures, this crowd of unknown forest monks who aspired and aspired in vain to sainthood. . . . It's true that the anonymous destiny of those who failed in their quest for sainthood remains much more difficult to grasp than the striking trajectory of the glorious victors."[28] One imagines that in early-first-century Roman Palestine there were innumerable would-be messiahs, each believing himself the fulfillment of the ancient Judaic prophecy.[29] Yet the cult of only one, Jesus of Nazareth, later became institutionalized as a world religion.

Charisma is, above all, a specific cultural relationship between a would-be prophetic figure and his or her potential following. And because it is a relationship or an interpersonal resonance, we cannot claim that an individual has charisma in the same way we might say that someone has a gold coin in his pocket. What constitutes a charismatic connection is always somewhat elusive, but what is charismatic in one cultural setting is unlikely to be charismatic in another, and what is charismatic at one historical moment might well be merely incomprehensible at another. Underpinning the individual gifts or radiant personality of a single figure, then, lie the more durable cultural expectations and desires that create, as it were, a kind or repertoire into which a prophet might fit. Thus from this perspective, a charismatic connection might be conceived as a specific congregation looking for a preacher whose message it can wholeheartedly embrace and whom it believes it can trust. It is as if the destination is largely known and specified (however ambitious it may be), and the congregation is in search of reliable transportation. The prophet is, in this sense, a vehicle. By the same token, a specific prophecy—for example, a new world will arrive when fifty white pagodas are built—is less interesting, since it is always disconfirmed, than is the underlying readiness to entertain certain kinds of futures. This readiness, having structural and historical causes, is likely to outlive the failure of a specific prophecy and to surface again in a new form. Why is it, in other words, that certain groups appear to have a vocation for millenarian expectations? Why are so many societies in the hills veritable cottage industries for the manufacture of utopian futures? There would seem to be something generic about many upland societies that is generative of prophecy.

It is the society within which a successful prophet appears that, in effect, lays down the basic script that shapes the prophet's repertoire. We saw, in this connection, that it was possible to set out something like a standard career pattern for a Lahu prophet. How this process of reciprocal influence might work can be likened to the influence that an audience might have on a medieval bard. Let us imagine a bard who lives exclusively by the voluntary contributions of ordinary people in the marketplace. And let us assume, for the sake of argument, that each of those who like what he sings gives him an identical small "copper." Having conjured up a bard who wants to please a large audience, let us further imagine that this bard has a repertoire of, say, a thousand songs and stories from which to select. Assuming that his audience has definite tastes, I imagine that, little by little, as the bard comes to know his audience, the actual songs he sings in the market square—perhaps even the order and style in which he sings them—will come to more closely approximate the distribution of tastes among his audience. Even if our bard is not adept at reading the expressions and enthusiasms of the crowd, the size of the pile of coppers at the close of the market will provoke adjustments in his repertoire.

Like any analogy, this one has its limitations. It allows too little for the creativity of the prophet and his capacity to add to the repertoire and to change tastes. By using the rather banal activity of singing in the public square as an analogy, I most certainly miss the huge stakes and high passions that animate a prophetic movement. Nonetheless, the analogy does illustrate the way in which the cultural expectations and historical understanding of a charismatic public—often misunderstood as mere putty in his hands—can play a decisive role in influencing the script of a successful prophet. This stochastic process of successive adjustment is familiar enough; it is the stock in trade of most successful politicians and preachers.[30]

"Sooner or Later . . ."

Any social hierarchy creates, by its very existence, a stratification of wealth, privilege, and honor. Each principle of stratification may yield a slightly different ranking: the Confucian scholar or the Buddhist abbot may top the ranking for prestige but may be materially poor. For most societies, of course, the correlations of rankings are high and, over time, many rankings are, to use the financial term, fungible. This social hierarchy is manifested by a pattern of ceremony, ritual, and consumption, often glossed as civilized conduct. Certain ways of celebrating marriages and funerals, certain clothes, housing styles, certain patterns of feasting, of ritual and religious behavior, of entertainment come to be seen as proper and worthy. Those who have the means to acquit themselves honorably by these standards come to see themselves, and are usually seen, as more exemplary and honorable than those who lack the means to emulate them.[31]

When Max Weber writes of the "religion of non-privileged classes," he has this sort of social and cultural distinction in mind. The stigma and dishonor experienced by the nonprivileged in a stratified order is less a question of calories and cash than one of standing and social esteem. They are daily reminded that their diet, their rites, their funerals, and by extension they themselves are inferior to the privileged. "It is immediately evident," as Weber notes, "that a need for salvation in the widest sense of the term has as one of its foci . . . dis-privileged classes." In contrast, "Turning to the 'sated' and privileged strata, the need for salvation is remote and alien to warriors, bureaucrats, and the plutocracy."[32]

The disprivileged have the least interest in maintaining the current distribution of status and wealth and potentially the most to gain from a radical reshuffling of the social order. Little wonder, then, that they should be disproportionately attracted to movements and religions that promise a completely new dispensation. The lively interest of the disprivileged strata in a "world turned upside down" is, as it were, formally recognized in the Jewish tradition of the Jubilee Year, when debts are forgiven, slaves redeemed, and prisoners released. This message of the Old Testament, as well as the idea of an escape from Egyptian bondage and a Promised Land, was taken to heart by North American slaves, for whom a Jubilee Year and redemption were taken literally. This interest is also manifested in annual rituals of reversal such as Carnival in Catholic countries, the feast of Holi in Hindu India, and the Water Festivals of Southeast Asia, where, for a brief period, the normal social order is suspended or reversed. Far from being mere safety valves serving harmlessly to release tension, the better to impose hierarchy the rest of the year, these ritual sites have always been zones of struggle, threatening to spill over into actual revolt.[33]

Weber tried to be more precise in specifying those among the disprivileged who would be most likely to believe that "sooner or later there would arise some tremendous hero or god who would place his followers in the positions they truly deserved in the world." He believed that among the peasantry, for example, the appeal of a revolutionary religion was greatest for those at the edge, those "threatened by enslavement or proletarianization, either by domestic forces (financial, agrarian, seigneurial) or by some external political power." That is, it was not so much penury that led peasants to radical religious sects as the imminent prospect of losing their status as independent smallholders and falling into abject dependence as landless laborers or, worse, someone's serf. Not particularly religious to begin with, let alone orthodox, peasants (etymologically, the term *pagan*, meaning nonbeliever, comes to us directly from the Latin *paganus*, meaning country-dweller) turned to antiestablishment revolutionary sects when their economic and social independence was menaced. Among others, Weber pointed to the Donatist sects of Roman North Africa, the Taborites (aka Hussites) of early-fifteenth-century Bohemia, the Diggers of the English Civil Wars, and Russian peasant sectarians as examples of the prophetic tradition of agrarian radicalism.[34]

Weber's insight will prove useful when it comes to a close discussion of prophetic movements in the hills. For the moment, it is sufficient to note that peasant communities already incorporated into a state-based order are prone to support radical prophetic movements whenever their relatively autonomous village order (local dispute settlement, managing grazing rights and common land, selecting their own leaders) is threatened by an intrusive centralizing state. Again, it appears to be less a question of income and food supply than one of autonomy.[35]

Religious heterodoxy and prophetism with millenarian overtones are, historically at least, as common in the lowlands and within populations already part of lowland states as they are in the hills. In fact, as indicated earlier, the millenarian ideas circulating in the hills are, for the most part, assembled from fragments that have been imported from valley states.

If we take Burma as our Theravada example, it is clear that it has the full complement of heterodox practices and beliefs. There is a long tradition of *weikza* (adepts at alchemy, magic, flying, and immortality), hermit monks (*yà thè*), healers by possession and trance, astrologers (*bedin saya*), black magic practitioners (*auk lan saya*), and wonder-working monks, any of whom might be taken for an embryo-Buddha, Chakaveddi, Mettreya.[36]

One of the basic oppositions within lowland Theravada Buddhism is that between the forest or hermit monk on the one hand and, on the other, the settled clergy living under the monastic discipline of one of the (nine) recognized orders.[37] The monk who decides to pursue a personal quest for spiritual powers as a hermit, a quest often accompanied by great austerities, rigorous fasting, and meditation in cemeteries and over cadavers, not only leaves the area of settled agriculture and government; he also enters the dangerous world of powerful spirits and nondomesticated nature. Those forest monks who become the objects of popular veneration, and are therefore known to us, are believed to have thereby acquired miraculous powers: to predict the future (including the winning lottery number!), to ward off death until the arrival of the next Buddha, to devise powerful medicines and protective talismans, to master alchemy and the ability to fly, and to confer merit on their faithful devotees. The fact that these powers are seen by settled lowlanders to have been acquired only by leaving, as it were, state space and the landscape of irrigated-rice cultivation for the forest and wilderness is something of an implicit tribute to the powers thought to reside outside the ambit of the padi state. The fact that a great many forest monks are themselves of non-Burman ethnicity is also a recognition of the appeal of hill heterodoxy.[38]

All these roles might collectively be seen as the charismatic, heterodox wing of Buddhist practice. Precisely because they depend on inspiration and a charismatic connection, they have always been discouraged as a threat to the institutional, hierarchical clergy (*sangha*). Just as the Roman authorities looked with favor on the oracles of Apollo (who moved only in the best society) and banned the tumultuous revelries of the cult of Dionysus, much favored by women and lower-class men, so have Theravada authorities proscribed charismatic threats.[39] That such activities have constituted an ever-present danger is implied in the warning in the Buddhist ordination ceremony: "Again no member of our brotherhood can ever arrogate to himself extraordinary gifts or supernatural perfections, or through vainglory give himself out as a holy man, for instance, as to withdraw into solitary places or on pretense of enjoying ecstasies like the Ariya, afterwards presume to teach others the way to uncommon spiritual attainments."[40] The founder of the Kon-baung Dynasty in the eighteenth century, Alaunghpaya, was concerned enough about this threat that those who failed to finish the prescribed course of study for the monkhood were tattooed and expelled "so that their hetero-doxy could be verified by a mark."[41]

How might we understand the logic behind Burmese religious syn-cretism within the lowland state? We might, I think, begin with Michael Mendelson's observation that the Buddhist clergy is most densely clustered wherever wealth and padi cultivation are concentrated — that is to say, in the spaces most suitable for state-building. The wealthy lay public, officialdom, and the centers of official monastic learning gravitated to these same locations. Add to this close linkage another observation by Mendelson that the strength of Buddhism vis-à-vis other indigenous religious traditions (for example, ani-mism) is directly related to the strength of royal authority — that is to say, the monarchical state. If we then read noncanonical Buddhism, the practices for-bidden in the ordination ceremony, nat worship, and other animist practices as reflecting the seams, the ruptures, the fissures in the historical process of state-building, a certain logic is discernible. These variant religious practices and their practitioners represent zones of resistant difference, dissent, and, at the very least, failures of incorporation and domestication by state-promoted religion.

Just as the opposition party in the British Parliament has a shadow cabi-net that replicates — in waiting — the actual cabinet, so does official canonical Buddhism have a set of alternative institutions that both shadow and bedevil it. In place of the iconic monastic school, there are the hermit and the forest monk, outside the state, who escape monastic discipline. In place of the offi-cial millennial expectations of Buddhism, there are the curers, the would-be mín laún, Mattreya, Setkyamin . . . who promise a double-quick utopia to their followers. In place of central pagodas and shrines, there are the local nat pwes (spirit ceremonies). In place of merit-making for salvation, there are mundane, here-and-now techniques for improving one's luck in the world. In place of the bureaucratic, exam-passing sangha, there are charismatic monks assembling independent followings. Most Burman Buddhists move easily and quite unself-consciously between their household nat shrine and a read-ing of the Tripitika at a pagoda; the distinction I am making is thus, largely, an analytical one.

The warrant for seeing alternative forms of worship as representing the sutured-but-still-evident seams in the historical process of state-making is most evident in nat worship. Most nats are believed to be the spirits of real existing persons who died "green" or premature deaths and therefore have left behind powerful spirits that can protect or harm people. What is striking about many of the best known nats is that the legends surrounding their earthly lives are emblematic of disobedience or rebellion against the king.[42] Two of the best known, "the Taungbyon brothers," were said to have been fun-loving Muslims who, though they had helped the king acquire an important Buddhist relic, were too busy playing marbles to bring their two bricks to help build the pagoda to house it. For this act of lèse-majesté, the king had them killed by having their testicles crushed. The annual festival honoring them in Taungbyon village, twenty miles north of Mandalay, is a veritable bacchanal of eating, drinking, gambling, and open sexuality, threatening always to get out of hand. Speculating that the nats may represent the guardian spirit of different groups and localities conquered by the centralizing kings, Melford Spiro notes the political and religious oppositional tone of the Taungbyon cult: The nats "symbolize opposition to authority. Here in performing their cultus . . . the people are expressing their opposition to authority. But the nat[s] . . . also symbolize opposition to religious authority. . . . The nat devotees are afforded the opportunity to express their hostility to Buddhism and to satisfy needs which are prohibited by it."[43] Other nats include those who were unjustly put to death by the king (the Mahagiri nats, brother and sister, for whom most households maintain a shrine), at least three regicides, and several libertines exemplifying anti-Buddhist behavior.

There is a central pantheon of thirty-seven nats (the number is the cosmologically correct one for devas and subordinate tributary kingdoms), which, in part, was centrally established. Mendelson believes that the pantheon represents an effort to appropriate a series of local cults under a monarchical Buddhist umbrella, much as the cults of particular saints in Catholic countries are often associated with pre-Christian deities. The purpose was to harness these powerful but essentially fissiparous spirits to a centralized monarchy.[44] And yet the desired alliance has been an uneasy one, with nat worship continuing to represent a spirit of resistance both to canonical Buddhism and to the unified state. As Mendelson summarizes it, "There is evidence for believing that, whenever Buddhism was strong, the nat cult was weakened — say, by measures prohibiting local nat cults — thus Buddhism goes along with a strong central monarchy while Animism coincides with the triumph of the forces of locality and rebellion."[45] The ritual life of the Burmans, then, continues to reflect the still unresolved conflicts of state-making.

Quite apart from the nat cults, the cleavage between the bureaucratized, registered, exam-taking clergy—Weber's routinization of charisma—on the one hand and the wonder-working, healing, amulet dispensing clergy on the other is still very much in evidence. Many village pongyi are, in keeping with the expectations of their lay supporters, hybrids of the two. At times of national crisis, it has been the prophetic stream that has represented lay aspirations. It would be impossible, in fact, to write a credible history of twentieth-century Burmese nationalism without this prophetic tradition. From the time, shortly after the colonial conquest, when U Ottama declared himself a pretender (*mín gyi*) and was hanged for his defiance by the British, there stretches an all but unbroken skein of would-be Buddhist world emperors (*setkyamin*) preparing for the Buddha's return, up to the Saya San revolt in 1930. Although that revolt enters the archives under his name and he has become a state-sanctioned hero, presumably for his protonationalism, it is well to remember that he was one of three or four "would-be kings" in that rebellion.[46] Today, of course, it is the "undomesticated" clergy that represents the democratic aspirations of the lay public, while the captive clergy is kept in line by lavish personal and monastic gifts from the military high brass.[47] Ne Win, when he was alive and in power, banned any film featuring nat worship. Nat worship and prophetic forms of Buddhism are to the organized and tamed sangha, one might say, as swiddening and root crops are to irrigated padi cultivation. The former are illegible and resist state incorporation, while the latter lend themselves to centralization.

High-Altitude Prophetism

Lowland prophetic movements have, until recently, been as common as those in the hills. What distinguishes them, perhaps, from highland movements is that they represent a protest against oppression and inequality within an agreed cultural matrix. Such strategies may be, for all that, no less bitter and protracted, but they are, in a sense, lovers' quarrels. That is, they are, to use a Western concept, about the terms of the social contract, not about whether there should be a social contract in the first place. The growing cultural, linguistic, and religious flattening of valley society since at least the twelfth century—a hard-won state effect—has left its scars, but there is rarely a naked bid for cultural or political secession. Within this cultural matrix, radical options are still imaginable for those who are impoverished and/or stigmatized. A radical reshuffling of the cards in which existing class and status distinctions might be abolished is thinkable. But it is, to pursue the metaphor, a question of redistributing the cards in an existing card game, not a question of whether to sit at the table at all or, for that matter, to throw the table over.[48]

The sorts of precipitating conditions that seem associated with prophetic and millenarian activity are so varied as to defy easy accounting. Suffice it to say that each involves a sense of overwhelming collective peril to which the prophecy and the actions taken to realize that prophecy constitute an attempted remedy. The peril in question can take the form of a natural disaster—floods, crop failures, epidemics, earthquakes, cyclones—though the agency of the spirits or gods is typically seen at work, as in the case of the Old Testament Israelites. The perils may also be eminently man-made—as in the case of war, invasion, crushing taxes, or corvée—and integral to the history of most state peoples.

What relatively autonomous hill peoples have historically faced, however, are the ominous choices forced on them by encroaching state power. This might mean the choice between enslavement and headlong flight, between the loss of direct control of their communities or subsistence activities and open revolt, between forced sedentarization and breaking up and scattering. Compared with the choices that valley populations face, these seem far more draconian, not to say revolutionary, and the information that hill peoples have on which to base their choices is often minimal. Imagine, to take a more contemporary example, the fateful choice of Hmong groups in the 1960s, between allying themselves with the Americans, supporting the Pathet Lao, or moving away. Hill peoples are by no means naïve when dealing with valley powers, but they often confront threats that are both hard to comprehend and fraught with grave consequences for their way of life.

Something of the difference can be appreciated from the different sorts of revolts along the Siamese-Lao borders from the late seventeenth century on. Revolts at the close of the seventeenth century were caused by commoner resentment over taxes, poor harvests, and an influx of Chinese tax collectors working for the Siamese. These revolts, though led by "miracle-working holy men with visions of local autonomy and social equality," were rebellions of state populations determined to force a renegotiation of the terms of their incorporation.[49] By the early nineteenth century, however, the expansionist Chakkri kings were extending their power to the hills—enslaving large numbers of people, massacring those who resisted, and imposing direct administration on hill peoples. Prophetic rebellions broke out and set the stage for Anauvong's massive 1827 revolt, centered in Vientiane, against Siamese rule. These later rebellions, unlike the earlier ones by commoners (*phrai*), might be termed "virgin-land revolts" in the sense that many relatively independent populations were being threatened with absorption by the state for the first time. The issue at stake was not reforming the terms of incorporation but whether these populations would be administered at all.

Lest the hill peoples invoked here seem like the native peoples of the New World suddenly, in the sixteenth century, confronted by the organization and weaponry of a more technically advanced state, it must be emphasized that these populations were not naïve. They had long been acquainted with lowland states. Recall, in this context, the important distinction between the symbolic, the economic, and the political reach of the state. These people so vigorously resisting political incorporation had long been enthusiastic consumers of lowland cosmology—so much so that they had borrowed its traditions to create their own rebellious traditions. Symbolic commerce, perhaps because its goods are weightless and less impeded by the friction of distance, circulates most briskly. Economic exchange was nearly as brisk owing to the fact that hills and valleys are complementary ecological zones: each has products that the other needs. They are natural partners. Hill peoples had long enjoyed the advantages of voluntary symbolic and economic exchange while evading, if possible, the inconveniences of political subordination, most often in the form of slavery. It was this and only this involuntary "import" from the state they were resisting.

Prophetic, holy-man revolts were, parenthetically, not only deployed against lowland state intrusion. They were also deployed within the hills, often in the same ethnic group as a state-prevention measure. This much is implicit in Edmund Leach's analysis of revolts against tyrannical village heads among the Kachin. It is also apparent in Thomas Kirsch's account of a syncretic Chin "democratic" cult that successfully repudiated the community feasts monopolized by the chiefs and restored "private" feasts that allowed everyone to compete for ritual status. The cultural technique of prophetic movements can be as useful for state prevention as for state evasion.

Holy-man revolts in the hills might well be considered one of several techniques for thwarting state incorporation. The standard, lower-risk techniques we have discussed at great length: swiddening, escape crops, social fissioning and dispersal, and perhaps oral traditions might be together considered one-half the hill armory for state evasion. The other, perhaps last-ditch, high-stakes technique in the armory is rebellion and the prophetic cosmology that goes with it. This is precisely what Mikael Gravers intriguingly suggests for the Karen. As he put it,

> The ambiguity of the Karen strategy between valley and hills can be described as a double strategy with a defensive dimension avoiding taxes, corvée and political suppression [and] subsisting on swidden agriculture, hunting, and collecting; or an offensive dimension emulating royal powers to resist state administration and coercion and also to construct their own polity. Both dimensions look for a moral leadership founded on Buddhist ethics and contain an emulation of the Buddhist states as well as a cultural (ethnic) critique of neighboring monarchies and states.[50]

Dialogue, Mimicry, and Connections

The legends, rituals, and politics of hill societies can be usefully read as a contentious dialogue with the valley state that looms largest in its imagination. The closer and larger that state, the more of the conversation it will usurp. Most of the origin myths of hill societies assert a hybridity or connection that implies kinship. In some cases a stranger/foreigner arrives and forms a union with an autochthonous woman. Their joint progeny are this hill people. In other legends, hill and valley people are hatched from different eggs—of the same parentage—and are, hence, brother and sister. Already, a certain original equality between highland and lowland becomes part of the narrative. In the same fashion, the claim in many hill legends that their people once had a king, books, and writing, and that they planted wet rice in the valleys, is a claim of an original equal status that has been lost, treacherously withheld, or stolen. One of the central promises of many a prophet is precisely that he will be the king who will right this injustice and restore this equality, or perhaps even turn the tables. The Hmong version is a particularly strong one. Their king Chih-yu was, by legend, murdered by the founder of the Chinese state. A new king will arise one day to liberate the Hmong and inaugurate a golden age.[51]

The presumption of a cultural dialogue between hill and valley has at least two additional sources. First, both hill and valley societies were planets in a larger galactic system (Indic or Sinic) of mutual influence. Hill peoples may not have been political subjects of valley states, but they were active participants in the economic system of exchange and in the even wider cosmopolitan circulation of ideas, symbols, cosmology, titles, political formulas, medical recipes, and legends. As has been said of folk culture, hill peoples "continually incorporate into their fabrics significant parts of the sophisticated intellectual traditions . . . which are part of a super cultural area."[52] More frictionless than economic exchange, cheaper, and completely voluntary, this cultural buffet allowed hill societies to take just what they wanted from it and put it to precisely the use they chose.

Hill and valley are also firmly joined by a shared history. We must not forget that many hill peoples are descendants—in some cases fairly recent— of valley-dwelling state populations. They brought with them much of the culture and beliefs that prevailed in the places they left. Just as isolated Appalachian valleys have preserved older English and Scottish dialects, music, and dance long after they have disappeared from their place of origin, so do hill societies constitute something of a living historical archive of beliefs and rituals their ancestors brought with them or picked up en route in their long migrations. Hmong geomancy, for example, appears to be a faithful replica of Han practices several centuries ago. Their formulas of authority, insignia of rank, titles, and chiefly costumes might be museum pieces in a valley exhibit. Curiously enough, the valley prejudice that hill peoples represent "our past" turns out to be partly true, but not at all in the way imagined. Rather than being social fossils themselves, hill people have brought and often kept antique practices from the valleys. When one adds to this the constant flight to the hills of persecuted religious sects, hermit monks, dissident political factions, royal pretenders and their entourages, and outlaws, one can see how hill society did come to reflect back aspects of the valley's often repressed past.

When it comes to cosmology and religion in particular, there would seem to be a plausible connection between dissident, charismatic religious movements in the hills and the disprivileged strata within state populations. Remarking that highlanders had remained largely aloof from the religions of the state cores in Southeast Asia (Buddhism, Islam), Oscar Salemink also astutely noted that highland religion "often labeled 'animism' has many beliefs and practices in common with lowland folk religion."[53] If we in turn take note of the fact that when valley religions do make it to the hills—for example, Karen and Shan Buddhism—they are likely to take heterodox and charismatic forms, then something of a continuum between symbolic dissent by subaltern state populations and relatively independent hill societies emerges. It is among these peoples, dispossessed and marginal, respectively, that the more revolutionary, "world-upside-down" prophetic message makes

its greatest appeal. And of course, it is with the fringes of the valley population that hill peoples are likely to have most contact. Arriving in the valleys
for trade and work, hill visitors are in closest contact with the bottom of the
valley social hierarchy. The lower echelons of the valley population, along
with the "lumpen intelligentsia" of monks and hermits, are also the most
likely to drift into the hills. Thus, in terms of structural position as well as of
social contact, we should probably treat radical valley religious movements
as different in degree but not in kind from hill prophetic movements. Both
emphasize the mundane functions of salvation religion; both share myths of
a just king or returning Buddha who will restore justice; and both have ample
reasons (though not the same ones) to resent the valley state. Each is, finally,
something of a social and historical archive of state-breaking cosmologies and
practices.

Making a new state, a new order, which is exactly what nearly all prophetic movements aim at, requires, logically, breaking an existing order. On
the surface of it, such movements are rebellions. They appropriate the power,
magic, regalia, and institutional charisma of the valley state in a kind of symbolic jujitsu in order to attack it. The nature of the utopia a new king or
Mettreya will bring can be read as the negation of state oppressions: all will
be equal, there will be no corvée, taxes, or tribute, no one will be poor, wars
and killing will cease, the Burman or Han or Tai oppressor will withdraw or
be destroyed, and so forth. One can infer what is wrong with the present by
the content of the promised future. Those expecting a new utopia, far from
being passive, often prepare themselves ritually, announce their withdrawal
of allegiance, refuse to hand over taxes, and launch attacks. The mobilization around a prophet is the idiom of both state formation and rebellion in
premodern Southeast Asia, an ominous sign known well by rulers and their
pundits.

A fair amount of ink has been spilled wondering whether the use of the
dominant ritual discourse—say, by Karen millennial Buddhist sects opposing
Burman rule, or by the Hmong opposing imperial Han rule—can be taken
as subversive if it is so symbolically indebted to state rituals.[54] The question
is, I think, a mere debater's point, for reasons that will become clear. It is
true, surely, that the only existing discourse for political order beyond a small
league of villages was the discourse of monarchy—human or divine. But this
was no less true of European rebellions until the late eighteenth century.[55]
Virtually all states were monarchies, and the remedy for a bad king was a
better king.

The precolonial, colonial, and postcolonial states of mainland Southeast Asia (and China as well) were in no doubt about the threat posed by wonder-working pretenders and their entourages. They have acted with dispatch to stamp out such movements wherever they arose and to support, in their place, a formal, orthodox, clerical hierarchy that could be supervised from the center. As Max Weber would have forecast, they have been implacably hostile to all charismatic inspiration with political overtones. In this respect, the fact that potential rebels deploy Buddhist cosmology and Han imperial insignia is not in the least reassuring to state officials.[56]

We have often noted what might be called the great chain of mimicry that extends from Angkor and Pagan through pettier and pettier states right down to hamlet chiefs with the slightest pretentions among, say, the Lahu or Kachin. The classical states similarly modeled themselves after the states of South Asia in a process one might call the "localization of imperial ritual."[57] It is pervasive as a process, although the proximate model for imitative palace architecture, titles, regalia, and ritual was generally the nearest larger political domain. What is important for our purposes is that the mimicry bore no relationship to the scope of power actually wielded. Clifford Geertz goes so far as to suggest that "what was high centralization representationally was enormous dispersion institutionally," as if symbolic centralization could serve as a counterweight to the limits of "hard" power.[58]

Much the same process, I suggest, is at work in the symbolic languages of rebellion as in local claims to rulership. It is as if there is "open-access software" freely available to any rebel claiming to be the "once and future king." Whether he gathers a large following is another matter. Structurally, however, the chances of a Lahu prophet becoming the universal monarch are no greater than the Wa hamlet chief becoming emperor, despite the fact that they have the cosmology for it. The dispersal of populations and agricultural production, coupled with a geography that impedes, if it does not absolutely prevent, social mobilization on a large scale, work decisively against it.[59] F. K. Lehman aptly notes the "marked disparity between what the supra-local political system attempts to be, on the models provided it by its civilized neighbors, and what its resources and organizational capacity really permit it to achieve."[60] Petty states can be and have been founded in the hills by charismatic figures (for example, the Kayah State in Burma), and larger kingdoms by valley prophets (Alaunghpaya), but they are the exceptions that prove the rule. The cosmological bluster is the dialect, the only idiom in which a claim to supralocal authority can be phrased. As an idea, it is surely an imperial legacy, an "as if" state whose essence remains unchanged, even as it rarely if ever corresponds to empirical reality. The "as if" state that lays claim to a cosmological hegemony as a center—a claim that typically obscures a fragmented and tenuous political situation on the ground—was by no means confined to highland strongmen. Such ritual sovereignty was typical of the valley kingdoms as well. In fact, it appears to have been the usual situation in South India, the locus classicus from which Southeast Asian valley kingdoms derived much of their cosmology.[61]

In the invocation of the "as if" state, in the mimicry of palace architecture, of ritual formulas, of getting the cosmology right, there is undeniably a kind of sympathetic magic at work. For those populations largely out of range of direct imperial power, the great state centers arrive in symbolic fragments that seem eminently appropriable. Their situation is not much different from that of the Japanese officials who toured the West at the beginning of the Meiji Restoration and who imagined that the key to Western progress was the constitution. If they got the constitution right, they reasoned, progress would more or less automatically follow. The formula itself was deemed efficacious. In this belief, highlanders were not one whit different than the founders and usurpers of lowland states whose Brahmin handlers made sure that their palaces, regalia, genealogies, and oaths were scrupulously correct down to the minutest detail. Like a magic spell, it had to be "word-perfect."

Perhaps because of the symbolic magnetism of the valley state, charismatic leaders in the hills, rebellious or not, have been expected to demonstrate a knowledge of this wider world and a connection with it. They have been, virtually without exception, local cosmopolitans. That is, they have local roots but typically have traveled widely, speak many languages, have contacts and alliances elsewhere, know the sacred formulas of valley religions, and are skilled speakers and mediators. In one way or another, frequently many ways, they are savvy, to use the Native American pidgin term to capture the same qualities. It is quite extraordinary, in fact, how far this generalization travels. In the great Taiping Rebellion, in the hundreds of cargo-cult uprisings in the Pacific Islands, in the rebellions of New World prophets against Europeans, the key figures are often culturally amphibious translators who move relatively easily between the worlds they inhabit. The conclusion of Stuart Schwartz and Frank Salomon, writing of early colonial revolts in South America, is fairly representative: "With amazing regularity, the leaders of messianic or millenarian frontier uprisings turned out to be mestizos who had opted for Indian life ways or, in the Andes, bi-cultural Indians whose social circumstances resembled that of mestizos."[62]

The function of translation between cultures can sometimes be understood more literally, given the diversity of vernacular languages in the hills. Nicholas Tapp describes a powerful Hmong village chief in northern Thailand who was widely admired for his linguistic command of Karen, Lahu, Chinese, Shan, and northern Thai.[63] Just as often, however, the cosmopolitanism derives from a knowledge of the lowland religions and their cosmologies. This helps explain why monks, ex-seminarians, catechists, healers, traders, and peripheral local clergy are vastly overrepresented in the ranks of prophets. They are, in the Gramscian sense, the organic intellectuals of the dispossessed and marginal in the premodern world. This too, as a generalization, travels well. Marc Bloch notes the prominent role of the country priests in peasant uprisings in medieval Europe. Their "plight was often no better than that of their parishioners but [their] minds could better encompass the idea that their miseries were part of a general ill, [they were] men well-fitted to play the time-honoured role of the intellectual."[64] Max Weber termed this class "pariah intellectuals" and noted that it stood "on the point of Archimedes in relation to social convention . . . and was capable of an original attitude toward the meaning of the cosmos."[65] In the highlands such religious figures play much the same role, articulating the aspirations of the community and, at the same time, able to command, or at least neutralize, the symbolic technology of the state.

The amphibious position of such leaders, with one foot in each of the two worlds, makes them potentially dangerous. They can, structurally, become a fifth column serving outside interests. Erik Mueggler describes a Yi village in Yunnan that, realizing this danger, took quite exceptional ritual and practical steps to contain it.[66] The crucial and potentially ruinous responsibility for hosting and feeding Han officials, sometimes accompanied by hundreds of troops, was rotated annually among a handful of prosperous families. During their year of service, the host couple was required to act as ur-Lahu and abjure anything culturally coded as Han. They wore clothing thought to have been worn by Lahu ancestors; they ate and drank from wooden vessels rather than ceramic ones; they drank only homemade wheat beer; they ate no meat associated with lowland diets (dogs, horses, cattle); and they were never to speak Chinese throughout their year of service. One could scarcely imagine a more comprehensive set of prohibitions designed to keep the host family hyper-Lahu and to keep the Han at arm's length. Almost all social contact with the Han was relegated to a "speaker" who lodged free at the host's house for the year. He, by contrast, drank and ate with the guests, dressed well and had cosmopolitan manners, spoke fluent Chinese, and generally entertained the dangerous guests. The speaker was, one could say, a village-level minister of foreign affairs whose job was to placate the guests, minimize their demands, and serve as a kind of cultural barrier between the Han and the internal affairs of the village. Knowing that a powerful and cosmopolitan local intermediary could as easily be a liability as an asset, the Lahu took pains to split the two roles and thus minimize the danger.

Turning on a Dime: The Ultimate Escape Social Structure

I am determined, in what follows, to "deexoticize" prophetic movements in upland Southeast Asia. Commonly, such movements are often treated as a phenomenon sui generis, a radical break with normal reasoning and action and therefore suggestive of a kind of collective derangement, if not psychopathology.[67] This is unfortunate for two reasons. First, it ignores the rich history of millenarian movements in the West that continues to this day. Second, and more germane in this context, it misses the degree to which prophetic activity is continuous with traditional healing practices and with village decisions about moving or splitting up. Prophetic activity can, I believe, fruitfully be seen as a strong and more collective version of these more quotidian activities—different in degree but not necessarily in kind.

The shaman or traditional healer treats patients who are troubled or ill, typically through trance and/or possession. The shaman identifies what is out of whack and then conducts rituals to persuade the spirit troubling the patient to withdraw. In the case of the prophet, however, it is the entire community that is, as it were, out of whack. Often the crisis and threat are such that the normal cultural paths to dignity and respect—diligence as a cultivator, bravery, successful feasting, good hunting, marriage and children, and locally honorable behavior generally—are no longer adequate to an exceptional situation. It is in this context that a whole community's life world is at stake and cannot be made whole with minor adjustments. As Tapp has expressed it, "If the shaman is concerned with the health and well-being of individual patients and their families . . . the messianic prophet is ultimately concerned with the salvation of Hmong society as a whole."[68] The role is more grandiose, the patient is a collectivity, and the stakes are far greater, but the prophet is, or proposes to be, the shaman for a whole community in trouble.

Treating prophetism as something altogether exceptional overlooks what is essentially a "minor league" version of prophet-inspired change: that associated with the fissioning or movement of an existing village site. Though it is hardly a daily occurrence, it is common enough to be the object of what might be called cultural routinization. Any number of perfectly reasonable circumstances might lead to the breakup or movement of a village and its fields: soil exhaustion, population growth, crop failures, political pressure by neighboring groups or states, an unpropitious death or miscarriage, an epidemic, factional rivalry, visitation by malevolent spirits, and so forth. Whatever the underlying reasons, two aspects of a potential move are important. First, it is always accompanied by a great deal of uncertainty, anxiety, and social tension. Even if, as is usually the case, a new site has already been selected, the potential dangers are still considerable—as they were historically in making alliances and choosing whether or not to go to war. For this reason, in most cases, the choice was made or announced via a prophetic dream. Among the Hmong, for example, a prominent woman or man, often a shaman, would have a dream telling her to move to a new place. If it were a question of fission, the "dreamer" would, with his or her followers, pick up and leave, sometimes founding a "daughter" village nearby.[69] For the Hmong, with their strong belief in geomancy, every change in landscape was, by definition, a change of luck.

Karen villages are likely to move or split in much the same way. If anything, Karen villages, like those of the Lahu, seem to be exceptionally fragile and apt to break up for any number of reasons. The breakup is, as in the Hmong case, typically announced via a prophetic vision, dream, or sign. It is not the case, then, that prophets come either in the form of world conquerors or not at all. Prophetism is a comparatively ordinary experience tied to important but less earthshaking decisions. On this reading, the prophets who make it into the archives are not the only prophets; they are, rather, the "major league" prophets with larger followings and more audacious goals.

What distinguishes a major league millenarian movement from small-scale prophetism is that its followers so frequently, as their prophet instructs, burn their bridges. Unlike relocating villagers who hope to restore, under better conditions, many of the routines they left behind, the followers of millenarian movements are both awaiting and instituting a new world. They often completely cease their previous practices. They may stop planting, sell their rice and land, give away their money, slaughter their livestock, radically change their diet, don new clothes and amulets, burn their houses, and break sacred taboos. After this kind of bridge-burning, there is no easy way back.[70] It also follows that revolutionary acts of this magnitude completely change the social hierarchy of a village community. Previous standing and prestige mean nothing in the new order, and the prophet and his acolytes, many of them perhaps of low status in the old order, are now elevated. Whether it brings a revolution in the external world, there is no doubt that it is revolutionary, in the full sense of the word, for the community that experiences it.

As a social process, millenarianism of this kind is escape social structure of a high order. And although it is not sufficient to explain millenarian movement by the functions they may perform, one is driven to wonder whether such movements facilitate a rapid and massive adaptation to radically changed circumstances. Lehman seems to suggest as much: "The traditional habit of the Sgaw Karen . . . of throwing up millennial movements and leaders seems to function to permit these people to reorient themselves radically to new contexts of social and cultural relations." He also notes that millennial movements among the Karen set in motion a kind of ethnogenesis: "To change their religion almost totally is exactly this, an alteration in ethnic identity in response to changing intergroup relations."[71]

In his account of the rise of a recent Karen Buddhist sect under U Thuzana in southeastern Burma, Mikael Gravers emphasizes that it had the effect of repositioning these Karen in a zone of war and massive relocation: "These movements signify a continuous revaluation of cosmology and ethnic identity, aiming at creating order and overcoming crisis."[72] For every would-be prophet who manages to lead his followers to a zone of relative peace and stability—and subsistence—many others fail. But the coincidence of such movements with economic, political, and military crises suggests that they can be seen as desperate social experiments, a throw of the dice in a setting where the odds of a very favorable outcome are long.

We know, in fact, that charismatic movements can and have resulted in the creation of new states and new ethnic and political identities. The most striking and best documented is the founding, in the nineteenth century, of the two major Kayah states of Bawkahke and Kantarawaddy, the first later to form the basis of a new territory and realigned ethnic identity in the Kayah/ Kerenni State in Burma. What we know about this history "clearly indicates that the founders both came out of the south and that they were typically charismatic personages capitalizing on the knowledge of the outside world. They founded a religious cult, on which the Kayah polity was explicitly based, strikingly reminiscent of the millennial ideology . . . among Mon and

Burman Buddhist and plains Karen, both Buddhist and animist during this era."[73] There were mundane considerations involved as well, not least, as we noted earlier, the fact that this area contained one of the last great stands of valuable teak. Nevertheless, it was a major ethnic repositioning within Karennic groups, and it was inaugurated by a charismatic prophet.

The Lahu, like a great many hill peoples, are subdivided into smaller factions usually identified by colors: the Red Lahu, Yellow Lahu, Black Lahu, and so on. The origin of these factions is lost in the mists of time and legends, but Anthony Walker believes that "some almost certainly originated with messianic leaders."[74] It is probable that the prophetic movement has historically been the dominant mode of collective ethnic reformulation in the hills. If so, this process could be seen as resembling village fission on a far grander and more dramatic scale, but one not fundamentally different in kind.

As in the case of village fissioning, such political reshufflings nearly always involve a repositioning vis-à-vis adjacent ethnic groups and valley states. The Karen Buddhist sect leader U Thuzana sought to create a zone of peace for his followers. He was also decisively repositioning them closer to the Burmese state to the point where his fighters (the Democratic Karen Buddhist Army, DKBA) became little more than mercenaries and profiteers under Burmese military supervision. Other fissioning, other charismatic movements, have led people to push farther into the hills, to move long distances, and to modify their culture to accommodate a new situation.

There is, at the very least, an elective affinity, to use Max Weber's term, between the existential situation faced by many hill peoples in Zomia and the remarkable plasticity and adaptability of their social organization, ethnic affiliation, and religious identity. Such mobile, egalitarian, marginal peoples have, for the most part, long histories of defeat and flight and have faced a world of powerful states whose policies they had little chance of shaping. Just as petty sellers in the market are "price takers" rather than price givers or setters, so have these people had to thread their way through shifting and dangerous constellations of powers in which they have largely been pawns. Faced with slave raids, demands for tribute, invading armies, epidemics, and occasional crop failures, they appear to have developed not just the subsistence routines to keep the state at arm's length but a shape-shifting social and religious organization admirably adapted to cope with a turbulent environment. The concentration of heterodox sects, hermit monks, pretenders, and would-be prophets in most hill societies has provided, in effect, the agency that allows many of them to substantially reinvent themselves when the situation requires it.[75]

To stand back and take all this in, to wonder at the capacity of hill peoples to strike out, almost overnight, for new territory—socially, religiously, ethnically—is to appreciate the mind-boggling cosmopolitanism of relatively marginal and powerless people. Far from being a backward, traditional people in the presumptive grip of custom and habit, they seem positively protean (even Californian) in imagining themselves anew.

Cosmologies of Ethnic Collaboration

The first thing that strikes any observer of hill societies is their bewildering linguistic and political complexity over comparatively small distances. On a "stop-action" snapshot that freezes the historical flux, it is diversity that seems to dominate this scene as compared with that of the valleys. What was said originally about Balkan nationalisms—that they represented the narcissism of small differences—would be even more appropriate for Zomia. And in fact, all the valley powers—from the classical states to the colonial regimes to the U.S. Special Forces, the Central Intelligence Agency, and the Burmese ruling junta today—have exploited these differences for their own purposes.

The major and apparently long-standing exception to this rule is the mobilization of people across ethnic lines by charismatic figures deploying fragments of lowland, millenarian cosmologies. Charisma is, in this context, a qualitatively different form of social cohesion from the glue provided by custom, tradition, kinship, and ancient ritual. Thus before his death in 2007, the famous Pa'an-based monk Sayadaw Thamanya gathered around him some twenty thousand adherents of many ethnicities. He was born into a PaO family, but his followers were Karen, Shan, Mon, and Burman as well, all eager to participate in the powerful Buddhist field of merit he had created. Although his opposition to the military regime then in Rangoon was carefully coded, his movement was, for a time, the largest expression of mass antiregime sentiment seen since the democratic uprising of 1988. In this case, as in hundreds of others reported in the archives and colonial records, it appears that only charismatic religious prophets are capable of overcoming the innumerable divisions of hill societies and attracting a mass following that transcends ethnicity, lineage, and dialect.

Some of the greatest challenges to Han state expansion in southwest China and to colonial control of highland areas were posed by just such interethnic coalitions, each animated by a prophet announcing a just king and/or a golden age. Three exemplary rebellions illustrate the potentially massive dimensions of such mobilization.

The mid-nineteenth-century so-called Miao Rebellion in Guizhou (1854–73) was, in fact, a multiethnic uprising involving millions of people over nearly twenty years and claiming as many as five million lives. It coincided with an unparalleled outbreak of risings against Ming rule, all of them inflected by syncretic religious cults: the Nien Rebellion centered on Kiangsi, 1851–68; the "Muslim Rebellion" in Yunnan, 1855–73; and the great Taiping peasant rebellion, 1951–64. Given its duration and extent, the Miao Rebellion was inevitably decentralized and involved many disparate elements, including bandits, adventurers, ruined Han officials, and others. Nearly half the participants may have been nominally Han, with most of the rest drawn from ethnic hill minorities, among whom the Miao were the most numerous. Muslim Chinese (Hui) participated as well. It is clear that the main ideological element fusing this unwieldy coalition was a shared belief in a worldly religious redemption: "A final element that affected rebels of both Han and minority extraction was millenarian religion. To some degree, adherence to folk religious groups crossed ethnic lines. Quite a few Miao belonged to sects led by Han and, to a lesser extent, the reverse was true."[76] Here we seem to have a manifestation of the appeal of radical prophetic religion to both lower strata of state populations (in this case, especially Han miners) and marginal hill populations. No doubt the content of their utopian expectations was different, but both groups hoped for an imminent emancipation.

A second example of a pan-ethnic prophetic movement was the so-called Dieu-python Rebellion, which convulsed the Central Highlands of Vietnam and parts of Cambodia in 1937.[77] What united the rebels was the belief that the python-god, a shared highland deity, had returned to earth to inaugurate a golden age. The dieu-python would destroy the French, and hence all taxes and corvée burdens, while those who followed the ritual prescriptions would enter the golden age and share French goods among themselves. Although the movement had a prophet of sorts, Sam Bram, who distributed holy charts and magic water, it spread throughout the highlands zone where the prophet had never been. Many hill groups, particularly the Jarai, stopped cultivating altogether for a time.

What took the French utterly by surprise was the pronounced multiethnic character of the uprising and its shared cosmology. Colonial ethnographers had invested great effort in cataloguing the different "tribes" of the Central Highlands, and the idea that these disparate peoples (some of whom were nominally Catholic!) would actually share a mobilizing cosmology was both astounding and troubling. The prophetic dimension of the rebellion did not prevent the geography of its incidence from following certain fracture lines of socioeconomic difference. Thus the violence was concentrated in those highland areas where French pacification efforts had been most brutal, where Theravada Buddhist influence was most pronounced, and among hill peoples whose livelihood was directly threatened. Ideologically speaking, however, Salemink shows that it was part of a longer lineage of "holy man" revolts that extended back well before the arrival of the French. Pan-highland messianic revolts against Lao princes inspired by a Buddhist monk from Laos had erupted in 1820. And in the years immediately before the dieu-python outbreak, two prophetic rebellions had been crushed: a Buddhist holy man's revolt led by Ong Kommodam (inventor of a secret script) and also called the Kha Rebellion in the Boloven Plateau and a second uprising on the Cambodian-Cochin-Annam border, whose forces attacked French posts.[78] This last was crushed by a scorched-earth policy and aerial bombardment. Nor did the continuity of the rebellions end there. Many of the leaders in all three uprisings can be traced to the Pathet Lao and the Vietminh a generation later. The arrival of socialism in Vietnam did not signal the end of millenarian agitation. After the great military victory of the Vietminh at Dien Bien Phu over the French (with help from highland forces), a broad millenarian movement erupted among highland minorities in 1956 that took two years for the Vietminh to crush. Whole villages stopped work, sold off cattle, attacked government offices, and moved en masse into Laos and awaited an imminent king.[79]

Finally, virtually every one of the numerous Karen prophetic movements that have been documented has had a multiethnic following. Such was the case, for example, in the precolonial Karen-Mon rising in 1740 near Pegu/Bago, which included Burmans, Shan, and PaO; in the early colonial rebellion of 1867 near Papun that brought together Kayah, Shan, Mon, and PaO; in the multiethnic "White monk" anti-Thai movement in the 1970s; and, most recently, in the Hsayadaw Thamanya movement near Pa'an, led by a PaO but drawing in many hill and valley groups. When it comes to holy-man movements, the boundary markers of ethnicities and language groups so beloved of anthropologists and administrators appear to present no obstacle to cooperation.

Here it is worth noting that the leaders of prophetic movements are typically above, or at least outside, the normal kinship order. Shamans and monks are, by virtue of their special gifts and status, elevated above familial and lineage politics. Unlike others, they are not typically seen to be working for the parochial self-interest of their social group.[80] In a few cases, the Hmong and the Karen in particular, the role of the orphan as hero and eventually king may play a similar role. As someone who has no family and who rises by his wits alone, the orphan is uniquely positioned to be a unifier across lineage and even ethnicity.

Again and again, in the hills of Zomia and elsewhere, one encounters interethnic holy-man revolts as a characteristic form of resistance. Although I have not made anything like a systematic survey, there seems to be a strong association between stateless frontiers and such movements. We saw in the case of South America that frontier rebellions among displaced people normally took a messianic form with bicultural leaders. For the Middle East, the historian Ira Lapidus insists that for conquest movements, "kinship was a secondary phenomenon." Lapidus writes: "Such movements were not based on lineage but on the agglomeration of diverse units, including individuals, clients, religious devotees, and fractions of clans . . . and the most common form of agglomeration was religious chieftainship under a charismatic, religio-political leader."[81] Noticing the same phenomenon of interethnic holy men–led rebellions, Thomas Barfield adds: "In the ethnically fragmented regions of Afghanistan and Pakistan's North West Frontier Province, the typical uprising was led by religious visionaries who claimed to be acting on God's command to bring about some divinely inspired change. . . . Charismatic clerics . . . exploded on the political scene by rousing the tribes to resistance, asserting their success had been pre-ordained."[82]

In settings that range from Buddhist to Christian to Muslim to animist, messianic holy-man rebellions seem prevalent. It is surely worth considering the proposition that such movements are the characteristic form of resistance among small, divided, acephalous societies that have no central institutions that might help coordinate joint action. More centralized societies can and do organize resistance and rebellion through their existing institutions.[83] Acephalous societies, especially those that are egalitarian, porous, and dispersed, either do not resist collectively — perhaps the commoner situation — or, if they do, their resistance is likely to be temporary, ad hoc, and charismatic.

To put it somewhat differently, one might say that the shape-shifting and simplified forms of escape social structure among egalitarian groups had the consequence of stripping them of the structural means for concerted action. Mobilization was possible only through charismatic prophets who stood above and outside kinship and lineage rivalries. And the only cosmological grid, the only ideational architecture, as it were, for such ad hoc co-operation came from the idea of a universal monarchy appropriated, gener-ally, from lowland salvation religion.

Spirit worship, by contrast, is not portable; once one is away from a familiar landscape, the spirits are alien and potentially dangerous. Only the universal valley religions claim a placeless refuge, infinitely portable.[84] Most hill societies have been shaped by escape—by dispersal, swiddening, collect-ing, fissioning—but the ubiquity of potentially violent prophetic movements suggest that when "cornered," with their normal modes of escape closed to them, they have appropriated enough cosmological architecture to serve as the necessary glue for pan-ethnic rebellions. The heterodox and oppositional purposes to which they put this "as if" state—namely to resist actual incor-poration into lowland polities—hardly permits us to imagine that they are in the hegemonic grip of lowland cosmology.

Christianity: A Resource for Distance and Modernity

With the arrival of Christian missionaries in the hills around the turn of the century, upland peoples gained access to a new salvation religion. Many of them seized it. It had two great advantages: it had its own millenarian cos-mology, and it was not associated with the lowland states from which they might want to maintain their distance. It was a powerful alternate, and to some degree oppositional, modernity. Christianity enjoyed remarkable suc-cess in converting hill peoples in Zomia, a success that it could never repeat, with the partial exception of Vietnam, among valley populations.

Throughout much of South and Southeast Asia it has long been com-mon for hill peoples, scheduled castes, and marginal and minority popula-tions to maintain or adopt a religious identity at variance with that of core-state populations, whose culture they associate with their stigmatization. Thus where we find Hinduism in the valleys, we might find animism, Islam, Christianity, or Buddhism in the hills. Where, as in Java, we might find Islam in the valleys, we are likely to find Christianity, animism, or Hinduism in the hills. In Malaysia, where the rulers are Muslim, many of the minority hill peoples are Christian, animist, or Baha'i. Where hill peoples do adopt the prevailing lowland religion, it is often a heterodox version of lowland doctrine. In most cases, then, upland populations, while borrowing lowland cosmologies for their own purposes, have chosen to mark themselves off reli-giously from the lowlands.

For our particular purposes, Christianity in the hills bears on hill-valley relations in two ways. First, it represents a modern identity that confers the "uniqueness and dignity which the wider world . . . refused to acknowledge."[85] This new identity, as we shall see, promises literacy and education, modern medicine, and material prosperity. It has, furthermore, a built-in millenarian cosmology that promises its own version of a conquering king who will destroy the wicked and uplift the virtuous. Second, the presence of Christianity as an institution as well as an ideology ought to be seen as an additional vector, another resource, for group formation. It allows a group or a fraction of a group to reposition itself in the ethnic mosaic. Like village fissioning or more modern techniques of social identity—the political party, the revolutionary cell, the ethnic movement—Christianity offers a powerful way of creating a place for new elites and an institutional grid for social mobilization. Each of these techniques can be put to the service of maintaining and emphasizing hill-valley distinctions—sometimes a kind of proxy for hill nationalism—or, more rarely, for minimizing them.

Until the arrival of Christian missionaries, Hmong prophetic rebellions drew on their own rich legend of a great king who would one day return to save his people, supplemented with elements of popular (Mahayana) Buddhism and Taoism that were compatible with these expectations. As substantial numbers of Hmong became familiar with the Christian scriptures, Jesus Christ, Mary, and the Holy Trinity were easily assimilated into the Hmong view of a coming liberation. It became as common for prophets in some areas to claim to be Jesus, Mary, or the Holy Ghost, or all three as to claim to announce the arrival of Huab Tais, the ancient Hmong king.[86] The eschatological message of scriptural Christianity mapped closely enough on Hmong millenarian beliefs that little adjustment was required.

The promise of literacy and the return of the Book (the Bible) were enormous attractions for the Hmong. Having had their book stolen, according to legend, by the Chinese, or having lost it, they looked to its recovery to lift the contempt in which they were held by such lowland peoples as the Chinese and the Thai. Largely for this reason, the American Baptist missionary Samuel Pollard, who devised a Hmong script still used today, was regarded as something of a messiah himself. The Hmong now had not just a script but a script of their own. Inasmuch as Hmong identity is understood as a series of negated contrasts with the Chinese, Pollard's achievement allowed them to be, in principle, equally literate, but in a non-Chinese script. Previously the route to the secular trinity of modernity, cosmopolitanism, and literacy led through the Chinese and Thai lowlands. Now Christianity offered the opportunity to be modern, cosmopolitan, literate, and still Hmong.

On almost any view, the Hmong, from the extermination campaigns waged against them by the Qing and Ming, to large-scale pell-mell migration, to their ill-starred alliance with the American CIA's Secret War, have had an astoundingly long run of catastrophic bad luck. For the past five centuries, the chances of premature death and/or forced flight must have been as great for the Hmong as for any identifiable people in the region.[87] In light of this history it is perhaps not so surprising that they have been so adept at moving at the drop of a hat, reshuffling their social organization, and shape-shifting between various forms of millenarian dreams and revolt. These are, in a sense, high-stakes experiments in social identity by a people hoping to change their luck. As their situation has worsened, they have developed escape social structure into something of an art form.

Lahu have converted as well in substantial numbers to Christianity in Yunnan, Burma, and Thailand, beginning around the turn of the twentieth century. According to Lahu legend, the first missionary, William Young, was prophesied by a Wa-Lahu religious leader a decade or so before his arrival. God and Jesus were immediately assimilated to the Lahu creator-god Gui-sha, whose return was anticipated. This amalgamation of pre-Christian deities with biblical figures was based in part on a Lahu appropriation of the Christian narrative and in part on the missionaries' efforts to work their own deities into what they knew of Lahu legends. The Lahu, like African slaves in the New World, identified with the plight of the Israelites, their wandering, their subjugation, and, of course, their ultimate emancipation.[88]

The second coming of Jesus was read as heralding the imminent liberation of the Lahu people. Shortly after the missionaries' first successes in Burma and Thailand, a Lahu prophet, inspired by the Christian message and Mahayana prophesies, announced that 1907 would be the last year the Lahu would pay tribute to the Shan sawbwa of Kengtung, because the Lahu had a new Lord. He brought many Lahu into the church fold, but when he claimed to be a god and took several wives, he was "deposed" by church authorities and ended by leading a countermovement against Christianity.[89] Thus the cultural appropriation of Christianity as a set of beliefs and as an institution, to make it serve hill needs, often against valley adversaries and even the missionaries themselves, is obvious in the case of the Lahu, the Hmong, and the

Karen. The following much-abbreviated account of the Christian nativity story in a Lahu (or Lahu-Wa) pamphlet shows the flavor of this mutual appropriation:

> Jesus Christ . . . [was] a man whose mother was a widow. Before he was born some fortune tellers told his mother that she was going to have a son who would be strong enough to conquer the whole world. When the chief heard that, he was so angry that he decided to kill Jesus' mother. With the help of the villagers, Mary escaped to a horse stable where Jesus was born in a horse manger. His mother took him home, and he jumped down from his mother's arms. No sooner had he stepped on the floor . . . than there appeared a golden chair for him to sit in.[90]

Stepping back from this historically deep and remarkably widespread incidence of millenarian activity, there is a realist school that would regard the entire record as an abject failure of essentially magical solutions. After all, the promised millennium never arrived, and those who answered the call were defeated, ruined, and scattered, if not killed. From this vantage point, the endless litany of prophetic movements over the centuries is itself testimony enough to their repeated futility. Surveying this ideological landscape of frustrated hopes and trying to draw something positive from it, many historians and anthropologists have found in it a protonationalism or even a protocommunism that paves the way for secular movements with many of the same objectives but a less magical, and hence more promising, idea of how to get there. This is the assessment of Eric Hobsbawn in his classic *Primitive Rebels*, where he notes that the revolutionary program of the Christian millenarian movements lacked only this element of realism.[91] Replace Gui-sha, God, Mettreya, Buddha, Huab Tais, or the Mahdi with the vanguard party of the proletariat, and you would have the real thing.

If we see millenarian fervor as only the most comprehensive and ambitious form of escape social structure, it appears in a different light. It represents an audacious poaching of the lowland ideological structure to fashion movements that aim at warding off or destroying the states from which they are poached. To be sure, the millennium is never reached. Nevertheless, such movements have created new social groups, reshuffled and amalgamated ethnicities, assisted the founding of new villages and new states, provoked radical shifts in subsistence routines and customs, set off long-distance moves, and, not trivially, kept alive a reservoir of hope for a life of dignity, peace, and plenty in the teeth of very long odds.

Hill people have, in a sense, seized whatever ideological materials were available to them to make their claims and take their distance from the lowland states. At first, the raw materials were confined to their own legends and deities, on the one hand, and, on the other, the emancipatory messages they could make out in the lowland religions, especially Mahayana and Theravada Buddhism. When Christianity became available as a framework for dreaming, it was infused with the same prophetic messages. At different times, both socialism and nationalism have offered the same apparent promise. Today, "indigenism," backed by international declarations, treaties, and well-heeled NGOs, offers some of the same prospects for framing identities and claims.[92] Much of the destination remains the same, but the means of transportation has changed. All of these imagined communities have been charged with utopian expectations. Most have failed, and some have ended at least as badly as millenarian uprisings. Mimicry, fetishism, and utopianism are not a highland monopoly.

CHAPTER 9

Conclusion

Savagery has become their character and nature. They enjoy it, because it means freedom
from authority and no subservience to leadership. Such a natural disposition is the
negation and antithesis of civilization.
—Ibn Khaldun on nomads

As quaint customs and exotic hill tribes are celebrated in museums, the media and
tourism, the populace—or perhaps only the urban middle class—comes to know itself
by what they once were and who they are not.
—Richard O'Connor

The world I have sought to describe and understand here is fast
disappearing. For virtually all my readers it will seem a very far
cry indeed from the world they inhabit. In the contemporary
world, the future of our freedom lies in the daunting task of taming Leviathan, not evading it. Living in a fully occupied world, one with
increasingly standardized institutional modules, the two most hegemonic of
which are the North Atlantic modules of individual freehold property and
the nation-state, we struggle against the enormous disparities in wealth and
power spawned by the former and the ever more intrusive regulation of our
interdependent lives by the latter. Populations have never, as John Dunn tell-
ingly puts it, depended "more abjectly for their security and prosperity on
the skills and good intentions of those who rule them."[1] And, he adds, the
only frail instrument we have for taming Leviathan is another North Atlantic
module—via Greece: representative democracy.

The world evoked here is, by contrast, one in which the state has not
come so close, as it now has, to sweeping all before it. That world, on a long
view, was the world most of mankind inhabited until quite recently. Simplifying greatly, we might identify four eras: 1) a stateless era (by far the longest),
2) an era of small-scale states encircled by vast and easily reached stateless
peripheries, 3) a period in which such peripheries are shrunken and beleaguered by the expansion of state power, and finally, 4) an era in which virtually the entire globe is "administered space" and the periphery is not much
more than a folkloric remnant. The progression from one era to the next has

been very uneven geographically (China and Europe being more precocious than, say, Southeast Asia and Africa) and temporally (with peripheries growing and shrinking depending on the vagaries of state-making). But about the long-run trend there can be not a shred of doubt.

It just so happens that the upland border area we have chosen to call Zomia represents one of the world's longest-standing and largest refuges of populations who live in the shadow of states but who have not yet been fully incorporated. In the past half-century or so, however, the combination of technological prowess and sovereign ambitions has so compromised even the relative autonomy of Zomian populations that my analysis here has far less applicability to the situation after the Second World War. Since then, throughout Zomia, there has been a truly massive transfer, both planned and spontaneous, of lowland populations of Han, Kinh, Thai, and Burmese to the hills. There they serve the dual purpose of peopling the frontiers with a presumably loyal population and producing cash crops for export, while relieving population pressure in the valleys. Demographically, it represents a conscious strategy of engulfment and eventual absorption.[2]

Until very recently, however, the massif has signified the basic political choice confronting much of mankind before the hegemony of the nation-state. The choice was not how to tame the inevitable Leviathan but rather how to position oneself vis-à-vis valley states. The options ranged from remote, egalitarian, ridge-top swiddening and foraging—staying as far from state centers as possible—to settling in more hierarchical groups close to valley states to take advantage of the tributary, trading, and raiding possibilities. None of these choices was irreversible. A group could adjust its distance from the state by altering its location, social structure, customs, or subsistence patterns. Even if it altered none of its practices or customs, its distance from an adjacent state could shift under its feet, so to speak, by the collapse or rise of a dynasty, a war, or demographic pressure.

Who were the Zomians? Initially, of course, the entire population of mainland Southeast Asia, whether in the highlands or lowlands, were Zomians in the sense of not being the subjects of any state. Once the first, small, Hinduizing mandala states were formed, the vast majority of those not yet incorporated as subjects became, ipso facto, the first self-governing peoples in an environment that now included (small) states. As it happens, we know something about these nonstate populations on the basis of archeological research. These findings suggest widespread craft specialization and complexity, but in a context that appears politically decentralized and relatively egalitarian (suggested by a rough equality in "grave goods"). The findings are consistent with what some archeologists have called "heterarchy": social and economic complexity without unified, hierarchical ranking.[3] What evidence we have indicates that the hills were sparsely populated and that the bulk of these nonstate populations lived on arable plateaus or in the lowlands, though rarely on the vulnerable flood plains.

As the early states, especially the Han, expanded into the valley lands suitable for wet-rice cultivation, they created at least two kinds of "refugees" who came, over time, to dominate the population in the hills. The first were the hitherto stateless peoples of the plains (many of whom may well have been shifting cultivators), who lay in the path of the padi state's horizontal expansion. It was from among such groups that the padi state's original subjects had been gathered. Those who for whatever reason wished to evade incorporation as subjects had to place themselves out of range either on the plains at greater remove from the core or in the less accessible hills. There was, on this reading, a segment of the nonsubject population—those already in the hills and those avoiding the early states—who had never been directly incorporated into state structures. Over the long haul, however, it is clear that the hills were populated increasingly by pulses of migration by state subjects fleeing valley kingdoms for any one of several reasons—corvée labor, taxes, conscription, war, struggles over succession, religious dissent—all having directly to do with state-making. It could also happen that a subject population could find itself suddenly stateless when war, crop failure, or epidemic destroyed the state or impelled people to move to save their lives. On a time-lapse photograph, these pulses of migration might look like a maniacal game of bumpercars, with each new pulse exerting its own jolt on earlier migrants and they, in turn, resisting or moving into the territory of still earlier migrants. It is this process that has created "shatter zones" and that goes a long way toward explaining the crazy-quilt pattern of constantly reformulated identities and locations in the hills.

Zomia was, in all these senses, a "state effect," or, more precisely, an effect of state-making and state expansion. Shatter zones and regions of refuge are, then, the inescapable "dark twin" of state-making projects in the valleys. The state and its resulting shatter zone are mutually constituted in the full sense of that much-abused term; each stands in the other's shadow and takes its cultural bearings from the other. The valley state's elites define their status as a civilization by reference to those outside their grasp, while at the same time depending on them for trade and to replenish (by capture or inducements) their subject population. The hill peoples, in turn, are dependent on the valley state for vital trade goods and may position themselves cheek by jowl with valley kingdoms to take full advantage of the opportunities for profit and plunder, while generally remaining outside direct political control. Other hill peoples, more remote and/or egalitarian, appear to have structured themselves as something of an antithesis of valley hierarchy and authority. Valley and hill peoples represent two contrasting political spheres, one rather concentrated and homogeneous, the other dispersed and heterogeneous, but each unstable and each constituted of human material pulled, at one time or another, from the other.

Upland societies, far from being the original, primal "stuff" from which states and "civilizations" were crafted, are, rather, largely a reflexive product of state-making designed to be as unappealing as possible as a site of appropriation. Just as nomadic pastoralism is now generally recognized as a secondary adaptation by populations wishing both to leave the sedentary agrarian state and yet take advantage of the trading and raiding opportunities it afforded, so is swiddening largely a secondary adaptation. Like pastoralism, it disperses population and lacks the "nerve centers" that a state might seize. The fugitive nature of its production frustrates appropriation. Hill societies with their deliberate out-of-the-way locations, with their mixed portfolio of linguistic and cultural identities, with the variety of subsistence routines at their disposal, with their capacity to fission and disperse like the "jellyfish" tribes of the Middle East, and with their capacity, thanks in part to valley cosmologies, to form new resistant identities at the drop of a hat, are constituted as if they were intended to be a state-maker's or colonial official's worst nightmare. And indeed, they are largely so.

We are, analytically speaking, forced back to the terrain of the elementary units of hill society: the hamlet, the segmentary lineage, the nuclear family, the swiddening group. The uniqueness, plurality, and fungibility of identities and social units in the hills are poor raw material for state-making. Such elementary units may, from time to time, aggregate in small confederations and alliances for war and trade, and under the leadership of a charismatic prophet, but they are likely to lapse, just as soon, into their constituent units. If would-be state-makers found them unpromising, historians and anthropologists have found them equally frustrating. Noting this fluidity and, in particular, the chimerical nature of the major ethnic identities, François Robinne and Mandy Sadan have recently suggested that it would be more ethnographically correct to focus analysis on villages, families, and exchange networks and no longer privilege ethnicity as "a kind of superior artifact, covering other cultural markers; it would become as cultural marker among others."[4] Given the porosity of ethnic boundaries, the bewildering variation within any particular identity, and the historical vagaries of what it has meant to be a "Kachin" or a "Karen," a healthy agnosticism about the category itself seems just the right move. If we follow Robinne and Sadan's wise advice, I suspect that much of the flux and apparent disorder is resolved once we examine hill social order and reformulations of identity as strategic repositionings of various villages, groups, and networks vis-à-vis the gravitational force—political, economic, and symbolic—of the nearest valley state.

State Evasion, State Prevention: Global-Local

I have come to see this study of Zomia, or the massif, not so much as a study of hill peoples per se but as a fragment of what might properly be considered a global history of populations trying to avoid, or having been extruded by, the state. Such a task is clearly beyond me and, ideally, it would be a collaborative undertaking by a great many scholars. In the Southeast Asian context alone, it would encompass far more than I have able to examine here. It would, minimally, cover the history of the sea gypsies (*orang laut*), whose nonstate option was to take to their boats. Dispersed on the water, they could evade slavers and states amid the complex waterways of the archipelago while raiding, slaving, and occasionally serving as mercenaries themselves. They were, for a time, to the Malay Sultanate of Melaka, a watery version of what the Cossacks were to the tsarist armed forces. Their history would intertwine with that of the inhabitants of the mangrove coasts and of the constantly shifting deltas of the great rivers of Southeast Asia. Each of these locations has presented daunting obstacles to state administration and has therefore served as a zone of refuge.

Other peoples and other geographies that might belong to such a global history of extrastate spaces have been mentioned in passing by way of illustration. The Gypsies, the Cossacks, the Berbers, the Mongols, and other pastoral nomads would be essential to a broad history of state peripheries. Maroon communities wherever unfree labor was an integral part of state-building—as it was in most of the New World, Russia, and the Roman and Islamic worlds—would form another part of that global history, not to mention Africans like the Dogon, who evaded capture in the first place. And of course, all those areas of colonial conquest where indigenous peoples were menaced with extermination or were run out of their previous habitats to new locations would form a large chapter of this story.[5] The comparative study of such zones of refuge would, despite their geographical, cultural, and temporal dispersion, share a few common, diagnostic characteristics. If they were of any historical depth, they would, like most shatter zones to which various groups have repaired over time, display something of the ethnic and linguistic complexity and fluidity we have found in Zomia. Aside from being located in remote, marginal areas that are difficult of access, such peoples are also likely to have developed subsistence routines that maximize dispersion, mobility, and resistance to appropriation. Their social structure as well is likely to favor dispersion, fission, and reformulation and to present to the outside world a kind of formlessness that offers no obvious institutional point of entry for would-be projects of unified rule. Finally, many, but by no means all, groups in extrastate space appear to have strong, even fierce, traditions of egalitarianism and autonomy both at the village and familial level that represent an effective barrier to tyranny and permanent hierarchy.

Most of the peoples dwelling in the massif seem to have assembled a fairly comprehensive cultural portfolio of techniques for evading state incorporation while availing themselves of the economic and cultural opportunities its proximity presented. Part of this portfolio is the very flux and ambiguity of the identities they may assume over time. So striking is this characteristic—and so vexing to state administrators—that Richard O'Connor has suggested that while we usually start with the assumption that a group has an ethnic identity, in Southeast Asia, "where people change ethnicity and locality rather frequently, we might better say that *an ethnicity has a people.*"[6] It is perhaps one of the features of shatter zones located at the interstices of unstable state systems that there is a premium on the adaptability of identities. Most hill cultures have, as it were, their bags already packed for travel across space, across identities, or across both. Their broad repertoires of languages and ethnic affiliations, their capacity for prophetic reinvention, their short and/or oral genealogies, and their talent for fragmentation all form elements in their formidable travel kit.

We might, in this light, want to consider Fernand Braudel's assertion about mountain peoples: namely that their "history is to have none, to remain always on the fringes of the great waves of civilization."[7] For Zomia, at least, one would want to recast this argument radically. Better put, they have multiple histories they can deploy singly or in combination depending on the circumstances. They can, as in the case of the Akha and the Kachin, create long, elaborate genealogies or, as in the case of the Lisu and Karen, have minimally short genealogies and migration histories. If they appear to be without a definite history, it is because they have learned to travel light, not knowing what their next destination might be. They are not outside of time nor historyless. Rather like tramp steamers and Gypsies working the seams of the great trade routes and states, respectively, their success depends on maximizing their agility. It is in their interest to keep as many of their options open as possible, and what kind of history to have is one of those options. They have just as much history as they require.

These cultural positionings, along with geographical remoteness, mobility, choice of crops and cultivation techniques, and, frequently, a "no-handles" acephalous social structure, are, to be sure, measures of state evasion. But it is crucial to understand that what is being evaded is not a relationship per se with the state but an evasion of subject status. What hill peoples on the periphery of states have been evading is the hard power of the fiscal state, its capacity to extract direct taxes and labor from a subject population. They have, however, actually sought, sometimes quite eagerly, relationships with valley states that are compatible with a large degree of political autonomy. In particular, a tremendous amount of political conflict has been devoted to the jockeying for advantage as the favored trading partner of one lowland emporium or another. Hills and valleys were, as we have seen, complementary as agro-ecological niches. This meant in effect that adjacent valley states typically competed with one another to acquire hill products and populations.

A favored relationship might, once secured, be formalized by a tributary relationship that, however asymmetrical it might appear ceremonially or in the valley records, might in practice give the hill partner the upper hand. The point is that we must not take valley representations at face value. Beyond the narrow arc of hard tax-and-corvée power, then, lay a very much larger penumbra of economic exchange often expressed in the idiom of tribute. This zone represented a durable link of mutually advantageous trade that, with very few exceptions, did not imply anything in the way of permanent political subordination. The greater the value of the commodities and the smaller their size and weight, the greater the circumference of this penumbra; in the case of gems, rare medicinals, and opium, for example, it could be enormous.[8]

When it comes to the symbolic and cosmological reach of the great valley states, their influence is both vast and, at the same time, shallow. Whether Sinitic or Indic or, in some cases, an exotic hybrid, virtually all the ideas that might legitimate authority beyond the level of a single village are on loan from the lowlands. Such ideas are, however, cast loose from their lowland moorings and are reformulated in the hills to serve local purposes. The term *bricolage* is particularly apt for this process, inasmuch as lowland fragments of cosmology, regalia, dress, architecture, and titles are rearranged and assembled into unique amalgams by prophets, healers, and ambitious chiefs. The fact that the symbolic raw materials may be imported from the lowlands does not prevent them from being confected by highland prophets into millenarian expectations that may be used to oppose lowland cultural and political hegemony.[9]

The role of lowland cosmology in facilitating collective action and overcoming what some social scientists would call the transaction costs associated with social fragmentation may, more speculatively, be related to the overall argument about state evasion. The very features of hill societies that help them evade incorporation—dispersal, mobility, ethnic complexity, small swiddening groups, and egalitarianism—encourage disunity and place enormous obstacles in the way of corporate organization and collective action. The only social resource for such cooperation came, ironically, from the lowland, where social hierarchy and the cosmology that goes with it are taken for granted.

Virtually all hill societies exhibit a range of state-evading behavior. For some, such characteristics are compatible with a degree of internal hierarchy and, from time to time, imitative state-making. For other groups, however, state evasion is coupled with practices that might be termed the prevention of internal state-making. Relatively acephalous groups with strong traditions of equality and sanctions against permanent hierarchy, such as the Akha, Lahu, Lisu, and Wa, seem to belong to this category. State-preventing societies share some common characteristics. They are likely to prevent the emergence of any permanent ranking of lineages through marriage alliances; they are more likely to have cautionary legends about the assassination or expulsion of overreaching headmen; and, finally, their villages and lineages are likely to divide into smaller and more egalitarian fragments when inequalities do threaten to become permanent.

Gradients of Secession and Adaptation

There is a paradox in trying to describe a shatter zone or region of refuge such as Zomia. In order to portray the flux and plasticity of hill societies one has, necessarily, to stand somewhere, even if that "somewhere" is itself in motion. I have surely done this by talking about "the Karen," "the Shan," and "the Hmong" as if they were solid, static units of social organization. They are not, particularly when observed over any considerable period of time. So at the risk of further dizzying the reader and myself, we ought to recall just how radical this flux is. Valley runaways have been replenishing the hill population for as long as we can tell. Hill people have been assimilating into valley-state societies also for as long as we can tell. The essentialized "line" between hill and valley peoples remains in place despite quite massive traffic back and forth in each direction. Hill societies themselves are porous; gradients of identity make any firm "identity frontier" quite arbitrary. While hill societies reformulate themselves, so do individuals, kin groups, and whole communities. And while hill societies are positioning themselves vis-à-vis state projects in the valley, they are also positioning themselves vis-à-vis their hilly neighbors in this complex constellation of peoples.[10] There is nothing particularly unusual about this; the process of positioning and mutual adaptation is, to a large degree, the leitmotif of hill politics. If it makes our heads swim, it is some consolation that while it perplexes colonizers and state officials, the actors themselves are neither confused nor mystified about who they are and what they are doing.

Adaptation to the dangers or temptations of neighboring polities is hardly a practice confined to peoples at the periphery of states. Core peasantries as well have developed routines to take advantage of favorable developments at the political center and to shield themselves from the worst effects of turmoil. The repertoires deployed by the Chinese peasantry during the Ming and Qing dynasties to cope with dynastic collapse and with order and prosperity have been elaborated in some detail by G. William Skinner.[11] What is distinctive about these repertoires, for our purposes, is that they represent defensive measures by a peasantry that remains where it is and continues to practice sedentary agriculture. It illustrates a pattern of self-defense under very constrained circumstances. Seeing how core peasantries adapt in this fashion will help us appreciate how the far wider options open to peoples on the state periphery operate.

In periods of dynastic consolidation, peace, and buoyant trade, Skinner explains, the local community opens and adapts to the opportunities these conditions afford. Economic specialization, trade, and administrative and political links flourish as the community takes advantage of the opportunities in the wider world. By contrast, in periods of dynastic collapse, economic depression, and civil strife and banditry, the local community withdraws increasingly into its own shell as a self-protective measure. The withdrawal was patterned, according to Skinner: first a normative withdrawal, then an economic closure, and, finally, a defensive military closure. Specialists and traders returned home, economic specialization diminished, the local food supply was guarded, outsiders were expelled, crop-watching societies were formed, stockades built, and local militias created.[12] When flight and rebellion apparently were not available options, what the local community did in the face of a threatening external environment was to secede normatively, economically, and militarily. It tried, without budging, to create an autonomous, autarkic space—in effect declaring its independence from the larger society while the danger lasted. And when the threat subsided, the local community reopened in the reverse order: first militarily, then economically, and finally, normatively.

Zomia's hill societies have, in a comparable but far more expansive fashion, a large bandwidth of configurations among which they can move to integrate themselves more closely with the neighboring polities or, alternatively, to keep them at a distance. Unlike Skinner's stuck-in-the-rice-padi-mud Chinese peasantry, uplanders are physically mobile, capable of moving considerable distances, and in possession of a range of subsistence techniques they can deploy singly or in combination as the circumstances dictate. Upland society itself, after all, was created largely by a series of secessionists who, however, are capable of adjusting or modulating the degree of their secession in one direction or another. Such adjustments can take place along one or several dimensions not easily available to the core peasantry. The first of these dimensions is location; the higher and more remote their dwelling, the farther they generally are from state centers, slave raids, and taxes. A second dimension is scale and dispersal; the smaller and more dispersed their settlements the less tempting a target they represent for raiders and states. Finally, they can and do modulate their subsistence techniques, each of which embodies a position vis-à-vis states, hierarchy, and political incorporation.

Hjorleifur Jonsson, in this context, contrasts three subsistence strategies: 1) foraging–hunting and gathering, 2) swiddening, and 3) fixed-field agriculture.[13] Foraging is virtually appropriation-proof and permits little in the way of social inequality. Swiddening is appropriation resistant, though it may generate a surplus and some, usually temporary, internal hierarchy.[14] Fixed-field agriculture, especially of the wet-rice variety, is appropriable and raidable and is associated with large settlements and durable social hierarchies. These techniques could be combined in various proportions and adjusted over time, but it was quite clear to the Yao/Mien making such choices that any adjustment expressed a political option. Foraging and swiddening were both understood by those who practiced them as forms of political secession from the lowland state, with foraging the more radical, distancing choice.[15]

Upland groups have, then, a large bandwidth of possible locations as well as social and agro-ecological configurations available to them. They run the gamut all the way from, say, taking up padi cultivation on the plains and inviting incorporation as peasants into the valley state to the other extreme of foraging and swiddening in remote, fortified, ridge-top settlements while cultivating a reputation for killing intruders. Between these stark polar opposites lie a host of hybrid possibilities. Which of these options is actually exploited at any particular time will depend, in part, as with Skinner's Chinese peasants, on external conditions. At times of peace, economic expansion, and state encouragement of settlement, hill groups are more likely to take up sedentary cultivation, move closer to state centers, seek tributary and trade relations, and drift ethnically and linguistically toward valley cultures. At times of war, turbulence, and rapacious taxes and slave raids, hill groups would drift in the opposite direction and, in all likelihood, be joined by refugees fleeing the state cores.

Any particular hill people will appear, at any moment, to have adopted a particular configuration, say, as hilltop swiddeners and opium growers. Their culture may even appear to confine them to that configuration. But over long stretches of time there is likely to have been considerable movement, often by various fragments of the same ethnic group who have found themselves in different situations. Nor is there any reason whatever why the movement should be in a single direction.[16] On the contrary, on any long view, there is every reason to imagine a history of dozens of reformulations and adjustments toward and away from valley states, all assimilated successfully as "tradition" within a pliable oral culture.

Here it is worth recalling that most foragers and nomadic peoples—and perhaps swiddeners as well—were not aboriginal survivals but were rather adaptations created in the shadow of states. Just as Pierre Clastres supposed, the societies of many acephalous foragers and swiddeners are admirably designed to take advantage of agro-ecological niches in trading with nearby states yet manage to avoid subordination as subjects. If one were a social Darwinian, one might well see the mobility of hill peoples, their spare dispersed communities, their noninherited rankings, their oral culture, their large port-folio of subsistence and identity strategies, and perhaps even their prophetic inclinations as brilliantly suited to a tumultuous environment. They are better adapted to survival as nonsubjects in a political environment of states than to making states themselves.

Civilization and Its Malcontents

British and French colonial administrators, justifying the novel tax burdens they were imposing on their subjects, often explained that taxes were the inevitable price one paid for living in a "civilized society." By this discur-sive legerdemain they neatly managed three tricks: they described their sub-jects as effectively "precivilized," they substituted imperial ideals for colonial reality, and above all, they confounded "civilization" with what was, in fact, state-making.

The "just-so" story of civilization always requires a wild untamed an-tagonist, usually just out of reach, to eventually be subdued and incorporated. The hypothetical civilization in question—whether French, Han, Burman, Kinh, British, or Siamese—is defined by this negation. This is largely why tribes and ethnicity begin, in practice, where sovereignty and taxes stop.

One can see in a flash why these just-so stories, concocted largely to improve the self-confidence and cohesion of the rulers, might be less than convincing at the frontiers of empire. Imagine, for example, an education in the Confucian classics—filial piety, observance of the rituals, the obligations of rule, benevolent care for the well-being of the subjects, honorable con-duct, rectitude—in the context of, say, the mid-nineteenth-century frontier in Yunnan or Guizhou. How could one not be struck by the chasm between these imperial imaginings on the one hand and the realities of the Ming and Qing frontier on the other? The "lived" frontier, as distinct from the dis-cursive frontier, was rife with corrupt civil magistrates selling justice to the highest bidder, military adventurers and bandits, exiled officials and crimi-nals, land grabbers, smugglers, and desperate Han settlers.[17] Small wonder that the ideals of Han civilization had little traction on the ground. On the contrary, the contradiction between ideal and reality was sufficient reason both for local people and for reflective imperial officials to conclude that the civilizational discourse was mere humbug.[18]

The Han and Theravada polities of China and Southeast Asia had some-what different perceptions of the ideal, "civilized" subject. In the Han case there was no religious test for civilization, although the patriarchal family, ancestral tablets, and knowledge of the characters presupposed ethnic assimilation. In the Burman or Thai case, Buddhism and the veneration of the *sangha* did constitute a religious test although, on the other hand, the manpower-starved states of mainland Southeast Asia could not afford to be ethnic snobs. The Indic-style classical kingdoms were hierarchical, like the Han, but ethnically quite inclusive.

All such states, however, were, for impelling fiscal and military reasons, padi states. In practice, therefore, the padi state did everything in its power to encourage densely concentrated settlement and the irrigated wet rice that fostered it. To the degree that its subjects grew the same grains in roughly the same way, in communities that were roughly homogeneous, the tasks of land valuation, taxation, and administration were that much easier. In the Han case, the codification of the patriarchal household as the basic unit of property and administration further facilitated social control. The ideal subject of the padi state also represented a vision of landscape and human settlement in which the cleared plains of irrigated rice fields and their human communities came to represent an ideal that was, at once, cultivated and cultured.

The padi state's officials had, on the other hand, every incentive to discourage all form of settlement, subsistence, and social organization that represented an inappropriable landscape. They discouraged and, when they could, prohibited dispersed settlement, foraging, swiddening, and migration away from the core. If the padi fields had come to mean civilized landscape of properly organized subjects and their production, then by extension those who lived in remote places, in the hills or in the forests, who shifted their fields and often shifted themselves, who formed and re-formed small egalitarian hamlets were uncivilized. What is most striking here, of course, is how closely the ideal of a civilized landscape and demography coincides with a landscape and demography most suitable for state-making and how closely a landscape unsuitable for state appropriation, as well as the people who inhabit it, is understood as uncivilized and barbaric. The effective coordinates, from this perspective, for figuring out who is civilized and who is not, turn out to be not much more than an agro-ecological code for state appropriation.

The tight correlation is unmistakable between life at the margins of the state on the one hand and primitiveness and backwardness on the other, in the view of valley elites. One has only to list the most salient characteristics of landscapes and peoples beyond the state's easy grasp to produce, simultaneously, a catalogue of primitiveness. Dwelling in inaccessible forests and on hilltops codes as uncivilized. Foraging, forest collecting—even for commercial gain—and swiddening also code as backward. Scattered living and small settlements are, by definition, archaic. Physical mobility and transient, negotiable identities are both primitive and dangerous. Not following the great valley religions or not being the tax- and tithe-bearing subjects of monarchs and clergy places one outside the pale of civilization.

In the valley imagination, all these characteristics are earlier stages in a process of social evolution at the apex of which elites perch. Hill peoples are an earlier stage: they are "pre-" just about everything: pre–padi cultivation, pre-towns, prereligion, preliterate, pre–valley subject. As we have seen at some length, however, the characteristics for which hill peoples are stigmatized are precisely those characteristics that a state-evading people would encourage and perfect in order to avoid surrendering autonomy. The valley imagination has its history wrong. Hill peoples are not pre- anything. In fact, they are better understood as post–irrigated rice, postsedentary, postsubject, and perhaps even postliterate. They represent, in the longue durée, a reactive and purposeful statelessness of peoples who have adapted to a world of states while remaining outside their firm grasp.

There's nothing particularly wrong with the valley understanding of the agro-ecology, social organization, and mobility of the peoples who elude them. They've sorted these people, as it were, into the right bins. In addition to radically misunderstanding the historical sequence, however, they have got their labels wrong. If they merely substituted "state-subject" for "civilized" and "not-a-state-subject" for "uncivilized," they'd have it just about right.

Notes

CHAPTER 1. Hills, Valleys, and States

1. *Guiyang Prefectural Gazetteer,* quoted in Mark Elvin, *The Retreat of the Elephants: An Environmental History of China* (New Haven: Yale University Press, 2004), 236–37.

2. *Gazetteer of Upper Burma and the Shan States,* compiled from official papers by J. George Scott, assisted by J. P. Hardiman, vol. 1, part 1 (Rangoon: Government Printing Office, 1893), 1: 154.

3. Elizabeth R. Hooker, *Religion in the Highlands: Native Churches and Missionary Enterprises in the Southern Appalachian Area* (New York: Home Missions Council, 1933), 64–65.

4. Valley peoples and states may make further vernacular distinctions between those who are sedentary and live in villages and those who live in the forest and are presumptively nomadic.

5. The relationship between Bedouin pastoralists and urban Arabs, as it concerns state-making and civilization, pervades the writings of the great fourteenth-century Arab historian and philosopher Ibn Khaldun.

6. Recent archeological evidence appears to indicate that widespread copper mining and metallurgy on an industrial scale, associated elsewhere with state formation, was practiced in northeast Thailand without any evidence of state centers. It appears to have been an off-season craft of agriculturists on a surprising scale. See Vincent Pigott, "Prehistoric Copper Mining in Northeast Thailand in the Context of Emerging Community Craft Specialization," in *Social Approaches to an Industrial Past: The Archaeology and Anthropology of Mining,* ed. A. B. Knapp, V. Pigott, and E. Herbert (London: Routledge, 1998), 205–25. I am grateful to Magnus Fisk-esjö for bringing this to my attention.

7. Anthony Reid, *Southeast Asia in the Age of Commerce, 1450–1680,* vol. 1, *The Lands Below the Winds* (New Haven: Yale University Press, 1988), 15. China, less Tibet, at 37 persons per square kilometer was more densely populated than the South Asian subcontinent at 32 per square kilometer. Europe at that time had roughly 11 persons per square kilometer.

8. Richard A. O'Connor, "Founders' Cults in Regional and Historical Perspective," in *Founders' Cults in Southeast Asia: Polity, and Identity,* ed. Nicola Tannenbaum and Cornelia Ann Kammerer, Yale Southeast Asia Monograph Series no. 52 (New Haven: Yale University Press, 2003), 269–311, quotation from 281–82. For a quite different and largely unilinear account of the rise of states generally, see Allen W. Johnson and Timothy Earle, *The Evolution of*

Human Societies: From Foraging Group to Agrarian State, 2nd ed. (Stanford: Stanford University Press, 2000).

9. Richard A. O'Connor, "Agricultural Change and Ethnic Succession in Southeast Asian States: A Case for Regional Anthropology," *Journal of Asian Studies* 54 (1995): 968–96.

10. See, in this connection, Michael Mann, *The Sources of Social Power* (Cambridge: Cambridge University Press, 1986), 63–70.

11. Charles Tilly, *Coercion, Capital, and European States, AD 990–1992* (Cambridge, Mass.: Blackwell, 1990), 162.

12. Encouragement of sedentarism is perhaps the oldest "state project," a project related to the second-oldest state project of taxation. It was at the center of Chinese statecraft for millennia through the Maoist period, when People's Liberation Army soldiers by the thousands were digging terraces to get the "wild" Wa to plant irrigated wet rice.

13. Hugh Brody, *The Other Side of Eden: Hunters, Farmers, and the Shaping of the World* (Vancouver: Douglas and McIntyre, 2000).

14. Sanjay Subramanyum, "Connected Histories: Notes toward a Reconfiguration of Early Modern Eurasia," *Modern Asian Studies* 31 (1997): 735–62.

15. For an excellent account of this process in Vietnam and Indonesia, see Rodolphe de Koninck, "On the Geopolitics of Land Colonization: Order and Disorder on the Frontier of Vietnam and Indonesia," *Moussons* 9 (2006): 33–59.

16. The colonial and early postcolonial regimes, like the classical states, had considered these areas *terra nullius* or *inutile* — as in the traditional distinction between *La France utile* and *La France inutile* — in the sense that they did not repay the costs of administration in terms of grain or revenue. Though forest and hill products might be valuable and though their populations might be captured as slaves, they were considered to lie well outside the directly administered, profitable grain core on which state power and revenue depended. These areas were, under colonialism, typically governed by so-called indirect rule, whereby traditional authorities were supervised and made tributary rather than replaced. Under Han administration from the Yuan Dynasty through much of the Ming, such zones were governed, as we shall see, under the tusi system, a Chinese form of indirect rule.

17. Hill populations have in quite a few cases, and for their own reasons, adopted lowland religions as their own. The symbolic appropriation of lowland religions has, however, not necessarily implied incorporation in the lowland state. See, for example, Nigel Brailey, "A Reinvestigation of the Gwe of Eighteenth Century Burma," *Journal of Southeast Asian Studies* 1, no. 2 (1970): 33–47. See also the discussion in Chapter 8.

18. Patricia M. Pelley, *Post-Colonial Vietnam: New Histories of the National Past* (Durham: Duke University Press, 2002), 96–97.

19. This official account has been effectively contradicted in Keith Taylor's "Surface Orientations in Vietnam: Beyond Histories of Nation and Region," *Journal of Asian Studies* 57 (1998): 949–78.

20. These four groups, each now represented by a nation-state, have absorbed all of the many earlier states of the region with the exception of Cambodia and Laos, which have, for their part, incorporated nonstate spaces of their own.

21. Geoff Wade, "The Bai-Yi Zhuan: A Chinese Account of Tai Society in the 14th century," paper presented at the 14th IAHA Conference, Bangkok, May, 1996, appendix 2, 8. Cited in Barbara Andaya, *The Flaming Womb: Repositioning Women in Early Modern Southeast Asia* (Honolulu: University of Hawai'i Press, 2006), 12.

22. Willem van Schendel, "Geographies of Knowing, Geographies of Ignorance: Southeast Asia from the Fringes," a paper for the workshop Locating Southeast Asia: Genealogies, Concepts, Comparisons and Prospects, Amsterdam, March 29–31, 2001.

23. Jean Michaud, *Historical Dictionary of the Peoples of the Southeast Asian Massif* (Lan-

ham, Md.: Scarecrow, 2006), 5. See also Jean Michaud, ed., *Turbulent Times and Enduring Peoples: Mountain Minorities in the Southeast Asian Massif* (Richmond, England: Curzon, 2000).

24. Michaud, *Historical Dictionary*, 2. Adding the lowland populations now in the hills would raise the figure by perhaps another fifty million, a figure that is increasing daily.

25. Ernest Gellner, "Tribalism and the State in the Middle East," in *Tribes and State Formation in the Middle East*, ed. Philip Khoury and Joseph Kostiner (Berkeley: University of California Press, 1990), 109–26, quotation from 124. Analogies to the Pashtuns, Kurds, and Berbers are less apposite because, in these three cases, the people in question have—or better, are assumed to have—a common culture. No such cultural cohesion is presumed for the great mountain kingdom discussed here, although some of its peoples (for example, Dai, Hmong, Akha/Hani) are far flung across the region. But for a perceptive account of Islamic sectarianism in the hills, see Robert LeRoy Canfield, *Faction and Conversion in a Plural Society: Religious Alignments in the Hindu-Kush*, Anthropological Papers, Museum of Anthropology, University of Michigan, 50 (Ann Arbor: University of Michigan, 1973).

26. Laos is a partial exception inasmuch as, like Switzerland, it is largely a "mountain state" with a small valley plain along the Mekong that it shares with Thailand.

27. See, in this connection, Sidney Pollard's suggestive *Marginal Europe: The Contribution of Marginal Lands since the Middle Ages* (Oxford: Clarendon, 1997).

28. Other explicit proponents of a systematic view from the periphery include Michaud, *Turbulent Times and Enduring Peoples*, especially the Introduction by Michaud and John McKinnon, 1–25, and Hjorleifur Jonsson, *Mien Relations: Mountain Peoples, Ethnography, and State Control* (Ithaca: Cornell University Press, 2005).

29. F. K. L. Chit Hlaing [F. K. Lehman], "Some Remarks upon Ethnicity Theory and Southeast Asia, with Special Reference to the Kayah and Kachin," in *Exploring Ethnic Diversity in Burma*, ed. Mikael Gravers (Copenhagen: NIAS Press, 2007), 107–22, esp. 109–10.

30. Fernand Braudel, *The Mediterranean and the Mediterranean World in the Age of Philip II*, vol. 1, trans. Sian Reynolds (New York: Harper and Row, 1966).

31. Reid, *Southeast Asia in the Age of Commerce*, vol. 1.

32. Van Schendel, "Geographies of Knowing," 10, puts it nicely: "If seas can inspire scholars to construct Braudelian regional worlds, why not the world's largest mountain ranges?" But this did not happen. Instead, excellent studies of various parts of Zomia continued to be done, but these did not address an audience of fellow "Zomianists," nor did they have the ambition to build up a Zomia perspective that could offer a new set of questions and methodologies to the social sciences.

33. The "anarchy," of course, was entirely in the eye of the beholder. Hill peoples were in no doubt about who they were, even if, for the colonial official, they were illegible.

34. E. R. Leach, "The Frontiers of Burma," *Comparative Studies in Society and History* 3 (1960): 49–68.

35. For a fine analysis of gender relations among the Lahu, see Shanshan Du, *Chopsticks Only Work in Pairs: Gender Unity and Gender Equality among the Lahu of Southwest China* (New York: Columbia University Press, 2002).

36. Nan Chao/Nan-zhuao and its successor, the Dali Kingdom in southern Yunnan, from roughly the ninth century to the thirteenth; Kengtung/Chaing-tung/Kyaing-tung, a trans-Salween/Nu kingdom in the Eastern Shan States of Burma, independent from roughly the fourteenth century until its conquest by the Burmese in the seventeenth; Nan, a small independent kingdom in the Nan River Valley in northern Thailand; Lan-na, near the present site of Chiang Mai in Thailand, and independent from roughly the thirteenth to the eighteenth century, allowing for a Burmese conquest in the mid-sixteenth century. It is diagnostic that each of these kingdoms was dominated by the padi-planting, Tai-speaking peoples most frequently associated with state-making in the hills.

37. Janet Sturgeon, "Border Practices, Boundaries, and the Control of Resource Access: A Case from China, Thailand, and Burma," *Development and Change* 35 (2004): 463-84.

38. Van Schendel, "Geographies of Knowing," 12.

39. Braudel, *The Mediterranean*, 1: 32, 33. Braudel fails here, I think, to note those peoples who carry, as it were, their civilizations on their backs wherever they go: Roma (Gypsies) and Jews, for example.

40. Ibn Khaldun, *The Muqaddimah: An Introduction to History*, 3 vols., trans. Franz Rosenthal, Bollinger Series 43 (New York: Pantheon, 1958), 1: 302.

41. O. W. Wolters, *History, Culture, and Region in Southeast Asian Perspectives* (Singapore: Institute for Southeast Asian Studies, 1982), 32. Wolters's citation is from Paul Wheatley, "Satyanrta in Suvarnadvipa: From Reciprocity to Redistribution in Ancient Southeast Asia," in *Ancient Trade and Civilization*, ed. J. A. Sabloff et al. (Albuquerque: University of New Mexico Press, 1975), 251.

42. Quoted in Andrew Hardy, *Red Hills: Migrants and the State in the Highlands of Vietnam* (Honolulu: University of Hawai'i Press, 2003), 4.

43. Owen Lattimore, "The Frontier in History," in *Studies in Frontier History: Collected Papers, 1928-1958* (Oxford: Oxford University Press, 1962), 469-91, quotation from 475.

44. Edmund Leach, *The Political Systems of Highland Burma: A Study of Kachin Social Structure* (Cambridge: Harvard University Press, 1954).

45. Thomas Barfield, "The Shadow Empires: Imperial State Formation along the Chinese-Nomad Frontier," in *Empires: Perspectives from Archaeology and History*, ed. Susan E. Alcock, Terrance N. D'Altroy, et al. (Cambridge: Cambridge University Press, 2001), 11-41. Karl Marx identified such parasitic, militarized peripheries engaged in slave-raiding and plunder on the fringe of the Roman Empire as "the Germanic mode of production." For the best account of such secondary state formation by the Wa people, see Magnus Fiskesjö, "The Fate of Sacrifice and the Making of Wa History," Ph.D. thesis, University of Chicago, 2000.

46. I borrow the term from Gonzalo Aguirre Beltrán, who argues that much of the post-conquest indigenous population of Spanish America could be found "in areas that are particularly hostile or inaccessible to human movement" and marginal to the colonial economy. For the most part, he has in mind rugged mountainous areas, although he includes tropical jungles and deserts. Aguirre Beltrán tends to see such areas more as "survivals" of precolonial populations rather than environments to which populations fled or were pushed. *Regions of Refuge*, Society of Applied Anthropology Monograph Series, 12 (Washington, D.C., 1979), 23 and passim.

47. Michaud, *Historical Dictionary*, 180, quotation from 199. Elsewhere, writing about the hill populations of Vietnam (the "montagnards"), he echoes the theme. "To some extent montagnards can be seen as refugees displaced by war and choosing to remain beyond the direct control of state authorities, who sought to control labor, tax productive resources, and secure access to populations from which they could recruit soldiers, servants, concubines, and slaves. This implies that montagnards have always been on the run." Michaud, *Turbulent Times and Enduring Peoples*, 11.

48. See Christine Ward Gailey and Thomas C. Patterson, "State Formation and Uneven Development," in *State and Society: The Emergence and Development of Social Hierarchy and Political Centralization*, ed. J. Gledhill, B. Bender, and M. T. Larsen (London: Routledge, 1988), 77-90.

49. Fiskesjö, "Fate of Sacrifice," 56.

50. The classic texts elaborating this argument include Pierre Clastres, *Society against the State: Essays in Political Anthropology*, trans. Robert Hurley (New York: Zone, 1987); Aguirre Beltrán, *Regions of Refuge;* Stuart Schwartz and Frank Salomon, "New Peoples and New Kinds of People: Adaptation, Adjustment, and Ethnogenesis in South American Indigenous

Societies (Colonial Era)," in *The Cambridge History of Native Peoples of the Americas*, ed. Stuart Schwartz and Frank Salomon (Cambridge: Cambridge University Press, 1999), 443–502. For a review of recent evidence, see Charles C. Mann, *1491: New Revelations of the Americas before Columbus* (New York: Knopf, 2005).

51. Felix M. Keesing, *The Ethno-history of Northern Luzon* (Stanford: Stanford University Press, 1976); William Henry Scott, *The Discovery of the Igorots: Spanish Contacts with the Pagans of Northern Luzon*, rev. ed. (Quezon City: New Day, 1974).

52. See, for example, Bruce W. Menning, "The Emergence of a Military-Administrative Elite in the Don Cossack Land, 1708–1836," in *Russian Officialdom: The Bureaucratization of Russian Society from the Seventeenth to the Twentieth Century*, ed. Walter MacKenzie Pinter and Don Karl Rowney (Chapel Hill: University of North Carolina Press, 1980), 130–61.

53. Leo Lucassen, Wim Willems, and Annemarie Cottaar, *Gypsies and Other Itinerant Groups: A Socio-historical Approach* (London: Macmillan, 1998).

54. Martin A. Klein, in "The Slave Trade and Decentralized Societies, *Journal of African History* 42 (2001): 49–65, observes that rather more centralized African societies often became predatory slave-raiders themselves (further reinforcing centralizing tendencies) and that decentralized societies often retreated to hills and forest zones of refuge when they were available, as well as fortifying their settlements to evade slave raids. See also J. F. Searing, "'No Kings, No Lords, No Slaves': Ethnicity and Religion among the Sereer-Safèn of Western Bawol (Senegal), 1700–1914," *Journal of African History* 43 (2002): 407–29; Dennis D. Cordell, "The Myth of Inevitability and Invincibility: Resistance to Slavers and the Slave Trade in Central Africa, 1850–1910," in *Fighting the Slave Trade: West African Strategies*, ed. Sylviane A. Diouf (Athens: Ohio University Press, 2003), 50–61; and for an attempt at a statistical analysis, Nathan Nunn and Diego Puga, "Ruggedness: The Blessing of Bad Geography," special section of the *American Historical Review* devoted to "Geography, History, and Institutional Change: The Causes and Consequences of Africa's Slave Trade," March 2007.

55. The term *mandala*, borrowed from south India, describes a political landscape of court centers radiating power outward through alliances and charisma, but having no fixed frontiers. It is an inherently plural term in the sense that it conjures up a number of contending mandalas jockeying for tribute and allies, with each mandala's sway waxing and waning—or disappearing altogether—depending on the circumstances. See I. W. Mabbett, "Kingship at Angkor, *Journal of the Siam Society* 66 (1978): 1058, and, especially, Wolters, *History, Culture, and Region*.

56. Scholarship on Southeast Asia as a whole is far less guilty of this charge than, say, scholarship on India or China. As a crossroads and contact zone, the borrowing and adaptations of religious beliefs, symbols of authority, and forms of political organization that originated elsewhere could hardly be overlooked. Mandala elites themselves flaunted such trappings. The "hill effects" on valley culture and social organization, however, are typically ignored.

57. The cases of the Minagkabau and the Batak on Sumatra, who long cultivated irrigated rice and developed an elaborate culture but did not create states, reminds us that while irrigated rice is nearly always a precondition of state formation, it is not sufficient.

58. The same process is roughly applicable, it seems, to our understanding of the formation of the Han system at a much earlier period.

59. Gilles Deleuze and Felix Guattari, *A Thousand Plateaus: Capitalism and Schizophrenia*, trans. Brian Massum (Minneapolis: University of Minnesota Press, 1987), 360.

60. Clastres, *Society against the State*. There are many such shatter zones in Africa that developed as populations threatened with capture for the slave trade fled into areas of relative safety. One such area is the Lamé-speaking zone along the current Guinea-Liberian border. Michael McGovern, personal communication, November 2007.

61. M. P. Griaznov, *The Ancient Civilization of Southern Siberia*, trans. James Hogarth

(New York: Cowles, 1969), 97–98, 131–33, cited in Deleuze and Guattari, *A Thousand Plateaus*, 430.

62. Lattimore, "Frontier in History," 472.

63. Ernest Gellner, *Saints of the Atlas* (London: Weidenfeld and Nicolson, 1969), 1–2.

64. Ibid., 1–2, 14, 31.

65. Quoted in Richard Tapper, "Anthropologists, Historians, and Tribespeople on Tribe and State Formation in the Middle East," in *Tribes and State Formation in the Middle East*, ed. Philip Khoury and Joseph Kostiner (Berkeley: University of California Press, 1990), 48–73, quotation from 66.

66. The stripping down of social structure to simpler, minimal forms, just as the resort to variable and mobile subsistence practices and fluid identities, has been shown to enhance adaptability to a capricious natural and political environment. See in this connection Robert E. Ehrenreich, Carole L. Crumley, and Janet E. Levy, eds., *Heterarchy and the Analysis of Complex Societies*, Archeological Papers of the American Anthropological Society, no. 6 (1995).

67. This point is missed, I think, in the perennial debates about whether Southeast Asian classical states were more dependent on trade or on manpower. A positional advantage at a river junction, a mountain pass, a jade or ruby mine had to be held militarily against rival claimants.

68. Georges Coedès, *The Indianized States of Southeast Asia* (Honolulu: East-West Center Press, 1968), originally published in France in 1948.

69. J. C. van Leur, *Indonesian Trade and Society* (The Hague: V. van Hoeve, 1955), 261.

70. John Smail, "On the Possibility of an Autonomous History of Modern Southeast Asia," *Journal of Southeast Asian History* 2 (1961): 72–102.

71. Peter Bellwood, "Southeast Asia before History," chapter 2 of *The Cambridge History of Southeast Asia*, ed. Nicholas Tarling, vol. 1, *From Early Times to 1800* (Cambridge: Cambridge University Press, 1992), 90.

72. Compared with other cultural zones, the maritime states of Southeast Asia, located at or near the estuary of rivers, left little in the way of physical evidence behind. The long search for the remains of Srivijaya is perhaps the most striking case in point. See in this context Jean Michaud, *Historical Dictionary*, 9, who notes that both building materials and burial practices in the hills leave little in the way of archeological traces. In this connection it should be added that, even in the lowlands, commoners were often forbidden to build structures with brick, stone, or even teak, lest it become a potential fortification in a rebellion. Hjorleifur Jonsson, personal communication, June 6, 2007.

73. The obverse of this fact is that a kingdom that does not leave a paper trail is unlikely to appear in the record at all. Georges Condominas notes that the Lua' kingdom(s) of highland and Khmer Southeast Asia, despite leaving ruins and oral legends of its founding by the marriage of a Lawa king and a Mon queen who brought Buddhism to the hills, has left hardly a trace because it apparently had no writing system. *From Lawa to Mon, from Saa' to Thai: Historical and Anthropological Aspects of Southeast Asian Social Spaces*, trans. Stephanie Anderson et al., an Occasional Paper of Anthropology in Association with the Thai-Yunnan Project, Research School of Pacific Studies (Canberra: Australian National University, 1990).

74. Such chronicles do, then, the symbolic work of the state. I am indebted to Indrani Chatterjee for pointing this out to me.

75. One major exception is found in the Burmese *Sit-tans*, administrative records that are devoted largely to providing an inventory of taxable property and economic activity and population according to their tax status. See Frank N. Trager and William J. Koenig, with the assistance of Yi Yi, *Burmese Sit-tàns, 1784–1826: Records of Rural Life and Administration*, Association of Asian Studies monograph no. 36 (Tucson: University of Arizona Press, 1979).

76. Richard A. O'Connor, "Review of Thongchai Winichakul, *Siam Mapped: A History*

of the Geo-body of a Nation" (Honolulu: University of Hawai'i Press, 1994), *Journal of Asian Studies* 56 (1997): 280. A telling example is the official Burmese court version of a diplomatic letter from the Chinese emperor in which it appears that the Chinese emperor as the emperor of the East is addressing the Burmese king as the emperor of the West and that the two are coequals bestriding the civilized world. As Than Tun remarks, "In all probability, this Burmese version of the address from China is quite different from its original though it is the one acceptable to the Burmese king who admits no other monarch as his superior." *Royal Orders of Burma, A.D. 1598–1885*, part 1, *A.D. 1598–1648*, ed. Than Tun (Kyoto: Center for Southeast Asian Studies, 1983), 3: 1. Official court histories remind me of my high school newspaper, *The Sun Dial*, whose motto was "We Mark Only the Hours That Shine."

77. One of the first efforts to correct this myopia may be found in Taylor, "Surface Orientations." It should be noted that the important work of demystifying nationalist histories is, finally, well under way in Southeast Asia.

78. Walter Benjamin, "Theses on the Philosophy of History," in *Illuminations*, ed. Hannah Arendt (New York: Schocken, 1968), 255–56. I am grateful to Charles Lesch for bringing this to my attention in his unpublished paper "Anarchist Dialectics and Primitive Utopias: Walter Benjamin, Pierre Clastres, and the Violence of Historical Progress," 2008.

79. See Herman Kulke, "The Early and Imperial Kingdom in Southeast Asian History," in *Southeast Asia in the 9th to 14th Centuries*, ed. David G. Marr and A. C. Milner (Singapore: Institute for Southeast Asian Studies, 1986), 1–22. Bronson makes a related point that the northern two-thirds of South Asia has, over the past three millennia, produced "exactly two moderately durable, region-spanning states: the Gupta and the Mughal. Neither of these nor any of the smaller states lasted longer than two centuries and anarchical interregna were everywhere prolonged and severe." Bennett Bronson, "The Role of Barbarians in the Fall of States," in *The Collapse of Ancient States and Civilizations*, ed. Norman Yoffee and George L. Cowgill (Tucson: University of Arizona Press, 1988), 196–218.

80. Anthony Day, "Ties That (Un)Bind: Families and States in Pre-modern Southeast Asia," *Journal of Asian Studies* 55 (1996): 398. Day is here criticizing the state-centric aspect of the important historiographic work by Anthony Reid and Victor Lieberman.

81. See Taylor, "Surface Orientations." Taylor imaginatively examines several periods in the early history of the area now called Vietnam, while scrupulously avoiding reading back modern national or regional narratives for which there is no contemporary evidence.

82. See in this connection Sara (Meg) Davis's critique of Condominas, "Premodern Flows and Postmodern China: Globalization and the Sipsongpanna Tai," *Modern China* 29 (2003): 187: "Villagers shifted between villages and towns, federations of villages and states split and reformed, and the nobility was sometimes compelled to travel far and wide to hold a constituency together. . . . Such continual and steady movement and change make the region difficult to characterize, though we can note three constants: Village affiliation, strong traditions of independence, and freedom of movement."

83. Anthony Reid, "'Tradition' in Indonesia: The One and the Many," *Asian Studies Review* 22 (1998): 32.

84. Akin Rabibhadana, "The Organization of Thai Society in the Early Bangkok Period, 1782–1873," Cornell University, Thailand Project, Interim Report Series, no. 12 (July 1969), 27.

85. Richard White, *The Middle Ground: Indians, Empires, and Republics in the Great Lakes Region, 1650–1815* (Cambridge: Cambridge University Press, 1991).

86. Thucydides, *The Peloponnesian War*, trans. Rex Warner (New York: Penguin, 1972).

87. Basile Nikitina, quoted, in French, by Tapper in "Anthropologists, Historians, and Tribespeople," 55; my translation.

88. Sir Stamford Raffles, cited by Reid in "'Tradition' in Indonesia," 31.

CHAPTER 2. State Space

1. Quoted in Yong Xue, "Agrarian Urbanization: Social and Economic Changes in Jiangnan from the 8th to the 19th Century," Ph.D. diss., Yale University, 2006, 102. The logic invoked here is derived directly from the standard formulations of "central-place theory" as elaborated by Johann Heinrich von Thünen, Walter Christaller, and G. W. Skinner. The logic, precisely because it is so schematic, is also occasionally faulty. For example, what if free spring pasture is available along the transportation route? In this case the draft animals might grow fatter at no cost along the way and, for that matter, may be themselves part of the cargo, as it were, if they are sold at the destination!

2. As Peter Bellwood notes, the density of population in wet-rice cultivation is roughly ten times as great as swidden/slash-and-burn, rain-fed, hill rice: a decisive advantage, as we shall see, for the state. "Southeast Asia before History," in *The Cambridge History of Southeast Asia*, ed. Nicholas Tarling, vol. 1, *From Early Times to 1800* (Cambridge: Cambridge University Press, 1992), 1: 90.

3. Should they wish to, of course, officials can also punish the cultivator or the entire village by burning the dry, ripe crops to the ground.

4. Notice, as well, that a store of grain allows armies to march long distances (Julius Caesar's legions, for example) while feeding themselves, and, in turn, it allows besieged defenders of a fortified state core to hold out longer. Premodern invasions were often planned to coincide with the grain harvest so that the army could provision itself en route rather than having to carry all its rations in its pack train.

5. See, in general, Jonathan Rigg, *The Gift of Water: Water Management, Cosmology, and the State in Southeast Asia* (London: School of Oriental and African Studies, 1992), and, especially, in that volume, Philip Stott, "Ankor: Shifting the Hydraulic Paradigm," 47–58, and Janice Staargardt, "Water for Courts or Countryside: Archeological Evidence from Burma and Thailand Revisited," 59–72. The point of that volume is, in part, to lay permanently to rest the thesis of hydraulic societies proposed by Karl Wittfogel in *Oriental Despotism: A Comparative Study of Total Power* (New Haven: Yale University Press, 1976, 9th ed.), for Southeast Asia at any rate. Among other things, the demographic realities and the possibility of flight prevented any large-scale mobilization of forced labor. The scholarly consensus is best expressed by Clifford Geertz in his examination of the complex Balinese system of terracing and irrigation. "In fact the state role in . . . construction seems to have been minor at best. . . . In the first place, the growth of the subak system was almost certainly a very gradual, piecemeal process, not an all-at-once collective effort demanding authoritative coordination of huge masses of men. By the nineteenth century, the system was essentially complete, but even before the nineteenth century its expansion was slow, steady, and almost imperceptible. The notion that impressive irrigation works need highly centralized states to construct them rests on ignoring this fact: such works are not built at one blow." *Negara: The Theatre State in Nineteenth-Century Bali* (Princeton: Princeton University Press, 1980), 197. See also the references in Geertz and, also for Bali in particular, Stephen Lansing, *Priests and Programmers: Technologies of Power and the Engineered Landscape of Bali* (Princeton: Princeton University Press, 1991).

6. Barbara Watson Andaya, "Political Development between the Sixteenth and Eighteenth Centuries," in Tarling, *Cambridge History*, 1: 402–59, quotation from 426.

7. Jan Wisseman Christie, "Water from the Ancestors: Irrigation in Early Java and Bali," in Rigg, *Gift of Water*, 7–25, quotation from 12.

8. Andaya, "Political Development," 426.

9. I owe this insight to Edward Whiting Fox, *History in Geographical Perspective: The Other France* (New York: Norton, 1971), 25.

10. One imagines that the "shock and awe" effect of elephants in a military campaign

might have been more decisive than their value as pack animals. I am grateful to Katherine Bowie for reminding me of the use of elephants in war.

11. *The Man Shu (Book of the Southern Barbarians)*, trans. Gordon H. Luce, ed. G. P. Oey, data paper no. 44, Southeast Asia Program, Cornell University, December 1961, 4–11.

12. See table 1. I am grateful to Alexander Lee for assembling and calculating this information. C. Ainslie, *Report on a Tour through the Trans-Salween Shan States, Season 1892–'93* (Rangoon: Superintendent, Government Printing, 1893).

I have selected two parallel routes surveyed by Ainslie from Pan Yang to Man Pan. "There is another," he writes, "via Long Lawk which runs high up among the hills and is said to be a very bad road, even for loaded men."

Ainslie also notes the presence or absence of camping sites. Many of the good ones (clear, flat areas near to a water source) are flooded in the wet season. The standard unit of the table is the "stage" or day's march.

13. The figures for travel by foot and the carrying capacities of porters and bullock carts are taken from Anthony Reid, *Southeast Asia in the Age of Commerce, 1450–1680*, vol. 2, *Expansion and Crisis* (New Haven: Yale University Press, 1993), 57. Jeremy Black, writing about military movements in seventeenth-century Europe, gives fifteen miles (twenty-four kilometers) a day as the upper limit for an army on the march. *European Warfare, 1660–1815* (New Haven: Yale University Press, 1994), 37. A larger army requiring a baggage train would average only ten miles (sixteen kilometers) a day (hence the tactical importance of swift-moving cavalry). John A. Lynn, ed., *Feeding Mars: Logistics in Western Warfare from the Middle Ages to the Present* (Boulder: Westview, 1993), 21.

14. See the calculations for a cart pulled by a team of four horses in Lynn, *Feeding Mars*, 19. Perhaps because of the famed roads of the Roman Empire, Peter Heather calculates that an oxcart traveling over level terrain could cover forty kilometers a day (nearly twenty-five miles). Diocletian's Prices Edict, however, records that the price of a wagon of wheat doubled for every fifty miles (eighty kilometers) it traveled. See Peter Heather, *The Fall of the Roman Empire: A New History of Rome and the Barbarians* (Oxford: Oxford University Press, 2006), 107, 111.

15. Fox, *History in Geographical Perspective*, 25.

16. F. K. Lehman [Chit Hlaing], "Burma: Kayah Society as a Function of the Shan-Burma-Karen Context," in *Contemporary Change in Traditional Society*, 3 vols., ed. Julian Steward (Urbana: University of Illinois Press, 1967), 1: 1–104, quotation from 13.

17. Reid, *Southeast Asia in the Age of Commerce*, 2: 54.

18. Charles Tilly, "War Making and State Making as Organized Crime," in *Bringing the State Back In*, ed. Peter Evans, Dietrich Rueschmeyer, and Theda Skocpol (Cambridge: Cambridge University Press, 1985), 178.

19. George Fitzherbert, review of Melvyn C. Goldstein, *A History of Modern Tibet*, vol. 2, *The Calm before the Storm, 1951–1955* (Berkeley: University of California Press, 2008), *Times Literary Supplement*, March 28, 2008, 24.

20. The simile "as the crow flies" is a nearly perfect expression of relatively frictionless movement through the air, though, of course, with its storms, drafts, and prevailing winds, the air is hardly a frictionless medium.

21. Thongchai Winichakul, *Siam Mapped: A History of the Geo-Body of a Nation* (Honolulu: University of Hawai'i Press, 1994), 31.

22. Fernand Braudel, *The Mediterranean and the Mediterranean World in the Age of Philip II*, 2 vols., trans. Sian Reynolds (New York: Harper and Row, 1966).

23. Here William's invasion of Great Britain is the exception that proves the rule, inasmuch as most of Great Britain is close to the navigable routes to the sea.

Table 1 Walking Times in Eastern Shan State, 1892–93

Stage	Distance (km)	# of Rivers to Cross	Major Elevation Changes	Comments
Pang Yang to Nam Nge Lam	11.25	1	760-meter drop 215-meter rise 365-meter drop	Due to elevation changes: "Difficult march in wet weather."
Nam Nge Lam to Man Kat	15.25	3 (ferry needed for 1)	550-meter rise "very steep" descent 120-meter rise 120-meter fall	"This march would be very difficult in wet weather," due to the necessity of crossing streams.
Man Kat to Lau Kiu	14.5	3	1,200 meters up 1,200 meters down ? rise 275-meter rise "very steep" "very easy descent"	Rivers: "Very rapid and impassible in flood."

Lau Kiu to Ta Pong	19.25	2	Along the river, so no major change. However, several steep gullies.	
Ta Pong to Man Pan	7.25	1	Small rise; large drop	Entrance to the capital of a small Shan state.
Ta Mat Long to Pang Wo	13.25	1	"Easy" 850-meter rise. (90-meter descent and climb to get water)	"No road when the Salween rises."
Pang Wo to Pak Long	13.25	0	150-meter descent 150-meter "gradual rise" 2,400-meter descent "rather steep in places"	A good deal of rice stored in village.
Pak Long to Nam Wa	10.5	1	350-meter drop 245-meter rise 335-meter drop "rather steep"	
Nam Wa to Nam Nge Lam	14.5	2	455-meter rise "very steep at first" 610-meter descent	

24. Andaya, "Political Development," 427. Andaya cites similarly impressive figures for the armed manpower of Mataram (Java) and Ava (Burma).

25. Flood retreat agriculture was, and is, practiced along such rivers, but it appears less stable and reliable than irrigation on smaller perennial streams. See Staargardt, "Water for Courts or Countryside." It is an ironic comment on Karl Wittfogel's widely discredited thesis that while extensive irrigation can, and has, been constructed independent of the state, the extensive drainage required to open deltaic lowlands to cultivation may, in fact, require a different sort of "hydraulic-state" and the provision of credit to pioneers.

26. E. R. Leach, "The Frontiers of Burma," *Comparative Studies in Society and History* 3 (1960): 49–68, quotation from 58.

27. Ibid.

28. Ibid., 56.

29. Relevant here is G. William Skinner's development of the standard market area, from the work of von Thünen and Christaller, as a unit of social and cultural integration; see "Chinese Peasants and the Closed Community: An Open and Shut Case," *Comparative Studies in Society and History* 13 (1971): 270–81. Since Skinner's model is based on a standardized flat terrain, it would have to be corrected for the varying influence of navigable rivers, on the one hand, or for that of swampy or mountainous terrain on the other. For a telling example of a religious movement that traveled more easily downriver than laterally across the hills, see Charles F. Keyes's description of the Telakhon, Karen, prophetic movement in the hills behind Moulmein/Mawlemyain. Keyes, ed., *Ethnic Adaptation and Identity: The Karen on the Thai Frontier with Burma* (Philadelphia: ISHII, 1979), 66–67.

30. Leach, "Frontiers of Burma," 58.

31. Benedict Anderson, "The Idea of Power in Javanese Culture," in *Culture and Politics in Indonesia*, ed. Claire Holt et al. (Ithaca: Cornell University Press, 1972).

32. *Royal Orders of Burma, A.D. 1598–1885*, part 1, *A.D. 1598–1648*, ed. Than Tun (Kyoto: Center for Southeast Asian Studies, 1983), 72.

33. O. W. Wolters, *History, Culture, and Region in Southeast Asian Perspectives*, rev. ed. (Ithaca: Cornell University Press, in cooperation with the Institute of Southeast Asian Studies, Singapore, 1999), 28.

34. Thongchai, *Siam Mapped.*

35. Thongchai, ibid., 88, claims that this was Cambodia's strategy as a tributary to both Siam and Vietnam in the nineteenth century.

36. Ibid., 73, 86. Thongchai also notes that the small kingdom of Lai paid tribute simultaneously to China, Tonkin, and Luang Prabang (100). The now classic study of such zones of fractured sovereignty and the social and political flux of identities they throw up is Richard White, *The Middle Ground: Empires and Republics in the Great Lakes Region, 1650–1815* (Cambridge: Cambridge University Press, 1991).

37. See *Royal Orders of Burma*, 3: vii.

38. One might imagine river travel to be a major exception to this rule. During the months of high rainfall, however, major rivers were often in spate and difficult to navigate, not to mention the added difficulty of a return voyage against a swift current.

39. Desawarnana (Nagarakartagama), quoted in Wolters, *History, Culture, and Region,* 36.

40. See, for example, "Glass Palace Chronicle: Excerpts Translated on Burmese Invasions of Siam," compiled and annotated by Nai Thein, *Journal of the Siam Society* 5 (1908): 1–82 and 8 (1911): 1–119.

41. *Gazetteer of Upper Burma and the Shan States*, compiled from official papers by J. George Scott, assisted by J. P. Hardiman, vol. 1, part 1 (Rangoon: Government Printing Office, 1893), 136.

42. Perhaps the most striking colonial example was the strangulation of the French fort at Bien Bien Phu by North Vietnamese forces with help from hill peoples. But for a more representative example, see William Henry Scott's fine account of Igorot strategies against the Spanish in Northern Luzon, *The Discovery of the Igorots: Spanish Contacts with the Pagans of Northern Luzon*, rev. ed. (Quezon City: New Day, 1974), 31–36, 225–26.

CHAPTER 3. Concentrating Manpower and Grain

Epigraph from Nicholas Gervaise, *The Natural and Political History of the Kingdom of Siam*, trans. John Villiers (Bangkok, 1987), 27, quoted in Victor B. Lieberman, *Strange Parallels: Southeast Asia in Global Context, c. 800–1830*, vol. 1, *Integration on the Mainland* (Cambridge: Cambridge University Press, 2003), 27.

1. Anthony Reid, *Southeast Asia in the Age of Commerce, 1450–1680*, vol. 1, *The Lands Below the Winds* (New Haven: Yale University Press, 1988), 20. Owen Lattimore, in a discussion of state cores and frontiers, suggests a graded series of subsistence patterns from most extensive to most intensive: hunting-gathering, pastoral nomadism, rain-fed agriculture, and irrigated agriculture. The last, by virtue of the concentration of manpower and grain it represents, is, he believes, most hospitable to state-making. "The Frontier in History," in *Studies in Frontier History: Collected Papers, 1928–1958* (Oxford: Oxford University Press, 1962), 469–91, esp. 474.

2. Richard A. O'Connor, "Agricultural Change and Ethnic Succession in Southeast Asian States: A Case for Regional Anthropology," *Journal of Asian Studies* 54 (1995): 988n11. O'Connor credits F. K. Lehman [Chit Hlaing], "Empiricist Method and Intentional Analysis in Burmese Historiography: William Koenig's *The Burmese Polity, 1752–1819*, a Review Article," *Crossroads: An Interdisciplinary Journal of Southeast Asian Studies* 6 (1991): 77–120.

3. In practice, padi farmers might have rain-fed fields and swiddens as well as irrigated rice fields. For the cultivators, this mixed portfolio of subsistence routines offered some flexibility. They could ease some or all their tax burden by planting less land to heavily taxed padi and shifting to less heavily taxed crops.

4. Georges Condominas, *From Lawa to Mon, from Saa' to Thai: Historical and Anthropological Aspects of Southeast Asian Social Spaces*, trans. Stephanie Anderson et al., an Occasional Paper of the Department of Anthropology in Association with the Thai-Yunnan Project, Research School of Pacific Studies (Canberra: Australian National University, 1990). Michael Mann, in *The Sources of Social Power*, employs a strikingly similar metaphor of "social cageing" to describe the efforts of the earliest states to circumscribe a population (Cambridge: Cambridge University Press, 1986), 54–58.

5. Quoted in Mark Elvin, *The Retreat of the Elephants: An Environmental History of China* (New Haven: Yale University Press, 2004), 104.

6. See Frank N. Trager and William J. Koenig, with the assistance of Yi Yi, *Burmese Sit-tàns, 1784–1826: Records of Rural Life and Administration*, Association of Asian Studies monograph no. 36 (Tucson: University of Arizona Press, 1979). Trager and Koenig point out that even district histories in precolonial Burma focus on what they term "the shadow of the throne," where "the hinterland appears but mainly to serve the purpose of the royal center" (1). The notable exception to this are the *sit-tàns* (usually translated as "inquests"), which consist of locality-by-locality reports by headmen of their area of jurisdiction, the land and the crops sown on it, and, above all, the sources of annual revenue it provides to the crown. They are essentially a revenue inventory with particular attention devoted to the most lucrative land: irrigated riceland bearing one or two crops annually.

7. Quoted ibid., 77–78.

8. The term is Robert Elson's in "International Commerce, the State, and Society: Eco-

nomic and Social Change," chapter 3 of *The Cambridge History of Southeast Asia*, ed. Nicholas Tarling, vol. 2, *The Nineteenth and Twentieth Centuries* (Cambridge: Cambridge University Press, 1992), 131.

9. R. L. Carniero, "A Theory of the Origin of the State," *Science* 169 (1970): 733–38.

10. Clifford Geertz, *Negara: The Theatre State in Nineteenth-Century Bali* (Princeton: Princeton University Press, 1980), 24.

11. Thongchai Winichakul, *Siam Mapped: A History of the Geo-Body of a Nation* (Honolulu: University of Hawai'i Press, 1994), 164.

12. Barbara Watson Andaya, "Political Development between the Sixteenth and the Eighteenth Centuries" in Tarling, *Cambridge History*, vol. 1, *From Early Times to 1800*, 402–59, esp. 422–23. The term *Dato/Datu* in the Malay world meant "lord with vassals." Burmese officials above the level of village chiefs were often designated the beneficiaries of a locality's revenue (the often cited town-eater or *myó-sà*). This was not the same as ruling the district, and such revenue was often given in fractional shares to many dignitaries. Nor was such an entitlement generally inheritable. It also seems that those officials who did rule a locality or benefit from its revenue retained jurisdiction over such people or claimed their taxes after they had moved to another location. Hence the puzzlement of the British to discover that the subjects of a single locality owed allegiance or taxes to several different claimants.

13. J. Kathirithamby-Wells, "The Age of Transition: The Mid-eighteenth Century to Early Nineteenth Centuries," in Tarling, *Cambridge History*, 1: 883–84.

14. Reid, *Southeast Asia in the Age of Commerce*, vol. 2, *Expansion and Crisis* (New Haven: Yale University Press, 1993), 108.

15. Quoted ibid., 1: 129.

16. See in this connection the remarkable evidence assembled by Kenichi Kirigaya in "The Age of Commerce and the Tai Encroachments on the Irrawaddy Basin," draft paper, June 2008, and the models of center-periphery relations in Noboru Ishikawa's "Centering Peripheries: Flows and Interfaces in Southeast Asia," Kyoto Working Papers on Area Studies no. 10, JSPS Global COE Program, Series 7, *In Search of Sustainable Humanosphere in Asia and Africa*, Subseries 8, Center for Southeast Asian Studies, Kyoto University, December 2008.

17. Lieberman, *Strange Parallels*, 1: 88.

18. Amar Siamwalla, "Land, Labour, and Capital in Three Rice-growing Deltas of Southeast Asia, 1800–1840," Yale Economic Growth Center, discussion paper 150 (July 1972), emphasizes the efforts of the core states centered in Mandalay, Bangkok, and Hanoi to prevent mass migration to southern delta areas outside their control. In the crudest "transportation-economy" terms, it nearly always makes sense to move people to fertile land rather than the products of fertile land to the capital. People are easier to move than grain; for one thing, they walk and, once resettled, they produce a surplus that does not have to be moved far.

19. See, for example, Charles Tilly, *Coercion, Capital, and European States, AD 990–1992* (Cambridge, Mass.: Blackwell, 1990), chapter 5; Jeremy Black, *European Warfare, 1660–1815* (New Haven: Yale University Press, 1994), 9–15; and Richard Whiting Fox, *History in Geographical Perspective: The Other France* (New York: Norton, 1971), chapter 2. England is, of course, the glaring exception. Its success as a largely maritime power rested, Black suggests, on its massive wealth from trade, which allowed it to subsidize others to do much of its fighting for it.

20. Quoted in Akin Rabibhadana, "The Organization of Society in the Early Bangkok Period, 1782–1873," Cornell University Thailand Project, Interim Report Series, no. 12 (July, 1969), 16–18.

21. *The Glass Palace Chronicle of the Kings of Burma*, trans. Pe Maung Tin and G. H. Luce, issued by the Text Publication Fund of the Burma Research Society (Oxford: Oxford University Press, Humphrey Milford, 1923), 177.

22. Quoted in Rabibhadana, "Organization of Society," 16–18.

23. *Glass Palace Chronicle*, 177, 150.

24. See, for example, the long list of retainers of Queen Thirusandevi ibid., 95.

25. The ruler of Palembang in 1747 observed: "It is very easy for a subject to find a lord, but it is much more difficult for a lord to find a subject." For an illuminating discussion and a list of adages (including some quoted here), see Anthony Reid, "'Closed' and 'Open' Slave Systems in Precolonial Southeast Asia," in *Slavery, Bondage, and Dependency in Southeast Asia*, ed. Anthony Reid (New York: St. Martin's, 1983), 156–81, esp. 157–60.

26. Thucydides, *The Peloponnesian War*, trans. Rex Warner (New York: Penguin Books, 1972), e.g., 67, 96, 221, 513, and 535. Thucydides goes out of his way to praise the Spartan general Brasidas for negotiating the peaceful surrender of cities so as to increase the Spartan tax and manpower base at no cost in Spartan lives.

27. Elvin, *Retreat of the Elephants*, 104, quoting the late-fourth-century BCE Guanzi jiping.

28. Ibid. 104, quoting from *The Book of the Lord of Shang*.

29. Jeffrey Herbst, *States and Power in Africa: Comparative Lessons in Authority and Control* (Princeton: Princeton University Press, 2000), 18.

30. Igor Kopytoff, *The African Frontier: The Reproduction of Traditional African Societies* (Bloomington: Indiana University Press, 1987), 40. Kopytoff's excellent essay is very suggestive for understanding manpower-starved political systems.

31. Quoted ibid., 62, 53.

32. Ibid., 62.

33. Richard A. O'Connor, "Rice, Rule, and the Tai State," in *State Power and Culture in Thailand*, ed. E. Paul Durrenberger, Yale Southeast Asia monograph no. 44 (New Haven, 1996), 68–99, quotation from 81.

34. Thant Myint U, "The Crisis of the Burmese State and the Foundations of British Colonial Rule in Upper Burma," Ph.D. diss., Cambridge University, 1995, 46–47.

35. For more on this theme, see my *Seeing Like a State: How Certain Schemes for Improving the Human Condition Have Failed* (New Haven: Yale University Press, 1998), especially chapters 1 and 2.

36. The sit-tàns provide evidence of the agro-ecological specialization by ethnic group. Thus the Karen population of Hanthawaddy/Pegu were mostly swiddeners and foragers, taxed as much for their honey and silver production as for their small grain yields. See Toshikatsu Ito, "Karens and the Kon-baung Polity in Myanmar," *Acta Asiatica* 92 (2007): 89–108.

37. John S. Furnivall, *The Fashioning of Leviathan: The Beginnings of British Rule in Burma*, ed. Gehan Wijeyewardene (1939; Canberra: Department of Anthropology, Research School of Pacific Studies, Australian National University, 1991), 116.

38. A homely analogy from beekeeping may be helpful here. Until roughly a century ago, the gathering of honey was a difficult affair. Even if captured swarms were kept in straw hives, extracting the honey usually meant driving off the bees with fire or smoke and often destroying the colony in the process. The arrangement of brood chambers and honey cells followed complex patterns that varied from hive to hive, making the harvest complex and wasteful. The modern beehive, in contrast, is designed to solve the beekeeper's problem. A device called the queen-excluder separates the brood chambers below from most of the honey supply above, by preventing the queen from entering and laying eggs above a certain level. Furthermore, the cells are arranged neatly in vertical frames, nine or ten to a box, which allow easy, frame-by-frame extraction of honey, wax, and propolis. Harvesting is made possible by observing "bee space"—the precise distance between frames (three-eighths of an inch) that bees will leave open rather than bridging the frames with honeycomb. From the beekeeper's point of view, the modern hive is an orderly, "legible" hive allowing him or her to inspect the condition of the

colony and the queen, judge the honey production (usually by weight), enlarge or contract the size by standard units, move it to a new location, and, above all, extract just enough honey (in temperate climates) to ensure that the colony will overwinter successfully. And just as the beekeeper raids the hive when it is heavy with honey, so were invasions timed seasonally to coincide with the beginning of the dry season and crops ripe for plunder and provisions. (Thucydides noted that invasions occurred when the grain on the route of march was ripe and that it was a potentially fatal miscalculation to invade too early, when the grain was green. In the case of a punitive raid, an invading army could also burn the ripe grain [impossible in the case of root crops] and thereby scatter or render destitute an enemy population. *Peloponnesian War*, 173, 265, 267.) Without pushing this analogy further than it merits, the concentration and uniformity of monoculture—in this case padi rice—does for the tax man and military recruiter roughly what the modern hive does for the beekeeper.

39. Andrew Hardy, *Red Hills: Migrants and the State in the Highlands of Vietnam* (Honolulu: University of Hawai'i Press, 2003), 288. Hardy is citing both a work in Vietnamese by Mai Khac Ung and, among others, Masaya Shiraishi, "State, Villagers, and Vagabonds: Vietnamese Rural Society and the Phan Ba Vanh Rebellion," Senri Ethnological Studies 13 (1984): 345–400.

40. Quoted in Hardy, *Red Hills*, 240–55. Hardy also has a good discussion of French policy, as does Oscar Salemink, *The Ethnography of Vietnam's Central Highlanders: A Historical Contextualization, 1850-1990* (London: Routledge-Curzon, 2003). See also Jean Michaud, ed., *Turbulent Times and Enduring Peoples: Mountain Minorities in the Southeast Asian Masssif* (Richmond, England: Curzon, 2000), and Pamela McElwee, "Becoming Socialist or Becoming Kinh: Government Policies for Ethnic Minorities in the Socialist Republic of Vietnam," in *Civilizing the Margins: Southeast Asian Government Policies for the Development of Minorities*, ed. Christopher R. Duncan (Ithaca: Cornell University Press, 2004), 182–21. For an account of the resettlement policy of the ill-starred Saigon regime, see Stan B-H Tan, "Dust beneath the Mist: State and Frontier Formation in the Central Highlands of Vietnam, the 1955–1961 Period," Ph.D. diss., Australian National University, 2006.

41. Pamela Kyle Crossley, Helen Siu, and Donald Sutton, eds., *Empire at the Margins: Culture and Frontier in Early Modern China* (Charlottesville: University of Virginia Press, 2006). See especially the contributions by John E. Herman, David Faure, Donald Sutton, Anne Csete, Wing-hoi Chan, and Helen Siu and Lui Zhiwei.

42. Grant Evans, "Central Highlands of Vietnam," chapter 2 of *Indigenous Peoples of Asia*, ed. R. H. Barnes, Andrew Gray, and Benedict Kingsbury, Association of Asian Studies monograph no. 48 (Ann Arbor: University of Michigan Press, 1995).

43. Nicholas Tapp, *Sovereignty and Rebellion: The White Hmong of Northern Thailand* (Singapore: Oxford University Press, 1990), 38. See also William Robert Geddes, *Migrants of the Mountains: The Cultural Ecology of the Blue Miao [Hmong Njua] of Thailand* (Oxford: Clarendon, 1976), 259.

44. Tapp, *Sovereignty and Rebellion*, 31, 34.

45. The pattern in mainland Southeast Asia is repeated in the Malay world to the south. Sultans in Perak (Malaysia) have constantly insisted that the lowland but highly mobile Semai form permanent settlements. In Sarawak the Malaysian government has tried consistently "to make the Punan conform to the norms of farming peoples." "Progress and development mean standardization on the model of the farmers: rice farming to the point of self-sufficiency." See Geoffrey Benjamin and Cynthia Chou, eds., *Tribal Communities in the Malay World: Historical, Cultural, and Social Perspectives* (Singapore: Institute of Southeast Asian Studies, 2002), 47. See also Robert Knox Denton, Kirk Endicott, Alberto Gomes, and M. B. Hooker, *Malaysia and the Original People: A Case Study of the Impact of Development on Indigenous Peoples, Cul-*

tural Survival Studies in Ethnicity and Change (Boston: Allyn and Bacon, 1997); John D. Leary, *Violence and the Dream People: The Orang Asli and the Malayan Emergency, 1948–1960*, Ohio University Center for International Studies, Monographs in International Studies, Southeast Asian Studies no. 95 (Athens: Center for International Studies, Ohio University, 1995); and Bernard Sellato, *Nomads of the Borneo Rainforest: The Economics, Politics, and Ideology of Settling Down*, trans. Stephanie Morgan (Honolulu: University of Hawai'i Press, 1994), 171–73.

46. Kevin Malseed, "'We Have Hands the Same as Them': Struggles for Local Sovereignty and Livelihoods by Internally Displaced Karen Villagers in Burma," unpublished research paper, Karen Human Rights Group, 2006, 9.

47. O. W. Wolters, *History, Culture, and Region in Southeast Asian Perspectives*, rev. ed. (Ithaca: Cornell University Press, in cooperation with the Institute of Southeast Asian Studies, Singapore, 1999), passim, esp. 58–67.

48. Crossley, Siu, and Sutton, *Empire at the Margins*, especially Helen Siu and Liu Zhiwei, "Lineage, Market, Pirate, and Dan: Ethnicity in the Pearl River Delta," 285–331. The authors suggest that the way in which the "Dan" became "Han" is a process that typifies early Han state-building as well.

49. Wolters, *History, Culture, and Region*, 86.

50. The Tai linguistic family incorporates a large number of peoples all the way from northern Vietnam to northeastern India. In eastern Burma (the Shan states), much of northern Thailand, and southern Yunnan, they tend to be a padi-planting, state-forming, Buddhist people. It is these Tai I am referring to here. There are Tai peoples throughout the region (sometimes called "hill Tai") who are non-Buddhist swiddeners living outside state structures.

51. David Wyatt, quoted in Wolters, *History, Culture, and Region*, 128n10.

52. Lieberman, *Strange Parallels*, 1: 271–73, 318–19.

53. Ibid., 1: 319. Here I believe Lieberman may imply too much in the way of ethnic and religious consciousness. It is more likely that identities were more fluid, their bearers versed in two or more languages, and more identified, perhaps, with a place of origin or residence rather than having a firm linguistic or ethnic identity.

54. Peter Heather, *The Fall of the Roman Empire: A New History of Rome and the Barbarians* (Oxford: Oxford University Press, 2006), 201. Heather, with this example, endeavors to show that the Romans at the Celtic periphery of their empire could nevertheless prevail culturally despite their small numbers.

55. Condominas, *From Lawa to Mon*, 65–72.

56. Ibid., 41.

57. Mentioned in passing by Mandy Sadan in "Translating *gumlau:* History, the 'Kachin,' and Edmund Leach," in *Social Dynamics in the Highlands of Southeast Asia: Reconsidering Political Systems of Highland Burma by E. R. Leach*, ed. François Robinne and Mandy Sadan, Handbook of Oriental Studies, section 3, Southeast Asia (Leiden: Brill, 2007), 76.

58. Edmund Leach, *The Political Systems of Highland Burma: A Study of Kachin Social Structure* (1954; Boston: Beacon Press, 1968), 39.

59. "In the Tay [Tai] social formation only the chiefs and the free peasants have wet rice fields and the non-Tay may not have them." Condominas, *From Lawa to Mon*, 83.

60. See the insightful analysis of Jonathan Friedman, "Dynamique et transformations du système tribal, l'exemple des Katchins," *L'homme* 15 (1975): 63–98. In southwest China, the numerous small Tai states that arose were invariably based on a fertile plateau that might be at a fairly high altitude. Such plateaus were called *bazi* by the Chinese, a term that might be translated as "valley basin" or "flatland on mountainous plateau." I am grateful to Shanshan Du for her explanation of these terms.

61. The Malay state, if one were comparing precolonial Southeast Asian states in terms of their thirst for manpower, would qualify almost as a limiting case. It was exceptionally open, pluralistic, and assimilative, with the formula for assimilation being more of a state affiliation than a thick, cultural identity. Speaking Malay (a language of trade like Swahili), professing Islam, and being a subject of a Malay state was virtually all it took. Inclusion in this hyper–manpower state did not preclude coercion. Melaka and the other Malay states were responsible for most of the enormously rich slave trade in the region. Though the classical Malay state was, typically, a trading port mediating between forest products and international trade, the most valuable cargoes in its ships' holds were human captives sold or kept as slaves.

Just how cosmopolitan the Malay state was at the beginning of the sixteenth century (just before the Portuguese conquest) is reflected in Tome Pires's claim that eighty-four distinct languages could be heard on the streets of Melaka. It not only rivaled and perhaps surpassed Venice and Constantinople for sheer diversity, but it was a social and political system open to talent. The greatest of Melaka's rulers, Sultan Mansur, appointed to manage his finances a "heathen king" from India who converted and founded a famous dynasty of court counselors. The same Sultan also elevated one of his non-Muslim slaves from Palembang, who, in turn, founded the powerful Laksamana Dynasty. As Reid emphasizes, outsiders could quickly be incorporated and rise to prominence. "Some foreign traders, sharing religion and language, could cross the boundary into the local aristocracy very quickly, while all could do so within a generation if willing to accept the dominant religion and culture."

Like the Tai padi state, the Malay *negeri* was an effective centripetal population machine. One consequence of its success was the fact that most Malays were—in contemporary parlance—"hyphenated Malays": Bengali-Malays, Javanese-Malays, Chinese-Malays, Minagkabau-Malays, and so on. Even the earliest settlements in the Malay world appear to have been drawn from diverse ethnic sources and established to take advantage of trading opportunities. Thus each Malay negeri had its own cultural flavor, determined in large part by the local populations it had absorbed, not to mention the slaves and merchants who had been incorporated. Malayness was, in these terms, something of an achieved status, a performance (sometimes under compulsion!): less an ethnic identity than the minimal cultural and religious conditions for membership in the trading state and its hierarchy. If anything, Malay identity was even more fluid than Tai identity, but at the core of each was becoming the subject of a state that had every incentive to absorb as many subjects as possible.

62. See Michael Aung-Thwin, "Irrigation in the Heartland of Burma: Foundations of the Precolonial Burmese State," Center for Southeast Asian Studies, Northern Illinois University, occasional paper 15 (1990), and Reid, *Southeast Asia in the Age of Commerce*, 1: 20, 22.

63. Lieberman, *Strange Parallels*, 1: 90.

64. Ibid. Here, as well, I wonder whether Lieberman isn't retrospectively assigning identities that, owing to bi- and trilingualism and physical mobility, may have been far more indeterminate than this list implies. He suggests as much elsewhere when he discusses Burmese and Mon identities in the eighteenth century, "Ethnic Politics in Eighteenth-Century Burma," *Modern Asian Studies* 12 (1978): 455–82.

65. Lieberman, *Strange Parallels*, 1: 114.

66. See, for example, Thant Myint-U, "Crisis of the Burmese State," 35.

67. Reverend Father Sangermano, *A Description of the Burmese Empire*, trans. William Tandy (Rome: John Murray, 1883).

68. Lieberman, "Ethnic Politics in Eighteenth-Century Burma."

69. The case can be, and has been, made for the historical origins of cultural distinctions that are, today, represented as both essential and of great antiquity. Thus Ernest Gellner asserts that many of the Arabic-speaking regions of North Africa also contain populations composed "in large part of Arabized Berbers." *Saints of the Atlas* (London: Weidenfeld and Nicol-

son, 1969), 13. Nicholas Tapp, with respect to southwest China, claims that the "Sinicization process . . . was not so much the result of an invasion of southwest China by Han Chinese from the north as it was the result of indigenous peoples, especially in lowland areas, becoming Chinese." Tapp writes, "Thus many of the 'Chinese' in this area were not descendants, in a biological sense, of groups of northern Han Chinese; rather, they had adopted the Chinese role when it became advantageous to do so." *Sovereignty and Rebellion*, 172.

70. Richard A. O'Connor, "Agricultural Change and Ethnic Succession," passim.

71. Reid, Introduction to *Slavery, Bondage, and Dependency*, 27.

72. Thomas Gibson, "Raiding, Trading, and Tribal Autonomy in Insular Southeast Asia," in *An Anthropology of War*, ed. Jonathan Hess (New York: Cambridge University Press, 1990), 125–45.

73. This discussion comes from Katherine Bowie's fine article "Slavery in Nineteenth-Century Northern Thailand: Archival Anecdotes and Village Voices," in Durrenberger, *State Power and Culture*, 100–138.

74. Ibid., 110.

75. Between 1500 and 1800 there was a steady flow of African slaves, many of them skilled artisans and seamen, moving eastward across the Indian Ocean. This little-known aspect of the non-Atlantic slave trade has only recently been examined.

76. Bowie, "Slavery in Nineteenth-Century Northern Thailand," quoting Archibald Ross Colquhoun, *Amongst the Shans* (London: Field and Tuer, 1885), 257–58.

77. Insular Southeast Asia was an analogous case with two variations. First, maritime slaving expeditions swept the small islands and the coastal strands clean of captives, forcing others to retreat inland, often upstream and into the hills. Watchtowers were commonly erected on the beaches to warn the strand residents of pirate-slavers. Second, Muslims were forbidden to enslave other Muslims, though this stricture was often breached. To my knowledge, the role of this prohibition in encouraging conversion to Islam has not been examined; it must have been a powerful incentive. Early-seventeenth-century Mataram followed the mainland script; it destroyed rebellious tributaries (for example, Pajang, Surabaya) and moved their populations to Mataram. It raided the hills. "As a non-Islamic population, the Tengger highlands were fair game for enslavement. . . . Between 1617 and 1650 Mataram forces made repeated forays into the mountain territories . . . to seize slaves." Hefner, *Political Economy*, 37.

78. *Gazetteer of Upper Burma and the Shan States*, compiled from official papers by J. George Scott, assisted by J. P. Hardiman, vol. 1, part 1 (Rangoon: Government Printing Office, 1893), 432.

79. Gibson, "Raiding, Trading, and Tribal Autonomy," works this out nicely for insular Southeast Asia, describing the Buid (Philippines) as an example of a society preyed upon and the Iban as organized slave raiders. For the best treatment of maritime slaving, see James Francis Warren, *The Sulu Zone, 1768–1898: The Dynamics of External Trade, Slavery, and Ethnicity in the Transformation of a Southeast Asian Maritime State* (Singapore: Singapore University Press, 1981).

80. Charles Crosthwaite, *The Pacification of Burma* (London: Edward Arnold, 1912), 318.

81. Condominas, *From Lawa to Mon*, 53.

82. Salemink, *Ethnography of Vietnam's Central Highlanders*, 28; Grant Evans, "Tai-ization: Ethnic Change in Northern Indochina," in *Civility and Savagery: Social Identity in Tai States*, ed. Andrew Turton (Richmond, England: Curzon, 2000), 263–89, quotation from 4. See also Karl Gustav Izikowitz, *Lamet: Hill Peasants in French Indochina* (Gothenburg: Ethnografiska Museet, 1951), 29.

83. Peter Kunstadter, "Ethnic Group, Category, and Identity: Karen in North Thailand," in *Ethnic Adaptation and Identity: The Karen and the Thai Frontier with Burma*, ed. Charles F. Keyes (Philadelphia: ISHI, 1979), 154.

84. Izikowitz, *Lamet*, 24.

85. Leo Alting von Geusau, "Akha Internal History: Marginalization and the Ethnic Alliance System," chapter 6 in Turton, *Civility and Savagery*, 122–58. In insular Southeast Asia, most if not all of those groups called "hill tribes" today bear a cultural memory in which the fear of abduction and slavery is powerful. What we know about the Penan/Punan and the Moken (the boat people, or "sea gypsies" of Burma's west coast) suggests that avoiding capture is at the center of their pattern of livelihood. The most documented case is that of the so-called *Orang Asli* (Semai, Semang, Jakun, Batek, Senoi, Temuan), who were actively hunted until the 1920s. They had reason to flee again during World War II and the subsequent Emergency, when they risked capture by those who wished to turn them into auxiliary soldiers, trackers, and porters or, just as they feared, to round them up forcibly and settle them in guarded camps. Many of these groups had earlier devised forms of silent barter and were careful, when trading with lowlanders, to conceal the route back to their location in the forest, lest they be followed by slave-raiders.

86. "Glass Palace Chronicle: Excerpts Translated on Burmese Invasions of Siam," compiled and annotated by Nai Thein, *Journal of the Siam Society* 8 (1911): 1–119, esp. 15.

87. It is hard to know exactly what to make of the numbers reported, for example, in the Glass Palace Chronicle. Its account of the late-sixteenth-century invasion of Siam claims that more than half a million troops set out from Hanthawaddy. This claim seems, from what we know about premodern warfare, preposterous on its face. It is perhaps a case of the "cosmological bluster" we shall examine below. Elsewhere an invasion of Chiang Mai, not much later, reports an army of 630,000, with 120,000 coming from the king of Ava and his Shan tributaries, 120,000 from Hanthawaddy, 120,000 from Prome, 150,000 from Anawrata's column, plus another 120,000 (origin unspecified). The coincidence in numbers is surely exaggerated and reflects, I suspect, some combination of diplomacy, conventions of chronicle writing, and astrologically auspicious numbers. *Journal of the Siam Society* 5 (1908): 1–82, esp. 20, 32.

88. Ronald Duane Renard, "Kariang: History of Karen-Tai Relations from the Beginnings to 1923," Ph.D. diss., University of Hawai'i, 1979, 143–44.

89. See Trager and Koenig, *Burmese Sit-tàns*, and Victor B. Lieberman, *Burmese Administrative Cycles: Anarchy and Conquest, 1580–1760* (Princeton: Princeton University Press, 1984).

90. James Z. Lee, *The Political Economy of a Frontier Region: Southwest China, 1250–1800* (Cambridge: Harvard University Press, 2000).

91. William J. Koenig, *The Burmese Polity, 1752–1819: Politics, Administration, and Social Organization in the Early Kon-baung Period*, Center for South and Southeast Asian Studies, University of Michigan Papers on South and Southeast Asian Studies, no. 34 (Ann Arbor, 1990), 160.

92. For the richest documentation, see Lieberman, *Burmese Administrative Cycles*, esp. 152–77.

93. Koenig, *Burmese Polity*, 224.

94. Quoted in A. Thomas Kirsch, "Cosmology and Ecology as Factors in Interpreting Early Thai Social Organization," *Journal of Southeast Asian Studies* 15 (1984): 253–65.

95. R. R. Langham-Carter, "The Burmese Army," *Journal of the Burma Research Society* 27 (1937): 254–76.

96. King Taksin (1768–82) introduced the tattooing of subjects of the crown to prevent them from being reappropriated by princes and nobles as "private property." On the subject of technologies of identification in general in the Thai context, see the fine article by Pingkaew Laungaramsri, "Contested Citizenship: Cards, Colours, and the Culture of Identification," manuscript, 2008.

97. Koenig, *Burmese Polity*, especially chapter 5, "The Officials."

98. Lieberman, *Strange Parallels*, 1: 61; Wolters, *History, Culture, and Region*, 141.

99. Quoted in Malseed, "'We Have Hands the Same as Them,'" 14.

100. Ibid., 14.

101. The argument is most carefully and convincingly elaborated in Lieberman's *Burmese Administrative Cycles*. See also Koenig, *Burmese Polity*, and Rabibhadana, "Organization of Society."

102. Lieberman, *Strange Parallels*, 1: 156.

103. Thant Myint-U, "Crisis of the Burmese State," 5.

104. Andaya, "Political Development," 447.

105. At an earlier stage, when its population was both smaller and had easy access to a land frontier, China faced similar dilemmas of statecraft. See the discussion of population control in the Han Dynasty in Patricia Buckley Ebery, *The Cambridge Illustrated History of China* (Cambridge: Cambridge University Press, 1996), 73–75.

106. For more detail see James Scott, *The Moral Economy of the Peasant: Subsistence and Rebellion in Southeast Asia* (New Haven: Yale University Press, 1976), especially chapter 4.

107. There is also no easy, rational accounting for General Than Shwe's brusque decision in 2006 to move Burma's capital from Yangon to remote Nay Pyi Daw.

CHAPTER 4. Civilization and the Unruly

Epigraphs from Charles Richard, "Etude sur l'insurrection du Dahra (1845–46)," in *Recognizing Islam: Religion and Society in the Modern Arab World*, ed. Michael Gilsenen (New York: Pantheon, 1982), 142, cited in Timothy Mitchell, *Colonizing Egypt* (Berkeley: University of California Press, 1988), 95; Mann to superintendent of Indian Affairs, September 28, 1865, rpt. in Dale Morgan, "Washakie and the Shoshone: A Selection of Documents from the Records of the Utah Superintendency of Indian Affairs," *Annals of Wyoming* 29 (1957): 215; Karl Jacoby, *Crimes against Nature: Squatters, Poachers, Thieves, and the Hidden History of American Conservation* (Berkeley: University of California Press, 2001), 87.

1. These claims were above all cosmological; they constituted the idiom in which monarchical claims were asserted. Thus the comical spectacle of two petty, would-be universal monarchs ruling adjacent kingdoms that held sway over a few villages beyond what each understood to be his palace walls.

In Burma and Thailand the influence of Brahminical arts, especially astrology, is still widespread both among popular classes and among elites, including Burma's military rulers. See, for example, A. Thomas Kirsch, "Complexity in the Thai Religious System: An Interpretation," *Journal of Asian Studies* 36 (1972): 241–66. As Kirsch claims, popular Brahminism and *nat/phi* worship have come to represent the "this-worldly," secular side of an otherwise resolutely salvational Theravada Buddhism. See also Ni Ni Hlaing, "History of the Myanmar Ponna," M.A. thesis, University of Mandalay, 1999.

2. F. K. Lehman (Chit Hlaing) points out that the Thai and Lao states were "galactic" in the sense that the paramount king had, in principle, lesser kings beneath him, on the model of Indra having thirty-two devatas (lesser deities), while Burma was a more unified imperial state. Personal communication, January 2008.

3. The major exception to this pattern is the Han-Chinese state, which did not have a religious criterion for membership unless one counts what passes as Confucianism as a state religion.

4. Patricia M. Pelley, *Post-Colonial Vietnam: New Histories of the National Past* (Durham: Duke University Press, 2002), 89. Durong goes on to explain that the Miao/Hmong, living at the highest altitudes, were the most uncivilized.

5. Leo Alting von Geusau, "Akha Internal History: Marginalization and the Ethnic Alli-

ance System," chapter 6 in *Civility and Savagery: Social Identity in Tai States,* ed. Andrew Turton (Richmond, England: Routledge-Curzon, 2000), 122–58, quotation from 141–42.

6. In Great Britain, for example, students are said to "go up" to Oxford or Cambridge even if they are coming from the Welsh or Scottish hills.

7. Originally, of course, the term refers to Muhammad's flight to Medina from Mecca. It came to mean a migration and the adoption of a new way of life and hence, in the Berber context, settling permanently.

8. Eric A. Havelock, *The Muse Learns to Write: Reflections on Orality and Literacy from Antiquity to the Present* (New Haven: Yale University Press, 1986), 105.

9. One is reminded of Robert Frost's description of home, in "The Death of the Hired Man," as "the place where, when you have to go there, they have to take you in."

10. Andrew Hardy, *Red Hills: Migrants and the State in the Highlands of Vietnam* (Honolulu: University of Hawai'i Press, 2003), 25.

11. In the Kon-baung dynasty such vagrancy was associated with the leakage of people away from the crown's service units (*ahmudan*) into private service. It had, originally, for this reason a strong fiscal and administrative rationale behind it. Lehman (Chit Hlaing), personal communication January 2008.

12. Pascal Khoo Thwe, *From the Land of the Green Ghosts* (London: HarperCollins, 2002), 184–85.

13. Quoted in Charles Patterson Giersch, "Qing China's Reluctant Subjects: Indigenous Communities and Empire along the Yunnan Frontier," Ph.D. thesis, Yale University, 1998, 75.

14. It is perhaps due to the fact that the padi core was surrounded by foragers and swiddeners that Burmese kings referred to their territories as being surrounded by a "ring of fire." Barbara Andaya, *The Flaming Womb: Repositioning Women in Early Modern Southeast Asia* (Honolulu: University of Hawai'i Press, 2006), 25.

15. Quoted in Anthony R. Walker, *Merit and the Millennium: Routine and Crisis in the Ritual Lives of the Lahu People* (Delhi: Hindustan Publishing, 2003), 69–71, 88, et seq. See also Richard von Glahn, *The Country of Streams and Grottoes: Expansion, Settlement, and the Civilizing of the Sichuan Frontier in Song Times* (Cambridge: Harvard University Press, 1987).

16. The Burmese equivalent for "raw" (Chinese *shang*) is *lu seín* (လူ စိမ်း) and for "cooked" (Chinese *shu*) is *lu c'eq* (လူ ချက်). The former is translatable as greenhorn or stranger and the latter as cooked or mature.

17. Gonzalo Aguirre Beltrán makes the same observation about New World populations fleeing Spanish colonization for the remote, hilly regions. *Regions of Refuge,* Society of Applied Anthropology Monograph Series, 12 (Washington, D.C., 1979), 87.

18. Neither reverence for one's (paternal) ancestors, an essentially private lineage ritual, nor the more public, Confucian code of conduct operates in anything like the same manner.

19. Giersch, "Q'ing China's Reluctant Subjects," 125–30.

20. Susan D. Blum, *Portraits of "Primitives": Ordering Human Kinds in the Chinese Nation* (Oxford: Rowman and Littlefield, 2001). Blum's surveys among Han in Kunming shows that nomadism, living in the hills, not growing wet rice, going barefoot, and geographical remoteness are associated both with minority status and with a lack of civilization or development, which, in turn, is read as emulating the Han. There are "folkloric" minorities such as the Dai who are seen as "on their way" to becoming Han, as opposed to the Wa, who are seen as undesirable and the rawest of the raw. The most difficult minorities to classify were the Hui (Muslims) and the Zang (Tibetans), who, rather like the Jews in early modern Europe, are manifestly literate and civilized but have rejected assimilation.

21. Richard A. O'Connor, "Agricultural Change and Ethnic Succession in Southeast

Asian States: A Case for Regional Anthropology," *Journal of Asian Studies* 54 (1995): 968–96, quotation from 986.

22. As we have seen, the padi state, as a manpower state, could not afford to be choosy about whom it incorporated as subjects. Hilly subjects, it was assumed, would gradually assimilate into Burman lowland ways. At the level of the court, however, the crown readily welcomed Hindus, Portuguese, Armenians, and Chinese as civilized foreigners and made no special effort to convert them.

23. The literature on this subject is vast and sophisticated. For a schematic description of the pattern, see Bennet Bronson, "Exchange at the Upstream and Downstream Ends: Notes toward a Functional Model of the Coastal State in Southeast Asia," in *Economic Exchange and Social Interaction in Southeast Asia: Perspectives from Prehistory, History, and Ethnography,* ed. Karl Hutterer (Ann Arbor: Center for Southeast Asian Studies, University of Michigan, 1977). Here we concentrate on upstream-downstream because the pattern is more analogous to inland-mainland systems of exchange. Nevertheless, it is worth noting that the coastal (*pasir*) state was often just as much a collection point for products foraged by seafaring people (the famous *orang laut* or sea gypsies) as for products from the hills.

24. Ronald Duane Renard, "The Role of the Karens in Thai Society during the Early Bangkok Period, 1782–1873," *Contributions to Asian Studies* 15 (1980): 15–28.

25. Oscar Salemink, *The Ethnography of Vietnam's Central Highlanders: A Historical Contextualization, 1850–1990* (London: Routledge-Curzon, 2003), 259–60.

26. F. K. Lehman [Chit Hlaing], "Burma: Kayah Society as a Function of the Shan-Burma-Karen Context," in *Contemporary Change in Traditional Society,* 3 vols., ed. Julian Haynes Steward (Urbana: University of Illinois Press, 1967), 1: 1–104, esp. 22–24.

27. J. G. Scott provides a more complete list at the turn of the century for imports to Kengtung, an eastern Shan state polity, from various adjacent states. From Burma: cheap cloth from Manchester and India, rugs, velvet, satin, aniline dyes, mirrors, matches, kerosene, condensed milk, colored paper, candles, soap, lead pencils, enameled ware. From western Shan states: all kinds of iron implements, lacquer boxes, fish paste, and leaves for cheroot wrappers. From China: salt, straw hats, copper and iron pots, silk, satin, opium requisites, pigments, tea, lead, percussion caps. *Gazetteer of Upper Burma and the Shan States,* compiled from official papers by J. George Scott, assisted by J. P. Hardiman, vol. 1, part 2 (Rangoon: Government Printing Office, 1893), 424.

28. Most of the work on Malay history over the past two decades converges around this interpretation. See, among others, Bernard Sellato, *Nomads of the Borneo Rainforest: The Economics, Politics, and Ideology of Settling Down,* trans. Stephanie Morgan (Honolulu: University of Hawai'i Press, 1994); Jane Drakard, *A Malay Frontier: Unity and Duality in a Sumatran Kingdom,* Studies on Southeast Asia (Ithaca: Cornell Southeast Asia Program, 1990); J. Peter Brosius, "Prior Transcripts: Resistance and Acquiescence to Logging in Sarawak," *Comparative Studies in Society and History* 39 (1997): 468–510; Carl L. Hoffman, "Punan Foragers in the Trading Networks of Southeast Asia," in *Past and Present in Hunter Gatherer Studies,* ed. Carmel Shrire (Orlando: Academic Press, 1984), 123–49. Hoffman claims, persuasively I think, that *Punan* is a portmanteau term covering many groups that are more closely tied to their respective downriver trading partners than to one another. He further claims that their subsistence activities are in the service of their essentially commercial collecting role rather than the other way around. They are, in other words, commercial speculators—hoping for the lucrative find.

29. Ronald Duane Renard, "Kariang: History of Karen-Tai Relations from the Beginnings to 1923," Ph.D. diss., University of Hawai'i, 1979, 22.

30. The tradition, throughout much of the region, of "founders' cults" recognizes the

ritual (not political) primacy of the first settlers/clearers of the land, on whose relationship with the spirits of the place its auspiciousness and fertility depend. See F. K. Lehman [Chit Hlaing]'s "The Relevance of the Founders' Cults for Understanding the Political Systems of the Peoples of Northern Southeast Asia and its Chinese Borderlands," in *Founders' Cults in Southeast Asia: Ancestors, Polity, and Identity*, ed. Nicola Tannenbaum and Cornelia Ann Kammerer, monograph no. 52 (New Haven: Council on Southeast Asian Studies, 2003), 15–39.

31. See, for example, Geoffrey Benjamin and Cynthia Chou, eds., *Tribal Communities in the Malay World: Historical, Cultural, and Social Perspectives* (Singapore: Institute of Southeast Asian Studies, 2002), 50; Sellato, *Nomads of the Borneo Rainforest*, 29, 39; William Henry Scott, *The Discovery of the Igorots: Spanish Contacts with the Pagans of Northern Luzon*, rev. ed. (Quezon City: New Day, 1974), 204.

32. A banal but telling contemporary example: the automobile bumper sticker reading "Proud to be an American" can be understood only as a reply to the unstated, but implicit, assertion: "Ashamed to be an American," without which it would have no reason for being.

33. Owen Lattimore, "The Frontier in History," in *Studies in Frontier History: Collected Papers, 1928–1958*, 469–91, quotations from 472–75. What Lattimore appears to miss in his account is the astonishing degree to which nonstate populations migrated over time from China south of the Yellow River to the west and southwest. The most striking, but hardly the only case, appears to be the Miao. See Herold J. Wiens, *China's March toward the Tropics: A Discussion of the Southward Penetration of China's Culture, Peoples, and Political Control in Relation to the Non-Han-Chinese Peoples of South China in the Perspective of Historical and Cultural Geography* (Hamden, Conn.: Shoe String, 1954).

34. Lattimore, as noted, makes this point about the northern Great Wall(s). For the Miao walls, see the astute article by Magnus Fiskesjö, "On the 'Raw' and the 'Cooked' Barbarians of Imperial China," *Inner Asia* 1 (1999): 139–68. Once again, it is crucial to recall that Han culture was itself a confection, an alloy of many cultural elements. Just as it was taken for granted that the Han changed nature while the barbarians "lived in it," Mencius said that he had heard of Chinese changing barbarians but never of barbarians changing the Chinese. It is this last contention that Fiskesjö convincingly refutes (140).

35. Hjorleifur Jonsson, "Shifting Social Landscape: Mien (Yao) Upland Communities and Histories in State-Client Settings," Ph.D. diss., Cornell University, 1996, 231.

36. Michael Dove, "On the Agro-Ecological Mythology of the Javanese and the Political Economy of Indonesia," *Indonesia* 39 (1985): 11–36, quotation from 35.

37. Benjamin and Chou, *Tribal Communities in the Malay World*, 44.

38. Paul Wheatley, *The Golden Khersonese: Studies in the Historical Geography of the Malay Peninsula before A.D. 1500* (Kuala Lumpur: University of Malaya Press, 1961), 186.

39. Georges Coedès, *The Indianized States of Southeast Asia*, trans. Susan Brown Cowing (Honolulu: East-West Center, 1968), 33. What did spread, however, were Brahminical rituals and astrology in popular divination and the epic stories of the Ramayana and the Mahabharata. F. K. Lehman (Chit Hlaing) believes, to the contrary, that Buddhist cosmology may have acquired, through Indian traders, an early popular authority such that anyone aspiring to kingship found it advantageous to adopt the rituals of Buddhist/Hindu kingship. Personal communication, January 2008. Others, such as Wolters and Wheatley, believe that the cosmology appealed initially to ambitious leaders as a way of enhancing their claims to authority—in a kind of theatrical self-hypnosis—that only later became rooted in popular culture.

40. Oliver Wolters, *History, Culture, and Region in Southeast Asian Perspective* (Singapore: Institute for Southeast Asian Studies, 1982), 64.

41. M. C. Ricklefs, *Jogjakarta under Sultan Mangkubumi, 1749–1792* (London: Oxford University Press, 1974).

42. Sheldon Pollack, "India in the Vernacular Millennium: Literature, Culture, Polity," *Daedalus* 197 (1998): 41–75.

43. Wolters, *History, Culture, and Region,* rev. ed. (Ithaca: Cornell University Press, in cooperation with the Institute of Southeast Asian Studies, Singapore, 1999), 161.

44. Ibid., quoting Ian Mabbett in Ian Mabbett and David Chandler, *The Khmers* (Oxford: Blackwell, 1995), 26.

45. Wolters, *History, Culture, and Region* (1999), 12n45, quoting David Chandler, *A History of Cambodia* (Boulder: Westview, 1992), 103.

46. For the phenomenon on the coastal plains, see Wheatley, *Golden Kheronese,* 294.

47. Jonsson, "Shifting Social Landscape," 133.

48. G. E. Mitton [Lady Scott], *Scott of the Shan Hills: Orders and Impressions* (London: John Murray, 1936), 246. Bamboo, given its watertight properties and strength, was a common storage container for letters of appointment kept by lowland officials as well.

49. Edmund Leach, *The Political Systems of Highland Burma: A Study of Kachin Social Structure* (Cambridge: Harvard University Press, 1954), 281.

50. Maurice Collis, *Lords of the Sunset* (London: Faber and Faber, 1938), 83. See also comparable descriptions of the Shan palace at Mong Mit (203) and Kengtung (277).

51. Leach, *Political Systems of Highland Burma,* 286.

52. Lehman [Chit Hliang], "Burma," 1: 15–18.

53. Leach, *Political Systems of Highland Burma,* 112–14.

54. Von Geusau, "Akha Internal History," 151.

55. Patricia Buckley Ebrey, *The Cambridge Illustrated History of China* (Cambridge: Cambridge University Press, 1999), 67.

56. Quotation from Pelley, *Post-Colonial Vietnam,* 92. See also Keith Taylor, "On Being Muonged," *Asian Ethnicity* 1 (2001): 25–34. Taylor notes that early French ethnographers first saw the Muong as a kind of proto-Kinh. See also Salemink, *Ethnography of Vietnam's Central Highlanders,* 285.

57. Pelley, *Post-Colonial Vietnam,* 92. Lest this claim seem exotic, it is worth recalling that at the turn of the twentieth century it was common for American scholars to think of the hill population of Appalachia as "our contemporary ancestors." Dwight Billings and Kathleen Blee, *The Road to Poverty: The Making of Wealth and Hardship in Appalachia* (Cambridge: Cambridge University Press, 2000), 8.

58. Quoted in Ebrey, *Cambridge Illustrated History,* 57.

59. Quoted in "Autonomy, Coalition, and Coerced Coordination: Themes in Highland-Lowland Relations up through the Vietnamese American War," mimeo; emphasis added.

60. Quoted in Victor B. Lieberman, *Strange Parallels: Southeast Asia in Global Context, c. 800–1830,* vol. 1, *Integration on the Mainland* (Cambridge: Cambridge University Press, 2003), 431, in turn quoting Chandler, *History of Cambodia,* 126, 130. The featherbed metaphor perhaps meets its hill riposte in the saying of the Kachin: "Stone cannot be used as a pillow; the Han cannot become friends." Quoted in Zhushent Wang, *The Jingpo Kachin of the Yunnan Plateau,* Program for Southeast Asian Studies, Monograph Series (Tempe: Arizona State University Press, 1997), 241.

61. See David Faure, "The Yao Wars in the Mid-Ming and Their Impact on Yao Ethnicity," in *Empire at the Margins: Culture and Frontier in Early Modern China,* ed. Pamela Kyle Crossley, Helen Siu, and Donald Sutton (Charlottesville: University of Virginia Press, 2006), 171–89, and Ebrey, *Cambridge Illustrated History,* 195–97.

62. Alexander Woodside, "Territorial Order and Collective-Identity Tensions in Confucian Asia: China, Vietnam, Korea," *Daedalus* 127 (1998): 206–7. Compare this with John Stuart Mill on why the Basque or the Breton should wish to join civilized France as a citizen,

rather "than to sulk on his own rocks, a half savage relic of past times, revolving in his own little mental orbit, without participation or interest in the general movement of the world." *Utilitarianism, Liberty, and Representative Government* (London: Everyman, 1910), 363–64, quoted in E. J. Hobsbawm, *Nations and Nationalism since 1780,* 2nd ed. (Cambridge: Cambridge University Press, 1990), 34.

I want to express my deep thanks to Shanshan Du for her careful explanation of the history and workings of the *tusi* system in southwestern China; personal communication, July 2008.

63. Quoted in Wiens, *China's March toward the Tropics,* 219.

64. Quoted ibid., 251–52.

65. It is this hypocrisy to which George Orwell's jaded protagonist in *Burmese Days* (New York: Harcourt-Brace, 1962), Flory, most objects: "The pukka sahib pose . . . the slimy white man's burden humbug. . . . It's so simple. The official holds the Burman down while the businessman goes through his pockets" (39–40).

66. Nicholas Tapp, *Sovereignty and Rebellion: The White Hmong of Northern Thailand* (Singapore: Oxford University Press, 1990), 38.

67. The term *social fossils* is from Magnus Fiskesjö, "Rescuing the Empire: Chinese Nation-Building in the 20th Century," *European Journal of East Asian Studies* 5 (2006): 15–44. As Fiskesjö observes, the absorption of such societies is, above all, hastened by the demographic envelopment of millions of Han settlers in the highlands.

68. One could discern, I believe, for the numerous language groups scattered across Zomia, something of a rough cultural watershed, north and east of which polities were drawn into a Han-Chinese civilizational orbit and south and west of which they were drawn into a Theravada-Sanskritic orbit. Presumably, as dynasties and states waxed and waned, this line shifted, but when and where the two orbits overlapped, the cultural and political room for maneuver left to hill peoples was larger.

69. Leach, *Political Systems of Highland Burma,* 39, and O'Connor, "Agricultural Change and Ethnic Succession," 974–75.

70. Lieberman, *Strange Parallels,* 1: 114.

71. Fiskesjö, "On the 'Raw' and the 'Cooked' Barbarians," 143, 145, 148. I am very much in debt to Fiskesjö's lucid and subtle analysis of these terms on Han-Chinese statecraft.

72. Ebrey, *Cambridge Illustrated History,* 56.

73. Anne Csete, "Ethnicity, Conflict, and the State in the Early to Mid-Qing: The Hainan Highlands, 1644–1800," in Crossley, Siu, and Sutton, *Empire at the Margins,* 229–52, quotation from 235.

74. A fifteenth-century document, for example, referring to the Yi on the Yunnan-Burmese borderlands, claims that these barbarians would "rejoice the day prefectures and counties are enumerated in their areas and they are *finally* governed by [Ming] officials." Quoted in John E. Herman, "The Cant of Conquest: Tusi Offices and China's Political Incorporation of the Southwest Frontier," in Crossley, Siu, and Sutton, *Empire at the Margins,* 135–68, quotation from 145; emphasis added.

75. Fiskesjö, "On the 'Raw' and the 'Cooked' Barbarians," 153.

76. Faure, "Yao Wars in the Mid-Ming." See also David Faure, "The Lineage as a Cultural Invention: The Case of the Pearl River Delta," *Modern China* 15 (1989): 4–36. The Yao claim a special dispensation from the Chinese emperor, recorded on a decree they preserve, that exempts them from corvée labor and taxes and recognizes their right to move at will within their territory.

77. Norma Diamond, "Defining the Miao: Ming, Qing, and Contemporary Views," in *Cultural Encounters on China's Ethnic Frontiers,* ed. Steven Harrell (Seattle: University of Washington Press, 1995), 92–119.

78. Gordon H. Luce, trans., *The Man Shu (Book of the Southern Barbarians)*, 37.

79. Wing-hoi Chan, "Ethnic Labels in a Mountainous Region: The Case of the *She* Bandits," in Crossley, Siu, and Sutton, *Empire at the Margins*, 255–84. Chan also makes the case that the ethnogenesis of the famously peripatetic Hakka may be explained similarly. *She* also means unirrigated hill rice fields, and thus the "ethnic" name also describes a mode of subsistence and a "hilly" habitat.

80. Benjamin and Chou, *Tribal Communities in the Malay World*, 36.

81. Anna Lowenhaupt Tsing, *In the Realm of the Diamond Queen: Marginality in an Out-of-the-Way Place* (Princeton: Princeton University Press, 1993), 28. The hill swiddens of the Meratus are also described as an agriculture that is not-yet-ordered (*pertanian yang tidak terator*).

82. Felix M. Keesing, *The Ethno-history of Northern Luzon* (Stanford: Stanford University Press, 1962), 224–25.

83. Ernest Gellner, *Saints of the Atlas* (London: Weidenfeld and Nicolson, 1969), chapter 1.

84. Lois Beck, "Tribes and the State in 19th- and 20th-Century Iran," in *Tribes and State Formation in the Middle East*, ed. Philip Khoury and Joseph Kostiner (Berkeley: University of California Press, 1990), 185–222.

85. Bennet Bronson, "The Role of Barbarians in the Fall of States," in *The Collapse of Ancient States and Civilizations*, ed. Norman Yoffee and George L. Cowgill (Tucson: University of Arizona Press, 1991), 203–10, quotation from 200. Much of this paragraph is an elaboration of Bronson's argument.

86. This and the following two paragraphs are drawn from Thomas S. Burns's excellent *Rome and the Barbarians, 100 BC–AD 400* (Baltimore: Johns Hopkins University Press, 2003).

87. Stephen T. Driscoll, "Power and Authority in Early Historic Scotland: Pictish Symbol Stones and other Documents," in *State and Society: The Emergence and Development of Social Hierarchy and Political Centralization*, ed. J. Gledhill, B. Bender, and M. T. Larsen (London: Routledge, 1988), 215.

88. Burns, *Rome and the Barbarians*, 182. A far darker vision of Roman expansion as it might have looked to the barbarians is evident in the words Tacitus puts in the mouth of the defeated British chief Calgacus: "To robbery, slaughter, and plunder they give the lying name of empire; they make a solitude and call it peace." Cited ibid., 169.

89. Quoted in Charles Patterson Giersch, "Q'ing China's Reluctant Subjects: Indigenous Communities and Empire along the Yunnan Frontier," Ph.D. diss., Yale University, 1998, 97.

90. Crossley, Siu, and Sutton, Introduction to *Empire at the Margins*, 6.

91. Wing-hoi Chan, "Ethnic Labels in a Mountainous Region," 278.

92. Donald S. Sutton, "Ethnicity and the Miao Frontier in the Eighteenth Century," in Crossley, Siu, and Sutton, *Empire at the Margins*, 469–508, quotation from 493.

93. The same tight association between direct rule by Han authorities and civilized status held in the Pearl River Delta. Household registration itself (entering the map) "transformed identities from alien (yi) to commoner (mín). . . . In times of dynastic crisis, it was not uncommon to find households abandoning their registered status to avoid taxes and conscription. They became bandits, pirates, and aliens in the official records." Helen F. Siu and Liu Zhiwei, "Lineage, Marketing, Pirate, and Dan," in Crossley, Siu, and Sutton, *Empire at the Margins*, 285–310, quotation from 293.

94. Quoted in Woodside, "Territorial Order and Collective Identity Tensions," 213. For evidence that Vietnamese commonly moved into upland society and assimilated to its culture, see Taylor, "On Being Muonged," 28.

CHAPTER 5. Keeping the State at a Distance

First epigraph is quoted in Mark R. Woodward and Susan D. Russell, "Transformations in Ritual and Economy in Upland Southeast Asia," in *Ritual, Power, and Economy: Upland-Lowland Contrasts in Mainland Southeast Asia,* ed. Susan D. Russell, Monograph Series on Southeast Asia, Center for Southeast Asian Studies, Northern Illinois University, occasional paper no. 14 (1989), 1–26, quotation from 9. Compare the following passage from the *Tao Te Ching:*

> The great Way is very smooth
> but people love bypaths
>
> The court is very well kept
> the fields are very weedy
> the granaries very empty.

Michael LaFargue, *The Tao of the Tao Te Ching* (Albany: SUNY Press, 1992), 110.

Second epigraph is from Owen Lattimore, "The Frontier in History," *Studies in Frontier History: Collected Papers, 1928–58* (London: Oxford University Press, 1962), 469–91, quotation from 469–70. Lattimore continues: "The maximum of difference [in two distinct societies separated by a frontier] is to be sought near the center of gravity of each . . . and not at the frontier where they meet. A frontier population is marginal. . . . They inevitably set up their own nexus of social contact and joint interest. Men of both border populations . . . become a 'we' group to whom others of their own nationality, and especially the authorities, are 'they.' . . . It is often possible to describe the border populations . . . as a joint community that is functionally recognizable though not institutionally defined" (470).

1. See *New York Times,* July 23, 2004, and the *Final Report of the National Commission on Terrorist Attacks upon the United States* (Washington, D.C.: Government Printing Office, 2004), 340, 368, http://www.gpoaccess.gov/911/index.html.

2. Jean Michaud, ed., *Turbulent Times and Enduring Peoples: Mountain Minorities in the Southeast Asian Massif* (Richmond Surrey: Curzon, 2000), 11. Michaud goes on to note that hill peoples have occasionally launched state-making projects of their own.

3. Guerrilla resistance in the zone of direct state expansion is seldom successful over the longer term unless the guerrillas have powerful state allies. French military backing, for example, allowed many Native American groups to resist the expansion of English colonists for a time.

4. Gonzalo Aguirre Beltrán, *Regions of Refuge,* Society of Applied Anthropology Monograph Series, no. 12 (Washington, D.C., 1979), 23, 25. When mountainous terrain held valuable resources, like the silver deposits of Potosí, they were seized.

5. Ibid., 39.

6. Stuart Schwartz and Frank Salomon, "New Peoples and New Kinds of People: Adaptation, Adjustment, and Ethnogenesis in South America Indigenous Societies (Colonial Era)," in *The Cambridge History of Native Peoples of the Americas,* ed. Stuart Schwartz and Frank Salomon (Cambridge: Cambridge University Press, 1999), 443–502, quotation from 448. See also the recent attempt to summarize our demographic understanding of the Conquest that bears directly on such migration and social structure in Charles C. Mann, *1491: New Revelations of the Americas before Columbus* (New York: Knopf, 2005). Although the demographic facts are the subject of heated debate, it seems evident that the population of the New World was far larger than previously assumed. It was anything but an empty continent and just may have been "fully occupied." It is important to note in this context that if the epidemic-driven

demographic collapse was anything like as dramatic as now seems to be the case, foraging and swiddening would have become far more advantageous as an agro-ecological strategy, promising a higher return per unit of labor than fixed-field agriculture, now that so much land was unoccupied. Jared Diamond makes an analogous claim that the Australian "aboriginal" population was originally located more densely in the most productive regions of the country (for example, the Darlington River system of the Southeast) and was driven into drier areas that the Europeans didn't want. *Guns, Germs, and Steel: The Fate of Human Societies* (New York: Norton, 1997), 310.

7. Schwartz and Salomon, "New Peoples," 452.

8. Ibid., 452. For more detailed accounts of Andean flight from Spanish forced settlement, see Ann M. Wightman, *Indigenous Migration and Social Change: The Forasteros of Cuzco, 1570–1720* (Durham: Duke University Press, 1990), and John Howland Rowe, "The Incas under Spanish Colonial Institutions," *Hispanic American Historical Review* 37 (1957): 155–99.

9. Mann, *1491*, 225.

10. Schwartz and Salomon, "New Peoples," 460.

11. Richard White, *The Middle Ground: Indians, Empires, and Republics in the Great Lakes Region, 1650–1815* (Cambridge: Cambridge University Press, 1991), 1, 14. Here too, epidemics played a key role, along with the warfare of competitive state-building in displacing people.

12. See the remarkable study by Leo Lucassen, Wim Willems, and Annemarie Cottaar, *Gypsies and Other Itinerant Groups: A Socio-historical Approach,* Centre for the History of Migrants, University of Amsterdam (London: Macmillan, 1998).

13. Ibid., 63. Such hunted groups, not surprisingly, often banded together to raid settlements in this zone as more refugees poured in. Local authorities responded by hunting and killing gypsies and other vagrants. The authors document a similar pressure on Gypsies (Bohemians) in France, where they were rounded up for the galleys.

14. There are interesting parallels between this "outlaw" corridor and what has been described as the "Wa corridor," or the heartland between the upper reaches of the Mekong and the Salween/Nu, which has the further advantage of being deeply fissured. Magnus Fiskesjö, "The Fate of Sacrifice and the Making of Wa History," Ph.D. thesis, University of Chicago, 2000, 51.

15. I rely entirely here on Robert W. Hefner's fine account in *The Political Economy of Mountain Java: An Interpretive History* (Berkeley: University of California Press, 1990). For a detailed cultural analysis, see his earlier *Hindu Javanese: Tengger Tradition and Islam* (Princeton: Princeton University Press, 1985).

16. Hefner, *Political Economy*, 9.

17. Quoted ibid., 182; *ngoko* refers to "low" Javanese, in which the elaborate, power-coded terms of address are dispensed with.

18. Unlike Zomia, Tengger dissent is not ethnically coded. Had Tengger been even more isolated, and for a longer time, Hefner notes, the difference might well have been "ethnicized." Instead, the people of the Tengger highlands think of themselves as Javanese: they dress as Javanese (though deliberately without ostentation); they speak Javanese (but avoid using its rank-laden terms of address in the village). They think of themselves as *wong gunung* (mountain) Javanese and therefore a very distinct subset of Javanese. Hefner suggests (personal communication, February 2008) that other more recently incorporated autonomous peoples in insular Southeast Asia still retain a strong sense of being a distinct, often more egalitarian, society, without this distinctiveness necessarily taking on strong ethnic characteristics. See in this connection Sven Cederroth, *The Spell of the Ancestors and the Power of Mekkah: A Sasak Community on Lombok* (Göteborg: Acta Universitatis Gothoburgensis, 1981), and

Martin Rössler, *Striving for Modesty: Fundamentals of Religion and Social Organization of the Makassarese Patuntung* (Dordrecht: Floris, 1990).

19. Felix M. Keesing, *The Ethnohistory of Northern Luzon* (Stanford: Stanford University Press, 1976), 4. This and the next paragraph rely heavily on Keesing's argument.

20. William Henry Scott, *The Discovery of the Igorots: Spanish Contacts with the Pagans of Northern Luzon*, rev. ed. (Quezon City: New Day, 1974), 75, argues along the same lines: "Such *reducciones* naturally required the relocation of scattered tribes and semi-sedentary agriculturalists into settled communities where they could . . . be reached by clergy, tribute collections, and road foremen."

21. Keesing, *Ethnohistory of Northern Luzon*, 2, 304. This view accords in its broad outlines with the historical account of Scott in *Discovery of the Igorots*, 69–70.

22. Keesing qualifies his argument by allowing that there were other reasons to head for the hills: the search for gold, the desire to collect and trade hill products, escape from lowland feuds and wars, and epidemics. He is clear, however, that the overwhelming reason for flight was the colonial labor system of the Spanish. This view in endorsed in Scott, *Discovery of the Igorots*, who would extend it beyond Northern Luzon to the Philippines as a whole; see 69–70.

23. Keesing, *Ethnohistory of Northern Luzon*, 3.

24. The culminating event for the Yao/Mien was their defeat at the battle of Great Vine Gorge in Guizhou in 1465. The victors sent eight hundred captives to Beijing to be beheaded there. It was not long after, in 1512, that the scholar-soldier Wang Yangming proposed to revive the Yuan policy of "using barbarians to rule barbarians," a policy of indirect rule that became known as the *tusi* system.

25. C. Pat Giersch, "A Motley Throng: Social Change on Southwest China's Early Modern Frontier, 1700–1880," *Journal of Asian Studies* 60 (2001): 67–94, quotation from 74.

26. Richard von Glahn argues persuasively that acephalous groups are less likely to revolt than more centralized "tribes," such as the Dai or Yi, who can mobilize large-scale resistance. This does not imply, however, that they are more likely to be absorbed, only that they are more likely to scatter and flee rather than holding their ground. In fact, the more centralized and hierarchical the social structure of a group, the closer it is to lowland norms and the easier it may be for it to assimilate en masse. *The Country of Streams and Grottoes: Expansion Settlement, and the Civilizing of the Sichuan Frontier in Song Times,* Council on East Asian Studies, Harvard University (Cambridge: Harvard University Press, 1987), 213. See also Mark Elvin, *The Retreat of the Elephants: An Environmental History of China* (New Haven: Yale University Press, 2004), 88, who notes that "emigration" is often the only means of escape from corvée and domination.

27. Wiens, *China's March toward the Tropics,* 186. I believe it is more plausible, contrary to Wiens's assumption, to believe that many contemporary hill peoples were long ago valley dwellers who became hill farmers as a consequence of adaptation. It is also worth pointing out that for much of the time the Han-Chinese were pressing to the south and southwest, they were, in turn, being pressed from the north by Mongolian armies.

28. Ibid., 69.

29. Ibid., 81–88, 90. This is in marked contrast to Wiens's usual placid, evenhanded tone throughout his survey.

30. Ibid., 317.

31. Those who elect to stay will often be absorbed into the arriving hill society in the same fashion as the Han absorbed the groups whom they enveloped.

32. C. Backus, *The Nan-chao Kingdom and Tang China's Southwestern Frontier* (Cambridge: Cambridge University Press, 1981). The "Tainess" of Nan Chao has, since the publication of Backus's book, been heavily contested. Jean Michaud, personal communication, April 2008.

33. G. E. Harvey, cited in David Wyatt, *Thailand: A Short History* (New Haven: Yale University Press, 1986), 90.

34. It also happened, occasionally, that militarily expansive padi states in the hills drove other hill peoples into the lower valleys. From the thirteenth century on, the Ahom, a Tai group, drove the people of the rival Dimasa kingdom into the valleys, where they eventually merged into the Bengali majority. The Ahom themselves later conquered the lowlands of the Brahmaputra Valley and acculturated to the Hindu-Assamese. See Philippe Ramirez's fine article "Politico-Ritual Variation on the Assamese Fringes: Do Social Systems Exist?" in *Social Dynamics in the Highlands of Southeast Asia: Reconsidering Political Systems of Highland Burma by E. R. Leach,* ed. François Robinne and Mandy Sadan, Handbook of Oriental Studies, section 3, Southeast Asia (Leiden: Brill, 2007), 91–107.

35. *Gazetteer of Upper Burma and the Shan States,* compiled from official papers by J. George Scott, assisted by J. P. Hardiman, 5 vols. (Rangoon: Government Printing Office, 1893). The epigraph of this section is from Reverend Father Sangermano, *A Description of the Burmese Empire,* trans. William Tandy (Rome: John Murray, 1883), 81, emphasis added.

36. This is amply confirmed in seventeenth-century decrees warning fighting men on the march not to "kill birds and beasts to eat," "loot and plunder," or "molest girls and married young women." *Royal Orders of Burma, A.D. 1598–1885,* part 1, *A.D. 1598–1648,* ed. Than Tun (Kyoto: Center for Southeast Asian Studies, 1983), 1: 87.

37. Robert E. Elson, "International Commerce, the State, and Society: Economic and Social Change," chapter 3 of *The Cambridge History of Southeast Asia,* ed. Nicholas Tarling, vol. 2, *The Nineteenth and Twentieth Centuries* (Cambridge: Cambridge University Press, 1992), 164.

38. One of the first historians to identify this practice as a widespread form of political protest was Michael Adas. See his pathbreaking analysis in "From Avoidance to Confrontation: Peasant Protest in Pre-colonial and Colonial Southeast Asia," *Comparative Studies in Society and History* 23 (1981): 217–47.

39. Scott, *Gazetteer of Upper Burma,* vol. 1, part 2, 241.

40. J. G. Scott [Shway Yoe], *The Burman: His Life and Notions* (1882; New York: Norton, 1963), 243.

41. Scott, *Gazetteer of Upper Burma,* vol. 1, part 1, 483.

42. The most comparable historical setting of which I have seen a description is that of a zone of refuge in the Great Lakes region in nineteenth-century North America so perceptively and painstakingly described by Richard White in *The Middle Ground.*

43. Paul Wheatley, *The Golden Kheronese: Studies in the Historical Geography of the Malay Peninsula before A.D. 1500* (Kuala Lumpur: University of Malaya Press, 1961), xxiv.

44. But not out of reach of other forms of power such as warring factions, bandits, and slave-raiders taking advantage of the vacuum to sweep up an exposed population.

45. Scott, *Gazetteer of Upper Burma,* vol. 1, part 2, 508. The epigraph of this section is from *The Glass Palace Chronicle of the Kings of Burma,* trans. Pe Maung Tin and G. H. Luce, issued by the Text Publication Fund of the Burma Research Society (Oxford: Oxford University Press, London: Humphrey Milford, 1923), 177.

46. Or, to put it another way, the condition of being and remaining taxable was a central qualifying feature of Burmese, Thai, or Chinese ethnicity. Only, I believe, in this context does the Mien/Yao treasuring of purportedly imperial scrolls from the emperor granting them perpetual immunity from the tax and corvée burdens of Han subjects and the right to move as they wish in the hills, make sense. A large part of Mien/Yao ethnicity is, precisely, non-subjecthood. See, for example, the fine study by Hjorleifur Jonsson, *Mien Relations: Mountain People and State Control in Thailand* (Ithaca: Cornell University Press, 2005). Jean Michaud speculates that the Mien/Yao may long ago have been pushed westward, out of Hunan, by the

coastal Han. *Historical Dictionary of the Peoples of the Southeast Asian Massif* (Latham, Maryland: Scarecrow Press, 2006), 264.

47. Hjorleifur Jonsson, "Shifting Social Landscape: Mien (Yao) Upland Communities and Histories in State-Client Settings," Ph.D. diss., Cornell University, 1996, 274.

48. Oscar Salemink, *The Ethnography of Vietnam's Central Highlanders: A Historical Contextualization, 1850-1990* (London: Routledge-Curzon, 2003), 298. See also his "Sedentarization and Selective Preservation among the Montagnards in the Vietnamese Central Highlands," in Michaud, *Turbulent Times and Enduring Peoples,* 138-39.

49. An example of this shift is given by Yin Shao-ting in his description of De'ang swiddeners in Yunnan. *People and Forests: Yunnan Swidden Agriculture in Human-Ecological Perspective,* trans. Magnus Fiskesjö (Kunming: Yunnan Educational Publishing, 2001), 68.

50. Charles Tilly, *Coercion, Capital, and European States, AD 990-1992* (Cambridge, Mass.: Blackwell, 1990), 14 and chapter 3. The first epigraph in this section is quoted by Hazel J. Lang, *Fear and Sanctuary: Burmese Refugees in Thailand,* Studies in Southeast Asia no. 32 (Ithaca: Cornell Southeast Asia Program Publications, 2002), 79. Compare this to the Bugis text from Sulawesi: "We are like birds sitting on a tree. When the tree falls we leave it and go in search of a large tree where we can settle." Quoted in Leonard Andaya, "Interactions with the Outside World and Adaptation in Southeast Asia Society, 1500-1800," Tarling, *Cambridge History of Southeast Asia,* 1: 417. The second epigraph is from Scott [Shway Yoe], *The Burman,* 533.

51. Anthony Reid, "Economic and Social Change, 1400-1800, in Tarling, *Cambridge History of Southeast Asia,* 1: 460-507, esp. 462.

52. Charles Keeton III, *King Thibaw and the Ecological Rape of Burma: The Political and Commercial Struggle between British India and French Indo-China in Burma, 1878-1886* (Delhi: Mahar Book Service, 1974), 3.

53. Jeremy Black, *European Warfare, 1600-1815* (New Haven: Yale University Press, 1994), 99, and Martin van Crevald, *Supplying War: Logistics from Wallenstein to Patton* (Cambridge: Cambridge University Press, 1977), cited in Charles Tilly, *Coercion, Capital, and European States,* 81. See also John A. Lynn, ed., *Feeding Mars: Logistics in Western Warfare from the Middle Ages to the Present* (Boulder: Westview, 1993).

54. Lynn, *Feeding Mars,* 21.

55. William J. Koenig, *The Burmese Polity, 1752-1819: Politics, Administration, and Social Organization in the Early Kon-baung Period,* Center for South and Southeast Asian Studies, University of Michigan Papers on South and Southeast Asian Studies, no. 34 (Ann Arbor, 1990), 34.

56. Scott, *Gazetteer of Upper Burma,* vol. 1, part 2, 231, part 1, 281.

57. Ronald Duane Renard, "Kariang: History of Karen-Tai Relations from the Beginnings to 1923," Ph.D. diss., University of Hawai'i, 1979, 78, 130 et seq.

58. Pierre du Jarric, *Histoire des choses plus memorables advenues tant ez Indes Orientales que autres païs de la descouverte des Portugois, en l'etablissement et progrez de la foy crestienne et catholique* (Bordeaux, 1608-14), 1: 620-21, cited in Reid, "Economic and Social Change," 462.

59. "Glass Palace Chronicle: Excerpts Translated on Burmese Invasions of Siam," compiled and annotated by Nai Thein, *Journal of the Siam Society* 8 (1911): 1-119, quotation from 43.

60. Scott [Shway Yoe], *The Burman,* 494. Mutiny was more dangerous and therefore less common than desertion, although it did occur. See Koenig, *Burmese Polity,* 19, for a brief account of a mutiny by Mon troops in the Burmese army in the 1772 campaign against the Thais. It is, in my view, a fine thing to see an army that has decided it has had enough and wants no further part of the war and drifts away. The Confederacy in the War between the States was undone largely by desertion. One of the most inspiring things I have ever seen was a large

papiermâché statue of a running figure, a "Monument to the Deserters of Both World Wars" (Denkmal an den Unbekannten Deserteurs der Beiden Weltkriegen) assembled by German anarchists shortly after the fall of the Berlin Wall and taken, via flatbed truck, to the cities of the former German Democratic Republic. It was chased from city to city by the local authorities until it came to rest, briefly, in Bonn.

61. Most recruits in such armies were press-ganged in the first place and would have seized any opportunity to desert. Jeremy Black reports a desertion rate of 42 percent from the Saxon infantry during 1717–28. *European Warfare*, 219.

62. This is especially true when the troops are already far from home. Thucydides' account of the disintegration of the Athenian-led forces in Sicily is instructive. "With the enemy now on equal terms with us, our slaves are beginning to desert. As for the foreigners in our service, those who were conscripted are going back to their cities as quickly as they can; those who were initially delighted with the idea of high pay and thought they were going to make some money rather than do any fighting . . . are either slipping away as deserters or making off in one way or another—*which is not difficult, considering the size of Sicily.*" *The Peloponnesian War*, trans. Rex Warner (New York: Penguin, 1972), 485, emphasis added.

63. Khin Mar Swe, "Ganan: Their History and Culture," M.A. thesis, University of Mandalay, 1999.

64. Scott, *Gazetteer of Upper Burma*, vol. 1, part 1, 205–7.

65. Charles F. Keyes, ed., *Ethnic Adaptation and Identity: The Karen on the Thai Frontier with Burma* (Philadelphia: ISHI, 1979), 44.

66. F. K. Lehman [Chit Hlaing], "Empiricist Method and Intensional Analysis in Burmese Historiography: William Koenig's *The Burmese Polity, 1752–1819,* a Review Article," *Crossroads: An Interdisciplinary Journal of Southeast Asian Studies* 6 (1991): 77–120, esp. 86.

67. Renard, "Kariang," 44.

68. Leo Alting von Geusau, "Akha Internal History: Marginalization and the Ethnic Alliance System," chapter 6 in *Civility and Savagery: Social Identity in Tai States,* ed. Andrew Turton (Richmond, England: Curzon, 2000), 130.

69. Scott, *Gazetteer of Upper Burma*, vol. 1, part 2, 282–86.

70. Ibid., 49.

71. As a late-nineteenth-century visitor to the Shan states observed, "From what we have learnt, there is little doubt that the sparsity of the hill tribes in the hills neighboring Zimmé [Chiang Mai] has been chiefly caused by their having been, in olden time, systematically hunted like wild cattle to supply the slave market." Archibald Ross Colquhoun, *Amongst the Shans* (London: Field and Tuer, 1885), 257.

72. In western India, hill raids on the plains were so extensive that by the early nineteenth century only 1,836 of the 3,492 former villages were populated, and the sites of 97 villages could not even be remembered. Ajay Skaria, *Hybrid Histories: Forests, Frontiers, and Wildness in Western India* (Delhi: Oxford University Press, 1999), 130. I have encountered no inventory of loot in the Burmese materials, but perhaps this inventory of booty from western Indian hill raids on the plains is suggestive: 77 bullocks, 106 cows, 55 calves, 11 female buffaloes, 54 brass and copper pots, 50 pieces of clothing, 9 blankets, 19 iron ploughs, 65 axes, ornaments, and grain. Ibid., 132.

73. For an important examination of slaving across the Sunda Shelf, see Eric Tagliacozzo, "Ambiguous Commodities, Unstable Frontiers: The Case of Burma, Siam, and Imperial Britain, 1800–1900," *Comparative Studies in Society and History* 46 (2004): 354–77.

74. Scott, *Gazetteer of Upper Burma*, vol. 1, part 2, 315.

75. The Wa were well known for their ridgetop fortifications built to deter raiders for "heads" and slaves. Fiskesjö, "Fate of Sacrifice," 329. There was a maritime version of this

manpower capture and trade in insular Southeast Asia. A number of peoples, most notably Malays, Illanu, Bugis, and Bajau, scoured seaward settlements throughout the archipelago, capturing slaves to incorporate into their own society or selling them on. As a result, vulnerable maritime communities evaded capture by retreating inland and up the watershed or took to their boats to become sea nomads. The *orang laut* (sea people), who live largely on their boats and specialize in collecting (sea foraging), are the maritime equivalent of the small hill groups that retreated to the ridgelines. In fact, the Jakun (a forest-dwelling people linguistically related to the "sea nomads") are suspected of having come from the same stock—some fleeing to the hills, others taking to their boats. See in this connection the illuminating book by David E. Sopher, *The Sea Nomads: A Study Based on the Literature of the Maritime Boat People of Southeast Asia*, Memoirs of the National Museum, no. 5 (1965), Government of Singapore; and Charles O. Frake, "The Genesis of Kinds of People in the Sulu Archipelago," in *Language and Cultural Description: Essays by Charles O. Frake* (Stanford: Stanford University Press, 1980), 311–32.

76. Andrew Hardy, *Red Hills: Migrants and the State in the Highlands of Vietnam* (Honolulu: University of Hawai'i Press, 2003), 29.

77. Salemink, *Ethnography of North Vietnam's Central Highlanders*, 37.

78. Thongchai Winichakul, *Siam Mapped: A History of the Geo-Body of a Nation* (Honolulu: University of Hawai'i Press, 1994), 102.

79. See Christian Culas and Jean Michaud, "A Contribution to the Study of Hmong (Miao) Migration and History," in *Hmong/Miao in Asia*, ed. N. Tapp, J. Michaud, C. Culas, and G. Y. Lee (Chiang Mai: Silkworm, 2004), 61–96; and Jean Michaud, "From Southwest China to Upper Indochina: An Overview of Hmong (Miao) Migrations," *Asia-Pacific Viewpoint*, 38 (1997): 119–30. In fact, the most comprehensive source for the nineteenth-century and twentieth-century migrations from southwest China into mainland Southeast Asia (especially Vietnam, Laos, and Thailand) is Jean Michaud's edited volume *Turbulent Times and Enduring Peoples*, especially the chapters by Christian Culas and Michaud.

80. See the fine analysis of "small border powers" in Janet Sturgeon, *Border Landscapes: The Politics of Akha Land Use in China and Thailand* (Seattle: University of Washington Press, 2005).

81. Fiskesjö, "The Fate of Sacrifice," 370.

82. Charles Crosthwaite gives an example of such fusion between rebellion and princely pretenders shortly after the British conquest of upper Burma. A Shan ruler, confirmed by the British as sovereign in his district, seized several adjacent districts and was dismissed. He was then joined by "the two sons of the Hmethaya Prince, one of King Mindon's numerous progeny. . . . Their cause was taken up by a noble guerilla leader Shwe Yan, who raised their standard in the Ava District. . . . The elder [son] Saw Naing, escaped to Hsen-wi, and, failing to get help there, retired to the mountains and very difficult country on the border of Tawnpeng and Mong-mit." Charles Crosthwaite, *The Pacification of Burma* (London: Edward Arnold, 1912), 270.

83. See E. Michael Mendelson, "The Uses of Religious Skepticism in Burma," *Diogenes* 41 (1963): 94–116, and Victor B. Lieberman, "Local Integration and Eurasian Analogies: Structuring Southeast Asian History, c. 1350–c. 1830," *Modern Asian Studies* 27 (1993): 513.

84. There is an interesting parallel here between the rich valley abbeys of French Catholicism and the poor clergy of the *bocage* at the time of the French Revolution. The former, for its avarice and failure to aid the indigent with tithes, was the object of popular wrath (arson and plunder), whereas the poor, marginal clergy of the bocage were popular and eventually crucial participants in the counterrevolutionary uprising in the Vendée. See Charles Tilly, *The Vendée* (Cambridge: Harvard University Press, 1964).

85. The literature is vast. See, for example, Stanley Tambiah, *Buddhist Saints of the Forest and the Cult of Amulets* (New York: Cambridge University Press, 1984), and Kamala Tiyavanich, *Forest Recollections: Wandering Monks in Twentieth-Century Thailand* (Honolulu: University of Hawai'i Press, 1997). Forest sects and hermitages were "an extension of the early Buddhist practice of 'going forth' . . . distancing oneself from society in order to achieve a strict disciplining of the mind and body demanded by the eightfold path." Reynaldo Ileto, "Religion and Anti-colonial Movements," in Tarling, *Cambridge History of Southeast Asia*, 2: 199. See also the valuable and more recent study of contemporary, charismatic forest monks in Burma by Guillaume Rozenberg, *Renoncement et puissance: La quête de la sainteté dans la Birmanie contemporaine* (Geneva: Editions Olizane, 2005).

86. E. Michael Mendelson, *Sangha and State in Burma: A Study of Monastic Sectarianism and Leadership*, ed. John P. Ferguson (Ithaca: Cornell University Press, 1975), 233. For a more contemporary and exceptionally illuminating analysis of "sainthood," forest monks, and their entourages, see Rozenberg, *Renoncement et puissance*.

87. Mendelson, *Sangha and State in Burma*, 233. See also Lehman [Chit Hlaing], "Empiricist Method and Intensional Analysis," 90, who writes of monks and chapters falling from favor and taking refuge in "the remote towns and villages."

88. Edmund Leach, *The Political Systems of Highland Burma: A Study of Kachin Social Structure* (Cambridge: Harvard University Press, 1954), 30.

89. That is to say, on the east bank of the Salween River rather than the west bank. Scott, *Gazetteer of Upper Burma*, vol. 1, part 1, 320.

90. Bertil Lindner, *Land of Jade: A Journey through Insurgent Burma* (Edinburgh: Kiscadale and White Lotus, 1990), 279. For a comparable account a century earlier of Shan Buddhist heterodoxy, see Archibald Ross Colquhoun, *Amongst the Shans* (London: Field and Tuer, 1885), p. 103.

91. Charles Tilly, *Contention and Democracy in Europe, 1650–2000* (Cambridge: Cambridge University Press, 2004), 168, et seq.

92. Robert LeRoy Canfield, *Faction and Conversion in a Plural Society: Religious Alignments in the Hindu—Kush*, Museum of Anthropology, University of Michigan, no. 50 (Ann Arbor: University of Michigan, 1973), quotation from 13. I am greatly indebted to the insights and fine-grained ethnographic detail provided by this monograph, brought to my attention by Thomas Barfield.

93. Such diseases, as they killed off the less resistant, became endemic to such populations. When they encountered immunologically naïve populations (initially far healthier) in the New World, the mortality rates were devastating. Another great urban scourge should be noted: fire. Premodern cities—made from combustible materials, and their light and cooking fuel provided by open flame—burned regularly, and the historical record is full of references to devastating fires in Southeast Asian cities. See, for example, Anthony Reid, *Southeast Asia in the Age of Commerce, 1450–1680*, vol. 2, *Expansion and Crisis* (New Haven: Yale University Press, 1993), 91; Scott, *Gazetteer of Upper Burma*, vol. 1, part 2, 1, on Amarapura; Koenig, *Burmese Polity*, 34–35, on fires in Amarapura and Rangoon. The epigraph from this section is from Jared Diamond, *Guns, Germs, and Steel* (New York: Norton, 1997), 195, and the first paragraph draws on Diamond's arguments about epidemic diseases.

94. Reid, *Southeast Asia in the Age of Commerce*, 2: 291–98. Reid here aggregates the effects of drought and subsequent famine with disease. The connection between drought and famine are obvious enough, but epidemics often come unaccompanied by famine.

95. David Henley, *Fertility, Food, and Fever: Population, Economy, and Environment in North and Central Sulawesi, 1600–1930* (Leiden: Kitlv, 2005), chapter 7 and p. 286.

96. Scott, *Discovery of the Igorots*, 90. Scott does not tell us how frequently the fleeing

Igorots brought the epidemics with them or how often they arrived at the passes to find them already blocked.

97. Michael Aung-Thwin, in his otherwise fine study of irrigation in Burma's heartland during the Pagan period, emphasizes this advantage to the exclusion of the vulnerabilities of crowding and monocropping. *Irrigation in the Heartland of Burma: Foundations of the Precolonial Burmese State,* occasional paper no. 15 (DeKalb: Council of Southeast Asian Studies of Northern Illinois University, 1990), 54.

98. Nai Thein, "Glass Palace Chronicle," 53.

99. Thant Myint-U, *The Making of Modern Burma* (Cambridge: Cambridge University Press, 2001), 43.

100. Koenig, *Burmese Polity,* 43.

101. Keeton, *King Thibaw and the Ecological Rape of Burma.*

102. Lieberman, *Strange Parallels,* 1: 163, 174, 318–19.

103. Broadly understood, the concentration of population in the state core—also known as "government"—is a major cause of famine, fire, and epidemics, not to mention war. All of them, then, are in part state effects. The royal decrees specifying a series of steps that all inhabitants of the capital must take to be prepared to prevent fires and to extinguish them when they did occur are evidence of this concern. See Than Tun, *Royal Orders of Burma,* 3: xiv, 49–50.

104. Imagine, for example, a New Orleans that every twenty or thirty years experienced a crisis evacuation on the order of the one occasioned by Hurricane Katrina. In such circumstances, an array of crisis routines would be deeply embedded in the popular memory.

105. Lieberman, *Strange Parallels,* 1: 369, 394, 312.

106. Aung-Thwin, *Irrigation in the Heartland of Burma,* 34.

107. This is the pattern described in some detail for Chinese villages by G. William Skinner in "Chinese Peasants and the Closed Community: An Open and Shut Case," *Comparative Studies in Society and History* 13 (1971): 270–81.

108. Once again, the hills are meant literally but also metaphorically as a state-resistant space.

109. Nai Thein, "Glass Palace Chronicle," 17. The epigraph for this section is quoted in Scott, *Discovery of the Igorots,* 141.

110. Scott, *Gazetteer of Upper Burma,* vol. 1, part 1, 148.

111. Hardy, *Red Hills,* 134.

112. G. E. Mitton [Lady Scott], *Scott of the Shan Hills: Orders and Impressions* (London: John Murray, 1930), 182. Scott goes out of his way to play up the Wa's head-hunting proclivities.

113. Martin Smith, *Burma: Insurgency and the Politics of Ethnicity* (London: Zed, 1991), 349.

114. Sociolinguists will recognize this as analogous to the way in which isolated migrants, especially those isolated from their point of origin, may preserve antique dialects long after they have been lost in the culture from which they originally departed. Quebec French, Boer Dutch, and Appalachian English are cases in point.

115. Crosthwaite, *Pacification of Burma,* 116.

116. Smith, *Burma,* 231.

117. In March 2006 I attempted with a friend to make a trip by motorcycle into the southern reaches of the Pegu Yoma, east of Tharawaddy town. Within less than two hours, the track became so sandy that is was impassible for our motorcycle. We continued on foot. We met a few bullock carts loaded with firewood and charcoal from the hills. After half a day's walk we came to a settlement of eight or nine rough houses, many of whose trees seemed from a distance to

be festooned with white gauze. We quickly realized that the white gauze effect was made by mosquito nets. All the villagers were sleeping in the trees after marauding elephants from the hills had broken into their small granaries and eaten all their young banana saplings. Elephants, no less than rebels, found the location advantageous for raiding.

118. Scott, *Gazetteer of Upper Burma*, vol. 1, part 1, 133.

119. Elvin, *Retreat of the Elephants*, 190.

120. *Shih Nai-an*, trans. J. H. Jackson (Cambridge: C&T, 1976), originally published in Shanghai.

121. Wilfred Thesiger, *The Marsh Arabs* (Harmondsworth: Penguin, 1967), 99. Arash Khazeni, in an excellent thesis on nineteenth-century Qajar, Iran, notes that a defeated Bakhitari military leader fled with his family to these marshes near the Shatt-al-Arab. "Opening the Land: Tribes, States, and Ethnicity in Qajar Iran, 1800–1911," Ph.D. diss., Yale University, 2005.

122. Consider, for example, the huge Pripet Marshes (covering one hundred thousand square kilometers of Poland, Belarus, and northwestern Ukraine), which the Nazis had grandiose plans for draining, or the Pontine Marshes near Rome, finally drained by Mussolini. It is no mere coincidence, I think, that much the same civilizational discourse was applied to stateless swamp dwellers as to stateless hill peoples. They were seen as a primitive, even degenerate, population who could be redeemed only by radically changing their environment or by removing them altogether.

123. See, for example, Robert Rimini, "The Second Seminole War," chapter 16 of *Andrew Jackson and His Indian Wars* (New York: Viking, 2001), 272–76. In an interesting parallel to the supposition that some groups in the Malayan peninsula evaded the Malay state and slavery by heading to the hills while others took to their boats, some of the fleeing Cherokee went to the swamps while a small group "hid away in the uppermost reaches of the mountains" of North Carolina.

124. Bland Simpson, *The Great Dismal: A Carolinians Swamp Memoir* (Chapel Hill: University of North Carolina Press, 1990), 69–73.

125. Mariana Upmeyer, "Swamped: Refuge and Subsistence on the Margin of the Solid Earth," term paper for graduate seminar, The Comparative Study of Agrarian Societies, Yale University, 2000.

126. Stan B-H Tan, "Dust beneath the Mist: State and Frontier Formation in the Central Highlands of Vietnam, the 1955–61 Period," Ph.D. diss., Australian National University, 2006, 191.

127. Smith, *Burma*, 262.

128. Sopher, *Sea Nomads*, 42–43.

129. For a good account of piracy, see James Warren, *Sulu Zone, 1768–1868: The Dynamics of External Trade, Slavery, and Ethnicity in the Transformation of a Southeast Asian Maritime State* (Kent Ridge: Singapore University Press, 1981), and Nicholas Tarling, *Piracy and Politics in the Malay World: A Study of British Imperialism in Nineteenth-Century Southeast Asia* (Melbourne: F. W. Cheshire, 1963). For a broader study of maritime contraband, smuggling, and the sea as a state-resistant zone, see Eric Tagliacozzo, *Secret Trades, Porous Borders: Smuggling and States along a Southeast Asian Frontier, 1865–1915* (New Haven: Yale University Press, 2005).

130. Owen Lattimore, *Nomads and Commissars: Mongolia Revisited* (Oxford: Oxford University Press, 1962), 35.

131. Magnus Fiskesjö, "Rescuing the Empire: Chinese Nation-Building in the 20th Century," *European Journal of East Asian Studies* 5 (2006), 15–44, quotations from 38.

132. In his study of the "Miao Rebellion," Robert D. Jenks concluded that Han representation was numerically greater than minority representation. It was in the interest of the au-

thorities never to admit this because, while it was to be expected that barbarians would rebel no matter how well ruled, the only explanation for Han rebellion was misrule—a condition for which the provincial authorities would be held responsible. *Insurgency and Social Disorder in Guizhou: The "Miao" Rebellion, 1854-1873* (Honolulu: University of Hawai'i Press, 1994), 4. For a perceptive account of Han participation in a "Miao" revolt in the late eighteenth century, see Daniel McMahon, "Identity and Conflict in a Chinese Borderland: Yan Ruyi and Recruitment of the Gelao during the 1795-97 Miao Revolt," *Late Imperial China* 23 (2002): 53-86.

133. Geoffrey Benjamin and Cynthia Chou, eds., *Tribal Communities in the Malay World: Historical, Cultural, and Social Perspectives* (Singapore: Institute of Southeast Asian Studies, 2002), 34. For a more elaborate description, see Geoffrey Benjamin, "The Malay World as a Regional Array," paper presented to the International Workshop on Scholarship in Malay Studies, Looking Back, Striding Forward, Leiden, August 26-28, 2004.

134. Nicholas Tapp, *Sovereignty and Rebellion: The White Hmong of Northern Thailand* (Singapore: Oxford University Press, 1990), 173-77.

135. Michaud, *Turbulent Times and Enduring Peoples,* 41.

136. Shanshan Du, *Chopsticks Only Work in Pairs: Gender Unity and Gender Equality among the Lahu of Southwest China* (New York: Columbia University Press, 2002), 115.

137. Charles F. Keyes, ed., *Ethnic Adaptation and Identity: The Karen on the Thai Frontier with Burma* (Philadelphia: ISHI, 1979), 30-62. This crude gloss can hardly do justice to the complexities of the Karen diaspora as explained by Keyes. The Karenni (Red Karen)/Kayah are perhaps a major exception inasmuch as they have made a stab at state formation themselves, taking on the features of Shan statecraft and earning a reputation as much feared slave-raiders.

138. A more complex and accurate historical account would have to show the oscillation between approach and avoidance, depending on political and economic conditions. Nonstate peoples may, under favorable circumstances, seek closer lowland affiliations, and by the same token state populations may under unfavorable circumstances seek to leave the valley state. The choices we have outlined earlier should not be seen as necessarily "once and for all" choices.

Throughout maritime Southeast Asia there are numerous societies that are virtually defined by their avoidance of the lowland state. The Senoi and Semang, among the scattered *orang asli* population of Malaysia, have structured their subsistence practices in order to avoid becoming peasants. In Sulawesi the Wana fled to the deep interior to avoid forced settlement under the Dutch. The Penan of Sarawak, beloved by antilogging environmentalists, have a history of foraging designed to keep themselves outside the lowland state while trading profitably with it. Many such groups have a reputation of fleeing from most contact with lowlanders, perhaps the result of long experience with slaving expeditions. And, as the Ming Dynasty's volume *Description of the Hundred Barbarians* reports of the Wa: "Their nature is soft and weak and they fear government." See, in order, Robert Knox Denton, Kirk Endicott, Alberto Gomes, and M. B. Hooker, *Malaysia and the Original People: A Case Study of the Impact of Development on Indigenous Peoples, Cultural Survival Studies in Ethnicity and Change* (Boston: Allyn and Bacon, 1997); Jane Monnic Atkinson, *The Art and Politics of Wana Shamanship* (Berkeley: University of California Press, 1989); Peter Brosius, "Prior Transcripts, Divergent Paths: Resistance and Acquiescence to Logging in Sarawak East Malaysia," *Comparative Studies in Society and History* 39 (1997): 468-510; and Yin, *People and Forests,* 65.

139. Von Geusau, "Akha Internal History," 134.

140. Ibid., 135.

CHAPTER 6. State Evasion, State Prevention

1. The material for this section comes from the detailed reporting of the Karen Human Rights Group (hereinafter KHRG) in "Peace Villages and Hiding Villages: Roads, Relocations, and the Campaign for Control of Toungoo District," October 15, 2000, KHRG report 2000–05.

2. Ibid., 24. Military portering is especially dreaded. It has been common for porters to be worked to exhaustion on maneuvers and then executed so that they cannot return home, to be forced to walk ahead of Burmese troops through suspected minefields, and, occasionally, to be forced to wear uniforms and precede the troops in order to draw insurgent fire. Porters are seized wherever people concentrate: relocation sites, villages, markets, video parlors, bus stations, ferry crossings, and so on.

3. KHRG, "Free Fire Zones in Southern Tenasserim," August 20, 1997, KHRG report 97–09, 7.

4. Not surprisingly, the sanitation and water supply conditions in relocation zones are often such as to pose a major health threat as well. In this respect, they mimic the epidemiological hazards of state cores more generally.

5. KHRG, "Free Fire Zones," 7, 10.

6. The question of whether pure foraging in tropical rainforests is a viable subsistence strategy was explored by a variety of experts in *Human Ecology* 19 (1991), an issue entirely devoted to the matter. On balance the answer appears to be yes.

7. KHRG, "Abuses and Relocations in the Pa'an District," August 1, 1997, KHRG report 97–08, 8. These villagers were also hoping that they might be able to return to their fields to plant a new crop.

8. For early colonial accounts of hiding villages that are "usually cunningly concealed and are as difficult to find as the *ovis Ammon*," see *Gazetteer of Upper Burma and the Shan States*, compiled from official papers by J. George Scott, assisted by J. P. Hardiman, vol. 1, part 2 (Rangoon: Government Printing Office, 1893), 195, 416. The pacification campaign of the British in the Kachin hills in the early twentieth century bore a family resemblance to contemporary Burmese military rule in minority areas. British troops burned hostile villages, destroying all their grain supplies and crops, exacted tribute and forced labor, and insisted on a formal act of submission and the confiscation of weapons. Ibid., vol. 1, part 1, 336.

9. "Glass Palace Chronicle: Excerpts Translated on Burmese Invasions of Siam," compiled and annotated by Nai Thein, *Journal of the Siam Society* 5 (1908): 1–82 and 8 (1911): 1–119, quotation from 5: 74–75. The account is of Anawhrata's seventeenth-century expedition against Linzin (Vientiane).

10. Clifford Geertz, *Negara: The Theatre State in Nineteenth-Century Bali* (Princeton: Princeton University Press, 1980), 23.

11. Robert D. Jenks, *Insurgency and Social Disorder in Guizhou: The "Miao" Rebellion, 1854–1873* (Honolulu: University of Hawai'i Press, 1994), 11, 21, 131.

12. See, for example, Geoffrey Benjamin and Cynthia Chou, eds., *Tribal Communities and the Malay World: Historical, Cultural, and Social Perspectives* (Singapore: Institute for Southeast Asian Studies, 2002), especially chapter 2, "On Being Tribal in the Malay World," 7–76.

13. Ibid. Benjamin's position on "tribality" in general, a position that increasingly finds favor among anthropologists and historians, is that states, in effect, create tribes. He writes, "On this view, all historically and ethnologically reported tribal societies are secondary formations, characterized by the positive steps they have taken to hold themselves apart from incorporation into the state apparatus (or its more remote tentacles), while often attempting to suppress the knowledge that their way of life has been shaped by the presence of the state, or

whatever represents its complexifying effects." Ibid., 9. See also Leonard Y. Andaya, "Orang Asli and Malayu in the History of the Malay Peninsula," *Journal of the Malaysian Branch of the Royal Asiatic Society* 75 (2002): 23–48.

14. For a fine general treatment of patterns of nomadism, see Thomas J. Barfield, *The Nomadic Alternative* (Englewood Cliffs, N.J.: Prentice-Hall, 1993).

15. William Irons, "Nomadism as a Political Adaptation: The Case of the Yomut Turkmen," *American Ethnologist* 1 (1974): 635–58, quotation from 647.

16. A. Terry Rambo, "Why Are the Semang? Ecology and Ethnogenesis of Aboriginal Groups in Peninsular Malaysia," in *Ethnic Diversity and the Control of Natural Resources in Southeast Asia,* ed., A. T. Rambo, K. Gillogly, and K. Hutterer (Ann Arbor: Center for South and Southeast Asia, 1988), 19–58, quotation from 25. For an analogous treatment of the Punan/Penan of Sarawak, see Carl L. Hoffman, "Punan Foragers in the Trading Networks of Southeast Asia," in *Past and Present in Hunter-Gatherer Studies,* ed. Carmel Shrire (Orlando: Academic Press, 1984), 123–49.

17. *The Man Shu (Book of the Southern Barbarians),* trans. Gordon H. Luce, ed. G. P. Oey, data paper no. 44, Southeast Asia Program, Cornell University, December 1961, 35.

18. David Christian, *Maps of Time: An Introduction to Big History* (Berkeley: University of California Press, 2004), 186. The archeological evidence is clear. "John Coatesworth writes, 'Bioarcheologists have linked the agricultural transition to a significant decline in nutrition and to increase in disease, overwork and violence in areas where skeletal remains make it possible to compare human welfare before and after the change.' Why would one prefer a lifeway based on the painful cultivation, collection and preparation of a small variety of grass seeds, when it was so much easier to gather plants or animals that were more varied, larger, and easier to prepare" (223). This analysis lends further support to Ester Boserup's thesis, in *The Conditions of Agricultural Growth* (Chicago: Aldine-Atherton, 1972), that sedentary grain agriculture was a painful adaptation to crowding and land shortage. This evidence is also in keeping with Marshall Sahlins's description of foraging society as "the original affluent society." *Stone Age Economics* (London: Tavistock, 1974), 1.

19. William Henry Scott, *The Discovery of the Igorots: Spanish Contacts with the Pagans of Northern Luzon,* rev. ed. (Quezon City: New Day, 1974), 90.

20. Graeme Barker, "Footsteps and Marks: Transitions to Farming in the Rainforests of Island Southeast Asia," paper prepared for the Program in Agrarian Studies, Yale University, September 26, 2008, 3. The epigraph for this section is quoted in Arash Khazeni, "Opening the Land: Tribes, States, and Ethnicity in Qajar Iran, 1800–1911," Ph.D. diss., Yale University, 2005, 377. Although the poem ends with dreams of state conquest typical of militarized pastoral-nomads (in this case the Bakhtiari of Iran), it is the association of fixed cultivation with oppression to which I wish to call attention here. I am grateful for Khazeni's research assistance and for the many insights of his thesis.

21. Pierre Clastres, *Society against the State: Essays in Political Anthropology,* trans. Robert Hurley (New York: Zone, 1987). Originally published as *La société contre l'état* (Paris: Editions de Minuit, 1974).

22. The evidence now suggests that the New World was far more densely populated before the Conquest than previously imagined. We now know, in large part through archeological evidence, that agriculture was practiced in most areas where it was technically feasible and that the population of the New World may actually have been more numerous than that of Western Europe. For a broad review of the evidence, see Charles C. Mann, *1491: New Revelations of the Americas before Columbus* (New York: Knopf, 2005).

23. A. R. Holmberg, *Nomads of the Longbow: The Siriono of Eastern Bolivia* (New York: Natural History, 1950).

24. For a reconstruction of the Siriono history, based in part on a closer study of a closely related group, see Allyn Mclean Stearman, "The Yukui Connection: Another Look at Siriono Deculturation," *American Anthropologist* 83 (1984): 630–50.

25. Clastres, "Elements of Amerindian Demography," in *Society against the State*, 79–99. The movement from settled agriculture to hunting and foraging could be documented as well in North America, where a similar demographic collapse made foraging territory more abundant, and European metal tools, firearms, and horses made it less laborious. See Richard White, *The Middle Ground: Indians, Empires, and Republics in the Great Lakes Region, 1650–1815* (Cambridge: Cambridge University Press, 1991), passim.

26. A fine general survey is Richard Price's edited collection *Maroon Societies: Rebel Slave Communities in the Americas*, 2nd ed. (Baltimore: Johns Hopkins University Press, 1979).

27. Yin Shao-ting, *People and Forests: Yunnan Swidden Agriculture in Human-Ecological Perspective*, trans. Magnus Fiskesjö (Kunming: Yunnan Education Publishing House, 2001), 351.

28. Richard A. O'Connor, "A Regional Explanation of the Tai Müang as a City-State," in *A Comparative Study of Thirty City-States*, ed. Magnus Herman Hansen (Copenhagen: Royal Danish Academy of Sciences and Letters, 2000), 431–47, quotations from 434. O'Connor also cites Georges Condominas's *From Lawa to Mon, from Saa' to Thai: Historical and Anthropological Aspects of Southeast Asian Social Spaces*, trans. Stephanie Anderson et al., an Occasional Paper of Anthropology in Association with the Thai-Yunnan Project, Research School of Pacific Studies (Canberra: Australian National University, 1990), 60, and E. P. Durrenberger and N. Tannenbaum, *Analytical Perspectives on Shan Agriculture and Village Economics* (New Haven: Yale University Southeast Asian Monographs, 1990), 4–5, in support of his position.

29. Jean Michaud, *Historical Dictionary of the Peoples of the Southeast Asian Massif* (Lanham, Md.: Scarecrow, 2006), 180.

30. See, for example, Herold J. Wiens, *China's March toward the Tropics: A Discussion of the Southward Penetration of China's Culture, Peoples, and Political Control in Relation to the Non-Han-Chinese Peoples of South China in the Perspective of Historical and Cultural Geography* (Hamden, Conn.: Shoe String, 1954), 215, and Jan Breman, "The VOC's Intrusion into the Hinterland: Mataram," unpublished paper. To the political and tax advantages of shifting cultivation, one must add the relative flexibility of swiddeners to take advantage of new opportunities for trade and exchange. Bernard Sellato, in the Bornean context, claims in effect that swiddening is both safer and more adaptable. It offers a more reliable and diversified diet as well as fitting easily into "commercial collecting" of profitable forest products. In all, Sellato believes, "the flexibility of the system, finally, allows for a more efficient response to the opportunities presented by the modern world (short-term wage-labor, for instance) while rice farmers are chained to their work in the fields." *Nomads of the Borneo Rainforest: The Economics, Politics, and Ideology of Settling Down*, trans. Stephanie Morgan (Honolulu: University of Hawai'i Press, 1994), 186.

31. The most convincing, fine-grained demonstration of this fact is to be found in the work of the great Chinese agronomist Yin Shao-ting, now available to English readers in *People and Forests;* see especially 351–52.

32. Jan Wisseman Christie, "Water from the Ancestors: Irrigation in Early Java and Bali," in *The Gift of Water: Water Management, Cosmology, and the State in Southeast Asia*, ed. Jonathan Rigg (London: School of Oriental and African Studies, 1992), 7–25. See also J. Steven Lansing, *Priests and Programmers: Technologies of Power in the Engineered Landscape of Bali*, rev. ed. (Princeton: Princeton University Press, 1991, 2007).

33. Edmund Leach, *The Political Systems of Highland Burma: A Study of Kachin Social Structure* (Cambridge: Harvard University Press, 1954), 236–37.

34. The celebrated Dogon of Benin fit this pattern. They fled to the hills and there, on rocky soil, constructed permanent field agriculture by carrying up soil basket by basket. It was hardly efficient, but it meant the difference between freedom and capture. Once they were safe from attack, however, they spread out and returned to shifting cultivation.

35. Michaud, *Historical Dictionary,* 100.

36. In fact, swiddening is, from this perspective, a more locationally stable mode of subsistence than grain growing when the danger of raiding is high. Grain growers, once their crops and granaries have been confiscated or destroyed, must move away to find food. Swiddeners, by contrast, are likely to have enough root crops still in the ground, as well as different aboveground crops maturing, that they can more readily move back and manage to subsist after the immediate physical danger has passed.

37. The converse is not necessarily the case. As noted much earlier, irrigated rice has been cultivated both in state and nonstate contexts.

38. Michael Dove, "On the Agro-Ecological Mythology of the Javanese and the Political Economy of Indonesia," *Indonesia,* 39 (1985): 11–36, quotation from 14.

39. Hjorleifur Jonsson, "Yao Minority Identity and the Location of Difference in the South China Borderlands," *Ethnos* 65 (2000): 56–82, quotation from 67. In his thesis, "Shifting Social Landscape: Mien (Yao) Upland Communities and Histories in State-Client Settings," Cornell University, 1996, Jonsson phrases the matter in a slightly more cultural vein: "I propose that up-landness was premised on the state's takeover of the lowland domain. . . . Uplanders who explicitly stand outside states, and do not share the worldview of state populations, act on the ecological division of the lowlands and the forests in a way that reproduces it, and this is the background I propose for upland adaptations to farming in the forest, not an unmediated nature, but an environment that has been prefigured by the state" (195).

40. Nicholas Tapp, *Sovereignty and Rebellion: The White Hmong of Northern Thailand* (Singapore: Singapore University Press, 1990), 20, quoting from F. M. Savina, *Histoire des Miao* (Hong Kong: Imprimerie de la Société des Missions-Etrangères de Paris, 1930), 216.

41. A close description of the range of subsistence activities in such a complex requires a brilliant and meticulous ethnography. The first such example for Southeast Asia is Harold Conklin's celebrated study *Hanunoo Agriculture: A Report on an Integral System of Shifting Cultivation in the Philippines* (Rome: Food and Agriculture Organization of the United Nations, 1957). It's hard to know how to apportion equitably the awe this report inspires between the knowledge and skill of the Hanunoo on the one hand and the observational powers of their ethnographer on the other.

42. Scott, *Gazetteer of Upper Burma,* vol. 1, part 2, 416. Scott does observe that hill people are of note when they do pay taxes or "grow produce the Shan is too lazy to grow himself," but then writes: "Payment is only enforced with difficulty in the face of passive resistance and there is always the risk of the people leaving en masse" (416).

43. Thus it is that there is always grain—usually a single grain such as wheat, maize, rice, or rye—at the center of any "civilization's" diet: its emblematic staple. For the Romans, the striking thing about the barbarians was the relative absence of grain in their diet—as opposed to meat and dairy products. Thomas Burns, *Rome and the Barbarians, 100 BC–AD 400* (Baltimore: Johns Hopkins University Press, 2003), 129.

44. An alternative, but one which requires high levels of state power, is to reduce complexity by forcing a village to plant on specific fields a state-mandated crop, which the officials can then confiscate. This was the essence of the "cultivation system" the Dutch imposed in colonial Java.

45. Mya Than and Nobuyoshi Nishizawa, "Agricultural Policy Reforms and Agricultural Development," in *Myanmar Dilemmas and Options: The Challenge of Economic Transition in the*

1990s, ed. Mya Than and Joseph L. H. Tan (Singapore: Institute of Southeast Asian Studies), 89–116, quotation from 102. See also the striking account of a village leader during the Great Leap Forward in China who advised his fellow villagers to plant turnips because, unlike grains, they were not taxed or confiscated. The village thereby managed to avoid the starvation that affected neighboring villages. Peter J. Seybolt, *Throwing the Emperor from His Horse: Portrait of a Village Leader in China, 1923–1995* (Boulder: Westview, 1996), 57.

46. Grain-growing peasants, menaced repeatedly by raiders and armies in search of provisions, are practiced at burying their grain in small lots; the advantage of root crops is that they are already buried in small lots! William McNeill, "Frederick the Great and the Propagation of Potatoes" in *I Wish I'd Been There: Twenty Historians Revisit Key Moments in History*, ed. Byron Hollinshead and Theodore K. Rabb (London: Pan Macmillan, 2007). 176–89.

47. Geoffrey Benjamin notes that the orang asli of Malaysia prefer crops that require relatively little in the way of labor (millets, tubers, sago, coconut, and banana), as this facilitates their mobility. See his "Consciousness and Polity in Southeast Asia: The Long View," in *Local and Global: Social Transformation in Southeast Asia, Essays in Honour of Professor Syed Hussein Alatas*, ed. Riaz Hassan (Leiden: Brill, 2005), 261–89.

48. One of the tactical errors of the Communist forces in the jungle during the Emergency in Malaya was to have cleared and planted rice padis which could easily be spotted from the air. I am grateful to Michael Dove for this point.

49. For the New World this debate is summarized in Mann's *1491*. For Southeast Asia, see Sellato, *Nomads of the Borneo Rainforest*, 119 et seq. For a more skeptical view, see Michael R. Dove, "The Transition from Stone to Steel in the Prehistoric Swidden Agricultural Technology of the Kantu' of Kalimantan, Indonesia," in *Foraging and Farming*, ed. David Harris and Gordon C. Hillman (London: Allen and Unwin, 1989), 667–77.

50. Hoffman, "Punan Foragers."

51. Ibid., 34, 143.

52. See Michael Adas, "Imperialist Rhetoric and Modern Historiography: The Case of Lower Burma Before the Conquest," *Journal of Southeast Asian Studies* 3 (1972): 172–92, and Ronald Duane Renard, "The Role of the Karens in Thai Society during the Early Bangkok Period, 1782–1873," *Contributions to Asian Studies* 15 (1980): 15–28.

53. Condominas, *From Lawa to Mon*, 63.

54. Sellato, *Nomads of the Borneo Rainforest*, 174–80.

55. John D. Leary, *Violence and the Dream People: The Orang Asli in the Malayan Emergency, 1848–1960*, Monographs in International Studies, Southeast Asian Studies, no. 95 (Athens, Ohio: Center for International Studies, 1995), 63.

56. See David Sweet, "Native Resistance in Eighteenth-Century Amazonia: The 'Abominable Muras,' in War and Peace," *Radical History Review* 53 (1992): 49–80. The Muras were masters of twenty-five hundred square kilometers of labyrinthine waterways that shifted with the annual flooding. They were a magnet for runaways from the Portuguese forced labor system, and, in fact, the term *Mura* was less an ethnic identity that a portmanteau term for "outlaws." In the dry season they planted short-term crops on flood-retreat land, as well as maize and manioc.

57. For the bulk of the discussion on roots and tubers and on maize, I am much indebted to Peter Boomgaard's remarkable historical surveys. See, in particular, "In the Shadow of Rice: Roots and Tubers in Indonesian History, 1500–1950," *Agricultural History* 77 (2003): 582–610, and "Maize and Tobacco in Upland Indonesia, 1600–1940," in *Transforming the Indonesian Uplands: Marginality, Power, and Production*, ed. Tania Murray Li (Singapore: Harwood, 1999), 45–78.

58. Sago occupies a nether space, as do many plants, between a fully domesticated crop

and a naturally occurring "wild" species. It came to the mainland apparently from eastern Indonesia and spread in areas suitable to its propagation, where it is both encouraged and tended. It surpasses even cassava in terms of caloric yield per unit of labor.

59. Boomgaard, "In the Shadow of Rice," 590.

60. Scott, *Discovery of the Igorots*, 45.

61. I am grateful to Alexander Lee for having assembled the widely scattered data to make these comparisons possible.

62. I rely throughout this section on Peter Boomgaard's foundational work "Maize and Tobacco."

63. Ibid., 64.

64. Boomgaard, "Maize and Tobacco," 65.

65. Robert W. Hefner, *The Political Economy of Mountain Java* (Berkeley: University of California Press, 1990), 57. If Hefner's claim has more general applicability and if it also true that steel implements transformed swiddening, then modern swiddening cannot be used to generalize about earlier swiddening practices without a great many qualifications.

66. Maize and potatoes also made it possible for dominant ethnic groups to move out of the valleys and colonize the hills. Thus in Southwest China, Han populations adopting maize and potato cultivation spread farther up the slopes, with Han administrators not far behind. The effect was to impel many non-Han populations even farther into the hills and higher into the watershed. See, in this connection, Norma Diamond, "Defining the Miao: Ming, Qing, and Contemporary Views," in *Cultural Encounters on China's Ethnic Frontier*, ed. Steven Harrell (Seattle: University of Washington Press, 1995), 92–119, quotation from 95, and Magnus Fiskesjö, "On the 'Raw' and the 'Cooked' Barbarians of Imperial China," *Inner Asia* 1 (1999): 139–68, esp. 142.

67. In this section, again, Boomgaard, "In the Shadow of Rice," is my valuable guide.

68. Mann reports meeting a Brazilian woman from Santarém who claimed that when an asphalt street, laid some years before, was torn up, there was a crop of manioc beneath it. *1491*, 298.

69. James Hagen (personal communication, February 2008) alerts me to the fact that in the Maluku context, at least, wild pigs are not picky about the tubers they root out and eat and than any differences are probably marginal.

70. Marc Edelman, "A Central American Genocide: Rubber, Slavery, Nationalism, and the Destruction of the Guatusos-Malekus," *Comparative Studies in Society and History* 40 (1998): 356–90, quotation from 365. For a post–U.S. Civil War account of the development and subsequent curtailment of a free-peasant economy of emancipated slaves that depended on common property, see Steven Hahn, "Hunting, Fishing, and Foraging: Common Rights and Class Relations in the Postbellum South," *Radical History Review* 26 (1982): 37–64.

71. This argument is brilliantly elaborated by Richard O'Connor in, "Rice, Rule, and the Tai State," in *State Power and Culture in Thailand*, ed. E. Paul Durrenberger, Southeast Asia Monograph no. 44 (New Haven: Yale Southeast Asian Council, 1996), 68–99.

72. F. K. Lehman [Chit Hlaing], "Burma: Kayah Society as a Function of the Shan-Burma-Karen Context," in *Contemporary Change in Traditional Society*, ed. Julian Steward (Urbana: University of Illinois Press, 1967), 1: 1–104, quotation from 59. It is worth noting that Lehman sees the political environment in which the Kayah position themselves as a kind of solar system in which Burman, Shan, and Karen societies each exercise both attracting and repelling influences.

73. Ira Lapidus, "Tribes and State Formation in Islamic History," in *Tribes and State Formation in the Middle East*, ed. Philip S. Khoury and Joseph Kostiner (Berkeley: University of California Press, 1990), 48–73, quotation from 52.

74. Prominent exceptions would include the Hmong, the Karen, and the Kachin: the last two militarized and Christianized under British rule. The single most striking instance is the great "Miao (Hmong) Rebellion" in Guizhou, Southwest China, from 1854 to 1973. Retreat is, of course, often accompanied by defensive military measures.

75. Ernest Gellner, *Saints of the Atlas* (London: Weidenfeld and Nicholson, 1969), 41–49; Malcolm Yapp, *Tribes and States in the Khyber, 1838–1842* (Oxford; Clarendon, 1980), quoted in Richard Tapper, "Anthropologists, Historians, and Tribespeople on the Tribe and State Formation in the Middle East," in Khoury and Kostiner, *Tribes and State Formation*, 48–73, quotation from 66–67.

76. See Karen Barkey's fine study, *Empire of Difference: The Ottomans in Comparative Perspective* (Cambridge: Cambridge University Press, 2008), 155–67. The difficulties the Ottomans had with the Dervish orders were, she suggests, analogous to the troubles the tsarist authorities had with the Old Believers and Uniates.

77. Lois Beck, "Tribes and the State in 19th- and 20th-Century Iran," in Khoury and Kostiner, *Tribes and State Formation*, 185–222, quotations from 191, 192.

78. Owen Lattimore, "On the Wickedness of Being Nomads," *Studies in Frontier History: Collected Papers, 1928–1958* (London: Oxford University Press, 1962), 415–26, quotation from 415.

79. White, *Middle Ground*, writes, "What is clear is that socially and politically, this was a village world. . . . The units called tribes and nations and confederacies were only loose leagues of villages. . . . Nothing resembling a state existed in the *pays d'en haut*" (16).

80. Stuart Schwartz and Frank Salomon, "New Peoples and New Kinds of People: Adaptation, Adjustment, and Ethnogenesis in South American Indigenous Societies (Colonial Era)," in *The Cambridge History of Native Peoples of the Americas*, ed. Stuart Schwartz and Frank Salomon (Cambridge: Cambridge University Press, 1999), 443–502, esp. 460.

81. Irons, "Nomadism as a Political Adaptation," and Michael Khodarkovsky, *When Two Worlds Met: The Russian State and the Kalmyk Nomads, 1600–1771* (Ithaca: Cornell University Press, 1992).

82. Marshall Sahlins, *Tribesmen* (Englewood Cliffs, N.J.: Prentice-Hall, 1968), 45–46, quoted ibid., 64.

83. For a persuasive illustration of intensification and deintensification of agriculture in the precolonial Andes as a political option, see Clark Erickson, "Archeological Approaches to Ancient Agrarian Landscapes: Prehistoric Raised-Field Agriculture in the Andes and the Intensification of Agricultural Systems," paper presented to the Program in Agrarian Studies, Yale University, February 14, 1997.

84. Leach, *Political Systems of Highland Burma*, 171.

85. Scott, *Gazetteer of Upper Burma*, vol. 1, part 2, 246.

86. Charles Crosthwaite, *The Pacification of Burma* (London: Edward Arnold, 1912), 236, 287.

87. A. Thomas Kirsch, "Feasting and Society Oscillation, a Working Paper on Religion and Society in Upland Southeast Asia," data paper no. 92 (Ithaca: Southeast Asia Program, 1973), 32.

88. Leach, *Political Systems of Highland Burma*, 171. In most cases, a political choice to mark oneself off from state subjects or lowland societies involves a cultural agenda as well. In this connection, see Geoffrey Benjamin's description of Semang and Senoi egalitarianism as an "abreaction" to Malay identity, prompting "dis-assimilation" from its cultural markers. Benjamin and Chou, *Tribal Communities in the Malay World*, 24, 36.

89. Magnus Fiskesjö, "The Fate of Sacrifice and the Making of Wa History," Ph.D. thesis, University of Chicago, 2000, 217.

90. Alain Dessaint, "Lisu World View," *Contributions to Southeast Asian Ethnography*, no. 2 (1998): 27–50, quotation from 29, and Alain Dessaint, "Anarchy without Chaos: Judicial Process in an Atomistic Society, the Lisu of Northern Thailand," *Contributions to Southeast Asian Ethnography*, no. 12, special issue *Leadership, Justice, and Politics at the Grassroots*, ed. Anthony R. Walker (Columbus, Ohio: Anthony R. Walker, 2004), 15–34.

91. Jacques Dournes, "Sous couvert des maîtres," *Archive Européen de Sociologie* 14 (1973): 185–209.

92. Jonathan Friedman, "Dynamics and Transformation of a Tribal System: The Kachin Example," *L'Homme* 15 (1975): 63–98; Jonathan Friedman, *System, Structure, and Contradiction: The Evolution of Asiatic Social Formations* (Walnut Creek, Calif.: Altimira, 1979); David Nugent, "Closed Systems and Contradiction: The Kachin in and out of History," *Man* 17 (1982): 508–27.

93. François Robinne and Mandy Sadan, eds., *Social Dynamics in the Highlands of Southeast Asia: Reconsidering the Political Systems of Highland Burma by E. R. Leach*, Handbook of Oriental Studies, section 3, Southeast Asia (Leiden: Brill, 2007). For a searching critique of Leach's misunderstanding of the terms *gumsa* and *gumlao* see especially the contributions by La Raw Maran, "On the Continuing Relevance of E. R. Leach's *Political Systems of Highland Burma* to Kachin Studies," 31–66, and F. K. L. Chit Hlaing [F. K. Lehman], Introduction, "Notes on Edmund Leach's Analysis of Kachin Society and Its Further Applications," xxi–lii.

94. Maran, "Continuing Relevance," shows that there are many gumsa arrangements, only one of which (the *gumshem magma* variant of *gumchying gumsa*) approximates the strict hierarchy verging on tyranny that Leach associated with the gumsa system tout court. He claims further that there were no "true" gumlao (gumlau) but rather more or less democratic variations on gumsa. Strictly speaking, the most egalitarian gumsa-gumlao systems are actually competitive oligarchies of feasting open to anyone who can successfully build a substantial following. Where Leach, with his structuralist orientation, apparently went wrong is in assuming that a combination of a segmentary lineage system and asymmetric marriage alliance necessarily lead to fixed rank and hierarchy. Maran shows that this is not the case, as does Chit Hlaing [Lehman] in his Introduction. Cornelia Ann Kammerer, "Spirit Cults among Akha Highlanders of Northern Thailand," in *Founders' Cults in Southeast Asia: Ancestors, Polity, and Identity*, ed. Nicola Tannenbaum and Cornelia Ann Kammerer, monograph no. 52 (New Haven: Council on Southeast Asian Studies, 2003), 40–68, also shows that chiefly ritual monopolies and asymmetric marriage-alliance systems are compatible with a high degree of egalitarianism.

95. The more authoritarian forms of Kachin hierarchy, as Nugent and others have stressed, were not confined to the internal tensions it generated among lower-ranked lineages and noninheriting sons. The opium boom and the ensuing scramble for new opium lands, and the British efforts to curtail chiefly taxes (in lieu of raiding) on caravan trade and to eliminate slaving as a source of Kachin revenue and manpower, played perhaps a more decisive role in undermining the more hierarchical variants of Kachin social organization. See, in this connection, Vanina Bouté, "Political Hierarchical Processes among Some Highlanders of Laos," in Robinne and Sadan, *Social Dynamics in the Highlands*, 187–208.

96. One reason that Leach may have systematically overestimated the authoritarian characteristics of the gumsa system is that the gumsa chief, when representing himself to the Shan, adopted the princely titles and the conduct of a Shan lord. The same gumsa chief, among his own people, might have few or no subjects and would not be countenanced as a hereditary aristocratic chief; Leach may well have mistaken the bluster for the substance. See Chit Hlaing [Lehman], Introduction.

97. Allowing for the Southeast Asian context, the ideology of the gumlao and of gumsa villages is reminiscent of the most egalitarian (Anabaptist) sects in the Reformation and in the English Civil War. There is the same insistence on ritual equality, the rejection of tribute, the refusal of servitude and the deferential terms of address that accompany it, and the idea of individual autonomy and individual rank, in this case, earned through feasting.

98. Scott, *Gazetteer of Upper Burma*, vol. 1, part 2, 414.

99. The most penetrating analysis of the feasting system is that of Thomas Kirsch, who, in "Feasting and Social Oscillation," contrasts the gumlao/democratic emphasis on the ritual autonomy of feasting with the gumsa/autocratic emphasis on lineage hierarchy in feasting. For the democratizing (at least initially) impact of opium farming on feasting, see Hjorleifur Jonsson, "Rhetorics and Relations: Tai States, Forests, and Upland Groups," in Durrenberger, *State Power and Culture*, 166–200.

100. Leach, *Political Systems of Highland Burma*, 198–207.

101. E. Paul Durrenberger, writing about the Lisu, puts the matter of more and less hierarchical forms of social organization in a more materialist, and to me more convincing, context: "In highland Southeast Asia there is an ideology of honor and wealth that can be translated into rank and prestige under certain circumstances. Where wealth and access to valuable goods are scarce, hierarchic forms will develop; where they are widespread, egalitarian forms will develop." "Lisu Ritual: Economics and Ideology," in *Ritual, Power, and Economy: Upland-Lowland Contrasts in Mainland Southeast Asia*, ed. Susan D. Russell, Monograph Series on Southeast Asia, Center for Southeast Asian Studies, Northern Illinois University, occasional paper no. 14 (1989), 63–120, quotation from 114.

102. Leach, *Political Systems of Highland Burma*, 199, quoting "Expeditions among the Kachin Tribes of the North East Frontier of Upper Burma," compiled by General J. J. Walker from the reports of Lieutenant Eliot, Assistant Commissioner, Proceedings R.G.S. XIV.

103. Leach, *Political Systems of Highland Burma*, 197–98, cites H. N. C. Stevenson, *The Economics of the Central Chin Tribes* (Bombay, [c. 1943]); two works by J. H. Hutton, *The Agami Nagas* (London, 1921) and *The Sema Nagas* (London, 1921); and T. P. Dewar, "Naga Tribes and Their Customs: A General Description of the Naga Tribes Inhabiting the Burma Side of the Paktoi Range," *Census* 11 (1931): report, appendixes.

104. For the Karen see Lehman [Chit Hlaing], "Burma."

105. Quoted in Martin Smith, *Burma: Insurgency and the Politics of Ethnicity* (London: Zed, 1991), 84.

106. Leach, *Political Systems of Highland Burma*, 234. I am skeptical of this claim once one figures in the cost of dependence in terms of tribute, corvée, and grain. In any event, Leach provides no figures that would substantiate his assertion.

107. F. K. Lehman [Chit Hlaing], *The Structure of Chin Society: A Tribal People of Burma Adapted to a Non-Western Civilization*, Illinois Studies in Anthropology no. 3 (Urbana: University Illinois Press, 1963), 215–20.

108. I compress what I take to be the argument of Nicholas Tapp, in *Sovereignty and Rebellion*, especially chapter 2. See also Kenneth George, *Showing Signs of Violence: The Cultural Politics of a Twentieth-Century Headhunting Ritual* (Berkeley: University of California Press, 1996). George's uplanders give coconuts to their lowland neighbors to remind them both that they were headhunters and that they have abandoned the practice.

109. Lehman [Chit Hlaing], "Burma," 1: 19.

110. Jonsson, "Shifting Social Landscape," 384.

111. See, for example, Vicky Banforth, Steven Lanjuow, and Graham Mortimer, Burma Ethnic Research Group, *Conflict and Displacement in Karenni: The Need for Considered Responses* (Chiang Mai: Nopburee, 2000), and Zusheng Wang, *The Jingpo Kachin of the Yunnan*

Plateau, Program for Southeast Asian Studies Monograph Series (Tempe: Arizona State University, 1992).

112. E. Paul Durrenberger, "Lisu: Political Form, Ideology, and Economic Action," in *Highlanders of Thailand*, ed. John McKinnon and Wanat Bhruksasri (Kuala Lumpur: Oxford University Press, 1983), 215–26, quotation from 218.

113. One is reminded of hill peoples who either propagate, or take care not to scotch, stories of their headhunting and cannibalism as a way of keeping lowland intruders at bay.

114. Anthony R. Walker, *Merit and the Millennium: Routine and Crisis in the Ritual Lives of the Lahu People* (Delhi: Hindustani Publishing, 2003), 106, and Shanshan Du, *Chopsticks Only Work in Pairs: Gender Unity and Gender Equality among the Lahu of Southwestern China* (New York: Columbia University Press, 2002).

115. Leo Alting von Geusau, "Akha Internal History: Marginalization and the Ethnic Alliance System," chapter 6 in *Civility and Savagery: Social Identity in Tai States*, ed. Andrew Turton (Richmond, England: Curzon, 2000), 122–58, quotation from 140. Meanwhile, the Akha, a midslope people, are busy enacting their cultural superiority vis-à-vis groups such as the Wa, Palaung, and Khmu.

116. Leach, *Political Systems of Highland Burma*, 255. Eugene Thaike [Chao Tzang Yawnghwe], *The Shan of Burma: Memoirs of a Shan Exile*, Local History and Memoirs Series (Singapore: Institute of Southeast Asian Studies, 1984), 82, claims that the Shan were also free to move. And of course they were, and did often move away from a Sawbwa whom they thought oppressive. Leach's point is simply that the cost of moving was less for a swiddener.

117. Ronald Duane Renard, "Kariang: History of Karen-Tai Relations from the Beginning to 1933," Ph.D. diss., University of Hawai'i, 1979, 78. Another nineteenth-century instance of the Karen effort to separate tributary relationships from local autonomy is reported by Charles F. Keyes. Although Karen villages were attached to the Kingdom of Chiang Mai, "the authorities were never allowed to enter the village itself but shared a ritual meal with village elders at some place outside the village." Keyes, ed., *Ethnic Adaptation and Identity: The Karen on the Thai Frontier with Burma* (Philadelphia: ISHI, 1979), 49.

118. Raymond L. Bryant, *The Political Ecology of Forestry in Burma, 1824–1994* (Honolulu: University of Hawai'i Press, 1996), 112–17.

119. Anthony R. Walker, "North Thailand as a Geo-ethnic Mosaic: An Introductory Essay," in *The Highland Heritage: Collected Essays on Upland Northern Thailand*, ed. Anthony R. Walker (Singapore: Suvarnabhumi, 1992), 1–93, quotation from 50.

120. Keyes, *Ethnic Adaptation and Identity*, 143.

121. Walker, *Merit and the Millennium*. Much the same could be said about the "eternally footloose" Hmong. See William Robert Geddes, *Migrants of the Mountains: The Cultural Ecology of the Blue Miao [Hmong Njua] of Thailand* (Oxford: Clarendon, 1976), 230.

122. Walker, *Merit and the Millennium*, 44. In keeping with their cultural fleetness of foot, the Lahu-Nyi seem extremely negligent about their genealogies and "cannot even recall the names of their grandfathers." This, of course, allows them to make or discard a kinship connection with comparative ease. See Walker, "North Thailand as a Geo-ethnic Mosaic," 58. Such shallow genealogies and small, supple, household units have been called "neoteric" and seem to characterize many (but not all) marginal, stigmatized populations. See Rebecca B. Bateman, "African and Indian: A Comparative Study of Black Carib and Black Seminole," *Ethnohistory* 37 (1990): 1–24.

CHAPTER 6½. Orality, Writing, and Texts

1. Leo Alting von Geusau, "Akha Internal History: Marginalization and the Ethnic Alliance System," chapter 6 in *Civility and Savagery: Social Identity in Tai States*, ed. Andrew

Turton (Richmond, England: Curzon, 2000), 122–58, quotation from 131. Nicholas Tapp has suggested the term *alliterate* to describe peoples who lack writing but know of writing and texts. This has surely been the condition of all Southeast Asia hill peoples for as long as anyone can imagine. *Sovereignty and Rebellion: The White Hmong of Northern Thailand* (Singapore: Singapore University Press, 1990), 124.

2. Von Geusau, "Akha Internal History," 131, quoting Paul Lewis, *Ethnographic Notes on the Akha of Burma,* 4 vols. (New Haven: HRA Flexbooks, 1969–70), 1: 35.

3. Anthony R. Walker, *Merit and the Millennium: Routine and Crisis in the Ritual Lives of the Lahu People* (Delhi: Hindustan Publishing, 2003), 568. The relative success enjoyed by missionaries among the Lahu, Walker claims, arose from their promise to restore what the Lahu regarded as a lamentable loss of writing and texts.

4. Magnus Fiskesjö, "The Fate of Sacrifice and the Making of Wa History," Ph.D. thesis, University of Chicago, 2000, 105–6.

5. Jean-Marc Rastdorfer, *On the Development of Kayah and Kayan National Identity: A Study and a Bibliography* (Bangkok: Southeast Asian Publishing, 1994).

6. Fiskesjö, "Fate of Sacrifice," 129.

7. Isabel Fonseca, in her work on the Gypsies (Roma/Sinti), reports a Bulgarian story of their squandering their inheritance of literacy and Christianity by writing their god-given religion on cabbage leaves, which their donkey ate. A Romanian version has it that the Gypsies built a church of stone and the Romanians one of bacon and ham. The gypsies haggled, got the Romanians to exchange churches, and then proceeded to eat their church. Aside from the other rich interpretive possibilities here (transsubstantiation!), this story accomplishes the neat trick of simultaneously conveying greed, improvidence, illiteracy, irreligion, trading, and craftsmanship! *Bury Me Standing: The Gypsies and Their Journey* (New York: Knopf, 1995), 88–89.

8. Olivier Evrard, "Interethnic Systems and Localized Identities: The Khmu subgroups (*Tmoy*) in Northwest Laos," in *Social Dynamics in the Highlands of Southeast Asia: Reconsidering the Political Systems of Highland Burma by E. R. Leach,* ed. François Robinne and Mandy Sadan, Handbook of Oriental Studies, section 3, Southeast Asia (Leiden: Brill, 2007), 127–60, quotation from 151.

9. J. G. Scott [Shway Yoe], *The Burman: His Life and Notions* (1882; New York: Norton, 1963), 443–44.

10. Tapp, *Sovereignty and Rebellion,* 124–72. Tapp provides references for several other hill legends of the loss of writing.

11. If some of the Tai peoples in the Yangzi Valley were, long ago, a literate state-making people, their literacy would have been in another script than the Sanskrit-derived script linked to Theravada Buddhism they mostly use today.

12. Even here, the absence of written records from the period is not conclusive evidence that all writing ceased, though it is certain that virtually all the purposes to which it had been previously put had been snuffed out for the better part of four centuries.

13. Peter Heather, *The Fall of the Roman Empire: A New History of Rome and the Barbarians* (Oxford: Oxford University Press, 2006), 441.

14. It is nonetheless common for illiterate peoples to preserve documents that seem to guarantee them their land and freedoms: for example, the famous imperial decree allowing the Mien to move freely in the hills and make their swiddens, Russian peasants' copies of tsarist decrees believed to order the emancipation of the serfs, and the Spanish land titles the original Zapatistas brought to Mexico City to assert their claims against the haciendas.

15. Thus the Yao/Mien have their sacred written treaty with the Chinese emperor and a restricted Chinese script necessary for their preoccupation with geomancy adapted from Chinese practice. The Sui, a minority in the Chinese province of Guizhou, have a pictogram script

used in divination and geomancy rituals. Jean Michaud, *Historical Dictionary of the Peoples of the Southeast Asian Massif* (Lanham, Md.: Scarecrow, 2006), 224.

16. The Portuguese in the early seventeenth century encountered high rates of literacy evenly divided between men and women in the southern Philippines, Sumatra, and Sulawesi. What is striking is not only the fact that these peoples were far more literate than the Portuguese at that time but that their literacy was not associated with courts, texts, taxation, trade records, formal schooling, legal disputes, or written histories. It seemed to be deployed exclusively in the service of the oral tradition. People would, say, write down a spell or a love poem (the same thing, essentially!) on a palm leaf in order to memorize and declaim it or else to present the actual script to the loved one as a part of courtship ritual. This is a fascinating case of a form of literacy divorced entirely, it seems, from the state-making technologies with which it has usually been associated. See Anthony Reid, *Southeast Asia in the Age of Commerce, 1450-1680*, vol. 1, *The Lands Below the Winds* (New Haven: Yale University Press, 1988), 215-29.

17. Writing, Roy Harris argues convincingly, is not simply speech "written down" but something quite different. See his arguments in *The Origin of Writing* (London: Duckworth, 1986) and *Rethinking Writing* (London: Athlone, 2000). I am grateful to Geoffrey Benjamin for these references.

18. Even the Pict symbol stones found in northern England, never quite deciphered, have this character. They were clearly meant as assertions of permanent territorial authority. What precisely they conveyed to contemporaries is obscure, but to dispute the meaning of a symbol stone, one would have to produce a competing text, a competing symbol stone, that could be read against it.

19. James Collins and Richard Blot, *Literacy and Literacies: Text, Power, and Identity* (Cambridge: Cambridge University Press, 2003), 50 et seq. The most spectacular recent attempt to physically efface a history was the dynamiting by the Taliban of the two thousand–year–old Buddha statues in Bahmian, Afghanistan.

20. The convolutions required to efface an inconvenient physical record in writing or monuments is captured in the Roman tradition of *damnatio memoriae*, by which the Senate would destroy all written and monumental traces of a citizen or tribune who was considered a traitor or who had brought disgrace on the Republic. Of course, the damnatio memoriae was itself an official, written, and duly recorded act! The Egyptians destroyed the cartouches memorializing the pharaohs they wished to erase from the record. One is reminded of the Soviet practice of airbrushing out of photographs all those comrades who had fallen afoul of Stalin in the purges of the 1930s.

21. For the forms that much of this record keeping takes, see Frank N. Trager and William J. Koenig, with the assistance of Yi Yi, *Burmese Sit-tàns, 1764-1826: Records of Rural Life and Administration*, Association of Asian Studies monograph no. 36 (Tucson: University of Arizona Press, 1979).

22. Mogens Trolle Larsen, Introduction, "Literacy and Social Complexity," in *State and Society: The Emergence and Development of Social Hierarchy and Political Centralization*, ed. J. Gledhill, B. Bender, and M. T. Larsen (London: Routledge, 1988), 180. The remaining 15 percent appear to be lists of signs arranged on some taxonomic principle, presumably as an aid to learning the script.

23. Claude Lévi-Strauss, *Tristes Tropiques*, trans. John Weightman and Doreen Weightman (New York: Atheneum, 1968), 291. The relationship between writing and state formation seems to me to be one less of cause and effect than of elective affinity. As with wet-rice irrigation, one can find writing without states and, more rarely, states without writing, but the two normally go hand in hand. I thank Thongchai Winichakul for pressing me on this issue.

24. Von Geusau, "Akha Internal History," 133.

25. For the classic account see Christopher Hill, *The World Turned Upside Down: Radical Ideas during the English Revolution* (Harmondsworth: Penguin, 1975). A more contemporary, extreme example is the Khmer Rouge imprisonment and execution, as class enemies, of those who could read and write French. A curious variation is the suspicion of—and occasional persecution of—educated, literate Han by the two major non-Han dynasties of China: the Mongol/Yuan and the Manchu/Qing. See Patricia Buckley Ebery, *The Cambridge Illustrated History* (Cambridge: Cambridge University Press, 1996), chapter 9.

26. Mandy Joanne Sadan, *History and Ethnicity in Burma: Cultural Contexts of the Ethnic Category "Kachin" in the Colonial and Postcolonial State, 1824–2004* ([Bangkok], 2005), 38, quoting T. Richards, "Archive and Utopia," *Representations* 37 (1992), special issue: *Imperial Fantasies and Post-Colonial Histories,* 104–35, quotations from 108, 111.

27. The obvious exception, when the telling of histories, legends, and genealogies is confined to a small, specialized group of people, is examined below.

28. Eric A. Havelock, *The Muse Learns to Write: Reflections on Orality and Literacy from Antiquity to the Present* (New Haven: Yale University Press, 1986), 54. Havelock adds: "The audience controls the artist insofar as he still has to compose in such a way they [the audience] can not only memorize what they have heard but also echo it in everyday speech. . . . The language of the Greek classical theatre not only entertained its society, it supported it. . . . Its language is eloquent testimony to the functional purposes to which it is put, a means of providing a shared communication—a communication not casual but significant historically, ethnically, politically" (93).

29. This is why Socrates believed that writing out his teachings effectively destroyed their meaning and value, while it is just this instability, spontaneity, and improvisation of speech that made Plato so suspicious of drama and poetry.

30. Jan Vansina, *Oral History as Tradition* (London: James Currey, 1985), 51–52. The classic source on Serbian epics from which is derived a great deal of our knowledge about oral epic performance, including our suppositions about classical Greek epics, is Alfred Lord's *The Singer of Tales* (New York: Atheneum, 1960).

31. Barbara Watson Andaya, *To Live as Brothers: Southeast Sumatra in the Seventeenth and Eighteenth Centuries* (Honolulu: University of Hawai'i Press, 1993), 8.

32. Richard Janko notes that "unlettered Bosnian bards" were in the 1950s still singing the deeds of Suleiman the Magnificent from the 1550s, and that bards on the island of Keos remembered the great volcanic eruption of 1627 BCE on the nearby island of Santorini (which did not affect them). "Born of Rhubarb," review of M. L. West, *Indo-European Poetry and Myth* (Oxford: Oxford University Press, 2008), *Times Literary Supplement,* February 22, 2008, 10.

33. Von Geusau, "Akha Internal History," 132.

34. The story was, of course, sung in the PaO tongue (a Karennic language), then translated into Burmese and then into English. It is impossible to know how much the story has drifted from its 1948 version, but it would, in principle, be possible to compare the various extant versions currently being sung in the PaO hills to ascertain regional variations.

35. Edmund Leach, *The Political Systems of Highland Burma: A Study of Kachin Social Structure* (Cambridge: Harvard University Press, 1954), 265–66.

36. Ronald Duane Renard, "Kariang: History of Karen-Tai Relations from the Beginnings to 1923," Ph.D. diss., University of Hawai'i, 1979.

37. For those familiar with the Malay world, the same variation can be observed in the variant tellings of the classic stories about the Malay brothers Hang Tuah and Hang Jebat, which have radically different political meanings vis-à-vis the contemporary Malay state.

38. Swiddeners have a similarly rich portfolio of swiddening neighbors they have known in the course of their long agricultural history. This too is a kind of shadow community that can,

when necessary or useful, be invoked to establish new and advantageous alliances for trade or politics.

39. Vansina, *Oral History as Tradition*, 58. Igor Kopytoff notes that in African "societies without written records, many different groups could claim to be of the royal blood. . . . As the Africans put it, 'the slaves sometimes became masters and the masters slaves.'" *The African Frontier: The Reproduction of Traditional African Societies* (Bloomington: Indiana University Press, 1987), 47.

40. William Cummings, *Making Blood White: Historical Transformations in Early Modern Makassar* (Honolulu: University of Hawai'i Press, 2002).

41. Margaret R. Nieke, "Literacy and Power: The Introduction and Use of Writing in Early Historic Scotland," in Gledhill, Bender, and Larsen, *State and Society*, 237–52, quotation from 245.

42. Hjorleifur Jonsson, "Shifting Social Landscape: Mien (Yao) Upland Communities and Histories in State-Client Settings," Ph.D. diss., Cornell University, 1996, 136. Renato Rosaldo, *Ilongot Headhunting, 1883–1974: A Study in Society and History* (Stanford: Stanford University Press, 1980), 20, says much the same about the abbreviated oral histories of the Ilongot.

43. Vansina, *Oral History as Tradition*, 115. What seems debatable as a general matter with this argument is that a scattered, marginal, decentralized, egalitarian people could have, on that account, a history that amounted to an elaborate lament of defeat, victimization, treachery, and migrations, as do many hill peoples. Some modern national histories—for example, those of Ireland, Poland, Israel, and Armenia—take essentially this form.

44. See, in this context, Reinhart Kosseleck, *The Practice of Conceptual History: Timing, History, Spacing Concepts* (Stanford: Stanford University Press, 2002), which argues that a consciousness of history is uniquely a product of the Enlightenment.

CHAPTER 7. Ethnogenesis

1. *Gazetteer of Upper Burma and the Shan States*, compiled from official papers by J. George Scott, assisted by J. P. Hardiman, vol. 1, part 1 (Rangoon: Government Printing Office, 1893), 387.

2. Edmund Leach, *The Political Systems of Highland Burma: A Study of Kachin Social Structure* (Cambridge: Harvard University Press, 1954), 48.

3. *Census of India, 1931*, vol. 11, *Burma*, part 1, Report (Rangoon: Government Printing and Stationery, 1933), 173, 196.

4. Leach, *Political Systems of Highland Burma*, 46.

5. *Census of India, 1931*, vol. 11, part 1, 174, and J. H. Green, "A Note on Indigenous Races in Burma," appendix C, ibid., 245–47, quotation from 245. Green goes on to suggest body measurements and cultural inventories that, he believes, would help establish "stages of cultural evolution."

6. Leach, *Political Systems of Highland Burma*, 49. See also David E. Sopher, *The Sea Nomads: A Study Based on the Literature of the Maritime Boat People of Southeast Asia*, Memoirs of the National Museum, no. 5 (1965), Government of Singapore, 176–83, for a similar argument.

7. For this paragraph, I have drawn from Norma Diamond, "Defining the Miao: Ming, Qing, and Contemporary Views," in *Cultural Encounters on China's Ethnic Frontier*, ed. Steven Harrell (Seattle: University of Washington Press, 1995), 92–116; Nicholas Tapp, *The Hmong of China: Context, Agency, and the Imaginary* (Leiden: Brill, 2003); and Jean Michaud, ed., *Turbulent Times and Enduring Peoples: Mountain Minorities in the Southeast Asian Massif* (Richmond, England: Curzon, 2000). One episode of the exchange of population in the hills—a Yao village in which a majority of the adult males had been adopted from other ethnic groups—is

cited by Nicholas Tapp, *Sovereignty and Rebellion: The White Hmong of Northern Thailand* (Singapore: Oxford University Press, 1990), 169.

8. Martin Smith, *Burma: Insurgency and the Politics of Ethnicity* (London: Zed, 1991), 143. Smith also points to padi-planting, monolingual Burmese-speaking, self-identified Karen fighting with the Karen National Union (KNU) and presumably willing to die on behalf of this identity (35).

9. Charles F. Keyes, ed., *Ethnic Adaptation and Identity: The Karen on the Thai Frontier with Burma* (Philadelphia: ISHI, 1979), 6, 4.

10. François Robinne, "Transethnic Social Space of Clans and Lineages: A Discussion of Leach's Concept of Common Ritual Language," in *Social Dynamics in the Highlands of Southeast Asia: Reconsidering the Political Systems of Highland Burma by E. R. Leach*, ed. François Robinne and Mandy Sadan (Amsterdam: Brill, 2008), 283–97. This raises the question of the limits of absorption. As long as those being absorbed at any one time are only a small proportion of the "receiving" society, one imagines a fairly smooth process. In the case of a large pulse of migrants coming en masse in the wake of a war or famine, one imagines that the group might well maintain its distinctiveness. This appears to be the case for the Intha living on Inlay Lake in the Shan states, who, legend has it, were military deserters who came together in large numbers from the south.

11. Sanjib Baruah, "Confronting Constructionism: Ending India's Naga War," *Journal of Peace Research* 40 (2003): 321–38, quotation from 324, quoting Julian Jacobs et al., *The Nagas: The Hill People of Northeast India: Society, Culture, and the Colonial Encounter* (London: Thames and Hudson, 2003), 23.

12. Geoffrey Benjamin and Cynthia Chou, eds., *Tribal Communities in the Malay World: Historical, Cultural, and Social Perspectives* (Singapore: Institute of Southeast Asian Studies, 2002), 21.

13. Leach, *Political Systems of Highland Burma*, 244. J. G. Scott, when negotiating the border with Chinese officials at the turn of the century, was trying to untangle the tribes. "Rode out with General Liu to fix the line across the plain. No line could be found which would divide Kachin and Shan cultivation. The different fields were as completely mixed up as the blocks on a child's puzzle letter toy box." G. E. Mitton [Lady Scott], *Scott of the Shan Hills: Orders and Impressions* (London: John Murray, 1936), 262.

14. Michael Moerman, "Ethnic Identity in a Complex Civilization: Who Are the Lue," *American Anthropologist* 67 (1965): 1215–30, quotations from 1219, 1223.

15. Hjorleifur Jonsson, "Shifting Social Landscape: Mien (Yao) Upland Communities and Histories in State-Client Settings," Ph.D. diss., Cornell University, 1996, 44, subsequently published as *Mien Relations: Mountain People and State Control in Thailand* (Ithaca: Cornell University Press, 2005).

16. E. J. Hobsbawm, *Nations and Nationalism since 1780*, 2nd ed. (Cambridge: Cambridge University Press, 1990), 64.

17. Here, the Tai muang, or statelet, with its inevitable padi core, must be distinguished from the many so-called upland or "tribal" Tai, who may well be Buddhist but who are hill peoples largely outside state structures.

18. Leach, *Political Systems of Highland Burma*, 32.

19. Georges Condominas, *From Lawa to Mon, from Saa' to Thai: Historical and Anthropological Aspects of Southeast Asian Social Spaces*, trans. Stephanie Anderson et al., an Occasional Paper of Anthropology in Association with the Thai-Yunnan Project, Research School of Pacific Studies (Canberra: Australian National University, 1990), 41.

20. For the best survey and analysis see Anthony Reid, ed., *Slavery, Bondage, and Dependency in Southeast Asia* (New York: St. Martin's, 1983).

21. Leach, *Political Systems of Highland Burma*, 221–22.

22. Condominas, *From Lawa to Mon*, 69–72.

23. Scott, *Gazetteer of Upper Burma*, vol. 1, part 1, 478. Many of these marriages also represented alliances that helped protect the ruler against his princely rivals.

24. Leach, *Political Systems of Highland Burma*, chapter 7, 213–26. But see also, for a similar Lisu-to-Shan transformation, E. Paul Durrenberger, "Lisu Ritual, Economics, and Ideology," in *Ritual, Power, and Economy: Upland-Lowland Contrasts in Mainland Southeast Asia*, ed. Susan D. Russell, Monograph Series on Southeast Asia, Northern Illinois University, occasional paper no. 14 (1989), 63–120; and for a more formal analysis grounded in political economy, see Jonathan Friedman, "Tribes, States, and Transformations," in *Marxist Analyses and Social Anthropology*, ed. Maurice Bloch (New York: Wiley, 1975), 161–200.

25. See, for example, David Marlowe, "In the Mosaic: The Cognitive and Structural Aspects of Karen-Other Relationships," in Keyes, *Ethnic Adaptation and Identity*, 165–214, and Peter Kunstadter, "Ethnic Groups, Categories, and Identities: Karen in Northern Thailand," ibid., 119–63.

26. Kunstadter, "Ethnic Groups, Categories, and Identities," 162.

27. Katherine Palmer Kaup, *Creating the Zhuang: Ethnic Politics in China* (Boulder: Lynne Rienner, 2000), 45.

28. Leach, *Political Systems of Highland Burma*, 39.

29. Jonsson, "Shifting Social Landscape," 218.

30. Leach, *Political Systems of Highland Burma*, 40–41.

31. Scott, *Gazetteer of Upper Burma*, vol. 1, part 1, 274.

32. See, along these lines, Richard A. O'Connor, "Agricultural Change and Ethnic Succession in Southeast Asian States: A Case for Regional Anthropology," *Journal of Asian Studies* 54 (1995): 968–96.

33. See Victor B. Lieberman, *Strange Parallels: Southeast Asia in Global Context, c. 800–1830*, vol. 1, *Integration on the Mainland* (Cambridge: Cambridge University Press, 2003); and his "Reinterpreting Burmese History," *Comparative Studies in Society and History* 29 (1987): 162–94; and his "Local Integration and Eurasian Analogies: Structuring Southeast Asian History, c. 1350–1830," *Modern Asian Studies* 27 (1993): 475–572.

34. O. W. Wolters, *History, Culture, and Region in Southeast Asian Perspectives*, rev. ed. (Ithaca: Cornell University Press, in cooperation with the Institute of Southeast Asian Studies, Singapore, 1999), 52. Wolters specifically excludes Vietnam from this generalization.

35. Grant Evans, "Tai-ization: Ethnic Change in Northern Indochina," in *Civility and Savagery: Social Identity in Tai States*, ed. Andrew Turton (Richmond, England: Curzon, 2000), 263–89.

36. Jonsson, *Mien Relations*, 158–59. See also his "Yao Minority Identity and the Location of Difference in South China Borderlands," *Ethnos* 65 (2000): 56–82.

37. Ronald Duane Renard, "Kariang: History of Karen-Tai Relations from the Beginning to 1933," Ph.D. diss., University of Hawai'i, 1979, 18, makes this case for the Karen and Thai in Ratburi province, Thailand.

38. What is missing here is the issue of whether the performance is accepted by powerful others. Many Germans of Jewish ancestry in the 1930s were entirely assimilated into secular German culture and experienced themselves as Germans only to find, fatally, that Nazi "race science" classifications prevailed.

39. F. K. Lehman [Chit Hllaing] "Ethnic Categories in Burma and the Theory of Social Systems," in *Southeast Asian Tribes, Minorities, and Nations*, ed. Peter Kunstadter (Princeton: Princeton University Press, 1967), 75–92, quoted in Tapp, *Sovereignty and Rebellion*, 172.

40. Leach, *Political Systems of Highland Burma*, 287.

41. For persuasive accounts of the adaptive quality of plural identities in the Malay world,

see, for example, Anna Lowenhaupt Tsing, *In the Realm of the Diamond Queen: Marginality in an Out-of-the-Way Place* (Princeton: Princeton University Press, 1993); Jane Drakard, *A Malay Frontier: Unity and Duality in a Sumatran Kingdom*, Studies on Southeast Asia (Ithaca: Cornell University Press, 1990); Victor T. King, "The Question of Identity: Names, Societies, and Ethnic Groups in Interior Kalimantan and Brunei Darussalam," *Sojourn* 16 (2001): 1-36.

42. For the most convincing broadside against the term *tribe* in this context, see Morton H. Fried's little classic *The Notion of Tribe* (Menlo Park: Cummings, 1975).

43. Thomas S. Burns, *Rome and the Barbarians, 100 BC-AD 400* (Baltimore: Johns Hopkins University Press, 2003), 103.

44. Diamond, "Defining the Miao," 100-102.

45. Oscar Salemink, *The Ethnography of Vietnam's Central Highlanders: A Historical Contextualization, 1850-1990* (London: Routledge-Curzon, 2003), 21-29.

46. Tania Murray Li, ed., *Transforming the Indonesian Uplands: Marginality, Power, and Production* (Singapore: Harwood, 1999), 10.

47. For studies of this process in the Middle East, see Richard Tapper, *Frontier History of Iran: The Political and Social History of Shahsevan* (Cambridge: Cambridge University Press, 1998), and Eugene Regan, *Frontiers of the State in the Late Ottoman Empire* (Cambridge: Cambridge University Press, 1999).

48. Quoted in Fried, *Notion of Tribe*, 59.

49. This perspective is most lucidly elaborated in Fredrik Barth, ed., *Ethnic Groups and Boundaries: The Social Organization of Cultural Difference* (1969; Long Grove, Ill.: Waveland, 1998), 9-38, and shared by Leach, *Political Systems of Highland Burma;* F. K. Lehman [Chit Hlaing], "Burma: Kayah Society as a Function of the Shan-Burma-Karen Context," in *Contemporary Change in Traditional Society*, 3 vols., ed. Julian Steward (Urbana: University of Illinois Press, 1967), 1: 1-104; and Keyes, *Ethnic Adaptation and Identity*, although Keyes wishes (4) to emphasize the degree to which, once established, such groups acquire a more distinctive culture, structurally opposed to other groups.

50. Bruce W. Menning, "The Emergence of a Military-Administrative Elite in the Don Cossack Land, 1708-1836," in *Russian Officialdom: The Bureaucratization of Russian Society from the Seventeenth to the Twentieth Century*, ed. Walter McKenzie Pinter and Don Karl Rowney (Chapel Hill: University of North Carolina Press, 1980), 130-61, quotation from 133.

51. See Leo Tolstoy's fine novella *The Cossacks*, in *The Cossacks and Other Stories* (Harmondsworth: Penguin, 1960), 163-334. Here Tolstoy writes in particular about the Tarek River Cossacks, called the Greben Cossacks, who settled among the Chechens.

52. Cossacks also provided military forces to the Ottomans; see Avigador Levy, "The Contribution of the Zaporozhian Cossacks to Ottoman Military Reform: Documents and Notes," *Harvard Ukrainian Studies* 6 (1982): 372-413.

53. See Richard Price, Introduction to part 4, *Maroon Societies: Rebel Slave Communities in the Americas*, 2nd ed. (Baltimore: Johns Hopkins University Press, 1979), 292-97.

54. Fredrik Barth, "Ecological Relationships of Ethnic Groups in Swat, North Pakistan," *American Anthropologist* 58 (1956): 1079-89, and Michael T. Hannan, "The Ethnic Boundaries in Modern States," in *National Development and the World System: Educational, Economical, and Political Change, 1950-1970*, ed. John W. Meyer and Michael T. Hannan (Chicago: University of Chicago Press, 1979), 253-75, quotation from 260.

55. Manfred von Richthofen, *Letters* [to the Shanghai General Chamber of Commerce], 2nd ed. (Shanghai, 1903; Peking reprint, 1914), 119-20, quoted in Owen Lattimore, "The Frontier in History," in *Studies in Frontier History: Collected Papers, 1928-1958* (Oxford: Oxford University Press, 1962), 469-91, quotation from 473n2.

394 NOTES TO PAGES 262–63

56. Lattimore, "Frontier in History," 473n2.

57. The distinction between "Kayah" and "Karenni" (Red Karen) is an artifact of political relabeling, rather like the distinction between Myanmar and Burma for the name of the country as a whole. Since the previous term *Karenni* was associated with rebellion against the regime in Rangoon, the term *Kayah*—actually the name for the preponderant subdivision of the Karenni—was chosen instead because it did not carry these associations. Thus today the state is officially called Kayah State, though it might more accurately be called Karenni State. I use the term *Karenni* for shorthand. F. K. Lehman (Chit Hlaing), on whose fine analysis I rely here, uses the term *Kayah* in "Burma."

58. Ibid., 35.

59. F. K. L. Chit Hlaing [F. K. Lehman], "Some Remarks on Ethnicity Theory and Southeast Asia, with Special Reference to the Kayah and Kachin," in *Exploring Ethnic Diversity in Burma*, ed. Michael Gravers (Copenhagen: NIAS Press, 2007), 112.

60. For accounts of ethnicization having largely to do with control over trade privileges or land, see Lois Beck, "Tribes and the State in 19th- and 20th-Century Iran," in *Tribes and State Formation in the Middle East*, ed. Philip Khoury and Joseph Kostiner (Berkeley: University of California Press, 1990), 185–222; and, on the piratical Tausug in the Sulu Archipelago, James Francis Warren, *The Sulu Zone, 1768–1898: The Dynamics of External Trade, Slavery, and Ethnicity in the Transformation of a Southeast Asian Maritime State* (Singapore: Singapore University Press, 1981), and Charles O. Frake, "The Genesis of Kinds of People in the Sulu Archipelago," in *Language and Cultural Description: Essays by Charles O. Frake* (Stanford: Stanford University Press, 1980), 311–32. For an astute analysis of the invention of indigeneity in the late twentieth century, see Courtney Jung, *The Moral Force of Indigenous Politics: Critical Liberalism and the Zapatistas* (Cambridge: Cambridge University Press, 2008).

61. One of the most striking cases of this process concerns the Bushman of the Kalahari— also known as the san-Khoi—so often depicted as a peripheral, wild, Stone Age remnant from the dawn of human history. Though the historical facts are still in some dispute, it now appears that this understanding is radically mistaken. In Edwin Wilmsen's reconstruction, the Bushmen of the Kalahari are essentially a dispossessed class of mixed origin that has over time been relegated to serflike labor and foraging in bands in the arid sandveld. Comprising pastoralists, many of them Tswana, ruined by cattle raids, livestock epidemics, and war, escaped slaves, and military deserters (many of these in turn Europeans), they joined a small San-speaking population of foragers who had once prospered on sales of ivory, ostrich feathers, and hides. See Wilmsen's classic *Land Filled with Flies: A Political Economy of the Kalahari* (Chicago: University of Chicago Press, 1989). For some of the controversy surrounding this interpretation, see Jacqueline S. Solway's review of Wilmsen's book in *American Ethnologist* 18 (1991): 816–17.

The importance of the subsistence niche to the determination of ethnicity is revelatory. Speakers of non-San languages who have no livestock and who forage (or work as servants) are understood to be San-Bushmen. On the contrary, San speakers who have livestock and are well off are understood to be of Tswana ethnicity. As the two groups are, to use Wilmsen's term, "interdigitated," it is common for bilingual San speakers to routinely "pass" as Tswana. The San-Bushmen are, then, essentially a stigmatized class—or caste—relegated to the least desirable subsistence niche of foraging, and their identity has become synonymous with that niche. In relational terms it would be just as accurate to say that the keystone of Tswana ethnic self-making was the stigmatization of the San-Bushmen. The net effect of treating in homogeneous and stigmatizing terms what is in fact a diverse population is to have "aboriginalized" them. Wilmsen, *Land Filled with Flies*, 85, 108, 133.

62. Ibid., 275, 324, the latter quotation citing John Iliffe, *A Modern History of Tanganyika* (Cambridge: Cambridge University Press, 1979).

63. I am grateful to Shan-shan Du for her careful exposition of the evolution of the tusi system as it evolved, creating hereditary chiefdoms with territorially defined kingdoms to match throughout much of southwest China, especially in poor, inaccessible areas at high altitudes. The system was largely abandoned in favor of direct administration (*gai tui gui liu*, replacing tusi by mobile officials), with household registration and taxes starting in the mid-eighteenth century, under the Ming. Personal communication, August 2008.

64. Max Gluckman, *Order and Rebellion in Tribal Africa* (London: Cohen and West, 1963).

65. Benedict R. O'G. Anderson, *Imagined Communities: Reflections on the Origin and Spread of Nationalism*, 2nd ed. (London: Verso, 1991), 167–69.

66. Geoffrey Benjamin, "The Malay World as a Regional Array," paper presented to the International Workshop on Scholarship in Malay Studies, Looking Back, Striding Forward, Leiden, August 26–28, 2004; and Benjamin and Chou, *Tribal Communities in the Malay World*. See Salemink, *Ethnography of Vietnam's Central Highlanders*, 284, on the Jarai prohibition on the use of the plow.

67. For example, if one were inventing a set of taboos for a group to discourage mixing and commensuality, one could scarcely do better than the traditional high-caste ideas about pollution in India or the stricter versions of orthodox Jewish kosher dietary laws.

68. The epigraph of this section is from Fried, *Notion of Tribe*, 77.

69. Charles F. Keyes, "A People Between: The Pwo Karen of Western Thailand," in Keyes, *Ethnic Adaptation and Identity*, 63–80, and Renard, "Kariang," passim. It is important to recall, in this context, that it has been at least as common over time, and much more so in the past half-century, for the Karen to become Mon, Burman, Thai, Shan, and so on.

70. Leo Alting von Geusau, "Akha Internal History: Marginalization and the Ethnic Alliance System," chapter 6 in Turton, *Civility and Savagery*, 122–58, esp. 133–34, 147–50. I believe that von Geusau himself married into the Akha and was incorporated in the manner he describes. See also E. Paul Durrenberger's account of Yao/Mien household competition to attach outsiders to achieve economic and social success: "The Economy of Sufficiency," in *Highlanders of Thailand*, ed. John McKinnon and Wanat Bhruksasri (Kuala Lumpur: Oxford University Press, 1983), 87–100, esp. 92–93.

71. Leach, *Political Systems of Highland Burma*, 127–30. The social transaction, if it may be called that, redistributes food and goods—material equality—among the community, while concentrating status inequalities.

Officially, the youngest son succeeds to his father's chiefly title (ultimogeniture). Any other son, however, can become chief by successfully founding a new community, by purchasing the ritual rights from the youngest son, or by conquest—providing always that he can successfully make the claim stick. Ibid., 157.

72. Ibid., 164, 166, 167. See also Robinne, "Transethnic Social Space of Clans and Lineages."

73. The logic of feasting and oscillation between democratic (gumlao) and autocratic (gumsa) forms among hill peoples has been worked out brilliantly by A. Thomas Kirsch in "Feasting and Social Oscillation, a Working Paper on Religion and Society in Upland Southeast Asia," data paper no. 92 (Ithaca: Southeast Asia Program, 1973).

74. Lehman [Chit Hlaing], "Burma," 1: 17. Lehman also points out that in China and India, from which valley-state ideological forms are derived, "there was a regular ideology of usurpation that required the usurper and his descendants eventually to establish a real and an imaginary genealogy linking them either to a royal ancestor or a god" (17). A similar point is made by Clifford Geertz with respect to Bali. Although there was a rigid principle of direct descent, "genealogies . . . continually were manipulated in order to rationalize current power

realities." *Negara: The Theatre State in Nineteenth-Century Bali* (Princeton: Princeton University Press, 1980), 31.

75. Rudi Paul Lindner, *Nomads and Ottomans in Medieval Anatolia*, Indiana University Uralic and Altaic Series, ed. Stephen Halkovic, vol. 144 (Bloomington: Research Institute of Inner Asian Studies, Indiana University, 1983), 33.

76. To cite one final example, Robert Harms has shown in his study of the Nunu in the Congo that the "organic unity of the lineage model and the personal manipulations of the big-man ethos" were, structurally, in contradiction. In practice the contradictions were resolved by fabricating genealogies to make it appear as if the big man had been the rightful heir, even when his position was based on personal wealth and political maneuvering instead of on genealogical reckoning. *Games against Nature: An Eco-Cultural History of the Nunu of Equatorial Africa* (Cambridge: Cambridge University Press, 1987), 21.

77. Kirsch, "Feasting and Social Oscillation," 35.

78. Renard, "Kariang," chapter 2, esp. 3–32. Adaptability has in many cases meant absorption into valley societies. It is probably a safe assumption to claim that a majority of the "Karen" have, over the past millennium or so, assimilated to valley societies—a process considerably accelerated over the past half-century.

79. Jonsson, "Shifting Social Landscape," 238. Benjamin, in the Malayic context, makes a point of showing that groups have moved in and out of tribality over time. *Tribal Communities in the Malay World*, 31–34. For a recent analysis of a quasi-settled group (the Chewong) moving "back" into "tribality," see Signe Howell, "'We People Belong in the Forest': Chewong Recreations of Uniqueness and Separateness," ibid. 254–72.

80. Lehman [Chit Hlaing], "Burma," 1: 254, 272.

81. Jonsson, *Mien Relations*, 19–34.

82. For a detailed analysis of this dynamic in the South Asian context, see Sumit Guha's fine *Environment and Ethnicity in India, 1200–1991* (Cambridge: Cambridge University Press, 1999).

83. The cease-fire arrangements that the current military dictatorship in Burma has concluded with many hill rebels can be read in much the same way: a grant of armed autonomy and economic opportunities in return for an end to active hostilities.

In the Malay world it is virtually a historical truism that upstream populations were so vital to Malay coastal states that it was important to manage those relations well. See, in this connection, inter alia, Bernard Sellato, *Nomads of the Borneo Rainforest: The Economics, Politics, and Ideology of Settling Down*, trans. Stephanie Morgan (Honolulu: University of Hawai'i Press, 1994). More broadly, on the symbiosis between hill/steppe peoples and adjacent lowland centers, see David A. Chapell, "Ethnogenesis and Frontiers," *Journal of World History* 4 (1993): 267–75.

84. The last "lowland" ally of the Karen was, of course, the British colonial regime in whose army they—as well as the Kachin and Chin—were vastly overrepresented. They depicted themselves as an "orphaned" people, and their abandonment by the British only added to the legend. For more on Karen alliances to valley kingdoms, see Keyes, *Ethnic Adaptation*, chapter 3, 63–80; Mikael Gravers, "Cosmology, Prophets, and Rebellion among the Buddhist Karen in Burma and Thailand," *Moussons* 4 (2001): 3–31; and E. Walter Coward Jr., "Tai Politics and the Uplands," draft paper (March 2001).

85. Baruah, "Confronting Constructionism." Maritime kingdoms in the Malay world had watery barbarian allies. Melaka had its *orang laut*, the Bugis had the Bajau, and so on.

86. As noted earlier, Leach asserts that Shan culture and state-making is uniform and stable from place to place. If, however, each Shan statelet was largely created by the ingathering of adjacent hill peoples, then each Shan statelet should be somewhat different depending

upon the particular hill populations it absorbed, just as each Malay state was said to bear the marks of the stateless upstream people it had incorporated.

87. The difference, of course, is that the Han series is a formula for being absorbed by an existing state, while the Shan formula is, or can be, a formula for creating a state.

88. For citations, see Leach, *Political Systems of Highland Burma*, 197, and his bibliography, 313–18. The first and third epigraphs for this section are from Thomas Barfield, "Tribe and State Relations: The Inner Asian Perspective," in Khoury and Kostiner, *Tribes and State Formation*, 153–82, quotations from 163 and 164, respectively; the second is from Karl Gustav Izikowitz, *Lamet: Hill Peasants in French Indochina* (Gothenburg: Ethnografiska Museet, 1951), 113.

89. For the Karen see, for example, Lehman [Chit Hlaing], "Burma," 1: 35–36, and Smith, *Burma*, 31, 432n7; for the Wa, see Scott, *Gazetteer of Upper Burma*, vol. 1, part 1, 493–519; for the Lahu, see Anthony R. Walker, *Merit and the Millennium: Routine and Crisis in the Ritual Lives of the Lahu People* (Delhi: Hindustan Publishing, 2003), 72; and for the Karenni, see again Lehman [Chit Hlaing], "Burma," 1: 37–41.

90. Scott, *Gazetteer of Upper Burma*, vol. 1, part 1, 363.

91. Leach, *Political Systems of Highland Burma*, 199, excerpted from a 1929 handbook, "Advice to Junior Officers."

92. Scott, *Gazetteer of Upper Burma*, vol. 1, part 1, 370. Scott's prose is judicious. Such communities were permitted in tracts where they had been recognized and where it was felt that the imposition of a duwa would occasion new resistance. Furthermore, gumlao communities outside the administrative boundary but still within British Burma were left undisturbed—essentially left to their own devices. See also Vanina Bouté, "Political Hierarchical Processes among Some Highlanders of Laos," in Robinne and Sadan, *Social Dynamics in the Highlands*, 187–208, who notes that the Lao court and, subsequently, the French colonizers always preferred more hierarchical societies to egalitarian ones, as the former both were closer in form to their own state structures and provided them with a ready-made structure of control.

93. Lehman [Chit Hlaing], "Burma," 1: 38. This paragraph is drawn entirely from Lehman's astute analysis.

94. Jonsson, "Shifting Social Landscape," 116–20; Durrenberger, "Lisu Ritual, Economics, and Ideology"; and E. Paul Durrenberger, "Lisu: Political Form, Ideology, and Economic Action," in McKinnon and Bhruksasri, *Highlanders of Thailand*, 215–26.

95. The classic analysis is Eric R. Wolf's *Europe and the People without History* (Berkeley: University of California Press, 1982).

96. Durrenberger, "Lisu," 218. Related to this are the traditions for ferocity, savagery, and in particular headhunting, which are, it seems, actually promoted by certain stateless peoples to discourage state incursions into their territory. See, in this connection, Magnus Fiskesjö, "On the 'Raw' and the 'Cooked' Barbarians of Imperial China," *Inner Asia* 1 (1999): 139–68, esp. 146, and Renato Rosaldo, *Ilongot Headhunting, 1883–1974: A Study in Society and History* (Stanford: Stanford University Press, 1980), 155.

97. The literature from the Malay world is extensive, but perhaps the best-worked-out analysis of the contrast and oscillation between hierarchical state forms and acephalous egalitarian forms, both at the ideological level and at the level of social praxis, is Jane Drakard's *Malay Frontier*.

98. Robert Montagne, *Les Berbères et le Makhazen au Sud du Maroc* (Paris: F. Alcan, 1930), cited in Ernest Gellner, *Saints of the Atlas* (London: Weidenfeld and Nicolson, 1969), 26.

99. Michael Khodarkovsky, *Where Two Worlds Met: The Russian State and the Kalmyk Nomads, 1600–1771* (Ithaca: Cornell University Press, 1992), 47.

100. David Faure, "The Yao Wars in the Mid-Ming and Their Impact on Yao Ethnicity," in *Empire at the Margins: Culture and Frontier in Early Modern China,* ed. Pamela Kyle Crossley, Helen Siu, and Donald Sutton (Charlottesville: University of Virginia Press, 2006), 171–89.

101. Von Geusau, "Akha Internal History," 153.

102. Physical mobility is facilitated for many swiddening groups by the assiduous maintenance of a widely dispersed network of kinsmen and friends. The Hmong (Njua) of northern Thailand, for example, have marriage alliances that span great distances, facilitating migration to new areas of fertile lands and political safety. Their history of swiddening also gives them a shadow society of ex-swiddening neighbors that may be activated as the need arises. William Robert Geddes compares these social networks to "invisible telephone lines linking the household to areas near and far, and along any one of them may come a message of hope stimulating movement." *Migrants of the Mountains: The Cultural Ecology of the Blue Miao [Hmong Njua] of Thailand* (Oxford: Clarendon, 1976), 233.

103. Philippe Ramírez, writing of the Korbi people of Assam, notes that various political choices were freighted with consequences for ethnic identity. "Group identity—ascribed identity, at least—is determined not by certain cultural features but by allegiance to a political authority or a political order. . . . In this case, cultural heterogeneity does not prevent coherence of the group in terms of identity or social relationship." "Politico-Ritual Variations on the Assamese Fringes: Do Social Systems Exist?" in Robinne and Sadan, *Social Dynamics in the Highlands,* 91–107, quotations from 103–4.

104. Walker, *Merit and the Millennium,* 529.

105. Jonsson, "Shifting Social Landscape," 132.

106. The linguist Robert Blust believes that all Austronesian hunter-gatherers in the Malay world were once sedentary agriculturalists who knew rice cultivation techniques and who subsequently became nomadic by choice. Cited in Carl L. Hoffman, "Punan Foragers in the Trading Networks of Southeast Asia," in *Past and Present in Hunter-Gatherer Studies,* ed. Carmel Shrire (Orlando: Academic Press, 1984), 123–49, citation from 133. See also Sopher, *Sea Nomads,* 363–66.

107. Jonsson, "Shifting Social Landscape," 124, 185–86.

CHAPTER 8. Prophets of Renewal

Epigraphs are from, respectively, Guillaume Rozenberg, *Renoncement et puissance: La quête de la sainteté dans la Birmanie contemporaine* (Geneva: Editions Olizane, 2005), 274 (my translation); and John Dunn, *Setting the People Free* (London: Atlantic, 2006), 188.

1. See, especially, Christian Culas, *Le messianisme Hmong aux XIXème et XXème siècles* (Paris: Editions MSH, 2005). The Hmong, strictly speaking, are the largest of four linguistic subgroups of the Miao, and by far the most numerous in mainland Southeast Asian states.

2. Herold J. Wiens, *China's March toward the Tropics: A Discussion of the Southward Penetration of China's Culture, Peoples, and Political Control in Relation to the Non-Han-Chinese Peoples of South China in the Perspective of Historical and Cultural Geography* (Hamden, Conn.: Shoe String, 1954), 66–91, and Nicholas Tapp, *Sovereignty and Rebellion: The White Hmong of Northern Thailand* (Singapore: Oxford University Press, 1990), 151.

3. The Yao/Mien have no happier a history. They were defeated by Han troops and auxiliaries at Great Vine Gorge in Guangxi in 1465. It took 160,000 troops to defeat them; 7,300 Yao were decapitated and 1,200 taken prisoner. Mark Elvin, *The Retreat of the Elephants: An Environmental History of China* (New Haven: Yale University Press, 2004), 226.

4. Wiens, *China's March toward the Tropics,* 90.

5. Robert D. Jenks, *Insurgency and Social Disorder in Guizhou: The "Miao" Rebellion,*

1854-1873 (Honolulu: University of Hawai'i Press, 1994), 90; Wiens, *China's March toward the Tropics*, 90.

6. Hmong had moved earlier into northern Siam and rebelled in 1796 and 1817 against Thai slaving raids and administrative controls: the so-called "red-iron policy." See Victor B. Lieberman, *Strange Parallels: Southeast Asia in Global Context, c. 800-1830*, vol. 1, *Integration on the Mainland* (Cambridge: Cambridge University Press, 2003), 300 et seq. As late as 1967, the rumor that a new Hmong king had been born set off a large-scale migration by refugees in Laos to walk to the king's court. Nicholas Tapp, "Ritual Relations and Identity: Hmong and Others," in *Civility and Savagery: Social Identity in Tai States*, ed. Andrew Turton (Richmond, England: Curzon, 2000), 84-103.

7. Quoted in Mikael Gravers, "Cosmology, Prophets, and Rebellion among the Buddhist Karen in Burma and Thailand," *Moussons* 4 (2001): 3-31, quotation from 13.

8. Jonathan Falla, *True Love and Bartholomew: Rebels on the Burmese Border* (Cambridge: Cambridge University Press, 2006), 375.

9. I am indebted for much of this analysis to the perceptive work of Mikael Gravers, for example, "Cosmology, Prophets, and Rebellion"; "Conversion and Identity: Religion and the Formation of Karen Ethnic Identity in Burma," in *Exploring Ethnic Diversity in Burma*, ed. Mikael Gravers (Copenhagen: NIAS Press, 2007), 227-58; and "When Will the Karen King Arrive? Karen Royal Imaginary in Thailand and Burma," manuscript, 28 pp., 2008.

10. Quoted in Gravers, "When Will the Karen King Arrive?" 7.

11. This account is drawn from Gravers's "Cosmology, Prophets, and Rebellion"; "When Will the Karen King Arrive?"; Theodore Stern, "Ariya and the Golden Book: A Millenarian Buddhist Sect among the Karen," *Journal of Asian Studies* 27 (1968): 297-328; and the "Glass Palace Chronicle: Excerpts Translated on Burmese Invasions of Siam," compiled and annotated by Nai Thein, *Journal of the Siam Society* 5 (1908): 1-82 and 8 (1911): 1-119.

12. The meaning of the term *Gwe*, as Gravers explains, is the subject of much discussion. References to "Gwe Mon" and "Gwe Shan" at the time suggest that it is not an ethnic term. Gravers believes that it may refer to Gwae Gabaung, a mountain famous as a refuge after the fall of Pegu. Other mín laún adopted the prefix Gwe as well.

13. Mon, Shan, and Burmese followed his banner, as well as Kayah and PaO (Taungthu), these last two also Karennic-speaking groups. One commentary suggests that Tha Hla was either the son, by a concubine, of the Burman king, Pagan Mín, or the son of Pagan Mín's uncle, who had revolted and fled. If so, it would have been a fairly typical move for a pretender or rebel prince to seek backing at the periphery in order to seize power. Nai Thein, "Glass Palace Chronicle," 8: 98.

14. This and the next two paragraphs are based on Gravers's "Cosmology, Prophets, and Rebellion," 10-12.

15. Stern, "Ariya and the Golden Book."

16. It is indicative of the importance of millenarian themes in Karen politics that Martin Smith's detailed and comprehensive history of insurgency in Burma after World War II contains but a single appendix: "Millenarianism," devoted almost entirely to the Karen. *Burma: Insurgency and the Politics of Ethnicity* (London: Zed, 1991), 426-28.

17. This account of Lahu millenarianism is based almost exclusively on Anthony R. Walker's extraordinarily rich, insightful, and learned book *Merit and the Millennium: Routine and Crisis in the Ritual Lives of Lahu People* (Delhi: Hindustan Publishing, 2003). This landmark volume and Walker's translation of a Lahu creation epic, *Mvuh Hpa Mi Hpa: Creating Heaven, Creating Earth* (Chiang Mai: Silkworm, 1995), deserve to be far more widely known than they are currently.

18. Quoted in Walker, *Merit and the Millennium*, 80, plate 17.

19. Ibid., 78.

20. The male part of the dual Gui-sha was responsible for the sky and the female part for the earth. As the male was lazier than the female, there was too much earth and not enough sky. Gui-sha rectified this by squeezing the earth so that it protruded more into the sky to balance the proportions. The result was a wrinkled earth with mountains and valleys.

21. Walker, *Merit and the Millennium*, 505.

22. These clashes were almost certainly related to the Cold War machinations of the U.S. Central Intelligence Agency and its missionary collaborator William Young, grandson of the revered first Baptist missionary to the Lahu. See Alfred McCoy, *The Politics of Heroin: C.I.A. Complicity in the Global Drug Trade*, rev. ed. (Chicago: Lawrence Hill, 2003), 342–45, 372–74.

23. Both uprisings are described in Walker, *Merit and the Millennium*, 524–33, quotation from 524. Also useful are Walker's account of a Lahu prophet contemporary with his own fieldwork in the 1970s and a study of the same prophet by Sorot Sisisai, a Thai scholar.

24. S. C. Peoples and Howard Campbell, "The Lahu: Paper Prepared for the Joint Commission of Baptists and Presbyterians to Consider the Mission Problems in the Kengtung Field" (Chiang Mai: American Presbyterian Mission, typescript, Chiang Mai Payab Archives, 1907), quoted in Walker, *Merit and the Millennium*, 587.

25. Karl Marx, Introduction to *Contribution to Critique of Hegel's Philosophy of Right* (1843). It is impossible to read the *Communist Manifesto* without being struck by how much it owes, normatively and structurally, to Christian eschatological thinking: a debased world of oppression and sin, a deepening crisis, a final clash between good and evil, the triumph of good, the perfect society, and the end of history. In this context, the appeal of socialism to the Western working class must have rested, in some part, on how neatly it tracked the millenarian narrative of Christianity they were already familiar with.

26. Marc Bloch, *French Rural History: An Essay in Its Basic Characteristics*, trans. Janet Sondheimer (Berkeley: University of California Press, 1970), 169.

27. For an analysis that teases out the major strands of Buddhist practice in Thailand, see A. Thomas Kirsch, "Complexity in the Thai Religious System: An Interpretation," *Journal of Asian Studies* 36 (1972): 241–66.

28. Rozenberg, *Renoncement et puissance*, 276.

29. There are clearly "millenarian situations" in which an unprecedented set of circumstances renders untenable the ordinary past understandings about conduct, status, security, and how a worthy life should be lived. Richard White describes such a situation for Native Americans. Writing of Tenswatawa, a famous Algonquin prophet, he claims that "the Algonquin and white villages of the backcountry teemed with visionaries and God seemed to scatter revelations across the land with abandon." *The Middle Ground: Indians, Empires, and Republics in the Great Lakes Region, 1650–1815* (Cambridge: Cambridge University Press, 1991), 503. One location even called itself "Prophetstown" (513).

30. Franklin Roosevelt's first campaign for the presidency in 1932 could usefully be studied in this fashion. He began as a conservative Democrat, and yet as he gauged the tremendous hopes the unemployed working classes placed in him and adjusted his "stump" speech accordingly from whistle-stop to whistle-stop, his speech (not to mention FDR himself) was increasingly infused with the promises of secular salvation his hearers reposed in him. For a similar understanding of Martin Luther King Jr.'s preaching following the same stochastic process, even within the same sermon, see Taylor Branch, *Parting the Waters: America in the King Years, 1954–63* (New York: Simon and Schuster, 1988).

31. Such distinctions were reinforced in precolonial Burma and Siam by sumptuary laws governing the kinds of clothes, houses, and entourages people of a certain status could have.

32. Max Weber, *The Sociology of Religion*, trans. Ephraim Fischoff (Boston: Beacon, 1963),

101. In the elided section of the quotation, Weber implies that other classes—for example, artisans, the lower middle classes, lower clergy—may be in even greater need of immediate salvation, a theme to which he later returns.

33. I have discussed this theme at much greater length in "Protest and Profanation: Agrarian Revolt and the Little Tradition," *Theory and Society* 4 (1977): 1–38 and 211–46, and in *Domination and the Arts of Resistance: Hidden Transcripts* (New Haven: Yale University Press, 1990). For a detailed historical account of Carnival spilling over into revolt, see Emmanuel Le Roy Ladurie, *Carnival in Romans*, trans. Mary Feney (Harmondsworth: Penguin, 1981).

34. Weber, *Sociology of Religion*, 139, 80, 81. Weber actually uses the term "agrarian communism," which seems inappropriate here inasmuch as the sects he invoked, though they insisted on popular local control over land distribution, were defending a peasant smallholding tradition.

35. This helps explain why, say, the reigns of the absolutist French kings, determined to rule provincial France systematically and impose a homogeneous civil order, were the occasions for widespread revolts, many with millenarian overtones. See Boris Porchnev, *Les soulèvements populaires en France au XVIIème siècle* (Paris: Flammarion, 1972).

36. For ethnographic details of an actual wonder-working monk and the kind of entourage he attracted, see E. Michael Mendelson, "Observations on a Tour in the Region of Mount Popa," *France-Asie* 179 (1963): 786–807, and his "A Messianic Buddhist Association in Upper Burma," *Bulletin, School of Oriental and African Studies (SOAS)* 24 (1961): 560–80. For a more general description of popular religious syncretism, see Melford Spiro, *Burmese Supernaturalism: A Study in the Explanation and Reduction of Suffering* (Englewood Cliffs, N.J.: Prentice-Hall, 1967).

37. Here I rely heavily upon a recent study of eight renowned forest monks by Guillaume Rozenberg, *Renoncement et puissance*.

38. When asked to what monastic order he belonged, the famous contemporary forest monk Hsayadaw Thamanya, of PaO ethnicity, is reported to have replied, "I don't belong to any branch (*gaing*), I belong to the 'gone-to-the-forest' branch." Ibid., 35.

39. I. M. Lewis, *Ecstatic Religions: A Study of Shamanism and Spirit Possession*, 2nd ed. (London: Routledge, 1989), 91.

40. Quoted in J. G. Scott [Shway Yoe], *The Burman: His Life and Notions* (1882; New York: Norton, 1963), 118.

41. Barbara Wilson Andaya, "Religious Development in Southeast Asia, 1500–1800," chapter 9 in *The Cambridge History of Southeast Asia*, ed. Nicholas Tarling, vol. 1, *From Early Times to 1800* (Cambridge: Cambridge University Press, 1992), 565.

42. Mendelson, "Messianic Buddhist Association."

43. Spiro, *Burmese Supernaturalism*, 139.

44. Mendelson believes that many of the nats actually represent murdered royal relatives. Since the king was himself so often a usurper of the throne, making the dead relative (who anyway was powerful for dying a "green" or premature death) into a nat cult was a way of appeasing its spirit and persuading it, by a kind of symbolic jujitsu, to protect the king himself. Saya San, in the same spirit, during his revolt in 1930 invoked the spirit of an Englishman his forces had just slain to protect his following. "Observations," 786.

45. Ibid., 785.

46. E. Michael Mendelson, *Sangha and the State in Burma: A Study of Monastic Sectarianism and Leadership*, ed. John P. Ferguson (Ithaca: Cornell University Press, 1975), 207.

47. For a fine account of an important lay meditation movement, see Ingrid Jordt, *Burma's Mass Lay Meditation Movement: Buddhism and the Cultural Construction of Power* (Athens: Ohio University Press, 2007).

48. For the sorts of revolutionary moves that are available within a social order (that is to

say, without any external knowledge of other possibilities), see my *Domination and the Arts of Resistance*, 77–82.

49. Lieberman, *Strange Parallels*, 1: 328.

50. Gravers, "When Will the Karen King Arrive?" 2.

51. Tapp, "Ritual Relations and Identity," 91.

52. George M. Foster, "What Is Folk Culture?" *American Anthropologist* 55 (1953): 159–73, quotation from 104.

53. Oscar Salemink, *The Ethnography of Vietnam's Central Highlanders: A Historical Contextualization, 1850–1990* (London: Routledge-Curzon, 2003), 73–74.

54. Tapp, "Ritual Relations and Identity."

55. The exception in Europe was the free city-state, a model not available in Southeast Asia, unless the Malay trading port be seen as a partial equivalent.

56. See the interesting argument along these lines in Paul Stange, "Religious Change in Contemporary Southeast Asia," in Tarling, *Cambridge History of Southeast Asia*, vol. 2, *The Nineteenth and Twentieth Centuries* (Cambridge: Cambridge University Press, 1992), 529–84. An interesting parallel is the adoption by Berbers of Sufism in contrast to Arab Sunni orthodoxy. They acknowledge, as it were, participation in the overarching Islamic culture, with its emphasis on brotherhood and equality, while dissenting from the Arab state and its hierarchy. See Philip Khoury and Joseph Kostiner, eds., *Tribes and State Formation in the Middle East* (Berkeley: University of California Press, 1990).

57. Edmund Leach, *The Political Systems of Highland Burma: A Study of Kachin Social Structure* (Cambridge: Harvard University Press, 1954), 112–13.

58. Clifford Geertz, *Negara: The Theatre State in Nineteenth-Century Bali* (Princeton: Princeton University Press, 1980), 132. For maritime Southeast Asia, J. D. Legge notes that M. C. Ricklefs and C. C. Berg interpret the centralist cosmology of Javanese power as functioning as a counterweight to the practical diffusion of power. "The Writing of Southeast Asian History," chapter 1 in Tarling, *Cambridge History of Southeast Asia*, 1–50, esp. 33.

59. Charles Tilly has noted that the geography of Switzerland resulted in a Protestant Reformation that was contentious and fractured between Zwingli (Basel) and Calvin (Geneva) as well as against Catholic holdouts. *Contention and Democracy in Europe, 1650–2000* (Cambridge: Cambridge University Press, 2004), 169.

60. F. K. Lehman [Chit Hlaing], "Burma: Kayah Society as a Function of the Shan-Burma-Karen Context," in *Contemporary Change in Traditional Society*, 3 vols., ed. Julian Steward (Urbana: University of Illinois Press, 1967), 1: 1–104, quotation from 34.

61. Hermann Kulke, "The Early and Imperial Kingdom in Southeast Asian History," in *Southeast Asia in the 9th to 14th Centuries*, ed. David G. Marr and A. C. Milner (Singapore: Institute for Southeast Asian Studies, 1986), 1–22. Surely this should come as no surprise to Europeans for whom the Roman Empire and Holy Roman Empire lived on as ideas in political claims and jurisprudence long after the eternal city had become a ruin amid feuding warlords. Alexander Woodside, "The Centre and the Borderlands in Chinese Political Thinking," in *The Chinese State and Its Borders*, ed. Diana Lary (Vancouver: University of British Columbia Press, 2007), 11–28, esp. 13. Much the same could be said about the Ottoman Empire. See Karen Barkey, *Empire of Difference: The Ottomans in Comparative Perspective* (Cambridge: Cambridge University Press, 2008), 13, 82.

62. Stuart Schwartz and Frank Salomon, "New Peoples and New Kinds of People: Adaptation, Adjustment, and Ethnogenesis in South American Indigenous Societies (Colonial Era)," in *The Cambridge History of Native Peoples of the Americas*, ed. Stuart Schwartz and Frank Salomon (Cambridge: Cambridge University Press, 1999), 443–502, quotation from 486. Gonzalo Aguirre Beltrán also characterized such shatter zones as privileged locations of nativistic and messianic religions. *Regions of Refuge*, Society of Applied Anthropology Mono-

graph Series, 12 (Washington, D.C., 1979), 49. See also, along these lines, Barkey, *Empire of Difference,* 42, on the Ottoman case, as well as Richard White, *Middle Ground;* Peter Worsley, *The Trumpet Shall Sound: A Study of Cargo Cults in Melanesia* (New York: Schocken, 1968); Kenelm Burridge, *New Heaven, New Earth: A Study of Millenarian Activities* (New York: Schocken, 1969); and Jonathan Spence, *God's Chinese Son: The Taiping Heavenly Kingdom of Hong Xiuquan* (New York: Norton, 1996).

63. Tapp, *Sovereignty and Rebellion,* 57.

64. Bloch, *French Rural History,* 169.

65. Weber, *Sociology of Religion,* 126.

66. Erik Mueggler, "A Valley House: Remembering a Yi Headmanship," in *Perspectives in the Yi of Southwest China,* ed. Steven Harrell (Berkeley: University of California Press, 2001), 144–69, esp. 158–61.

67. Peter Worsley's *The Trumpet Shall Sound* and Kenelm Burridge's *New Heaven, New Earth,* for all their sympathy for cargo-cult participants and understanding of the material conditions that set off such rebellions, fall into this trap. Such Southeast Asianists as Mikael Gravers, Anthony R. Walker, and Nicholas Tapp largely avoid it.

68. Tapp, "Ritual Relations and Identity," 94.

69. This is often how a new, charismatic "big man" in the hills gets his start.

70. As students of cults and conversion have emphasized, the more demanding and radical the cult, the greater the importance of a public severing of ties with the old order; that is to say, a burning of bridges so that one cannot return is a mark of complete commitment to the new order.

71. F. K. Lehman [Chit Hlaing], "Who Are the Karen, and If So, Why? Karen Ethnohistory and a Formal Theory of Ethnicity," in *Ethnic Adaptation and Identity: The Karen on the Thai Frontier with Burma,* ed. Charles F. Keyes (Philadelphia: ISHII, 1979), 215–53, quotations from 240, 248.

72. Gravers, "Cosmology, Prophets and Rebellion," 24.

73. Lehman [Chit Hlaing], "Who Are the Karen?" 224.

74. Anthony R. Walker, "The Lahu People: An Introduction," in *Highlanders of Thailand,* ed. John McKinnon and Wanat Bhruksasri (Kuala Lumpur: Oxford University Press, 1983), 227–37, quotation from 231.

75. Fredrik Barth, in his introduction to *Ethnic Groups and Boundaries: The Social Organization of Culture Difference* (1969; Long Grove, Ill.: Waveland, 1998), which emphasizes human agency in the social organization of boundaries, writes that one of the strategies open to elites in nonindustrial nations is to "choose to emphasize ethnic identity, using it to develop new positions and patterns, to organize activities in these sectors formerly not found in their societies or inadequately developed, for the new purpose. . . . The third strategy generates many of the interesting movements that can be observed today, from nativism to new states" (33). Squinted at long enough, I think Barth is making more or less the same argument we are proposing here. Hugh Brody suggests that societies in which shamanism is widely practiced is, because of the indistinct line between dreaming and consciousness, between good and bad, and between playful and serious, a society that is uniquely flexible. *The Other Side of Eden: Hunters, Farmers, and the Shaping of the World* (Vancouver: Douglas and McIntyre, 2000), 245.

76. Jenks, *Insurgency and Social Disorder in Guizhou,* 6.

77. This account is taken from Salemink, *Ethnography of Vietnam's Central Highlanders,* chapter 4, 100–129, and Geoffrey Gunn, *Rebellion in Laos: Peasant and Politics in a Colonial Backwater* (Boulder: Westview, 1990).

78. On the Ong Kommodam uprising see Gunn, *Rebellion in Laos.*

79. See Christian C. Lentz, "What Revolution? Calling for a King in Dien Bien Phu,"

paper prepared for the Annual Meeting of the Association of Asian Studies, April 3–6, 2008, Atlanta. Lentz's much awaited thesis will treat these themes at greater length.

80. As William Robert Geddes notes for the Hmong group he studied, "It is partly for this reason the persons who often do become the most important in large communities are the shamans, the basis of whose authority is religious and therefore not confined to a particular social group." *Migrants of the Mountains: The Cultural Ecology of the Blue Miao [Hmong Njua] of Thailand* (Oxford: Clarendon, 1976), 256. The importance of figures who are above reproach may be related to the common phenomenon of the stranger-king in Southeast Asia, explored in David Henley's "Conflict, Justice, and the Stranger-King: Indigenous Roots of Colonial Rule in Indonesia and Elsewhere," *Modern Asian Studies* 38 (2004): 85–144.

81. Ira Lapidus, "Tribes and State Formation in Islamic History," in Khoury and Kostiner, *Tribes and State Formation in the Middle East*, 25–47, quotation from 29.

82. Thomas Barfield, "Political Legitimacy in Afghanistan," manuscript, 53.

83. This is what is also suggested by Peter Worley in *The Trumpet Shall Sound*, 227. It is a conclusion I resisted, owing to its functionalist mode of reasoning, but which is nonetheless hard to reject on the evidence.

84. Richard A. O'Connor, "Sukhothai: Rule, Religion, and Elite Rivalry," paper presented at the Forty-first Annual Conference of the Association of Asian Studies, Washington, D.C., 1989, cited in Anthony Reid, *Southeast Asia in the Age of Commerce, 1450–1680*, vol. 2, *Expansion and Crisis* (New Haven: Yale University Press, 1993), 151.

85. Here I use the formulation of James Hagen in his fine study of the Maneo community of Maluku, *Community in the Balance: Morality and Social Change in an Indonesian Society* (Boulder: Paradigm, 2006), 165.

86. Tapp, *Sovereignty and Rebellion*, 95–97. Tapp reports such rebellions in the 1950s as well. Jesus was sometimes confused with Sui Yi, the premier shaman historically, who is also prophesied to return to earth one day.

87. Outside the region, of course, the indigenous peoples of the New World far outstrip this lamentable history. For the period of the Indochina War, see Alfred McCoy's fine detailed account in chapter 7, "The Golden Triangle," in *The Politics of Heroin: CIA Complicity in the Global Drug Trade*, rev. ed. (Chicago: Lawrence Hill, 2003), 283–386.

88. See the fine book on the oral tradition of the Christian Bible among African Americans by Allen Dwight Callahan, *The Talking Book: African Americans and the Bible* (New Haven: Yale University Press, 2007).

89. This account is drawn from Walker, *Merit and the Millennium*, 580–86.

90. Quoted ibid., 791.

91. E. J. Hobsbawm, *Primitive Rebels: Studies in Archaic Forms of Social Movement in the 19th and 20th Centuries* (New York: Norton, 1965).

92. See Courtney Jung, *The Moral Force of Indigenous Politics: Critical Liberalism and the Zapatistas* (Cambridge: Cambridge University Press, 2008).

CHAPTER 9. Conclusion

Second epigraph is from Richard A. O'Connor, "Founders' Cults in Regional and Historical Perspective," in *Founders' Cults in Southeast Asia: Ancestors, Polity, and Identity*, ed. Nicola Tannenbaum and Cornelia Ann Kammerer, Yale Southeast Asian Monograph Series no. 52 (New Haven: Yale University Press, 2003), 269–313, quotation from 297.

1. John Dunn, *Setting the People Free: The Story of Democracy* (London: Atlantic, 2005), 182.

2. See, for example, Magnus Fiskesjö, "Rescuing the Empire: Chinese Nation-Building in the 20th Century," *European Journal of East Asian Studies* 5 (2006): 15–44.

3. Joyce C. White, "Incorporating Heterarchy into Theory on Socio-political Development: The Case from Southeast Asia," in *Heterarchy and the Analysis of Complex Societies,* ed. Robert M. Ehrenreich, Carole L. Crumley, and Janet E. Levy, Archeological Papers of the American Archeological Association, no. 6 (1995): 103–23.

4. François Robinne and Mandy Sadan, Postscript, "Reconsidering the Dynamics of Ethnicity through Foucault's Concept of 'Spaces of Dispersion,'" in *Social Dynamics in the Highlands of Southeast Asia: Reconsidering Political Structures of Highland Burma by E. R. Leach,* ed. François Robinne and Mandy Sadan, Handbook of Oriental Studies, section 3, Southeast Asia (Leiden: Brill, 2007), 299–308.

5. In East and Southeast Asia, this would include the Austronesian populations of Taiwan and Hainan, as well as previous state-bearing Malayic peoples like the Cham.

6. O'Connor, "Founders' Cults," 298–99.

7. Fernand Braudel, *The Mediterranean and the Mediterranean World in the Age of Philip II,* vol. 1, trans. Sian Reynolds (New York: Harper and Row, 1966), 33.

8. The great maritime states of Southeast Asia such as Pegu/Bago, Srivijaya, and Melaka, owing to the great advantage of low friction of terrain across water, had a far greater and more vital penumbra than did the more agrarian states of Pagan, Ava, Ayutthaya, or Tongkin, though they were militarily weaker.

9. Slaves in North America made similar use of Christianity and the Bible—especially the Old Testament—to confect a message of liberation and emancipation.

10. Nor is the whole constellation a self-contained system. External shocks have, from time to time, provoked a wholesale realignment of its structure. The colonial conquest and the Japanese occupation in World War II, not to mention the subsequent wars of national liberation fought by lowland majorities and now, often, by upland minorities, are striking cases in point. These shocks completely transformed the constellation of power relations and the options available to each ethnic group in repositioning itself advantageously in the new order.

11. G. William Skinner, "Chinese Peasants and the Closed Community: An Open and Shut Case," *Comparative Studies in Society and History* 13 (1971): 270–81.

12. The pattern of preserving the local food supply is reminiscent of the market customs in eighteenth-century-England at times of food shortage. See E. P. Thompson's famous article "The Moral Economy of the English Crowd in the Eighteenth Century," *Past and Present* 50 (1950): 76–136.

13. Hjorleifur Jonsson, "Shifting Social Landscape: Mien (Yao) Upland Communities and Histories in State-Client Settings," Ph.D. diss., Cornell University, 249, 380–84.

14. Permanent inequalities can arise under contemporary conditions where land is scarce and modern forms of freehold property have been instituted, allowing some families to accumulate land and others to become landless tenants or laborers. Where land is plentiful and open property forms prevail, inequality, when it arises, is usually linked to the family cycle and how many able-bodied workers a family disposes.

15. Georges Condominas makes the same point in *From Lawa to Mon, from Saa' to Thai: Historical and Anthropological Aspects of Southeast Asian Social Spaces,* trans. Stephanie Anderson et al., an Occasional Paper of Anthropology in Association with the Thai-Yunnan Project, Research School of Pacific Studies (Canberra: Australian National University, 1990), 60.

16. Once again, there is a "watery" version of this readjustment. David E. Sopher points out that many groups of orang laut/sea gypsies have become sedentary and then returned to their seafaring ways only to become sedentary once again. The widespread idea that once nomads settle, it is for good, is without foundation. *The Sea Nomads: A Study Based on the Literature of the Maritime Boat People of Southeast Asia,* Memoirs of the National Museum, no. 5 (1965), Government of Singapore, 363–66.

17. One could, of course, easily work this out for any imperial project. In the French case,

the contrast between the ideals of the French Revolution, the rights of man, the idea of citizenship, and the civic discourse of Victor Hugo would, say, confront the realities of colonial Saigon or Algiers. As a little thought experiment, try comparing the discourse of "development" (today's euphemism for civilization) with the unseemly NGO scramble for turf and loot in, say, Vientiane.

18. Flory, the tragic hero of George Orwell's first novel, *Burmese Days,* is a memorable depiction of someone driven to suicide by this contradiction.

Glossary

Much of this glossary is taken with permission, nearly verbatim, and with profound thanks, from Jean Michaud's valuable *Historical Dictionary of the Peoples of the Southeast Asian Massif* (Latham, Md.: Scarecrow, 2006).

Akha The generic name given by specialists of the massif to an extensive Tibeto-Burman-speaking group originating in southern Yunnan, otherwise called Ikaw in Thailand, Kaw in Burma, Ko in Laos, Ha Nhi in Vietnam, and Hani in China. The total number of Akha defined in this way is approximately 1,750,000, of whom 80 percent live in China.

Ava Ava, the capital of Burma off and on from 1364 to 1841, was founded by King Thadominbya on an artificial island at the confluence of the Irrawaddy and the Myitnge created by digging a canal to link the two rivers. Before this, Sagaing had been capital, but after Sagaing fell to the Shan, the court moved across the river to Ava. The kings of Ava set about restoring Burmese supremacy, which had disintegrated after the collapse of Pagan at the time of the Mongol invasion under Kublai Khan, which ended the First Burmese Empire, founded by King Anawrahta in 1057.

Chin A Tibeto-Burman-speaking group in the lower western Burma border area, in the Chin Hills, part of the Arakan Range, often called Khyang in Burmese texts (pronounced "tchng"). The estimated Chin population in Burma for 2004 was 258,000. Most Chin of Burma dwell in the Chin state, which starts at the western limit of the Irrawaddy plain.

Chin Hills A range in northwestern Burma that extends into India's Manipur state. They are also known as the Arakan Yoma range.

Guizhou The "Flower Country" in Chinese. Guizhou's total population in 2000 was 35 million. It is one of four core mountainous provinces in southwest China.

The 2000 census yields the figure of 34.7 percent of province population, or about 12 million people, officially recognized as minorities, who in turn belong to twenty designated minority peoples. Among these, the Miao is the most numerous group.

Han Ethnic Chinese who, after the name of the influential Han Dynasty (202 BCE–222 CE), refer to themselves as *Han minzu*, the "Han nationality" (more than 1.1 billion in 2001, or 91.5 percent of China's population). The Han all speak one or another of the languages of the Sinitic branch of the Sino-Tibetan language family, which subdivides into such parent languages as Mandarin (commonly called Chinese), Cantonese, Hakka, Wu, Yue, Xian, and so on.

Hani Also called Woni, they form an important Tibeto-Burman-speaking minority in China. They officially numbered more than 1.4 million in 2000. The Hani live in the southeast Yunnan in the Honghe Hani-Yi autonomous prefecture, which includes Hinghe, Yuanyang, Luchun, and Jinping counties, along the Red River and its tributaries. The Hani also spill over the border into Southwest Asia, where they are generally known as the Akha.

Hmong Pronounced "mong" in English. With an estimated population of 4 million, the Hmong are one of the major mountain minority groups of the mainland Southeast Asian massif. Moreover, along with the much larger family of Tai-speakers, the Hmong are the only highland minority group found today in all six countries of the massif. They are the most numerous subgroup of the Miao.

Kachin The name used in Burma for the group called Jingpo (Jinghpaw) in adjacent Chinese territory, where they constitute a minority nationality registered under that name. The Burmese Kachin, many of whom live in the Kachin state of northern Burma, estimated at 446,000 individuals in 2004, are, however, three times more numerous than the Jingpo in China. Part of the Tibeto-Burman language family, the Kachin language gave its name to the Kachinic language branch.

Karen A major Tibeto-Burman-speaking group of more than 4.3 million, found chiefly in Burma (an estimated 3.9 million in 2004), with a significant presence in Thailand (438,000 in 2002, twice that number if refugees from Burma are counted). Their language is part of the Karennic branch of the Tibeto-Burman family.

Kayah/Karenni This Tibeto-Burman-speaking group dwells in Burma and, residually, in Thailand. In Burma the group nominally heads the Kayah state—the name having been changed from Karenni state in 1952—traversed by the Salween River, with Loikaw as its capital.

Khmer The ethnic Cambodians proper, making up more than 90 percent of that country's population. They form the bulk of the Khmer branch within the Mon-Khmer linguistic family. Khmer and Khamen are also the names officially attributed to the Khmer-speaking minorities in Vietnam, Laos, and Thailand.

Khmu A Mon-Khmer-speaking group, part of the Khmuic branch named after them, 568,000 of whom inhabit the mainland Southeast Asian massif. The Khmu dwell chiefly in Laos (88 percent of the group) with a presence in Vietnam (10 percent) and Thailand (2 percent). A noteworthy number of alternative spellings for this name have been used through time, including Khamu, Khmu, Kho-mu, Kmhmu, Khmou, Khomu, Kamu and Khamuk.

Kinh/Viet The word literally means "capital," and by extension, "people of the capital." The official ethnonym of the most numerous "nationality" (*Dan toc*) in the Socialist Republic of Vietnam (SRV) (more than 65 million in 1999, or 87 percent of the country's population). Kinh is the name most ethnic Vietnamese prefer to call themselves, to distinguish themselves from other dominant lowland identities in the region, such as Han in China, the Thai in Thailand, the Lao in Laos, and so on. Among these other groups, however, Viet is commonly preferred to Kinh to name the Kinh minorities in neighboring countries sharing the massif.

Lahu A speaker of the Tibeto-Burman language family, originating from southern China, from where some have migrated into the massif over the past two to three centuries. Today the Lahu are found in five countries in mainland Southeast Asia and total approximately 650,000 individuals. In China, where 70 percent of them live (450,000 in 2000), the Lahu dwell in southern Yunnan between the Nu (Salween) and Lancing (Mekong) rivers.

Lamet Mon-Khmer speakers belonging to Palaungic branch, the Lamet were reported to number 16,740 in Laos in 1995, evenly spread between the provinces of Luangnamtha and Bokeo in the northwest of the country. This group, also called Kha Lamet in the past and Rmeet today, is known to Western social scientists thanks in particular to the classic monograph *Lamet: Hill Peasants in French Indochina* published in 1951 by the Swedish anthropologist Karl Gustav Izikowitz.

Lan Na/Lanna Literally, "the million rice fields." An important Tai kingdom, flourishing from the fourteenth century to the sixteenth and centered on the town of Chiang Mai at the heart of the domain of the Tai Yuan, covering most of what constitutes Thailand today. In the highlands of the Kingdom of Lan Na resided many highland groups politically and economically dependent on this Tai muang.

Lao As an ethnic label, Lao applies to all speakers of the Lao (southwest) branch of the Tai-Kadai language family, spread over several countries. Thailand accounts for the vast majority of 28 million or so Lao speakers in Asia, with approximately 25 million of them clustered under the northeastern Isan umbrella identity. There are also Lao minorities officially registered in neighboring northwestern Vietnam (11,611 in 1999) and northern Cambodia (19,819 in 1995).

Lawa (Lua) In Thailand, where they are also called Lua (Lua'), the Lawa constitute an official highland minority, with a population of 22,000 (2002) distributed over five provinces, the majority living in Chiang Mai, Mae Hong Son, and Chiang Rai. Linguists and ethnologists have suggested that the Lawa are to be grouped with the Mon-Khmer-speaking Wa of China and Burma, within the Palaung-Wa linguistic subfamily, with whom they share similarities.

Lisu (Lisaw) A minority, perhaps numbering a million, speaking forms of the Tibeto-Burman language family, the Lisu are found in China, where they originate and where nearly 83 percent of them live today, with a smaller number in Burma (10 percent) and Thailand (7 percent).

Lue (Lu, Lü, Leu, Pai-i) A Tai-speaking group, and one of the few highland minorities found in five countries of the Southeast Asian massif. Linguists believe that the Lue language is spoken in southern China by about 260,000 people, who are also known locally as Pai-i (Dai); another estimated 87,000 Lue-speakers live in Burma, and approximately 70,000 in Thailand. There are 119,000 (1995) Lue registered in Laos and 4,000 (1999) in Vietnam; both countries recognize them as official minority groups.

Mandalay Mandalay is the second-largest city in Burma, with a population of 927,000 (2005 census) and a metropolitan agglomeration of 2.5 million. It was the last royal capital (1860–85) of an independent Burmese kingdom before annexation by the British, in 1885, and is capital of the current Mandalay Division. The city is bounded by the Irrawaddy River to the west and is located 716 kilometers (445 miles) north of Rangoon, the capital until 2007 and Burma's largest city.

Miao One of the largest official minority groups in China, with almost 9 million members in 2000, all speaking forms of the Miao-Yao language family. Nearly half of the Miao are located in Guizhou, where they form the most important minority nationality. They also make up significant proportions of the minority population in Yunnan, Hunan, Guangxi, Sichuan, and Hubei. The Hmong form the most numerous subgroups of the Miao within Southeast Asia, especially in Thailand, Vietnam, and Laos.

Mien The autonym used in several areas of the mainland Southeast Asian massif to designate subgroups of Yao speakers. In Thailand and Laos, for example, most Yao refer themselves as In Mien (Yu Mien), while in Vietnam they use Kim Mien (Kim Mum). American linguists have suggested that since the Mien subgroup is the most important of all Yao groups numerically, it should replace the term *Yao* in the linguistic category "Miao-Yao language family."

Mon People of the kingdom of Pegu in what is now lower Burma.

Muong The Muong of Vietnam speak forms of the Muongic branch of the Viet-Muong subfamily within the Austro-Asiatic languages family. The Muong numbered 1.1 million in the 1999 national census, making them the third-largest minority of Vietnam, after the Tay and the Thai.

Nan Chao (Chau) The "southern prince" or "southern kingdom." Between the eighth and thirteenth centuries CE, a feudal highland kingdom that thrived in the region of the adjacent headwaters of the Yangzi, Red (Yuan), Mekong (Lancang), Salween (Ni), and Irrawaddy rivers, a territory that is today split between western Yunnan and northeastern Burma.

Orang Asli "Original" or "first" peoples in the Malay language. A generic construct used in Malaysia to identify all minority Austro-Asiatic (Aslian, Semang-Senoi branch) and Austronesian (Malay branch) groups once considered aboriginal to the Malaysian peninsula, who together number approximately 100,000 people.

Padaung A Karennic-speaking Tibeto-Burman subgroup, part of the Burmese Kayah (Red Karen, Karenni), not to be confused with the Mon-Khmer Palaung. Although the Padaung ethnic category is not officially recognized in Burma, it is believed that Burma is where a vast majority of them currently live. In Thailand the tentative figure of 30,000 Padaung has been suggested, all dwelling in Mae Hong Son province. Some Padaung have been exploited as tourist curiosity, owing to the stacked brass necklaces their women wear.

Palaung A Mon-Khmer-speaking group found in Burma (an estimated 400,000 in 2004) in two separate clusters at the extreme north of the Shan state, in regions of high altitude. The Palaung call themselves Ta-ang. Although evidence is scarce, historians believe that the Palaung preceded Shan and Kachin settlement in that region.

Pegu Yoma Mountain range of south-central Burma, extending 435 kilometers (270 miles) north-to-south between the Irrawaddy and Sittang rivers and ending in a ridge at Rangoon. The range averages about 600 meters (2,000 feet) in elevation, reaching its highest point in the north at Popa Hill, an extinct volcano (1,518 meters [4,981 feet]). Ethnic minorities (hill peoples) practice shifting agriculture in these mountains, growing upland rice, corn (maize), and millet. During the 1960s the Pegu Yoma Mountains were a refuge for Karen and Communist insurgents.

Shan A major Tai-speaking group of the southwest branch living in upper Burma, where their number was estimated in 2004 to be 2.6 million. The Shan in Burma are associated with the Shan state, which has Taunggyi as its capital. However, it is estimated that the Shan themselves account for only half of the population of their namesake state. The bulk of the Shan in Burma call themselves Tai Yi ("Great Tai"). All Shan settlements in Burma and its periphery are remnants of the thirteenth-to-sixteenth-centuries CE—possibly older—Tai feudal kingdoms or muang, which quickly spread from China across most of the midaltitude lands in the massif, where they established feudal domains based on a wet-rice economy. In 1947 a single Shan state, absorbing the former Wa states and incorporating also significant numbers of Kachins, Lahu, Akha, and Palaung, among

others, was established by the new independent Burmese constitution, along
with most of the other *pyi ne,* or highland ethnic states, that still exist today.

Shan state Shan state is an administrative division of Burma, which takes its name
from the Shan people, one of several ethnic groups that inhabit the area. It is the
largest of the fourteen administrative divisions by land area. Shan state is largely
rural, with only three cities of significant size: Lashio, Kengtung, and the capital,
Taunggyi. Shan state borders China to the north, Laos to the east, and Thailand
to the south. It also shares borders with five administrative divisions of Myanmar. Shan state covers 155,800 square kilometers (60,000 square miles), almost
a quarter of the total area of Myanmar. Most of the Shan state is a hilly plateau;
there are higher mountains in the north and south. The gorge of the Salween
River cuts across the state.

Tai/Thai Not to be confused with the far more numerous Thai who form the
dominant ethnic group of Thailand, the Tai are a southwest Tai-speaking group
and the second-most-numerous national minority in Vietnam. In 1999 there
were officially 1.3 million Thai in northwestern Vietnam, in the upper valleys of
the Da (Black) and Ma rivers, with extensions into the western Red River basin.
The group occupies most of the midregions along the Laotian border from
China to southern Nghe An province. It is generally believed that the Thai of
Vietnam migrated from China at least a thousand years ago and have inhabited
northwest Vietnam ever since.

Wa A Mon-Khmer-speaking group of the Palaung-Wa branch located in the
China-Burma-Laos-Thailand border area. In China 396,000 (2000) Wa dwell
in southwestern Yunnan, in particular in the Xishuangbanna Dai autonomous
prefecture. Some believe the group called Lawa in northern Thailand (15,711 in
1995) should also be included in the Palaung-Wa linguistic cluster.

Yao (Mien) With the Miao, the Yao form the bulk of the population speaking
forms of the Miao-Yao language family. They total approximately 3.3 million
across the mainland Southeast Asian massif. Originating from China, possibly in
southern Hunan, the Yao have gradually dispersed westward under demographic
pressure from coastal Han.

Yi The official name used in China for the group otherwise called Lolo or Lo Lo
in Southeast Asia. In China the number of Yi officially accounted for in the 2000
national census was a considerable 7.7 million. With such a demographic weight,
the Yi are thus the most numerous and most widespread of the sixteen Tibeto-
Burman-speaking nationalities in China.

Yunnan "South of the clouds." The southwesternmost province of China, Yunnan
(population 43 million in 2000) has common international borders with Vietnam,
Laos, and Burma, as well as provincial borders with Tibet, Sichuan, Guizhou,
and Guangxi. Geographically as much as culturally, Yunnan can be considered to
lie at the very heart of the mainland Southeast Asian massif. It has a large num-

ber of highland minority population and is officially home to more than twenty-five of China's national minorities.

Zhuang Pronounced "'tchuang." China's largest minority nationality and the largest highland minority in the whole of the mainland Southeast Asian massif. The Zhuang officially number a staggering 16 million individuals (2000), more than three times the total population of Laos, or equal to the populations of Laos and Cambodia combined.

Index

Yale Agrarian Studies Series

Bill Winders, *The Politics of Food Supply: U.S. Agricultural Policy in the World Economy*

James C. Scott, *The Art of Not Being Governed: An Anarchist History of Upland Southeast Asia*